Travellers

in

Switzerland

'The Matterhorn looks like a sea-lion couchant or a sphinx, and again like the hooded-snake frontal worn by the Egyptian Kings'

(*Paul Popper*)

GERARD MANLEY HOPKINS, 1868; Riffel

Travellers in Switzerland

G. R. de BEER, F.R.S.

GEOFFREY CUMBERLEGE
OXFORD UNIVERSITY PRESS
London New York Toronto
1949

Oxford University Press, Amen House, London E.C.4
GLASGOW NEW YORK TORONTO MELBOURNE WELLINGTON
BOMBAY CALCUTTA MADRAS CAPE TOWN
Geoffrey Cumberlege, Publisher to the University

PRINTED IN GREAT BRITAIN

CONTENTS

ILLUSTRATIONS

The Publishers acknowledge their thanks to the sources listed for permission to reproduce the illustrations.

EXPLANATION

This book is composed of three parts.

In the CHRONOLOGICAL SECTION travellers are arranged year by year and alphabetically within the year. Under each traveller is his itinerary and, where appropriate, a quotation or anecdote showing his reactions to the scenery or the people. Readers requiring further information can find bibliographical details of the sources in the Alphabetical Section.

In the TOPOGRAPHICAL SECTION, under the names of some two dozen places, visitors are enumerated under the years of their visits.

In the ALPHABETICAL SECTION each traveller is listed with bibliographical references to his works and the dates of his travels in black type which refer back to the Chronological Section.

INTRODUCTION

SHORTLY before the start of the Second German War a friend asked me if I would help him to edit a manuscript, which he had discovered, of a journey through Switzerland in 1765. Although reasonably familiar with the literature of travel in Switzerland I found it difficult to recall then and there who had travelled in that country in or about the year 1765, or where they went. I decided accordingly to prepare a chronological list of itineraries of travellers, and the result is the present work.

I am very grateful to this friend, for at that time I was prevented by military service from any coherent pursuit of my normal scientific work, or indeed of any work other than that involved in my duties. But as a result of his suggestion I found myself provided with a pleasant background of thoughts in whatever moments of leisure that I had. During the four and a half years which I spent at the War Office I usually had in my pocket one book from my alpine library, and in periods of enforced idleness in air-raid shelters or on night-duty, or when fire-watching, I gradually worked through all my books with Switzerland or Alps in their titles. Whenever possible I spent my luncheon interval in the London Library and devoted the time to a perusal of its admirable travel and biography sections. It was astonishing how much interesting material was hidden away in memoirs, journals, letters, and biographies, as well as in more general books of travel in Europe. The War Office Library also provided a little grist for my mill, and I paid occasional visits to the libraries of the Royal Society, the Linnean Society, the Royal Geographical Society, the Geological Society, the Alpine Club, and the British Museum. I am grateful to the librarians and authorities of all these.

There was something delightfully soothing in the mechanical nature of the task which I had set myself. Apart from a few simple decisions on method of recording and type of stationery to be used, no thought was required at all. All that I had to do was to read, note the itineraries, and make some short extract which characterized the traveller. I lived in a Switzerland of fancy, and I attribute to its serene influence a large part of the peace of mind which I enjoyed during a time of great mental strain. When the invasion of Europe came I carried my fever with me across the Channel and found new books to buy in Normandy and old books to read in my officers' billets in Belgium, Holland, and Germany, containing accounts of travels.

My friends entered into the spirit of my wild ghost chase and helped me greatly by suggesting references of books. Foremost among these is Miss May Nugent, who took as much interest in the search as myself, and without whose constant help there would be many gaps in my lists. I am also indebted to my wife, to Major H. Pearce, Major D. Batchelor, and Major C. H. Glover, as well as to Mr. Arnold Lunn, Mr. Michael Roberts, Canon Raven, Miss Y. ffrench, M. Ernest Giddey, Mr. E. S. de Beer, Mr. John Russell, Miss M. Jarrett, Dr. R. H. D. Short, and the late Mr. Logan Pearsall Smith for giving me references. One of the most pleasant memories which I cherish of a visit to the headquarters of the 12th United States Army Group immediately after the German offensive in the Ardennes was a conversation in Colonel Powell's mess with a member of his staff, Mr. Bishop, who pointed out that Joachim Du Bellay was a man for me. Mr. J. Monroe Thorington has very kindly given me numerous references to American travellers. Mr. C. W. Nettleton has not only put me on to books but has found them for me.

I also owe a debt to some published works. Chief among these are Count Leopold Berchtold's *Essay to direct and extend the Inquiries of Patriotic Travellers*, W. A. B. Coolidge's *Swiss Travel and Swiss Guide Books*, G. Bettex and E. Guyon's *Les Alpes Suisses dans la littérature et dans l'art*, Mlle C.-E. Engel's *Littérature alpestre en France et en Angleterre*, Dr. G. Schirmer's *Die Schweiz im Spiegel englischer und amerikanischer Literatur*, L. Mazuchetti and A. Lohner's *L'Italia e la Svizzera*, E. Ziehen's *Die deutsche Schweizerbegeisterung*, and A. Dreyer's *Geschichte der alpinen Literatur*. I have also made use of A. Wäber's splendid *Bibliographie der schweizerischen Reiselitteratur*. Knowing well, however, from my own experience, how difficult it is to avoid errors in bibliographies and quotations, I have not relied on the works mentioned for either; every book quoted in this work has been handled by me.

I have given the itineraries by citing the essential places as points outlining the routes. The word 'Pass' after the name of a pass means that the traveller crossed it; where it is omitted the traveller went to the top and back on the same side. Some itineraries, which were not fully described by the travellers, I have been able to complete when there was no doubt possible of the route which they took; others are left incomplete. So far as possible, however, I have taken the traveller (and the reader) from entry into to exit from Switzerland, and I suppose that this requires an explanation of the reason why I have imposed this geographical limit on myself.

In the first place, this limit is not politically absolute, for I could not separate Chamonix and its district from Geneva, and I have included those regions of Italy which would be traversed by a traveller making the tour of Mont Blanc, Monte Rosa, or Piz Bernina. The same reasons doubtless actuated J. G. Ebel, John Murray, Karl Baedeker, and Adolphe Joanne when they compiled their Swiss handbooks and guides.

But the fact remains that I have centred myself in Switzerland, because I know it and its travel-literature best, because it is associated with human experience in a way which differentiates it from neighbouring regions, and because I suppose that I was not interested to catalogue the traffic over the Mont Cenis, Little St. Bernard, and Brenner passes.

I think it was Emerson who remarked on the ability of a beautiful face to give pleasure without effort. Like many such truths, this one is half true. To give pleasure, a face requires a certain regularity and proportion of features which are beyond the control of its owner to produce. But what really attracts us in a beautiful face is the expression which reflects benevolent qualities in the personality of its possessor and for which it is responsible. It may be effortless, but it is not automatic. I think that the same is true of Switzerland. Its features are superb, and its people have added to them an expression of charm by the love which they bear to their own mountains, lakes, and valleys, the care with which they tend them, the generosity with which they share them, and the general principles of freedom and right of asylum with, and for, which they have endowed and protected them. Without any desire to disparage other regions, I think that my analogy applies most to Switzerland.

I have dealt as well as I could with the men and women who have recorded their experiences and impressions in print or who have had it done for them. From 941 to 1945 they cover a thousand years, during the last two hundred of which the yearly record is complete, except for the period of anaesthesia of the Second German War.

Since human interest plays such a part in the attractiveness of the country, I have endeavoured wherever possible to clothe the bones of my who-went-where-when dictionary with a little of the flesh and blood of the travellers themselves in the form of quotations, anecdotes, or indications of the works, literary, artistic, or musical, to which they were inspired by their surroundings or on which they were engaged. French quotations I have left as they are, but those in other languages are translated into English. I have, however, to confess to a certain lack of interest in the early German emperors who were perpetually leading armies or escaping across the Swiss passes, and, except for a very few, I have omitted them. They contributed nothing to the human interest of the places through which they passed, and, as Mr. J. E. Tyler's interesting work on the *Alpine Passes* shows, their itineraries are in many cases uncertain and conjectural.

I have restricted the sources on which I have drawn to printed books, accessible to anyone who wants to know more about where any given person went, what he was doing, or the conditions of the places themselves at different times. Three times I have cheated; by including some details of the Duke of Connaught's itinerary from his private scrap-book which I was once privileged to see; by including details of Gibbon's Tour from his Swiss journal which I am about to publish, and by making use of Mr. F. Oughton's continuation of the late A. L. Mumm's *Alpine Club Register* for the dates of Mr. Geoffrey Winthrop Young's climbs. I am most grateful to Mr. Oughton. A further restriction which I have thought necessary to make has been to exclude accounts of journeys and climbs published in contemporary issues of the various alpine journals. This work is not a record of mountaineering and there would have been no end to it had I chosen any other course. On the other hand, I have been careful to include books, and those by such eminent mountaineers as Wills, Moore, Whymper, Winthrop Young, Lunn, Smythe, and Graham Brown provide intense human interest in the places visited. Some of these writers lend themselves easily to chronological and topographical recording of their tracks; others defy such a mechanical analysis of their sagas.

In many cases it has been an exercise of some interest and ingenuity to determine the actual dates of the journeys, for these are not always given. Possibly for the first time in his life or since, Voltaire has been a veritable godsend; for everyone who visited him at Ferney was usually careful to give his age which can be used as a ready reckoner. In other cases the deaths of rulers such as George II, Frederick the Great, or Robespierre have enabled the dates to be determined. Sometimes the travellers meet one another, which is helpful. Catastrophes like landslides, fires, and floods have also been useful. In yet other cases a perpetual calendar has revealed the year in which a particular day of the week fell on a particular date of the month. When all these methods failed, I have fallen back on the expedient of the date of publication or of the preface of the first edition of the work as the nearest possible approximation. These cases are denoted by a (*c*) after the traveller's name.

It might be said that I should have included maps in my book. I believe that if there is anything worse than having no maps, it is having maps which do not show what is wanted. Some itineraries are interesting in their local detail, and to provide maps for them I should have had to emulate Murray's or Baedeker's handbooks. I have preferred to refer the reader to these.

Perhaps I should say a word about how my book is constructed. The first part is a chronological section in which the travellers are arranged year by year, and alphabetically within each year. I have purposely omitted the day and the month (when known), for if the reader requires detail to this extent he must be referred to the original source. This he will find in the third, alphabetical and bibliographical section. The references are there given, and also in dark type the years of the travels, which will enable the reader to find his traveller's itinerary and an anecdote or quotation in the chronological section. In the second, or topographical, section, I have simply selected some two dozen places and enumerated their visitors under the years of their visits, which enables the reader to refer both to the chronological and alphabetical sections.

It will be seen that the travellers cover practically every walk of life. They include writers, poets, historians, and philosophers, artists and composers, scientists, divines, crowned heads, soldiers and politicians, revolutionaries and refugees, charlatans and scoundrels, and simple ordinary people. They come from Switzerland, England, America, France, Belgium, the Netherlands, Germany, Italy, Spain, Denmark, Sweden, Russia, South Africa, India, and Japan. A surprising number of travellers published their impressions anonymously and I have had, so to speak, to identify the anonymous with numbers.

It can also be seen how places now well known came gradually to be included in an itinerary, such as Grindelwald, Chamonix, Zermatt, and Eggishorn. Others like Einsiedeln have dropped out. It is also possible to see how itineraries themselves have developed. While journeys in Switzerland were at first merely passages through the country, the urge for scientific and philosophical observations, and the spread of the romantic movement, soon led to intricate circuitous tours, like those of J. J. Scheuchzer, William Coxe, Wordsworth, or Baron de Frenilly. The methods of travel available have also played their part in the shaping of itineraries. These could be extensive and complicated when the traveller went on foot, while they have tended to become simpler when he relied on railways to take him to selected places. These places then became centres.

The travels also reflect major events of European history, and the post-war rushes can be seen after the Seven Years War in 1764, the Wars of the French Revolution in 1802, and the Napoleonic Wars in 1814 and 1815.

I have no doubt that many interesting travellers and journeys have been omitted, and I hope so, for otherwise a great source of my enjoyment will have dried up. At all events I trust that my book contains enough, and that the population of travellers in Switzerland which I have revived is sufficiently dense, to help and encourage any persons who may have or find manuscripts of Travels in Switzerland to edit them.

Now that I have no more time for this play and have closed my lists, I find that the uses of my work are wider than I had originally imagined. When Dr. J. Monroe Thorington suggested to me that I should turn my attention to unveiling the anonymity of the four Englishmen who were reported to have made an attempt on Mont Blanc and had an accident in 1792, I turned to my Topographical Section; and, looking at the entries under 'Chamonix 1792' and the cross-references to the chronological section, I immediately found that Thomas Whaley was the leader of the wanted party. This was the sort of thing for which I expected my work to be useful, and it was. But in addition to this purely objective research, there is another use to which it can be put. This follows from the canalization imposed on ordinary travellers by the paths through and passes over the Alps and Jura. It is possible to stand within a few feet of where Wordsworth was when he first saw Mont Blanc, or where Mr. Hilaire Belloc stood when he first descried the whole range of the Alps, or to stay in the inns where Goethe stayed, or to follow on the ground the routes of the armies led by the Duc de Rohan, General Lecourbe, or Marshal Suvorof. Examples such as these could be prolonged indefinitely, and such topographical contacts with the past have given me an insight into the works and deeds of predecessors which I feel is closer than ordinary study and could not be obtained in any other way.

Switzerland has played a large part in the development of ideas associated with the romantic movement, one of the origins of which may be attributed to Albrecht von Haller's journey of 1728 and to the poem, *Die Alpen*, to which it inspired him. Students of the romantic movement could do worse than to retrace the steps of his tour; and countless others suggest themselves. Admirers of Wagner will find that the sound of the alp-horn on the Rigi at sunrise was his source of inspiration for the cor anglais tune which the herdsman plays in the third act of *Tristan and Isolde*. I have in my *Escape to Switzerland* suggested the possibility that the silhouette of the

Bernese Oberland may have influenced Brahms in his composition of the Double Concerto. Nietzsche had one of his major thoughts near the source of the Inn, and Sénancour drew his inspiration wholesale from Bex and the Dent du Midi. I like to think of future students going to travel agencies and booking for a 'Jean-Jacques Rousseau 1754', or a 'Shelley 1814'.

Scientists can also benefit from visiting the scenes of the labours of their predecessors. The late Dr. R. T. Gunther once told me that it was quite easy to understand why William Coys was the first English botanist to distinguish the ordinary elm from the wych elm, for on visiting the house where Coys had lived he found magnificent specimens of each species standing immediately in front of it. The Mer de Glace was the glacier most assiduously studied by de Saussure, and by looking at it now it can be seen how he was misled to an erroneous interpretation of the method of origin of median moraines. For as that glacier rounds the foot of the Aiguille du Dru, all its median moraines are deflected to its right-hand side, and give the impression of an almost continuous mass of rubble edging out from the border on that side.

Marshal von Moltke once said that of former battles only the battlefield remains. This is, of course, not true; in addition to the field there is the tradition of the warriors. Indeed, some warriors like William Tell are very real and potent forces to-day in spite of the possibility that they may never have lived at all. However this may be, if military historians visit battlefields to advance their science, other and more peaceful studies may surely derive advantage from an application of the same method of pilgrimage. It is not new, for in the eighteenth century visitors flocked to the scenes of Rousseau's characters in *La Nouvelle Héloïse*; Matthew Arnold devoted himself similarly to a literary pilgrimage to the haunts of Sénancour's *Obermann*.

Lastly I find that I have provided myself with one answer to a question which has long puzzled me: why are people so fond of Switzerland? Clearly it cannot be for a single reason, but for many. There are, of course, its accessibility to all nations of Europe in normal times, the sterling qualities of its inhabitants, the striking nature of the scenery, the association of the Alps with pleasurable activities, recovery of health, holidays from work, walking, climbing, and ski-ing.

I believe that an additional reason why people are so fond of Switzerland is because so many people have been so fond of Switzerland, and that it is the human interest of past events, thoughts, and deeds in particular places which produces a subsequent attraction to those places. The recognition of this idea appears in the works of many writers. I may cite Byron's Sonnet:

Rousseau—Voltaire—our Gibbon—and de Staël—
  Leman! these names are worthy of thy shore,
  Thy shore of names like these, wert thou no more,
Their memory thy remembrance would recall:
To them thy banks were lovely as to all,
  But they have made them lovelier, for the lore
  Of mighty minds doth hallow in the core
Of human hearts the ruin of a wall
  Where dwelt the wise and wondrous; but by *thee*
How much more, Lake of Beauty! do we feel,
  In sweetly gliding o'er thy crystal sea,
The wild glow of that not ungentle zeal,
  Which of the heirs of immortality
Is proud, and makes the breath of glory real!

Logan Pearsall Smith has drawn attention to the effect produced on Stendhal when, in Napoleon's army, he passed through Clarens and the scenes of *La Nouvelle Héloïse*; 'the sound of church-bells, descending from the mountain, mingled with his thoughts of Clarens and gave him a moment of divine felicity which was of itself enough, he said, to render life worth living, and which, he wrote long after, was the nearest approach to perfect happiness, to *le bonheur parfait*, that he had ever known'.

Similar expressions are to be found in the writings of Matthew Arnold, John Addington Symonds, John Ruskin, Sainte-Beuve, Jules Michelet, Leslie Stephen, and Frederic Harrison from whom I should like to quote a passage:

There is hardly a spot round this most poetic and historic corner of Europe, this Lake Leman and its neighbouring valleys and mountains, but what recalls to us some line of poetry, some passage of romance, a great literary triumph, a memorable conflict, an illustrious career, an heroic death. Poets made the charm of Greece. But poets, romancers, dramatists, moralists, historians, theologians, artists—all combine to give a special halo of romance to the Alps and the Alpine world at large. Byron, Rousseau, Voltaire, Gibbon, Shelley, Coleridge, Turner, Ruskin, Schiller, Manzoni, Scott—have all stamped on the mind of Europe their special ideas of this region.

Lastly, to quote once more from Logan Pearsall Smith:

Strange, as another sentimental pilgrim, Henry James, has expressed it, strange and special the effect of the empty places we stand and wonder in to-day for the sake of these vanished people; 'the irresistible reconstruction, to the all but baffled vision, of irrevocable presences and aspects, the conscious, mocking void, sad somehow with excess of serenity'.

It is as if the places themselves had become impregnated with some relic of the life, emotions, and thoughts of their former visitors. This relic, provided only it be known, makes its appeal to those interested in life and lives. Many are not susceptible to it. But enough have enjoyed it to establish a fashion and create a general feeling which infects others. I hope that my book will enable more to succumb to the epidemic, simply by letting them know the names of a few interesting people who were where they are before them.

G. R. de B.

November 1948

CHRONOLOGICAL SECTION

Itineraries and Anecdotes of Travellers

941

WILLA OF IVREA. BELLINZONA, MESOCCO, SAN BERNARDINO PASS, THUSIS, COIRE

Liudprand wrote: 'The woman was with child and near her confinement when she crossed the San Bernardino pass, and I cannot marvel enough that she succeeded in going on foot by a way so rough and impassable.'

972

MAYOL, SAINT. AOSTA, GRAND ST. BERNARD PASS, ORSIÈRES

On his way back from Rome, the Abbot of Cluny was kidnapped by the Saracens while crossing the bridge at Orsières, and held to ransom.

990

SIGERIC OF CANTERBURY. AOSTA, GRAND ST. BERNARD PASS, MARTIGNY, LAUSANNE, YVERDON, VALLORBE, JOUGNE

1125

BERNARD OF CLAIRVAUX, SAINT. GENEVA

Although the great saint once said 'do not the mountains drop sweetness, and the hills flow with milk and honey?', after spending a day in riding along the shore of the lake of Geneva his companions spoke about 'the lake', to which he replied 'what lake?'

1128

RUDOLF DE ST. TROND. AOSTA, GRAND ST. BERNARD PASS, MARTIGNY

One priest was not sufficient to hear the confessions of the travellers, so numerous were they although it was early January.

1151

SEEMUNDARSON, NICHOLAS. BASLE, SOLEURE, AVENCHES, VEVEY, MARTIGNY, GRAND ST. BERNARD PASS, AOSTA

1176

PHILIP OF COLOGNE. CONSTANCE, COIRE, DISENTIS, LUKMANIER PASS, BELLINZONA, COMO

1188

JOHN DE BREMBLE. MARTIGNY, GRAND ST. BERNARD PASS, AOSTA

'Pardon me for not writing. I have been on the mount of Jove; on the one hand looking up to the heavens of the mountains, on the other shuddering at the hell of the valleys, feeling myself so much nearer heaven that I was more sure that my prayer would be heard. "Lord", I said, "restore me to my brethren, that I may tell them, that they come not to this place of torment . . .".'

1231

BONIFACE OF BRUSSELS. BASLE, LAUSANNE, MARTIGNY, GRAND ST. BERNARD PASS, AOSTA

1236

ALBERT DE STADE. LUGANO, BELLINZONA, ST. GOTTHARD PASS, ALTDORF, LUCERNE, ZOFINGEN, BASLE

'When thou reachest Basle, be kind to thy feet, and take ship.'

1254

ODO OF ROUEN. VALLORBE, LAUSANNE, MARTIGNY, SION, BRIG, SIMPLON PASS, DOMODOSSOLA

1331

CHARLES IV, EMPEROR. LAUSANNE, MARTIGNY, SION, BRIG, SIMPLON PASS, DOMODOSSOLA

1356

PETRARCA, FRANCESCO. MILAN, ? ST. GOTTHARD PASS, BASLE

'Who would have told me that I who, when young, had seen the Rhine where it is old from the length of its course, should now that I am old see it near its source where it is young? Whereas when my life had run half its course I saw that river where its tired waters divide into two, now, in my declining years, I shall see it again at the roots of the mountains from which it gushes and grows as it goes on its way.'

1402

ADAM OF USK. BASLE, BERNE, LUCERNE, ALTDORF, ST. GOTTHARD PASS, BELLINZONA, LUGANO, COMO

He passed through 'Basle, Berne, Lucerne and its wonderful lake, Mount St. Gotthard and the hermitage on its summit, where I was drawn in an ox-waggon half dead with cold and with mine eyes blindfold lest I should see the dangers of the pass; on the eve of Palm Sunday I arrived at Bellinzona' . . .

1432

PIUS II, POPE (AENEAS SYLVIUS PICCOLOMINI). MILAN, BELLINZONA, ST. GOTTHARD PASS, ALTDORF, LUCERNE, BASLE

'By way of the St. Gotthard Alps, steep mountains towering to the skies and covered deep with snow and ice.'

1435

PIUS II, POPE (AENEAS SYLVIUS PICCOLOMINI). AOSTA, GRAND ST. BERNARD PASS, MARTIGNY, THONON, RIPAILLE

1438

TAFUR, PERO. MILAN, BELLINZONA, ST. GOTTHARD PASS, ALTDORF, LUCERNE, BASLE

Seated on a rough sledge of trees 'like a Castilian threshing machine', drawn by oxen and followed by his horse which he led by the reins, he was comforted by the fact that if anything went over the edge it would be the oxen, and he would be safe.

1460

EPTINGEN, HANS BERNHARD VON. COMO, LUGANO, BELLINZONA, AIROLO, ST. GOTTHARD PASS, HOSPENTHAL, FLUELEN, BRUNNEN, SCHWYZ, EINSIEDELN, ZUG, CHAM, MÜNSTER, ZOFINGEN, PRATTELEN, BASLE

1462

WEY, WILLIAM. BASLE, RHEINFELDEN, SCHAFFHAUSEN, CONSTANCE, ARBON, RHEINECK

1468

PIATTI, PIATTINO. MILAN, BELLINZONA, ST. GOTTHARD PASS, LUCERNE

'Relying on thy piety, we began to place faith in our cattle and were drawn over the high pass in a bullock-cart' (Prayer to Holy St. Gotthard).

1481

GÜGLINGEN, PAUL WALTHER VON. BASLE, LUCERNE, FLUELEN, WASSEN, HOSPENTHAL, ST. GOTTHARD PASS, AIROLO, BELLINZONA, LUGANO, COMO

1492

ANONYMOUS I. CONSTANCE, FELDKIRCH, MAIENFELD, COIRE, LENZERHEIDE, TIEFENKASTEL, BIVIO, SEPTIMER PASS, CHIAVENNA

DÜRER, ALBRECHT. CONSTANCE, SCHAFFHAUSEN, SCHWYZ, LUCERNE, BASLE

Dürer's itinerary is deduced partly from documents, and partly by identification of the landscapes that form the background to many of his paintings. That in the portrait of Hans Tucher suggests the Mythen, behind Schwyz.

1494

MÜNZER, JEROME. CONSTANCE, ZURICH, EINSIEDELN, BADEN, SOLEURE, BERNE, MORAT, FRIBOURG, LAUSANNE

Eighteen years after the battle of Morat, Münzer was appalled at the pile of bones, which were still being washed up by the lake.

1504

PELLIKAN, KONRAD. LUCERNE, SCHWYZ, ALTDORF, ST. GOTTHARD PASS, BELLINZONA, LOCARNO, ST. GOTTHARD PASS, ALTDORF, SISIKON, FROHNALP, MORSCHACH, LUCERNE, BADEN, BASLE

1507

MACHIAVELLI, NICCOLO. GENEVA, FRIBOURG, LUCERNE, MELLINGEN, SCHAFFHAUSEN, CONSTANCE

'Between Geneva and Constance I put up four times in the lands of the Swiss and during the journey I gathered intelligence of their condition and quality with what diligence I possess.'

1508

PLATTER, THOMAS (*c*). GRÄCHEN, STALDEN, VISP, OBERGESTELEN, GRIMSEL PASS, MEIRINGEN, LUCERNE, BASLE

1509

ERASMUS OF ROTTERDAM. CHIAVENNA, SPLÜGEN PASS, THUSIS, COIRE, CONSTANCE

During this journey he thought out his 'Praise of Folly'.

1514

PLATTER, THOMAS (*c*). GRÄCHEN, STALDEN, VISP, KIPPEL, LÖTSCHEN PASS, KANDERSTEG, ENTLIBUCH, ZURICH

'When now I went away with my two brothers and crossed over the Lötschen mountains towards Gastern, my two brothers sat down on the slope of the snow and slid down the mountain. I also wished to do this, and as I did not quickly put my feet apart, the snow threw me over, so that I fell down the mountain, head over heels. It would have been no wonder if I had slid to my death, by striking my head on a tree, for there were no rocks. This happened to me three times, so that I shot down the comb of the ridge head foremost and the snow fell in heaps on my face.'

1515

PACE, SIR RICHARD. CONSTANCE, ZURICH, LUCERNE

'To whomsoever the Swiss incline, he is like in time to be lord of all . . . undoubtedly, if I had brought money with me, the King's grace, and none other, had had the Swiss surely.'

1517

HOLBEIN, HANS. BASLE, LUCERNE, ALTDORF

One of Holbein's drawings of the Virgin and Child has, as a background, a landscape which is unmistakably taken from Lucerne with its lake, covered bridges, walls, and towers.

1518

WATT, JOACHIM VON. LUCERNE, PILATUS

'The shepherd who acted as our guide made us promise on oath that we would not throw anything into the lake nor do any rash thing, for, he assured us, he was answerable with his life, and he persisted in repeated recommendations to us to observe modesty and silence, as if he were leading us to a holy place.'

1522

ERASMUS OF ROTTERDAM. BASLE, SCHAFFHAUSEN, CONSTANCE, BASLE

'The situation of the place itself is pleasing. Hard by is the wonderfully beautiful lake of Constance, stretching many miles in either direction and always lovely. The wooded mountains showing themselves everywhere, some afar, others near by, add charm to the scene. For there the Rhine, as though wearied with his journey through the rough and rugged Alps, refreshes himself as it were in a pleasant inn, and, slipping softly through the middle of the lake, recovers at Constance his channel and his name together, for the lake prefers to owe its name to the city. . . . The Alps smiling down upon me close at hand beckoned me on. My friends dissuaded me, but they would have done so in vain, if the gravel, that potent orator, had not persuaded me to go back to Basel and fly up into my nest again.'

1524

PLATTER, THOMAS (*c*). BASLE, SCHAFFHAUSEN, CONSTANCE, ST. GALL, RAPPERSWIL, SCHWYZ, ALTDORF, ANDERMATT, REALP, ALTDORF, BECKENRIED, BRUNIG PASS, MEIRINGEN, GRIMSEL PASS, OBERGESTELEN, VISP, GRÄCHEN

With his friend Heinrich Billing, Platter was making a tour of Switzerland. They reached Realp and proposed crossing the Furka pass, but, 'when Heinrich saw the mountain, he was so afraid in the night that he was doubtful whether he wished to go over the mountain on the morrow'. So they went back, and 'we came again to Uri and went on the lake; then came a wind, so that Heinrich was very much terrified, and said to the boatman: "row to the land, I will not travel further." He said "there is no danger". But he behaved so troublesomely that he had to row to the land not far from the place where William Tell sprang out of the boat.'

TSCHUDI, AEGIDIUS. GRAND ST. BERNARD PASS, ST. THEODUL PASS, FURKA PASS, ST. GOTTHARD PASS, OBERALP PASS, LUKMANIER PASS, SAN BERNARDINO PASS, SPLÜGEN PASS, SEPTIMER PASS

'I wandered over many Alpine passes, . . . and visited the places on each side of them. . . . Those who journey in spring through the Valpelline to the Great St. Bernard are usually forbidden to let off musket-shots or to give loud cries or song, lest by the sound the snow slide down and harm men and goods on the road; this I experienced myself in the year of Grace 1524 when I travelled that way.'

1532

PLATTER, THOMAS. ZURICH, LUCERNE, BRUNIG PASS, MEIRINGEN, GRIMSEL PASS, OBERGESTELEN, VISP, GRÄCHEN

On the way up the Grimsel pass 'it began to dawn upon my wife that it would go roughly, for we were compelled to eat very coarse bread. There were also some men who wished to cross the mountain on the next day who spoke to me: "You dare not take the woman over the mountain." There my wife had good living. She must needs lie in the straw to which she was not accustomed. On the next day we arose and God helped us over the mountain, although her clothing was frozen to her body.'

1535

PARACELSUS, PHILIP VON HOHENHEIM. TIRANO, BERNINA PASS, ST. MORITZ, PFÄFERS

'Of all the mineral springs in Europe known to me, I give preference to that which I found at St. Moritz, the water of which is in August as acid as vinegar. He who takes this water medicinally regains his health, and will never be troubled by stone or gravel, gout or arthritis. It strengthens the stomach so that it can digest tartar even as an ostrich digests iron and a blackbird sand. And not only tartar but everything else in food and drink which might bring about a disorder.'

1536

RHELLICANUS, JOHANNES MÜLLER. BERNE, ERLENBACH, STOCKHORN, ERLENBACH, BERNE

'We reached the summit of the Stockhorn. From there, to the east, marshes, lakes, the impetuous course of the Simme and of the Aare, towns, plains and green pastures, strike the eye; while on the side where Phoebus bathes his horses in the waters of the west, we see innumerable mountains, like the waves of a huge sea. Our eyes are satiated, but our stomachs cry out. . . .'

1537

CELLINI, BENVENUTO. TIRANO, BERNINA PASS, PONTE, ALBULA PASS, COIRE, WALLENSTADT, WESEN, ZURICH, SOLEURE, LAUSANNE, GENEVA—GENEVA, MARTIGNY, SION, BRIG, SIMPLON PASS, DOMODOSSOLA

The Bernina and Albula, still under the snow, were crossed 'at the utmost hazard of their lives'. At Wallenstadt, 'when I saw the barks I was terribly frightened, because they were made of deal boards, neither well nailed together nor even pitched; and if I had not seen four German gentlemen, with their horses, in one of them I should never have ventured on board, but have turned back directly.'

1541

RABELAIS, FRANÇOIS (*c*). GENEVA, BERNE, THUN, SION

'Quand la neige est sus les montaignes, la fouldre, l'esclair, les lancis, le maulubec, le rouge grenat, le tonnoire, la tempeste, tous les diables sont par les vallées. En veulx-tu veoir l'expérience? Va on pays de Souisse et consydère le lac de Wunderberlich, à quatre lieues de Berne, tirant vers Sion.'

TURNER, WILLIAM. CHIAVENNA, SPLÜGEN PASS, THUSIS, COIRE, WALLENSTADT, ZURICH, BASLE

1542

MAROT, CLÉMENT. GENEVA

'Amour de prendre auec femmes esbatz
Pour y iouster sans selle ne sans baz
T'auroit-il fait habiter à Genèue?
Je croy que non, car Venus y a tresue,
Et n'ose plus user de priuaulté . . .'

(MALINGRE)

1544

STUMPF, JOHANN. ZURICH, LUCERNE, ENGELBERG, JOCH PASS, INNERTKIRCHEN, GRIMSEL PASS, OBERGESTELEN, BRIG, SION, MARTIGNY, LAUSANNE, FRIBOURG, BERNE, ZOFINGEN

The red wine that he was given near Sion was 'so dark and thick that you could write with it'.

1545

FRIES, HANS. ZURICH, WESEN, COIRE, THUSIS, SPLÜGEN PASS, CHIAVENNA

The earliest recorded journey through the Alps undertaken expressly for fun. At Campo Dolcino, Fries and his friends had to sleep in a fowl-house; at another place there was only one bed for all six of them.

1546

MÜNSTER, SEBASTIAN. BASLE, LAUSANNE, MARTIGNY, SION, LEUK, GEMMI PASS, LEUK, BRIG, FURKA PASS, ANDERMATT

The Gemmi path 'goes up in the form of a snailshell or screw with continual turns and bends to right and left; it is a narrow path and dangerous, especially to drunkards and persons who are subject to giddiness, for whichever way the eye looks, there are only precipices and deep sheer drops, so that even those whose heads are steady cannot regard them without horror. . . . This I know full well, for I climbed the mountain from Leukerbad to inspect it, and quaked to my very heart and bones.'

1549

VERGERIO, PIERPAOLO. TIRANO, POSCHIAVO, BERNINA PASS, PONTRESINA, MALOJA PASS, CASACCIA, VICOSOPRANO

'He lodged a night at Pontresina, a town situate on the northern base of Mount Bernina. It happened that the parish priest had died that day, and the inhabitants assembled in the evening at the inn to converse with the landlord, who was judge of the village, about choosing a successor. After engaging their attention by conversing on the subject which had called them together, Vergerio asked them if they would not hear a sermon from him. The greater part objecting to this, "Come", said the judge, "let us hear what this new-come Italian will say." So highly gratified were the people with his sermon that they insisted on his preaching to them again before his departure. Accordingly he did preach . . . with such effect that the inhabitants soon after agreed harmoniously in abolishing the mass and giving a call to a protestant minister.'

1550

LEMNIUS, SIMON (*c*). PFÄFERS, SARGANS, WALLENSTADT, ZURICH, BADEN, BRUGG, SÄCKINGEN, BASLE

1552

CARDANO, GERONIMO. DOMODOSSOLA, SIMPLON PASS, BRIG, SION, MARTIGNY, VILLENEUVE, GENEVA—BASLE, BERNE, COIRE, CHIAVENNA

The celebrated doctor's journey to Edinburgh to treat the Archbishop of St. Andrews.

LAMBIN, DENYS. EDOLO, APRICA PASS, TIRANO, BERNINA PASS, COIRE, ZURICH, BADEN, LAUSANNE, GENEVA

'Depuis mon départ de Padoue, j'ai tout le temps été en voyage! Difficile, pénible, affligeant, surtout dans le temps où nous avons trainé dans les rochers et les montagnes de la Rhétie.'

PLATTER, FELIX. BASLE, SOLEURE, FRIBOURG, LAUSANNE, GENEVA

At an inn at Messières, near Fribourg, he and his companions had to barricade themselves in, sword in hand, and to get away in the middle of the night to escape from bandits.

1553

BALE, JOHN. BASLE, ZURICH, GENEVA

'I must mention what Zurich has done for us Englishmen. When I was with you and enjoyed your hospitality, Bullinger, and the good wishes of others, I saw with what love you took unto yourselves those of us who were and are with you.'

DU BELLAY, JEAN, CARDINAL. GENEVA, SOLEURE, WIEDLISBACH, ZURICH, COIRE, CHIAVENNA

1554

KNOX, JOHN. GENEVA, ZURICH

'Travelled through all the congregations of Helvetia and reasoned with all the pastors and many other excellently learned men.'

1555

GESNER, CONRAD. LUCERNE, PILATUS

'We are of opinion that journeys in the Alps, undertaken with friends, provide pleasures and enjoyment of every kind to each of the senses, provided that there be no disturbance in the temperature of the air, nor in the state of body or mind, for these excursions are not designed for a sick man nor for a debilitated constitution.'

1556

MAGNY, OLIVIER DE. EDOLO, APRICA PASS, TIRANO, BERNINA PASS, PONTRESINA, ALBULA PASS, COIRE

'J'aimeroy mieux avoir sur mer un grand oraige,
Trente jours tout de reng en danger de naufraige,
Mais que de ce danger n'advinsent les effects:

Que passer aux Grisons la Vrigue et la Berline,
Le pont de Camogasc, et le pont Arrasine,
Avecques leurs marrons et leurs poiles infectz.'

1557

BRANTÔME, PIERRE DE BOURDEILLE DE. GENEVA, COIRE

'. . . à Genève la première fois que je fus en Italie, parceque pour lors ce chemin par là estoit commun pour les François, et par les Suisses et Grisons, à cause des guerres.'

DU BELLAY, JOACHIM. COMO, COIRE, GENEVA

> 'Ilz ont force beaux lacs et force sources d'eau,
> Force prez, force bois. J'ai du reste (Belleau)
> Perdu le souvenir, tant ilz me firent boire. . . .'

MARTI, BENEDIKT. BERNE, STOCKHORN, ERLENBACH, NIESEN

'I noticed the following inscription in Greek, carved by a scholar who had succumbed to the charm of mountains: "Love of mountains is best." I think that it would be difficult to find a mountain as charming as this one [Niesen], not only on account of the view which extends in all directions, but also because of the diversified flora which is so abundant.'

1559

BRUSCHIUS, GASPAR (*c*). ZURICH, BADEN, WINDISCH, HABSBURG, KÖNIGSFELD, BRUGG, SCHAFFHAUSEN, CONSTANCE

'Saw many worthy objects, rocks, houses, castles, rivers, churches and lakes, with a joyful heart. . . . This famous region of Switzerland is a match for all others, even if you consider the resources of the whole world.'

FABRICIUS, JOHANN. COIRE, CALANDA

'I wish, my dear Gesner, that you had been with us for an hour or two; we all of us said the same.'

1561

GESNER, CONRAD. ZURICH, COIRE, THUSIS, ALBULA PASS, SCHULS, STA. MARIA, UMBRAIL PASS, BORMIO

1562

PLATTER, FELIX. BASLE, THUN, ZWEISIMMEN, LENK, RAWYL PASS, SION, LEUKERBAD, VISP, GRÄCHEN

1563

BAUHIN, JOHANN. BASLE, NEUCHATEL, CREUX DU VAN, MONT SUCHET, THOIRY, GENEVA, SALÈVE

1564

SMITH, RICHARD. COMO, LUGANO, BELLINZONA, ST. GOTTHARD PASS, ALTDORF, LUCERNE, BASLE

'This mountaine is from the fote to the topp 2 leages and very stepe the way narow stony and dangerous snow lyenge uppon the mountaine both winter and somer / uppon the top of this hil is an osterye / al our way unto this mountaine the hills ar very full off chestnutt tres and very abundant of chestnuts / but this mountaine bereth nothinge but snow and stones / we ffound extrem cold uppon this hill / we decended this hill still untill we came to a littel towne called olsera [Andermatt] from there rode an enlyshe myle plaine ground and descended agen / from olsera aboute ii enlyshe myles is a brydge which is called ponte inferno / it standeth in a straite betwene the mountaines the beginninnge of the ryver of rehin cometh from mount godard and at this brydge hath such a fale amonge the huge stones that is merveylous.'

1566

PENNY, THOMAS. ZURICH, WÄGGITAL, BOCKMÄTTLI, MORAT, GENEVA, SALÈVE

1573

RAUWOLFF, LEONHART. FELDKIRCH, MAIENFELD, COIRE, THUSIS, SPLÜGEN PASS, CHIAVENNA, COMO

1575

CHYTRAEUS, NATHAN (*c*). COMO, LUGANO, BELLINZONA, MESOCCO, SAN BERNARDINO PASS, THUSIS, COIRE, ZURICH, BASLE

'. . . Narrow and sinuous is the road yonder, and from the rocks all around deep snow threatens to fall. Just as a flying bird, however light, imparts motion to a twig, so the snow, falling as a great compacted mass violently tears out the mountain-ash from the heights and wrenches off all in its path. Great is the din, and this causes a new mass of snow to become detached, which follows and makes for the depths in a swift whirlwind. Just as the heavens tumble, so the mountain roars back in reply. Luckless is he who is obliged to take the road at such a time, and to cross the awe-sounding Alps. Neither home nor friends will he see again. I avoided these dangers, however, with God's guidance. . . .'

1577

BAUHIN, CASPAR. BASLE, ZURICH, RAGAZ, PFÄFERS, COIRE, THUSIS, SPLÜGEN PASS, CHIAVENNA

1580

MONTAIGNE, MICHEL DE. BASLE, BADEN, SCHAFFHAUSEN, CONSTANCE

'Eus ne ferment guiere les vitres mesmes la nuit.'

1586

LINDEBERG, PETER (*c*). COMO, BELLINZONA, MESOCCO, SAN BERNARDINO PASS, THUSIS, COIRE, PFÄFERS, WALLENSTADT, ZURICH, BADEN, BASLE

'. . . Sleepless, we tire with our weary feet at some distance from great Mount San Bernardino, its peaks surrounded by the highest vaults of heaven, congealed with cold and covered with white frost which neither the course of fiery Apollo, nor high summer, nor the burning Dog-star can touch, but only cold and the Boreal wind. . . .'

1587

RYFF, ANDREAS. BASLE, LUCERNE, ALTDORF, ST. GOTTHARD PASS, BELLINZONA, LUGANO

'No man who comes round the corner of the rock and has to cross this high narrow bridge, if he has not seen it before, is man enough not to be terrified and somewhat upset, particularly as there is no other way round.'

1589

THOU, JACQUES AUGUSTE DE. TIRANO, POSCHIAVO, BERNINA PASS, PONTE, ALBULA PASS, COIRE, WALLENSTADT, ZURICH, SOLEURE, BASLE

Walensee: 'La barque n'était que de sapin; le patron y avait reçu très-imprudemment un allemand avec son cheval; cet animal, effrayé par le choc des ondes et s'abattant à tout moment des jambes de derrière risquait d'autant plus de chavirer le bâtiment, que la pluie et le vent ne faisaient qu'augmenter. . . .'

1591

RYFF, ANDREAS. BASLE, THUN, KANDERSTEG, GEMMI PASS, LEUK

1592

MORYSON, FYNES. CONSTANCE, SCHAFFHAUSEN, EGLISAU, ZURICH, BASLE

'The other day after dinner by your advice, I took my journey on foot, and with more sighes than paces, came in foure houres with much paine to the little city Eglisaw, and coming to the Inne, they offered me meat, but I did nothing but so crie out for my bed, as you would have said I was the eldest sonne of sloth.'

1593

MAXIMILIAN, DUKE OF BAVARIA. MILAN, BELLINZONA, ST. GOTTHARD PASS, FLUELEN, LUCERNE, ZURICH, BASLE

'Crossed the St. Gotthard pass under great danger, the peasants having been called up in groups to shovel away the snow that blocked the way.'

WOTTON, SIR HENRY. CHIAVENNA, SPLÜGEN PASS, THUSIS, COIRE, BERNE, GENEVA

'I took my course through the Grisons to Geneva, leaving a discreet country in my opinion too soon.'

1595

MORYSON, FYNES. TIRANO, BERNINA PASS, PONTE, ALBULA PASS, LENZERHEIDE, COIRE, WALLENSTADT, ZURICH, SOLEURE, MORAT, LAUSANNE, GENEVA, LAUSANNE, MORAT, BERNE, SOLEURE, BASLE

'I passed all alone, not so much as accompanied with a footeman, over the high Alpes, which I think very few have done besides myself.'

1597

HENTZNER, PAUL. BASLE, CONSTANCE, ZURICH, SOLEURE, BERNE, NEUCHATEL, YVERDON, GENEVA

1598

LUDWIG, PRINCE OF ANHALT KÖHTEN. BASLE, LIESTAL, WALDENBURG, SOLEURE, BERNE, MORAT, LUCENS, LAUSANNE, NYON, GENEVA, LAUSANNE, ROMONT, FRIBOURG, BERNE, HUTTWIL, WILLISAU, MALTERS, LUCERNE, KNONAU, ZURICH, BADEN, SCHAFFHAUSEN, CONSTANCE

'Should have liked to stay longer in Berne.'

1599

HENTZNER, PAUL. BASLE, ZURICH, WESEN, COIRE, THUSIS, SPLÜGEN PASS, CHIAVENNA, SONDRIO, APRICA PASS, EDOLO

'When we had stayed a few days at Basle, partly to rest and partly to prepare ourselves for our journey to Italy, having at last invoked the name of God that by His great mercy He might deign to bless this most dangerous journey, we departed. . . .' Presently he came to 'Thusis where starts a road very difficult and most dangerous on account of its extreme narrowness between enormous rocks and continual bridges suspended high above cascades of the Rhine, crossing which it is impossible to avoid trembling with constant fear lest you be thrown into the depths; indeed it is scarcely possible to avoid being terrified with extreme horror at the noise of the Rhine roaring between the rocks far below. . . .'

ISABEL CLARA EUGENIA, INFANTA. PONTE TRESA, TAVERNE, BELLINZONA, ST. GOTTHARD PASS, ALTDORF, LUCERNE, BASLE

'One crosses a bridge which is called after the Devil with much reason, for in spite of being little more than twenty paces across, it is most dangerous to pass, for so great is the depth to the bottom that you can scarcely see the water although it falls over a rock with such a noise that you cannot hear yourself speak. . . . But in spite of all these things, I would not like to have missed seeing this country, for at the time that we saw it I doubt if there can be a greater thing in the world, nor any more worthy to be seen though not to live in because of its asperity.'

RYFF, ANDREAS. CHIAVENNA, SPLÜGEN PASS, HINTERRHEIN

Would rather go twice over the St. Gotthard than once over the wicked and troublesome Splügen pass.

1600

REBMANN, HANS RUDOLF (*c*). THUN, NIESEN, STOCKHORN

The 18,000-line poem which Rebmann wrote to describe the visit which the old Stockhorn paid on 8 August 1600 to his dear neighbour the Niesen, clad in all his finery and accompanied by his household and court, to attend a princely banquet, and the conversation between them, shows that Rebmann had visited some places himself, and that others such as the Faulhorn near Grindelwald, the Schilthorn, Obersteinberg, and Stufensteinalp near Lauterbrunnen, the Kiental, Adelboden, Diemtigtal, Lenk, and the Turbachtal, were already well-known and frequented.

1604

VIRUES, CRISTOBAL DE. MILAN, PONTE TRESA, BELLINZONA, FAIDO, ST. GOTTHARD PASS, FLUELEN, BREMGARTEN

'A divine spectacle.'

WOTTON, SIR HENRY. COIRE, THUSIS, SPLÜGEN PASS, CHIAVENNA

'An honest man sent abroad to lie for his country.'

1606

SALES, SAINT FRANÇOIS DE. ANNECY, BONNEVILLE, CHAMONIX

'J'ai vu ces jours passés des monts épouvantables tout couverts d'une glace épaisse de dix ou douze piques et les habitants des vallées voisines me dirent qu'un berger allant pour secourir une sienne vache tomba dans une fente de douze piques de haut, en laquelle il mourut glacé! O Dieu! dis-je, l'ardeur de ce berger était-elle si chaude à la queste de sa vache que cette glace ne l'ait point refroidie.'

1607

BENTIVOGLIO, CARDINAL. VARESE, BELLINZONA, ST. GOTTHARD PASS, ALTDORF, LUCERNE, BASLE

... 'Everything as far as here is Alps, rocks, crags and precipices; one mountain on another, and the St. Gotthard which raises the snows to the skies and made me taste winter in midsummer, on the top of all. ... The Alps are for the Swiss and, conversely, the Swiss are made for the Alps.'

1608

CORYAT, THOMAS. BERGAMO, PIAZZA BREMBANA, SAN MARCO PASS, MORBEGNO, CHIAVENNA, SPLÜGEN PASS, THUSIS, COIRE, WESEN, ZURICH, BADEN, BASLE

'The ways are very offensive to foote travellers. For they are pitched with very sharp and rough stones that will very much punish and grate a man's feete.'

1610

GRASSER, JOHANN JAKOB (*c*). BASLE, LAUFENBURG, ZURZACH, SCHAFFHAUSEN, STEIN, CONSTANCE, ST. GALL, ZURICH, BADEN, LUCERNE, SOLEURE, BERNE, MORAT, PAYERNE, FRIBOURG, LAUSANNE, GENEVA

'If you value the gifts of nature aright, even the frozen fields of the valleys and the savageness of the mountain passes have their delightfulness; in horror itself you will find something that pleases. ... The marble masses of the mountains rise up like walls and towers of many wonderful architectural structures. ... The defiles through the rocks, the tortuous mountain paths, the springs, the flow, now impetuous, now languid of the streams, the surface of the lakes, the colours of the meadows, the height of the trees, lastly the novel appearance of the earth and the sky on all sides, ravish the eye of the spectator and arrest his attention.'

1612

LESCARBOT, MARC. LAUSANNE, BERNE, FRIBOURG, THUN, LUCERNE, ZUG, GLARUS, ZURICH, ST. GALL, APPENZELL, COIRE, DISENTIS, OBERALP PASS, ANDERMATT, FURKA PASS, BRIG, SION, GENEVA, PORRENTRUY, BASLE

'Lucerne belle en soy et dedans son enclos,
Mais hideuse au deuant, aux côtés, et à dos,
Par le prochain aspect de ces Alpes chenuës,
Et des monts qui par tout tiennent ses auenuës . . . .'

OWEN, JOHN. GENEVA

'Genevese minister—thou would'st punish adultery with death?—I do not wonder at it!—Thou art in the right; for thy wife is beautiful.'

1613

LITHGOW, WILLIAM. BASLE, ORBE, GENEVA

'Glance, Glorious Geneve, Gospell-Guiding Gem;
Great God Governe Good Geneves Ghostly Game.'

1616

WOTTON, SIR HENRY. BASLE, LAUSANNE, THONON, CHAMBÉRY

'Infection hindered us to pass the nearest way to Chambéry, and forced us to put our horses and selves at hazard over the Leman Lake, and so to traverse Savoy, by such rocks and precipices as I think Hannibal did hardly exceed it when he made his way (as poets tell us) with fire and vinegar.'

1617

BUSINO, HORATIO. BERGAMO, PIAZZA BREMBANA, SAN MARCO PASS, MORBEGNO, CHIAVENNA, SPLÜGEN PASS, THUSIS, COIRE, WALLENSTADT, RAPPERSWIL, ZURICH, BADEN, BASLE

1620

BURSER, JOACHIM (*c*). BASLE, WASSERFALL, BADEN, LUCERNE, PILATUS, SCHWYZ, EINSIEDELN, SCHINDELLEGI, PFÄFERS, COIRE, DISENTIS, ST. GOTTHARD, SION, LEUKERBAD, GEMMI, ST. NIKLAUS, ST. THEODUL PASS, AOSTA, GRAND ST. BERNARD PASS, GENEVA

HAGENBACH, JOHANN JAKOB (*c*). INTERLAKEN, GRINDELWALD, LAUTERBRUNNEN

HUYGENS, CONSTANTIJN. SCHAFFHAUSEN, EGLISAU, ZURICH, RAPPERSWIL, SARGANS, COIRE, THUSIS, SPLÜGEN PASS, CHIAVENNA, MORBEGNO, SAN MARCO PASS, PIAZZA BREMBANA, VENICE, PIAZZA BREMBANA, SAN MARCO PASS, MORBEGNO, CHIAVENNA, SPLÜGEN PASS, THUSIS, COIRE, RAPPERSWIL, ZURICH, BADEN, BASLE

The party passed through the Valtelline three days before the massacre and noticed that all guards had been doubled in anticipation of trouble.

1621

HOWELL, JAMES. GENEVA

'Being so near the Lake of Geneva, curiosity would carry any one to see it.'

WARD, MARY. BASLE, LUCERNE, FLUELEN, ALTDORF, ST. GOTTHARD PASS, BELLINZONA, MILAN

'In her pilgrim's attire, with four companions, a maid, a priest, a gentleman and a serving-man, two horses, one to carry the baggage and another to ease who should be weary.'

1623

WOTTON, SIR HENRY. CHIAVENNA, SPLÜGEN PASS, THUSIS, COIRE, ZURICH, BASLE

'A miserable passage of the Alpes.'

1626

BELLI, FRANZESCO. COMO, LUGANO, BELLINZONA, ST. GOTTHARD PASS, ALTDORF, BRUNNEN, ZUG, BREMGARTEN, MELLINGEN, BRUGG, AARAU, RHEINFELDEN, BASLE

'The dangers in crossing this mountain are neither few nor small . . . some get themselves drawn across in a bullock cart, others wish to enjoy a ride on horseback. I, rejecting both these methods, considered that there was less risk in using my judgment and my feet than in trusting myself to the vagaries and accidents of an animal.'

1635

ROHAN, HENRI DUC DE. BASLE, AARAU, REGENSBURG, WINTERTHUR, ST. GALL, COIRE, THUSIS, SPLÜGEN PASS, CHIAVENNA, TIRANO, CHIAVENNA, MALOJA PASS, SCANFS, CASANNA PASS, LIVIGNO, FORCOLA DI LIVIGNO, POSCHIAVO, TIRANO, BORMIO, CHIAVENNA

'Lettre de M. le Cardinal de Richelieu à M. le duc de Rohan. Monsieur, je ne sçaurois assez vous témoigner le contentement que le Roi a eu de la victoire que vous avez remportée sur ses ennemis au pays où vous êtes. . . .'

1637

LASSELS, RICHARD (*c*). GENEVA, LAUSANNE, MORAT, SOLEURE, ZURICH, RAPPERSWIL, COIRE, BERNINA PASS, TIRANO

'Others, to auoid the snow of Berlino, are forced now and then (as I was once) to pass ouer the mountain Splug, which is hill enough for any traveller.'

1639

MILTON, JOHN. MILAN, ? SIMPLON PASS, BRIG, MARTIGNY, GENEVA

'Through Verona and Milan and the Pennine Alps and then by the Lake Leman I arrived at Geneva';

'Ah! what roaming whimsey drew my steps to a distance,
Over the rocks hung in air and the Alpine passes and glaciers.'

1641

BOYLE, THE HON. ROBERT. GENEVA, LAUSANNE, SOLEURE, ZURICH, COIRE, THUSIS, SPLÜGEN PASS, CHIAVENNA, PLURS, MORBEGNO, SAN MARCO PASS, PIAZZA BREMBANA, BERGAMO

'There is three wayes from hence [Geneva] into Italy by Sweetserland and ye Grisons, by Turin, and by Marseilles. The first is to peinefull because of ye great quantity of snow that couereth ye mountaines; ye second is to Dangerous because of ye armys that are both in piedmon and upon the state of Milan; the third is ye Longest indeed but ye sweetest. . . .'

1643

BRACKENHOFFER, ELIE. BASLE, OLTEN, AARAU, ZURICH, ALBIS, LUCERNE, SURSEE, ST. URBAN, SOLEURE, BERNE, MORAT, LAUSANNE, GENEVA, VOIRONS, GENEVA

'From Zurich we reached the great mountain Albis. It is a mountain very high and very steep. . . .'

1646

BRACKENHOFFER, ELIE. CONSTANCE, SCHAFFHAUSEN, ZURZACH, ZURICH, BASLE

EVELYN, JOHN. DOMODOSSOLA, SIMPLON PASS, BRIG, SION, MARTIGNY, BOUVERET, GENEVA

'Thro' almost unaccessible heights we came in prospect of Mons Sempronius, now Mount Sampion, which has on its sum'it a few huts and a chapell. . . . Arriv'd at our cold harbour (tho' the house had a stove in every roome) and supping on cheese and milk with wretched wine, we went to bed in cupbords so high from the floore that we climb'd them by a ladder; we were covered with feathers, that is we lay between two ticks stuff'd with them, and all little enough to keepe one warme.'

1647

RAYMOND, JOHN. DOMODOSSOLA, SIMPLON PASS, BRIG, SION, MARTIGNY, ST. MAURICE, BOUVERET, GENEVA

'Having with much paines, yet delight, because of the variety, crouded through some of the Alpes, wee came to dinner at *Sampion*, at the top of the Mountaine. . . .'

1650

HUYGENS, CONSTANTIJN, Jun. GENEVA, ROLLE, MORGES, YVERDON, PAYERNE, MORAT, BERNE, MORGES, GENEVA

Huygens visited the Canal d'Entreroche which his father had promoted.

1653

VINNE, VINCENT LAURENTSZ VAN DER. BASLE, BALSTHAL, WIEDLICHSBACH, BASLE, DELÉMONT, MOUTIER, BIENNE, YVERDON, COSSONAY, MORGES, GENEVA

With his companions, van der Vinne ran into the Peasants' War and was held captive by the peasant army at Wiedlichsbach and narrowly escaped execution at their hands, until allowed to return to Basle, whence they started out afresh by another route.

1654

DURY, JOHN. BASLE, ZURICH, AARAU, BERNE, BASLE, SCHAFFHAUSEN, ST. GALL, HERISAU, LAUSANNE, GENEVA, BERNE, AARAU

'Sir,—I am spoken to by the Lords of Zurich who are here [Aarau], to entreat you to help, by your letters to his highness, to second their request unto the Duke of Savoy, in behalf of the poor distressed Protestants of the Piedmont, who are commanded to be gone out of their native country (where they have lived so many hundred years), if they will not go to mass.'

1655

HACKAERT, JAN. BASLE, SCHAFFHAUSEN, ZURICH, GLARUS, COIRE, ILANZ, THUSIS, SPLÜGEN, ZILLIS, AVERS CRESTA, THUSIS, REICHENAU, ZURICH

1656

PELL, JOHN. GENEVA, BERNE, ZURICH

'Sought ways free from the danger of the popish soldiers, to which end I hired guides in the Country of Berne.' (Allusion to the Civil War.)

RERESBY, SIR JOHN. GENEVA, LAUSANNE, BERNE, SOLEURE, ZURICH, COIRE, BERGÜN, ALBULA PASS, PONTRESINA, TIRANO, APRICA PASS, EDOLO

'From Chur we had ten hours to Borgon, where we rather chose to lie upon benches than in nasty beds. . . . We came to our lodging at Pontrazin, a very mean one.'

1659

MORTOFT, FRANCIS. EDOLO, APRICA PASS, SONDRIO, CHIAVENNA, SPLÜGEN PASS, THUSIS, COIRE, RAPPERSWIL, ZURICH

'After dinner wee had 8 or 10 miles of extreame bad way, being constrained to goe up mountaines and Rockes even until night, and so lay at the foote of a greate Mountaine that seperates the country of the Valtolines from that of the Grisones. May the 1st, wee rose at 3 a clocke in the Morning to passe this most dangerous Mountaine, being about 7 howers before we could get to the topp of it, this Mountaine being counted by all 9 miles up to it, and as many before one can get to the bottom of it againe. The way here was very slippery and excessive cold, soe that being at the topp of it, the wind was so excessive and the snow so thicke, that it made one feele a great extreamity of cold, but by 12 a clocke wee gott of from this horrible mountaine.'

1660

LUDLOW, EDMUND. GENEVA.

'In the house where I lodged, the mistress being an English woman, I found good beer, which was a great refreshment to me, after the fatigue of my journey.'

1661

MANCINI, MARIE. GENEVA, MARTIGNY, SION, BRIG, SIMPLON PASS, DOMODOSSOLA

She was carried in a litter over the Simplon pass, during the crossing of which several members of her escort are said to have perished.

1662

LUDLOW, EDMUND. GENEVA, LAUSANNE, VEVEY

'Thinking it too hazardous to remain any longer at Geneva, I departed the next day, accompanied by a particular friend, for Lausanne, where we found Mr. Lisle and Mr. Cawley. . . . We had considerable addition to our company by the arrival of Mr. William Say, Colonel Bisco, Mr. Serjeant Dendy, Mr. Nicholas Love, Mr. Andrew Broughton, Mr. Slingsby Bethel, and Mr. Cornelius Holland at Lausanne.'

1663

BROWN, EDWARD. GENEVA, LAUSANNE, BERNE, ZURICH

'The city of Geneva is as pleasantly situated as its inhabitants can wish, surrounded by Mountains, which defend it from the East and West winds, and by which as they have many openings on the North and South, the Inhabitants are prevented from being incommoded with a thick and moist Air.'

RAY, JOHN. BASLE, BADEN, ZURICH, SCHAFFHAUSEN, CONSTANCE

Baden:—'the poor people put a Cheat upon strangers, bringing them to sell (as they pretend) *fossile Dice*, which they say, they dig out of the Earth naturally so figured and marked. But I am well assured, such as they brought us were artificial Dice, and if they dig'd them out of the Earth, they first buried them there themselves.'

SYDNEY, ALGERNON. VEVEY, BERNE

1665

LOCATELLI, SEBASTIANO. GENEVA, THONON, EVIAN, MARTIGNY, SION, BRIG, SIMPLON PASS, DOMODOSSOLA

RAY, JOHN. STA. MARIA, OFEN PASS, ZERNEZ, PONTE, ALBULA PASS, BERGÜN, COIRE, WALLENSTADT, GLARUS, EINSIEDELN, SCHWYZ, ALTDORF, STANS, LUCERNE, ZUG, ZURICH, AARAU, SOLEURE, BERNE, FRIBOURG, LAUSANNE, GENEVA, SALÈVE, RECULET, LA DOLE

The Swiss 'are so honest that one may travel their countrey with a bag of gold in his hand. . . . They would be troubled if we distrusted them so far as to take our portmanteau's into the lodging chambers and not leave them in the common dining-room.'

SCHELLINK, WILLEM. BASLE, SCHAFFHAUSEN, ZURICH, BADEN, LUCERNE, WILLISAU, BURGDORF, BERNE, SOLEURE, BALSTHAL, BASLE

1666

MURALT, JOHANN VON (*c*). BASLE, REIGOLDSWIL, WASSERFALL, SOLEURE, BERNE, SION, SARNEN, LUCERNE, PILATUS, ST. GOTTHARD PASS, LUKMANIER PASS, COIRE, PFÄFERS, APPENZELL, ST. GALL, CONSTANCE, SCHAFFHAUSEN, ZURICH, EGLISAU, BADEN, BASLE

'Not without forethought has a learned hand engraved in the rock of the highest summit of the Niesen, facing the Stockhorn in the so-called Andreas district of the puissant Lords of Berne, the words *ὁ τῶν ὀρῶν ἔρως ἄριστος* which is translated "Love of mountains most delights the heart". It is not otherwise, for joy and love of mountains grows nowhere higher and greater than where the plants show themselves in greatest splendour, luxuriance and multiplicity of kinds.'

1668

MAZARIN, HORTENSE MANCINI DUCHESSE DE. LES VERRIÈRES, NEUCHÂTEL, AARBURG, LUCERNE, ALTDORF, ST. GOTTHARD PASS, BELLINZONA, MILAN

'Passant par un village de Suisse où il y avait quelque garnison, nous faillimes d'être tous assommés, faute d'entendre la langue; et pour comble de bonne fortune, nous apprimes en arrivant à Altdorf, qu'il fallait y faire quarantaine avant que d'entrer dans l'état de Milan.'

MURALT, JOHANN VON. GRINDELWALD

1669

LE PAYS, RENÉ. CHAMONIX

'Depuis quinze jours j'ai monté et descendu les plus dangereuses montagnes de Savoye, j'ai passé sur les bords de mille précipices et jusqu'ici je ne me suis point précipité.'

PATIN, CHARLES. CONSTANCE, SCHAFFHAUSEN, BADEN, ZURICH, SOLEURE, BERNE, MORAT, PAYERNE, GENEVA

'Solothurn is one of the most pleasant countries in Switzerland: the mountains seem to stoop as it were on purpose to give passage to the Waters, and to afford a most delightful prospect with all manner of necessary Conveniences. . . . There are bears in those Parts, my Lord.'

1673

MANCINI, MARIE. AOSTA, GRAND ST. BERNARD PASS, MARTIGNY, LAUSANNE, BASLE

'Nous étions bien éloignés de passer si agréablement notre temps sur les montagnes de Saint-Bernard, allant parmi les neiges et des précipices si affreux que c'étaient des abîmes.'

1676

WAGNER, JOHANN JAKOB. ZURICH, LUCERNE, PILATUS

. . . 'This place is rarely visited except by shepherds and by those who ascend the mountain for the joy of their souls, since the prospect thence onto the lower regions is most vast and pleasing, and from the summit more than 16 lakes and rivers can be seen with the utmost wonder and delight.'

1682

FAESCH, HANS JAKOB. BASLE, LUCERNE, FLUELEN, HOSPENTHAL, ST. GOTTHARD PASS, BELLINZONA, LUGANO, MENDRISIO, LOCARNO, BELLINZONA, ST. GOTTHARD PASS, FLUELEN, LUCERNE, BRUGG, BASLE.

'The way down Monte Ceneri is so bad and the descent so troublesome that if we had not sat down where we were and inhaled fresh air, we should hardly have got down the mountain in our fatigue.'

1683

MABILLON, JEAN. BASLE, BADEN, MURI, ZUG, AEGERI, EINSIEDELN, RAPPERSWIL, ST. GALL

'La forme de leurs lits est excessivement incommode pour les Français, car ils sont plus courts que le corps, et tellement chargés d'oreillers, qu'on y est plus assis que couché: la matière n'en vaut pas mieux que la forme, parce qu'en été même, au lieu d'être sous une couverture légère, vous êtes sous une pesante couëtte de plume . . .'

1684

TAVERNIER, JEAN BAPTISTE. GENEVA, ROLLE, AUBONNE, YVERDON, SOLEURE, BASLE

The great traveller considered that only Constantinople could be compared with Aubonne, his home.

1685

BURNET, GILBERT. GENEVA, LAUSANNE, BERNE, ZURICH, COIRE, THUSIS, SPLÜGEN PASS, CHIAVENNA, COMO, LUGANO, LOCARNO, BELLINZONA, MILAN

'They are extream civil to strangers, but it seems in all commonwealths innkeepers think that they have a right to exact upon strangers.'

LABRUNE, M. GENEVA, LAUSANNE, MORAT, BERNE, SOLEURE, LIESTAL, BASLE, SCHAFFHAUSEN, CONSTANCE, ZURICH, BADEN, AARAU, BERNE, AARBERG, NEUCHÂTEL, YVERDON, LAUSANNE, GENEVA

From Zurich to Berne, Labrune was accompanied by three Scotsmen, Messrs. Baillie, Hay, and Cuninghame.

1686

BURNET, GILBERT. GENEVA, AVENCHES, MORAT, BERNE, BASLE

'I left *Geneva* with a Concern that I could not have felt in leaving any Place out of the Isle of *Britain*.'

1688

MISSON, MAXIMILIEN. GENEVA, LAUSANNE, BERNE, SOLEURE, BASLE

'Their summits covered with snow merge into the clouds and resemble the foaming waves of an angry sea. If one admires the courage of those who first risked themselves upon that element, there is room for wonder that anyone dared to venture among the rocks of these horrible mountains.'

1689

ARNAUD, HENRI. NYON, YVOIRE, BOEGE, VIUZ, ST. JEOIRE, CLUSES, SALLANCHES, MÉGÈVE, COL DE HAUTE LUCE, ST. NICOLAS EN VEROCE, COL DU BONHOMME, SEEZ, VAL D'ISÈRE, COL D'ISERAN, LANSLEVILLARD, COL DU CLAPIER

This was the 'glorious return' of the Waldenses to their valleys.

1690

ARANTHON D'ALEX, JEAN D'. ANNECY, CHAMONIX

'Autant de fois que l'Evêque alloit faire ses visites en ces quartiers là, les Peuples le prioient d'aller exorciser et bénir ces Montagnes de glace. . . . Ils assuroient que depuis sa dernière visite, les glaciers s'étoient retirés de plus de quatre-vingts pas.'

COXE, THOMAS. ZURICH, BERNE, THUN, INTERLAKEN, GRINDELWALD

'The whole towne rang wth joy y^t^ whole day and night, and I should have told y^r^ Lop: sooner y^t^ at my entry into it they shutt up all their shops and thousands of spectators of all ages and sexes crowded at ye windows from ye cellar to ye garetts, and saluted me so continually and civilly as I pass't, y^t^ I could not putt on my hatt from one gate of ye city to ye other.'

1693

SHERARD, WILLIAM (*c*). GENEVA, SALÈVE, LA DOLE

When travelling in the Alps, Sherard was mistaken by a peasant for a wolf as he was creeping in search of plants, and narrowly missed being shot.

1702

ADDISON, JOSEPH. GENEVA, LAUSANNE, FRIBOURG, BERNE, SOLEURE, ST. GOTTHARD PASS, ZURICH, ST. GALL

He wrote to William Congreve a letter which 'comes to you from the top of the highest mountain in Switzerland where I am now shivering among the Eternal frosts and snows. . . . I am here entertained with the prettiest variety of snow-prospects that you can imagine.'

SCHEUCHZER, JOHANN JAKOB. ZURICH, EINSIEDELN, SCHWYZ, ALTDORF, SURENEN PASS, ENGELBERG, JOCH PASS, MEIRINGEN, BRUNIG PASS, LUCERNE, ZURICH

'I stayed two weeks in the monastery at Engelberg to help the fathers and brothers, who were suffering from cramp and colic accompanied by fevers which traversed the body and limbs and other evil effects. The chief cause of the disease was probably the bad conditions of the pots and pans . . .'

1703

HOTTINGER, JOHANN HEINRICH. GRINDELWALD

'I wish to bring forward a matter which I have learned with my own eyes, and which nobody else has observed hitherto. There may be seen in glaciers certain lines which we usually call strata, to the number of seven, eight, or nine, and from these it is possible to make an accurate estimate of their years, just as natural philosophers allege that they can tell the years of trees from the growth-rings.'

SCHEUCHZER, JOHANN JAKOB. ZURICH, WALLENSTADT, RAGAZ, KUNKELS PASS, REICHENAU, THUSIS, SPLÜGEN PASS, CHIAVENNA, MALOJA PASS, ST. MORITZ, JULIER PASS, TIEFENKASTEL, THUSIS, REICHENAU, SEGNES PASS, ELM, GLARUS, ZURICH

The waters of St. Moritz 'taste almost like ink'.

1704

CAVALIER, JEAN. PORRENTRUY, LA CHAUX DE FONDS, NEUCHÂTEL, BOUDRY, YVERDON, LAUSANNE, MARTIGNY, GRAND ST. BERNARD PASS, AOSTA

The leader of the Camisard huguenot rebellion in the Cevennes had to travel in disguise through the catholic Valais while his men made their way from the Val d'Abondance to that of Aosta across 'les terribles montagnes de la Suisse, du côté de St. Maurice'.

SCHEUCHZER, JOHANN JAKOB. ZURICH, WALLENSTADT, RAGAZ, PFÄFERS

Taking the waters at Pfäfers, becoming 'dizzy and dazed'.

1705

BLAINVILLE, M. DE. SCHAFFHAUSEN, ZURICH, EINSIEDELN, BADEN, AARAU, BERNE, MORAT, FRIBOURG, LAUSANNE, GENEVA

'The country about Berne is very pleasant, being adorned with many castles and pleasure-houses. Throughout the canton in general the Air is none of the best, because of the Forests and Lakes with which it abounds.'

SCHEUCHZER, JOHANN JAKOB. ZURICH, GLARUS, KLAUSEN PASS, ALTDORF, ST. GOTTHARD PASS, AIROLO, PIORA, UOMO PASS, LUKMANIER PASS, DISENTIS, SEDRUN, OBERALP PASS, ANDERMATT, FURKA PASS, BRIG, LEUK, GEMMI PASS, KANDERSTEG, THUN, BERNE, BRUGG, ZURICH

'If the whole of Switzerland were a single mountain we should be the most unfortunate inhabitants of Europe, for on the northern side we should be plagued by the north wind which would wither the grass and fruit so that we would be obliged to live elsewhere, and only the southern and western sides would be fertile. But as our country is divided into mountains and valleys, the former hold off the bitter winds and prevent them from sweeping in full blast through the valleys just as in England the fertility of gardens is increased by high walls which keep away the salt sea air.'

1706

BODMER, SAMUEL. THUN, INTERLAKEN, MEIRINGEN, GADMEN, STEIN, MEIRINGEN, GRIMSEL PASS, MEIRINGEN, GRINDELWALD, LAUTERBRUNNEN, KANDERSTEG, ZWEISIMMEN, GSTAAD, ROUGEMONT

SCHEUCHZER, JOHANN JAKOB. ZURICH, ZUG, LUCERNE, ENGELBERG, JOCH PASS, MEIRINGEN, INTERLAKEN, THUN, BERNE, FRIBOURG, MORAT, NEUCHÂTEL, BIENNE, SOLEURE, AARBURG, AARAU, MELLINGEN, ZURICH

1707

BLAINVILLE, M. DE. GENEVA, LAUSANNE, MORAT, AARBERG, SOLEURE, BALSTHAL, BASLE

'This whole tract of land between Nyon and Morges, is called La Côte, and produces white Wines, which are famous among the inhabitants of that Canton, who never find the least inconveniency to whatever excess they drink them. . . .'

SCHEUCHZER, JOHANN JAKOB. ZURICH, WALLENSTADT, COIRE, THUSIS, SAN BERNARDINO PASS, MESOCCO, FORCOLA PASS, CHIAVENNA, MALOJA PASS, ST. MORITZ, PONTE, ALBULA PASS, BERGÜN, LENZERHEIDE, COIRE, ZURICH

'I have not myself climbed the high Piz Beverin, but after my departure Herr von Rosenroll went up it and gave me the following description: "it takes 6 hours from Thusis to the top . . . the view from this mountain is very extensive and pleasant".'

1708

BURNET, WILLIAM. ZURICH, GRINDELWALD

1709

SCHEUCHZER, JOHANN. ZURICH, COIRE, THUSIS, ANDEER, PIZ LA TSCHERA, SPLÜGEN

SCHEUCHZER, JOHANN JAKOB. ZURICH, ZUG, LUCERNE, BRUNIG PASS, BRIENZ, INTERLAKEN, GRINDELWALD, INTERLAKEN, KANDERSTEG, GEMMI PASS, LEUK, SION, MARTIGNY, GENEVA, NEUCHÂTEL, MORAT, ZURICH

'I must speak of the usefulness of glaciers, and will treat, not of the fact that, like the snows, they act as coolers to condense the vapours rising from the mountains, nor of the subterranean warmth that they keep in and guard from dissipation, nor again of the rivers such as the Rhone, Rhine, etc., and innumerable streams to which they give rise; but I will deal only with the use of their waters for drinking. Who would have thought that the waters from melting glaciers are the most precious and health-giving of all the waters of Switzerland?'

1710

SCHEUCHZER, JOHANN JAKOB. ZURICH, GLARUS, RATZMATT, BLEITSTOCK, ELM, GLARUS, WALLENSTADT, SARGANS, ALTSTÄTTEN, TROGEN, HERISAU, LICHTENSTEIG, ALT ST. JOHANN, KYBURG, ZURICH

1711

SCHEUCHZER, JOHANN JAKOB. ZURICH, SOLEURE, BERNE, THUN, WERDENSTEIN, ZURICH

1712

ROUSSEAU, JEAN-BAPTISTE. SOLEURE, AARAU, BADEN, LAUSANNE

One of his 'Allégories', written at Soleure, refers to the surrounding scenery and the wood of Attisholz, near Soleure:

> 'Ainsi, non loin de ces rives fécondes,
> Où l'Aar répand ses libérales ondes,
> Au fond d'un bois dont le nom révéré
> Au jeune Atys est encor consacré . . .'

1717

CAPPELER, MAURITZ ANTON. LUCERNE, PILATUS

An excursion by the founder of crystallography.

1720

ANONYMOUS 2. GENEVA, LAUSANNE, BERNE, ZURZACH, ZURICH, BADEN, BASLE

'On ne peut traverser sans peur ces chemins affreux et bordez de précipices d'une hauteur démesurée.'

BREVAL, JOHN DURAND. GENEVA, LAUSANNE, MORAT, BERNE, SOLEURE, BADEN, ZURICH, WINTERTHUR, ST. GALL, ARBON

'The first remarkable Place in the Pais de Vaud, as you follow the old Roman way from Geneva to Lausanne is the castle of Copet; the greatest merit of which consists in the Prospect of the vast Bason before it, and of the Pennine Alps on the opposite side of the Lake, that rise one behind another, as far as it is possible for the Eye to reach, in a thousand irregular Figures.'

PÖLLNITZ, CHARLES LEWIS BARON DE. GENEVA

'On each side are the mountains of Savoy, the tops of which being covered with snow, form a very agreeable view.'

1722

SAINT-MAURE, CHARLES DE. GENEVA, NYON, ROLLE, AUBONNE, MORGES, LAUSANNE, VEVEY, BEX, MARTIGNY, LAUSANNE, ROMAINMOTIER, MOUDON, BERNE, FRIBOURG, AVENCHES, MORAT, PAYERNE, NEUCHÂTEL, YVERDON, ORBE, NEUCHÂTEL, BIENNE, SOLEURE, AARAU, BADEN, ZURICH, LUCERNE, MEGGEN, LÜTZELAU, DEMMEN, PILATUS, WILLISAU, ROTENBURG,

SEMPACH, GERSAU, ALTDORF, ANDERMATT, ST. GOTTHARD PASS, AIROLO, ST. GOTTHARD PASS, HOSPENTHAL, FURKA PASS, ANDERMATT, OBERALP PASS, ANDERMATT, ALTDORF, SCHWYZ, EINSIEDELN, BASLE, SCHAFFHAUSEN, BASLE, PORRENTRUY, MONTBELIARD, ST. IMIER, TAVANNES, BELLELAY, DELÉMONT, LANDSKRON, BASLE, BRUGG, HABSBURG, BASLE

'I clambered up to the Top of the celebrated Mountain *Pilate*, . . . and the People peaceably enjoy, from the Summit thereof, a most delightful prospect: Nor do I ever remember to have met with a finer, or more curious one . . .'

1723

MANN, SIR HORACE. GENEVA, GRINDELWALD

'Four years previously, the glacier had advanced so much that the inhabitants were considering a petition to their government for permission to make use of the services of an exorcist to drive the glacier back, in accordance with the prescription of a gentleman of Vaud, but they took this action in secret and the glacier did in fact recede, though doubtless for other reasons.'

1724

BREVAL, JOHN DURAND. PONTARLIER, STE. CROIX, YVERDON, GRANDSON, NEUCHÂTEL, BIENNE, SOLEURE, FRAUENBRUNN, BERNE, AVENCHES, KÖNIZ, BERNE, ST. URBAN, BADEN, ZURICH, KLOTEN, EGLISAU, SCHAFFHAUSEN, BASLE

'That very learned Naturalist Dr. *Scheutzer*, F.R.S. in a long Conversation we had together, told me of several new Botanick Discoveries made among the *Swiss* and *Grison* Mountains, as likewise of many strange Phenomena found upon Fossils, Effects of Petrification, or Monuments of the Deluge in these Parts, that were as yet unpublish'd by him.'

1725

SAUSSURE, CÉSAR DE. LAUSANNE, YVERDON, NEUCHÂTEL, NIDAU, SOLEURE, WANGEN, AARAU, BIBERSTEIN, BRUGG, WALDSHUT, LAUFENBURG, BASLE

From Yverdon, this journey was made by boat to Basle and took seven days. It took one whole day to cross the lake of Neuchatel, and while going down the Aar the boat struck a rock.

1726

GAGNEBIN, ABRAHAM. LA FERRIÈRE, CHASSERAL, TÊTE DE RANG, CREUX DU VAN, LUCERNE, PILATUS, BERNE, FRIBOURG, GRUYÈRES, VEVEY, DENT DE JAMAN

GESNER, JOHANN. BASLE, ZURICH, COIRE, ALBULA PASS, ST. MORITZ, JULIER PASS, BIVIO, SEPTIMER PASS, CHIAVENNA, SPLÜGEN PASS, HINTERRHEIN, VALS, ILANZ, PANIXER PASS, ELM, GLARUS, ZURICH

'I had indeed intended to push on from Hinterrhein to the St. Gotthard, but there was no way which would not strike terror into my then young mind.'

1727

HAGENBUCH, JOHANN KASPAR. ZURICH, AARAU, SOLEURE, BIENNE, NEUCHÂTEL, YVERDON, FRIBOURG, MORAT, BERNE, BURGDORF, LUCERNE, SARNEN, STANS, KÜSSNACHT, ZUG, EINSIEDELN, SCHWYZ, BRUNNEN, ALTDORF, KLAUSEN PASS, LINTHAL, GLARUS, PFÄFERS, COIRE, ALTSTÄTTEN, APPENZELL, TROGEN, ST. GALL, CONSTANCE, SCHAFFHAUSEN, ZURICH

The party of students ascended Pilatus to enjoy the view of the surrounding lowlands, a view only spoilt by the mountains which unfortunately limited the horizon.

SULZBACH, PRINCE OF. CHAMONIX

1728

HALLER, ALBRECHT VON. BASLE, MOUTIER, BIENNE, NEUCHÂTEL, ORBE, LAC DE JOUX, LAUSANNE, GENEVA, MARTIGNY, SION, LEUK, GEMMI PASS, KANDERSTEG, INTERLAKEN, MEIRINGEN, JOCH PASS, ENGELBERG, LUCERNE, ZURICH, BADEN, BERNE

It was during this journey, undertaken with Johann Gesner 'pour voir la nature et non pas les hommes', that Haller conceived his poem 'Die Alpen'.

1729

AISSÉ, MLLE. GENEVA

KEYSLER, JOHANN GEORG. BASLE, SOLEURE, BERNE, FRIBOURG, MORAT, LAUSANNE, GENEVA

1730

GESNER, JOHANN. ZURICH, BILTEN, GLARUS, LINTHAL, PANTENBRÜCKE, BLATTENBERG

'Of alpine plants I found many of the rarest . . .'

HALLER, ALBRECHT VON. BERNE, THUN, WEISSENBURGBAD

'I took advantage of my stay to explore the steep rocks and precipices that surround Weissenburgbad, and climbed the Alps of Waach and Gemsengrat. From this time on, I was able to go to the most difficult places without feeling giddy as previously had been the case.'

ROUSSEAU, JEAN-JACQUES. GENEVA, NYON, FRIBOURG, MOUDON, LAUSANNE, VEVEY, LAUSANNE

Rousseau was escorting Mme de Warens' maid, Mlle Merceret, from Annecy to her home at Fribourg.

1731

GESNER, JOHANN. ZURICH, APPENZELL, KAMOR, ZURICH

HALLER, ALBRECHT VON. BERNE, BELP, GURNIGEL, BÜRGLEN, MORGETENGRAT, WEISSENBURGBAD, ERLENBACH, STOCKHORN, KANDERSTEG, GEMMI PASS, LEUKERBAD, GEMMI PASS, KANDERSTEG, THUN, BERNE, CHASSERAL, MORAT, BERNE

'In 1730 I crossed a flat piece of snow which did not appear to present any danger. I passed by the same way in 1731: now my hair stood on end when I realised that I had crossed by a snow bridge over a deep gully into which I now had to climb down but which the snow had concealed from me the previous year.'

ROUSSEAU, JEAN-JACQUES. LAUSANNE, NEUCHÂTEL, BOUDRY, FRIBOURG, BERNE, SOLEURE

Rousseau was acting as interpreter to the Archimandrite Athanasius Paulus, whom he had met at Boudry on his begging tour.

SCHMUZ, JOHANN. ZURICH, GLARUS, KLAUSEN PASS, ALTDORF, SCHWYZ, EINSIEDELN, ZUG, STANS, LUCERNE, ESCHOLTZMATT, THUN, BERNE, MORAT, NEUCHÂTEL, BIENNE, SOLEURE, AARAU, ZURICH

1732

HALLER, ALBRECHT VON. BERNE, THUN, INTERLAKEN, LAUTERBRUNNEN, GRINDELWALD, GROSSE SCHEIDEGG, MEIRINGEN, GRIMSEL PASS, MEIRINGEN, BRIENZERROTHORN, INTERLAKEN, BERNE, ORBE, MONT SUCHET, LAC DE JOUX

Haller had proposed crossing the Grimsel to visit the Valais, but the popular disturbances arising out of the exploitation of a mine in the valley of Binn by two Englishmen, Mandel and Aston, caused him to change his plans.

1733

HALLER, ALBRECHT VON. BERNE, THUN, NIESEN, FRUTIGEN, KANDERSTEG, GEMMI PASS, LEUK, SION, MARTIGNY, AIGLE, COL DES MOSSES, CHÂTEAU D'OEX, ZWEISIMMEN, THUN, BERNE

1735

GESNER, JOHANN. ZURICH, LUCERNE, BRUNIG PASS, BRIENZ, INTERLAKEN, KANDERSTEG, GEMMI PASS, LEUKERBAD, GEMMI PASS, KANDERSTEG, BERNE, ZURICH

1736

HALLER, ALBRECHT VON. BERNE, THUN, INTERLAKEN, LAUTERBRUNNEN, GRINDELWALD, GROSSE SCHEIDEGG, MEIRINGEN, GENEVA, DOLE, ZURICH, ALTDORF, ANDERMATT, FURKA PASS, GRIMSEL PASS, MEIRINGEN, INTERLAKEN, BERNE

SEIGNEUX DE CORREVON, GABRIEL. LAUSANNE, VAULION, LAC DE JOUX, MONT TENDRE

'Perché sur la Cime la plus élevée, je me mis à observer le Monde & sa gloire.'

1738

HUBER, JOHANN JACOB. BASLE, ZURICH, RAGAZ, PFÄFERS, MONTELUNA, COIRE, FILISUR, ALBULA PASS, PONTE, MALOJA PASS, CHIAVENNA, BELLINZONA, ST. GOTTHARD PASS, HOSPENTHAL, FURKA PASS, GRIMSEL PASS, MEIRINGEN, BASLE

1739

HALLER, ALBRECHT VON. BERNE, SUMISWALD, BIENNE, NEUCHÂTEL, NOIRAIGUE, CREUX DU VAN, MORAT, BERNE, RIGGISBERG, GURNIGEL, BERNE, BALSTHAL, LIESTAL, BASLE

WALPOLE, HORACE. GENEVA

'I find there are many English in the town; Lord Brook, Lord Mansel, Lord Hervey's eldest son, and a son of — of Mars and Venus, or of Antony and Cleopatra, or, in short, of — . . . [presumably Charles Churchill] Gray and I return to Lyons in three days.' Of the Alps he added, 'I hope I shall never see them again'.

1740

CHRISTEN, WOLFGANG. BERNE, THUN, INTERLAKEN, MEIRINGEN, GROSSE SCHEIDEGG, GRINDELWALD, LAUTERBRUNNEN, INTERLAKEN, KANDERSTEG, FRUTIGEN, ADELBODEN, HAHNENMOOS PASS, LENK, ZWEISIMMEN, WIMMIS, THUN, BERNE

1741

MONTAGU, LADY MARY WORTLEY. GENEVA

'I think this air does not agree with my health. I have had a return of many complaints from which I had an entire cessation during my stay in Italy, which makes me inclined to return thither, though a winter journey over the Alps is very disagreeable.'

POCOCKE, RICHARD. BASLE, LIESTAL, WALDENBURG, SOLEURE, AARBERG, MORAT, LAUSANNE, NYON, GENEVA, CHAMONIX, GENEVA, THONON, EVIAN, AIGLE, BEX, VEVEY, FRIBOURG, MORAT, NEUCHÂTEL, BERNE, LUCERNE, WALCHWIL, ZUG, ZURICH, WINTERTHUR, SCHAFFHAUSEN, BASLE

'From Geneva I went to the glacieres in Savoy, an account of which has been lately published.'

STILLINGFLEET, BENJAMIN. GENEVA, CHAMONIX, GENEVA

'Mr. Stillingfleet, as well as his pupil, being inured to bodily exercises, and attracted by the wonders of Nature, they, with other Members of the Common Room, made frequent excursions into the valleys of the Alps, and in particular visited those icy regions which stretch at the foot of Mont Blanc.'

WINDHAM, WILLIAM. GENEVA, CHAMONIX, GENEVA

'Those who are desirous to undertake this Journey, ought not to set out till towards the Middle of August; they would at that time find not so much Snow on the Mountain. They might go to the Crystal Mines, and divert themselves with shooting of Bouquetins; the Oats would then be cut, and their Horses would not suffer so much. Although we met with nothing which had the Appearance of Danger, nevertheless I would recommend going well armed; 'tis an easy Precaution, and on certain Occasions very useful, one is never the worse for it, and oftentimes it helps a Man out of a Scrape.'

1742

MARTEL, PETER. GENEVA, CHAMONIX, GENEVA

'Vastly well satisfied with our Journey, and without any other regret than not having stayed longer at Chamouny, to have considered the Beauties of the Places thereabouts.'

POLIER DE BOTTENS. KANDERSTEG, HOHTHÜRLI PASS, SEFINENFURKE PASS, LAUTERBRUNNEN

When he arrived in Lauterbrunnen saying that he had come direct from Kandersteg, people were so incredulous that an inquiry was set up and affidavits taken.

SERERHARD, NICOLAS (*c*). SEEWIS, SCESAPLANA, LUNERSEE, CAVELLJOCH PASS, SEEWIS

'We reached the summit of the mountain and real wonderment began. We had already been astonished on the great glacier, for we found on it pieces of nutshells, horse's and human hair, and wood shavings, which puzzled us not a little. I attributed them to the wind. . . . The view from this place is something marvellous.'

SULZER, JOHANN GEORG. ZURICH, ALBIS, ZUG, RIGI, LUCERNE, PILATUS, STANSSTAD, ALTDORF, ANDERMATT, OBERALP PASS, DISENTIS, COIRE

The view from the Rigi was described by Sulzer as the most beautiful in the world.

1744

ROUSSEAU, JEAN-JACQUES. DOMODOSSOLA, SIMPLON PASS, BRIG, TURTMANN, SION, MARTIGNY, LAUSANNE, NYON, GENEVA

It was apparently on this journey that he obtained the material for the 'Lettres du Valais' in his *Nouvelle Héloïse*. 'Sur les hautes montagnes, où l'air est pur et subtil, on se sent plus de facilité dans la respiration, plus de légèreté dans le corps, plus de sérénité dans l'esprit.'

WAASER, JOSEPH EUGENIUS. ENGELBERG, TITLIS

1747

ANONYMOUS I A. BIENNE, MORAT, AVENCHES, MOUDON, LAUSANNE, VEVEY, AIGLE, BEX, ST. MAURICE, LAUSANNE, MORGES, ROLLE, COPPET, GENEVA, LAUSANNE, ECHALLENS, YVERDON, NEUCHÂTEL, BIENNE

STANHOPE, PHILIP. LAUSANNE, BEX, BERNE, EINSIEDELN

1748

ALTMANN, JOHANN GEORG. BERNE, THUN, INTERLAKEN, GRINDELWALD

'The ice-mountains of Switzerland are nothing other than a real and in every way complete sea of ice which the Omnipotent and Wise Creator has placed on these high mountains in order to purify the air of the neighbouring regions and to provide Switzerland and other countries of Europe with springs and rivers.'

HOLLIS, THOMAS. GENEVA, BERNE, ZURICH

'This tour which we made highly entertained and indeed surprised us. For instead of seeing (as we expected) a country generally wild, barren, and uncultivated, and a people generally poor, we observed lands, although by nature not fertile, yet made so with much art, even in many places to the tops of precipices; and a people, although none of them possessing vast riches, yet, as a body, wealthy, and without any that are absolutely poor.'

HUTTON, JAMES. SCHAFFHAUSEN, ST. GALL, ZURICH, AARAU, BERNE, NEUCHÂTEL, GENEVA

'The Lord loves Switzerland, and will save many who might not be suitable for the congregation.'

1749

COLLINI, COME ALEXANDRE. COMO, RIVA, CHIAVENNA, SPLÜGEN PASS, THUSIS, COIRE

'Nos guides nous recommandèrent de ne point frapper les chevaux, mais de les laisser marcher à volonté, parce qu'ils sont accoutumés à cette route; ils nous avertirent aussi de ne pas jeter des éclats de voix, soit pour nous appeler, soit pour essayer des échos. Dans ces montagnes la plus légère commotion donnée à l'air peut occasionner la chute d'une lavanche, et l'on sait que ces terribles éboulemens de neige ensevelissent quelquefois les voyageurs qui n'ont pas pris les précautions que nos guides nous prescrivaient. Nous entrâmes donc à cheval dans la Via Mala; jamais route (si on peut l'appeler ainsi) n'a été mieux nommée.'

1750

CASANOVA, JACQUES. GENEVA, LAUSANNE, MARTIGNY, GRAND ST. BERNARD PASS, AOSTA

'Je pris la route du Saint-Bernard que je franchis en trois jours avec sept mulets qui portaient moi, mon domestique, ma malle et la voiture qui avait été destinée à la femme charmante que je venais de perdre sans espoir de retour. Un homme accablé par une grande douleur a l'avantage que rien ne lui parait pénible. C'est une espèce de désespoir qui a aussi ses douceurs. Je ne sentais ni la faim, ni la soif, ni le froid qui gélait la nature sur cette affreuse partie des Alpes, ni la fatigue inséparable de ce pénible et dangereux passage.'

KLOPSTOCK, FRIEDRICH. SCHAFFHAUSEN, ZURICH

'Near the bend of the lake, you see a long row of Alps before you. I have never seen such a perfectly beautiful view.'

MAUGIRON, MARQUIS DE. CHAMONIX

'Ce qui me parait fort extraordinaire, c'est que ce soit dans les extrémités de chaudes vallées que ce [sic] trouvent ce qu'on appelle les glacières. Il y en a plusieurs, mais la plus belle est celle de Faucigny . . .'

WALSER, GABRIEL. BERNEGG, COIRE, ST. MORITZ

The water at St. Moritz 'acts very violently, makes one quite silly in the head and takes one's strength away; indeed, for the first few days one feels so slack and tired that one can scarcely cross the road.'

1751

ANONYMOUS 2 A. ZURICH, ZUG, LUCERNE, SARNEN, GERSAU, SCHWYZ, EINSIEDELN, GLARUS, ELM, SCHWANDEN, LINTHAL, KLAUSEN PASS, ALTDORF, ANDERMATT, OBERALP PASS, DISENTIS, COIRE, RORSCHACH, ST. GALL, HERISAU, CONSTANCE, SCHAFFHAUSEN, ZURICH

'. . . These wondrous mountains of ice that are piled up on one another many fathoms high and stand there, very pale, afford the traveller a vastly pretty prospect from their greenish blue colours, shimmering in the rays of the sun.'

NEEDHAM, JOHN TURBERVILLE. AOSTA, ST. REMY, GRAND ST. BERNARD, COL DE SÉRÉNA, COURMAYEUR, COL DE LA SEIGNE, BOURG ST. MAURICE

'. . . . Il est à présumer que le Mont Tourné [Mont Pourri] est la montagne la plus élevée de l'Europe.'

1752

GUETTARD, JEAN-ÉTIENNE (*c*). LUCERNE, ENGELBERG

'Le Canton de Lucerne que je viens de parcourir, est un des plus grands; il voisine celui d'Underwald, qui est à la vérité un des plus petits, mais qui n'est pas des moins fournis en fossiles; le seul district d'Engelberg renferme de l'or, de l'argent, du spath, du cristal, des pierres talcqueuses, du schiste, de l'ardoise et du marbre.'

1753

GIBBON, EDWARD. JOUGNE, LAUSANNE

SINNER, FRIEDRICH. INTERLAKEN, MEIRINGEN, GRIMSEL PASS, OBERGESTELEN, GRIES PASS, DOMODOSSOLA, LUGANO, BELLINZONA, ST. GOTTHARD PASS, ALTDORF, BUOCHS, SARNEN, BRUNIG PASS, INTERLAKEN, BRIENZ, BRUNIG PASS, SARNEN, STANS, ENGELBERG, JOCH PASS, MEIRINGEN, INTERLAKEN

'As a great amateur of mountain journeys, of which in the years 1751 and 1752 I have already made many as tiring as they were dangerous in the mountains around Interlaken and in neighbouring cantons, I undertook this year in August on the occasion of my official inspection of the Haslithal with my nephew Sinner de Balaigues yet another which took us far afield and was attended with all manner of mishaps.'

1754

ANONYMOUS 2 A. ZURICH, AARBURG, SOLEURE, BERNE, FRIBOURG, LAUSANNE, MARTIGNY, SION, BRIG, OBERGESTELEN, FURKA PASS, ANDERMATT, ALTDORF, ENGELBERG, LUCERNE, SCHWYZ, EINSIEDELN, RAPPERSWIL, ST. GALL, CONSTANCE, SCHAFFHAUSEN, ZURICH

ANONYMOUS 2 B. ZURICH, ZUG, LUCERNE, ENTLIBUCH, SARNEN, STANS, ALTDORF, ST. GOTTHARD PASS, FAIDO, PASSO PREDALP, LUKMANIER PASS, DISENTIS, COIRE, WALLENSTADT, GLARUS, SARGANS, UNTERWASSER, ST. GALL, CONSTANCE, SCHAFFHAUSEN, ZURICH

Crossing the Passo Predalp, 'our guide bade us pluck up courage, and we had to descend after dark, over stones and snow and through water. God be praised that the moon shone. At length, after many dangers, at 10 o'clock we reached a chalet where ten persons young and old were warming themselves at a fire. We asked for lodging, but they refused us because they thought that we were soldiers or otherwise dangerous people.'

DE LUC, JEAN-ANDRÉ, GENEVA, CHAMONIX, MARTIGNY, GENEVA

He was accompanied by his brother Guillaume Antoine De Luc, Mr. Jefferys, Mr. MacKinnon, and Captain Forbes.

ROUSSEAU, JEAN-JACQUES. GENEVA, HERMANCE, THONON, RIPAILLE, MEILLERIE, VILLENEUVE, VEVEY, CHILLON, CULLY, OUCHY, LAUSANNE, MORGES, NYON, GENEVA

'De tous ces amusements, celui qui me plut d'avantage fut une promenade autour du lac, que je fis en bateau avec Deluc père, sa bru, ses deux fils, et ma Thérèse. Nous mîmes sept jours à cette tournée, par le plus beau temps du monde. J'en gardai le vif souvenir des sites qui m'avaient frappé à l'autre extrémité du lac, et dont je fis la description quelques années après dans la *Nouvelle Héloïse*.'

WALSER, GABRIEL. BERNEGG, BLUDENZ, TSCHAGGUNS, PLATTEN PASS, ST. ANTÖNIEN, DAVOS

Davos has 'handsome, well-built men and women who are honest, friendly and polite to strangers. When you greet them they thank you kindly and say "Pass in God's name" and show you the way.'

1755

COLLINI, COME ALEXANDRE. GENEVA, PRANGINS, LAUSANNE, GENEVA

Collini was accompanying Voltaire who took a house, 'Monrion' near Lausanne as a winter residence, and another, 'Sur St. Jean' which he renamed 'Les Délices' near Geneva for summer.

GIBBON, EDWARD. LAUSANNE, YVERDON, NEUCHÂTEL, SOLEURE, BADEN, ZURICH, EINSIEDELN, BASLE, AARAU, BERNE, LAUSANNE

'The fashion of climbing the mountains and reviewing the glaciers had not yet been introduced by foreign travellers, who seek the sublime beauties of nature.'

GOLDSMITH, OLIVER. GENEVA, BERNE, BASLE, SCHAFFHAUSEN

Goldsmith travelled with his flute, singing for his supper. He 'ate a savoury dinner on the top of the Alps', and 'flushed woodcocks on Mount Jura'. His 'Animated Nature' contains many descriptions of the wonder of mountains, based on his experiences during this journey, and it was while he was in Switzerland that he wrote the first sketch of 'The Traveller'.

HALLER, ALBRECHT VON. BERNE, BIENNE, MORAT, LAC DE JOUX, DENT DE VAULION, MONT TENDRE

SINNER, FRIEDRICH. INTERLAKEN, KANDERSTEG, GEMMI PASS, LEUK, MARTIGNY, AIGLE, COL DES MOSSES, CHÂTEAU D'OEX, SAANEN, ZWEISIMMEN, INTERLAKEN

In Martigny Sinner states that he 'spent the night "more Vallesiaco" that is to say that it was expensive and dirty'.

1756

CHARLES EDWARD, PRINCE. BASLE

'Charles, accompanied by Miss Walkenshaw and the daughter that had been born three years ago, took up his abode at Basel in Switzerland. Here he passed himself off as a Dr. Thompson, an English doctor, anxious to recruit the health of himself and his wife and child by the mountain air.'

CONDAMINE, M. DE LA. GENEVA

Referring to 'ice-vallies', 'the most celebrated and most curious of these is at three days journey from Geneva, towards the sources of the Arve, at the foot of the White Mountain. The way to it is through the valley of Chamogny. I was on the point of quitting Geneva, when I was informed of these particulars: the tour demands at least eight days: it requires also preparations and conveniencies with which I was unprovided, and cannot be undertaken by one person only.'

GRUNER, GOTTLIEB SIEGMUND. BERNE, THUN, INTERLAKEN, MEIRINGEN, GROSSE SCHEIDEGG, GRINDELWALD, LAUTERBRUNNEN

'If we consider the ice-mountains in general and in particular their coverings of snow, the complaint against their presence is most unjustified; and it is quite certain that the snowy giants are more useful in a country than if they were covered with the richest pastures.'

HALLER, ALBRECHT VON. BERNE, THUN, INTERLAKEN, LAUTERBRUNNEN

'I found beside the ice which is called the Steinengletscher [Lauterbrunnen Breithorn glacier] some plants which were all the more delightful as I had not been in the Alps for twenty years.'

KEATE, GEORGE. GENEVA, MORAT, BERNE, SOLEURE, BASLE, SCHAFFHAUSEN, ZURICH, LUCERNE, ALTDORF, ST. MAURICE, GENEVA

Keate's journey is reflected in his poems, 'The Helvetiad', 'Verses occasioned by visiting in 1756 a small chapel on the lake of Lucerne in the canton of Uri, erected to the memory of the famous William Tell', and 'The Alps'. Referring to the last work, Voltaire wrote to Keate: 'J'en aime bien mieux mes montagnes depuis que vous les avez embellies. Vous rendez l'horreur agréable . . .'

VOLTAIRE, AROUET DE. GENEVA, LAUSANNE, BERNE, SOLEURE, LAUSANNE, GENEVA

'Nous irons à Soleure; de là nous retournerons à Monrion, et nous regagnons ensuite notre lac de Genève.'

1757

BULLINGER, BALTHAZAR. ZURICH, ALBIS, ZUG, LUCERNE, SACHSELN, STANS, BRUNNEN, ALTDORF, ANDERMATT, OBERALP PASS, DISENTIS, ILANZ, COIRE, ZURICH

'Stay at home and amuse yourself as best you can; a Swiss tour with young women is impossible. You know the heroes who are with me: to-day they nearly all lost their nerve.'

HALLER, ALBRECHT VON. BERNE, BEX, CHAMOSSAIRE, ORMONT-DESSUS, COUFFIN, AIGLE, MARTIGNY, BRANSON, BERNE

'notre Lac de Genève'

(*Swiss Federal Railways*) VOLTAIRE, 1756

'I am so delighted with the country and its inhabitants, that I could willingly take up my abode here for some time longer'

(*Swiss Federal Railways*) WILLIAM COXE, 1779; Schuls

WYSS, RUDOLF. BERNE, THUN, INTERLAKEN, LAUTERBRUNNEN, GRINDELWALD, GROSSE SCHEIDEGG, MEIRINGEN, GRIMSEL, MEIRINGEN, BERNE

'Ce voyage était infiniment pénible, quoique les chevaux chargés passent partout où j'ai voyagé, je n'aurais jamais osé risquer de m'en servir, et suis par conséquent marché à pied. Mais toutes les peines ont été adoucies par la contemplation des merveilles de la nature, qu'un amateur ne peut considérer d'un oeil indifférent, s'il fait réflexion à leurs destinations, à leurs utilités, et à la sagesse infinie du Créateur.'

1758

GIBBON, EDWARD. LAUSANNE, JOUGNE

GRIMM, SAMUEL HIERONYMUS. BERNE, THUN, INTERLAKEN, MEIRINGEN, GRIMSEL, MEIRINGEN, GROSSE SCHEIDEGG, GRINDELWALD, LAUTERBRUNNEN, THUN, BERNE

1759

HALLER, ALBRECHT VON. AIGLE, ANZEINDAZ, ENSEX, PERCHE, AIGLE

1760

CASANOVA, JACQUES. SCHAFFHAUSEN, ZURICH, EINSIEDELN, BADEN, LUCERNE, SOLEURE, BERNE, MORAT, ROCHE, LAUSANNE, GENEVA

CHAVANNES, GAUDARD DE. GENEVA, LAUSANNE, MORAT, BERNE, SOLEURE, LIESTAL, BASLE

HALLER, ALBRECHT VON. AIGLE, JAVERNAZ, PONT DE NANT, LE RICHARD, PANEYROSSAZ, ANZEINDAZ, SOLALEX

LACHENAL, WERNER. BASLE, LUCERNE, FLUELEN, WASSEN, ST. GOTTHARD PASS, BELLINZONA, LUGANO, MENDRISIO, MONTE GENEROSO, CHIAVENNA, SPLÜGEN PASS, THUSIS, COIRE, BASLE

SAUSSURE, HORACE-BÉNÉDICT DE. GENEVA, CHAMONIX

On this, de Saussure's first visit to Chamonix, he announced his offer of a prize to whoever would discover a way to the summit of Mont Blanc.

1761

GAGNEBIN, ABRAHAM. LA FERRIÈRE, BERNE, THUN, INTERLAKEN, LAUTERBRUNNEN, GRINDELWALD, GROSSE SCHEIDEGG, MEIRINGEN, GRIMSEL, ZINCKENSTOCK, MEIRINGEN, BRUNIG PASS, LUCERNE, ENGELBERG

In the previous year the great naturalist had asked for subscriptions towards a journey he would make in the Alps, after which the plants, fossils, and crystals which he found would be distributed among the subscribers. Lord Coventry was the subscriber on whose behalf Gagnebin travelled in this and the following two years.

HALLER, ALBRECHT VON. AIGLE, COL DES MOSSES, LAC LIOSON

'Since my age and corpulence no longer allow me to rise like a bird to the heights, I must content myself with crawling about the valleys like a worm.'

SAUSSURE, HORACE-BÉNÉDICT DE. GENEVA, CHAMONIX

1762

ROCHEFOUCAULD D'ENVILLE, LOUIS ALEXANDRE, DUC DE LA. GENEVA, CHAMONIX

ROUSSEAU, JEAN-JACQUES. VALLORBE, YVERDON, FIEZ, MAUBORGET, REDALLAZ, VUISSENS, MOTIERS-TRAVERS

Rousseau had been expelled from France, proscribed in Geneva. While at Yverdon he was expelled by the Government of Berne, and took refuge at Motiers-Travers under the protection of Marshal Lord Keith, Frederic the Great's Governor of Neuchâtel. It was there that he wrote his *Lettres de la montagne*.

1763

ANDREAE, JOHANN GERHARD. BASLE, SCHAFFHAUSEN, ZURICH, SCHINZNACH, LUCERNE, ALTDORF, ANDERMATT, ALTDORF, SARNEN, BRUNIG PASS, MEIRINGEN, GROSSE SCHEIDEGG, GRINDELWALD, LAUTERBRUNNEN, INTERLAKEN, THUN, BERNE, FRIBOURG, VEVEY, BEX, LAUSANNE, GENEVA, YVERDON, NEUCHÂTEL, SOLEURE, BALSTHAL, LIESTAL, BASLE

DICK, JACOB. ZURICH, RAPPERSWIL, COIRE, THUSIS, SPLÜGEN PASS, CHIAVENNA, TIRANO, BORMIO, UMBRAIL PASS, STA. MARIA, OFEN PASS, S. GIACCOMO DI FRAELE, LIVIGNO, FORCOLA DI LIVIGNO, MOTTA, BERNINA PASS, MALOJA PASS, SEPTIMER PASS, FORCELLINA PASS, AVERS, SPLÜGEN, SAN BERNARDINO PASS, MESOCCO, BELLINZONA, FORMAZZA, GRIES PASS, ULRICHEN, BRIG, MARTIGNY, AIGLE

GIBBON, EDWARD. JOUGNE, LAUSANNE

MORGAN, JOHN. GENEVA, LAUSANNE, GENEVA

The earliest known visit to Switzerland by an American.

PALMERSTON, HENRY TEMPLE, LORD. GENEVA, LAUSANNE

Of his visitor, Gibbon wrote: 'He seems to have a very right notion of travelling and I fancy will make very great improvements.'

ROUSSEAU, JEAN-JACQUES. MOTIERS-TRAVERS, ESTAVAYER, MOTIERS-TRAVERS

' . . . La contrariété des mauvais tems, qui nous ont retenus plusieurs jours dans un cabaret; ma foiblesse et la longueur du voyage m'ont fait renoncer à le poursuivre quelque désir que j'en eusse, et nous sommes revenus sur nos pas après une absence de dix jours, qui ne nous a pas menés plus loin qu'Estavayé.' Rousseau's intention had been to visit Zurich.

SCHINZ, HANS RUDOLF. ZURICH, SCHINDELLEGI, EINSIEDELN, SCHWYZ, FLUELEN, ANDERMATT, FURKA PASS, BRIG, LEUK, GEMMI PASS, KANDERSTEG, SPIEZ, INTERLAKEN, BRIENZ, BRUNIG PASS, LUCERNE, ZURICH

Crossing the lake of Brienz, 'if our boatman had not been a good talker and entertained us with descriptions of his journey to America and back, we should have fallen asleep.'

1764

ANONYMOUS 2 C. GENEVA, CHAMONIX

'Quand on a le soleil de dos, la vue de ce lac gelé, et de ce théâtre de pyramides bizarrement colorées, est des plus grands et des plus magnifiques spectacles que l'on puisse imaginer. . . . On croit voir les débris d'un magnifique palais, ou les ruines d'une ville superbe. Un poète dirait qu'on voit des tours de diamant, des colonnes d'émeraude.'

BECKFORD, PETER. GENEVA, LAUSANNE, MOTIERS-TRAVERS

'I passed several hours in his company very agreeably, but found the celebrated author of *Emile*, as I expected, differing as much in his manners, as in his writings, from his more fortunate rival.'

BOSWELL, JAMES. BASLE, SOLEURE, BERNE, NEUCHÂTEL, MOTIERS-TRAVERS, LAUSANNE, GENEVA

Boswell was on his way to Corsica, and while in Switzerland he paid his celebrated visits to Rousseau at Motiers-Travers and to Voltaire at Ferney.

BOUFFLERS, CHEVALIER DE. BASLE, SOLEURE, VEVEY, BEX, GENEVA

'Il y a des endroits ici où un enrhumé peut cracher à son choix dans l'Océan ou dans la Méditerranée.'

ESCHERNY, FRANÇOIS LOUIS D'. MOTIERS-TRAVERS, CHASSERON

'Nous [including J.-J. Rousseau] escaladâmes, au moyen d'une échelle, d'énormes tas de foin rassemblés dans la grange. Là, côte à côte, chacun s'endormit comme il put; la chose n'était pas aisée, car le foin, nouvellement fauché et très chaud, fermentait au dessous de nous; nous étions presque sur un volcan.'

GIBBON, EDWARD. LAUSANNE, GENEVA

MALTHUS, DANIEL. GENEVA, MOTIERS-TRAVERS

A visit to Jean-Jacques Rousseau by the father of the celebrated economist. He made the journey from England for this sole purpose and afterwards recalled his visit in the following terms: 'J'ai passé la journée avec vous, nous avons dîné ensemble, nous nous sommes promenés, le soir, dans les prairies. . . .'

OSTERWALD, SAMUEL FREDERIC D'. NEUCHÂTEL, MOTIERS-TRAVERS, LA BRÉVINE, LE LOCLE, LA CHAUX DE FONDS, LA SAGNE, LES PONTS, LA TOURNE, DOMBESSON, NEUCHÂTEL

ROUSSEAU, JEAN-JACQUES. MOTIERS-TRAVERS, CHASSERON, MOTIERS-TRAVERS, LA ROBELLAZ, MOTIERS-TRAVERS, YVERDON, GOUMOENS, MORGES, NYON, THONON, YVERDON, MOTIERS-TRAVERS, CHAMP DU MOULIN, CRESSIER, NEUCHÂTEL, MOTIERS-TRAVERS

Rousseau intended to take the waters at Aix les Bains, but did not feel well enough to go farther than Thonon, where he met and conferred with his supporters from Geneva.

SAUSSURE, HORACE-BÉNÉDICT DE. GENEVA, CHAMONIX

This, de Saussure's third journey to Chamonix, was made in March.

1765

BRYDONE, PATRICK. MOTIERS-TRAVERS

In company with 'Lord Kelmants, Mr. Millecken, Mr. Errington, and Mr. Kendrick', Brydone paid a visit to Jean-Jacques Rousseau.

DE LUC, JEAN-ANDRÉ. GENEVA, TANINGE, SAMOËNS, SIXT

The first attempt to climb Mont Buet.

DESMAREST, NICOLAS. CHAMONIX

ESCHERNY, FRANÇOIS LOUIS D'. MOTIERS-TRAVERS, COLOMBIER, LA TOURNE, PLAMBOZ, LA SAGNE, LE LOCLE, LES BRENETS, LA CHAUX DE FONDS, MOTIERS-TRAVERS, BROT, CREUX DU VAN, MOTIERS-TRAVERS

'On est surtout frappé de voir dans ces sites sauvages de jolies personnes, élégamment vêtues, parcourir ces inégalités, sauter d'un rocher à l'autre, gravir une colline, en descendre avec rapidité, errer dans ces forêts et y arborer des plumes, des guirlandes, et des chapeaux anglais.'

FLORIAN, JEAN PIERRE CLARIS DE. GENEVA

'Fernixo [Ferney] est entouré de montagnes couvertes de neige en tout temps; dès que les premiers rayons du soleil viennent les frapper, on voit l'or se répandre lentement et par degrés sur les sommets glacés que l'oeil peut à peine mesurer; cette vive lumière descend des montagnes pour venir éclairer un pays superbe, et se réflechir dans un lac qui couvre sept lieues d'étendue.'

HERVEY, FREDERICK AUGUSTUS. MOTIERS-TRAVERS

A visit to Jean-Jacques Rousseau by the future Earl of Bristol and his wife.

PENNANT, THOMAS. GENEVA, LAUSANNE, VEVEY, BEX, ST. MAURICE, VEVEY, CHATEL ST. DENIS, CHESOLLES, FRIBOURG, MORAT, BIENNE, BERNE, THUN, INTERLAKEN, LAUTERBRUNNEN, GRINDELWALD, GROSSE SCHEIDEGG, MEIRINGEN, BRUNIG PASS, LUCERNE, FLUELEN, ST. GOTTHARD, FLUELEN, BRUNNEN, SCHWYZ, EINSIEDELN, RAPPERSWIL, ZURICH, SCHAFFHAUSEN

'I visited that wicked wit Voltaire; he happened to be in good-humour.'

ROUSSEAU, JEAN-JACQUES. MOTIERS-TRAVERS, LA CHAUX DE FONDS, LA FERRIÈRE, MOTIERS-TRAVERS, BROT, CREUX DU VAN, MOTIERS-TRAVERS, NEUCHÂTEL, ILE ST. PIERRE, BIENNE, BASLE

Driven out of Motiers-Travers by popular agitation, Rousseau went to the Ile St. Pierre in the Lake of Bienne. Expelled again, Rousseau left Switzerland for England.

SHARP, SAMUEL. GENEVA

'I must confess to you that I have yet seen nothing which has afforded me so much pleasure as that extraordinary genius Mons. Voltaire. My principal motive for passing the Alps, by way of Geneva, was a visit to that Gentleman.'

THOMAS, ABRAHAM, & PETER. BEX, MARTIGNY, VISP, ZERMATT, ST. THEODUL PASS, BREUIL, CHATILLON, AOSTA, GRAND ST. BERNARD PASS, MARTIGNY, BEX

'Des Anglais ont découvert Chamounix; mais ce sont nos botanistes Suisses, et Thomas le premier, qui ont découvert Zermatt. La première fois qu'il y fut, avec je ne sais quels compagnons, la population s'effraya de ces étrangers armés de couteaux et de pioches, et munis d'énormes boîtes, telles qu'on n'en avait jamais vu dans le pays. Des groupes se formèrent, on se consulta, on chuchota; chacun fit part de ses observations et de ses soupçons, si bien que tout Zermatt fut convaincu que ces étrangers étaient des espions, qui venaient observer les passages de la vallée, dans l'intention évidente de les franchir au retour avec les moutons qu'ils pourraient voler sur les hauts alpages. Aussitôt la foule se porta devant la maison du curé, la seule du village où il fut alors possible de trouver un logement, et le somma de livrer les hommes qu'il venait de recevoir, attendu que ces hommes étaient des espions.'

WILKES, JOHN. GENEVA

'The Appenines are not near so high or so horrible as the Alps. On the Alps you see very few tolerable spots; and only firs, but very majestic.'

1766

BOURRIT, MARC-THÉODORE. GENEVA, CHAMONIX

DICK, JAKOB. SPIEZ, KIENTHAL, FRUTIGEN, KANDERSTEG

HERVEY, FREDERICK AUGUSTUS. SCHAFFHAUSEN, ZURICH, BERNE, PAYERNE, LAUSANNE, GENEVA

'So widely famed was the Bishop as a traveller, and so great was his reputation as a connoisseur of all good things, that Lord Bristol's Hotel—he was latterly known everywhere on the continent as Lord Bristol—came to be the best known and regarded in every city or town where he sojourned and was thus the precursor of the Hotels Bristol still to be found all over Europe.'

HERVEY, WILLIAM. SCHAFFHAUSEN, ZURICH, BERNE, PAYERNE, LAUSANNE, ORBE, VALLORBE

'Crossing the Mount Jura is a fine view of the two lakes of Neuchatel and Geneva; the country between the two lakes a well cultivated sloping hill, Geneva lake bounded by the Alps.'

HIRSCHFELD, C. C. L. BASLE, SOLEURE, BERNE, FRIBOURG, BIENNE, ILE ST. PIERRE, BERNE, THUN, INTERLAKEN, LAUTERBRUNNEN, GRINDELWALD, ZURICH, SCHAFFHAUSEN

'What struck me most in Switzerland among the curiosities of nature were those horrid structures the Alps. . . . Never can a view of nature be finer than that of a glacier at sunset. When the sun was no more to be seen on the horizon, we raised our eyes to the snow mountains where we saw the most wonderful colouring. . . . One is awe-stricken at this view, and longs to impart this pleasant sense of horror to all one's friends.'

JETZLER, CHRISTOPH. SCHAFFHAUSEN, GLARUS, LINTHAL, THIERFEHD, SANDALP, BIFERTENFIRN, KLAUSEN PASS, ALTDORF, ANDERMATT,

ST. GOTTHARD PASS, AIROLO, ST. GOTTHARD PASS, ANDERMATT, OBERALP PASS, DISENTIS, COIRE, PFÄFERS

'I should have liked to climb the Tödi although the hunter who was with me said that he had never been to the top and did not know if it could be done.'

RICOU, J. D. BEX, VISP, ZERMATT, SCHÖNBÜHL, OBERSTAFFEL, STOCKJE

'Comme les montagnes de Pratoborgno sont d'une étendue presque immense il n'est presque pas possible d'aller partout; c'est la raison pour laquelle je n'ai pas trouvé le géranium ni la petite linaire. Peut-être, les aurais-je trouvés si j'avais pu aller dans une montagne où Thomas avait été, mais une couche de neige fraîche tombée il n'y avait que quelques jours sur les glaciers a fait que mon guide n'a pas voulu y aller disant qu'il y avait du danger à les traverser à cause des fentes que la neige cachait.'

SAUSSURE, HORACE-BÉNÉDICT DE. GENEVA, LE MOLE, SAMOËNS, SIXT

1767

FUESSLI, JOHANN CONRAD. GERSAU, BECKENRIED, ENGELBERG, SURENEN PASS, ALTDORF

'Engelberg: what does one find there? Nothing but repulsive mountains and, between them, a fine monastery but a poor village; scattered houses and bare meadows. No gardens, no fruit trees, there are no fields to please the eye.'

SAUSSURE, HORACE-BÉNÉDICT DE. GENEVA, CHAMONIX, COL DU BONHOMME, COL DE LA SEIGNE, COURMAYEUR, AOSTA, GRAND ST. BERNARD PASS, MARTIGNY, GENEVA

1768

ANONYMOUS 3. BASLE, LUCERNE, SCHWYZ, BRUNNEN, ALTDORF, ST. GOTTHARD PASS, BELLINZONA, MILAN, DOMODOSSOLA, SIMPLON PASS, BRIG, SION, MARTIGNY, GENEVA

'Je grimpais à la cime du St. Gothard, d'où la vue s'égare sur les montagnes variées et majestueuses qui l'environnent. Là, j'eus le plaisir ineffable de voisiner avec le Ciel qui n'en est éloigné que de trois pas et un saut. . . .'

DERBY, ELIZABETH COUNTESS OF. GENEVA, CHAMONIX, GENEVA, LAUSANNE, MEILLERIE

'Lo! where Mont Blanc his silver columns rears,
And crowns with glitt'ring ice th'astonished spheres!
Ye unsunned Vallies of eternal snow,
Whose deep-imbosom'd rocks for ever grow;
Where seas of Alps on seas of Alps arise,
Till chrystal pyramids assail the skies . . .'

FOX, CHARLES JAMES. GENEVA

THOMAS, ABRAHAM (*c*). BEX, VISP, SAAS, ANTRONA PASS, DOMODOSSOLA, TOSA FALLS, GRIES PASS, OBERGESTELEN, GRIMSEL PASS, UNTERAAR GLACIER, BEX, SION, EVOLENA, FERPECLE, AROLLA, PRAZGRAS, ROUSSETTE, LA CRETAZ, VALTOURNANCHE, VAL DE BAGNES.

1769

BOURRIT, MARC-THÉODORE. GENEVA, CHAMONIX

CAMPBELL OF ARDKINGLAS, SIR JAMES. GENEVA

While dining with Voltaire, Campbell relates that his host carved a partridge, 'thrust his fork into it, and then put the fork into his mouth, apparently to ascertain if the fumette was as he would have it. He then proceeded to cut it up, and sent a part of it to me. I sent it away without eating of it; and on his asking the reason, I told him the true one, without any circumlocution, that in carving the partridge he had used a fork which had just been in his own mouth.'

CASANOVA, JACQUES. LUGANO

Casanova came to Lugano to get his book printed there, where there was no censorship. The book was *La Réfutation de l'Histoire de Venise d'Amelot de la Houssaye.*

COKE, LADY MARY. GENEVA

'Mountains, Valleys, woods, rivers, lakes and Vineyards, accompanies one all the way, & the situation of Geneva is far more beautiful then that of any other place I have yet seen. . .'

GORANI, COMTE JOSEPH. BASLE, MOUTRET, NEUCHÂTEL, ROMAINMÔTIER, LAC DE JOUX, GENEVA

ROLAND DE LA PLATIÈRE. BASLE, SOLEURE, BERNE, FRIBOURG, LAUSANNE, GENEVA

'Dans aucun pays que je connaisse, les auberges ne sont tenues comme en Suisse: propreté, honnêteté, abondance et délicatesse; tout s'y trouve au premier degré.'

STANHOPE, WALTER. BERNE, LAUSANNE

'From a Window where I sit at present I see one of ye most delicious prospects in ye World. Imagine everything that is rich and lovely near at hand, and ye snowy Alps peeping over ye Clouds at forty Miles distance.'

1770

BOURRIT, MARC-THÉODORE. GENEVA, MARTIGNY, SION, THUN, INTERLAKEN, LAUTERBRUNNEN, GRINDELWALD, CHAMONIX

DE LUC, JEAN-ANDRÉ. GENEVA, SAMOËNS, SIXT, MONT BUET

HERVEY, FREDERICK AUGUSTUS. GENEVA, COIRE, BONDO

Voltaire, hearing that Lord Bristol was going to Rome, asked him 'to bring back the ears of the Grand Inquisitor'.

PARS, WILLIAM. GENEVA, CHAMONIX, LAUTERBRUNNEN, GRINDELWALD, MEIRINGEN, GRIMSEL PASS, FURKA PASS, ANDERMATT

SAUSSURE, HORACE-BÉNÉDICT DE. GENEVA, CHAMONIX, MARTIGNY, SION, GRIMSEL PASS, MEIRINGEN, GRINDELWALD, VEVEY, DENT DE JAMAN.

For part of this tour de Saussure was accompanied by Lord Palmerston, Mr. Sloane, Mr. Hatsel, and William Pars the artist.

1771

BRYDONE, PATRICK. AOSTA, GRAND ST. BERNARD PASS, MARTIGNY, GENEVA

Left 'the parched fields of Italy for the delightful cool mountains of Switzerland, where liberty and simplicity, long since banished from polished nations, still flourish in their original purity—where the temperature and moderation of the climate and that of the inhabitants are mutually emblematic of each other. For whilst other nations are scorched by the heat of the sun, and the still more scorching heats of tyranny and superstition, here the genial breezes for ever fan the air, and heighten that alacrity and joy which liberty and innocence alone can inspire; here the genial flow of the soul has never yet been checked by the idle and useless refinements of art, but opens and expands to all calls of affection and benevolence.'

PEZAY, MASSON DE (*c*). BASLE, SOLEURE, BERNE, THUN, INTERLAKEN, LAUTERBRUNNEN, GRINDELWALD, THUN, BERNE, LAUSANNE

'A chaque pause de ma marche, je crois qu'il n'est rien de plus haut, de plus grand, de plus horrible que ce que je vois. Je fais un pas, nouvelles horreurs, gradation nouvelle dans le gigantesque des tableaux. La Nature ne se lasse point, & mon étonnement se fatigue. Ce que je vois est si grand, que mon imagination vaine n'ose rien au-delà. Cependant ce que j'ai vu s'abaisse devant ce que je vais voir; & ce que je vais voir, doit s'abaisser devant mille autres masses, qu'il ne m'est pas réservé de connoître.'

SAUSSURE, HORACE-BÉNÉDICT DE. GENEVA, MARTIGNY, SION, BRIG, SIMPLON PASS, DOMODOSSOLA, LOCARNO, LUGANO, MONTE BRÈ, CAPRINO, GANDRIA, COMO, AOSTA, GRAND ST. BERNARD PASS, MARTIGNY, GENEVA

TREMBLAYE, CHEVALIER DE LA. LOCARNO, BELLINZONA, ST. GOTTHARD PASS, ALTDORF, SCHWYZ, GLARUS, ZURICH, APPENZELL, ZURICH, LUCERNE, BERNE, THUN, INTERLAKEN, GRINDELWALD, BERNE, NEUCHÂTEL, VEVEY, GENEVA, MARTIGNY, SION, CHAMONIX, GENEVA

WYTTENBACH, JAKOB SAMUEL. BERNE, THUN, INTERLAKEN, LAUTERBRUNNEN, KLEINE SCHEIDEGG, GRINDELWALD, GROSSE SCHEIDEGG, MEIRINGEN, GRIMSEL PASS, OBERGESTELEN, MÜNSTER, BRIG, SION, MARTIGNY, VEVEY, BERNE

On this, the first tourist passage of the Kleine Scheidegg, Wyttenbach was accompanied by Karl Viktor von Bonstetten and by the Rev. Norton Nicholls, the friend of Thomas Gray.

1772

BORDIER, ANDRÉ CÉSAR. GENEVA, EVIAN, MARTIGNY, TÊTE NOIRE PASS, CHAMONIX, GENEVA

'Ice not as an entirely hard and solid mass, but as a mass of coagulated material, or as wax, softened, flexible, and ductile up to a certain point.' This was, therefore, the first enunciation of the plastic theory of glacier movement.

BOURRIT, MARC-THÉODORE. GENEVA, CHAMONIX

'Un petit chapeau blanc couvre mon chef; mon habillement est une veste d'été, par-dessus je mets un habit d'hiver que j'ôte ou que je remets selon la température ou les courses que j'entreprends; je porte des bottes avec lesquelles je suis moins sensible aux chutes et aux glissades et sous les talons je porte des crampons d'acier . . . le mulet est chargé pour sa part d'une valise, d'un portefeuille, d'un parapluie (rouge), d'une lunette et, par décoration seulement je laisse apercevoir une paire de pistolets, quoique je n'aie ni plomb, ni poudre pour les charger.'

DE LUC, JEAN-ANDRÉ. GENEVA, SAMOËNS, SIXT, COL D'ANTERNE, MONT BUET

'The mountain air has this salutary property that it spreads a kind of calm through all the organs, allowing the soul to enjoy itself very tranquilly.'

NORTHUMBERLAND, ELIZABETH DUCHESS OF. GENEVA, THONON, SALÈVE, LAUSANNE, PAYERNE, MORAT

'A rude kind of Magnificence appears in these stupendous works of Nature. The Clouds at Times were manifestly under our feet. At the same Time that one could not see, without a sentiment of Horror, Rocks suspended over one's head.'

1773

BJÖRNSTAHL, JACOB JONAS. GENEVA, CHAMONIX, GENEVA, LAUSANNE, MORAT, BERNE, BADEN, ZURICH, SCHAFFHAUSEN, BASLE

Lord Mahon accompanied Björnstahl to Chamonix.

BOURRIT, MARC-THÉODORE. GENEVA, GRAND ST. BERNARD, VALSOREY, CHAMONIX

He ascended the Brévent with William Hervey, and, on the way down, claimed to have saved his life: 'Mon compagnon étoit tué, si mes cris ne l'avoient averti à temps du danger qu'il couroit par la chute d'un bloc de rocher; il évita ce malheur, et me dit que de sa vie le cri de désespoir que je poussai ne s'effaceroit de son souvenir.'

BRIONNE, COMTESSE DE. LAUSANNE, LAC DE JOUX, DENT DE VAULION

'On parle encore du voyage que madame la comtesse de Brionne fit en 1773 dans ces lieux déserts. Une pareille course a quelque chose de romanesque: elle nous rappelle l'apparition de Vénus à Enée dans les forêts de Lybie.'

HERVEY, WILLIAM. GENEVA, CHAMONIX, MARTIGNY, EVIAN, GENEVA, LAUSANNE, BERNE, SOLEURE, BASLE

MOORE, JOHN. GENEVA, CHAMONIX, MARTIGNY, EVIAN, GENEVA, LAUSANNE, BERNE, BASLE

'The wonderful accounts I had heard of the glaciers had excited my curiosity a good deal, while the air of superiority assumed by some who had made this boasted tour, piqued my pride still more. One could hardly mention anything curious or singular, without being told by some of those travellers, with an air of cool contempt, "Dear Sir, that is pretty well; but, take my word for it, it is nothing to the glaciers of Savoy".' Moore was travelling with the Duke of Hamilton.

MÜLLER, JOHANNES VON. SCHAFFHAUSEN, SCHINZNACH, ORBE, VALEYRES, MONT SUCHET, LAC DE JOUX, NEUCHÂTEL, SCHAFFHAUSEN

The great historian's first visit to Bonstetten at Valeyres where he was inspired to conceive his History of Switzerland.

1774

ANONYMOUS 4 (*c*). BASLE, SOLEURE, BERNE, LAUSANNE, GENEVA

'From Basle, go to Schaffhouse, (eighteen leagues), to see the source of the Rhine, and the glacières or vallies of ice, which passage at certain times is very dangerous, particularly when the ice is thawing, as it falls down in great flakes, and destroys houses, lands, &c. If time, look into one or two of the Interior Cantons, but beware of impositions.'

BERNOULLI, JEAN. SCHAFFHAUSEN, BASLE, LIESTAL, HAUENSTEIN, OLTEN, SOLEURE, BIENNE, NEUCHÂTEL, YVERDON, LAUSANNE, GENEVA

'Dans la soirée nous passâmes le Hauenstein, une des plus hautes montagnes du canton de Bâle. Je fus enchanté des cascades et d'autres beaux spectacles que présente la nature quand on monte cette montagne et des charmants sites pitoresques qui se succèdent sur cette route.'

BOURRIT, MARC-THÉODORE. GENEVA, CHAMONIX, COL DU BONHOMME, COL DE LA SEIGNE, COURMAYEUR, AOSTA, GRAND ST. BERNARD PASS, MARTIGNY, GENEVA

DE LUC, JEAN-ANDRÉ. LAUSANNE, MARTIGNY, SION, LAUSANNE, BERNE, THUN, INTERLAKEN, LAUTERBRUNNEN, GRINDELWALD, THUN, BERNE, NEUCHÂTEL, CHAUMONT, LAC DE JOUX, LAUSANNE

'C'est par ces chemins amusans que nous atteignîmes, sans nous en appercevoir, le sommet de la montagne.'

FERGUSON, ADAM. GENEVA, CHAMONIX

In 'face of a snowy mountain in Savoye, higher than all the mountains of Scotland piled upon one another, and containing more ice in its recesses than is to be found in all Scotland in the hardest winter. The bottom of this ice is continually melting in the valleys, like the bottom of a roll of butter placed on end in a frying pan.' Ferguson was acting as tutor to Lord Chesterfield.

MÜLLER, JOHANNES VON. SCHAFFHAUSEN, WINTERTHUR, ZURICH, ZUG, SCHWYZ, BRUNNEN, ALTDORF, LUCERNE, SURSEE, OLTEN, BERNE, FRIBOURG, VEVEY, LAUSANNE, GENEVA

Staying in Jean Tronchin's house in Geneva, Müller met Richard Neville.

PILATI DI TASSULLO, CARLO ANTONIO. BORMIO, UMBRAIL PASS, STA. MARIA, OFEN PASS, ZERNEZ, ST. MORITZ, ALBULA PASS, BERGÜN, COIRE, BERNE, GENEVA

Pilati relates that at St. Moritz there was a fine of one hundred écus for saying mass, even in private rooms.

ROLAND DE LA PLATIÈRE. LE LOCLE, LA CHAUX DE FONDS, NEUCHÂTEL, GENEVA

'Je me suis voué aux montagnes. . . . S'il est encore sur la terre un pays où l'homme avec la simplicité de la nature ait conservé la dignité de son être, où la liberté vivement sentie, toujours en action, toujours sans effort, ne soit point une chimère, . . . un pays enfin que le philosophe puisse contempler avec émotion, c'est la Suisse.'

SAUSSURE, HORACE-BÉNÉDICT DE. GENEVA, ST. GERVAIS, COL DU BONHOMME, COL DE LA SEIGNE, COURMAYEUR, AOSTA, GRAND ST. BERNARD PASS, MARTIGNY, GENEVA

Descending a narrow path to Courmayeur, de Saussure found himself behind a man on a mule, but when he asked if he might pass, the man replied that he should possess his soul in patience, for it was but natural that pedestrians should suffer from those who rode.

SCHINZ, CHRISTIAN SALOMON. ZURICH, UETLIBERG

'We all of us enjoyed our first station on the mountain; we rested for a quarter of an hour, and then went on to the utmost summit of the mountain. Our tiring journey was now richly rewarded by the wide prospect.'

1775

BLAIKIE, THOMAS. GENEVA, BOURDIGNY, ST. GENIS, SALÈVE, ST. CERGUE, LA DOLE, GENEVA, THONON, EVIAN, CHATEL, PAS DE MORGINS, MONTHEY, BEX, LES PLANS, PONT DE NANT, COL DES ESSETS, ANZEINDAZ, PAS DE CHEVILLE, SION, LEUK, GEMMI PASS, KANDERSTEG, LEISSIGEN, INTERLAKEN, GRINDELWALD, INTERLAKEN, THUN, BERNE, BIENNE, ST. IMIER, LA FERRIÈRE, TÊTE DE RANG, LA TOURNE, NOIRAIGUE, VALLORBE, LAC DE JOUX, MONT TENDRE, BALLENS, AUBONNE, COTTENS, ST. CERGUE, LES ROUSSES, LA DOLE, GEX, ST. GENIS, BOURDIGNY, GENEVA, CHAMONIX, COL D'ANTERNE, SIXT, TANINGES, MOLE, MONNETIER, GENEVA, LA DOLE, ST. CERGUE, LAC DE JOUX, ST. CERGUE, ROLLE, LAUSANNE, VEVEY, AIGLE, BEX, GRAND 'VIRE, MORCLES, FULLY, HAUT D'ALESSES, BEX, MONTHEY, EVIAN, GENEVA

At Taninges he narrowly escaped being murdered as some German travellers had been. During his tour Blaikie met J.-L. Garcin, Abraham Thomas, S. Engel, Abraham Gagnebin, Abraham-Louis de Coppet among fellow-botanists, Dr. Paccard, H.-A. Gosse, and P. Gaussen among other celebrities. He called on H.-B. de Saussure, and, one day, Voltaire came to see him and his plants.

BOURRIT, MARC-THÉODORE. GENEVA, CHAMONIX, MONT BUET

GOETHE, JOHANN WOLFGANG. SCHAFFHAUSEN, CONSTANCE, ZURICH, EINSIEDELN, SCHWYZ, RIGI, ALTDORF, ANDERMATT, ST. GOTTHARD, ALTDORF, BRUNNEN, ZUG, ZURICH, BASLE

'Switzerland at first made so deep an impression on me that I was bewildered and restless. Only in later years, when I was concerned with mountains as a mineralogist was I able to consider them with composure.'

GUALANDRIS, ANGELO. COMO, LUGANO, BELLINZONA, AIROLO, ST. GOTTHARD PASS, ALTDORF, BRUNNEN, ZUG, ALBIS, ZURICH, BADEN, SOLEURE, LIESTAL, BASLE

'In a situation sufficiently horrible from the height of the mountains, the depth, narrowness and inequality of level, there is the bridge named after the Devil . . . Between all these horrors, the situation of the bridge is most pleasing.'

MÜLLER, JOHANNES VON. GENEVA, LAUSANNE, BULLE, GRUYÈRES, CHÂTEAU D'OEX, ROUGEMONT, ZWEISIMMEN, SPIEZ, THUN, INTERLAKEN, BRIENZ, BRUNIG PASS, SARNEN, LUCERNE, GERSAU, BRUNNEN, EINSIEDELN, ZURICH, SCHAFFHAUSEN, ZURZACH, BASLE, SOLEURE, BERNE, FRIBOURG, BULLE, VEVEY, GENEVA

A tour with Francis Kinloch, in the course of which they met Patrick Brydone at Lausanne.

SAUSSURE, HORACE-BÉNÉDICT DE. GENEVA, MARTIGNY, SION, MÜNSTER, FURKA PASS, ANDERMATT, ST. GOTTHARD PASS, AIROLO, ST. GOTTHARD PASS, ALTDORF, LUCERNE, LANGNAU, BERNE, GENEVA

On the St. Gotthard pass, de Saussure met Charles Greville making his way across the pass in a cabriolet; this was the first occasion on which a wheeled carriage crossed it.

SHUCKBURGH, SIR GEORGE. GENEVA, SALÈVE, ST. JEOIRE, MOLE, CHAMONIX

'Before me an immediate precipice, *a pic* of above 1,000 feet, and behind me the very steep ascent I had just now mounted. I was imprudently the first of the company; the surprise was perfect horror, and two steps further had sent me headlong from the rock.'

SULZER, JOHANN GEORG. BASLE, LANGENBRUCK, SOLEURE, BERNE, MORAT, LAUSANNE, VEVEY, NYON, GENEVA

'Berne has a view of the High Alps which, because of their bare cliffs which rise above the clouds and of the eternal snows which crown their summits and appear quite loose, present a wonderful spectacle that certainly no one can see without a kind of delight.'

1776

BOURRIT, MARC-THÉODORE. GENEVA, CHAMONIX

COXE, WILLIAM. SCHAFFHAUSEN, ST. GALL, APPENZELL, ALTSTÄTTEN, SARGANS, WALLENSTADT, GLARUS, EINSIEDELN, RAPPERSWIL, ZURICH, ALBIS, ZUG, LUCERNE, ALTDORF, ANDERMATT, FURKA PASS, MÜNSTER, GRIMSEL PASS, MEIRINGEN, GROSSE SCHEIDEGG, GRINDELWALD, LAUTERBRUNNEN, INTERLAKEN, KANDERSTEG, GEMMI PASS, LEUK, SION, MARTIGNY, TÊTE NOIRE PASS, CHAMONIX, GENEVA, LAUSANNE, LAC DE JOUX, YVERDON, NEUCHÂTEL, LA CHAUX DE FONDS, LE LOCLE, MORAT, FRIBOURG, BERNE, LANGNAU, BERNE, MORAT, LAUSANNE, GENEVA, LAUSANNE, YVERDON, NEUCHÂTEL, BIENNE, SOLEURE, BASLE

On the Montenvers Coxe refers to 'a hovel, where those, who make expeditions towards Mont Blanc, frequently pass the night'. This was before the erection of Blair's Folly in 1779, and shows that the tourist traffic at Montenvers was already heavy.

COZENS, JOHN ROBERT. GENEVA, CHAMONIX, MARTIGNY, BEX, BERNE, LAC DE JOUX, BERNE, THUN, INTERLAKEN, LAUTERBRUNNEN, GRINDELWALD, MEIRINGEN, JOCH PASS, ENGELBERG, SURENEN PASS, ALTDORF, KLAUSEN PASS, GLARUS, COIRE, THUSIS, SPLÜGEN PASS, CHIAVENNA, BONDO

Cozens was accompanying Richard Payne Knight as artist.

HOWARD, JOHN. GENEVA, LAUSANNE, BERNE, SOLEURE, BASLE

Visiting the prisons of Switzerland, 'and found them generally untenanted'.

KÜTTNER, KARL GOTTLOB. BASLE, BADEN, ZURICH, EINSIEDELN, RAPPERSWIL, GREIFENSEE, ZURICH, BASLE

'If you were to come here, you would marvel and say "I have never seen mountains before; all this is quite new to me." And the lake, that great mass of water surrounded by mountains reflected in its surface! I stood there, and could not take in all the sights before me. . .'

MALESHERBES, CHRÉTIEN GUILLAUME DE LAMOIGNON DE. BERNE, THUN, INTERLAKEN, LAUTERBRUNNEN

MIRABEAU, GABRIEL-HONORÉ DE. LES VERRIÈRES, MORGES, GENEVA, THONON—AOSTA, GRAND ST. BERNARD PASS, MARTIGNY, LAUSANNE, NEUCHÂTEL, LES VERRIÈRES, STE. CROIX, YVERDON, BERNE, SOLEURE, BASLE

Mirabeau had escaped from prison and, after passing through Switzerland to Provence, he returned to elope with the Marquise de Monnier.

ROLAND DE LA PLATIÈRE. BASLE, LUCERNE, ALTDORF, ANDERMATT, ST. GOTTHARD PASS, BELLINZONA, LUGANO, COMO

Roland's menu at Andermatt consisted of Bologna sausage, soup, a stew, lamb, brocolis, roast veal, roast chamois, salad, dessert and fruit; all of which confirmed his already favourable opinion of Swiss inns.

ROQUE, M. DE LA. GENEVA, CHAMONIX, MARTIGNY, BEX, LAUSANNE, YVERDON, MORGES, GENEVA

Sallanche: 'les chambres et les Lits y sont d'une mal-propreté à faire passer la plus violente envie de dormir.'
Chamonix: 'l'auberge est bonne, propre, et ordinairement bien approvisionnée, et à un prix raisonnable.'
Martigny: 'l'auberge, appelée, la Grande Maison (la seule où l'on puisse s'arrêter) est dénuée de meubles; du moins de bons Lits: d'ailleurs elle est propre et bien aérée, les vivres n'y manquent point.'

SAUSSURE, HORACE-BÉNÉDICT DE. GENEVA, CHAMONIX, MONT BUET

Accompanying de Saussure on his visit to Chamonix was Sir William Hamilton. De Saussure also made an expedition to the Mole with Sir George Shuckburgh of which the latter wrote, concerning a chalet on the mountain: 'on entering we found a comfortable fire, and the little *cabane* inhabited by a couple of Alpine shepherdesses and their two cows, on whose whey and some very coarse bread they wholly subsisted, not discontented but even proud of their lot; and who, out of a singular species of contempt, call the inhabitants of the plain, *mange-rôtis*, that is eaters of meat.'

SHERLOCK, MARTIN. GENEVA

To Sherlock, Voltaire made one of his rare observations on the beauties of the Alps. 'From his gardens you see the Alps, the Lake, the city of Geneva, and its environs, which are very pleasant. He said, "it is a beautiful prospect".'

SULZER, JOHANN GEORG. COMO, LUGANO, BELLINZONA, ST. GOTTHARD PASS, ALTDORF, LUCERNE, ALBIS, ZURICH, SCHAFFHAUSEN

From Lugano 'the way is truly one of romantic beauty. . . . The lovely morning and the keen mountain air which makes the sunshine brighter and the sky darker contributed with other pleasant impressions. I felt suddenly as if I had recovered my health.'

WYTTENBACH, JAKOB SAMUEL. BERNE, THUN, INTERLAKEN, LAUTERBRUNNEN, GRINDELWALD

At Lauterbrunnen Wyttenbach and his friends measured the height of the Staubbach fall by means of ropes knotted together. They found it to be 900 feet of Berne.

1777

BECKFORD, WILLIAM. GENEVA, SALÈVE

'Were I not to go to Voltaire's sometimes and to the mountains very often I should die.'

BESSON, HENRI. GENEVA, LAUSANNE, MARTIGNY, SION, GLETSCH, ULRICHEN, NUFENEN PASS, AIROLO, ST. GOTTHARD PASS, ALTDORF, LUCERNE, BERNE, THUN, INTERLAKEN, LAUTERBRUNNEN, GRINDELWALD, GROSSE SCHEIDEGG, MEIRINGEN, JOCH PASS, ENGELBERG, STANS, BRUNNEN, SCHWYZ, EINSIEDELN, RAPPERSWIL, GLARUS, ELM, PANIXER PASS, ILANZ, TSCHAMUTT, COIRE, ALTSTÄTTEN, ST. GALL, ZURICH, SCHAFFHAUSEN, BASLE

Besson noticed crescentic mounds below the Rhone glacier and interpreted them as moraines deposited during previous periods of greater glacial extension. To study glacier movement he suggested that stakes be planted across glaciers, and their displacement observed.

BOURRIT, MARC-THÉODORE. GENEVA, CHAMONIX, MONT BUET

DEFELLER, ABBÉ. BASLE, LAUFENBURG, SCHAFFHAUSEN, ZURICH, ALBIS, ZUG, LUCERNE, WILLISAU, BURGDORF, BERNE, SOLEURE, BALSTHAL, LIESTAL, BASLE

'Il y a là je ne sais quoi de terrible et d'agréable. On est charmé de voir une chose si extraordinaire, et d'avoir sous les yeux de si grandes opérations de la nature; et en même tems on ressent quelqu'inquiétude, comme à l'aspect de tout objet monstrueux et insolite.'

DESJOBERT, LOUIS-CHARLES-FELIX. BASLE, LANGENBRUCK, SOLEURE, BERNE, THUN, INTERLAKEN, LAUTERBRUNNEN, KLEINE SCHEIDEGG, GRINDELWALD, GROSSE SCHEIDEGG, MEIRINGEN, GRIMSEL PASS, OBERGESTELEN, FURKA PASS, ANDERMATT, ALTDORF, LUCERNE, LANGNAU, BERNE, KÖLLIKEN, BADEN, ZURICH, SCHAFFHAUSEN, BASLE, MOUTIER, BIENNE, ILE ST PIERRE, NEUCHÂTEL, LA CHAUX DE FONDS, MOTIERS-TRAVERS, YVERDON, LAUSANNE, EVIAN, VEVEY, BEX, LAUSANNE, GENEVA

Desjobert obtained much information on Rousseau's life at Motiers-Travers from Montmollin, the pastor.

JOSEPH II, EMPEROR. GENEVA, LAUSANNE, MORAT, BERNE, SOLEURE, BALSTHAL, LANGENBRUCK, BASLE

'At the last post house before Geneva, a gentleman came to my carriage and asked if I were the emperor. When I agreed and asked him why it interested him, he replied that he would be glad to know when the emperor proposed to go to Ferney to see Voltaire or to Geneva. On my inquiring whether Voltaire himself had charged him with this investigation, he replied in the affirmative. I then told him that this was the first occasion during the whole of my journey that I have been called upon to give an account of my intentions to any one.'

LENZ, JAKOB MICHAEL REINHOLD. BASLE, SCHAFFHAUSEN, ZURICH, EINSIEDELN, GRINDELWALD, OBERGESTELEN, FURKA PASS, ANDERMATT, ZURICH, BASLE, NEUCHÂTEL, SION, BERNE, COIRE, TIRANO, BERNINA PASS, PONTE, ALBULA PASS, COIRE, GLARUS, ST. GALL, APPENZELL.

MÜLLER, JOHANNES VON. VALEYRES, ORBE, PAYERNE, BERNE, THUN, INTERLAKEN, MEIRINGEN, SUSTEN PASS, WASSEN, ANDERMATT, ST. GOTTHARD PASS, BELLINZONA, LOCARNO, ISOLA BELLA, MERGOZZO, DOMODOSSOLA, SIMPLON PASS, BRIG, SIERRE, LEUK, GEMMI PASS, ENGSTLIGENGRAT, ADELBODEN, HAHNENMOOS PASS, LENK, ZWEISIMMEN, SAANEN, ROUGEMONT, ROSSINIÈRE, MONTBOVON, COL DE JAMAN, VEVEY, LAUSANNE, VALEYRES

A journey by the celebrated historian in company with Karl Victor von Bonstetten and Jean Trembley.

QUERINI, ANGELO. GENEVA, LAUSANNE, YVERDON, NEUCHÂTEL, BERNE, THUN, INTERLAKEN, LAUTERBRUNNEN, GRINDELWALD, THUN, BERNE, SOLEURE, ZOFINGEN, LUCERNE, ZURICH, BASLE, SCHAFFHAUSEN

'We reached Lauterbrunnen at last and went to the house of the village parson, to whom we had been directed. He was surprised at the large size of our party, and having greeted us a thousand times as "magnificent sirs" in a barbarous tongue, he wished us to the inn, alleging insufficiency of beds and the fact that his wife suffered from her feet. But in the end he did not refuse to take us in, and he treated us with the hospitality and good will that characterises Swiss parsons.'

RAMOND DE CARBONNIÈRES, L. E. BASLE, SCHAFFHAUSEN, ZURICH, EINSIEDELN, SCHWYZ, LUCERNE, ENGELBERG, JOCH PASS, MEIRINGEN, GROSSE SCHEIDEGG, GRINDELWALD, LAUTERBRUNNEN, INTERLAKEN, THUN, BERNE, LAUSANNE, GENEVA, MARTIGNY, SION, BRIG, FURKA PASS, ANDERMATT, ALTDORF, KLAUSEN PASS, GLARUS, ZURICH, SOLEURE, BASLE

'J'ai voyagé dans les montagnes, ou, pour mieux dire, j'ai erré sans tenir de route déterminée, à pied, avec un seul compagnon, né dans la région que nous parcourions.'

SAUSSURE, HORACE-BÉNÉDICT DE. GENEVA, MARTIGNY, SION, LEUKERBAD, GEMMI PASS, KANDERSTEG, INTERLAKEN, LAUTERBRUNNEN, KLEINE SCHEIDEGG, GRINDELWALD, GROSSE SCHEIDEGG, MEIRINGEN, GRIMSEL PASS, OBERGESTELEN, GRIES PASS, TOSA FALLS, DOMODOSSOLA, LUGANO, CHIAVENNA, SPLÜGEN PASS, THUSIS, COIRE, ZURICH, BERNE, GENEVA

SCHINZ, HANS RUDOLF. ZURICH, ALTDORF, ST. GOTTHARD PASS, LUGANO

From the St. Gotthard pass Schinz ascended the Cima di Fieudo. '... I glanced down at the way by which I had come, and the thought of my return journey began to distress me, for I could not make out how

I was going to find my way down safely . . . At last, after I had lain upon a rock, breathless, tired, and with trembling knees, I was rewarded for the hardships of my journey with a view over a wealth of peaks and passes . . . I found myself on this dizzy height as in another world in which all the impressions and sentiments of the life of society, human artificiality, and the amenities of domestic felicity, pale into insignificance.'

VOLTA, ALESSANDRO. COMO, LUGANO, BELLINZONA, ST. GOTTHARD PASS, ALTDORF, LUCERNE, EINSIEDELN, ZURICH, SCHAFFHAUSEN, BASLE, SOLEURE, BERNE, THUN, INTERLAKEN, LAUTERBRUNNEN, GRINDELWALD, THUN, BERNE, NEUCHÂTEL, LAUSANNE, GENEVA

'The eye is struck and the heart quickened by the magnificent contrast between a delightful open valley with rich pastures and fat cattle, and the immediately following dark gorge, narrow and deep, the sight of which dismays the traveller.'

1778

BECK, JEAN JOSEPH. GRESSONEY-ST-JEAN, LAVETZ, COL DE SALZA, HOHESLICHT, LYSJOCH

'Hardly had we got to the summit of the rock than we saw a grand—an amazing spectacle. We sat down to contemplate at our leisure the lost valley, which seemed to us to be entirely covered with glaciers. We examined it carefully, but could not satisfy ourselves that it was an unknown valley, seeing that none of us had ever been in the Valais.' The 'lost' valley was, of course, that of Zermatt.

BOURRIT, MARC-THÉODORE. GENEVA, MARTIGNY, CHERMONTANE, MARTIGNY, SION, SIERRE, VISSOYE, MEIDEN PASS, TURTMANN, BRIG, OBERGESTELEN, FURKA PASS, ANDERMATT, ALTDORF, LUCERNE, INTERLAKEN, LAUTERBRUNNEN, KLEINE SCHEIDEGG, GRINDELWALD

As a result of his visit to the Anniviers and Turtman valleys Bourrit concluded that these were the sites described by Rousseau in the 'Lettre du Valais' of his *Nouvelle Héloïse.*

DE LUC, GUILLAUME-ANTOINE. GENEVA, ST. GERVAIS, COL DU BONHOMME, COL DE LA SEIGNE, COURMAYEUR, AOSTA, GRAND ST. BERNARD PASS, MARTIGNY, BEX, MEILLERIE, GENEVA

'Quelle situation *romantique* que celle des bains [de Courmayeur]! Ce mot anglois m'échappe; car je ne sais que lui substituer. . . .'

FRISI, PAOLO. DOMODOSSOLA, SIMPLON PASS, BRIG, SION, MARTIGNY, GENEVA, MARTIGNY, GRAND ST. BERNARD PASS, AOSTA

KÜTTNER, KARL GOTTLOB. BASLE, OLTEN, AARBURG, LUCERNE, ALTDORF, ST. GOTTHARD PASS, BELLINZONA, LUGANO, COMO, MILAN,

LOCARNO, AIROLO, NUFENEN PASS, OBERGESTELEN, GRIMSEL PASS, MEIRINGEN, GROSSE SCHEIDEGG, GRINDELWALD, LAUTERBRUNNEN, INTERLAKEN, THUN, BERNE, BASLE

'Everyone who travels in Switzerland (and to travel through Switzerland and to make a journey in the Alps are two different things) wants to see Grindelwald and then says that he has been in the Alps. The truth is that few, even among the Swiss themselves, see more of the Alps than Grindelwald.'

MARTYN, THOMAS. GENEVA, VANDOEUVRE, LAUSANNE, VEVEY, BEX, GENEVA

'Vandoeuvre, Oct. 1, 1778.

'Our parlour windows have the mountains of Savoy in full front, with the glaciers towering over them, exhibiting a most august view at sunset, in a clear evening.'

MÜLLER, JOHANNES VON. GENEVA, ORBE, VALEYRES, GRUYÈRES, ROUGEMONT, ZWEISIMMEN, THUN, FRIBOURG, VEVEY, EVIAN, GENEVA, ROUGEMONT, ZWEISIMMEN, THUN, INTERLAKEN, BRIENZ, BRUNIG PASS, KRIENS, ENGELBERG, SURENEN PASS, ALTDORF, ANDERMATT, FLUELEN, SCHWYZ, LUCERNE, ESCHHOLZMATT, BERNE, VALEYRES, GENEVA

'At Rougemont I met two Englishmen: Garnet (cousin and friend of Gates the American General) and Randolph. . . .'

PICTET, MARC-AUGUSTE. GENEVA, CHAMONIX, MONT BUET, COL DU BONHOMME, COL DE LA SEIGNE, COURMAYEUR, AOSTA, GRAND ST. BERNARD PASS, MARTIGNY, VEVEY, GENEVA

RANDOLPH, —. BASLE, BERNE, LANGNAU, SOLEURE, AARAU, ZURICH, EINSIEDELN, ZURICH, SCHAFFHAUSEN, BERNE, THUN, INTERLAKEN, LAUTERBRUNNEN, GRINDELWALD, ROUGEMONT, BERNE, BIENNE, NEUCHÂTEL, PORRENTRUY, DELÉMONT, MOUTIER, LA CHAUX DE FONDS, LE LOCLE, MOTIERS-TRAVERS, YVERDON, VALLORBE, LAC DE JOUX, GENEVA

'To behold, from the Dent de Vaullion, the sun rising in all its splendor, and discovering to the astonished eye near half of Switzerland, nine considerable lakes, the fertile country of Franche Compté, and the noble Glacieres of Savoy bounding the rich borders of the lake of Geneva, are images which the pencil is unable to represent, and which the most daring flights of poetry would fail in their attempts to encircle.'

ROQUE, M. DE LA. LUGANO, BELLINZONA, ST. GOTTHARD PASS, ALTDORF, LUCERNE, GENEVA, LAUSANNE, BERNE, LANGNAU, THUN, INTERLAKEN, LAUTERBRUNNEN, GRINDELWALD, BERNE, SOLEURE, ZURICH, SCHAFFHAUSEN, BASLE

Thun: 'l'auberge ici est très bonne; celle d'Unterseen est détestable.' Lauterbrunnen: 'le moins de mal que l'on puisse dire de l'auberge est de convenir qu'elle est mauvaise: le meilleur parti est celui d'aller

directement mettre pied à terre chez le curé du lieu; sa maison peut recevoir trois ou quatre maitres à la fois: elle est communément assez bien approvisionnée.'
Grindelwald: 'le cabaret est très propre, mais communément assez vide de provision: il est bon de s'en assurer (de transportables) avant que de quitter Thun.'

SABRAN, MME DE. BASLE, SOLEURE, LUCERNE, LANGNAU, BERNE, LAUSANNE, GENEVA

'Ah! le beau pays que la Suisse, mon frère; mais quel dommage de ne pouvoir le voir plus en détail. . . . Vous n'avez pas idée de mon enthousiasme au milieu de ces superbes montagnes, dont les cimes menacent les cieux. . . . J'en veux au sort de ne pas m'avoir fait naître Suissesse. Je ne forme pas d'autres désirs que d'habiter ce charmant pays.'

SAUSSURE, HORACE-BÉNÉDICT DE. GENEVA, CHAMONIX, MONT BUET, COL DU BONHOMME, COL DE LA SEIGNE, COURMAYEUR, AOSTA, GRAND ST. BERNARD PASS, MARTIGNY, LAUSANNE, GENEVA

STUDER, SAMUEL EMANUEL. BERNE, GENEVA, CHAMONIX

VERNET, JOSEPH. GENEVA, CHAMONIX, EVIAN, LAUSANNE, GSTEIG, LAUENEN, INTERLAKEN, LAUTERBRUNNEN, SCHAFFHAUSEN

In 1763 Vernet had painted 'La Bergère des Alpes' to illustrate Marmontel's Tale, but without ever having been to Switzerland. Now he was remedying that omission, and among the pictures that he made on this visit were 'Caverne des dragons près St. André', 'Pont près du rocher de Balin', 'Glaciers de Breithorn', and 'Montagne de Getten [Gelten] dans le Canton de Berne'.

1779

BONSTETTEN, KARL VIKTOR VON. ROUGEMONT, GSTAAD, GSTEIG

'Ici [Rougemont] rien ne me trouble, rien ne me peine et je sens combien ces montagnes et ces rochers calment l'âme et la disposent à la sérénité.'

BOURRIT, MARC-THÉODORE. GENEVA, CHAMONIX

BRIDEL, LOUIS. CHIAVENNA, SPLÜGEN PASS, THUSIS, COIRE, WALLENSTADT, ZURICH

'En regardant cette immense montagne que je devois traverser le lendemain, je fus un peu effrayé.'

COXE, WILLIAM. CHIAVENNA, BONDO, MALOJA PASS, ST. MORITZ, ZUOZ, SCHULS, NAUDERS, RESCHEN-SCHEIDECK, STA. MARIA, UMBRAIL PASS, BORMIO, TIRANO, BONDO, CHIAVENNA, SPLÜGEN PASS, THUSIS, COIRE, LENZERHEIDE, WIESEN, DAVOS, KLOSTERS, LANDQUART, COIRE, DISENTIS, OBERALP PASS, ANDERMATT, ALTDORF, BRUNNEN, SCHWYZ, GERSAU, STANS, LUCERNE, ZURICH

St. Moritz; 'I am lodged in one of the boarding-houses, which abound in this place, for the accommodation of persons who drink the waters. The company at table consists, at present, of only two merchants of Appenzel, who are established at Genoa, and a clergyman of Lower Engadina.'

GERCKEN, PHILIPP WILHELM. BASLE, SOLEURE, BERNE, AARBURG, BADEN, ZURICH, SCHAFFHAUSEN, ST. GALL

From Berne 'one sees the distant snow mountains rise up in all their glory over the clouds. No view could be more splendid, these awful products of nature in the distance, and, near by, fine villages, fields, forests, and country houses.'

GOETHE, JOHANN WOLFGANG. BASLE, MOUTIER, BIENNE, BERNE, THUN, INTERLAKEN, LAUTERBRUNNEN, GRINDELWALD, GROSSE SCHEIDEGG, MEIRINGEN, INTERLAKEN, BERNE, LANGNAU, BERNE, PAYERNE, LAUSANNE, LAC DE JOUX, LA DOLE, ST. CERGUE, NYON, GENEVA, CHAMONIX, COL DE BALME, MARTIGNY, SION, BRIG, OBERGESTELEN, FURKA PASS, ANDERMATT, ALTDORF, LUCERNE, ALBIS, ZURICH, CONSTANCE, SCHAFFHAUSEN

'It grew darker, and only the larger masses were visible. One after another the stars rose over the scene. Above the summit of the mountains we saw a light we could not explain. It was clear, and without lustre, like the light of the Milky Way, yet more dense; something like the Pleiades, but much greater. We gazed upon it continually, until, changing our position, we beheld it as a huge pyramid, pervaded by some inward mystic light, something like that of the glow-worm, rising far above the dark mountain tops. We then saw it was the vast summit of Mont Blanc.'

GORANI, COMTE JOSEPH. GENEVA, NYON, BURSINEL, LAC DE JOUX

'Il alla visiter la vallée de Joux et traversa de grands bois où l'on n'entrait alors qu'armé jusqu'aux dents, "car ils fourmillaient de loups".'

HERVEY, FREDERICK AUGUSTUS. AOSTA, GRAND ST. BERNARD PASS, MARTIGNY, BERNE

'Very well, very much amus'd, and not the worse for having pass'd Mt. St. Bernard up to the knees in snow.'

KÜTTNER, KARL GOTTLOB. BASLE, MOUTIER, SOLEURE, BERNE, MORAT, AVENCHES, LAUSANNE, VEVEY

'There are splendid swimmers here; I see people a quarter of a league away from land.'

MARTYN, THOMAS. GENEVA, BOSSEY, SALÈVE, MORNEX, CHÈNE, GENEVA, LAUSANNE, VEVEY, AIGLE, BERNE, SOLEURE, BASLE, SCHAFFHAUSEN, CONSTANCE, ZURICH, LUCERNE, BERNE, BIENNE, NEUCHÂTEL, BERNE, THUN, INTERLAKEN, BRIENZ, MEIRINGEN, GROSSE SCHEIDEGG, GRINDELWALD, KLEINE SCHEIDEGG, LAUTERBRUNNEN, INTERLAKEN, THUN, BERNE, FRIBOURG, VEVEY, MARTIGNY, TÊTE NOIRE PASS, CHAMONIX, COL DE BALME, MARTIGNY, VEVEY, NEUCHÂTEL, GENEVA

This journey provided Martyn with the material for his *Sketch of a Tour through Swisserland*, published in London in 1787, the earliest English guide-book to Switzerland.

MÜLLER, JOHANNES VON. GENEVA, MEILLERIE, AIGLE, COL DES MOSSES, ROUGEMONT, BERNE, GENEVA

At Geneva Müller started his great friendship with Charles Abbot.

MURITH, L. LIDDES, BOURG ST. PIERRE, MONT VELAN

SAUSSURE, HORACE-BÉNÉDICT DE. GENEVA, ROLLE, GIMEL, COL DE MARCHAIRUZ, LAC DE JOUX, DENT DE VAULION, VALLORBE, YVERDON, NEUCHÂTEL, BIENNE, ILE ST. PIERRE, MORAT, LAUSANNE, GENEVA

Of the source of the Orbe, de Saussure wrote: 'Ah! si Pétrarque avoit vu cette source, et qu'il y eût trouvé sa Laure, combien ne l'auroit-il pas préférée à celle de Vaucluse, plus abondante peut-être et plus rapide; mais dont les rochers stériles n'ont ni la grandeur, ni la riche parure qui embellit la notre!'

SHERLOCK, MARTIN. GENEVA, LAUSANNE

'Everybody is seldom in the right; but everybody is in the right in saying, the Swiss are good people. . . . You are not mistaken, Sir, in your opinion about the beauties of Switzerland.'

SPALLANZANI, LAZZARO. GENEVA, LAUSANNE, BERNE, SOLEURE, BASLE, ZURICH, LUCERNE, BERNE, MORAT, VEVEY, MARTIGNY, GRAND ST. BERNARD PASS, AOSTA

STUDER, GOTTLIEB SIEGMUND. BERNE, THUN, INTERLAKEN, LAUTERBRUNNEN, GRINDELWALD, MEIRINGEN, GRIMSEL PASS, FURKA PASS, ANDERMATT, LUCERNE

Studer relates the legendary origin of the names of Lauterbrunnen and Grindelwald: 'Before these valleys were inhabited, explorers were sent in, of whom one reported on his return that he had seen nothing but waterfalls (lauter Brunnen); the other had found only forests (Grindel Wald).'

1780

BOURBONNE, CLAUDE CHARTRAIRE DE. CHAMONIX

'Chamouny est un très joli village pour un païs aussi près du Royaume des glaces.'

BOURRIT, MARC-THÉODORE. GENEVA, CHAMONIX

BRAND, THOMAS. CHAMONIX

'A little hut which Mr. Blair, an English gentleman, whose claret, hounds and fortune had run so fast in Dorsetshire that he himself was obliged to quit England, had built as a shelter against a storm or to preserve his wine from the sun on his frequent excursions to Chamouny. This is dignified with the inscription Chateau Blair, the paysans call it the Chateau de Montanvert, and sometimes the Chateau de Folie.'

BRIDEL, PHILIPPE. LAUSANNE, BULLE, ROUGEMONT, GESSENAY, GRUYÈRES, MOLÉSON, AVENCHES, LAUSANNE

'O montagnes de l'Helvétie!
Berceau de l'antique valeur,
Du vif amour de la patrie
Et de la naïve candeur!
Recevez mon sincère hommage;
Souffrez que j'élève mes yeux
Jusqu'aux sommets glacés de ces rocs sourcilleux,
Qui des Helvétiens terminant l'héritage;
Comme un rempart majestueux,
Bien loin de leur enceinte écartent l'esclavage.'

BÜRDE, SAMUEL GOTTLIEB. SCHAFFHAUSEN, ZURICH, WALLENSTADT, COIRE, THUSIS, SPLÜGEN PASS, CHIAVENNA, GENEVA, LAUSANNE, MORAT, BERNE, LENZBURG, BADEN, ZURICH, SCHAFFHAUSEN

At Morat 'I stayed behind to bathe in the lake, but I had chosen a bad time of day at noon, and was bitten by flies and other insects all over my body before I could get into my clothes again.'

CATANI, J. B. LUZEIN, ST. ANTÖNIEN, VIERECKER PASS, GARGELLEN, MATSCHUNERJOCHL PASS, HOCHMADERJOCH PASS, SCHLAPPINER PASS, MADRISHORN, ST. ANTÖNIEN, LUZEIN

A peasant to whom they applied for hospitality insisted that they should share his bed, which, in spite of their protests, they were obliged to do.

HEINSE, J. J. W. SCHAFFHAUSEN, ZURICH, ZUG, RIGI, LUCERNE, ALTDORF, ANDERMATT, FURKA PASS, GRIMSEL PASS, MEIRINGEN, GROSSE SCHEIDEGG, GRINDELWALD, LAUTERBRUNNEN, INTERLAKEN, THUN, BERNE, FRIBOURG, VEVEY, LAUSANNE, GENEVA

On the Rigi, 'bathed in the sparkling rays of the new sun rising like a young God behind the mountains of Glarus', Heinse felt 'exhilaration and sensual joy enter into him like light. . . . At a fearful depth beside precipitous rocks, night covers the silent smooth lakes, as far as the eye could see, grey clouds pass by like formless armies; it is the thousand-headed night, the night mother of things, quick with unborn life.'

RAYNAL, GUILLAUME-THOMAS. GENEVA, LAUSANNE, NEUCHÂTEL, ANET, BERNE, LUCERNE

Raynal wanted to erect a monument on the Grütli to commemorate the three founders of the Swiss Confederation, and his own name. Permission was refused, but four years later he succeeded in being allowed to build a little obelisk on the Altstad island near Lucerne. It was destroyed by lightning in 1796.

SALIS, ULYSSES VON (*c*). BONADUZ, VERSAM, TENNA, SAFIEN, GLASS PASS, TSCHAPPINA, THUSIS, COIRE, ILANZ, VALS

'We went to visit the worthy Johann Evangelista Bertsch, chaplain of St. Peter, of whom I had heard that he had this year succeeded in hatching out hens' eggs in an oven.'

WYTTENBACH, JAKOB SAMUEL. BERNE, THUN, REICHENBACH, KIENTHAL, GAMCHILÜCKE, DÜNDENGRAT

'A beautiful view over the entire ice amphitheatre of Lauterbrunnen.'

1781

GARCIN, JEAN-LAURENT. COTTENS, AUBONNE, MARTIGNY, CHAMONIX

Garcin literally caught his death of cold at Chamonix and died shortly after his return to Cottens.

HACQUET, BALTHAZAR. EDOLO, APRICA PASS, TIRANO, BORMIO, LIVIGNO, FORCOLA DI LIVIGNO, LA MOTTA, FIENO PASS, BERNINA PASS, ST. MORITZ, MALOJA, LUNGHIN PASS, SILVAPLANA, JULIER PASS, BIVIO, STALLERBERG PASS, AVERS CRESTA, HINTERRHEIN, ANDEER, THUSIS, COIRE, LENZERHEIDE, BERGÜN, ALBULA PASS, PONTE, SCHULS

On entering the valley of Avers, a girl came up to him, shook him by the hand and bade him welcome. Somewhat astonished, he discovered that as the inhabitants of the valley saw scarcely one stranger in ten years, it was their custom, when he did come, to treat him as their best friend. Hacquet's works earned for him the title of 'the de Saussure of the Eastern Alps'.

LA BORDE, JEAN BENJAMIN DE. BASLE, SCHAFFHAUSEN, ZURICH, BERNE, SOLEURE, GENEVA, LAUSANNE, BERNE, LUCERNE, ZUG, GLARUS, ST. GALL, APPENZELL, SARGANS, PFÄFERS, GLARUS, EINSIEDELN, SCHWYZ, BRUNNEN, ALTDORF, ST. GOTTHARD PASS, AIROLO, NUFENEN PASS, OBERGESTELEN, GRIMSEL PASS, MEIRINGEN, GROSSE SCHEIDEGG, GRINDELWALD, LAUTERBRUNNEN, INTERLAKEN, THUN, BERNE, FRIBOURG, VEVEY, MARTIGNY, CHAMONIX, GENEVA, MARTIGNY, GRAND ST. BERNARD PASS, AOSTA

MERCIER, SÉBASTIEN. NEUCHÂTEL

'Ma fenêtre me présente en perspective les tableaux les plus magnifiques de la nature et ses grands monuments. Un horizon immense est sous mes regards et la chaine majestueuse des Alpes en ceint le contour. . . . C'est pour moi que le soleil, en se levant, dore ces hautes montagnes; c'est pour moi qu'à son coucher elles sont illuminées d'un feu rouge et vif.'

NICOLAI, FRIEDRICH. SCHAFFHAUSEN, ST. GALL, APPENZELL, ZURICH, BERNE, THUN, INTERLAKEN, GRINDELWALD, THUN, BERNE, MOUTIER, BASLE

'The great scenes of nature convey an impression that no human performance can equal, but nowhere are they more majestic than in mountainous country.'

POL, LUCIUS. SCANFS, CASANNA PASS, LIVIGNO, BORMIO, TIRANO, CHIAVENNA, MALOJA PASS, ST. MORITZ

'I made my way over the mountains to St. Moritz, visiting again those regions which I loved as a little boy, and drinking from the springs I liked so much. Pleasant, simple little valley! I stood there eighteen years ago and heard the cuckoo, living the day with the joy of a nomad. Hills, you still know me! I think that you are the most beautiful. May your clover and Astragalus and Anemones and sweet smelling orchids ever bloom and decorate the memories of my youthful solitude.'

ROMILLY, SIR SAMUEL. VALLORBE, LAUSANNE, GENEVA, CHAMONIX, TÊTE NOIRE PASS, MARTIGNY, BEX, VEVEY, GENEVA, LAC DE JOUX, EVIAN, MEILLERIE, DENT D'OCHE, LAUSANNE, GENEVA

'While I was in this enchanting country, I made several little excursions to see and admire its beauties; . . . and one, which more than all the rest made a deep impression on me, to the summit of the Dent d'Oche, a very high mountain of Savoy on the southern bank of the lake of Geneva. The ascent is very difficult, and for that reason, perhaps, it is seldom visited by strangers; but the prospect it affords is the most beautiful and the most sublime that I ever beheld . . .'

SAUSSURE, HORACE-BÉNÉDICT DE. GENEVA, CHAMONIX, MARTIGNY, VAL DE BAGNES, ORSIÈRES, VAL FERRET, COL FERRET, COURMAYEUR, COL DE LA SEIGNE, COL DES FOURS, COL DU BONHOMME, CHAMONIX, GENEVA

STORR, GOTTLIEB KONRAD CHRISTIAN. SCHAFFHAUSEN, ZURZACH, BERNE, THUN, INTERLAKEN, LAUTERBRUNNEN, GRINDELWALD, GROSSE SCHEIDEGG, MEIRINGEN, GRIMSEL PASS, FURKA PASS, ANDERMATT, FURKA PASS, BRIG, SION, MARTIGNY, AIGLE, GENEVA, BERNE, ZURICH, BASLE

Lauterbrunnen 'is mostly so unprovided and unacquainted with all requirements above those that are offered by a shepherd's hut, that it would be necessary to purchase the visual enjoyment of the magnificent sights of the neighbourhood at the cost of considerable privations, were it not that the Pastor's house provides the traveller with well-appointed hospitality according to long-established custom.'...

TOWNE, FRANCIS. LUGANO, DOMASO, CHIAVENNA, SPLÜGEN PASS, THUSIS, COIRE, GLARUS, LAUSANNE, GENEVA, CHAMONIX

Towne's journey was made with 'Warwick' Smith, and he found it full of 'terrible adventure'.

ZAPF, G. W. BASLE, RHEINFELDEN, ZURZACH, BADEN, ZURICH, RHEINAU, BISCHOFFSZELL, RORSCHACH

A tour of monasteries.

1782

AFSPRUNG, JOHANN MICHAEL. ST. GALL, HERISAU, GLARUS, KLAUSEN PASS, ALTDORF, ANDERMATT, ALTDORF, BRUNNEN, SCHWYZ, EINSIEDELN, RIGI, LUCERNE, ZUG, ZURICH, CONSTANCE

'On the top of a hill I settled and saw, to the North East the greater part of the lake of Constance, the Swabian shore, Constance and Meersburg, Thurgau spread out like a lovely garden, to the south east the villages of Speicher, Trogen, Wald and Rahtobel, but to the South West the magnificent rock wall of which the Säntis is the top. . . . I remained some hours in this place, and every minute fastened me more closely to it, and made my departure more difficult. Here I wept tears of sweetest joy.'

ANONYMOUS 5 (*c*). VERSAM, SAFIEN, SAFIERBERG PASS, HINTERRHEIN, SAN BERNARDINO PASS, MESOCCO

'A traveller, who has formerly visited Switzerland, must grieve indeed when he sees what this unfortunate country is, and remembers what it was.'

BOURRIT, MARC-THÉODORE. GENEVA, CHAMONIX, GRAND ST. BERNARD

BRISSOT DE WARVILLE, JACQUES-PIERRE. GENEVA, LAUSANNE, BERNE, NEUCHÂTEL, LE LOCLE, LA CHAUX DE FONDS, ILE ST. PIERRE, MOTIERS-TRAVERS, LES VERRIÈRES

'Le mois que je passai dans cet adorable séjour me parut le temps le plus court de ma vie.'

CATANI, J. B., & POL, LUCIUS. LUZEIN, ST. ANTÖNIEN, PLASSECKEN PASS, SULZFLUH

'At 5 we stood on the summit of the Sulzfluh. What a glorious view! Deep, solemn stillness all around; the high air that we were breathing glimmering with the dawn; illuminated by the rising sun which now also shone on neighbouring peaks, leaving the deep valleys dark in a blue mist. Of all the mountains that I have climbed in the Grisons, I have never found one with a more glorious view than this.'

MEINERS, CHRISTOPH. CONSTANCE, SCHAFFHAUSEN, ZURICH, BADEN, BERNE, NEUCHÂTEL, LE LOCLE, LA CHAUX DE FONDS, NIDAU, BERNE, THUN, INTERLAKEN, LAUTERBRUNNEN, GRINDELWALD, GROSSE SCHEIDEGG, MEIRINGEN, BRUNIG PASS, SARNEN, STANS, ENGELBERG, BUOCHS, ALTDORF, ANDERMATT, ALTDORF, BRUNNEN, SCHWYZ, EINSIEDELN, ZUG, LUCERNE, HERZOGENBUCHSEE, NIDAU, MORAT, MOUDON, LAUSANNE, BEX, VEVEY, LAUSANNE, GENEVA, LAUSANNE, YVERDON, MOTIERS-TRAVERS, NEUCHÂTEL, NIDAU, MOUTIER, BASLE

'As I have no desire to become a martyr to my curiosity, I set bounds to the latter, although I should have liked to see the side of the Schreckhorn that is turned towards the Valais.'

MEISTER, LEONARD (*c*). ZUG, RIGI, LUCERNE, ZURICH, BASLE

'With every step I saw beneath me new woods and new valleys, new streams and heights. Like the breasts of all-nourishing Cybele, hills rose upon hills and mountains upon mountains. But on the summit! . . . Inspired, I raised my face to the sun; my eyes drank in infinite space; I was shaken by a divine shudder, and in deep reverence I sank down before God. . . .'

PAUL, CZAREVICH. ZURICH, BERNE, THUN, INTERLAKEN, GRINDELWALD

'Le comte et la comtesse du Nord regardèrent avec les yeux de Saint Preux et de Julie ces riantes campagnes de la Suisse où le chant des oiseaux a une tendresse infinie, où le murmure des eaux inspire une langueur amoureuse.'

PINI, ERMENEGILDO. MAGADINO, BELLINZONA, AIROLO, ST. GOTTHARD PASS, CIMA DI FIEUDO

SULZER, FRANZ JOSEPH. RORSCHACH, ST. GALL, CONSTANCE, SCHAFFHAUSEN, RHEINAU, ZURICH, BADEN, LAUFENBURG, BASLE

'I would not have missed my two days in Zurich for all the expenses of my six hundred mile tour.'

1783

BECKFORD, WILLIAM. GENEVA, CHAMONIX, GENEVA, EVIAN

Beckford was on his honeymoon.

BERRY, MARY. BASLE, LAUSANNE, MORGES, GENEVA, CHAMONIX, GENEVA

Miss Berry visited a museum kept by a peasant at Chamonix who 'remembered the arrival of Mr. Wyndham and Mr. Pococke the two first strangers that ever visited the glacier from curiosity, to whom his father served as guide'.

BOURRIT, MARC-THÉODORE. GENEVA, CHAMONIX, GRAND ST. BERNARD

Bourrit's first attempt on Mont Blanc was made in this year, in company with Dr. Paccard.

CATANI, J. B., & POL, LUCIUS. LUZEIN, ST. ANTÖNIEN, GRUBEN PASS, LUZEIN

ESPINCHAL, COMTE D'. BERNE, LUCERNE, ZURICH

It was on this journey that d'Espinchal witnessed a kind of mock battle involving combined land and aquatic operations on the lake of Zurich with two boats, each mounting twelve guns, and 1,200 men.

GIBBON, EDWARD. JOUGNE, LAUSANNE

HIRSCHFELD, C. C. L. BASLE, SOLEURE, BERNE

'Truly, it is not easy to find a country with so many attractions for the traveller as Switzerland. It has the magnificence and majesty of a mountainous country, the luxuriance of richly cultivated plains, and, above all, the awe of the Arctic regions and, in the Alps, the First Wonder of Nature.'

LENGEFELD, CHARLOTTE VON. SCHAFFHAUSEN, ZURICH, BADEN, KILCHBERG, BERNE, MORAT, PAYERNE, LAUSANNE, MORGES, AUBONNE, VEVEY

'Tyranny does not darken the hearts of the inhabitants of this blessed land. They are free, which gives a special significance to their existence, they are so kind and hospitable and wish well to all men.'

The impressions which Schiller's future wife gathered during this journey helped him to visualize the Switzerland of his *William Tell* but which he never himself saw.

RAZOUMOWSKY, COMTE GRÉGOIRE DE. LAUSANNE, BEX, ANZEINDAZ, BEX, MARTIGNY, SION, LEUK, GEMMI PASS, KANDERSTEG, THUN, BERNE, LAUSANNE, LUCERNE, ALTDORF

ROGET, MRS. CATHERINE. LAUSANNE, MOUDON, PAYERNE, BERNE, SOLEURE, WIEDLISBACH, BALSTHAL, LIESTAL, BASLE

SALIS, ULYSSES VON. BORMIO, ISOLACCIA, LIVIGNO, CASANNA PASS, SCANFS

SAUSSURE, HORACE-BÉNÉDICT DE. GENEVA, VEVEY, COL DE JAMAN, CHÂTEAU D'OEX, ZWEISIMMEN, INTERLAKEN, MEIRINGEN, GRIMSEL PASS, OBERGESTELEN, GRIES PASS, FORMAZZA, FURCA DEL BOSCO, CEVIO, BIGNASCO, LOCARNO, BELLINZONA, ST. GOTTHARD PASS, ALTDORF, LUCERNE, BERNE, GENEVA

At Obergestelen de Saussure was ill, and had trouble with the surly landlord of the inn who wanted to turn him out so as to use his room as a bar-parlour on the following day which was Sunday. De Saussure bought him off and cured himself by drinking an infusion of roasted oats, like coffee, the only remedy within his reach.

STUDER, SAMUEL EMANUEL. BERNE, THUN, INTERLAKEN, MEIRINGEN, GRIMSEL PASS, UNTERAAR GLACIER, INNERTKIRCHEN, GADMEN, STEIN

'We found ourselves close to the Finsteraarhorn, the largest and by far the most beautiful rock peak in the whole of our chain of Alps, which even surpasses in height its magnificent neighbours the Wetterhorn, Tossenhorn, Schreckhorn, Viescherhorns, both Eigers, and the Jungfrau, in the midst of which it rises up majestically like a white pointed flame of fire.'

1784

BERRY, MARY. GENEVA, CHAMONIX, COL DE BALME, MARTIGNY, BEX, LAUSANNE, GENEVA

At Geneva Miss Berry met Sir James Graham, Mr. Brand, Sir James Hall, and Mr. Dawkins, and, on the way to Chamonix, General O'Hara and Lady Pembroke.

BOURRIT, MARC-THÉODORE. GENEVA, CHAMONIX

Bourrit made his second attempt on Mont Blanc, from La Griaz. Starting during the night,

'Nous voilà en marche, précédés d'un flambeau. Cette façon de gravir les montagnes a ses avantages: l'on ne voit pas les précipices . . .'

BRIDEL, LOUIS. TRONS, THUSIS, SPLÜGEN PASS, CHIAVENNA, PLURS

CHÉNIER, ANDRÉ. GENEVA, CHAMONIX, MARTIGNY, THUN, INTERLAKEN, MEIRINGEN, JOCH PASS, ENGELBERG, LUCERNE, ZURICH

> 'O Lac, fils des torrents! O Thun, onde sacrée!
> Salut, monts chevelus, verts et sombres remparts
> Qui contenez ses flots pressés de toutes parts!
> Salut, de la nature admirables caprices,
> Où les bois, les cités, pendent en précipice.'

GUIBERT, COMTE DE. VALLORBE, YVERDON, BERNE, THUN, INTERLAKEN, LAUTERBRUNNEN, GRINDELWALD, THUN, BERNE

'Une jeune et jolie dame angloise ayant eu la fantaisie d'aller se mettre sous sa chute [Staubbach] et de s'y faire doucher, appuyée contre le rocher pendant une ou deux secondes, elle en sortit comme de raison trempée jusqu'aux os. Ses beaux cheveux, m'ajouta le ministre, étoient abattus et ruisseloient de tous côtés. Deux hommes étoient avec elle: l'un étoit son mari, et la grondoit de sa folie; l'autre plus jeune ne disoit mot et ne se lassoit pas de la regarder: je ne sais comment un homme du monde eût raconté plus délicatement cette petite histoire.'

LANGLE, MARQUIS DE. SOLEURE, LANGENBRUCK, LIESTAL, BASLE, LE LOCLE, MOTIERS-TRAVERS, BIENNE, ILE ST. PIERRE, BERNE, THUN, LUCERNE, ZUG, EINSIEDELN, GLARUS, RAPPERSWIL, ZURICH, SCHAFFHAUSEN, CONSTANCE, BERNE, MORAT, LAUSANNE, VEVEY, MORGES, GENEVA

'Artist! wherever you may be, go and sail upon the lake of Thun. The day I first saw that charming lake, had nearly been my last. My soul seemed to wish for its escape;—I was about to die from the pleasure arising from the excess of sensibility and enjoyment—I actually was on the point of fainting away. But as it happened to be the cool of the evening—the influence of the stars—the silence of nature—and the absence of day, restored me to myself, refreshed my blood—and thus the night, as it were, saved my life.'

LA ROCHE, SOPHIE VON. EGLISAU, ZURICH, ALBIS, KNONAU, LUCERNE, SURSEE, MURGENTHAL, BERNE, MORAT, LAUSANNE, GENEVA, CHAMONIX, GENEVA, VEVEY, LAUSANNE, MOUDON, PAYERNE, MORAT, BERNE, SOLEURE, BALSTHAL, BASLE

Before descending from Montenvers, Frau von Laroche's guide insisted on knocking off the heels from her shoes, which was apparently a routine mutilation.

MAYER, CHARLES JOSEPH DE. BASLE, CONSTANCE, ST. GALL, APPENZELL, ZURICH, EINSIEDELN, LUCERNE, ALTDORF, KLAUSEN PASS, ALTDORF, ANDERMATT, FURKA PASS, GRIMSEL PASS, MEIRINGEN, INTERLAKEN, LAUTERBRUNNEN, GRINDELWALD, THUN, KANDERSTEG, GEMMI

PASS, KANDERSTEG, BERNE, BIENNE, MORAT, AVENCHES, BIENNE, SONCEBOZ, NEUCHÂTEL, LA CHAUX DE FONDS, LE LOCLE, MOTIERS-TRAVERS, NEUCHÂTEL, YVERDON, LAC DE JOUX, ORBE, LAUSANNE, GENEVA, MARTIGNY, SION

Grindelwald: 'the ladies' glacier, much visited by beaux with sash knotted at the waist'. From the Grimsel de Mayer rhapsodized: 'My eye wandered over the Valais, over the Milanese, stopped at Mont Blanc, and doubled back to the St. Gotthard and Furka close by. How great was I! So many giants at my feet. What a sublime level!'

MERCIER, SÉBASTIEN. NEUCHÂTEL, GENEVA, LAUSANNE, BERNE, LUCERNE, ZURICH, SOLEURE, NEUCHÂTEL

'Heureuse terre, coupée de mille fontaines, terre qui me fut hospitalière quand je fuyais trois lettres de cachet, je te salue et je rafraîchis souvent ma pensée en me rappelant tes eaux abondantes et pures, charme de la vue, plaisir de la respiration, gage de la santé, tes belles eaux éternellement courantes, tombantes ou jaillissantes.'

PARSONS, WILLIAM. GENEVA, CHAMONIX, MARTIGNY, CHILLON, GENEVA

'Elegiac Ballad occasioned by the unhappy Fate of a young gentleman of Geneva, who perished by a Fall from a Precipice in Savoy, the Author having accompanied him to Chamouni. . . .' 'The author hopes this dreadful accident will be a warning to his exploring countrymen not to venture among dangerous precipices without a guide.'

ROBERT, F. BASLE, PORRENTRUY, MOUTIER, SOLEURE, ZURICH, SCHAFFHAUSEN, CONSTANCE, ST. GALL, APPENZELL, ALTSTÄTTEN, COIRE, DISENTIS, OBERALP PASS, ANDERMATT, FURKA PASS, MÜNSTER, GRIMSEL PASS, MEIRINGEN, GROSSE SCHEIDEGG, GRINDELWALD, LAUTERBRUNNEN, INTERLAKEN, ZWEISIMMEN, ROUGEMONT, COL DE JAMAN, VEVEY, LAUSANNE, MORAT, FRIBOURG, YVERDON, LAC DE JOUX, VALLORBE, STE. CROIX, MOTIERS-TRAVERS, LE LOCLE, LA CHAUX DE FONDS, NEUCHÂTEL, BERNE, LUCERNE, BRUNNEN, SCHWYZ, EINSIEDELN, GLARUS, KLAUSEN PASS, ALTDORF, STANS, BRUNIG PASS, BRIENZ, INTERLAKEN, KANDERSTEG, GEMMI PASS, LEUK, SION, MARTIGNY, GENEVA

'Vous êtes étranger, vous êtes notre frère; c'est la communauté qui vous reçoit dans le lieu le plus sacré et le plus respectable: elle vous y prend sous sa sauve-garde! C'est un témoignage de bienveillance universelle. C'est d'après ces principes et ces sentiments que, dans toute la Suisse, la principale auberge est ordinairement à l'hôtel de ville, dans une partie des batimens qui y est spécialement affectée.'

SAUSSURE, HORACE-BÉNÉDICT DE. GENEVA, LUCERNE, ENGELBERG, JOCH PASS, OCHSENSTOCK, ZURICH, ST. GALL, CONSTANCE, BASLE, GENEVA, CHAMONIX

At Chamonix de Saussure met and took tea with Mr. Blair, who had built the hut on the Montenvers.

STORR, GOTTLIEB KONRAD CHRISTIAN. SCHAFFHAUSEN, ZURICH, EINSIEDELN, LUCERNE, ALTDORF, ANDERMATT, OBERALP PASS, DISENTIS, REICHENAU, KUNKELS PASS, PFÄFERS, SARGANS, ALT ST. JOHANN, APPENZELL, ST. GALL, CONSTANCE

'At first glance the region of the St. Gotthard is undoubtedly terrible, yet everything combines to make of it an exceptionally picturesque landscape: a mill on the Mayenbach which throws itself into the Reuss which it equals in size, a little agriculture, the road built through this wild region, the village on the height with its church on the highest point, and, above all, the configuration of the mountains which assume remarkable shapes so that some look deceptively like ruins.'

WHALLEY, THOMAS SEDGWICK. CHAMBÉRY, ST. PIERRE, MIOLAN, CONFLANS, MOUTIERS, PEZEY, TAMIER, BELLEVEAUX, ALLEZON, CHAMBÉRY, GENEVA, LAUSANNE, CHAMONIX, GENEVA

'The glaciers themselves fell far short of my expectation, though certainly vast and wonderful objects; and, from their singularity, amply worth all the pains that curiosity takes to visit them, yet not deserving of all the praises that the overheated imaginations of some authors have bestowed on their sublimity and splendour. Conceive narrow arms of a tempestuous sea, rushing down in the hollow between stupendous rocks, and suddenly arrested in its fury by a mighty frost, and you have them before your eyes. But I fondly expected that the congealed billows would present all the *éclat* to the sight of pure ice, and imagined them sparkling in the sunbeams with the most radiant lustre. No such thing, my dear girl!'

1785

BECKFORD, WILLIAM. VEVEY, LA TOUR DE PEILZ

With his wife Beckford settled at the Château de la Tour de Peilz.

BOURRIT, MARC-THÉODORE. GENEVA, CHAMONIX

Bourrit made his third attempt on Mont Blanc in company with de Saussure.

BRICHE, MME DE LA. BASLE, SCHAFFHAUSEN, CONSTANCE, ZURICH, BERNE, FRIBOURG, LAUSANNE

A tragic journey during the course of which Mme de la Briche's husband died of small-pox at Zurich.

COXE, WILLIAM. SCHAFFHAUSEN, ZURICH, BASLE, MOUTIER, BIENNE, SOLEURE, BERNE, LANGNAU, LUCERNE, STANS, ENGELBERG, SURENEN PASS, ALTDORF, ANDERMATT, FURKA PASS, GRIMSEL PASS, MEIRINGEN, GROSSE

SCHEIDEGG, GRINDELWALD, LAUTERBRUNNEN, INTERLAKEN, KANDERSTEG, GEMMI PASS, LEUK, SION, MARTIGNY, COL DE BALME, CHAMONIX, TÊTE NOIRE PASS, MARTIGNY, BEX, VEVEY, LAUSANNE, GENEVA, LES VERRIÈRES, NEUCHÂTEL, MORAT, FRIBOURG, BIENNE, PORRENTRUY, BASLE

'I ascended, in company with three Englishmen and a Swiss gentleman, from Blair's Cabin, about an hour and a half, over the bare and rugged rocks, to a summit under the *Aiguille des Charmox,* near the spot from which a Genevan unfortunately fell and was dashed to pieces. On this summit, at the very edge of the fearful precipice which overlooks the Vale of Chamouny, stood a collection of stones, about three feet high, called by the natives *le bonhomme.* We immediately raised this heap to the height of six feet, and piled up another of the same elevation, which we styled, in the language of the country, *le monument de quatre Anglois,* in memory of the four Englishmen who amused themselves in forming it. (Mr. Whitbread, the two Mr. Cliffords, and myself. We were accompanied and assisted by M. Exchaquet.)'

FREYGRABEND, DR. ENGELBERG, TITLIS

'The prospect was on all sides open and unbounded. This sublime, yet dreary scene, though it surpasses all description, made an impression on my mind which I shall never forget. Here the painter and poet would find endless employment, if the colours of the painter, and the conceptions of the poet, could resist the effects of the extreme cold.'

HOBHOUSE, SIR BENJAMIN. GENEVA, LAUSANNE, JOUGNE

MARCARD, HEINRICH MATTHIAS. LAUSANNE, BELLEVUE, MEILLERIE, EVIAN, THONON, LAUSANNE, VEVEY, ALLAMAN, AUBONNE, NYON, GENEVA

'An Englishman, Mr. Beckford and his family were living at La Tour de Peilz.' Near Aubonne an English lady had lived alone for many years, banished from England by a mother jealous of her looks.

SAUSSURE, HORACE-BÉNÉDICT DE. GENEVA, MARTIGNY, GENEVA, CHAMONIX

De Saussure made an attempt on Mont Blanc in company with Bourrit, but it was not a success in either sense.

STORR, GOTTLIEB KONRAD CHRISTIAN. MARSCHLINS, LANDQUART, KÜBLIS, ST. ANTÖNIEN, RÄTSCHENHORN, LANDQUART, COIRE, REICHENAU, THUSIS, HINTERRHEIN, SAN BERNARDINO PASS, MESOCCO, BELLINZONA, MAGADINO, VARESE, LUGANO, PORLEZZA, CHIAVENNA, CASACCIA, SEPTIMER PASS, BIVIO, TIEFENKASTEL, LENZERHEIDE, COIRE

1786

BECKFORD, WILLIAM. LA TOUR DE PEILZ, EVIAN, GENEVA, SALÈVE, NEUCHÂTEL, ZURICH

Lady Beckford died at the Château de la Tour de Peilz. 'I lived in Switzerland among the Alps at twenty six, under a bitter domestic calamity. I found their solitudes soothe me as nothing else would—I have loved solitude more since.'

BOURRIT, MARC-THÉODORE. GENEVA, CHAMONIX

Green with envy at being overtaken in the race to the summit of 'his' Mont Blanc, Bourrit first suggested that the real summit might not have been reached, and next declared that the real hero of the ascent was not Dr. Paccard who, like himself, was an amateur, but Jacques Balmat, a guide and professional.

BRAND, THOMAS. CHAMONIX

'Two or 3 days before our arrival a Dr. Packard & a young man of the name of Balma achieved the long wish'd for adventure of gaining the highest summit of the Mont Blanc.'

BRAUNSCHWEIGER, N. CONSTANCE, SCHAFFHAUSEN, CONSTANCE, RHEINECK, ST. GALL, HERISAU, ZURICH, EINSIEDELN, SCHWYZ, LUCERNE, ALTDORF, ANDERMATT, FURKA PASS, OBERWALD, GRIMSEL PASS, MEIRINGEN, GROSSE SCHEIDEGG, GRINDELWALD, LAUTERBRUNNEN, INTERLAKEN, KANDERSTEG, GEMMI PASS, LEUK, SION, MARTIGNY, VEVEY, GENEVA, LAUSANNE, YVERDON, NEUCHÂTEL, LA CHAUX DE FONDS, NEUCHÂTEL, AARBERG, SOLEURE, BERNE, AARBURG, BADEN, BASLE

'It is incomparably beautiful, the lake of Zurich; not too broad that one cannot see each lovely shore from the other. It is really sublime here. Beauty is here unaccompanied by poverty, and were I to weep a tear it would be one of joy. How blessed man can be on earth!'

BRIDEL, PHILIPPE. BEX, ANZEINDAZ, PAS DE CHEVILLE, SION

'Il vaut la peine de naître et de vivre dans notre patrie . . . je voudrois que chacun en fût aussi intimement pénétré qu'un vieillard de nos Alpes, à qui je demandois un jour s'il étoit Suisse: il me répondit—Oui, par la grace de Dieu.'

CHANDLER, RICHARD. VEVEY, ROLLE

Chandler was now living in Switzerland.

COXE, WILLIAM. VALLORBE, ORBE, NYON, GENEVA, MORGES, YVERDON, NEUCHÂTEL, ILE ST. PIERRE, MORAT, FRIBOURG, BERNE, MURGENTHAL, LUCERNE, ALBIS, ZURICH, CONSTANCE, BASLE

'I made several excursions across the lake, to an insulated ridge between the lakes of Neuchatel and Morat, and enjoyed many delightful points of view. Of these various prospects, the most remarkable is from the summit of Mount Vuilly, where I seated myself on the edge of an abrupt precipice. . . . But what renders this charming spot more particularly striking is, that it is perhaps the only central point from which the eye can at once comprehend the vast amphitheatre formed, on one side, by the Jura stretching from the environs of Geneva as far as Basle, and, on the other, by that stupendous chain of snowy alps, which extends from the frontiers of Italy to the confines of Germany.'

GERSDORF, BARON ADOLF TRAUGOTT VON. CONSTANCE, SCHAFFHAUSEN, WINTERTHUR, ZURICH, BADEN, LUCERNE, BERNE, THUN, INTERLAKEN, LAUTERBRUNNEN, KLEINE SCHEIDEGG, GRINDELWALD, GROSSE SCHEIDEGG, MEIRINGEN, INTERLAKEN, THUN, BERNE, LAUSANNE, GENEVA, CHAMONIX, GENEVA, VEVEY, LAUSANNE, YVERDON, NEUCHÂTEL, NIDAU, BIENNE, BASLE

Baron von Gersdorf was an eye-witness of Paccard's and Balmat's first ascent of Mont Blanc. He watched them through his telescope and wrote an account of the climb which ranks as the chief authority.

KROCK, ANNA HELENA VON. SCHAFFHAUSEN, ZURICH, ALBIS, ZUG, LUCERNE, SURSEE, BERNE, THUN, INTERLAKEN, LAUTERBRUNNEN, GRINDELWALD, THUN, BERNE, FRIBOURG, MORAT, LAUSANNE, BEX, GENEVA, CHAMONIX, GENEVA, YVERDON, NEUCHÂTEL, LE LOCLE, LA CHAUX DE FONDS, BIENNE, SOLEURE, MOUTIER, DELÉMONT, BASLE

On the return from Chamonix, in drenching rain, the carriage upset and the mules escaped. Prince Galitzin lost his way in the dark, and M. Bourrit waded the river to set him on the right course.

PANGE, FRANÇOIS DE. BASLE, SCHAFFHAUSEN, ZURICH, OLTEN, FRAUENFELD, APPENZELL, HERISAU, MEIRINGEN, GRIMSEL, MEIRINGEN, NEUCHÂTEL, GENEVA, CHAMONIX, TÊTE NOIRE PASS, MARTIGNY, GENEVA

'Je poursuis ma route, elle reprend sa vigueur, le pin élève près d'elle son feuillage plus vert, la nature renaît devant moi. Chacun de mes pas semble l'animer, la rappèler à la vie. Qu'on pardonne cette illusion au voyageur des Alpes.'

PLOUCQUET, WILHELM GOTTFRIED. SCHAFFHAUSEN, BADEN, AARAU, BERNE, THUN, INTERLAKEN, LAUTERBRUNNEN, GRINDELWALD, THUN, BERNE, MORAT, LAUSANNE, MORAT, BIESONNE, LEURE, BALSTHAL, BASLE

'At Morat as we were eating, pleasant music burst on us from the lake, and there appeared two large boats sailing slowly round, one of them full of musicians. In the other was Lord Northampton, who has lived in this neighbourhood for some years, and who still mourns for his late wife. She lies embalmed at Avenches and he visits her every day.'

SAUSSURE, HORACE-BÉNÉDICT DE. GENEVA, CHAMONIX, MARTIGNY, SORNIOT, MARTIGNY, CHAMONIX, GENEVA

Another attempt by de Saussure on Mont Blanc was frustrated by bad weather.

SMITH, JOHN ('WARWICK'). GENEVA, CHAMONIX, MARTIGNY, GRAND ST. BERNARD, SION, GLETSCH, BRIG, SIMPLON PASS, DOMODOSSOLA

'The first who successfully aimed at producing that form in water-colours which assumed the appearance of a picture, properly designated.'

STANLEY, SIR JOHN THOMAS. NEUCHÂTEL, GENEVA, CHAMONIX, COL DE BALME, MARTIGNY

'We were joined on the glacier by some countrymen, one of whom struck me by his choosing to come upon it with his spurs on . . . at the same time had the mortification of seeing a French nobleman who had set out with us for the glacier, dressed in trousers, and good thick shoes with nails in their soles.'

TSCHARNER, JOHANN BAPTIST VON. PONTRESINA

'To the practised eye of the hunter, white streaks in the snow spell deathly danger; he avoids these places lest he should share the fate which, eighty years before, overtook an English Lord on the Muretto glacier (where you cross everlasting ice going from Malenco to Maloja, on the watershed of Bregaglia near the source of the Inn). Boldly and alone he hurries up the fearsome mountain, climbs on to the glacier and laughs at the rabbit-hearted hunter; he jumps over crevasses as one would leap over a board, and steps confidently onto the hard snow; he thinks he is secure and—falls suddenly into the abyss. In vain he emits a cry of despair, for no one hears him. Alone he travels, he dies alone. And even now the eye of the wiser hunter can descry him there in scarlet—for he sleeps in a red shroud.'

WHALLEY, THOMAS SEDGWICK. CONSTANCE, FRAUENFELD, ZURICH, LUCERNE, ALBIS, ZURICH, EINSIEDELN, SCHAFFHAUSEN, ZURICH, BERNE, SOLEURE, BALSTHAL, BASLE

'I do not agree with Mr. Coxe. The situation of Lucerne appears less beautiful to me, than that of Zurich. It is true that the mountains are piled in grand confusion, round the part of the lake one sees from the town, but that part is very narrow and insignificant, and frequently hides itself behind the advancing rocks between which it winds. As one sails up it, indeed, the scenery becomes sublimely savage, and the rocks and mountains are varied with all the bold angles, points, swells, woods, different colouring, barrenness and fertility, that form the enchantment of the Alps, and fill the mind with awe and admiration; and the lively and recent impression of these successive pictures naturally made Lucerne appear to Mr. Coxe, as he approached it from the lake, in a point of view unusually favourable. The enthusiasm excited in his mind had not begun to subside, and what he saw was united to what he had seen in too near a relation to be divided from each other. As I entered Lucerne by land, and with calm ideas, its position towards the lake, though picturesque, fell far short of my expectations.'

1787

BEAUFOY, MRS. MARK. NEUCHÂTEL, BERNE, THUN, INTERLAKEN, LAUTERBRUNNEN, GRINDELWALD, THUN, BERNE, NEUCHÂTEL, GENEVA, CHAMONIX

'I attended the Curate and his wife, set out to see the lead and silver mines which lie at the Southern Extremity of this Valley [Lauterbrunnen] . . . My maid mounted first, and from the height of her horse, the breadth of his back etc. together with her dress, I thought she never would have accomplished it. However, after about 5 Minutes in the most risible postures imaginable, I saw her safely seated close to his tail . . . I had lost my strength in laughing at her.' Arrived at the mine, 'There was no honor they did not show us, and to finish with they gave us the Mineurs Dance . . .'
Colonel Beaufoy's ascent of Mont Blanc, the fourth altogether, was the first by an Englishman.

BOURRIT, MARC-THÉODORE. GENEVA, CHAMONIX, COL DU GÉANT, COURMAYEUR

Baulked of the honour of being the first to ascend Mont Blanc, Bourrit recouped himself by crossing the Col du Géant.

BOWLES, WILLIAM LISLE. LUCERNE, LAUSANNE

'I was a child of sorrow when I passed,
Sweet country, through your rocky valleys last.'

CAGLIOSTRO, COUNT. BASLE, BIENNE

Giuseppe Balsamo, quack alchemist, mystic, and adventurer, was visited at Bienne by the Duke of Kent.

DZIEDUSZYCKI, LAURENT MARTIN. LAUSANNE, GENEVA, CHAMONIX, GENEVA, LAC DE JOUX, DENT DE VAULION, ST. AUBIN, NEUCHÂTEL, FRIBOURG, BERNE, HINDELBANK, LUCERNE, ZURICH, CONSTANCE, BIENNE, GENEVA

Kosciusko's future adjutant was at Chamonix on the day of de Saussure's return from the summit of Mont Blanc. During his tour

Dzieduszycki also met Lavater and Cagliostro, and only missed Mesmer by one day.

EXCHAQUET, CHARLES-FRANÇOIS. SERVOZ, CHAMONIX, COL DU GÉANT, COURMAYEUR

Exchaquet was the first tourist to cross the Col du Géant.

FONTANES, JEAN PIERRE LOUIS DE. GENEVA, CHAMONIX, COL DE BALME, MARTIGNY, VILLENEUVE, VEVEY, GENEVA

'Ah! mon ami, je vous appelle. Que n'êtes-vous à Vevey pour admirer, pour pleurer, pour rire, pour recevoir toutes les émotions douces de l'âme? Je viens de voir le Mont-Blanc. J'ai traversé les deux plus fameux glaciers de la Savoie, le glacier des Bossons et la mer de glace. Les trois pointes du Mont Blanc m'ont offert le plus magnifique spectacle dont mon imagination ait encore joui. Mais tout cela n'est rien. Les hauteurs effrayantes des montagnes m'avaient écrasé: je me suis enfoncé par le col de Balme dans le Valais. Non, l'âge d'or n'est point un rêve. Cette délicieuse vallée réfute tous ceux qui n'y croient pas.'

FRÉNILLY, FRANÇOIS AUGUSTE DE. LES VERRIÈRES, MOTIERS-TRAVERS, NEUCHÂTEL, BIENNE, BERNE, SOLEURE, BASLE, SCHAFFHAUSEN, CONSTANCE, ST. GALL, APPENZELL, SÄNTIS, ZURICH, EINSIEDELN, GLARUS, COIRE, BERGÜN, ALBULA PASS, ST. MORITZ, BERNINA PASS, TIRANO, CHIAVENNA, SPLÜGEN PASS, THUSIS, REICHENAU, DISENTIS, OBERALP PASS, ANDERMATT, FURKA PASS, OBERGESTELEN, GRIMSEL PASS, FURKA PASS, REALP, FLUELEN, SCHWYZ, RIGI, LUCERNE, BRUNIG PASS, MEIRINGEN, GRINDELWALD, LAUTERBRUNNEN, INTERLAKEN, KANDERSTEG, GEMMI PASS, LEUK, MARTIGNY, COL DE BALME, CHAMONIX, TÊTE NOIRE PASS, MARTIGNY, VEVEY, GENEVA

'We slept at Chamonix, where there was only one inn. The table d'hote supper charmed me: the company was a mixed one of men and women from every country in Europe, including a certain M. Bourrit who surpassed them all. He was, I believe, Precentor of St. Peter's at Geneva, and had published two large books on Switzerland. A man of volcanic imagination, he gave us at dessert a description of a sunrise. Dr. Paccard had just made the first ascent of Mont Blanc. Everybody was excited, I included, and I believe that I listened to Bourrit for half an hour without falling asleep. But at last fatigue got the better of me, and I know not if he succeeded in getting the sun to rise.'

MATTHISSON, FRIEDRICH. RORSCHACH, CONSTANCE, SCHAFFHAUSEN, ZURICH, ALBIS, ZUG, RIGI, EINSIEDELN, RICHTERSWIL, MORAT, NYON

'Klopstock had recently said to me: "the falls of the Rhine can be seen and heard, but neither painted nor sung".'

MICHAUD, JOSEPH. CHAMONIX

'Un grand nombre de savants et un plus grand nombre encore de ceux qui prétendent l'être arrivaient de toutes parts; je suivis la foule.'

MOROZZO DELLA ROCCA, COMTE (*c*). DOMODOSSOLA, FORMAZZA, GRIES PASS, CORNO PASS, AL ACQUA, AIROLO, BELLINZONA, MAGADINO, GOZZANO, MACUGNAGA, ALAGNA

'. . . Macognaga au pied du Mont Rose, qui se présente à l'ouest en tête de la vallée. J'ai même tenté de le gravir, mais j'avoue que je ne croyois pas l'entreprise aussi difficile. J'ai cependant monté le premier glacier d'où l'Anza tire sa source, et d'après une évaluation approchante, j'étois à 1500 toises environ d'élévation, mais mes guides m'assurant l'entreprise impossible, il a fallu y renoncer.'

MUIRHEAD, LOCKHART. JOUGNE, LA SARRAZ, LAUSANNE

'From the terrace on which this cathedral is seated, you may patiently survey the bold and elevated contour of the Alps, with their hoary and rocky peaks reflected in the lake, Mont Blanc domineering in the distance, the wavy luxuriance of shelving shores, and the frequent and comfortable dwellings of a contented peasantry.'

PENNINGTON, THOMAS. GENEVA, CHAMONIX, COL DE BALME, MARTIGNY, EVIAN, GENEVA, LAUSANNE, BERNE, SOLEURE, BASLE

... 'When we were on the glacier, the scene was very solemn; we could almost fancy ourselves out of the world, hemmed in as we were with mountains, and upon an immense body of ice: it was so awful that we were not sorry to quit it, for scenes of civilised life; in which, though perhaps curiosity might be less gratified, more comfort was to be obtained.'

ROLAND, MME. GENEVA, LAUSANNE, MORAT, BERNE, THUN, INTERLAKEN, LAUTERBRUNNEN, GRINDELWALD, THUN, ST. URBAN, LUCERNE, ALBIS, ZURICH, SCHAFFHAUSEN, BASLE

'Une femme qui peut aller à cheval, qui sait marcher quatre ou cinq heures au besoin, qui ne craint pas de brûler son teint au soleil, ou de se laisser mouiller à la pluie, peut encore se promettre de visiter assez en détail l'intérieur de la Suisse, pour peu qu'elle ait dans l'âme de cette énergie que développent les difficultés, et de ce sentiment qui s'enflamme au grand spectacle de la nature.'

SAUSSURE, HORACE-BÉNÉDICT DE. GENEVA, CHAMONIX, MONT BLANC

'Malgré l'admiration que me causait ce superbe spectacle, j'éprouvai le sentiment pénible de ne pas en tirer tout le parti possible et de savoir encore ma faculté contemplative affaiblie par la difficulté de la respiration. J'étais comme un gourmet invité à un superbe festin et qu'un dégoût extrême empêche d'en profiter.'

SMITH, JAMES EDWARD. GENEVA, CHAMONIX, COL DE BALME, MARTIGNY, LAUSANNE, BERNE, BASLE

'Often had I, in various places, imagined I had found scenes equal to anything Switzerland could present; but when I came to this celebrated country itself, I was obliged to own it far surpassed my expectations.'

STEINBRENNER, WILHELM LUDWIG. SCHAFFHAUSEN, ZURICH, EINSIEDELN, SCHWYZ, LUCERNE, SEMPACH, BERNE, MORAT, LAUSANNE, BEX, GENEVA, CHAMONIX, GENEVA, EVIAN, GENEVA, YVERDON, NEUCHÂTEL, LA CHAUX DE FONDS, BIENNE, SOLEURE, BASLE

'Who does not wish fervently to climb these Alps, to get a couple of thousand feet nearer to God?'

VOLTA, ALESSANDRO. COMO, DOMODOSSOLA, SIMPLON PASS, BRIG, SION, MARTIGNY, LAUSANNE, GENEVA

'The expences are much heavier than I had calculated; louis go just like écus; two louis for horses from Domodossola to Sion, without counting the tip to the guide; 2 louis for the coach from Sion to Lausanne. Altogether, to get to Geneva it will cost us 20 sequins.'

WATKINS, THOMAS. GENEVA, CHAMONIX, COL DE BALME, MARTIGNY, SION, BRIG, FURKA PASS, ANDERMATT, ALTDORF, LUCERNE, ZUG, ZURICH, ST. GALL, SCHAFFHAUSEN, BASLE, MOUTIER, BIENNE, NEUCHÂTEL, BERNE, FRIBOURG, LAUSANNE, GENEVA

'I beheld above us, at an immense height, the Aiguille de Charmeaux, which I thought, from its very superior elevation, would command a much fuller prospect of the object of our curiosity than Blair's Castle. I therefore quitted my company, and after an hour and a half's walking, climbing, and creeping along a ridge of sharp rocks, arrived under the second point of this Aiguille de Charmeaux, which, I believe, no mortal ever touched before. Indeed I must acknowledge, now the danger is over, it was extremely young in me to have attempted it.'

WYTTENBACH, JAKOB SAMUEL. BERNE, GENEVA, CHAMONIX, TÊTE NOIRE PASS, MARTIGNY, SION, BRIG, OBERGESTELEN, FURKA PASS, HOSPENTHAL, ST. GOTTHARD, ANDERMATT, ALTDORF, FLUELEN, LUCERNE, BERNE

Wyttenbach was accompanied by 'three stout Englishmen', of whom one was a Mr. Hawkins.

YOUNGE, W. DOMODOSSOLA, SIMPLON PASS, BRIG, SION, MARTIGNY, VILLENEUVE, VEVEY, LAUSANNE, GENEVA, BASLE

'The common accidents in mountainous countries was our lot.'

1788

BOURRIT, MARC-THÉODORE. GENEVA, CHAMONIX

Bourrit made his last attempt on Mont Blanc, in company with Mr. Woodley (later Governor of New South Wales) and Mr. Camper (son of the distinguished Dutch anatomist). Woodley alone reached the summit.

BRICHE, MME DE LA. GENEVA, CHAMONIX, GENEVA, VEVEY, BEX, BERNE, THUN, INTERLAKEN, GRINDELWALD, LAUTERBRUNNEN, INTERLAKEN, MEIRINGEN, INTERLAKEN, BERNE, LUCERNE, ZUG, SOLEURE, BIENNE, LE LOCLE

The country round Zug convinced Mme de la Briche that Milton must have passed that way before writing his description of Eden.

BRIDEL, PHILIPPE. BASLE, MOUTIER, BIENNE

'En voyageant en Suisse, le peintre trouve à chaque pas un tableau, le poète une image et le philosophe une réflexion.'

CAMBRY, JACQUES. GENEVA, CHAMONIX, GENEVA, LAUSANNE, VEVEY, BEX, MARTIGNY, COL DE BALME, MARTIGNY, BEX, VEVEY, GRUYÈRES, BULLE, FRIBOURG, BERNE, THUN, INTERLAKEN, LAUTERBRUNNEN, GRINDELWALD, THUN, BERNE, MORAT, YVERDON, NEUCHÂTEL, ILE ST. PIERRE, LA CHAUX DE FONDS, LE LOCLE, BIENNE, SOLEURE, MURGENTHAL, LUCERNE, FLUELEN, ALTDORF, ST. GOTTHARD PASS, AIROLO, BELLINZONA, LOCARNO, MILAN—RORSCHACH, ST. GALL, APPENZELL, CONSTANCE, SCHAFFHAUSEN, BASLE, ZURICH, LACHEN, EINSIEDELN, ZUG, LUCERNE, SURSEE, MURGENTHAL, BERNE, MORAT, PAYERNE, MORGES, GENEVA

At Brienz the innkeeper seriously proposed that Cambry should share a bed with a woman of eighty-three. At Le Locle he stayed 'dans l'hotel où le prince Edouard [Duke of Kent] et sa suite se livroyent à la gaieté bruyante des repas anglois. Une vapeur de rhum et de citron parfumoit nos appartemens.'

CLÉMENT, JEAN-MAURICE. CHAMPÉRY, DENT DU MIDI

The peak climbed by him seems to have been the Eperon which he says was higher than those at either end of the ridge. Since that date a fall of rock may have reduced the height of Clément's peak.

FERBER, JOHANN JAKOB. BERNE, NEUCHÂTEL, LE LOCLE, LA CHAUX DE FONDS, MOTIERS-TRAVERS, LES VERRIÈRES

FLORIAN, JEAN PIERRE CLARIS DE. GENEVA, CHAMONIX

'Tout cela m'a frappé de terreur et pénétré de tristesse: j'ai cru voir l'effrayante image de la nature sans soleil, abandonnée au dieu des tempêtes. En regardant ces belles horreurs, j'ai remercié l'Etre tout-puissant de les avoir rendues si rares; j'ai désiré mon départ pour repasser dans la vallée, la délicieuse vallée de Maglan.'

FOX, CHARLES JAMES. BIENNE, BERNE, LAUSANNE

Windham met Fox at Berne and wrote: 'Among the observations Fox was making, one was the extreme mildness of the government of this canton, and at the same time the great power lodged in the aristocracy, and again, the example given here lately of the greater prudence sometimes of peoples in the administration of public money than in that of their own.'

GOETHE, JOHANN WOLFGANG. CHIAVENNA, SPLÜGEN PASS, THUSIS, COIRE, FELDKIRCH

Being now 'concerned with mountains as a mineralogist', he was 'able to consider them with composure'.

MATTHISSON, FRIEDRICH. GENEVA, CHAMONIX, TÊTE NOIRE PASS, MARTIGNY, BEX

'We called on Dr. Paccard who described his ascent of Mont Blanc to us very simply and modestly. He appears to set very little store by this bold undertaking and insists that anybody of similar physical strength could reach the top of this mountain as well as he.'

MEINERS, CHRISTOPH. SCHAFFHAUSEN, ZURICH, BUREN, ST. GALL, HERISAU, APPENZELL, GAIS, KAMOR, SENNWALD, COIRE, DISENTIS, OBERALP PASS, ANDERMATT, FURKA PASS, GRIMSEL PASS, MEIRINGEN, INTERLAKEN, THUN, BERNE, MORAT, LAUSANNE, GENEVA, CHAMONIX, GENEVA, ROLLE, YVERDON, NEUCHÂTEL, LA TOURNE, LE LOCLE, LA CHAUX DE FONDS, NEUCHÂTEL, BIENNE, MOUTIER, BASLE

REYNIER, LOUIS (*c*). LAUSANNE, BEX, ANZEINDAZ, PANEYROSSAZ, PAS DE CHEVILLE, SION, SIERRE, VAREN, LEUKERBAD, GEMMI, TORRENTHORN

'Je me rappellerai toujours un habitant des Alpes, avec qui je faisais une course: nous avions suivi la belle plaine du Vallais, et nous parvenions, au milieu d'une journée très-chaude, au pied d'une montée roide et nue, où la chaleur se faisoit sentir avec force; mais ce chemin nous conduisoit dans les Alpes. Mon compagnon, avec un mouvement de joie qu'il ne peut retenir, s'écrie, *je suis heureux, nous allons monter*.'

SAUSSURE, HORACE-BÉNÉDICT DE. GENEVA, CHAMONIX, COL DU GÉANT, COURMAYEUR, COL FERRET, MARTIGNY, CHAMONIX, GENEVA

With his son, de Saussure spent 17 days on the Col du Géant making observations. He intended to stay longer but the guides put an end to the party by deliberately destroying the provisions so that a return to the lower regions became imperative.

WINDHAM, WILLIAM. SCHAFFHAUSEN, BASLE, SOLEURE, BIENNE, BERNE, THUN, INTERLAKEN, BERNE, LAUSANNE

'Nothing could be more beautiful than the valley, separated rather from the rest, at the end of which Meyringen lies. . . .'

WYTTENBACH, JAKOB SAMUEL. BERNE, THUN, INTERLAKEN, MEIRINGEN, GRIMSEL PASS, OBERGESTELEN, FURKA PASS, HOSPENTHAL, ST. GOTTHARD PASS, AIROLO, ST. GOTTHARD PASS, ANDERMATT, WASSEN, SUSTEN PASS, GADMEN, MEIRINGEN, INTERLAKEN, THUN, BERNE

1789

BEAUMONT, SIR ALBANIS (*c*). GENEVA, MARTIGNY, SION, BRIG, ULRICHEN, NUFENEN PASS, AIROLO, ST. GOTTHARD PASS, ANDERMATT, FURKA PASS, OBERGESTELEN, BRIG, MARTIGNY, GENEVA

'I found myself on the side of the Furca; then, keeping along its glacier for about three English miles, by the most frightful and terrific road that can possibly be imagined, exhibiting a continual chaos, nature all around me being *rudis indigestaque moles*; while my sensations were alternately assailed by the freezing cold of Siberia, and the intense and suffocating heat of the torrid zone, for the space of fourteen hours incessant walking, till we gained Obergestlin, which I reached absolutely exhausted. . . .'

BECKFORD, WILLIAM. EVIAN, LAUSANNE, BASLE

Beckford's most sumptuous season at Evian.

BOURRIT, MARC-THÉODORE. GENEVA, CHAMONIX

CONDÉ, LOUIS JOSEPH, PRINCE DE. SCHAFFHAUSEN, BRUGG, BERNE, THUN, INTERLAKEN, LAUTERBRUNNEN, GRINDELWALD, THUN, BERNE, SURSEE, LUCERNE, BADEN, ZURICH, CONSTANCE

Condé's intention was to cross into Italy by the Great St. Bernard, but this would have necessitated travelling along the shore of the lake of Geneva, and as rumour had it that republicans from the French shore of the lake were lying in wait for him, he reached Italy through Tyrol.

DAVALL, EDMUND. ORBE, MONT SUCHET, LAC DE JOUX, LAUSANNE, MARTIGNY, VALSOREY, GRAND ST. BERNARD

ESPINCHAL, COMTE D'. SCHAFFHAUSEN, MURGENTHAL, BERNE, ZOFINGEN, LUCERNE, ALTDORF, ST. GOTTHARD PASS, BELLINZONA, LOCARNO

In the first stream of refugees, d'Espinchal found himself with the Comte d'Artois and the Prince de Condé. While these made their way to Italy through Tyrol, he crossed the St. Gotthard with the Duc de

Bourbon. En route they picked up a man who seemed to have done everything everywhere and whom they made their servant 'pour les commissions secrètes et galantes', and dubbed him 'Figaro'.

GAUTHIER, MME DE. BASLE, SCHAFFHAUSEN, ZURICH, ST. GALL, CONSTANCE, ZURICH, EINSIEDELN, SCHWYZ, LUCERNE, MURGENTHAL, BERNE, THUN, INTERLAKEN, LAUTERBRUNNEN, GRINDELWALD, THUN, BERNE, SOLEURE, BERNE, MORAT, FRIBOURG, BULLE, GRUYÈRES, VEVEY, LAUSANNE, EVIAN, GENEVA, ROLLE, AUBONNE, LA SARRAZ, ORBE, YVERDON, VALLORBE, JOUGNE

Evian: 'un détachement de la troupe de comédie de Genève vient s'y etablir pendant la saison des eaux, qu'un Anglois nommé Becfort rendoit cette année très brillante.'

GROB, GREGORIUS (*c*). ST. GALL, ZUG, LUCERNE, SCHWYZ, RIGI

'For a Swiss the Rigi is a holy place; one feels that one is at the altar of Freedom; surrounded by high, awe-inspiring objects, one wants to take one's shoes off, bare one's head, fold one's hands, and offer thanks to the shadows of those great men who on this scene have wrought great deeds, the results of which have persisted throughout the centuries down to us.'

KARAMSIN, NICOLAI. BASLE, BRUGG, ZURICH, EGLISAU, SCHAFFHAUSEN, ZURICH, BADEN, AARAU, BERNE, THUN, INTERLAKEN, LAUTERBRUNNEN, KLEINE SCHEIDEGG, GRINDELWALD, GROSSE SCHEIDEGG, MEIRINGEN, INTERLAKEN, BERNE, MORAT, LAUSANNE, GENEVA

On the Kleine Scheidegg the Russian traveller wrote: 'I arrived at the top of the mountain, where a most wonderful alteration at once took place with me. I lost all sensation of fatigue, my strength returned, I breathed with ease and freedom, and an uncommon tranquillity and joy took possession of my heart. I sunk upon my knees, and, looking towards heaven, I offered up my adoration to Him who has so plainly stamped the seal of His omnipotence, grandeur, infinity, upon these masses of rock and snow.'

LAGE DE VOLUDE, BÉATRIX-STÉPHANIE DE. PORRENTRUY, BASLE, BERNE, LAUSANNE, GENEVA

A short flight from the revolution, not as is commonly believed accompanied by the Princesse de Lamballe.

MATTHISSON, FRIEDRICH. ROLLE, ST. CERGUE, LAUSANNE, GENEVA

At Rolle Matthisson met and discoursed with Richard Chandler, 'a small, stocky man with fiery eyes and glowing complexion'.

MCTAGGART, MRS. GENEVA, CHAMONIX, COL DE BALME, MARTIGNY, LAUSANNE, BERNE, LUCERNE, ZUG, ALBIS, ZURICH, SCHAFFHAUSEN

'There were two young gentlemen travelling with their tutors, one, young Mr. Dawson, since Lord Cremorne, with a Mr. Antrobus; the name of the others I forget. After our early dinner, for we conformed to the customs of the country, we used to dance, and there has seldom been so merry a party at the foot of Mont Blanc.'

MEYER, J. H. FLUELEN, ALTDORF, ST. GOTTHARD PASS, BELLINZONA, LOCARNO, LUVINO, PONTE-TRESA, LUGANO, PORLEZZA, MENAGGIO, CHIAVENNA, SPLÜGEN PASS, THUSIS, COIRE, WALLENSTADT, ZURICH

'For a traveller who does not fear fatigue, how much more agreeable are the narrow and tortuous paths of the Alps than the wide roads of the low country, drawn as straight as a die.'

MÜLLER, JOHANN GEORG. ZURICH, ALBIS, LUCERNE, STANS, SARNEN, BRUNIG PASS, MEIRINGEN, GROSSE SCHEIDEGG, MEIRINGEN, ENGSTLENALP

'. . . we feared to find no room in Grindelwald, and turned back.'

PENNINGTON, THOMAS. GENEVA, LAUSANNE, MORAT, BERNE, SOLEURE, BALSTHAL, BASLE

'The inns in this country are very expensive, you cannot dine for less than twenty batz a head, which is half a crown, nor sup for less than fifteen, wine excepted, and this is a dear article. Unless in great towns there is no table d'hote, and the innkeepers have such firmness, not to say obstinacy, that they hear all you have to say with the greatest composure, but hardly ever abate in their charges.'

PLACIDUS A SPESCHA. DISENTIS, SOMVIX, TENIGERBAD, DIESRUT PASS, VRIN, RUMEIN, VALS, VALSERBERG PASS, HINTERRHEIN, RHEINWALDHORN, THUSIS, VERSAM, DISENTIS

After the first ascent of the Rheinwaldhorn, 'when I presented myself before the Abbot [of Disentis] to receive his blessing, he made over me a quick "Kribis-Krabis" and said only "go". For several days I could not show myself in public. The skin peeled off my face and hands; I grew a new one and was well. Observe, readers, Providence made me physically blind like Paul in order to give me moral vision.'

RIGBY, EDWARD. GENEVA, CHAMONIX, COL DE BALME, MARTIGNY, BEX, VEVEY, LAUSANNE, MORAT, BERNE, SOLEURE, BALSTHAL, BASLE

'I have seen many prospects which have more excited my wonder—the vast height of the Alpine mountains, the huge and broken masses of rock, the immense tracts of snow and ice—but neither the eye nor the mind can dwell long on such prodigies of nature without something like fatigue, and as they are not connected with the idea of human residence, or, at least, of a comfortable existence, the continued view of them would be oppressive. The scene at Lausanne is the very reverse of this. Almost every one would say, "I wish I could live here".'

SABRAN, MME DE. BASLE, ZURICH, EINSIEDELN, LUCERNE, ALTDORF, ST. GOTTHARD, AIROLO, BELLINZONA, MILAN, LAUSANNE, BERNE, BASLE

'In spite of my sad forebodings and my conviction that in a very short time dreadful events will happen in France and at Paris, I am leaving Switzerland, and I leave it with as much regret as if I were going out of harbour into the middle of a storm and defying the tempest.'

SAUSSURE, HORACE-BÉNÉDICT DE. GENEVA, MARTIGNY, SION, BRIG, SIMPLON PASS, DOMODOSSOLA, MACUGNAGA, COL D'EGUA, ALAGNA, COL DE VALDOBBIA, GRESSONEY, BETTA FURKA, ST. JACQUES D'AYAS, COL DES CIMES BLANCHES, BREUIL, ST. THEODUL PASS, ZERMATT, VISP, SION, MARTIGNY, GENEVA

At Zermatt the priest refused to receive de Saussure's party in his house or to have anything to do with them.

SPAZIER, KARL. BASLE, SOLEURE, BERNE, BIENNE, LAUSANNE, EVIAN, LAUSANNE, BERNE, THUN, INTERLAKEN, LAUTERBRUNNEN, KLEINE SCHEIDEGG, GRINDELWALD, GROSSE SCHEIDEGG, MEIRINGEN, INTERLAKEN, THUN, LUCERNE, ZUG, ZURICH, SCHAFFHAUSEN, BASLE

Spazier attended one of William Beckford's parties at Evian. The sideboards were groaning under their loads of food and drink, and any person decently turned out was allowed to help himself *ad lib.* There was such a crowd that Spazier could find nothing to sleep on except straw.

TRALLES, JOHANN GEORG. BERNE, THUN, INTERLAKEN, HABKERN, HOHGANT, INTERLAKEN, SAXETEN, MORGENBERGHORN, MÜLENEN, ERLENBACH, STOCKHORN, NIESEN

A journey to make trigonometrical observations on the height of the mountains of the Bernese Oberland from a base near Thun and from the summits of the Hohgant, Stockhorn, and Niesen. At a later date, Tralles also ascended the Oldenhorn and the Diablerets to make further observations.

WYTTENBACH, JAKOB SAMUEL. BERNE, YVERDON, LAC DE JOUX, BERNE, KANDERSTEG

An excursion to the Lac de Joux with Edmund Davall.

1790

ANONYMOUS 5 A. SION, EVOLENA, FERPECLE, AROLLA

This visitor was taken by the peasants of the Val d'Herens for a spy or a sorcerer, and had great difficulty in getting a bed.

AUGERD, VICTOR. GENEVA, CHAMONIX, COL DE BALME, MARTIGNY, GRAND ST. BERNARD, MARTIGNY, LAUSANNE, GENEVA

'En me rapprochant et à la vue de ces coupoles hardies et brillantes de lumière, de ces voûtes de cristal transparentes dans l'intérieur desquelles on entendait mugir le fougueux Arveyron, qui se précipitait écumant à travers l'amoncellement d'énormes blocs de granit, je tombai dans une admiration silencieuse et extatique.'

BOURRIT, MARC-THÉODORE. GENEVA, CHAMONIX

'Or, un jour qu'il était sur le Montanvert avec une foule d'étrangers, et que chaque nation y formait ses groupes, il fut appelé par des Anglaises, et l'une d'entre elles lui parla de Myladi Craven; dans son enthousiasme, il en montrait une lettre, lorsque cette dame de son côté lui en fit voir aussi qu'il avait écrites; que l'on juge de sa surprise — c'était Myladi Craven elle-même.'

BRIDEL, PHILIPPE. BASLE, ZURICH, EINSIEDELN, SCHWYZ, ZUG, BREMGARTEN, BASLE

'La meilleure manière d'apprendre à connoitre la Suisse, n'est point de la parcourir tout d'une traite; mais c'est de faire chaque année un voyage dans quelqu'une de ses parties, suivant le conseil et la manière du célèbre Scheuchzer: il ne faut pas non plus la traverser sur la ligne droite des grands chemins: qui veut bien la voir, doit préférer les sentiers aux routes battues, entrer dans les vallées écartées, et visiter ces peuplades isolées, que des lacs et des chaines de montagnes séparent des quartiers plus fréquentés.'

GAUTHIER, MME DE. LES VERRIÈRES, LA BRÉVINE, LE CHATELET, CHASSERON, MOTIERS-TRAVERS, LA BRÉVINE, LE LOCLE, LA CHAUX DE FONDS, LA FERRIÈRE, LE LOCLE, LES BRENETS, LA BRÉVINE, LA TOURNE, NEUCHÂTEL, FONTAINE-ANDRÉ, ILE ST. PIERRE, NEUCHÂTEL, ILE ST. PIERRE, LA NEUVEVILLE, NEUCHÂTEL

'Mad. de B. . . . nous conta en chemin, que née dans le tems où parut Émile, ses sœurs & elles avoient été élevées d'après ce système: elle passa pour son compte les neuf premières années de sa vie dans les bois, presque nue, où elle se nourrissoit en partie de genièvre & de fruits sauvages. . . .'

GRASS, CARL. COIRE, DISENTIS, OBERALP PASS, ANDERMATT, FURKA PASS, GRIMSEL PASS, MEIRINGEN, GROSSE SCHEIDEGG, GRINDELWALD,

LAUTERBRUNNEN, INTERLAKEN, KANDERSTEG, GEMMI PASS, LEUK, MARTIGNY, TÊTE NOIRE PASS, CHAMONIX

At Lauterbrunnen 'the parson spoke to us of a certain Duc de Guise who passed through there with twelve young women a few days ago, and paid only two thalers for two bottles of wine'.

HALEM, G. A. VON. SCHAFFHAUSEN, CONSTANCE, ZURICH, ALBIS, THALWIL, EINSIEDELN, SCHWYZ, BRUNNEN, LUCERNE, BRUNIG PASS, MEIRINGEN, GROSSE SCHEIDEGG, GRINDELWALD, LAUTERBRUNNEN, INTERLAKEN, THUN, BERNE, BIENNE, ILE ST. PIERRE, NEUCHÂTEL, MOTIERS-TRAVERS, LA BRÉVINE, LE LOCLE, LA CHAUX DE FONDS, NEUCHÂTEL, MORAT, MOUDON, VEVEY, LAUSANNE, MORGES, GENEVA, CHAMONIX, TÊTE NOIRE PASS, MARTIGNY, BEX, EVIAN, THONON, GENEVA

'A man appeared before us with a badge on his chest. At first we thought that we were having to deal with local police, but it turned out that this was a Monsieur Paccard who offered us his services as guide to the valley of Chamonix. As proof of his credentials he pointed to his badge with the Arms of England, given to him by the Duke of Gloucester whom he had guided thither.'

HEIGELIN, J. F. (*c*). COIRE, THUSIS, SPLÜGEN PASS, CHIAVENNA, MALOJA PASS, ST. MORITZ, PONTRESINA, ZUOZ, SCALETTA PASS, DAVOS, KLOSTERS, LANDQUART, ZURICH

'Although the [St. Moritz] spring has been provided with a little house and thereby brought under cover, we found everything wretched and falling to pieces; not even the slightest comforts for cure-guests, and, except for the narrow and marshy valley of the Inn, the well-stocked lake and the beautiful road to Samaden and Zuoz, nothing to entertain and distract a stranger.'

HÉRAULT DE SÉCHELLES. BASLE, OLTEN, ZURICH, ST. GALL, APPENZELL, GLARUS, LUCERNE, GENEVA, CHAMONIX, MARTIGNY, GRAND ST. BERNARD

Chamonix, 'la plus belle nature de toutes les natures du monde'.

MATTHISSON, FRIEDRICH. NYON, CHILLON, GRANDCLOS, AIGLE, LEYSIN, TOUR DE MAYEN, BEX, ANZEINDAZ

The poet got into difficulties in trying to get down from the Tour de Mayen; completely exhausted, he sank into a deep sleep and was awakened before nightfall by an eagle, and eventually found his way down through the snow.

SÉNANCOUR, PIVERT DE. GENEVA, YVERDON, NEUCHÂTEL, MOTIERS-TRAVERS, BIENNE, MORAT, VEVEY, GLION, FRIBOURG, SCHWARZSEE, THUN, LUCERNE, ENGELBERG, JOCH PASS, MEIRINGEN, GRIMSEL PASS, KANDERSTEG, GEMMI PASS, LEUK, MARTIGNY, GRAND ST. BERNARD, BEX

'Je ne veux point parcourir la Suisse en voyageur, ou en curieux. Je cherche à être là, parce qu'il me semble que je serais mal ailleurs . . .' The author of *Obermann*.

SERRANT, M. DE. CHAMONIX, COL DU GÉANT, COURMAYEUR

'Nous touchâmes à la cabane de Mr. de Saussure que nous trouvâmes délabrée, découverte par les vents, et où il ne restait pour tout meuble qu'un mauvais tabouret de bois: je crus voir un temple élevé à l'amour des sciences.'

TOUR DU PIN, MARQUISE DE LA. VALLORBE, NYON, GENEVA, CHAMONIX, GENEVA, LAUSANNE, BERNE, SOLEURE, BASLE

'Je rencontrai aussi un personnage célèbre, M. Gibbon, dont la figure grotesque me donnait une envie de rire que j'avais bien de la peine à maîtriser.'

WORDSWORTH, WILLIAM. GENEVA, LAUSANNE, MARTIGNY, COL DE BALME, CHAMONIX, MARTIGNY, SION, BRIG, SIMPLON PASS, DOMODOSSOLA, COMO, SAMOLACO, FORCOLA PASS, SOAZZA, SAN BERNARDINO PASS, THUSIS, REICHENAU, DISENTIS, OBERALP PASS, ANDERMATT, ALTDORF, LUCERNE, ZURICH, EINSIEDELN, GLARUS, WALLENSTADT, ALTSTÄTTEN, APPENZELL, CONSTANCE, SCHAFFHAUSEN, LUCERNE, BRUNIG PASS, MEIRINGEN, GRINDELWALD, LAUTERBRUNNEN, INTERLAKEN, THUN, BERNE, NEUCHÂTEL, BASLE

'We are now, as I observed above, upon the point of quitting these most sublime and beautiful parts; and you cannot imagine the melancholy regret which I feel at the idea . . . I have looked upon, and as it were conversed with, the objects which this country has presented to my view so long, and with such increasing pleasure, that the idea of parting from them oppresses me with a sadness similar to what I have always felt in quitting a beloved friend . . . Ten thousand times in the course of this tour have I regretted the inability of my memory to retain a more strong impression of the beautiful forms before me; again and again, in quitting a fortunate station, have I returned to it with the most eager avidity, in the hope of bearing away a more lively picture. At this moment, when many of these landscapes are floating before my mind, I feel a high enjoyment in reflecting that perhaps scarcely a day of my life will pass in which I shall not derive some happiness from these images.'

1791

BLOCK, BARON VON. GENEVA, CHAMONIX, BERNE, THUN, INTERLAKEN, LAUTERBRUNNEN, ZURICH

'On the 17th of August, late in the evening, Block arrived at Lauterbrunn, when the people of the inn were all asleep; and probably his arrival prevented the landlord and the landlady, with their domestics from perishing. Soon after the landlady came to his chamber, and called on him to save himself. He hurried out, opened the house door, and was met by the waves.'

BOURRIT, MARC-THÉODORE. GENEVA, CHAMONIX, BEX

BRUN, FRIEDERIKE. GENEVA, CHAMONIX, GENEVA, LAUSANNE, BERNE, THUN, INTERLAKEN, LAUTERBRUNNEN, KLEINE SCHEIDEGG, GRINDELWALD, MEIRINGEN, BRUNIG PASS, LUCERNE, ZURICH, HERISAU, CONSTANCE

Friederike Brun addressed to Klopstock a poem entitled 'Chamouny beim Sonnenaufgang', which led Coleridge to write his 'Hymn before sunrise, in the Vale of Chamouny'.

CURTI, LÉOPOLD DE. BASLE, OLTEN, LUCERNE, SARNEN

'Les auberges sont si mauvaises, dans l'une et l'autre partie du canton d'Underwald, qu'il faut avoir les plus pressantes affaires pour se résoudre à y passer la nuit.'

ESPINCHAL, COMTE D'. EVIAN, LAUSANNE, GENEVA, LAUSANNE, BERNE, SOLEURE, BASLE

GRAY, ROBERT. BASLE, SCHAFFHAUSEN, CONSTANCE, ST. GALL, GAIS, APPENZELL, ALTSTÄTTEN, RAGAZ, WALLENSTADT, GLARUS, ZURICH, ZUG, SCHWYZ, BRUNNEN, ALTDORF, ANDERMATT, ALTDORF, LUCERNE, ZURICH, BADEN, AARAU, BERNE, FRIBOURG, BULLE, VEVEY, MARTIGNY, COL DE BALME, CHAMONIX, TÊTE NOIRE PASS, MARTIGNY, VEVEY, MOUDON, MORAT, BERNE, THUN, INTERLAKEN, LAUTERBRUNNEN, THUN, BERNE, NEUCHÂTEL, LE LOCLE, LA CHAUX DE FONDS, NEUCHÂTEL, YVERDON, ORBE, LAUSANNE, GENEVA

The inn at Glarus provided the spectacle of an old soldier of whom 'the landlord assured me that he has drunk twenty-nine bottles of a thin white wine this day, and he does not appear to be intoxicated'.

HOLROYD, MARIA JOSEPHA. LAUSANNE, GENEVA, CHAMONIX, COL DE BALME, MARTIGNY, LAUSANNE, BERNE, THUN, BERNE, BIENNE, ILE ST. PIERRE, MOUTIER, BASLE

'It was a tremendous scene: the darkness relieved by frequent flashes of lightning, the roaring of the torrent, and nearly fifty of the country people assembled round us, all talking at once, some magnifying the danger, others assuring us there was none at all. You cannot think how well Mama bore it! Lady W. thought hysterics becoming.'

JACOBI, GEORG ARNOLD. CONSTANCE, SCHAFFHAUSEN, ZURICH, ZUG, LUCERNE, THUN, INTERLAKEN, MEIRINGEN, GROSSE SCHEIDEGG, GRINDELWALD, LAUTERBRUNNEN, THUN, BERNE, BIENNE, ILE ST. PIERRE, NEUCHÂTEL, LE LOCLE, LA CHAUX DE FONDS, YVERDON, LAUSANNE, GENEVA, CHAMONIX, GENEVA

'Right and left of Chamonix, Nature, with mighty hand, has thrown down two magnificent glaciers. Here from the glorious Aiguille du

Dru comes the great glacier des Bois; there, from the Aiguille du Midi comes the beautiful Glacier des Bossons. They rise up the mountains as if to Heaven.'

LA ROCHE, SOPHIE VON. BASLE, SOLEURE, BERNE, LAUSANNE, GENEVA, NYON, LAUSANNE

The rent at Lausanne for four rooms, kitchen, and maids' room, furnished but not including bed linen, was 5 Carolins or £5 a month.

MATTHISSON, FRIEDRICH. MARTIGNY, GRAND ST. BERNARD PASS, AOSTA

OWEN, JOHN. BASLE, SOLEURE, BERNE, MORAT, LAUSANNE, GENEVA, CHAMONIX, COL DE BALME, MARTIGNY, GRAND ST. BERNARD, MARTIGNY, LAUSANNE, GENEVA

'What a wonderful country is this! He who has sojourned on the banks of the Leman Lake, will tell you, that the scenery around presents an ever-fruitful, ever-varied picture to the eye. The wonders of the universe seem here to be combined in one magnificent group, and all the sublimities of nature collected into a focus. Each recurring day gives birth to some new beauty.'

SNEEDORF, N. SCHAFFHAUSEN, ZURICH, BADEN, BRUGG, BASLE, MOUTIER, BIENNE, BERNE, THUN, INTERLAKEN, GRINDELWALD, THUN, BERNE, PAYERNE, LAUSANNE, GENEVA

'A traveller in Switzerland is sure to find tasty food and good sleeping quarters every day; according to the fashion, therefore, there is greater merit in crossing the St. Gotthard than in having been to Dover'. 'I took a boat across the Lake of Thun. Never have I made a more enjoyable trip; nothing is more divine than this lake and its surroundings.'

STOLLBERG, FRIEDRICH LEOPOLD. CONSTANCE, ZURICH, ALBIS, ZUG, LUCERNE, STANSTAD, ALTDORF, LUCERNE, ZOFINGEN, THUN, INTERLAKEN, MEIRINGEN, GROSSE SCHEIDEGG, GRINDELWALD, LAUTERBRUNNEN, THUN, BERNE, BIENNE, ILE ST. PIERRE, NEUCHÂTEL, LE LOCLE, LA CHAUX DE FONDS, NEUCHÂTEL, YVERDON, LAUSANNE, GENEVA

'You will perceive we continue our circuitous mode of travelling: but who indeed would wish to travel otherwise, in a country like this? To examine it as it deserves, a man must not travel post; but as if he went to take a walk for his recreation.'

WATTENWYL, EMANUEL VON. BERNE, THUN, INTERLAKEN, LAUTERBRUNNEN, KLEINE SCHEIDEGG, GRINDELWALD, GROSSE SCHEIDEGG, MEIRINGEN, GRIMSEL PASS

'La Jungfrau, une des plus hautes, et sans contredire la plus belle montagne de toute cette chaine des Alpes: toutes les autres ont l'air d'avoir souffert ou par les tems ou par de violentes révolutions de la nature.'

WEBSTER, ELIZABETH, LADY. LAUSANNE, GENEVA, CHAMONIX, LAUSANNE, BERNE, LUCERNE, SOLEURE, NEUCHÂTEL, FRIBOURG, VEVEY, LAUSANNE, GENEVA

'Our party to Chamouny consisted of the Sheffields, Mr. Pelham, and some others whose names I have forgotten.' Of this expedition Maria Josepha Holroyd wrote: 'If anybody ever offends you so grievously that you do not recollect any punishment bad enough for them, only wish them on a party of pleasure with Lady Webster! The ceremony began with irresolution in the extreme whether they should or should not go! How and which way they should go? And everything that was proposed she decidedly determined on a contrary scheme, and as regularly altered her mind in a few hours.'

WILKINSON, JOSHUA LUCOCK. GENEVA, ROLLE, LAUSANNE, VEVEY, VILLENEUVE, MARTIGNY, TÊTE NOIRE PASS, CHAMONIX, COL DU BONHOMME, VAL D'ISERE, COL DE L'ISERAN, BONNEVAL, MONT CENIS PASS, MILAN, CHIAVENNA, SPLÜGEN PASS, ANDEER, THUSIS, COIRE, WESEN, ZURICH, ZUG, LUCERNE, SARNEN, BRUNIG PASS, BRIENZ, INTERLAKEN, THUN, KANDERSTEG, GEMMI PASS, LEUK, SION, MARTIGNY, VEVEY, FRIBOURG, MORAT, BERNE, SOLEURE, BIENNE, NEUCHÂTEL, YVERDON, MOTIERS-TRAVERS, LA CHAUX DE FONDS, ST. IMIER, BASLE, BESANÇON, ST. CERGUE, NYON, GENEVA—GENEVA, EVIAN, LAUSANNE, YVERDON, BIENNE, BASLE

'I was lost in amazement: the sublime, rocky, and white vastness of the mountains, whose enormous peaks towered above the clouds, appeared like the wrecks of nature . . .'
At Rolle, Wilkinson was arrested on suspicion of being the escaped Louis XVI.

WOLLASTON, CHARLES BYAM. SCHAFFHAUSEN, ZURICH, EINSIEDELN, RAPPERSWIL, ZURICH, BERNE, THUN, BERNE, LAUSANNE, CHAMONIX, COL DE BALME, MARTIGNY, LAUSANNE, NEUCHÂTEL, LUCERNE, ALTDORF, ST. GOTTHARD PASS, BELLINZONA, LUGANO, COMO

'In my opinion glaciers, though they are fine things with accompaniments, do not do any better by themselves than the base of Handel's music would do without the other parts.'

WYNNE, ELIZABETH. RORSCHACH, WARTEGG, ST. GALL, WARTENSEE, WARTEGG

'The castle of Wardeck is on a little hill well cultivated and surrounded with fruit trees, the view over the lake is superb and near Wardeck at the bottom of the hill is the village *Stadt* and a quarter of a league away the town of *Roschach*. I think we shall be very well here. The country is beautiful and the society which we shall enjoy will be delightful.' Elizabeth and her parents had come to stay at Wartegg with the marquise de Bombelles: a stay that was to last for three years.

WYTTENBACH, JAKOB SAMUEL. BERNE, GENEVA, ORBE, NEUCHÂTEL, BERNE, THUN, INTERLAKEN, LAUTERBRUNNEN

'On behalf of the Lauterbrunnen lead mine undertaking, I went to Trachsellauenen to see and investigate everything, and, if possible, to improve matters.'

1792

BECKFORD, WILLIAM. EVIAN, GENEVA, LAUSANNE, NEUCHÂTEL, BIENNE

'I have been obliged to cross over the lake in a violent hurry, for all Savoy is bedivelled and bejacobinized, and plundering, ravaging, etc., is going on swimmingly.'

BOURRIT, MARC-THÉODORE. GENEVA, CHAMONIX

Tête Noire: 'c'est là encore où je voyais arriver des mulets ayant de chaque côté des paniers où étaient de jeunes personnes qu'on avait couvertes d'un voile pour leur ôter la vue des précipices et des horreurs de cette route tandis que leurs mères la parcouraient à pied en chancelant à chaque pas.'

CLARKE, EDWARD DANIEL. BASLE, BERNE, LUCERNE, FLUELEN, ST. GOTTHARD PASS, BELLINZONA, TURIN

'Our carriages were drawn by oxen and peasants over high mountains of snow, where no European had ever dreamed of meeting a carriage before, among precipices, rocks, torrents and cataracts. The mountaineers beheld us with astonishment, the children ran away from us, and the men could not be kept from the wheels insomuch that they broke the blinds of Mr. Tufton's carriage in their eagerness to see the inside. At one place where we stopped the village assembled to salute "*The Prince of Wales*", because they happened to see on the inside of one of the trunks—"*H. Mortimer, trunk maker to his Majesty and the Prince of Wales*".'

CLONCURRY, VALENTINE LAWLESS, LORD. NEUCHÂTEL, BERNE, GENEVA, LAUSANNE

'During the period of my residence at Neufchâtel it was visited by Mr. Beckford, the well-known author of "Vathek" who made his journey in a style that would astonish the princes of the present degenerate days. His travelling menage consisted of about thirty horses, with four carriages, and a corresponding train of servants. Immediately upon his arrival, Mr. Beckford set up a fine yacht upon the lake.'

During his stay in Switzerland in this and the following year, Cloncurry met Lord Coleshill (afterwards Earl Digby), the Duke of Sussex, Lord Boringdon (afterwards Earl Morley), Lord Morpeth, the Duchess of Devonshire, the Duchess of Ancaster, Lord Carmarthen (afterwards Duke of Leeds), Lord Cholmondely, Mr. (afterwards Earl) Annesley, Robert Fowler Bishop of Ossory, and Lord Robert Fitzgerald.

DESNOUES, ABBÉ. ANNECY, UGINE, ERY, MÉGÈVE, CHAMONIX, TÊTE NOIRE PASS, MARTIGNY, VEVEY, CHATEL ST. DENIS

DEVONSHIRE, GEORGIANA, DUCHESS OF. GENEVA, YVERDON, LAUSANNE, MARTIGNY, GRAND ST. BERNARD PASS, AOSTA

'There is a very high mountain call'd Montblanc cover'd with Ice always, and so high that nobody for many centuries had reach'd its top—a person got to the top and Mr. de Saussure was desirous to go (tho' very dangerous) to try experiments on the Air. His Wife, tho' she dreaded his going, had courage and Love enough to tell him, as it had been done, he, as a great Philosopher, ought to try it.'

ESCHERNY, FRANÇOIS-LOUIS D' (*c*). RECONVILLIER, MORAT, BERNE, THUN, INTERLAKEN, MEIRINGEN, GROSSE SCHEIDEGG, GRINDELWALD, LAUTERBRUNNEN, INTERLAKEN

GLOVER, SAMUEL (*c*). LAUSANNE, ST. MAURICE, MARTIGNY, COL DE BALME, CHAMONIX

'You towering glaciers, which proudly advance into the vallies, aping a stately march, entomb the spirits of those sovereigns, who, forgetful of their first, great duty, the happiness of their subjects, abandon themselves to every vice disgraceful to humanity; the smaller glaciers, which precede and follow them, contain the spirits of Court parasites —of evil Counsellors,—of Ministers, who, blind to their country's good and deaf to the peoples' cries, were solely intent on the means of furthering their interest and advancing their ambition;—but their punishment is in the highest degree humiliating; the smaller glaciers, impregnated with a portion of these groveling spirits, instead of solid ice, are soft and porous;—in spring, to preserve the corn from sudden frosts, the Mountaineers strew their fields with the substance of these Glaciers; this disgraceful proceeding takes place in the vicinity of the towering glaciers, the receptacles of the spirits of kings, and makes them tremble for their fate.'

HESS, LUDWIG. ZURICH, INTERLAKEN, KANDERSTEG, GEMMI PASS, LEUK, SION, MARTIGNY, TÊTE NOIRE PASS, CHAMONIX, LAUSANNE

The first Swiss painter of the High Alps, Hess was the son of a butcher whose work took him into the mountains to buy cattle. His account-books were full of alpine sketches.

IFFLAND, A. W. BASLE, MOUTIER, BIENNE, BERNE, SURSEE, LUCERNE, ALBIS, ZURICH, SCHAFFHAUSEN

'The great beauty that surrounded me on all sides did not prevent me from looking sadly at the ice-covered mountains and calculating whether after all it might not be possible for me to go to them.'

LA VALLÉE, J. CHAMONIX

'Mais ce n'est qu'une demi-jouissance quand le soleil éclaire ces théâtres pompeux du sauvage désordre de la nature. C'est au sein des nuits qu'il faut surprendre le silence dans son véritable empire; on le redoute parmi les tombeaux; on le déteste parmi les cachots; ici, c'est un dieu paysible dont le pied repose sur la ceinture du monde, et dont le front majestueux laisse sans s'émouvoir les étoiles rouler autour de sa tête immobile. Transportez-vouz, ô mon ami! Transportez-vous s'il se peut un moment avec nous sur les vertèbres gigantesques de l'une de ces montagnes qui paroissent à l'œil étonné les colonnes du trône du Mont-Blanc. Admirez et frémissez . . .'

MATTHISSON, FRIEDRICH. CHÂTEAU D'OEX, ROUGEMONT, SAANÈN, VEVEY, BLONAY

On his journey to the Saanen valley, Matthisson got the botanist Abraham Thomas to accompany him so as not to miss any plants. Matthisson relates that Thomas was so expert in his knowledge of the habitats of rare plants that he could go and put his hand on them without needing to look.

MONTYON, AUGET DE. GENEVA, LAUSANNE, BASLE

OWEN, JOHN. CONSTANCE, SCHAFFHAUSEN, ZURICH, BERNE, LAUSANNE, GENEVA, CHAMONIX, GENEVA—GENEVA, LAUSANNE, BERNE, AARBURG, AARAU, BRUGG, SCHAFFHAUSEN

'Reason and humanity appear to discountenance, except for some definite purpose of utility, expeditions upon this hazardous mountain. Saussure was a philosopher, and his ascension of the Mont Blanc tended to ascertain some points of moment, respecting the altitudes of the mountains, the rarity of the air, and other physical phenomena. A recent attempt was made, by four English gentlemen, to climb this mountain; and the issue of their expedition ought to render this the last example of similar curiosity.'

REICHARD, H. A. O. BASLE, SCHAFFHAUSEN, ZURICH, ALBIS, ZUG, LUCERNE, ALTDORF, ST. GOTTHARD PASS, BELLINZONA, MAGADINO, DOMODOSSOLA, SIMPLON PASS, BRIG, LEUK, GEMMI PASS, KANDERSTEG, BERNE, THUN, INTERLAKEN, LAUTERBRUNNEN, KLEINE SCHEIDEGG, GRINDELWALD, GROSSE SCHEIDEGG, MEIRINGEN, GRIMSEL, BRIENZ, INTERLAKEN, BERNE, LAUSANNE, GENEVA, CHAMONIX, COL DE BALME, MARTIGNY, GRAND ST. BERNARD

SAUSSURE, HORACE-BÉNÉDICT DE. GENEVA, ST. GERVAIS, COL DU BONHOMME, BOURG ST. MAURICE, PETIT ST. BERNARD PASS, AOSTA, CHATILLON, BREUIL, ST. THEODUL PASS, BREUIL, COL DES CIMES BLANCHES, ST. JACQUES D'AYAS, VERRES, AOSTA, GRAND ST. BERNARD PASS, MARTIGNY, GENEVA

'Placés sur cette planète depuis hier, et seulement pour un jour, nous ne pouvons que désirer des connaissances que vraisemblablement nous n'atteindrons jamais.'

SCHLEICHER, JEAN-CHRISTOPHE. BEX, VISP, ZERMATT, ST. THEODUL PASS, BREUIL

TAYLOR, GENERAL SIR HERBERT. GENEVA, LAUSANNE, VEVEY, BERNE, ZURICH, SCHAFFHAUSEN

At Vevey 'Mr. C. Blair was the only other Englishman with the exception of the Duke of Sussex, then Prince Augustus, who was there a short time, and associated with us very freely'.

WHALEY, THOMAS 'BUCK'. GENEVA, CHAMONIX, EVIAN, LAUSANNE, BERNE, SOLEURE, ZURICH, SCHAFFHAUSEN

In his memoirs the Irish eccentric spoke of 'a resolution I had formed of making a tour round the glaciers, and endeavouring to ascend Mont Blanc . . . But whether it was not the proper season, or that the weather was unusually severe, we had not proceeded above two thirds of the ascent when, owing to a violent shower of hail, a mass of snow detached itself from the mountain and killed two of our guides, which so intimidated the rest that it was impossible to prevail on them to proceed one step further; as they affirmed that the snow would soon fall in such masses as would inevitably overwhelm us all. I was now left alone with Lord Charles.' This was Lord Charles Townsend.

WITTE, CARL. BASLE, SCHAFFHAUSEN, ZURICH, WALLENSTADT, COIRE, THUSIS, SPLÜGEN PASS, CHIAVENNA, SOGLIO

WYNNE, ELIZABETH. WARTEGG, RORSCHACH, ARBON, HORN, WARTENSEE, WEIHNACHTEN, APPENZELL, ST. GALL, BÜREN, WIL, WINTERTHUR, WARTEGG, ZURICH, RICHTERSWIL, BADEN, BRUGG, SCHINZNACH, LENZBURG, AARAU, ZURICH, WINTERTHUR, WARTEGG, ST. GALL, GOSSAU, OVERDACH, LACHEN, EINSIEDELN, RICHTERSWIL, ZURICH, SCHAFFHAUSEN, CONSTANCE, WARTEGG, EGGERSRIED, WARTEGG

'I was enchanted of this charming country, and I much regretted not to be able to draw the country views because I cannot remember of having ever seen a more rural fine and agreeable prospect as this was.'

WYTTENBACH, JAKOB SAMUEL. BERNE, THUN, INTERLAKEN, LAUTERBRUNNEN, GRINDELWALD, MEIRINGEN, GRIMSEL PASS, FURKA PASS, ANDERMATT, OBERALP PASS, DISENTIS, LUKMANIER PASS, PASO DEL UOMO, PIORA, AIROLO, ST. GOTTHARD PASS, FLUELEN, LUCERNE, BERNE

An excursion with Mr. John Gould and Mr. Nutcombe.

1793

BOIGNE, ADÈLE DE. MILAN, BELLINZONA, ST. GOTTHARD PASS, ALTDORF, LUCERNE, LAUSANNE, CONSTANCE

BOMBELLES, MARQUIS DE. ST. GALL, WARTEGG, COIRE

'A Coire, M. de Bombelles, considéré comme le chef des émigrés, avait retenu une chambre pour voir de la fenêtre les insultes dirigées contre nous.' (M. SÉMONVILLE.)

BOURRIT, MARC-THÉODORE. GENEVA, CHAMONIX

It was in this year that the French Ambassador, M. de Sémonville, suggested to Bourrit the building of a hut on the Montenvert.

BRÄKER, ULRICH. WATTWIL, ZURICH, ZUG, LUCERNE, MALTERS, BRÄMEGG, ENTLIBUCH, ESCHOLZMATT, TRUB, LANGNAU, BERNE, HINDELBANK, MURGENTHAL, ROTHRIST, KÖLLIKEN, AARAU, BIBERSTEIN, SCHINZNACH, BRUGG, BADEN, ZURICH, KLOTEN, RORBAS, IRCHEL, ANDELFINGEN, FRAUENFELD, WIL, LICHTENSTEIG, WATTWIL

'As I topped the crest [between Biberstein and Schinznach] I stopped, had to stop, for I was suddenly spellbound by the most beautiful view that I had ever seen in my life. The glorious sun was just going down. In front of me lay an endless countryside, in twilight and shade. Behind me and to my right I saw huge mountain chains of giants. I believed I was looking at a row from the Säntis to the furthest snows behind Grindelwald. Naturally, I could not recognize all these princes, although they were in full sunshine and seemed quite near. To my left the chain of the Jura, likewise gilded by the sun. No, I had never seen such a view. . . .'

DEVONSHIRE, GEORGIANA, DUCHESS OF. MAGADINO, BELLINZONA, ST. GOTTHARD PASS, ALTDORF, LUCERNE, INTERLAKEN, GRINDELWALD

'The Milanese was infested with a band of robbers that caused us some alarm, and obliged us to use some precautions, but from the moment we entered the mountains of Switzerland we travelled without any fear, and felt perfectly safe.'

Georgiana was accompanied by Lady Elizabeth Foster. For her children Georgiana wrote a poem on her crossing of the St. Gotthard, and on the 24th stanza Coleridge wrote his 'Ode to Georgiana Duchess of Devonshire'.

DOLOMIEU, DÉODAT DE. CHAMONIX, GENEVA

GENLIS, MME DE. BASLE, SCHAFFHAUSEN, ZURICH, ZUG, BREMGARTEN, SCHAFFHAUSEN

Mme de Genlis, Governess of the Duke of Orleans' children, deserted from France with General Dumouriez and reached Switzerland with Mlle d'Orléans, where they were joined by the latter's brother the duc de Chartres. In Switzerland the party came in for hostility both from royalist refugees and republicans. At Zug they received a volley of stones through their windows, and they decided that as the duc de Chartres was so easily recognized, the party should split up.

GIBBON, EDWARD. LAUSANNE, BASLE, SCHAFFHAUSEN

GORANI, COMTE JOSEPH. ST. CERGUE, NYON, GENEVA, CELIGNY

Gorani claimed that his activities preserved Geneva from annexation by France at this time.

HERVEY, FREDERICK AUGUSTUS. SCHAFFHAUSEN, ALTDORF, ST. GOTTHARD PASS, BELLINZONA

LOUIS-PHILIPPE. SCHAFFHAUSEN, ZURICH, ZUG, BASLE, LUCERNE, FLUELEN, ALTDORF, ST. GOTTHARD PASS, BELLINZONA, GORDOLA, REICHENAU, BREMGARTEN

The duc de Chartres took up a post as mathematics master at the school at Reichenau under the name of Chabos. He gave every satisfaction in this capacity except that he seduced the school cook, Marianne Banzori.

MATTHISSON, FRIEDRICH. ZURICH, WALLENSTADT, RAGAZ, PFÄFERS, COIRE, MALANS, ERMATTINGEN, GRANDCLOS

'Writers of travels in Switzerland have a wide field open to them as soon as they decide to tread unbeaten paths, particularly in the Valais, the Grisons, and the Italian bailiwicks.'

SÉMONVILLE, CHARLES LOUIS HUGUET DE MONTARAN DE. GENEVA, LAUSANNE, BERNE, BADEN, ZURICH, ST. GALL, RORSCHACH, SARGANS, COIRE, LENZERHEIDE, TIEFENKASTEL, BIVIO, SEPTIMER PASS, VICOSOPRANO, CHIAVENNA, NOVATE

The French Revolutionary Ambassador to Turkey with his colleague Hugues Bernard Maret, Ambassador to Naples, were waylaid at Novate and handed over to the Austrians.

TRANCHANT DE LAVERNE, LÉGER MARIE PHILIPPE. MONTAGNY, BULLE, MOLESON, CHATEL ST. DENIS, VEVEY, LAUSANNE, MOUDON,

YVERDON, GRANDSON, ST. SULPICE, MOTIERS-TRAVERS, ST. AUBIN, NEUCHÂTEL, ILE ST. PIERRE, BIENNE, MORAT, AVENCHES, PAYERNE, MONTAGNY

Lunched with Lord Northampton who lay on a bed in a hut in his garden, surrounded by his family, dogs, cats, monkeys, canaries, parrots, and other animals.

WEBSTER, ELIZABETH, LADY. MILAN, AOSTA, GRAND ST. BERNARD PASS, MARTIGNY, BEX, VEVEY, LAUSANNE, AVENCHES, MORAT, BERNE, HINDELBANK, LENZBURG, MELLINGEN, BADEN, KAISERSTUHL, LAUFEN, SCHAFFHAUSEN

'Upon my coming into Bex I met Prince Hatzfeldt and my tiresome Scotch lover, Mr. Douglas. We supped together at the inn.' At Vevey, 'the English here are the Cholmondeleys, the old Duchess of Ancaster, Ld Morpeth, his friend who travels with him, and various other English and the son of an Irish bishop'.

WYNNE, ELIZABETH. WARTEGG, RHEINECK, RORSCHACH, ST. GALL, WIL, WINTERTHUR, ZURICH, BÜREN, WARTEGG, ALTSTÄTTEN, STOSS, GAIS, WARTEGG, ST. GALL, WIL, WINTERTHUR, ZURICH, ALBIS, LUCERNE, DAGMERSELLEN, ZOFINGEN, BERNE, MORAT, MOUDON, LAUSANNE, YVERDON, NEUCHÂTEL, AARBERG, ST. URBAN, BRUGG, ZURICH, WINTERTHUR, WARTEGG

'Mr. de Semonville, Barbarossa Maret and others passed through here this morning. All our French Emigrants went to Stadt on purpose to see them and in the meantime to tell them a parcel of impudences. . . . I cannot express how happy this Swiss tour has made me on all accounts.'

1794

BECKFORD, WILLIAM (*c*). LAUSANNE

'I bought the library [Gibbon's] to have something to read when I passed through Lausanne. I shut myself up for six weeks from early in the morning until night, only now and then taking a ride.'

BONSTETTEN, KARL VIKTOR VON. BERNE, TRUBSCHACHEN, NAPF, LUCERNE

The Napf 'is not at all high, and quite easy to climb, but so felicitously situated that on one side all the land between the Savoy and Tyrol mountains is to be seen at its feet, and on the other side the whole amphitheatre of the Alps. Perhaps I shall buy the mountain, build a hut on it and then become master of the most beautiful view in Switzerland.'

BOUTERWECK, FRIEDRICH. SCHAFFHAUSEN, CONSTANCE, ZURICH, EINSIEDELN, ZURICH, OLTEN, BERNE, THUN, INTERLAKEN, LAUTER-

BRUNNEN, KLEINE SCHEIDEGG, GRINDELWALD, GROSSE SCHEIDEGG, MEIRINGEN, INTERLAKEN, THUN, BERNE, MORAT, LAUSANNE, GENEVA, ST. CERGUE, LA DOLE, LAUSANNE

'An elegant English lady, whose name is not unknown, had come to Grindelwald to see the glaciers, and wanted to hire four men to carry her over the Scheidegg to Meiringen for the normal fee of one new gold Louis. The four strongest men in the whole of Grindelwald were searched for. But however keen the Swiss is to earn an honest penny, no-one accepted the task of carrying so important a lady, even for a full-weight gold Louis. But the lady wished to be carried. Four other men, the next strongest, were sent for, and the hire money doubled. The eight stalwarts looked at one another and formed a plan. Divided into two shifts, relieving one another, they lifted the preposterous weight and strode towards the Scheidegg . . .

'When they had received their Louis which they had earned with all their might, eaten and drunk, they slept all night and all next day, and were still exhausted when they woke.'

CLARKE, EDWARD DANIEL. AOSTA, GRAND ST. BERNARD PASS, MARTIGNY, VEVEY, GENEVA, LAUSANNE, BERNE, BASLE

'Ye have no idea of the severe grandeur of the Alpine mountains, whose hoary tops drink the aeriel solitude of the skies, and pour forth all the rivers of Europe.'

DOLOMIEU, DÉODAT DE. CHAMONIX, MONT BUET, SIXT

Mont Buet 'n'a exigé de moi presqu'aucune fatigue pour être gravi jusqu'à son sommet, et je suis resté pendant plus d'une heure sur le glacier qui le recouvre sans être incommodé par le froid. Nous avons donc joui sur ce superbe belvédère de la plus belle vue que puisse présenter cet intérieur des Alpes.'

GORANI, COMTE JOSEPH. GENEVA, CELIGNY, NYON, VICH, ROLLE, MORGES, LAUSANNE, MOUDON, PAYERNE, MORAT, BERNE, SOLEURE, BASLE, BRUGG, AARAU, LENZBURG, ZURICH, WINTERTHUR, FRAUENFELD, BISCHOFFSZELL, ST. GALL, APPENZELL, GLARUS, SCHWYZ, LUCERNE, ZURICH, FRAUENFELD, WINTERTHUR, BUCH, SCHAFFHAUSEN, BASLE

Proscribed by every country in Europe, the adventurer was also dodging a gang of assassins sent after him by the Queen of Naples.

HENNEZEL, BÉAT DE. COMO, LUGANO, BELLINZONA, AIROLO, ST. GOTTHARD PASS, AMSTEG, ALTDORF, LUCERNE, BIENNE, NEUCHÂTEL, YVERDON

'Après avoir longuement cheminé par des rochers plus effrayants que les précédents, . . . nous arrivâmes à Amsteg . . . harassés de corps et d'esprit. J'avais un noir que je ne puis exprimer. S'il y a des agréments dans le voyage d'Italie, il y a bien des épines, et le passage des monts n'en est pas une petite.'

LASCELLES, ROWLEY. LAUSANNE, VEVEY, BEX, VEVEY, CHATEL ST. DENIS, CHÂTEAU D'OEX, ZWEISIMMEN, THUN, INTERLAKEN, MEIRINGEN, BRUNIG PASS, SARNEN, STANS, ENGELBERG, LUCERNE, FLUELEN, ANDERMATT, ST. GOTTHARD, FURKA PASS, MÜNSTER, BRIG, LEUK, GEMMI PASS, KANDERSTEG, INTERLAKEN, LAUTERBRUNNEN, INTERLAKEN, KANDERSTEG, GEMMI PASS, LEUK, SION, MARTIGNY, BEX, VEVEY, LAUSANNE, AUBONNE, LAC DE JOUX, DENT DE VAULION, LAUSANNE, VEVEY, BEX, MARTIGNY, SION, LEUK, GEMMI PASS, KANDERSTEG, THUN, BERNE, BURGDORF, LANGENTHAL, AARBURG, ZURICH, SCHAFFHAUSEN, ZURICH, HOCHSTETTEN, GRINDELWALD, GROSSE SCHEIDEGG, MEIRINGEN, INTERLAKEN, THUN, BERNE, NIDAU, ILE ST. PIERRE, NEUCHÂTEL, ORBE, AUBONNE, LAUSANNE, MARTIGNY, SION, BRIG, SIMPLON PASS, DOMODOSSOLA

'The valley of Grindelwald was poured in prospect around me, its spacious concave divided into three parts by the three glacier rivers. It appeared a profound sea, ebbed of its waters; the bottom indeed perfectly green with numberless cottages scattered over it shell-wise. The ealder Scheidec had retired a little behind, on my right hand, having its green tunic sashed by a fine cascade the Millibach.'

LISMORE, JAMES DANIEL O'BRIEN LORD. MARTIGNY

The son of one of the Old Pretender's Ministers, a Jacobite refugee from the Jacobins of the French revolution after the invasion of Savoy, Lismore was found destitute at Martigny.

MATTHISSON, FRIEDRICH. BERNE, BLUMENSTEIN, STOCKHORN, ERLENBACH, THUN, BERNE, BIENNE, ILE ST. PIERRE

PONTÉCOULANT, LOUIS-GUSTAVE LE DOULCET DE. LES VERRIÈRES, MOTIERS-TRAVERS, NEUCHÂTEL, ILE ST. PIERRE, MORAT, BERNE, LAUSANNE, GENEVA, LUCERNE, ALTDORF, ZURICH, ZUG, REICHENAU, BERNE, MORAT, NEUCHÂTEL, LES VERRIÈRES

While working as a carpenter at Zurich, the proscribed Conventionnel was visited by Louis Philippe, likewise in exile.

WILLIAMS, HELEN MARIA. BASLE, ZURICH, BASLE, LUCERNE, ALTDORF, ST. GOTTHARD PASS, BELLINZONA, LUGANO, BELLINZONA, ROVEREDO, VAL CALANCA, MESOCCO, SAN BERNARDINO PASS, THUSIS, COIRE, WALLENSTADT, GLARUS, ZURICH, LUCERNE, ENGELBERG, LUCERNE, ZUG, LUCERNE, BASLE, SOLEURE, BIENNE, NEUCHÂTEL, MORAT, LAUSANNE, GENEVA, VEVEY, MARTIGNY, SION, MARTIGNY, VEVEY, FRIBOURG, BERNE

On the St. Gotthard pass the monks told Miss Williams that the day before her arrival, 'a numerous retinue of horses, oxen, mules, and other cattle, had passed in the suite of a great man, whose carriage they had dragged, by his order, from the bottom of the mountain, that he might have the fame of crossing St. Gotthard in a vehicle with wheels. As our countrymen are known to be the only travelling philosophers who make experiments of this kind, the Monks had no difficulty in conjecturing on the approach of this long procession, that if it was not the Emperor, or the Burgo-master of Berne, the two greatest personages they had heard of, it must be an English Lord.'

WYNNE, ELIZABETH. WARTEGG, ROSSBÜCHEL, WEIHNACHTEN, RORSCHACH, WALZENHAUSEN, ST. GALL, CONSTANCE, WARTEGG, ALTSTÄTTEN, BUCHBERG-STEINTISCH, GRIMMENSTEIN, WARTEGG, BREGENZ

'Ever since I have read *Rudolphe of Wertenberg* I have more pleasure when I walk round this country, as it makes me remember on all that has happen in former times in this part of Switzerland.'

1795

BONSTETTEN, KARL VIKTOR VON. BERNE, LANGNAU, LUCERNE, ALTDORF, ST. GOTTHARD PASS, BELLINZONA, LUGANO, LOCARNO, PONTE BROLLA, VALLE MAGGIA, BIGNASCO, FUSIO, LOCARNO, LUGANO, MENDRISIO, LOCARNO, CENTOVALLI, MASERA, DOMODOSSOLA, SIMPLON PASS, BRIG, SION, MARTIGNY, BEX, VEVEY, YVERDON, VALEYRES

Bonstetten was officiating as Syndic for the Swiss confederation in the Italian bailiwicks.

BOURRIT, MARC-THÉODORE. GENEVA, CHAMONIX

Under Bourrit's direction the 'Temple de la Nature' was erected on Montenvert.

BRUN, FRIEDERIKE. COIRE, THUSIS, VIA MALA, COIRE, ALTSTÄTTEN, GAIS, ZURICH, ALBIS, ZUG, RIGI, ALTDORF, ST. GOTTHARD PASS, BELLINZONA, LUGANO, MENDRISIO, LOCARNO, CENTOVALLI, DOMODOSSOLA

With Bonstetten, Matthisson, and Princess Louise of Anhalt-Dessau, 'La main dans la main, nous promîmes fidélité, à toi, ô Nature, à toi ô Amitié! et remerciements d'enfants, à toi Maître puissant de nos destinées! Ô villa Pliniana! aucun cœur humain n'a encore sacrifié sur ton autel! Pour toi Ô Immortalité, nous voulons vivre et mourir!'

DOLOMIEU, DÉODAT DE. GENEVA, CHAMONIX, COL DU BONHOMME, BEAUFORT, COL DU CORNET D'ARÈCHES, MOUTIERS

'C'est pour m'arracher au spectacle funeste que me présente mon pays que je viens de visiter les glaciers qui environnent le Mont Blanc; et en voyant ces majestueuses proéminences, ces énormes rochers, ces neiges éternelles, j'ai pu oublier, quelques instants, les crimes des hommes et les viles passions qui les agitent.'

ESCHER, HANS CONRAD. ZURICH, ALBIS, ZUG, BRUNNEN, ALTDORF, WASSEN, ST. GOTTHARD

Escher's journey enabled him to make out the fundamental structure of the mountains of the St. Gotthard massif, and particularly the fact that the strata on the northern side dip towards the south while those on the southern side dip towards the north.

HUMBOLDT, ALEXANDER VON. SCHAFFHAUSEN, ZURICH, BERNE, LAUSANNE, GENEVA, CHAMONIX, LUCERNE, ALTDORF, ST. GOTTHARD

'No descriptions of the eternal snows of the Alps when tinged in the morning or evening with a rosy hue, or of the beauty of the blue glacier ice, or of any part of the grandeur of the scenery of Switzerland, have reached us from the ancients, although statesmen and generals, with men of letters in their train, were constantly passing through Helvetia into Gaul. All these travellers think only of complaining of the difficulties of the way; the romantic scenery never seems to have engaged their attention.'

LALANDE, JEROME. GENEVA, CHAMONIX

'On voit avec regret, dans ce voyage, la démolition que l'extravagance d'Albitte fit exécuter en 1794 dans le département du Mont-Blanc, ainsi que dans le département de l'Ain. J'ai rencontré le citoyen Nouet prenant des angles sur les montagnes, pour lier la carte générale de France à celle de Savoie du département du Mont-Blanc; il se plaignoit plus que personne de la difficulté qu'ajoutoit à son travail le manque des signaux que les clochers fournissoient autrefois.'

MATTHISSON, FRIEDRICH. FELDKIRCH, COIRE, THUSIS, ANDEER, COIRE, WALLENSTADT, RICHTERSWIL, SCHWYZ, BRUNNEN, ALTDORF, ST. GOTTHARD PASS, BELLINZONA, LUGANO

'A week before our arrival in Bellinzona, a reigning princess of Germany with a numerous retinue and sumptuous equipage, had thrown everybody from the Burgermaster to the crossing-sweeper into amazement. For instead of bargaining, she always paid more than the exorbitant bills of the greedy landlords demanded.'

SABRAN, MME DE. BASLE, ZURICH, BASLE, BERNE, THUN, INTERLAKEN, LAUTERBRUNNEN, GRINDELWALD, MEIRINGEN, ENGELBERG, EINSIEDELN, ZURICH

SERGENT-MARCEAU, ANTOINE. BASLE, MEIRINGEN, JOCH PASS, ENGELBERG

'Emira crossed a foaming torrent on the trunks of two trees thrown over it, as if she had been born and brought up in the mountains. I own I needed her encouragement to follow her. I could not do so when she walked over the Mer de Glace, for I turned giddy. She was the first woman to walk on the eternal snows of the Joch pass. On that day we walked ten leagues accompanied by four guides.'

STETTLER, RUDOLF. MEIRINGEN, GAULI PASS, GRIMSEL

This journey was undertaken with von Graffenried expressly to determine the topography of the glacial regions concerned.

THOMAS, ABRAHAM. BEX, PAS DE CHEVILLE, SION, VISP, SAAS FEE, STALDEN, ZERMATT, ST. THEODUL PASS, BREUIL, CHATILLON, AOSTA, GRAND ST. BERNARD PASS, MARTIGNY, BEX

'Le voyageur, saisi d'un respect religieux, entend en même temps le son des cloches et les éclats des glaciers qui imitent le bruit du tonnerre.'

WICKHAM, WILLIAM. BASLE, BERNE, LAUSANNE

The British Minister to Switzerland took a house, Fauxblanc, near Lausanne.

1796

ANONYMOUS 6. VALLORBE, LA SARRAZ, LAUSANNE, GENEVA

'Never shall I forget the magnitude of the objects that presented themselves at once most unexpectedly to my view, after ascending a steep and rugged hill, when I first discovered that great primordial chain of the Alps, in an extent of upwards of an hundred miles. The impression this had on my senses is beyond conception; for I cried out with ecstasy, and could scarcely contain myself, while beholding the chain of Glaciers, and Mont Blanc. . . .'

BEAUREGARD, HENRY COSTA DE. AOSTA, GRAND ST. BERNARD PASS, MARTIGNY, LAUSANNE

'Chamounix est charmant en été, et l'hiver, qui ne laisse pas d'y être long, nous aurons le plaisir d'être séparés du monde par d'énormes amas de neige. Ce sera charmant; qu'en dites-vous, mon amie? . . . Ah! je vous le répète, si nous pouvions avoir une cabane à Chamounix et de quoi n'y pas mourir absolument de faim, nous serions trop heureux. . . .'

BONSTETTEN, KARL VIKTOR VON. BERNE, THUN, INTERLAKEN, MEIRINGEN, GRIMSEL PASS, OBERGESTELEN, GRIES PASS, DOMODOSSOLA, ARONA, LUGANO, LOCARNO, VAL ONSERNONE, LOCO, RUSSO, COMOLOGNO, MILAN, AOSTA, GRAND ST. BERNARD PASS, MARTIGNY, BEX, LAUSANNE, YVERDON, VALEYRES

'These Italian valleys never have money for anything useful; they have no doctors or schools, no money for the poor, the roads or the bridges—only for lawsuits is everyone well off, for this passion is the only force that has actuated these people for centuries; Locarno with a population of 1074 has 33 lawyers, who provide a veritable "Factory of destruction" by means of which all life is methodically ruined.'

BRIDEL, LOUIS. NYON, LAUSANNE, MORAT, BERNE, AARAU, ZURICH, ALBIS, RIGI, SCHWYZ, EINSIEDELN, RAPPERSWIL, HERISAU, TROGEN, SARGANS, GLARUS, LINTHAL, RICHETLI PASS, ELM, SEGNES PASS, COIRE, LANDQUART, KLOSTERS, DAVOS, TIEFENKASTEL, BIVIO, SEPTIMER PASS, CASACCIA, MALOJA PASS, ST. MORITZ, ZERNEZ, OFEN PASS, STA. MARIA, UMBRAIL PASS, BORMIO, TIRANO, CHIAVENNA, SPLÜGEN PASS, THUSIS, REICHENAU, DISENTIS, OBERALP PASS, ANDERMATT, ALTDORF, LUCERNE, ENGELBERG, JOCH PASS, MEIRINGEN, GROSSE SCHEIDEGG, GRINDELWALD, LAUTERBRUNNEN, INTERLAKEN, THUN, BERNE, GURNIGEL, FRIBOURG, BULLE, CHÂTEAU D'OEX, COL DES MOSSES, AIGLE, BEX, VEVEY, LAUSANNE

'Voila donc 461 lieues que nous avons faites, en parcourant la majeure partie de la Suisse, et cela fort agréablement, sans danger ni accident quelconque.'

BRUN, FRIEDERIKE. LAUSANNE, ORBE, VALEYRES

'The amphitheatre of the Alps resounds with the harmonies of the most glorious concords of colour! And the scale of creation drops in majestic steps from the three summits of Mont Blanc, through all the snow, rock and ice peaks of Savoy, Valais and Berne, down to the Moléson in the Canton of Fribourg. Truly, it is a heathen hymn of creation when colours turn into sound, as here.'

DOUGLAS, A. BERNE, LEUKERBAD, BERNE, BIENNE, ILE ST. PIERRE, BERNE, LAUSANNE, GENEVA, NYON, ST. CERGUE, MOREZ

GRASS, CARL. ZURICH, GLARUS, KLÖNTHAL

'Mountains! mountains! On your summits, body and soul are fortified and the heart becomes great. I wish that I could spirit you onto a high mountain, you puny, weak and sybaritic men, and say to your souls: "be no longer small, rise to sublimity, to strength of spirit; be men! be natural"!'

HEGEL, GEORG WILHELM FRIEDRICH. BERNE, THUN, INTERLAKEN, LAUTERBRUNNEN, KLEINE SCHEIDEGG, GRINDELWALD, GROSSE SCHEIDEGG, MEIRINGEN, GRIMSEL PASS, FURKA PASS, ANDERMATT, ALTDORF, LUCERNE

'We saw these glaciers today from the distance of half an hour's walk, and their appearance presents no further interest. One can only call it a new kind of seeing which, however, does not impose on the mind any further activity other than to notice that, in spite of the great heat of summer, one is so very close to masses of ice which descend to a level where cherries, nuts and corn ripen.'

LESLIE, SIR JOHN. SION, BRIG, GRIMSEL PASS, MEIRINGEN, GRINDELWALD

'I regard it as highly probable, that the hillocks so frequent in Upper Valais are of the same nature, [as moraines]. There was perhaps a time, therefore, when glaciers descended more than 3,000 feet below their actual line, into the bottom of the valley.'

TWEDDELL, JOHN. SCHAFFHAUSEN, ZURICH, GLARUS, SCHWYZ, SCHWANAU, LUCERNE, ENGELBERG, TITLIS, JOCH PASS, MEIRINGEN, INTERLAKEN, WIMMIS, BERNE, BASLE, BIENNE, NEUCHÂTEL, LAUSANNE, GENEVA

'The other day I ascended a very high mountain called TITLISBERG. It is 10,710 feet above the level of the sea. It cost me nine hours to ascend it. I set out at a quarter after midnight, and reached the summit at half after nine.'

WEDGWOOD, THOMAS. LUCERNE, RIGI, SARNEN, BRUNIG PASS, MEIRINGEN, GRINDELWALD, LAUTERBRUNNEN, INTERLAKEN, THUN

The 'first photographer' was accompanied by Sir John Leslie.

1797

BAGGESEN, JENS IMMANUEL. BERNE, THUN, INTERLAKEN, LAUTERBRUNNEN, KLEINE SCHEIDEGG, GRINDELWALD, GROSSE SCHEIDEGG, MEIRINGEN

The Danish poet was known as 'the northern bard of the Jungfrau'.

BONAPARTE, NAPOLEON. GENEVA, LAUSANNE, MORAT, BERNE, SOLEURE, BASLE

Napoleon was on his way to the Congress of Rastatt. On seeing the battlefield of Morat he remarked: 'We would not have made our retreat by the lake.'

BONSTETTEN, KARL VIKTOR VON. LUGANO, SAN SALVATORE, LOCARNO, VALLE VERZASCA, VOGORNO, SAN BARTOLOMEO, VAL ONSERNONE, LOCO, BELLINZONA, ST. GOTTHARD PASS, BERNE

'I have returned safe and sound from the Valle Verzasca. The effects of the alpine air are unbelievable. I bounded like a chamois over the rocky path by the precipices, and feel less tired this evening than I was this morning.'

BOURRIT, MARC-THÉODORE. GENEVA, CHAMONIX

'Une stature longue et maigre, un teint hâle, comme celui d'un mulatre, un œil ardent, plein de génie et de vie, une bouche ornée par un trait de finesse et de bonhomie qui inspire la confiance. Tel est le tableau rapide de cet homme singulier.'

BRIDEL, PHILIPPE. CHÂTEAU D'OEX, MOCAUSAZ, CHARMEY, VALSAINTE, SCHWARZSEE, CHARMEY, JAUN, ABLÄNDSCHEN, ROUGEMONT, CHÂTEAU D'OEX

Bridel considered that if Ossian had lived in Switzerland he would have placed the spirit of Loda and the home of storms and blizzards in the valley of Abländschen.

CARNOT, LAZARE. GENEVA, COPPET, NYON, LAUSANNE, VEVEY, BERNE, AARAU

The great revolutionary leader was in flight from his colleagues of the Directoire.

CHÊNEDOLLÉ, CHARLES DE. BERNE, THUN, INTERLAKEN, LAUTERBRUNNEN, GRINDELWALD, CHAMONIX

DESAIX, GENERAL. BASLE, OLTEN, LUCERNE, ALTDORF, ST. GOTTHARD, AIROLO, BELLINZONA, LUGANO, COMO

DOLOMIEU, DÉODAT DE. CHAMONIX, COL DU BONHOMME, COL DE LA SEIGNE, COURMAYEUR, AOSTA, ALAGNA, MACUGNAGA, BAVENO, LUGANO, AIROLO, AL ACQUA, NUFENEN PASS, ULRICHEN, BRIG, MARTIGNY, CHAMONIX, GENEVA

'Je n'ai pas été très heureux au St. Gothard; j'y ai été précédé par trois marchands de minéraux qui avaient presque tout enlevé.'

ENGHIEN, DUC D'. CONSTANCE, ZURICH, ALBIS, ZUG, LUCERNE, ENGELBERG, JOCH PASS, MEIRINGEN, GROSSE SCHEIDEGG, GRINDELWALD, INTERLAKEN, THUN, BERNE, MURI, LUCERNE, FLUELEN, ANDERMATT, ST. GOTTHARD, ALTDORF, SCHWYZ, EINSIEDELN, RAPPERSWIL, FRAUENFELD, CONSTANCE

'Mon voyage en Suisse, dont je vous parle au commencement de ma lettre, m'a extrêmement amusé. Mon grand-père a eu de la peine à m'accorder la permission de le faire et effectivement peut-être pouvait-il y avoir quelque espèce de danger, s'il avait été public. Il a été tout au contraire tout à fait incognito, et l'on n'a su que j'y étais que lorsque j'en ai été revenu. Figurez-vous le duc d'Enghien en redinfrac gris, le chapeau rond, la bottine anglaise, les cheveux rabattus sur les yeux, le reste à l'avenant, suivi de Sérent, de Cheffontaines et de Charles de Mellet dans le même équipage; un domestique avec un petit cheval portant un seul porte-manteau pour eux quatre, voyageant à pied le long des routes et faisant leurs huit et dix lieues par jour.'

ESCHER, HANS CONRAD (*c*). WASSEN, SUSTEN PASS, MEIRINGEN

Escher had heard of the Susten pass by word of mouth only, and had seen no previous descriptions of it. He was accompanied by the son of the celebrated M. Mesmer.

GOETHE, JOHANN WOLFGANG. SCHAFFHAUSEN, ZURICH, EINSIEDELN, SCHWYZ, BRUNNEN, ALTDORF, ANDERMATT, ST. GOTTHARD, ALTDORF, BECKENRIED, STANS, KÜSSNACHT, ZUG, ZURICH, SCHAFFHAUSEN

It was after this journey that Goethe wrote to Schiller:—'What will you say when I confess to you that, amid all these prosaic matters, a poetic one has arisen which inspires me with a good deal of confidence? I feel almost sure that the story of Tell could be treated epically; and if I should succeed in what I contemplate, we shall have a curious instance of a story first attaining its full truth through poetry, in place of history being made a fable, as is the general rule.' However, it was not Goethe, but Schiller, who had never been in Switzerland, who wrote *William Tell.*

HARE, AUGUSTUS WILLIAM. BELLINZONA, ST. GOTTHARD PASS, ALTDORF, BRUNNEN, SCHWYZ, ZURICH, BASLE

'We stopped a moment at the chapel built in memory of William Tell, and Augustus kissed the ground on which he stood, when, escaping from tyranny and injustice, he had the boldness to throw himself with his child into the stormy lake, and brave the waves, less cruel than mankind.'

KRÜDENER, JULIE DE. CONSTANCE, LAUSANNE

LAGE DE VOLUDE, BÉATRIX-STÉPHANIE DE. SCHAFFHAUSEN, BASLE, LUCERNE, ALTDORF, ST. GOTTHARD PASS, BELLINZONA, LUGANO, MILAN

'Pendant vingt lieues, un chemin de trois et même de deux pieds de large, à cause des monceaux de neige. Sur cette glace, qui était comme un miroir, chaque craquement du pied de mon cheval me paraissait mon arrêt de mort . . . . Il n'y a pas un jour où, remontant à cheval, je n'aie cru que c'était le dernier de ma vie.'

1798

BONSTETTEN, KARL VIKTOR VON. BERNE, YVERDON, NYON, BERNE, GÜMLIGEN, GROSSHOCHSTETTEN, LANGNAU, TRUBSCHACHEN, TRUB, BERNE, MORAT, PAYERNE, YVERDON, VALEYRES, LAUSANNE, BERNE, LIESTAL, BASLE

At the time of the French invasion the Bailif of Nyon had to take refuge from the invaders and from the Bernese peasants, which he did by hiding at Trub at the foot of the Napf.

HERBART, JOHANN FRIEDRICH, BERNE, THUN, INTERLAKEN, LAUTERBRUNNEN, KLEINE SCHEIDEGG, GRINDELWALD, GROSSE SCHEIDEGG, MEIRINGEN, INTERLAKEN, BERNE

NECKER, LOUIS ALBERT. CHAMONIX

'Louis Necker, agé de douze ans et demi et petit-fils de M. de Saussure, accompagné de sa soeur agée de onze ans, est monté au Montenvers, vendredi 20 juillet 1798, sous la conduite de son père, et il a vu avec beaucoup de regrets ces montagnes que son grand-père ne pourra plus revoir.'

1799

BRIDEL, PHILIPPE. GESSENAY, CHÂTEAU D'OEX, COL DES MOSSES, LAC LIOSON, ETIVAZ, SAZIEMA, LAC D'ARNON, GSTEIG, KRINNEN PASS, LAUENEN, GESSENAY

DUPIN, MAURICE. BASLE, UZNACH, GLARUS, ZURICH, CONSTANCE, ST. GALL, APPENZELL, GAMS, ALTSTÄTTEN

'. . . je me suis fort amusé, à l'attaque de Glaris, de voir les Russes gravir les montagnes' (George Sand's father).

LECOURBE, GENERAL CLAUDE-JACQUES. LUCERNE, ALTDORF, ST. GOTTHARD PASS, BELLINZONA, MESOCCO, SAN BERNARDINO PASS, THUSIS, TIEFENKASTEL, FILISUR, ALBULA PASS, PONTE, ZUOZ, SCHULS, PONTE, ALBULA PASS, TIEFENKASTEL, THUSIS, SAN BERNARDINO PASS, BELLINZONA, ST. GOTTHARD PASS, ALTDORF, SEEDORF

'Zuoz, 23 ventôse an VII
(13 mars 1799)

'Au général en chef Masséna,
La journée d'hier, mon général, m'a procuré un avantage complet sur les Autrichiens. Si jusqu'à ce jour ma division n'a eu à combattre que les éléments et des montagnes de neige presqu'impraticables, elle n'en a pas moins mérité par sa patience et ses privations en tous genres. Je suis en Engadine depuis hier, mais mes têtes de colonnes n'ont pu ledit jour s'y maintenir que momentanément. J'ai débouché par les Alpes Juliennes et l'Albula, le général Mainoni par le premier chemin, et moi par l'autre, chacun avec trois bataillons. . . .'

LEQUINIO, J. M. (*c*). LES ROUSSES, LA DOLE, GENEVA

'. . . que cela est beau! mon dieu, comme cela est beau! voilà tout ce que je savais dire, et je le répétai mille fois.'

MAISTRE, XAVIER DE. AOSTA, COIRE

'Lorsque Suvvarow pour aller d'Italie sur le Rhin passa le Saint-Gothard, le commandant de l'Avant-garde, prince Pakrazion, fit chercher secrètement à Turin un officier d'état major qui connût la guerre de montagne. Celui à qui il s'adressa vint le proposer à mon frère [Xavier] qui partit dans la minute avec dix louis que nous eumes bien de la peine à rassembler.'
Xavier only caught up with Suvorof at Coire, and this was how the author of the *Voyage autour de ma chambre* came to go to Russia.

MONTGOLFIER, ÉLIE ASCENSION DE. GENEVA, CHAMONIX

An attempt on Mont Blanc, alone, at the age of 15.

NEUILLY, ANGE-ACHILLE-CHARLES, COMTE DE. ZURICH, ROSENBERG, SCHINDELLEGI, PFÄFFIKON, RAPPERSWIL, ST. GALL, ARBON

'On ne se figure pas la hauteur des montagnes que nous occupions; la tête tournait quand on regardait en bas.' Neuilly was serving in the Austrian army opposing Masséna.

SUVOROF, ALEXANDER RYMNIKSKI, MARSHAL. VARESE, LUGANO, TAVERNE, BELLINZONA, AIROLO, ST. GOTTHARD PASS, HOSPENTHAL, ALTDORF, BÜRGLEN, KINZIG KULM PASS, MUOTTATHAL, PRAGEL PASS, GLARUS, NÄFELS, ELM, PANIXER PASS, ILANZ, COIRE

'I left Italy sooner than I should have done; but I did so in conformity with a plan which I had adopted in good faith rather than from conviction. I arranged for the combinations for my march into Switzerland. I enclose the route. I crossed the St. Gotthard and surmounted the obstacles that opposed my passage. On the appointed day I reached the spot where a junction was to be effected with me, when I found myself simultaneously deficient of everything.'

WICKHAM, WILLIAM. SCHAFFHAUSEN, ZURICH, GLARUS, SCHWYZ, ZURICH, SCHAFFHAUSEN

'Mr Wickham to Field Marshal Suwarow, Zurich, 22nd August 1799. Confidential. Monsieur le Maréchal,—the events which are taking place in this Country are so extraordinary, that I should consider that I was wanting in duty if I did not inform your Excellency of them myself.'

1800

BÉTHENCOURT, GENERAL ANTOINE. SION, BRIG, SIMPLON PASS, DOMODOSSOLA

'Je vous observe, citoyen Consul, que depuis le Simplon jusqu'à Davedro des empêchements impossibles à lever s'opposent au passage, non pas seulement des pièces de 4, mais aussi des munitions de guerre à dos de mulets; car, citoyen Consul, il faut être combattant sous vos ordres pour oser franchir des obstacles, que tout homme sans manquer à l'honneur, pourrait redouter.'

BONAPARTE, NAPOLEON. GENEVA, LAUSANNE, MARTIGNY, GRAND ST. BERNARD PASS, AOSTA

'A quelques minutes au dessus du Bourg [St. Pierre], le mulet que montait le Consul buta dans un passage escarpé et fit trébucher le cavalier. Le guide, Pierre-Nicolas Dorsaz, qui avait soin de marcher à côté et de se tenir du côté des précipices, retint le Consul, qui ne laissa apercevoir aucune émotion.'

BRIDEL, LOUIS. GRINDELWALD, GROSSE SCHEIDEGG, MEIRINGEN, BRUNIG PASS, STANS, LUCERNE, ZUG, SCHWYZ, BRUNNEN, ALTDORF, ST. GOTTHARD PASS, AIROLO

BUCH, LEOPOLD VON. BASLE, NEUCHÂTEL, LA CHAUX DE FONDS, LE LOCLE, MOTIERS-TRAVERS, NEUCHÂTEL, BERNE, GENEVA, CHAMONIX, GENEVA, NEUCHÂTEL

The great geologist first came to Switzerland to investigate the alleged coal-deposits of Le Locle for the Prussian Government, the King of Prussia being the sovereign of Neuchâtel at that time.

CADE, GEORGE. GENEVA, CHAMONIX, TÊTE NOIRE PASS, MARTIGNY, GRAND ST. BERNARD PASS, AOSTA, CHATILLON, BREUIL, ST. THEODUL PASS, ZERMATT, VISP, TURTMAN, SION, MARTIGNY, VILLENEUVE, NYON, GENEVA

At Chamonix, 'we were in every respect as well off as if we were in London'. At Zermatt they received lurid accounts of the sufferings which the war had brought to the valley in the preceding year, while at St. Niklaus the priest asked them to show him in an atlas the country from which they came, as they were the first Englishmen that he had ever seen.

COIGNET, JEAN-ROCH. MOREZ, LES ROUSSES, ST. CERGUE, NYON, LAUSANNE, MARTIGNY, GRAND ST. BERNARD PASS, AOSTA

Coignet was in one of the infantry units whose duty it was to manhandle the guns over the St. Bernard pass.

LECHI, GENERAL. VEVEY, MARTIGNY, GRAND ST. BERNARD PASS, AOSTA, CHATILLON, COL DE JOUX, BRUSSONE, COL DE RANZOLA, GRESSONEY, COL DE VALDOBBIA, RIVA, VARALLO

'Je vous rends, mon Général, le rapport de mon arrivée à Brusson. Les chemins sont impraticables pour l'artillerie absolument; la cavalerie, quoiqu'avec danger, elle passe.'

MACDONALD, MARSHAL. GENEVA, LAUSANNE, BERNE, ZURICH, RORSCHACH, COIRE, THUSIS, SPLÜGEN PASS, CHIAVENNA

'Le général Macdonald au Premier Consul.

'Chiavenna, le 16 frimaire (7 décembre)

'C'est dans la saison la plus horrible, par un temps épouvantable et au milieu des dangers de toute nature, qu'une partie de l'armée marchant sur des abîmes de neige et à travers les tourmentes et les avalanches, est parvenue à franchir les grandes Alpes, sans autre secours que la persévérance des chefs et le courage des troupes.'

MEISNER, FRIEDRICH. BERNE, THUN, INTERLAKEN, LAUTERBRUNNEN, KLEINE SCHEIDEGG, GRINDELWALD, MEIRINGEN, INTERLAKEN, BERNE

A walking tour with his pupils.

MONCEY, GENERAL. BERNE, LUCERNE, ALTDORF, ANDERMATT, ST. GOTTHARD PASS, BELLINZONA, LUGANO, MILAN

'Ordre du Jour.
. . . J'ai vu avec déplaisir, sur la route que j'ai traversée à la suite des colonnes, que le désordre, le pillage des magazins à fourrage avaient été à leur comble. Comment se fait-il que soldats et officiers ne sentent pas que le pillage des magazins les expose à se voir privés de tout secours . . .'

MUSSET-PATHAY, VICTOR ANTOINE DONATIEN. GENEVA, LAUSANNE, MARTIGNY, GRAND ST. BERNARD PASS, AOSTA

The father of Alfred de Musset was serving as a staff officer in Napoleon's army on its way to Marengo.

REICHARD, H. A. O. ZURICH, LUCERNE, ALTDORF, ST. GOTTHARD PASS, BELLINZONA

Reichard crossed the St. Gotthard pass at the same time as Moncey's division of Napoleon's army on its way to Marengo. The number of pack animals available had shrunk so low that the stores and munitions had to be carried across the pass by the local inhabitants.

STENDHAL. GENEVA, LAUSANNE, MARTIGNY, GRAND ST. BERNARD PASS, AOSTA

Stendhal was serving in the army that was on its way to Marengo. Of the crossing of the Great St. Bernard pass, concerning which so much was and has been made, he wrote to his sister: 'Tout ce que je puis te dire c'est qu'on en a extraordinairement exagéré la difficulté. Il n'y a pas un instant de danger pour les hommes.'

1801

BOURRIT, MARC-THÉODORE. GENEVA, CHAMONIX

'Someone of the company who once knew Rousseau personally, whispered to me, "The man must have inherited Rousseau's eyes, for I have never seen a more striking similarity". Bourrit gave us a sample of his oratorical talent by describing to us some of his celebrated and difficult mountain adventures with a passion that would have done justice to a vast audience' (MATTHISSON).

BRIDEL, LOUIS. VEVEY, BEX, MARTIGNY, GRAND ST. BERNARD, MARTIGNY, VEVEY

Bridel relates that it was customary to sell marmots to 'petits Savoyards, qui vont de lieux en lieux promener *la marmotte en vie, la pièce curieuse*: je ne sais pourquoi le nombre de ces petits professeurs d'histoire naturelle diminue journellement'.

BRUN, FRIEDERIKE. BASLE, MOUTIER, BIENNE, MORAT, LAUSANNE, OUCHY, VEVEY, ORBE, GENEVA

'How gorgeous is the frame in which this uniquely beautiful lake is set! How longingly my mind wanders in the great mountain world of the Valais. Yes! I promise thee, my loud-beating heart, not to leave these shores without making an excursion to the Valais.'

CANDOLLE, AUGUSTIN PYRAME DE. CHAMPAGNE, YVERDON, GENEVA, SERVOZ, VILLY, COL DE BREVENT, CHAMONIX, COL DU BON-HOMME, COL DE LA SEIGNE, COURMAYEUR, COL DE CHAPY, COL DE MALA-TRA, COL DE ST. REMY, GRAND ST. BERNARD PASS, MARTIGNY, GENEVA

A peasant near Courmayeur protested that there were no fleas in his bed which he offered to de Candolle, for he was never bitten. He even offered to give de Candolle six francs for every flea-bite he might get. Had de Candolle accepted this offer he would have been in a position to buy his host out of house and home next day.

DOLOMIEU, DÉODAT DE. GENEVA, CHAMONIX, MARTIGNY, GRAND ST. BERNARD PASS, MARTIGNY, SION, BRIG, SIMPLON PASS, DOMO-DOSSOLA, FORMAZZA, SAN GIACOMO PASS, AIROLO, PIORA, UOMO PASS, LUKMANIER PASS, DISENTIS, OBERALP PASS, ANDERMATT, ALTDORF, LUCERNE, BRUNIG PASS, MEIRINGEN, GROSSE SCHEIDEGG, GRINDELWALD, INTERLAKEN, THUN, BERNE, BIENNE, NEUCHÂTEL, MOTIERS-TRAVERS, YVERDON, LAUSANNE, BEX, GENEVA

'La contemplation de la nature étant plus satisfaisante que celle des hommes, je vais visiter les Hautes-Alpes.'

GIORDANI, PIETRO. ALAGNA, MONTE ROSA (PUNTA GIORDANI)

'It is from the top of the Alps that I write to you. I have climbed higher than the level of all the highest mountains except Monte Rosa. . . . You cannot imagine my chagrin at finding myself in that Sanctuary of Nature, destitute of the proper instruments for measuring the altitude and for the various experiments in physics which I should have had a unique opportunity of making.'

HEGNER, ULRICH. WINTERTHUR, ZURICH, BADEN, AARAU, BASLE

HÖLDER, CHR. G. VON. BERNE, LANGNAU, LUCERNE, RIGI, ALT-DORF, ANDERMATT, ST. GOTTHARD PASS, BELLINZONA, MAGADINO, MILAN, COMO, LUGANO, LUINO, FORMAZZA, GRIES PASS, OBERGESTELEN, GRIMSEL PASS, MEIRINGEN, GROSSE SCHEIDEGG, GRINDELWALD, KLEINE SCHEIDEGG, LAUTERBRUNNEN, INTERLAKEN, THUN, BERNE

Hölder relates that Josephine Bonaparte 'had the fancy to have a handsome couple from the Oberland on a farm near Paris. They were to have seven cows and a bull with them, and a house modelled on the lines of an Emmenthal chalet. But when they presented a young man of the Oberland with the bride who was proposed for him, he could not at first be persuaded to marry her. "I will not be such a fool", he said, "as to take such a beautiful woman to the French." However, he did and Josephine in return presented the city of Berne with a service of porcelain.'

HÖLDERLIN, FRIEDRICH. SCHAFFHAUSEN, ST. GALL, HAUPTWYL, EINSIEDELN, SCHWYZ

'If the God of Might has a throne upon this earth, it must be on these magnificent mountains. I can only stand there like a child and wonder and enjoy myself in silence.'
During his stay in Switzerland the German poet wrote 'Unter den Alpen gesungen', and 'Kanton Schwyz'.

KRÜDENER, JULIE DE. GENEVA, COPPET, VEVEY

'How often in looking across at the Chablais coast or wandering amid the cliffs of Meilleraye, returning to all these places, once witnesses of Julie's devotion and now the substance of popular legend, was I overwhelmed with love and melancholia.'

MATTHISSON, FRIEDRICH. LAUSANNE, NYON, ST. CERGUE, GENEVA, CHAMONIX, TÊTE NOIRE PASS, MARTIGNY, GRAND ST. BERNARD PASS, AOSTA

'Mont Blanc was clear of clouds and suitably illuminated; it was therefore easy for Dr. Paccard to describe to me the entire route of his ascent with rigorous exactitude. Paccard's appearance is one of the most imposing and impressive that I have ever seen.'

SANSOM, JOSEPH. BASLE, BADEN, ZURICH, BADEN, BRUGG, BERNE, NEUCHÂTEL, MOTIERS-TRAVERS, ILE ST. PIERRE, BERNE, THUN, INTERLAKEN, BRIENZ, BRUNIG PASS, ALPNACH, ZUG, ZURICH, SCHWYZ, BRUNNEN, FLUELEN, ANDERMATT, OBERALP PASS, SEDRUN, OBERALP PASS, ANDERMATT, ST. GOTTHARD PASS, AIROLO, BELLINZONA, MAGADINO

'After having made a circuit of three hundred miles, the greatest part of which had been performed *on foot*, with an advantage of observation, richly worth *the purchase of fatigue*.'

VOLTA, ALESSANDRO. DOMODOSSOLA, SIMPLON PASS, BRIG, SION, MARTIGNY, GENEVA

1802

BOURRIT, MARC-THÉODORE. GENEVA, CHAMONIX

BRUN, FRIEDERIKE. GENEVA, EVIAN, BEX, MARTIGNY, LAUSANNE, ST. CERGUE, LA DOLE, LAUSANNE, MARTIGNY, GRAND ST. BERNARD PASS, AOSTA

'Could any frontier be more sternly demarkated by nature? Where are there boundary stones comparable in majesty to the Dent du Midi and Dent de Morcle?'

BUCH, LEOPOLD VON. NEUCHÂTEL, BERNE, THUN, INTERLAKEN, MEIRINGEN, SUSTEN PASS, WASSEN, ANDERMATT, ST. GOTTHARD PASS, AIROLO, DAZIO, PIORA, BELLINZONA, LUGANO, MILAN, DOMODOSSOLA, SIMPLON PASS, BRIG, VISP, SAAS, VISP, SION, MARTIGNY, ST. MAURICE, BEX, LAUSANNE, GENEVA, NEUCHÂTEL

'Il y a peu de montagnes en Suisse qui offrent un aspect si grand, si imposant et si sublime que la Dent du Midi vue depuis Bex. Sa belle forme pyramidale est l'emblème de la solidité et de la force; et sa hauteur prodigieuse, que l'œil mesure depuis son pied, couvert de noyers et de vignes, jusqu'à ses cimes, cachées dans une neige éternelle, surpasse les fictions de l'imagination la plus hardie.'

CLASON, FRANCIS LEWIS. LAUSANNE, BERNE, SOLEURE, BASLE

Clason arrived in Switzerland two days after the promulgation of Napoleon's ultimatum and was a witness to the consternation of the people.

EUSTACE, JOHN CHETWODE. MENAGGIO, PORLEZZA, LUGANO, VARESE, DOMODOSSOLA, SIMPLON, DOMODOSSOLA

'As the road was merely traced out, but not passable beyond *Gondo*, we stopped at a spot where the torrent, forcing its way between two lofty rocks, takes a sudden turn, because the scenery here appeared particularly magnificent.'

KLEIST, HEINRICH VON. BERNE, THUN

The poet settled in a little house on the Delosea island, where the Aar flows out of the lake of Thun. There he mused and gazed at the mountains, until his stay came abruptly to an end, for as a result of the new revolution, his friend Wieland was given 12 hours to leave the country 'because he and Kleist had stood in front of Headquarters and mocked'.

LEMAISTRE, J. G. GENEVA, CHAMONIX, COL DE BALME, MARTIGNY, LAUSANNE, FRIBOURG, BERNE, THUN, INTERLAKEN, LAUTERBRUNNEN, GRINDELWALD, THUN, BERNE, LANGENTHAL, LUCERNE, ZUG, BADEN, BASLE, DELÉMONT, BIENNE, ILE ST. PIERRE, NEUCHÂTEL, GENEVA

'The beauties of Switzerland are so various; there is such an extraordinary combination of the grand and mild features of Nature, of the sublime and lovely; of wild and cultivated scenery; that it is almost impossible to conceive unwitnessed the satisfaction which one enjoys in travelling through this delightful country.'

MACNEVIN, WILLIAM JAMES. SCHAFFHAUSEN, ZURICH, CONSTANCE, ARBON, GAIS, APPENZELL, RAPPERSWIL, EINSIEDELN, SCHWYZ, RIGI, ZUG, LUCERNE, SOLEURE, NEUCHÂTEL, BERNE, FRIBOURG, VEVEY, GENEVA, CHAMONIX, MARTIGNY, EVIAN, GENEVA

'If in consequence of a recluse life and sedentary habits, the health were impaired, the fibres relaxed, and a person disposed to nervous afflictions, or to a troublesome obesity, or to visceral obstructions, I would recommend to him a long journey on foot from having experienced the good effects of it on myself. At first it is painful, and on that account should be undertaken when there are most attractions to amuse the attention, and allure the traveller to farther progress. It is that kind of journey which should be performed in Swisserland.'

NOEL, GERARD THOMAS. GENEVA, MARTIGNY, SION, BRIG, SIMPLON PASS, GENEVA, CHAMONIX, GENEVA

'The distant Alps, the near blue waters of the lake, and the groves upon its banks, became familiar and dear to Arvendel, even as though they were *living* associates! The intense interest excited by the sunsets among these Alpine regions, no description can delineate. The illumined summits of Mont Blanc, the roseate fires which kindle upon those eternal snows long after the sun has quitted the valleys, often presented to the imagination of Arvendel the brightest images of God and of eternity . . .'

PHILIPS, JOHN BURTON. GENEVA, CHAMONIX, COL DE BALME, MARTIGNY, LAUSANNE, GENEVA

At Chamonix 'we always got up at three in the morning to avoid the heat'.

POLLEN, COLONEL. GENEVA, CHAMONIX

Pollen made an attempt to climb Mont Blanc. His party of friends at Chamonix included Lord Frederick Montagu.

REICHARD, H. A. O. ZURICH, RICHTERSWIL, SCHWYZ, GENEVA, CHAMONIX

TURNER, JOSEPH MALLORD WILLIAM. GENEVA, CHAMONIX, COL DU BONHOMME, COL DE LA SEIGNE, COURMAYEUR, AOSTA, GRAND ST. BERNARD PASS, MARTIGNY, VEVEY, COL DE JAMAN, CHÂTEAU D'OEX, SAANEN, ZWEISIMMEN, INTERLAKEN, GRINDELWALD, GROSSE SCHEIDEGG, MEIRINGEN, BRUNIG PASS, LUCERNE, ALTDORF, ANDERMATT, ZURICH, SCHAFFHAUSEN, BASLE

'Turner never rhapsodised about scenery, but at some distance from his companion—generally much higher—applied himself to work in a silent, concentrated frame of mind. The superior elevation he required for the purpose of obtaining greater distance and more of a bird's-eye view. The sketches were rapid, and with the aid of his tremendous memory were completed subsequently, at leisure, at the inn.' Four hundred sketches were made on this tour.

YOSY, A. AARAU

'I was present when this town surrendered to General d'Erlach. . . . The ladies flew from one quarter of the town to the other, to hide their treasures . . .'

1803

BERRY, MARY. GENEVA, ROLLE, LAUSANNE, MORAT, BERNE, SOLEURE, BALSTHAL, BASLE

With her father and sister, Miss Berry narrowly missed arrest in Geneva, and had considerable difficulty with the French Commandant at Soleure, consequent upon the resumption of hostilities between France and England.

BOURRIT, MARC-THÉODORE. GENEVA, CHAMONIX

On his sixty-fourth birthday Bourrit went up the Brévent and found there 'une aimable et jeune Anglaise [Miss Henrietta Eckershall of Bath] la première de son sexe qui y soit jamais parvenue'.

BRIDEL, PHILIPPE. GESSENEY, GSTAAD, TURBACHTAL, LAUENEN

'L'hospitalité amène la confiance: le vieillard me demanda ce que je venois faire dans ce coin perdu, où l'on ne voyoit jamais d'étrangers — chercher quelques plantes rares, et admirer les beautés de ce pays, si différent de la plaine — trouvez-vous cela beau? — Oui! surtout ce torrent du Geltenbach, qui fait tout à côté de votre maison une si riche cascade — Moi, je le trouve bien laid — Pourquoi donc? — C'est que mon fils cadet s'y est noyé il y a deux ans.'

BUCH, LEOPOLD VON. NEUCHÂTEL, LAUSANNE, BEX, CHAMOSSAIRE, LE SEPEY, COL DES MOSSES, CHÂTEAU D'OEX, MONTBOVON, BULLE, ROMONT, NEUCHÂTEL, SCHWYZ, PRAGEL PASS, GLARUS, ELM, SEGNES PASS, ILANZ, VALS, VALSERBERG PASS, HINTERRHEIN, SPLÜGEN PASS, CHIAVENNA.

CAZENOVE, H. GENEVA, CHAMONIX, GENEVA

A holiday as prisoner of war, under detention by the French.

HÖLDER, CHR. G. VON. BERNE, THUN, KANDERSTEG, GEMMI PASS, LEUK, SION, EVOLENA, SION, MARTIGNY, LAUSANNE, GENEVA, ST. CERGUE, ROLLE, ORBE, LAC DE JOUX, YVERDON, NEUCHÂTEL, BIENNE, ILE ST. PIERRE, BERNE

'Friendly Evolena, surrounded by meadows and well-tilled fields. The houses are built partly on the banks of the stream, and partly scattered over the plain, occasionally forming little hamlets. Pleasant, homely valley. How rich you are in dispensing with many things which have become indispensable to millions of mortals.'

KLEIST, HEINRICH VON. BERNE, THUN, ANDERMATT, ST. GOTTHARD PASS, BELLINZONA, MILAN, THUN, BERNE, GENEVA

MINUTOLI, MENU VON. ST. GALL, ZURICH, BADEN, BERNE, LAUSANNE, GENEVA

MURITH, L. MARTIGNY, SION, TURTMANN, AUGSTBORD PASS, ZERMATT, GRÄCHEN, SAAS FEE, SIRWOLTEN PASS, SIMPLON, SAFLISCH PASS, BINN

Zermatt: 'Nous logeames chez Joseph Breni, seul aubergiste de l'endroit. Nous eumes l'avantage d'y trouver Mr. Necker de Saussure.'

NECKER, LOUIS ALBERT. GENEVA, CHAMONIX, ZERMATT

Concerning this journey by Horace-Benedict de Saussure's grandson, J. D. Forbes wrote: 'I recollect to have seen in the visitors' book at Chamouni Louis Necker's own record of this visit, entered in a boyish hand.'

PHILIPS, JOHN BURTON. GENEVA, LAUSANNE, NEUCHÂTEL, SOLEURE, BRUGG, ZURZACH, RHEINHEIM

Philips, his brother, and their tutor, P. M. Roget, were caught at Geneva by the outbreak of war. They escaped in shabby clothes, avoiding speaking English, slipping past sentries, and giving judicious bribes.

ROGET, PETER MARK. GENEVA, NYON, MORGES, ORBE, NEUCHÂTEL, AARBERG, BUREN, SOLEURE, HERZOGENBUCHSEE, ROTHRIST, WILDEGG, BRUGG, ZURZACH, RHEINHEIM

Roget was tutor to the Philips boys whom he sent on to Neuchâtel when the French Commandant at Geneva threatened to arrest them with the other English visitors and send them to Verdun.

RUMFORD, BENJAMIN THOMPSON, COUNT. BERNE, THUN, INTERLAKEN, GRINDELWALD, GENEVA, CHAMONIX

On the Mer de Glace, Rumford observed the cylindrical pits, or baignoires, formed in the ice by the melting action of water. For the densest water, which sinks to the bottom of the pit, is that which is nearest the temperature of 39° Fahrenheit, so that melting takes place at the bottom rather than at the sides of the pits.

ZOLLIKOFER, CASPAR. ST. GALL, APPENZELL, WEISSBAD, SÄNTIS

'Who can describe the majestic view that opens out on all sides? Who can measure the horizon that spreads and loses itself in the dark distance? Who knows the mountains and valleys spread out as on a map? or the names of the mosaic of towns, villages and castles which attract the eye? Who can describe the impression of this bewildering scene in terms suitable for the beauties of Nature? and what language has expressions and metaphors to portray it adequately?'

1804

ALLSTON, WASHINGTON. LUCERNE, ALTDORF, ST. GOTTHARD PASS, BELLINZONA, LOCARNO

'Such a sunrise! The giant Alps seemed literally to rise from their purple beds, and putting on their crowns of gold to send up a hallelujah almost audible.'

BRIDEL, PHILIPPE. GESSENAY, GSTAAD, TURBACHTAL, ZWITZEREGG, LENK

'Il est impossible de peindre dans toute leur beauté cette source et ses alentours; tant ce morceau est étranger aux conceptions ordinaires, et hors du domaine de tout langage humain: aussi ce que je vais en dire lui est plus inférieur encore, que les premières esquisses d'un élève ne le sont au tableau fini d'un grand maitre.'

CAZENOVE, H. GENEVA, CHAMONIX, SERVOZ, MONT BUET, COL DE LA GLIERE, CHAMONIX, COL DE BALME, VALLORSINE, MONT BUET, CHAMONIX, GENEVA

In spite of Bourrit's dissuasion and Mlle Contat's attempts to take his guide, he succeeded in his ascent of the Buet.

CONTAT, LOUISE. GENEVA, CHAMONIX

To welcome the great actress, Marsollier wrote in the visitors' book:

'A Mademoiselle Contat qu'on attend aujourd'hui.

Contat, assez souvent on te loue, on t'admire,
Viens en ces lieux admirer à ton tour;
Mais souviens-toi que tout Paris désire,
Et tes talens et ton retour.'

HEGNER, ULRICH. ZURICH, AARAU, BERNE, THUN, INTERLAKEN, LAUTERBRUNNEN, GRINDELWALD, MEIRINGEN, INTERLAKEN, BERNE, SOLEURE, ZURICH

At the inn at Meiringen, Hegner was offered a bed, 'like a Turkish pasha', in a room already occupied by five women. Of Grindelwald he wrote: 'One wishes to call all those friends whom one likes to think of in such surroundings; make haste so that as Solon said of Sappho's song which he wished to learn in his old age, you may die more happy.'

KINLOCH, FRANCIS. GENEVA, CHAMONIX, GENEVA, EVIAN, YVERDON, GENEVA, MILAN, DOMODOSSOLA, SIMPLON PASS, BRIG, SIERRE, SION, MARTIGNY, BEX, MORGES, GENEVA, ST. CERGUE

At Sierre 'where the house was so full, that all the accommodation we could procure was a mattress spread upon the floor of a room, where there were already three beds with each two people in it, besides a large dog, who lay at the feet of one of the persons asleep. It would require the talents of Scarron to paint some of the adventures of such a night'.

KOTZEBUE, AUGUST VON. SCHAFFHAUSEN, ZURICH, BADEN, BERNE, MORAT, LAUSANNE, GENEVA

'A person ought to see Switzerland with his own eyes, just as he ought to hear a concert with his own ears. He who paints countries with words does still less than the person who hums a symphony: therefore I neither can nor will say anything of Switzerland, but that I have here and there seen spots, where the Almighty may perhaps have stood, when he surveyed the world, after the creation, and said: "it is good".'

MATTHISSON, FRIEDRICH. VEVEY, MARTIGNY, SION, ULRICHEN, GRIES PASS, FORMAZZA, DOMODOSSOLA, SIMPLON PASS, BRIG, LEUKERBAD, MARTIGNY, VEVEY

'Of all the mountain passes that I have crossed into Italy (St. Gotthard, Splügen, Simplon and Brenner), none I am convinced presents to the friend of great, majestic, awe-inspiring and terrible Nature, a higher interest from first to last than the route over the Gries pass into the Val Formazza.'

SCHOPENHAUER, ARTHUR, AND JOHANNA. GENEVA, CHAMONIX, SCHAFFHAUSEN

'The haziness so frequently recognised in highly gifted persons, has its counterpart in Mont Blanc whose summit is usually wrapped in cloud.'

WITTE, CARL. SIMPLON, SAN ROCCO, TOSA FALLS, CHAMONIX

Witte made all preparations to ascend Mont Blanc, but was defeated by the weather.

1805

BARRÈS, JEAN-BAPTISTE. DOMODOSSOLA, SIMPLON PASS, BRIG, SION, MARTIGNY, GENEVA

BÉDOYÈRE, HENRI DE LA. GENEVA, CHAMONIX, MONT BUET, COL DE BALME, MARTIGNY, GRAND ST. BERNARD PASS, AOSTA

CANDOLLE, AUGUSTIN PYRAME DE. CHAMPAGNE, NEUCHÂTEL, ILE ST. PIERRE, MOTIERS-TRAVERS, CREUX DU VAN, CHAMPAGNE, VALLORBE, LAC DE JOUX, GENEVA, CHAMONIX, COL DE BALME, MARTIGNY, GRAND ST. BERNARD PASS, AOSTA

CHATEAUBRIAND, FRANÇOIS RENÉ DE. GENEVA, CHAMONIX, COL DE BALME, MARTIGNY, BEX, GENEVA

'The grandeur of mountains about which so much fuss is made is based only on the fatigue which they occasion. . . . I was delighted with the shores of the lake [of Geneva], but not at all with Chamonix. High mountains suffocate me. I did not like to feel my puny existence shut in so tightly between those heavy masses.'

ESCHER, HANS CONRAD. INTERLAKEN, MÜLLINEN, NIESEN

'Young admirer and searcher into the insoluble wonders of Nature! If you would see these from near and in their true grandeur, get up; forsake for a time your puny collections of minerals, plants, flowers, birds, insects, and other things that have dropped or been torn away from the splendour of Nature; betake yourself to a peak of the Swiss Alps, and the great spectacle that you can contemplate to your heart's content is yours! Here you require no microscope to see wonders, and all that you observe is worthy of your marvelling and your attention.'

IRVING, WASHINGTON. MAGADINO, BELLINZONA, ST. GOTTHARD PASS, ANDERMATT, ALTDORF, GERSAU, LUCERNE, ZURICH, BASLE

Washington Irving was returning from Rome with Cabell. The cemetery at Gersau suggested to him material which he used in 'Rural Funerals' in *The Sketch Book.*

LAGNEAU, LOUIS-VIVANT. GENEVA, EVIAN, MARTIGNY, SION, BRIG, SIMPLON PASS, DOMODOSSOLA

REICHARD, H. A. O. LUCERNE, RIGI

STEWARTON, —. GENEVA, LAUSANNE, BERNE

'I have lately been upon a very interesting but very melancholy expedition. I have visited those fields of battle where the Helvetian patriots fell under the daggers of French banditti, who overpowered them by far superior numbers, and where bravery was vanquished by treachery. Of the party was a desirable young lady about twenty-four, who at the battle of Frauenbrun, on the 4th of March, 1798, was wounded in seven places, in fighting against the French.'

YOSY, A. (*c*). THUN, INTERLAKEN, LAUTERBRUNNEN, GRINDELWALD, GROSSE SCHEIDEGG, MEIRINGEN, BRIENZ, INTERLAKEN, WIMMIS, NIESEN

'. . . We were gratified by the fall of an avalanche. Some French officers, who had crossed the Scheidek at the same time as ourselves, were much alarmed on this occasion, and actually imagined that the world was at an end.'

1806

ESCHER, HANS CONRAD. INTERLAKEN, SAXETEN, SULEGG

'Up! I will away and see great Nature in the form in which, with all her diversity, she has presented herself to my wondering gaze. I have never yet seen her closely enough.'

GAUDIN, JEAN-FRANÇOIS-THÉOPHILE. NYON, HERZOGENBUCHSEE, HOCHWACHT, ZURICH, UFENAU, GLARUS, FROHNALP, KLÖNTHAL,

LINTHAL, KLAUSEN PASS, ALTDORF, ST. GOTTHARD PASS, BELLINZONA, LUGANO, MONTE GENEROSO, LUINO, DOMODOSSOLA, SIMPLON PASS, BRIG, SION, MARTIGNY, BEX, VILLENEUVE, NYON

LEJEUNE, DR. MARTIGNY, COL DE BALME, CHAMONIX, BONNEVILLE, GENEVA

MEYER, DANIEL. ST. GALL, ALTSTÄTTEN, COIRE, LENZERHEIDE, FILISUR, ALBULA PASS, ST. MORITZ, MALOJA PASS, CHIAVENNA, SPLÜGEN PASS, THUSIS, COIRE, ST. GALL

'What an eternal shame it is that more care is not taken of this health resort [St. Moritz]. At small expense what splendid establishments might be erected on the magnificent site near the spring! But of this there is no question, and the spring itself is barely covered.'

SALIS-MARSCHLINS, KARL ULYSSES VON. COIRE, PARPAN-ROTHORN, AROSA, MAIENFELDERFURKA, DAVOS, SCALETTA PASS, ZERNEZ, DAVOS, KLOSTERS, LANDQUART, MARSCHLINS

'We came past three unutilised lakes to Arosa. This real mountain village, surrounded by Alps, lies in a very picturesque region. The chalets spread over the fields, the church on a mound, the three lakes above the village, in the midst of the most beautiful meadows which are reflected in their crystal-clear surfaces, the two lakes below the village shaded by melancholy copses of pine woods, the muffled noise of the Plessur roaring in the deep valley, everything gives this little land a sadly attractive atmosphere that is endlessly pleasing. Happy he who can live his life in this retreat far from the world.'

THOMAS, LOUIS. BEX, ANZEINDAZ, PAS DE CHEVILLE, SION, SIERRE, ZINAL, COL DE SOREBOIS, COL DE TORRENT, EVOLENA, AROLLA, COL DE RIEDMATTEN, PRALONG, SION, MARTIGNY, BEX

1807

CONSTANT, ROSALIE DE. LAUSANNE, GENEVA, CHAMONIX, COL DE BALME, MARTIGNY, BEX, VEVEY, LAUSANNE

'Après avoir gravi les Alpes, que le repos est délicieux sur ces pelouses d'un gazon velouté, en cueillant les fleurs qui les décorent ! C'est ainsi qu'un herbier devient un mémorial de toute la vie. Chaque plante porte avec elle le souvenir du lieu où on l'a cueillie, de la personne qui l'a donnée. On aime surtout à penser que toutes sont nées en ce pays fortuné où les beautés et les richesses de la nature nous rappellent que l'or n'est pas le premier des biens.'

IRVING, PETER. GENEVA, CHAMONIX, GENEVA, LUCERNE, ALTDORF

Washington Irving's brother made the earliest known reference by an American to Mont Blanc.

PASSERAT, JOSEPH-AMAND. BREGENZ, COIRE, LUCERNE, BRÜNIG PASS, MEIRINGEN, GRIMSEL PASS, OBERGESTELEN, BRIG, VISP

SCHLEGEL, AUGUST-WILHELM. COPPET, LAUSANNE, BERNE, THUN, INTERLAKEN, LAUTERBRUNNEN, KLEINE SCHEIDEGG, GRINDELWALD, GROSSE SCHEIDEGG, MEIRINGEN, GRIMSEL PASS, FURKA PASS, ANDERMATT, ST. GOTTHARD PASS, FAIDO, ST. GOTTHARD PASS, ALTDORF, LUCERNE, RIGI, SCHWYZ, EINSIEDELN, RAPPERSWIL, ZUG, LUCERNE, ENTLIBUCH, BERNE, FRIBOURG, LAUSANNE

'Ces belles et bonnes physionomies bernoises ont été pour moi comme un type de ce que la nation allemande a été et devroit être.'

STAËL, MME DE. COPPET, CHAMONIX

The excursion to Chamonix was arranged to entertain Mme Récamier and M. de Sabran. She returned breathless and indignant, asking what crime she had committed that she had been taken into that terrible country.

VIGÉE-LEBRUN, ÉLISABETH LOUISE. BASLE, MOUTIER, BIENNE, ILE ST. PIERRE, BERNE, THUN, INTERLAKEN, LAUTERBRUNNEN, GRINDELWALD, THUN, BERNE, SCHAFFHAUSEN, ZURICH, RAPPERSWIL, GLARUS, SOLEURE, WEISSENSTEIN, VEVEY, GENEVA, CHAMONIX

'Ne vous est-il pas arrivé, Madame, de rêver des lieux où vous voudriez vivre et mourir? Moi c'est dans un endroit comme Vevey que j'aimerais à passer ma vie avec quelques amis; Vevey, c'est le site de mes rêves, c'est mon lieu de prédilection.'

1808

GAUDIN, JEAN-FRANÇOIS-THÉOPHILE. NYON, LUCERNE, ZURICH, WESEN, WALLENSTADT, COIRE, THUSIS, SPLÜGEN PASS, CHIAVENNA, COMO, MONTE GENEROSO, LUGANO, LUINO, LOCARNO, VAL MAGGIA, CEVIO, FURCA DI BOSCO, VAL FORMAZZA, GRIES PASS, OBERGESTELEN, GRIMSEL PASS, MEIRINGEN, GROSSE SCHEIDEGG, GRINDELWALD, INTERLAKEN, KANDERSTEG, GEMMI PASS, LEUK, SION, MARTIGNY, BEX, VILLENEUVE, NYON

KRÜDENER, JULIE DE. GENEVA, COPPET

'Krüdener has just flown through. She is quite mad and spoke to Mme de Staël of heaven and hell' (MATTHISSON).

STAËL, MME DE. COPPET, BERNE, THUN, INTERLAKEN

'Il étoit assez piquant de voir se promener dans la rue d'Unterseen de jeunes Parisiens tout à coup transportés dans les vallées de la Suisse; ils n'entendoient plus que le bruit des torrents; ils ne voyaient plus que des montagnes, et cherchoient si dans ces lieux solitaires ils pourroient s'ennuyer assez pour retourner avec plus de plaisir encore dans le monde.'

VIGÉE-LEBRUN, ÉLISABETH LOUISE. NEUCHÂTEL, ALBIS, LUCERNE, ZUG, LUCERNE, BERNE, THUN, INTERLAKEN

'Après la fête, madame de Staël alla se promener avec le duc de Montmorency; moi, je m'établis sur la prairie pour peindre le site et les masses de groupes. Le comte de Grammont tenait ma boîte au pastel.'

1809

COURIER, PAUL LOUIS. BASLE, ZURICH, LUCERNE, FLUELEN, ALTDORF, ST. GOTTHARD PASS, AIROLO, BELLINZONA, LUGANO, MILAN

'Je vois dans les grandes Alpes l'hiver au dessus du printemps; à droite d'autres montagnes entrecoupées de vallons, à gauche le lac et la ville [Lucerne], et puis encore des montagnes ceintes de feuillage et couronnées de neige. Ce sont là ces tableaux qu'on vient voir de si loin, mais auxquels nous autres Suisses nous ne faisons non plus d'attention qu'un mari aux traits de sa femme après quinze jours de ménage.'

GAUDIN, JEAN-FRANÇOIS-THÉOPHILE. NYON, VILLENEUVE, MARTIGNY, SION, BRIG, SIMPLON PASS, DOMODOSSOLA, MACUGNAGA, MONTE MORO PASS, SAAS, HANNIGALP, GRÄCHEN, ZERMATT, ST. THEODUL PASS, BREUIL, CHATILLON, AOSTA, GRAND ST. BERNARD PASS, MARTIGNY, VILLENEUVE, NYON

'Menacing in its stature, monstrous in its height, the Matterhorn takes the form of a triangular pyramid, or rather of a very beautiful obelisk sparkling everywhere with snow and ice, is recognisable from afar, and commands the highest admiration.'

KÖNIG, F. N. BERNE, THUN, INTERLAKEN, LAUTERBRUNNEN, KLEINE SCHEIDEGG, GRINDELWALD, FAULHORN, GROSSE SCHEIDEGG, GRINDELWALD

König describes the egg game, which used to be played at Unterseen. Eggs to the number of 101 were laid out in a straight line on the ground, and one player had to pick them up one after the other and throw them into a tub, while the other player ran to Neuhaus, drank a glass of wine and returned. If he got back before the other had picked up all the eggs he was the winner.

MALLET, GEORGE. GENEVA, MARTIGNY, SION, BRIG, SIMPLON PASS, DOMODOSSOLA

UKLANSKI, CARL THEODOR VON. ZURICH, ALBIS, ZUG, LUCERNE, LANGNAU, BERNE, MORAT, YVERDON, LAUSANNE, BULLE, JAUN PASS, ERLENBACH, INTERLAKEN, LAUTERBRUNNEN, GRINDELWALD, GROSSE SCHEIDEGG, MEIRINGEN, INTERLAKEN, BERNE, ST. URBAN, ZURICH, SCHAFFHAUSEN

At Avenches, 'behind the gate, close to the road to Payerne I found a fine country house with a park, called Grangeneuve, belonging to a Mlle Bonjour. Here an Englishman, tired of life, decided to pass the remainder of his days. His memory is dear to the inhabitants of Avenche because of his generosity.' This was Lord Northampton.

1810

BENZENBERG, JOHANN FRIEDRICH. BASLE, SCHAFFHAUSEN, ZURICH, WALLENSTADT, RAGAZ, PFÄFERS, COIRE, THUSIS, VIA MALA, REICHENAU, DISENTIS, OBERALP PASS, ANDERMATT, ST. GOTTHARD, ALTDORF, BRUNNEN, RIGI, LUCERNE, BRUNIG PASS, BRIENZ, GRIMSEL, MEIRINGEN, GROSSE SCHEIDEGG, GRINDELWALD, KLEINE SCHEIDEGG, LAUTERBRUNNEN, INTERLAKEN, THUN, BERNE, FRIBOURG, VEVEY, MARTIGNY, GRAND ST. BERNARD, MARTIGNY, COL DE BALME, CHAMONIX, GENEVA, LAUSANNE, YVERDON, NEUCHÂTEL, LA CHAUX DE FONDS, LE LOCLE, SOLEURE, AARAU, ZURICH, SCHAFFHAUSEN

Pierre Balmat explained to Benzenberg at Chamonix that the Empress Josephine whom he had recently guided to Montenvers was kindness personified, but that her ladies were 'frightful'.

CAZENOVE, H. GENEVA, ROLLE, LAUSANNE, PAYERNE, MORAT, AARBERG, SOLEURE, BRUGG, RHEINHEIM, SCHAFFHAUSEN

An escape from detention by the French.

DUCREST, MME. GENEVA, CHAMONIX

'Before I set out I made inquiries as to the most proper dress for such an excursion [to Chamonix]. My companions, two pretty women from Paris, did not adopt the same precaution, and they soon had cause to regret their want of foresight. As we ascended the mountains, a thick fog in which we were enveloped completely uncurled their feathers, which drooped over their hats in the most inconvenient way. Their light dresses, open at the throat, afforded no protection against the frost, and their thin-soled slippers were almost worn out before they reached the inn.'

GOTTSCHALK, FRIEDRICH. GENEVA, CHAMONIX, COL DE BALME, MARTIGNY, BEX, EVIAN, THONON, GENEVA

HORTENSE, QUEEN. VALLORBE, LAUSANNE, GENEVA

JOSEPHINE, EMPRESS. GENEVA, CHAMONIX, GENEVA, NEUCHÂTEL, LA CHAUX DE FONDS, BIENNE, ILE ST. PIERRE, BERNE, THUN, INTERLAKEN, BERNE, LAUSANNE, GENEVA

'Ah je sens qu'au milieu de ces grands phénomènes,
De ces tableaux touchans, de ces terribles scènes,
Tout élève l'esprit, tout occupe les yeux;
Le cœur seul, un moment, se repose en ces lieux.'

LESCHEVIN, P. X. GENEVA, CHAMONIX

Leschevin made a close study of the hotel registers and found that entries by distinguished visitors were copied from one to the other.

PLACIDUS A SPESCHA. DISENTIS, VAL MAIGELS, VAL CANARIA, AIROLO, PASSO SELLA, MAIGELSLÜCKE, DISENTIS

1811

CUSTINE, ASTOLPHE DE. BASLE, SCHAFFHAUSEN, APPENZELL, WILDKIRCHLI, ZURICH, LAUSANNE, GENEVA, CHAMONIX, COL DE BALME, MARTIGNY, SION, LEUK, GEMMI PASS, KANDERSTEG, ZWEISIMMEN, INTERLAKEN, LAUTERBRUNNEN, MEIRINGEN, JOCH PASS, ENGELBERG, SURENEN PASS, ALTDORF, ANDERMATT, BELLINZONA, LUGANO, BELLINZONA, AIROLO, SAN GIACOMO PASS, TOSA FALLS, GRIES PASS, OBERGESTELEN, GRIMSEL PASS, MEIRINGEN, BRUNIG PASS, STANS, LUCERNE, SCHWYZ, EINSIEDELN, GLARUS, WALLENSTADT, PFÄFERS, GENEVA, VEVEY, MARTIGNY, SION, BRIG, SIMPLON PASS, DOMODOSSOLA, ISOLA BELLA, DOMODOSSOLA, SIMPLON PASS, BRIG, MARTIGNY, GENEVA

'Rien n'est volontaire dans ce qu'on éprouve au milieu d'un pays qui, à chaque pas que vous y faites, vous anéantit, vous terrasse d'admiration. Mais les tableaux y sont trop gigantesques; c'est plus grand que nature, comme disait un enfant en apercevant la mer, et j'éprouve plus d'étonnement que de satisfaction.'

CUSTINE, DELPHINE, MARQUISE DE. BASLE, LUCERNE, ALTDORF, ANDERMATT, ST. GOTTHARD PASS, BELLINZONA, LUGANO, OBERGESTELEN, GRIMSEL PASS, MEIRINGEN, BRUNIG PASS, STANS, LUCERNE, EINSIEDELN, GLARUS, GENEVA, VEVEY, MARTIGNY, SION, BRIG, SIMPLON PASS, DOMODOSSOLA, ISOLA BELLA, SIMPLON PASS, BRIG, MARTIGNY, GENEVA

'Where the horses can pass I will go, even on the slope of some dreadful glacier; I have not the slightest fear. All the same I much prefer my own fireside and the pleasant talk of my friends.'

MEYER, JOHANN RUDOLF. AARAU, ENTLIBUCH, MEIRINGEN, GRIMSEL PASS, OBERGESTELEN, BRIG, BEICH PASS, GUGGISTAFFEL, LÖTSCHENLÜCKE PASS, JUNGFRAU, VIESCH, GRIMSEL PASS, MEIRINGEN

The first ascent of the Jungfrau.

PLACIDUS A SPESCHA. DISENTIS, OBERALP PASS, ANDERMATT, FURKA PASS, GRIMSEL PASS, INNERTKIRCHEN, SUSTEN PASS, WASSEN, GÖSCHENERALP, ANDERMATT, OBERALP PASS, DISENTIS

REICHARD, H. A. O. LUCERNE, RIGI, BERNE, MORAT, LAUSANNE, GENEVA, CHAMONIX, GENEVA, EVIAN, MARTIGNY, GRAND ST. BERNARD PASS

In his room at the hospice of the Great St. Bernard, Reichard thought of the touching story of Eliza Jennings. 'But what prevented me sleeping was not the sighs of an Eliza but a cold sweat brought on by the icy cold of room and bed.'

ROGER, ALEXANDRE SALOMON. NYON, MARTIGNY, SALANFE, MARTIGNY, SION, BRIG, OBERGESTELEN, GRIMSEL PASS, FURKA PASS, ANDERMATT, ALTDORF, LUCERNE, RIGI, GLARUS, ZURICH, BERNE, NEUCHÂTEL, NYON

SCHOBERL, FREDERICK (*c*). GENEVA, EVIAN, MARTIGNY, SION, BRIG, SIMPLON PASS, DOMODOSSOLA

'The valley of Visp . . . is inhabited by a German Alpine tribe, among whom the simple manners of the patriarchal ages still prevail. It is, however, but little visited and therefore almost unknown.'

SCHÜTZ, KARL VON. ARBON, ST. GALL, APPENZELL, ALTSTÄTTEN, WERDENBERG, SARGANS, PFÄFERS, WESEN, GLARUS, LINTHAL, KISTEN PASS, BRIGELS, RUERAS, OBERALP PASS, ANDERMATT, AMSTEG, ALTDORF, BRUNNEN, SCHWYZ

'These romantic Alpine valleys are unknown and unvisited; their fearful cliffs which for their extraordinary beauty, height, and the uninterrupted view from their summit, can compare favourably with any mountains in Switzerland, remain unclimbed. When will a Saussure find these Alps and publish his observations on them?'

STAËL, MME DE. COPPET, ORBE, FRIBOURG, VAL SAINTE, VEVEY, BEX, ST. MAURICE, COPPET

WEBER, CARL MARIA VON. CONSTANCE, SCHAFFHAUSEN, ZURICH, ALBIS, RIGI, LUCERNE, AARBURG, SOLEURE, BERNE, THUN, INTERLAKEN, LAUTERBRUNNEN, KLEINE SCHEIDEGG, GRINDELWALD, GROSSE SCHEIDEGG, MEIRINGEN, INTERLAKEN, BERNE, AARAU, BASLE

'The devil of composition was in me and giving me no rest; whether I wanted to or not I just had to write verses.' During this journey Weber wrote the Aria for *Athalia* and *Künstlers Liebesforderung*.

1812

BERNOULLI, CHRISTOPH. BASLE, SISSACH, LUCERNE, SARNEN, BRUNIG PASS, MEIRINGEN, GRIMSEL PASS, OBERGESTELEN, VIESCH, BINN, BRIG, SIMPLON PASS, DOMODOSSOLA, MILAN, CHIAVENNA, SPLÜGEN PASS, THUSIS, COIRE, CONSTANCE, BASLE

A mineralogical excursion.

BOURRIT, MARC-THÉODORE. GENEVA, CHAMONIX

BUCH, LEOPOLD VON. COIRE, PARPAN PASS, TIEFENKASTEL, FILISUR, BERGÜN, ALBULA PASS, PONTE, ST. MORITZ, PONTRESINA, BERNINA PASS, TIRANO-BERNINA PASS, ST. MORITZ, JULIER PASS, TIEFENKASTEL, PARPAN PASS, COIRE

CHAMISSO, ADALBERT VON. GENEVA, ST. GERVAIS, COL DU BONHOMME, COL DE LA SEIGNE, COURMAYEUR, VAL FERRET, COL FERRET, COL DE FENÊTRE, GRAND ST. BERNARD PASS, MARTIGNY, SION, LEUK, GEMMI PASS, KANDERSTEG, INTERLAKEN, LAUTERBRUNNEN, KLEINE SCHEIDEGG, GRINDELWALD, GROSSE SCHEIDEGG, MEIRINGEN, GRIMSEL PASS, FURKA PASS, ANDERMATT, ALTDORF, LUCERNE, ZURICH, SCHAFFHAUSEN

In the course of this journey, the author of *Peter Schlemihl or the Man Who sold His Shadow*, made a collection of botanical specimens which eventually formed the nucleus of the Royal Prussian Herbarium, of which Chamisso became keeper.

ESCHER, HANS CONRAD. ZURICH, HÖRNLI, GLARUS, ELM, SEGNES PASS, ILANZ, VRIN, DIESRUT PASS, GREINA PASS, BIASCA, GIORNICO, VAL CRAMOSINA, VAL VIGORNESSO, SONOGNO, VAL VERZASCA, LOCARNO, BIGNASCO, FUSIO, SASSELLO PASS, AIROLO, ST. GOTTHARD PASS, ALTDORF, BRUNNEN, SCHWYZ, ZUG, ZURICH

So little was known of the country to the west of the Val Leventina, that when Escher crossed the pass from Giornico it was some time before he knew which valley he had descended into.

GAUDIN, JEAN-FRANÇOIS-THÉOPHILE. NYON, ZURICH, WESEN, COIRE, PARPAN, FILISUR, BERGÜN, ALBULA PASS, PONTE, ST. MORITZ, ZERNEZ, OFEN PASS, STA. MARIA, UMBRAIL PASS, BORMIO, TIRANO, COLICO, COMO, MILAN, AOSTA, GRAND ST. BERNARD PASS, MARTIGNY, NYON

LAMARTINE, ALPHONSE DE. DOMODOSSOLA, SIMPLON PASS, BRIG, SION, MARTIGNY, LAUSANNE, GENEVA

MEYER, GOTTLIEB & RUDOLF. AARAU, BERNE, THUN, INTERLAKEN, MEIRINGEN, GRIMSEL PASS, OBERAARJOCH, MÄRJELENSEE, JUNGFRAU, GRIMSEL PASS, STRAHLEGG PASS, GRINDELWALD

The ascent of the Jungfrau by J. R. Meyer the previous year was disbelieved, so his sons set out to climb it again and vindicate the family honour.

PLACIDUS A SPESCHA. DISENTIS, SEDRUN, KRÜZLI PASS, MADERANERTAL, AMSTEG, ALTDORF, BRUNNEN, SCHWYZ, EINSIEDELN, SCHWYZ, BRUNNEN, ALTDORF, AMSTEG, KRÜZLI PASS, DISENTIS

'It has now become the custom for learned persons to visit the valleys and mountains of Switzerland, partly in order to gain health or to restore it, and partly to acquire useful knowledge and happiness . . . Englishmen, Frenchmen, Germans, Italians, come every year. What do they look for but pleasure and health? They go away but return again, and cannot enjoy it too much. . . . Rarely does anyone fall ill on a mountain tour; seldom does anybody die or come to grief. But the places where one may rest are few and far between, especially in the wilder parts; one is often badly received and looked after. On the tour one must often suffer hunger and thirst, heat and cold, snow and rain, but if one had the assured hope of finding a comfortable resting place, all the hardships endured would vanish, and one would think oneself in an earthly paradise.'

SCHINER, M. (*c*). SIERRE, VISSOYE, AYER, GRIMENTZ

STAËL, GERMAINE DE. COPPET, LAUSANNE, BERNE, ZURICH, ST. GALL, FELDKIRCH

'Cette Suisse encore si calme et toujours si belle, ces habitants qui savent être libres par leurs vertus, lors même qu'ils ont perdu l'indépendance politique, tout ce pays me retenait; il me semblait qu'il me disait de ne pas le quitter.'

STAPFER, PHILIP ALBERT (*c*). BERNE, THUN, INTERLAKEN, LAUTERBRUNNEN, KLEINE SCHEIDEGG, GRINDELWALD, GROSSE SCHEIDEGG, MEIRINGEN

WAHLENBERG, GEORGE. SCHAFFHAUSEN, ZURICH, EINSIEDELN, RIGI, LUCERNE, PILATUS, ENGELBERG, LICHTENSTEIG, HOCHALP, KAMOR, WILDHAUS, ANDERMATT, FURKA PASS, GRIMSEL PASS, MEIRINGEN, ENTLIBUCH, ZURICH, RAGAZ, PFÄFERS, MONTELUNA, WEISSTANNEN, RIESETEN PASS, GLARUS, LINTHAL, SANDALP, LUCERNE, PILATUS, ENGELBERG, SURENEN PASS, ALTDORF, ANDERMATT, OBERALP PASS, DISENTIS, COIRE, PFÄFERS, MONTELUNA, LICHTENSTEIG, HOCHALP, KAMOR, EBENALP, RIGI, ENGELBERG, ENTLIBUCH, TANNHORN, MEIRINGEN, ZURICH

The Swedish botanist was concerned not only in finding plants but in taking measurements of the temperature of the air and the ground, on the basis of which he established his alpine floral zones.

YOSY, A. THUN, ZWEISIMMEN, LENK, IFFIGENSEE, LAUENEN, KRINNEN PASS, GSTEIG, GSTAAD, SAANEN

'I continued to explore the valley, over dangerous and unfrequented paths, where the solitary goat was clinging to the rugged cliffs; and the stones rolling underneath my feet in many places, as I ascended, almost made me repent the resolution I had taken of proceeding; but I was gratified by the views which perpetually regaled my sight. One of the most striking (for it would occupy a volume to describe the whole), is the beautiful lake of Effingen, which burst upon me when I was least prepared for anything so sublime and truly magnificent.'

1813

BOURQUENOUD, F. CHARMEY, COL DE CHESALETTE, SCHWARZSEE, NEUSCHELS PASS, JAUN, SATTEL, HOCHMATT, GROS MONT, LES MORTEYS, GRANDVILLARD, MOLÉSON, PART-DIEU, BULLE, CHARMEY

'Les Alpes fribourgeoises sont moins souvent visitées que celles des autres cantons, et par conséquent moins connues; elles méritent cependant de l'être.'

DES LOGES, CHR. (*c*). ST. GINGOLPH, TROIS TORRENTS, MONTHEY, SALVAN, MARTIGNY, CHAMPEX, GRAND ST. BERNARD, LIDDES, CHABLE, ISERABLES, SION, EVOLENA, COL DE TORRENT, GRIMENTZ, SIERRE, LEUKERBAD

'Le vallon de Champé est curieux, son lac est poissonneux et il a joué un rôle principal dans l'histoire des sorciers, en battant ses eaux on provoquait la tempête . . .'

MAYNARD, HENRI. BREUIL, ST. THEODUL PASS, BREITHORN

RAMBUTEAU, CLAUDE-PHILIBERT DE. GENEVA, MARTIGNY, SION, BRIG, SIMPLON PASS, DOMODOSSOLA, SIMPLON PASS, BRIG, AERNEN, BINN, OBERWALD, VISP, ST. NIKLAUS, MARTIGNY, GRAND ST. BERNARD, MARTIGNY, CHAMPÉRY, SION, MARTIGNY, CHAMONIX, CHAMBÉRY

The last French Prefect of the Département du Simplon.

1814

BERNARD, RICHARD BOYLE. GENEVA, CHAMONIX, COL DE BALME, MARTIGNY, BEX, LAUSANNE, GENEVA, LAC DE JOUX, YVERDON, NEUCHÂTEL, BIENNE, ILE ST. PIERRE, MORAT, BERNE, SURSEE, LUCERNE, ZUG, ZURICH, SCHAFFHAUSEN

Outside the Château de Prangins 'we waited some time, but without success, in the hope of seeing his Majesty'. This was Joseph Bonaparte, who had bought the château.
Then, 'on my return to Geneva, I met the Ex-Empress, Maria Louisa'.

BREWSTER, SIR DAVID. GENEVA, CHAMONIX, VEVEY, LAUTERBRUNNEN

After descending from the Montenvers, 'when we reached the bottom we were accosted in English by an old man, who was one of the two cretins described by Saussure, and exhibited in England'.

BRIDGES, GEORGE WINDHAM. GENEVA, CHAMONIX, COL DE BALME, MARTIGNY, SION, LEUK, GEMMI PASS, KANDERSTEG, THUN, BERNE, HERZOGENBUCHSEE, BADEN, ZURICH, SCHAFFHAUSEN, BASLE

BRUCE, CHARLES LENNOX CUMMING. GENEVA, COPPET

Referring to Louis Albert Necker, Bruce wrote: 'I owed to him at that time my introduction to the society of Coppet, and the kind and sustained friendship of Madame de Staël. There, with Schlegel, Sismondi, Dupont, Sir H. and Lady Davy, Lady Charlotte Campbell and her daughter, Louis and I formed two of the *dramatis personae* in acting little plays arranged by our hostess from the lesser poems of Byron.'

BURY, LADY CHARLOTTE. GENEVA, COPPET

In Geneva Lady Bury met the Princess of Wales and Sir Humphry Davy.

CANNING, STRATFORD. ZURICH, BERNE, LAUSANNE, GENEVA, CHAMONIX, MARTIGNY, SION, LEUK, GEMMI PASS, KANDERSTEG, ZURICH

'Put on your spurs, mount your yacht, and come the shortest possible way to this delicious country. When once here you will acknowledge that you have spent twenty years of your life most unprofitably. In short, you are, and must be, an owl till you set foot in this land of liberty.'

CAROLINE, PRINCESS OF WALES. BASLE, MOUTIER, BERNE, LAUSANNE, GENEVA, CHAMONIX, GENEVA, LAUSANNE, MARTIGNY, SION, BRIG, SIMPLON PASS, DOMODOSSOLA

Sir James MacKintosh met her at Brig: 'On arrival there, found the best inn was occupied by the Princess of Wales' Courier. She herself arrived almost immediately in one royal coach, so prodigiously crowded with provisions for luggage as to resemble one of the heaviest stages. Her train came in a coach, a chariot allemand, and a chariot, with a baggage-wagon. As I was walking along the street with M. —, the princess put her head out of the window, and as soon as she observed me, cried out, "Oh how delightful! Come up." She insisted on my bringing my daughter with me to dinner. She was very communicative, very foolish, very good-natured, and very undignified;—but I rather like her. The dinner was the best I had seen for some time.'

CLAIRMONT, CLAIRE. LES VERRIÈRES, NEUCHÂTEL, SOLEURE, LUCERNE, BRUNNEN, LUCERNE, LAUFENBURG, BASLE

'Half way to Neuchâtel the lake is discovered—it is nine miles broad. First you see an indistinct line of hills that seems more like rising and uneven ground and bears no marked or peculiar character, then comes a second line still darker and more rugged and characteristic; behind these is a third line of very high dark hills, rude and broken. Then—oh then come the terrific Alps. I thought they were white flaky clouds and what was my surprise when after a long and steady examination I found them really to be the snowy Alps.'

COPLESTONE, EDWARD. GENEVA, MARTIGNY, GRAND ST. BERNARD, MARTIGNY, BRIG, SIMPLON PASS, DOMODOSSOLA

DAVY, SIR HUMPHRY. DOMODOSSOLA, SIMPLON PASS, BRIG, SION, MARTIGNY, GENEVA, LAUSANNE, VEVEY, PAYERNE, BERNE, ZURICH, SCHAFFHAUSEN

At Geneva Davy experimented on iodine in de Saussure's house, and on the solar spectrum in Pictet's house. His valet and amanuensis was Michael Faraday. Fifteen years later Davy died at Geneva, where he lies buried.

FARADAY, MICHAEL. DOMODOSSOLA, SIMPLON PASS, BRIG, SION, MARTIGNY, GENEVA, LAUSANNE, VEVEY, PAYERNE, BERNE, ZURICH, SCHAFFHAUSEN

'We entered Switzerland, and traversed that mountainous and extraordinary country with health and fine weather, and were much diverted with the curious dresses and customs of the country.'

FREDERICK WILLIAM III, KING OF PRUSSIA. LES VERRIÈRES, NEUCHÂTEL, LES BRENETS, LE LOCLE, LA CHAUX DE FONDS, BERNE, THUN, INTERLAKEN, GRINDELWALD, LAUTERBRUNNEN, THUN, BERNE, ZURICH, SCHAFFHAUSEN

At Grindelwald the innkeeper handed the king an eagle-quill pen wherewith to sign his name, with the words 'your Majesty will recognize the feather having recently plucked the bird'.

GENOUDE, EUGENE. ST. CERGUE, GENEVA, LAUSANNE, BERNE, THUN, INTERLAKEN, LAUTERBRUNNEN, KLEINE SCHEIDEGG, GRINDELWALD, GROSSE SCHEIDEGG, MEIRINGEN, INTERLAKEN, THUN, FRIBOURG

HOLLAND, SIR HENRY. BASLE, MOUTIER, BERNE, LAUSANNE, GENEVA, CHAMONIX, MARTIGNY, SION, BRIG, SIMPLON PASS, DOMODOSSOLA

Holland was in attendance on Caroline, Princess of Wales, as her physician. 'An old London and Dover mail-coach had been purchased for the conveyance of some of the servants and baggage of the Princess. It was a whimsical sight this coach offered when scaling the Simplon, with all the old English designations still upon its panels.'

MACKINTOSH, SIR JAMES. GENEVA, THONON, EVIAN, VEVEY, LAUSANNE, MOUDON, BERNE, LUCERNE, FLUELEN, ALTDORF, ST. GOTTHARD PASS, BELLINZONA, MAGADINO, BAVENO, DOMODOSSOLA, SIMPLON PASS, BRIG, SION, MARTIGNY, GENEVA

'Till this morning, I never thoroughly believed that any scenes could surpass those of Scotland and the Lakes: but they are nothing. . . . Just before Gersau we entered the second part of the lake. The third part of it may be called the Gulf of Uri. It is upon this that its superiority to all other lakes, or, as far as I know, scenes upon earth, depends. The vast mountains rising on every side and closing at the end, with their rich clothing of wood, the sweet, soft spots of verdant pasture scattered at their feet and sometimes on their breast, and the expanse of water unbroken by islands, and almost undisturbed by any signs of living men, make an impression which it would be foolish to attempt to convey by words.'

MARIE-LOUISE, EMPRESS. CONSTANCE, BADEN, AARAU, BERNE, PAYERNE, LAUSANNE, GENEVA, CHAMONIX, COL DE BALME, MARTIGNY, EVIAN, GENEVA, LAUSANNE, BERNE, THUN, INTERLAKEN, LAUTERBRUNNEN, LUCERNE, RIGI

On the Mer de Glace she wished to go to the Jardin, but when it was pointed out to her that she would have to bivouac there for the night, Meneval relates: 'Cela eût sans doute ajouté un nouveau lustre à notre voyage; mais la duchesse, malgré son ardeur, ne voulut pas acheter cette gloire au prix de quelque bon rhumatisme.'

MAYNE, JOHN. GENEVA, EVIAN, MARTIGNY, SION, BRIG, SIMPLON PASS, DOMODOSSOLA

Mayne saw the Princess of Wales at Geneva; and, on telling the people of Simplon, that she would shortly pass their way, 'they agreed among themselves that it was absolutely impossible for so great a princess to sleep in the Simplon inn'.

MILFORD, JOHN. GENEVA, THONON, ST. MAURICE, BEX, VEVEY, LAUSANNE, GENEVA, CHAMONIX, GENEVA

'We again reached St. Martin. I had almost forgot to mention that the daughter of our host at this place is a most charming girl, with the fairest complexion of any female I ever saw in these parts, and might well represent the heroine of the novel of Florian, to which I have referred above; but what still made this idea more striking was, that, on inquiry, I found she was called Claudine . . .'

'The vast mountains rising on every side and closing at the end, with their rich clothing of wood, the sweet, soft spots of verdant pasture scattered at their feet and sometimes on their breast, and the expanse of water unbroken by islands'

SIR JAMES MACKINTOSH, 1814; Gulf of Uri

'As if God were pelting the Devil from Heaven with snow-balls'

(*Paul Popper*)

BYRON, 1816; Wengernalp

MOULINIÉ, C. E. F. GENEVA, ST. GERVAIS, PRARION, CHAMONIX

'Quand on examine attentivement le plan incliné qui commence à la cime du Mont-Blanc, et qui sert de base à toutes ces Aiguilles, ces Aiguilles même rongées par le temps, et le vide qui se trouve entr'elles, on croit voir un squelette décharné, ou des pans de mur qui survivent à un édifice presque tout emporté par un torrent, ou dévoré par un incendie.'

ROGERS, SAMUEL. ST. CERGUE, NYON, GENEVA, CHAMONIX, GENEVA, LAUSANNE, BERNE, LUCERNE, BRUNNEN, SCHWYZ, ZUG, BIENNE, ILE ST. PIERRE, GENEVA, MARTIGNY, SION, BRIG, SIMPLON PASS, DOMODOSSOLA

'Everything perhaps has fallen a little short of my expectations but the Alps alone. They have exceeded them; and whenever they appear they affect me as much as if I was seeing them for the first time—I may almost say, as if I had never heard of them.'

SHELLEY, PERCY BYSSHE. LES VERRIÈRES, NEUCHÂTEL, SOLEURE, LUCERNE, BRUNNEN, LUCERNE, LAUFENBURG, BASLE

With Mary Godwin and Jane Clairmont, Shelley arrived at Brunnen on August 24 and took 'two unfurnished rooms in an ugly big house, called the château. These we hired at a guinea a month, had beds moved into them, and the next day took possession.' They then discovered that £28 was all they possessed or could count on until December. So on the following day they decided to return by the cheapest possible route to England.

TISDALL, JAMES THOMAS TOWNLEY. GENEVA, CHAMONIX, TÊTE NOIRE PASS, MARTIGNY, VEVEY, CHÂTEAU D'OEX, THUN, BERNE, THUN, INTERLAKEN, BRIENZ, BRUNIG PASS, SARNEN, ENGELBERG, RIGI, LUCERNE, ZURICH, EINSIEDELN, WALLENSTADT, ALTSTÄTTEN, APPENZELL, ST. GALL, CONSTANCE, SCHAFFHAUSEN, BASLE

On the Rigi 'by a fortunate coincidence Marie-Louise arrived on the summit at 9 o'clock, having slept on the mountain for that purpose the night before. . . . I insinuated myself into conversation . . . and by that means arrived at the honor of some words expressed in the most obliging way from the Emperatrice (who I took care to call so). The conversation was on the subject of the Princess of Wales at Berne, where they met, or supped together.'

WILSON, GENERAL SIR ROBERT. DOMODOSSOLA, SIMPLON PASS, BRIG, SION, MARTIGNY, GENEVA, LAUSANNE, MORAT, BERNE, SOLEURE, BASLE

'At 12 o'clock last night we reached the gates of Geneva. I was refused entrance, and obliged to sleep on the glacis until 5 o'clock, as the carriage cramped my legs.'

WYSS, JOHANN RUDOLF. BERNE, THUN, INTERLAKEN, LAUTERBRUNNEN, ISENFLUH, MÜRREN, SCHILTALP, SEFINENTAL, LAUTERBRUNNEN, KLEINE SCHEIDEGG, GRINDELWALD, FAULHORN

The author of the *Swiss Family Robinson* pronounced the Faulhorn as 'not within the reach of ladies'.

1815

CANNING, STRATFORD. ZURICH, INTERLAKEN, LAUTERBRUNNEN, GRINDELWALD, ST. GOTTHARD PASS, SIMPLON PASS

'One slides down the snow as the Gauls used to do; with this difference, that instead of a shield one has nothing better than what nature has given all of us, to slide on.'

CHARPENTIER, JEAN DE. BEX, MARTIGNY, CHANRION, LOURTIER, MILLE, LIDDES, GRAND ST. BERNARD, MARTIGNY, SION, VISP, ZERMATT

At Lourtier, Charpentier heard Jean Baptiste Perraudin's views that the glaciers had formerly extended farther down the valley, even as far as Martigny. He was for a long time incredulous before becoming converted.

FOSCOLO, UGO. COMO, LUGANO, COIRE, ZURICH, RICHTERSWIL, UFENAU, ZURICH

FRYE, W. E. GENEVA, THONON, EVIAN, MARTIGNY, SION, BRIG, SIMPLON PASS, DOMODOSSOLA, MILAN, DOMODOSSOLA, SIMPLON PASS, BRIG, SION, MARTIGNY, LAUSANNE, GENEVA

GALLATIN, JAMES. GENEVA, COPPET, VUFFLENS, CHILLON, GENEVA

Gallatin was taken to Ferney by his father and shown where Voltaire had made to him one of his rare remarks appreciative of mountain scenery. Looking at a sunset behind the Jura he exclaimed: 'Can anything be grander than that?'

GUSTAVUS ADOLPHUS IV. BASLE, ZURICH

'Mr. Canning . . . my purpose in coming to Zurich was to ask you to lay a proposal I wish to make before His Britannic Majesty's Government. My heart is set on it for many reasons. It is that His Britannic Majesty should exert his influence with his Brother-Sovereigns to let *me* have the sovereignty of the Island of Elba. Since Buonaparte left it that island really belongs to no one in particular.'

HORTENSE, QUEEN. GENEVA, LAUSANNE, PAYERNE, MORAT, BERNE, AARAU, BADEN, ZURICH, WINTERTHUR, CONSTANCE

KRÜDENER, JULIE DE. BASLE, BERNE

'Switzerland rests me; it is so lovely and so tranquil in the midst of this distracted Europe. . . . I do not despair of seeing you among the Alps, which are worth all the salons in the world.'

LAMARTINE, ALPHONSE DE. ST. CERGUE, VINCY, NEUCHÂTEL, LA CHAUX DE FONDS, BERNE, NYON, NERNIER, GENEVA

'I was intoxicated by the Alpine scenery of which I had for the first time had a glimpse some years previously. I halted at every turn of the steep descent; I rested at every spring, in the shade of the most beautiful chestnuts, to drink so to speak this splendid landscape through my eyes.'

LEAKE, WILLIAM MARTIN. BASLE, ZURICH

Foreign Office, May 8, 1815

'Sir,

I have the honour to acquaint you that His Royal Highness the Prince Regent has been graciously pleased to appoint you to reside at the head quarters of the Army of the Swiss Confederation, now assembling on the frontiers of France for the purpose of defending the Swiss frontier against any attack which may be made upon it by the French troops . . .

CASTLEREAGH.'

METTERNICH, PRINCE. GENEVA, MARTIGNY, SION, BRIG, SIMPLON PASS, DOMODOSSOLA

The innkeeper at Martigny, having discovered Metternich's identity, served him a meal of twenty-nine courses. Four hours later, at Sion, Metternich found himself obliged to sit down to an official dinner, the number of courses of which was seventy-nine.

MILFORD, JOHN. MENAGGIO, PORLEZZA, LUGANO, VARESE, LAVENO, BAVENO, DOMODOSSOLA, SIMPLON PASS, BRIG, SION, MARTIGNY, GENEVA, LAUSANNE, BERNE, SOLEURE, BASLE

'The Bed-room they gave me was dark and gloomy; but I could not find fault with it when the landlord informed me, that no less a personage than the Princess of Wales had slept in the same not long before.'

MOULINIÉ, C. E. F. GENEVA, ST. GERVAIS, PRARION, MÉGÈVE

ROMILLY, LADY ANNE, & SIR SAMUEL. SCHAFFHAUSEN, CONSTANCE, ZURICH, BERNE, LAUSANNE, GENEVA, CHAMONIX, GENEVA, MARTIGNY, SION, BRIG, SIMPLON PASS, DOMODOSSOLA

'The shattered walls of the cottages of Meillerie bore testimony to the action which, only a few months ago, took place there between a part of the French and Austrian Armies.'

STAËL, GERMAINE DE. COPPET, LAUSANNE, MARTIGNY, SION, BRIG, SIMPLON PASS, DOMODOSSOLA

TRANT, CLARISSA. DOMODOSSOLA, SIMPLON PASS, BRIG, SIERRE, SION, MARTIGNY, VEVEY, GENEVA, VEVEY, FRIBOURG, BERNE, SOLEURE, BASLE

'Our dinner at Simplon is worth recording; after vain attempts to demolish the remains of some venerable cow, we feasted on a dish of fritters, so delicate and tempting in appearance that they would have graced the table of an Alderman. We of course congratulated ourselves upon having found such young and tender chickens upon the top of Mont Simplon, when suddenly my Father exclaimed "Clara, you have been eating frogs".'

WELDEN, LUDWIG VON. ST. GERVAIS, AIGUILLE DU GOUTER, CHAMONIX

The Austrian colonel and his guides had to spend the night on the Aiguille du Gouter in a hole in the snow.

WOLFF, JOSEPH. BASLE, BERNE, FRIBOURG, VEVEY, MARTIGNY, BRIG, SIMPLON PASS, DOMODOSSOLA

'At the distance of nine miles from Vevay, I found two English ladies who were true christians, and persuaded me to go to England', but Wolff was on his way to Rome 'to see what my Pope believes'.

WYNNE, ELISABETH. GENEVA, LAUSANNE, MARTIGNY, SION, BRIG, SIMPLON PASS, DOMODOSSOLA

1816

ALISON, SIR ARCHIBALD. GENEVA, CHAMONIX, COL DE BALME, MARTIGNY, VEVEY, MORAT, BERNE, THUN, INTERLAKEN, LAUTERBRUNNEN, GRINDELWALD, MEIRINGEN, BRUNIG PASS, LUCERNE, RIGI, ZUG, SCHWYZ, BRUNNEN, ALTDORF, ANDERMATT, FURKA PASS, MÜNSTER, BRIG, SIMPLON PASS, DOMODOSSOLA, BAVENO, LUGANO, PORLEZZA, MENAGGIO, COMO

'Often I lay awake at night thinking of the Alps.' Then, from the heights of Tarare, 'breathless and hardly able to stand from fatigue, but unable to take my eyes from the mountains, I threw myself on the ground and drank in, gasping, the enchanting spectacle'.

BELL, ANDREW. GENEVA, LAUSANNE, YVERDON, FRIBOURG, BERNE, HOFWYL, BASLE

BROUGHAM, HENRY, LORD. LAUSANNE, GENEVA

'It is a country to be in for two hours, or two and a half, if the weather is fine, and no longer. Ennui comes on the third hour, and suicide attacks you before night. There is no resource whatever for passing the time, except looking at lakes and hills which is over immediately.'

BYRON, LORD. BASLE, LUCERNE, BERNE, MORAT, LAUSANNE, GENEVA, NERNIER, EVIAN, MEILLERIE, ST. GINGOLPH, CHILLON, VEVEY, OUCHY, GENEVA, CHAMONIX, GENEVA, VEVEY, COL DE JAMAN, CHÂTEAU D'OEX, SAANEN, ZWEISIMMEN, INTERLAKEN, LAUTERBRUNNEN, KLEINE SCHEIDEGG, GRINDELWALD, GROSSE SCHEIDEGG, MEIRINGEN, INTERLAKEN, THUN, BERNE, FRIBOURG, MORAT, YVERDON, GENEVA, MARTIGNY, SION, BRIG, SIMPLON PASS, DOMODOSSOLA

'Neither the music of the shepherd, the crashing of the avalanche, nor the torrent, the mountain, the glacier, the forest, nor the cloud, have for one moment lightened the weight upon my heart nor enabled me to lose my own wretched identity in the majesty, and the power, and the glory, around, above, and beneath me.'
Canto III of *Childe Harold*, *The Prisoner of Chillon*, and *Manfred* owe their inspiration to these journeys.

CLIFFORD, LADY DE. GENEVA, CHAMONIX, COL DE BALME, MARTIGNY, EVIAN, GENEVA, LAUSANNE, FRIBOURG, BERNE, THUN, INTERLAKEN, LAUTERBRUNNEN, MEIRINGEN, BRUNIG PASS, LUCERNE, ZUG, ALBIS, ZURICH, SCHAFFHAUSEN, BASLE

'On the day when we visited these icy wilds [the Mer de Glace] there were not less than thirty persons who came to indulge a similar curiosity. Almost all these were English.'

COCKBURN, JAMES. GENEVA, CHAMONIX, TÊTE NOIRE PASS, MARTIGNY, GRAND ST. BERNARD, MARTIGNY, SION, BEX, LAUSANNE, NEUCHÂTEL, FRIBOURG, BERNE, THUN, INTERLAKEN, LAUTERBRUNNEN, GRINDELWALD, GROSSE SCHEIDEGG, MEIRINGEN, BRUNIG PASS, LUCERNE, SCHWYZ, EINSIEDELN, ZURICH, SCHAFFHAUSEN, ZUG, BRUNNEN, ALTDORF, ST. GOTTHARD PASS, BELLINZONA, LUGANO, BELLINZONA, MESOCCO, FORCOLA PASS, CHIAVENNA, SPLÜGEN PASS, THUSIS, REICHENAU, KUNKELS PASS, VÄTTIS, RAGAZ, ALTSTÄTTEN, ST. GALL, CONSTANCE, BASLE

Major Cockburn is said to have been the first to use a camera lucida in making his drawings and sketches in the Alps.

COPLESTONE, EDWARD. SCHAFFHAUSEN, ZURICH, ZUG, ALTDORF, ANDERMATT, FURKA PASS, GRIMSEL PASS, MEIRINGEN, GRINDELWALD, INTERLAKEN, THUN, BERNE, COPPET, GENEVA

'. . . Nor mountain scenes alone exalt the mind
To blissful musing, but such incidents
As mountain wanderers meet with oft beguile
Their weary steps, and whisper better things
Than from the craggy steep of Grindelwald,
Or Grimsel can be gather'd . . .'

ESCHER, HANS CONRAD. ZURICH, GLARUS, LINTHAL, KISTEN PASS, BRIGELS, SOMVIX, GREINA PASS, OLIVONE, LUKMANIER PASS, UOMO PASS, PIORA, AIROLO

FRYE, W. E. JOUGNE, ORBE, LAUSANNE, NYON, GENEVA

GLENBERVIE, LORD. DOMODOSSOLA, SIMPLON PASS, BRIG, SION, MARTIGNY, GENEVA, ST. CERGUE

'Among more than sixty English travellers here, there is Lord Byron, who is cut by everybody. They tell a strange adventure of his, at Dejean's inn. He is now living at a villa on the Savoy side of the lake with that woman who it seems proves to be a Mrs. Shelley, wife to the man who keeps the Mount Coffee-House.'

HAGEN, FRIEDRICH HEINRICH VON DER. SCHAFFHAUSEN, ST. GALL, HERISAU, LICHTENSTEIG, ZURICH, ALBIS, ZUG, LUCERNE, ZOFINGEN, BERNE, FRIBOURG, PAYERNE, LAUSANNE, MARTIGNY, COL DE BALME, CHAMONIX, TÊTE NOIRE PASS, MARTIGNY, SION, BRIG, SIMPLON PASS, DOMODOSSOLA

HALDANE, ROBERT. GENEVA, LAUSANNE, BERNE, BASLE, GENEVA

Pointing one day to Haldane's quarters in Geneva, Merle d'Aubigné exclaimed: 'Voilà le berceau de la seconde Réforme de Genève.'

HOBHOUSE, JOHN CAM. SCHAFFHAUSEN, CONSTANCE, ZURICH, LUCERNE, BERNE, LAUSANNE, GENEVA, CHAMONIX, GENEVA, VEVEY, COL DE JAMAN, CHÂTEAU D'OEX, SAANEN, ZWEISIMMEN, INTERLAKEN, LAUTERBRUNNEN, KLEINE SCHEIDEGG, GRINDELWALD, GROSSE SCHEIDEGG, MEIRINGEN, INTERLAKEN, THUN, BERNE, FRIBOURG, YVERDON, GENEVA, EVIAN, MARTIGNY, SION, BRIG, SIMPLON PASS, DOMODOSSOLA

'It was on this visit to Chamouni that a circumstance occurred which has been so entirely distorted, and represented contrary to the fact, that I feel bound to mention it. At an inn on the road the travellers'-book was put before us, and Lord Byron, having written his name, pointed out to me the name of Mr. Shelley, with the words atheist and philanthropist, written in Greek opposite to it, and observing: "Do you not think I shall do Shelley a service by scratching this out?" he defaced the words with great care.'

HOOKHAM, THOMAS. LES VERRIÈRES, NEUCHÂTEL, LAUSANNE, MARTIGNY, COL DE BALME, MARTIGNY, SION, BRIG, SIMPLON PASS, DOMODOSSOLA

'Another day of sunshine and joy has passed, leaving such vivid traces of the delicious intensity of my happiness that my remembrance of it will be as inerasible as the wild and stupendous scenes through which I have passed. A current of transport has coursed my veins throughout the day. I have sighed, I have been motionless, I have been speechless with joy. I did not suppose that the human frame was capable, for hours in succession, of enjoyment so exquisite; and I feel confident, that the scenery of Switzerland alone can generate such emotions: even while I write, recollection realises my transports, and my eyes are filled with the tears of joy: may these sensations visit my frame in after years, when age shall rob my limbs of their vigour, and circumscribe the feeble efforts of exercise to a garden, and orchard, and its adjoining copse.'

KOSCIUSKO, THADDEUS. SOLEURE, LUCERNE, ALTDORF, ST. GOTTHARD PASS, BELLINZONA, LUGANO, DOMODOSSOLA, SIMPLON PASS, BRIG, SOLEURE

The Polish patriot was accompanied across the St. Gotthard by Colonel Lord Stewart.

LANGTON, THOMAS. YVERDON, ORBE, VALLORBE, LAC DE JOUX, CHASSERAL, YVERDON, LAUSANNE, GENEVA, YVERDON, NEUCHÂTEL, LES BRENETS, ST. IMIER, MOUTIER, WEISSENSTEIN, SOLEURE, BERNE, YVERDON, MORAT, BERNE, THUN, INTERLAKEN, GRINDELWALD, BRIENZ, BRUNIG PASS, LUCERNE, RIGI, YVERDON, GENEVA

At Champitet, near Yverdon, the Langtons stayed in the house of Mme du Peyrou who must have been Henriette-Dorothée, daughter of Colonel Abraham de Pury and widow of Pierre-Alexandre du Peyrou, both friends of Jean-Jacques Rousseau. Langton also struck up a firm friendship with Pestalozzi at Yverdon.

LEWIS, MATTHEW GREGORY. GENEVA

It was at Geneva that 'Monk' Lewis made his famous will concerning his Jamaican property, witnessed by Byron, Shelley, and Polidori.

MURCHISON, SIR RODERICK. GENEVA, VEVEY, CHAMONIX, GRINDELWALD

The great geologist met Byron walking from Vevey to Clarens on June 13, the day before the great thunderstorm described by Byron in *Childe Harold*.

PARROT, FREDERIC. VARALLO, RIVA, COL D'OLEN, GRESSONEY, BETTA FURKA PASS, ST. JACQUES D'AYAS, BETTA FURKA PASS, GRESSONEY, COL DE VAL DOBBIA, RIVA, VARALLO

PLATEN-HALLERMUENDE, AUGUST VON. CONSTANCE, SCHAFFHAUSEN, ZURICH, ALBIS, ZUG, RIGI, LUCERNE, STANS, SCHWYZ, ALTDORF, ANDERMATT, FURKA PASS, GRIMSEL PASS, MEIRINGEN, INTERLAKEN, LAUTERBRUNNEN, THUN, BERNE, AARBERG, BIENNE, SOLEURE, AARAU, ZURICH, GLARUS, RAPPERSWIL, APPENZELL, ST. GALL, RORSCHACH

'A house is to be built on the Rigi Kulm, to put up future visitors. We had to content ourselves with a hut that we found there, and had a fire lighted for us as it was cold. We breakfasted and stayed three hours on the top. In the hut was a visitors' book, as usual in Switzerland. The book was fairly new, and had few well known names and few good verses or epigrams. The most distinguished was the English Walter Scott, who, however, said little of the beauties of the Rigi, but gave advice concerning the ascent and sojourn, which in any case was of no use to anyone who was already on the top.'

PLAYFAIR, JOHN. LES VERRIÈRES, NEUCHÂTEL, BIENNE, SOLEURE, AARAU, BADEN, SCHAFFHAUSEN, ZURICH, LUCERNE, BERNE, MORAT, LAUSANNE, GENEVA, CHAMONIX, TÊTE NOIRE PASS, MARTIGNY, LAUSANNE, GENEVA, MARTIGNY, SION, BRIG, SIMPLON PASS, DOMODOSSOLA

'For the moving of large masses of rock, the most powerful engines without doubt which nature employs are the glaciers.'

POLIDORI, JOHN WILLIAM. BASLE, LIESTAL, SOLEURE, BERNE, MORAT, PAYERNE, LAUSANNE, GENEVA, CHAMONIX, GENEVA, EVIAN, ST. GINGOLPH, BOUVERET, MONTREUX, COL DE JAMAN, CHÂTEAU D'OEX, SAANEN, ZWEISIMMEN, THUN, INTERLAKEN, LAUTERBRUNNEN, GRINDELWALD, INTERLAKEN, GIESSBACH, MEIRINGEN, GRIMSEL PASS, OBERGESTELEN, BRIG, SIMPLON PASS, DOMODOSSOLA

'We arrived at Secheron—where L[ord] B[yron], having put his age down as 100, received a letter half-an-hour after from I K—a thing that seems worthy of a novel.'

SEDGWICK, ADAM. GENEVA, LAUSANNE, VEVEY, MARTIGNY, COL DE BALME, CHAMONIX, TÊTE NOIRE PASS, MARTIGNY, GRAND ST. BERNARD, MARTIGNY, SION, LEUK, GEMMI PASS, KANDERSTEG, INTERLAKEN, GRINDELWALD, THUN, BERNE, LUCERNE, ALTDORF, ANDERMATT, LUCERNE, BASLE

'A man can imagine a mountain four times as high as any he has seen; but of that exquisite perfection of scenery which arises from contrast and combination, no one can have any perfect notion who has not been in Switzerland.'

SHARP, RICHARD. GENEVA, THUN

'There are two mistakes often made by travellers in the North and on the Continent: that of loitering on the road to visit inferior places before they reach the Lakes, or the Alps; and that of wasting time and strength in hunting after novelty, instead of dwelling on the noblest scenes and getting them by heart. Much needless toil is undergone to fill the journal and the sketch book. Madame de Staël complained to me, at Coppet, that she was often annoyed by travellers, who, as they had nothing to say to her, must have come merely to record the visit in their diaries, or add a paragraph to their letters.' 'Conversation' Sharp also called on Byron.

SHELLEY, FRANCES LADY. LES VERRIÈRES, NEUCHÂTEL, YVERDON, LAUSANNE, GENEVA, CHAMONIX, TÊTE NOIRE PASS, MARTIGNY, VEVEY, FRIBOURG, BERNE, THUN, INTERLAKEN, LAUTERBRUNNEN, THUN, BERNE, ZOFINGEN, LUCERNE, ALTDORF, ANDERMATT, ALTDORF, BRUNNEN, RIGI, ZURICH, SCHAFFHAUSEN

'Mr. Brougham has joined us; and we have been driving in a barouche (if a clumsy, heavy, dirty sort of sociable deserves that name) to Mon Repos and Ouchy . . . Mr. Brougham throughout this expedition had made himself very agreeable, and we told him "that we had saved him from committing suicide".'

SHELLEY, PERCY BYSSHE. GENEVA, NERNIER, EVIAN, MEILLERIE, ST. GINGOLPH, CHILLON, VEVEY, OUCHY, GENEVA, CHAMONIX, GENEVA

'Mont Blanc was before us, but it was covered with cloud; its base, furrowed with dreadful gaps, was seen above. Pinnacles of snow intolerably bright, part of the chain connected with Mont Blanc, shone through the clouds at intervals on high. I never knew—I never imagined what mountains were before. The immensity of these aerial summits excited, when they suddenly burst upon the sight, a sentiment of ecstatic wonder, not unallied to madness.'

SHEPPARD, JOHN. DOMODOSSOLA, SIMPLON PASS, BRIG, SION, MARTIGNY, MONTREUX, GENEVA, CHAMONIX, TÊTE NOIRE PASS, MARTIGNY, LAUSANNE, NEUCHÂTEL, LA CHAUX DE FONDS, BIENNE, SOLEURE, BERNE, THUN, INTERLAKEN, LAUTERBRUNNEN, GRINDELWALD, GROSSE SCHEIDEGG, MEIRINGEN, BRUNIG PASS, LUCERNE, ZURICH, SCHAFFHAUSEN

'If Dean Swift had visited Chamouni, he would certainly have carried off a specimen for the Brobdignag museum.'

SPOHR, LUDWIG. BASLE, ZURICH, BERNE, THUN, THIERACHERN, SPIEZ, KANDERSTEG, INTERLAKEN, LAUTERBRUNNEN, FRIBOURG, THIERACHERN, KANDERSTEG, GEMMI PASS, LEUK, BRIG, SIMPLON PASS, DOMODOSSOLA

'Thierachern, Gasthaus zum Löwen.

The daily exercise in the beautiful pure balmy air strengthens our bodies, enlivens our spirits and makes us joyous and happy. In such a disposition of mind, one works easily and quickly, and several compositions lie already completed before me, namely a Violin Concerto in the shape of a Vocal-scena and a Duett for two violins.'

TEIGNMOUTH, LORD. ST. GALL, APPENZELL, WILDKIRCHLI, ZUG, SCHWYZ, BERNE, GENEVA, CHAMONIX, GENEVA, MARTIGNY, GRAND ST. BERNARD PASS, AOSTA

WILLIAMS, HUGH WILLIAM. BASLE, SOLEURE, BIENNE, NEUCHÂTEL, ORBE, LAUSANNE, GENEVA, CHAMONIX, TÊTE NOIRE PASS, MARTIGNY, SION, BRIG, SIMPLON PASS, DOMODOSSOLA

'Pictures give no idea of them, and I fear never can. The mind is struck with the wonderful work of God. Awe, solemn awe, fills the soul in looking at these sublime productions of his hand. When the sun was set to the world below, and the blue smoke of the peaceful cottage was ascending through gloomy shade, the Alps were glowing in the heavens!'

1817

ELLIOTT, HENRY VENN. BASLE, SCHAFFHAUSEN, CONSTANCE, ZURICH, ZUG, ARTH, RIGI, LUCERNE, MEIRINGEN, GRIMSEL, GIESSBACH, INTERLAKEN, LAUTERBRUNNEN, BERNE, LAUSANNE, MARTIGNY, GRAND ST. BERNARD PASS, AOSTA

'As for the Hotel on the Righi, the accommodations were sufficiently miserable; and, to tell the truth, many a time would I have been glad to change my bed for our coachman's over the stable, or to compound for anything clean and unmolested.'

FRYE, W. E. LAUSANNE, MOUDON, PAYERNE, NEUCHÂTEL, BERNE, LAUSANNE, MARTIGNY, SION, BRIG, SIMPLON PASS, DOMODOSSOLA

HARE, AUGUSTUS WILLIAM. SCHAFFHAUSEN, ZURICH, COIRE, LUCERNE, BRUNNEN, SCHWYZ

HEGER, THOMAS. JOUGNE, BALLAIGUES, LA SARRAZ, LAUSANNE, GENEVA, BONNEVILLE, GENEVA, LAUSANNE, JOUGNE

HEGNER, ULRICH. ZURICH, ZUG, RIGI, LUCERNE, ZURICH

On the Rigi, 'the new inn that was begun last year is now so nearly completed that it provides comfortable quarters for many. . . . The proprietor is now busy building on a wing, for in the spring the number of visitors was so great and only the dining room was ready, that masses of people dossed down in the cowstall which was a hole dug in the ground.'

HOG, ROGER. GENEVA, CHAMONIX, GENEVA, LAUSANNE, BERNE, NEUCHÂTEL, MOTIERS-TRAVERS, YVERDON, GENEVA, THONON, MARTIGNY, SION, BRIG, SIMPLON PASS, DOMODOSSOLA

' "Can my eyes
Reach thy size?"

as the Lilliputian poem addressed to Gulliver says, I applied to Mont Blanc in the Valley of Chamouny; in fact they cannot, of so gigantic and bulky a mountain.'

KRÜDENER, JULIE DE. BASLE, LAUFENBURG, ZURICH, BERNE, LUCERNE, SCHAFFHAUSEN

LANGTON, THOMAS. GENEVA, YVERDON, VEVEY, BEX, MARTIGNY, CREUX DU VAN, GROTTE AUX FÉES, STE. CROIX, BALLAIGUES, LAC DE JOUX, SION, BRIG, SIMPLON PASS, DOMODOSSOLA

Langton describes a visit to an ice-cave in the Jura in the neighbourhood of the house which Mme du Peyrou had built so as to be near her father; it was therefore probably in the region of Montlesi, near Motiers-Travers.

MOULINIÉ, C. E. F. LAUSANNE, BEX, MARTIGNY, GRAND ST. BERNARD, MARTIGNY, TÊTE NOIRE PASS, CHAMONIX, COL DE BALME, MARTIGNY

'C'est un singulier tableau pour le philosophe observateur, que Chamouny fourmillant d'étrangers dans les beaux jours d'été. Au milieu de cette affluence de gens de différentes nations, dont plusieurs ne s'entendent point les uns les autres, j'étais frappé péniblement de ce que l'unité de langage n'a pas lieu entre les hommes, comme elle a lieu entre les animaux de même espèce.'

PLAYFAIR, JOHN. LINDAU, ALTSTÄTTEN, COIRE, WALLENSTADT, ZURICH, LUCERNE, RIGI, SCHWYZ, BRUNNEN, ALTDORF, ST. GOTTHARD PASS, AIROLO, NUFENEN PASS, OBERGESTELEN, GRIMSEL PASS, MEIRINGEN, GRINDELWALD, LAUTERBRUNNEN, INTERLAKEN, BRIENZ, BRUNIG PASS, LUCERNE, GENEVA

RAFFLES, THOMAS. GENEVA, CHAMONIX, TÊTE NOIRE PASS, MARTIGNY, LAUSANNE, MORAT, BERNE, SOLEURE, BASLE

'A wretch has had the hardihood to avow and record his atheism, having written over against his name in the album at Montanvert "an atheist".' He was travelling with his cousin Sir Stamford Raffles.

REICHARD, H. A. O. ZURICH, BERNE, THUN, INTERLAKEN, LAUTERBRUNNEN, KLEINE SCHEIDEGG, GRINDELWALD, BRIENZ

'On the lake of Brienz there are sailor women who row the boats and assume all kinds of celebrated nautical names; for example, one of them was called Admiral Nelson.'

ROSE, STEWART. MARTIGNY, SION, BRIG, SIMPLON PASS, DOMODOSSOLA

'There is indeed no real cause for terror in passing the Simplon; but it is impossible to look down from the carriage, almost grazing the brinks of the precipices, often unfurnished with the slightest protection, without experiencing something which comes near it.'

SCOTT, JOHN BARBER. COMO, NESSO, FORMAZZA, GRIES PASS, OBERGESTELEN, AIROLO, BELLINZONA, LUGANO, CAPOLAGO, MILAN

SIMOND, L. VALLORBE, ORBE, GIEZ, STE. CROIX, MOTIERS-TRAVERS, CREUX DU VAN, GROTTE AUX FÉES, STE. CROIX, BALLAIGUES, LAC DE JOUX, DENT DE VAULION, YVERDON, NEUCHÂTEL, ILE ST. PIERRE, BIENNE, MOUTIER, BASLE, SCHAFFHAUSEN, ST. GALL, GAIS, ALTSTÄTTEN, SARGANS, PFÄFERS, WALLENSTADT, GLARUS, ZURICH, ZUG, RIGI, LUCERNE, SURSEE, BERNE, THUN, INTERLAKEN, LAUTERBRUNNEN, KLEINE SCHEIDEGG, GRINDELWALD, GROSSE SCHEIDEGG, MEIRINGEN, INTERLAKEN, BERNE, YVERDON, VEVEY, LAUSANNE, GENEVA, CHAMONIX, GENEVA

SOMERVILLE, MARY. GENEVA, LAUSANNE, MARTIGNY, SION, BRIG, SIMPLON PASS, DOMODOSSOLA

SOUTHEY, ROBERT. NEUCHÂTEL, YVERDON, LAUSANNE, GENEVA, LUGANO, DOMODOSSOLA, SIMPLON PASS, BRIG, SION, MARTIGNY, TÊTE NOIRE PASS, CHAMONIX, TÊTE NOIRE PASS, MARTIGNY, VEVEY, LAUSANNE, BERNE, THUN, INTERLAKEN, GRINDELWALD, RIGI, ZURICH

'Were I to settle anywhere on the continent, Switzerland should be the country, and probably Lausanne the place.'

SPOHR, LUDWIG. DOMODOSSOLA, SIMPLON PASS, BRIG, SION, MARTIGNY, BEX, VEVEY, LAUSANNE, GENEVA, BERNE, THUN, THIERACHERN, ZURICH, BASLE

STARKE, MARIANA. GENEVA, CHAMONIX, GENEVA, THONON, EVIAN, MARTIGNY, SION, BRIG, SIMPLON PASS, DOMODOSSOLA

'. . . Persons, however, who wish to see Switzerland to advantage, should travel on foot; a mode so commonly adopted that the Foot-passenger is as well received even at the best inns, as if he came in a splendid equipage.' Mariana Starke's book suggested to John Murray the idea of the 'Handbooks'.

TICKNOR, GEORGE. LAUSANNE, GENEVA, CHAMONIX, GENEVA, CHILLON, ST. GINGOLPH, MARTIGNY, GRAND ST. BERNARD, MARTIGNY, SION, BRIG, SIMPLON PASS, DOMODOSSOLA.

'The falls of Niagara where one sea precipitates itself into another, may surpass it; but I have never seen Niagara, and the Mer de Glace remains solitary in my recollections of the stupendous works and movements of nature.'

WALDIE, JANE. MENAGGIO, PORLEZZA, LUGANO, COMO, MILAN, DOMODOSSOLA, SIMPLON PASS, BRIG, SION, MARTIGNY, GRAND ST. BERNARD, MARTIGNY, BEX, LAUSANNE, GENEVA

At the Great St. Bernard hospice, Miss Waldie was waited on by an 'old serving man' who 'was the only person who accompanied Prior Murith to the summit of Mont Velan' in 1779. This was the hunter Genoud.

WARING, SAMUEL MILLER. PONTARLIER, YVERDON, GENEVA, CHAMONIX, COL DE BALME, MARTIGNY, GRAND ST. BERNARD, MARTIGNY, BEX, BERNE, THUN, INTERLAKEN, LAUTERBRUNNEN, GRINDELWALD, GROSSE SCHEIDEGG, MEIRINGEN, GENEVA, ROLLE, LAUSANNE, FRIBOURG, BULLE, VEVEY

WESTON, STEPHEN. LES VERRIÈRES, NEUCHÂTEL, YVERDON, LAUSANNE, MARTIGNY, SION, BRIG, SIMPLON, BRIG, MARTIGNY, ST. MAURICE, EVIAN, GENEVA, CHAMONIX, GENEVA, LAUSANNE, NEUCHÂTEL, LES VERRIÈRES

Chamonix: '. . . The grand business at this place is to mount the hills, which you may do after breakfast at your ease in your char de côté for one hour, then on mules for one more, and after that on foot two hours, and you will find yourself either on the Montenvert, or the Chapeau.'

1818

ALISON, SIR ARCHIBALD. GENEVA, MARTIGNY, TÊTE NOIRE PASS, CHAMONIX, COL DU BONHOMME, COL DE LA SEIGNE, COURMAYEUR, AOSTA, GRAND ST. BERNARD PASS, MARTIGNY, SION, BRIG, SIMPLON PASS, DOMODOSSOLA

ANONYMOUS 7 B. GENEVA, LAUSANNE, VEVEY, MARTIGNY, SION, BRIG, SIMPLON PASS, DOMODOSSOLA

BAILLIE, MARIANNE. DOMODOSSOLA, SIMPLON PASS, BRIG, SION, MARTIGNY, THONON, GENEVA, CHAMONIX, GENEVA, VEVEY, MOUDON, MORAT, BERNE, SOLEURE, BALSTHAL, BASLE

BERRY, MARY. DOMODOSSOLA, SIMPLON PASS, BRIG, SION, MARTIGNY, GENEVA

'We slept at Martigny. We left it the 16th of June, at five o'clock in the morning; that same day, before five o'clock in the evening the water was already in the town.'

BRIDEL, PHILIPPE. MONTREUX, MARTIGNY, CHABLE, LOURTIER, CHANRION, SEMBRANCHER, GRAND ST. BERNARD

'"Le grand pontife de Milton, qui jeta un si beau pont sur le chaos, pour arriver à notre planète, n'a certainement pas fait d'élèves dans le Val de Bagnes", me disait un Irlandais.'

HALL, CAPT. BASIL. GENEVA, THONON, MARTIGNY, TÊTE NOIRE PASS, CHAMONIX, ST. GERVAIS, COL DU BONHOMME, COL DE LA SEIGNE, COURMAYEUR, AOSTA, GRAND ST. BERNARD PASS, MARTIGNY, SION, BRIG, SIMPLON PASS, DOMODOSSOLA

'There will always be found, even in the most frequented parts of the Alps, abundant opportunities for the most hardy exertion, and quite enough of privation and sources of enterprise to try the fortitude and spirit of the most adventurous, and to gratify the taste of the greatest lover of roughing.'

KEAN, EDMUND. GENEVA, MARTIGNY, GRAND ST. BERNARD

At the Grand St. Bernard, 'observing an old spinnet in one of the apartments, he opened it, and accompanied a few melodies with such beautiful taste and expression that the monks, transported with delight, earnestly pressed him to prolong his stay with them'.

KENT, EDWARD, DUKE OF. BERNE, THUN, INTERLAKEN, LAUTERBRUNNEN, GRINDELWALD

Queen Victoria's father was on his honeymoon.

LYELL, SIR CHARLES. GENEVA, CHAMONIX, GENEVA, LAUSANNE, YVERDON, NEUCHÂTEL, BIENNE, MOUTIER, BASLE, SCHAFFHAUSEN, ZURICH, ALBIS, ZUG, RIGI, LUCERNE, BRUNIG PASS, MEIRINGEN, GRIMSEL, MEIRINGEN, GROSSE SCHEIDEGG, GRINDELWALD, KLEINE SCHEIDEGG, LAUTERBRUNNEN, INTERLAKEN, THUN, BERNE, MORAT, VEVEY, BEX, MARTIGNY, MAUVOISIN, SEMBRANCHER, GRAND ST. BERNARD, MARTIGNY, SION, BRIG, SIMPLON PASS, DOMODOSSOLA

At Grindelwald, in the travellers' book of the Hotel, Lyell found Southey's reference to 'la belle Batelière'—'R. S. recognizes in Elizabeth a striking resemblance to la Formarina of Rafael.'

MATTHEWS, HENRY. DOMODOSSOLA, SIMPLON PASS, BRIG, SION, MARTIGNY, LAUSANNE, BERNE, THUN, INTERLAKEN, LAUTERBRUNNEN, GRINDELWALD, INTERLAKEN, BRIENZ, BRUNIG PASS, LUCERNE, ZURICH, RIGI, LUCERNE, ZOFINGEN, BERNE, LAUSANNE, GENEVA, CHAMONIX, GENEVA

MATZEWSKI, COUNT. GENEVA, CHAMONIX, AIGUILLE DU MIDI, MONT BLANC

MEDWIN, THOMAS. GENEVA

Byron's boat 'was keeled and clinker-built, the only one of the kind on the lake; and which, although Mr. Moore says it "was fitted to stand the usual squalls of the climate", was to my mind ill-adapted for the navigation, for it drew too much water and was narrow and crank. I saw it two years after, lying a wreck, and half submerged, though (like Voltaire's pen, of which hundreds have been sold as original to Englishmen at Ferney) there was at that time a chaloupe at Geneva that went by the name of Byron's.'

MURRAY, JOHN. GENEVA, MARTIGNY, SION, BRIG, SIMPLON PASS, DOMODOSSOLA

SCOTT, JOHN. VALLORBE, ORBE, LAUSANNE, MARTIGNY, SION, BRIG, SIMPLON PASS, DOMODOSSOLA

SIMOND, L. GENEVA, LAUSANNE, NEUCHÂTEL, LE LOCLE, PORRENTRUY, ZURICH, GLARUS, PRAGEL PASS, SCHWYZ, EINSIEDELN, SCHWYZ, STANS, SARNEN, BRUNIG PASS, BRIENZ, INTERLAKEN, THUN, BERNE, FRIBOURG, GRUYÈRES, MONTBOVON, COL DE JAMAN, MONTREUX, MARTIGNY, SION, BRIG, SIMPLON PASS, DOMODOSSOLA

'Les aubergistes . . . accoutumés aux mylords anglais d'autrefois, ne trouvent plus que des Anglais pour rire, qui marchandent à la porte, avant d'entrer, le prix de l'omelette et du gigot de mouton, dont ils feront leur diner . . . Si les Anglais ne paraissent plus ce qu'ils étaient autrefois, c'est que ce n'est plus du tout la même classe qui voyage, mais bien toutes les classes, et non pas à beaucoup près ce qu'il y a de mieux dans toutes les classes.'

STANLEY, EDWARD. MARTIGNY, SEMBRANCHER, CHABLE, MAUVOISIN

Stanley's narrative of his adventures in the passage of a 'mauvais pas' in the Val de Bagnes 'was originally inserted anonymously in *Blackwood's Magazine*, soon after the publication of *Anne of Geierstein*, the fictitious adventure therein recorded,' bearing so close a resemblance to one which had really occurred to himself. He has, indeed, some reasons for believing that the details might have reached the ears of Sir Walter Scott, and furnished him with the groundwork of the incident.'

WARING, SAMUEL MILLER. GENEVA, COLLONGES, GEX, LES ROUSSES, LAC DE JOUX, VALLORBE, YVERDON, SCHWYZ, EINSIEDELN, RAPPERSWIL

1819

ANONYMOUS 7. ST. ANTOINE, MONT SUCHET, BAULMES, YVERDON, NEUCHÂTEL, BERNE, THUN, KANDERSTEG, GEMMI PASS, LEUK, SION, MARTIGNY, COL DE BALME, CHAMONIX, GENEVA, LAUSANNE, VALLORBE

BRYDGES, SIR EGERTON. GENEVA, NYON, LAUSANNE, VEVEY, VILLENEUVE, ST. GINGOLPH, MEILLERIE, EVIAN, THONON, GENEVA, ST. GERVAIS, CHAMONIX, GENEVA, EVIAN, MARTIGNY, SION, BRIG, SIMPLON PASS, DOMODOSSOLA

DE LA BECHE, HENRY T. GENEVA, NYON, THONON, MORGES, OUCHY, MEILLERIE, ST. GINGOLPH, VEVEY, CHILLON, ROLLE, YVOIRE, GENEVA, CHAMONIX, COL DE BALME, MARTIGNY

At Chamonix he made an attempt on Mont Blanc by the Aiguille du Gouter with M. d'Houdetot, but without success.

GRANVILLE, AUGUSTUS BOZZI. BASLE, BERNE, LUCERNE, NEUCHÂTEL, ILE ST. PIERRE, YVERDON, LAUSANNE, GENEVA

'At Geneva, by a mere chance, we fell in with Madame Patterson Bonaparte.' This was the American wife of Napoleon's brother Jerome.

HEGETSCHWEILER, JOHANN. ZURICH, STÄFA, LACHEN, WÄGGITAL, SCHWEINALP PASS, KLÖNTHAL, GLARUS, LINTHAL, KISTEN PASS, BRIGELS, WALTENSBURG, PANIXER PASS, ELM, GLARUS, ZURICH

LA GRANDVILLE, COMTESSE DE. BASLE, MOUTIER, BIENNE, ILE ST. PIERRE, BERNE, MURGENTHAL, SURSEE, LUCERNE, STANS, KÜSSNACHT, ZUG, LUCERNE, SUMISWALD, WALKRINGEN, BERNE, MORAT, LAUSANNE, GENEVA

MOORE, THOMAS. GENEVA, THONON, MARTIGNY, SION, BRIG, SIMPLON PASS, DOMODOSSOLA

' . . . Ascended the Simplon, which baffles all description. . . . Walked on by myself, and saw such a scene by sunset as I shall never forget. That mighty panorama of the Alps, whose summits there, indistinctly seen, looked like the top of gigantic waves, following close upon each other; the soft lights falling on those green spots which cultivation has conjured up in the midst of this wild scene; the pointed top of the Jungfrau [? Bietschhorn], whose snows were then pink with the setting sun; all was magnificent to a degree that quite overpowered me, and I alternately shuddered and shed tears as I looked upon it . . .'

MOULINIÉ, C. E. F. GENEVA, COSSONAY, LAC DE JOUX, DENT DE VAULION, VALLORBE, LA SARRAZ, LAUSANNE, NYON, ST. CERGUE, LA DOLE, GEX, GENEVA

'Nous passâmes quatre heures à visiter de l'œil et de la lunette tout ce vaste horizon, à parcourir les bords de notre lac, à admirer la cime du Mont-Blanc perçant les nuages comme la foi s'élance dans les cieux, et à abaisser avec complaisance nos regards sur notre patrie, comme le chrétien, au jour où il triomphe de la mort par son entrée dans le séjour de l'immortalité sur la montagne sainte, contemple de là avec une douce émotion le lieu qui fut ici-bas son berceau.'

MÜLLER, W. L. BASLE, MOUTIER, BIENNE, NEUCHÂTEL, YVERDON, LAUSANNE, GENEVA, CHAMONIX, GENEVA, EVIAN, ST. MAURICE, BEX, VEVEY, MOUDON, PAYERNE, AVENCHES, MORAT, BERNE, THUN, INTERLAKEN, LAUTERBRUNNEN, GRINDELWALD, THUN, BERNE, ZOFINGEN, LUCERNE, RIGI, ZUG, ZURICH, SCHAFFHAUSEN

The last visitor to see Marc-Théodore Bourrit.

NAPIER, GENERAL CHARLES JAMES. GENEVA, MARTIGNY, SION, BRIG, SIMPLON PASS, DOMODOSSOLA

'All that imagination can paint as landscape is to be found between Geneva and Milan, until the eye and the mind alike grow weary with admiring.'

RAOUL-ROCHETTE, DÉSIRÉ. LES VERRIÈRES, NEUCHÂTEL, BIENNE, BERNE, THUN, INTERLAKEN, LAUTERBRUNNEN, KLEINE SCHEIDEGG, GRINDELWALD, INTERLAKEN, BRIENZ, BRUNIG PASS, LUCERNE, RIGI, SCHWYZ, BRUNNEN, ALTDORF, ANDERMATT, FURKA PASS, GRIMSEL PASS, MEIRINGEN

'Le second soir que je soupai à l'auberge de Lauterbrunnen, vingt-quatre voyageurs, venus de divers endroits de la Suisse, étaient rassemblés autour de la même table; et parmi tous ces étrangers, dont dix-huit étaient Anglais, j'étais le seul de ma nation.'

RENNIE, SIR JOHN. GENEVA, CHAMONIX, GENEVA, MORAT, BIENNE, BERNE, THUN, INTERLAKEN, MEIRINGEN, GENEVA, EVIAN, MARTIGNY, SION, BRIG, SIMPLON PASS, DOMODOSSOLA

'On our way, being at Meyringen, and short of ready cash, we proposed either to return direct to Geneva, or to change one of Herries' circular notes; but on offering one of these notes to the landlord, he at once said there was no occasion for it, as we were Englishmen and that was enough. Having produced a large bag of five-franc pieces, he told us to help ourselves, and was with difficulty persuaded to take one of Herries' notes in exchange.'

RENSSELAER, JEREMIAH VAN. DOMODOSSOLA, SIMPLON PASS, BRIG, SION, MARTIGNY, EVIAN, GENEVA, CHAMONIX, MONT BLANC, GENEVA

Van Rensselaer and his companion W. Howard were the first Americans to ascend Mont Blanc.

SCHULTES, G. VON. SCHAFFHAUSEN, CONSTANCE, APPENZELL, SÄNTIS, WATTWIL, ZURICH, ZUG, RIGI, ALTDORF, ANDERMATT, FURKA PASS, GRIMSEL PASS, MEIRINGEN, GROSSE SCHEIDEGG, GRINDELWALD, KLEINE SCHEIDEGG, LAUTERBRUNNEN, INTERLAKEN, THUN, BERNE, SOLEURE, WEISSENSTEIN, MOUTIER, BASLE

'The mountains are majestic, but a wild austerity reigns over them. My imagination peoples them with creatures adapted to the greatness of nature. The gigantic race of cedars crowns their grey summits, while out of the depths climb the wonder animals of the past, mammoths.'

SPENCER, LAVINIA, COUNTESS. GENEVA, MARTIGNY, SION, BRIG, SIMPLON PASS, DOMODOSSOLA

'You are already apprized of our having passed the Simplon most gallantly; but how surfeited I am for life of sublimities! Oh may I never see rock, torrent, cascade, or snow-topped mountain again. We were thirteen hours in the carriage going over this eternal road, and what with bodily fatigue and mental fright, I never was so tired in all my life. However, *me voici, grâce à Dieu*; and I may rejoice in the certainty of never undergoing the Simplon again.'

UNDRELL, CAPT. J. GENEVA, CHAMONIX, MONT BLANC, TÊTE NOIRE PASS, MARTIGNY, BEX, LAUSANNE, BERNE

'Nothing can be fancied so beautiful as the ethereal concave, arching out, if I may so express it, into infinity, without any exhalation or impurity of earth to intercept its magnificence. There was a something in the scene and the situation—a feeling of high-wrought enthusiasm, to which the mind willingly lent itself, seeming to stretch beyond the wonders it contemplated towards Him who formed them.'

VINCENT, JOHANN NIKLAUS. GRESSONEY ST. JEAN, MONTE ROSA (VINCENTPYRAMIDE)

WOLFF, JOSEPH. FRIBOURG, VALSAINTE, BULLE, VEVEY, LAUSANNE, GENEVA

'The providence of God conducted me to Miss Greaves and other English Christians, who already knew me by report. They recommended me to an English clergyman, who was at that time at Lausanne, and was going to London, for which place they gave me letters of introduction, and I departed for London.'

1820

AMPÈRE, JEAN JACQUES. GENEVA, LAUSANNE, VEVEY, BERNE, BIENNE, ILE ST. PIERRE, GENEVA, CHAMONIX, GENEVA, ENGELBERG, JOCH PASS, MEIRINGEN, GRIMSEL PASS, FURKA PASS, HOSPENTHAL, ST. GOTTHARD PASS, BELLINZONA, LUGANO, DOMODOSSOLA, SIMPLON PASS, BRIG

BAKEWELL, R. ANNECY, BONNEVILLE, CHAMONIX, GENEVA, LAUSANNE, BERNE, THUN, INTERLAKEN, GRINDELWALD, KLEINE SCHEIDEGG, LAUTERBRUNNEN, THUN, BERNE, VEVEY, MARTIGNY, SION, BRIG, SIMPLON PASS, DOMODOSSOLA, SIMPLON PASS, BRIG, SION, MARTIGNY, GENEVA

BERRY, MARY. JOUGNE, VALLORBE, LAUSANNE, GENEVA

Miss Berry met the Princess of Wales at Geneva.

COLSTON, MARIANNE. DOMODOSSOLA, SIMPLON PASS, BRIG, SION, MARTIGNY, LAUSANNE, BERNE, THUN, INTERLAKEN, LAUTERBRUNNEN, GRINDELWALD, MEIRINGEN, INTERLAKEN, BERNE, AARBURG,

LUCERNE, RIGI, ZURICH, SCHAFFHAUSEN, BASLE, SOLEURE, BIENNE, ILE ST. PIERRE, LAUSANNE, GENEVA

At the inn at Simplon 'we dined together, and passed a most agreeable evening, with Mr. F. and his very intelligent and agreeable lady. We again breakfasted together the following morning, and being anxious to avail ourselves of the first opportunity of having our dear little girl baptized, by an English clergyman, we requested the favour of Mr. F. to perform the ceremony. He gratified our wishes with the most friendly politeness. . . . She is, probably, the first English child who has been baptized on the summits of the Simplon.'

COULMANN, J. J. CONSTANCE, ARENENBERG, LUCERNE, RIGI

DIGBY, KENELM HENRY (*c*). GENEVA, CHAMONIX, GRINDELWALD, GROSSE SCHEIDEGG, MEIRINGEN, LUCERNE, PILATUS, ENGELBERG

DORNFORD, J. BERNE, GENEVA, CHAMONIX, MONT BLANC

'A bottle of our best wine had been reserved to drink on the summit to the health of the King and the Emperor Alexander, as well as to the memory of Saussure. H[enderson] and myself, during a short absence of Dr. H[amel] were even arranging between us the etiquette of precedency between the two monarchs . . .' Shortly afterwards there occurred the accident in which three guides were lost in an avalanche.

EDGEWORTH, MARIA. GENEVA, CHAMONIX, GENEVA, YVERDON, FRIBOURG, BERNE, THUN, INTERLAKEN, LAUTERBRUNNEN, GRINDELWALD, INTERLAKEN, BRIENZ, BRUNIG PASS, LUCERNE, ZUG, LAUSANNE, VEVEY, GENEVA

'I did not conceive it possible that I should feel so much pleasure from the beauties of nature as I have done since I came to this country.'

GAY, JACQUES. ZERMATT

'Mr. Gay spent a whole month at the high village of Zermatt with his gentle wife and her amiable sister.'

HAMEL, DR. GENEVA, CHAMONIX, MONT BLANC

Hamel's party, which included Joseph Dornford and Gilbert Henderson, was overwhelmed by an avalanche and three guides were killed.

HEGETSCHWEILER, JOHANN. ZURICH, GLARUS, LINTHAL, SANDALP, GLARUS, ZURICH

'It is not yet possible to give a definite answer to the question whether there has been an absolute increase or decrease of ice in the high Alps, for the edge of the outermost moraine is unknown, as is the distance to which the glaciers formerly extended.'

LAMARTINE, ALPHONSE DE. GENEVA

It was in Geneva that Lamartine and Marianna Eliza Birch underwent the Church of England solemnization of their wedding. In the last Canto of his *Pèlerinage de Childe Harolde*, dedicated to his wife, Lamartine refers to his honeymoon:

'Te souviens-tu du jour où, gravissant la cime
Du Salève aux flancs azurés,
Dans un étroit sentier qui pend sur un abîme,
Nous posions en tremblant nos pas mal assurés?'

MEDWIN, THOMAS. GENEVA, LEUKERBAD

At Geneva, 'Medwin was the chief medium that impressed us [i.e. E. J. Trelawny, E. E. Williams, and G. Jervoise] with a desire to know Shelley'.

MONTÉMONT, ALBERT. GENEVA, CHAMONIX, TÊTE NOIRE PASS, MARTIGNY, GRAND ST. BERNARD, MARTIGNY, SION, BRIG, SIMPLON PASS, DOMODOSSOLA

MOUNTAIN, ARMINE, S. H. GENEVA, CHAMONIX, COL DE BALME, TRIENT, TÊTE NOIRE PASS, CHAMONIX, GENEVA, VEVEY, FRIBOURG, BERNE

'The last rays of the setting sun, which shed a fluctuating red over the partially clouded heavens, coloured with tints of rose and pink the whole tremendous chain of snow-capped Alps which bounded the horizon. I believe the veriest Jew on earth would have lost for a moment the thread of worldly gains and dealings, and given way to the sensations which such a scene inspires.'

PLACIDUS A SPESCHA. TRONS, SURRHEIN, TENIGERBAD, GREINA PASS, CAMPO, CHIRONE, MONTERASCIO PASS, DIESRUT PASS, VRIN, OBERSAXEN, DISENTIS

RAOUL-ROCHETTE, DÉSIRÉ. OUCHY, GRUYÈRES, MONTBOVON, COL DE JAMAN, VEVEY, MARTIGNY, SION, LEUK, GEMMI PASS, KANDERSTEG, INTERLAKEN, BRIENZ, BRUNIG PASS, STANS, LUCERNE, ZUG, EINSIEDELN, GLARUS, SARGANS, COIRE, ALTSTÄTTEN, APPENZELL, ST. GALL, CONSTANCE, SCHAFFHAUSEN

'C'est un spectacle parfois assez divertissant que de voir ces Anglais trainer partout, en ce pays, l'attirail de l'opulence du leur; parcourir les montagnes, parés et brillans comme à une fête, en nombreuses caravanes d'hommes et de laquais, de femmes et de chevaux; étaler, en presence du luxe de la nature, celui de leur toilette, et porter leurs pompons sur les glaciers.'

ROBINSON, HENRY CRABB. GENEVA, LAUSANNE, BERNE, SOLEURE, LUCERNE, WINKEL, ALPNACH, SARNEN, RIGI, SCHWYZ, BRUNNEN, ALTDORF, AMSTEG, HOSPENTHAL, ST. GOTTHARD PASS, AIROLO, BELLINZONA, LOCARNO, LUINO, PONTE TRESA, LUGANO, COMO, MILAN, DOMODOSSOLA,

SIMPLON PASS, BRIG, TURTMANN, LEUKERBAD, GEMMI, LEUK, MARTIGNY, COL DE BALME, CHAMONIX, TÊTE NOIRE PASS, MARTIGNY, VILLENEUVE, LAUSANNE, GENEVA

Mrs. Wordsworth wrote in her journal 'H. C. R. was drunk with pleasure, and made us drunk too.'

STEIN, BARON VON. BASLE, AARAU, CONSTANCE, GAIS, ST. GALL, ZURICH, THUN, INTERLAKEN, THUN, BERNE, LAUSANNE, GENEVA, CHAMONIX, GENEVA, MARTIGNY, SION, BRIG, SIMPLON PASS, DOMODOSSOLA

TRELAWNY, EDWARD JOHN. LAUSANNE, GENEVA

Captain Daniel Roberts returned to Trelawny's hotel at Lausanne with three travellers. 'I saw by their utilitarian garb as well as by the blisters and blotches on their cheeks and noses that they were pedestrian tourists fresh from the blazing sun and frosty air of snow-covered mountains. The man was evidently a denizen of the north; his accent harsh, skin white, of an angular and bony build, and self-confident and dogmatic opinions. But the precision and quaintness of his language, and his eccentric remarks on common things, stimulated my mind. Our icy islanders thaw rapidly when they have drifted into warmer latitudes. These, flushed with health, delighted with their excursion, and with appetites earned by bodily and mental activity, were in such high spirits that Roberts and I caught the infection of their mirth. We all talked as loud and fast as if under the influence of champagne instead of café au lait.' These three travellers were William, Mary, and Dorothy Wordsworth.

WESTON, STEPHEN. GENEVA, LAUSANNE, MOUDON, MORAT, BERNE, SOLEURE, BALSTHAL, LIESTAL, BASLE

WORDSWORTH, DOROTHY, & WILLIAM. SCHAFFHAUSEN, ZURICH, AARBURG, HERZOGENBUCHSEE, BERNE, THUN, INTERLAKEN, LAUTERBRUNNEN, KLEINE SCHEIDEGG, GRINDELWALD, GROSSE SCHEIDEGG, MEIRINGEN, BRUNIG PASS, ENGELBERG, LUCERNE, RIGI, ALTDORF, AMSTEG, HOSPENTHAL, ST. GOTTHARD PASS, AIROLO, BELLINZONA, LOCARNO, LUINO, PONTE TRESA, LUGANO, COMO, MILAN, DOMODOSSOLA, SIMPLON PASS, BRIG, SION, MARTIGNY, COL DE BALME, CHAMONIX, TÊTE NOIRE PASS, MARTIGNY, VILLENEUVE, LAUSANNE, GENEVA

Dorothy: 'The sunshine had long deserted the valley, and was quitting the summits of the mountains behind the village; but red hues, dark as the red of rubies, settled in the clouds, and lingered there after the mountains had lost all but their cold whiteness, and the black hue of the crags. The gloomy grandeur of this spectacle harmonized with the melancholy of the vale; yet it was *heavenly glory* that hung over those cold mountains.'

William: 'As to the arbitrary, pitiless, godless wretches, who have removed Nature's landmarks by cutting roads through Alps and Appenines, until all things are reduced to the same dead level, they will be arraigned hereafter with the unjust.' (To Trelawney.)

ZUMSTEIN, JOSEPH. GRESSONEY ST. JEAN, MONTE ROSA (ZUMSTEINSPITZE)

1821

ALISON, SIR ARCHIBALD. GENEVA, ST. GINGOLPH, MARTIGNY, SION, LEUK, GEMMI PASS, KANDERSTEG, INTERLAKEN, LAUTERBRUNNEN, GRINDELWALD, MEIRINGEN, GRIMSEL PASS, FURKA PASS, ANDERMATT, ALTDORF, ANDERMATT, ST. GOTTHARD PASS, BELLINZONA, MESOCCO, SAN BERNARDINO PASS, HINTERRHEIN, SPLÜGEN PASS, CHIAVENNA, SONDRIO, APRICA PASS, EDOLO, TONALE PASS, PONTE, ALBULA PASS, FILISUR, THUSIS, COIRE, WALLENSTADT, NÄFELS, ZURICH, SCHAFFHAUSEN

'He who would acquire a taste for the choicest beauties of nature, and open in his mind a vein of the purest and most delicious enjoyment, should devote every vacant hour, when youth renders fatigue a pleasure, to the study of Switzerland.'

ANONYMOUS 7 A. GENEVA, LAUSANNE, VEVEY, ST. GINGOLPH, GENEVA, CHAMONIX, TÊTE NOIRE PASS, MARTIGNY, GRAND ST. BERNARD, MARTIGNY, SION, BRIG, SIMPLON PASS, DOMODOSSOLA

'Oh Nature! Nature! where'er we court thee, how sublime, how expanding, how immeasurably grand, how microscopically beautiful!'

BANCROFT, GEORGE. GENEVA, CHAMONIX, MARTIGNY, SION, LEUK, GEMMI PASS, KANDERSTEG, INTERLAKEN, LAUTERBRUNNEN, INTERLAKEN, MEIRINGEN, GRIMSEL PASS, FURKA PASS, ANDERMATT, FLUELEN, LUCERNE, GENEVA, MARTIGNY, SION, BRIG, SIMPLON PASS, DOMODOSSOLA

'When I entered Switzerland I came with a heavy and desponding heart. One event after another had happened to crush everything like cheerfulness in my bosom, and though I had not yet gained my one and twentieth year, my mind seemed to be sear, and I almost thought I had the heart of an old man. But I have reposed on the bosom of nature, and have there grown young again: from her breasts gush the streams of life, and they who drink of them, regain cheerfulness and vigour. I travelled alone and like a pilgrim on his tour to the promised land. I was on foot. Yet I never felt fatigue, and solitude was delightful. I could sit undisturbed amid the beauties of nature, and give way to the delightful flow of feelings and reflections, which came hurrying on me, as I sat on the Alpine rocks and gazed on the Alpine solitudes. Never till now did I know how beautiful and how kind a mother Earth is . . .'

BESSBOROUGH, HENRIETTA, COUNTESS OF. GENEVA, CHAMONIX, ST. MARTIN

'An English Dr. travelling with the Minto family has sent us into the mountains for change of air and coolness. . . .' This was probably Dr. C. J. B. Williams who became an authority on alpine resorts for invalids.

BROCKEDON, WILLIAM. GENEVA, CHAMONIX, SION, BRIG, SIMPLON PASS, DOMODOSSOLA

BUCHON, J. A. C. SCHAFFHAUSEN, CONSTANCE ST. GALL, TROGEN, HEINRICHSBAD, RAGAZ, COIRE, THUSIS, SAN BERNARDINO PASS, MESOCCO, BELLINZONA, LUGANO, MAGADINO, BELLINZONA, AIROLO, ST. GOTTHARD PASS, FLUELEN, GERSAU, LUCERNE, ZURICH, CONSTANCE

CHARPENTIER, JEAN DE. BEX, SAAS

Charpentier relates that there were still persons living at Saas who remembered seeing the Mattmark erratic block while it was being carried by the Schwarzberg glacier.

CORRIE, GEORGE ELWES. BOURG, ST. MAURICE, PETIT ST. BERNARD PASS, AOSTA, GRAND ST. BERNARD PASS, MARTIGNY, SION, BRIG, SIMPLON PASS, DOMODOSSOLA, MILAN, LUGANO, BELLINZONA, ST. GOTTHARD PASS, ALTDORF, LUCERNE, RIGI, SCHWYZ, GLARUS, ZURICH, LUCERNE, LAUSANNE, GENEVA

COULMANN, J. J. LES VERRIÈRES, MOTIERS-TRAVERS, YVERDON, FERNEY, COPPET

HERSCHEL, SIR JOHN. BREUIL, ST. THEODUL PASS, BREITHORN

HOLMAN, JAMES. GENEVA, LAUSANNE, VEVEY, MORAT, BERNE, SOLEURE, BASLE

'I suggested the advantages of the steamboat, which the smoothness of the water seemed particularly adapted for; but it was objected that the intercourse between the two places [Geneva and Lausanne], was not sufficient to compensate the measure.'

JAMESON, MRS. ANNA. GENEVA, EVIAN, MARTIGNY, SION, BRIG, SIMPLON PASS, DOMODOSSOLA

'These Alps make me ill; almost they suffocate me. All the descriptions I ever heard or read give but a faint idea of the magnificent reality.'

KASTHOFER, KARL. BERNE, THUN, INTERLAKEN, MEIRINGEN, SUSTEN PASS, WASSEN, ST. GOTTHARD PASS, BELLINZONA, MESOCCO, SAN BERNARDINO PASS, THUSIS, TIEFENKASTEL, DAVOS, KLOSTERS, LANDQUART, COIRE, DISENTIS, OBERALP PASS, ANDERMATT, FURKA PASS, GRIMSEL PASS, MEIRINGEN, INTERLAKEN, THUN, BERNE

MOUNTAIN, ARMINE S. H. LUCERNE, ALTDORF, ST. GOTTHARD PASS, BELLINZONA, LOCARNO

'I cannot describe to you the effect it has, when sometimes, after walking for hours, perhaps, surrounded by rocks uninhabited by man or beast, in silence so dread that the sound of your own voice startles you, you see winding round the point of a cliff a train of sumpter mules with their drivers. The appearance of the caravan is picturesque beyond expression, and the jingling of the bells with which the animals are adorned and the cries of the muleteers remind you that you belong to a world which you had almost imagined to have left for ever.'

RAOUL-ROCHETTE, DÉSIRÉ. GENEVA, CHAMONIX, COL DE BALME, MARTIGNY, SION, BRIG, SIMPLON PASS, DOMODOSSOLA

'Un moment, j'ai pu prendre le Prieuré pour un faubourg de Londres, et l'Arveyron pour la Tamise; et je ne serais pas sûr, en me sauvant sur le Mont-Blanc, de n'y pas trouver des Anglais.'

ROGERS, SAMUEL. GENEVA, LAUSANNE, MARTIGNY, SION, BRIG, SIMPLON PASS, DOMODOSSOLA

At Geneva Rogers saw John Kemble and Mrs. Siddons. It was during this tour that he began to write his poem 'Italy'.

SHARP, RICHARD. BEX

The 'Epistle to a Brother' was written at Bex.

SIDDONS, SARAH. LAUSANNE, BERNE, THUN, INTERLAKEN, GRINDELWALD

'Mrs. Siddons was "dying to see Chamouny", but, the expedition being judged too fatiguing, she saw Berne instead. She ate "of" chamois, crossed a lake, mounted a glacier with two men cutting steps in the ice with a hatchet, and bore all these fatigues "much more wonderfully than" the others of the party.'

STENDHAL. COMO, LUGANO, BELLINZONA, AIROLO, ST. GOTTHARD PASS, ALTDORF, LUCERNE, BASLE

'Occupé du moral, la description du physique m'ennuie.'

TENNANT, CHARLES. SCHAFFHAUSEN, ZURICH, RIGI, LUCERNE, SURSEE, THUN, BERNE, MORAT, LAUSANNE, GENEVA, CHAMONIX, GENEVA, THONON, EVIAN, MARTIGNY, GRAND ST. BERNARD, MARTIGNY, VEVEY, OUCHY, LAUSANNE, GENEVA

Riding towards Lausanne from Vevey by the edge of the lake, Tennant found his progress impeded by walls bounding private properties, jutting out into the water. 'Determined that this ill-natured contrivance should not now stop me, I drove my horse into the water . . .' and so he continued, his horse often swimming under him, until he reached Ouchy. But that was not the end of his troubles, for although he could dismount on to the parapet of the quay, the horse was still in the water. He shouted for help until 'a plan occurred to me which I thought it would be better to execute alone and in the dark, viz., to make a breach in the wall. To work I therefore set with hands and feet, and in a few minutes I had accomplished not only the required breach, but with the wreck I had formed a sort of road whereby to mount . . .'

WELDEN, LUDWIG VON. ZERMATT, ST. THEODUL PASS, BREUIL, COL DES CIMES BLANCHES, ST. JACQUES D'AYAS, BETTA FURKA PASS, GRESSONEY, MACUGNAGA

YOUNG, CHARLES MAYNE. GENEVA, LAUSANNE

A visit to John Kemble at Lausanne.

1822

BERRY, MARY. LAUSANNE, VEVEY, MARTIGNY, SION, BRIG, SIMPLON PASS, DOMODOSSOLA

' . . . Called on Mr and Mrs Kemble, who have a very pretty house here, upon the road to Vevey.'

BLESSINGTON, COUNTESS OF. GENEVA, LAUSANNE, BERNE, BADEN, ZURICH, SCHAFFHAUSEN, ZURICH, LUCERNE, GENEVA

'It is at evening that Mont Blanc puts on its most brilliant aspect; when the rays of the setting sun tinge its snow-crowned summits, casting on them a rosy radiance, which they retain for a short period, even after the bright luminary that lent it has disappeared from our sight; like memory, which retains images after the reality has faded away.'

CHATEAUBRIAND, FRANÇOIS RENÉ DE. GENEVA, MARTIGNY, SION, BRIG, SIMPLON PASS, DOMODOSSOLA

'J'ai vu le Simplon, les Iles Borromées, l'enfer et le ciel, et tout cela m'a été à peu près indifférent.'

CLISSOLD, FREDERICK. ST. CERGUE, LA DOLE, GENEVA, CHAMONIX, MONT BLANC, COL DE BALME, MARTIGNY, GRAND ST. BERNARD PASS, AOSTA

On the day of Clissold's ascent of Mont Blanc a Mrs. and Miss Campbell crossed the Col du Gêant to Courmayeur.

DUPPA, R. GENEVA, LAUSANNE, GENEVA, CHAMONIX, TÊTE NOIRE PASS, MARTIGNY, GRAND ST. BERNARD PASS, AOSTA, COURMAYEUR, COL DE LA SEIGNE, COL DES FOURS, COL DU BONHOMME, SALLANCHES, GENEVA, LAUSANNE, FRIBOURG, BERNE, THUN, INTERLAKEN, LAUTERBRUNNEN, KLEINE SCHEIDEGG, GRINDELWALD, LUCERNE, RIGI, ZUG, ZURICH

'I have been wet through twice, could see very little when I arrived at the top, from the bad weather. It was, nevertheless, very well worth the trouble, though I was several times within a hair's breadth of falling down the most frightful precipices.' This was while crossing the Kleine Scheidegg.

GALLATIN, JAMES. GENEVA, ROLLE, MARTIGNY, TÊTE NOIRE PASS, CHAMONIX, GENEVA

'Very few tourists. Some English, who seem to be doing the ascents more as a task than a pleasure.'

HEGETSCHWEILER, JOHANN. ZURICH, GLARUS, LINTHAL, SANDALP, GLARUS, ZURICH

HIRZEL-ESCHER, H. ZURICH, ZUG, LUCERNE, ENGELBERG, JOCH PASS, MEIRINGEN, GRIMSEL PASS, OBERGESTELEN, BRIG, VISP, SAAS, MONTE MORO PASS, MACUGNAGA, TURLO PASS, ALAGNA, COL D'OLEN, GRESSONEY, BETTA FURKA PASS, ST. JACQUES D'AYAS, COL DES CIMES BLANCHES, ST. THEODUL PASS, ZERMATT, VISP, LEUK, GEMMI PASS, KANDERSTEG, ZURICH

At Gressoney Hirzel-Escher called on the priest, 'but when his housekeeper heard that we thought of crossing the Matterhorn glacier, she clasped her hands over her head and recommended us to the protection of the Almighty, and promised to pray for our safety.'

KASTHOFER, KARL. BERNE, THUN, INTERLAKEN, BRIENZ, BRUNIG PASS, STANS, BRUNNEN, SCHWYZ, PRAGEL PASS, GLARUS, WALLENSTADT, COIRE, LENZERHEIDE, WIESEN, DAVOS, FLUELA PASS, SÜS, TARASP, SCARL PASS, OFEN PASS, ZERNEZ, ST. MORITZ, MALOJA PASS, CHIAVENNA, SPLÜGEN PASS, THUSIS, COIRE, DISENTIS, OBERALP PASS, ANDERMATT, ALTDORF, LUCERNE, BRUNIG PASS, BRIENZ, INTERLAKEN, THUN, BERNE.

At St. Moritz, 'the spring, which is situated at a quarter of a league from the nearest house, flows into a sort of vault or reservoir, which has, quite wrongly, been given the pompous name of salle: it is there that the drinkers sit. The ground between the village and the spring is partly marshy, and the path leading to it is badly kept. It is therefore to be presumed that the invalids who visit the spring, exposed as they are to the inclemencies of the weather on the way to it, and to inevitable chills on the spot, must often purchase relief from their old sufferings at the cost of new complaints.'

LA GRANDVILLE, COMTESSE DE. JOUGNE, ORBE, LAUSANNE, MARTIGNY, SION, BRIG, SIMPLON PASS, DOMODOSSOLA

MATTHISSON, FRIEDRICH. BREGENZ, ST. GALL, LICHTENSTEIG, RAPPERSWIL, ZURICH, ZUG, RIGI, SCHWYZ, BRUNNEN, LUCERNE, BERNE, THUN, INTERLAKEN, BERNE, ILE ST. PIERRE, BIENNE, MOUTIER, BASLE, WALDSHUT, SCHAFFHAUSEN

MENDELSSOHN-BARTHOLDY, FELIX. APPENZELL, ZUG, BERNE, THUN, INTERLAKEN, LAUTERBRUNNEN, KLEINE SCHEIDEGG, GRINDELWALD, BULLE, GENEVA

'. . . Every Swiss knows how to jodel. It consists of notes which are produced from the throat and generally they are ascending sixths, . . . Certainly this kind of singing sounds harsh and unpleasant when it is heard near by or in a room. But it sounds beautiful when you hear it with mingling or answering echoes, in the valleys or on the mountains or in the woods, and there, such shouting and yelling seems truly to express the enthusiasm of the Swiss people for their country. And when one stands on a crest early in the morning, with a clear sky over-head, and hears the singing accompanied, now loudly, now softly, by the jingling of cowbells from the pastures below, then it sounds lovely.'

MOUNTAIN, ARMINE S. H. DOMODOSSOLA, SIMPLON PASS, BRIG, LE LOCLE, LA SAGNE, NEUCHÂTEL, SCHAFFHAUSEN

On the way to Neuchâtel, 'a spectacle so magnificent, so extraordinary, so unique, that all description would be vain, struck my astonished view. The newly risen sun shone over my head, and illumined an immense ocean of white vapour, that covered the lake of Neuchatel and the vast tract of country beneath me, and extended itself to the foot of the Alps, the whole chain of which, from the mountains of Unterwalden to those of Savoy and Piedmont, forming a line of fifty leagues in length, I distinctly discovered . . . Yielding to the impulse of the moment, I sank on my knees upon the rock and thanked my Maker that I was permitted to behold a scene, splendid beyond thought, and which perhaps it is not the lot of one traveller among hundreds to enjoy.'

WALSH, COMTE THEOBALD. BASLE, SCHAFFHAUSEN, ZURICH, EINSIEDELN, ZUG, RIGI, LUCERNE, ENGELBERG, SURENEN PASS, ALTDORF, ST. GOTTHARD PASS, BELLINZONA, LUGANO, DOMODOSSOLA, SIMPLON PASS, BRIG, SION, MARTIGNY, LAUSANNE, GENEVA, CHAMONIX, COL DE BALME, MARTIGNY, VEVEY, COL DE JAMAN, CHÂTEAU D'OEX, ZWEISIMMEN, INTERLAKEN, LAUTERBRUNNEN, KLEINE SCHEIDEGG, GRINDELWALD, GROSSE SCHEIDEGG, MEIRINGEN, GRIMSEL, BRIENZ, INTERLAKEN, THUN, BERNE, SOLEURE, BIENNE, ILE ST. PIERRE, MOUTIER, BASLE

'Il faut qu'il y ait un principe vivifiant dans l'air qu'on respire en Suisse, ou bien que les sensations nouvelles et toujours diverses que l'âme y éprouve, ainsi que les distractions sans nombre qui s'offrent aux yeux, aient le pouvoir de charmer les fatigues du corps, tout en tenant sans cesse en action les facultés de l'esprit.'

WELDEN, LUDWIG VON. GRESSONEY ST. JEAN, MONTE ROSA (LUDWIGSHÖHE)

1823

ANONYMOUS 8. GENEVA, CHAMONIX, COL DE BALME, MARTIGNY, GRAND ST. BERNARD PASS, AOSTA, COURMAYEUR, COL DE LA SEIGNE, COL DU BONHOMME, ST. GERVAIS, GENEVA

ANONYMOUS 8 A (*c*). GENEVA, LAUSANNE, VEVEY, ST. GINGOLPH, GENEVA, CHAMONIX, TÊTE NOIRE PASS, MARTIGNY, GRAND ST. BERNARD, MARTIGNY, SION, BRIG, SIMPLON PASS, DOMODOSSOLA

BELLOT, M. GENEVA, MOTIERS-TRAVERS, ST. AUBIN, NEUCHÂTEL, ILE ST. PIERRE, BIENNE

At Motiers-Travers, Bellot spoke to people who had personally known Jean-Jacques Rousseau.

BERRY, MARY. GENEVA, COPPET

'Went to Coppet. We found the Duc and Duchesse de Broglie, and Auguste de Staël and Miss Randall.'

CHAPUYS MONTLAVILLE, LOUIS ALCESTE DE. PORRENTRUY, DELÉMONT, MOUTIER, BIENNE, AARBERG, BERNE, THUN, INTERLAKEN, LAUTERBRUNNEN, KLEINE SCHEIDEGG, GRINDELWALD, INTERLAKEN, MEIRINGEN, GRIMSEL PASS, FURKA PASS, ANDERMATT, OBERALP PASS, DISENTIS, COIRE, PFÄFERS, SARGANS, ALTSTÄTTEN, GAIS, ST. GALL, SCHAFFHAUSEN, ZURICH, AARAU, BERNE, MORAT, LAUSANNE, GENEVA, VEVEY, MARTIGNY, COL DE BALME, CHAMONIX, GENEVA

Col de Balme:—'Les Anglais se reposent des heures entières aux chalets qui se trouvent sur ces pentes, et dans leur admiration, qui est aussi longue que profonde, souvent ils s'oublient jusqu'au soir; ils couchent alors sur la dure, à côté de l'humble berger, et le lendemain ils jouissent encore avec délices des effets brûlans des premiers rayons du jour.'

ERSKINE, THOMAS. GENEVA, MARTIGNY, SION, BRIG, SIMPLON PASS, DOMODOSSOLA

FORBES, MURRAY. BASLE, SOLEURE, NEUCHÂTEL, GENEVA, CHAMONIX, GENEVA, EVIAN, ST. MAURICE, BEX, VEVEY, MOUDON, FRIBOURG,

BERNE, THUN, INTERLAKEN, GRINDELWALD, LAUTERBRUNNEN, THUN, BERNE, MURGENTHAL, ZOFINGEN, SURSEE, LUCERNE, ZURICH, SCHAFFHAUSEN

'Pedestrian excursions are by no means uncommon in Switzerland, and it is most extraordinary, that they appear sometimes to be undertaken by persons to whom oeconomy need not be an object.'

GOBAT, SAMUEL. CREMINES, MOUTIER, BASLE, YVERDON, LAUSANNE, GENEVA

At Geneva the future Bishop of Jerusalem met Gerard Noel, Thomas Erskine, Daniel Wilson, and Miss Greaves.

HIRZEL-ESCHER, H. ZURICH, WÄGGITAL, REDETENSTOCK, LOCHLI PASS, KLÖNTAL, GLARUS, KÄRPFSTOCK, LINTHAL, STACHELBERG, RISELTSTOCK, RABÜTZLI PASS, SCHWYZ, EINSIEDELN, ZURICH

JACKSON, H. H. GENEVA, CHAMONIX, MONT BLANC, GENEVA

JOHNSON, JAMES. GENEVA, CHAMONIX, COL DE BALME, MARTIGNY, GRAND ST. BERNARD, MARTIGNY, EVIAN, GENEVA, LAUSANNE, NEUCHÂTEL, BERNE, THUN, INTERLAKEN, LAUTERBRUNNEN, GRINDELWALD, GROSSE SCHEIDEGG, MEIRINGEN, BERNE, ZOFINGEN, LUCERNE, ZUG, ZURICH, SCHAFFHAUSEN

'The Highland glens and valleys are not quite on a par with Grindelwald, Lauterbrunnen, and Meyringen; but they are not blotted and deformed by goitre and cretinism. Moreover, they have that which the Helvetian vales and cliffs are remarkably destitute of—a romantic tale—and historic event—or a legendary tradition connected with every step.'

LIEVEN, DOROTHEA CHRISTOPHEROVNA, PRINCESS. GENEVA, MARTIGNY, SION, BRIG, SIMPLON PASS, DOMODOSSOLA

'. . . Drowned at Geneva, had a narrow escape of an overturn [on the Simplon], and arrived at Milan half dead with fright.'

QUINET, EDGAR. GENEVA, NYON, LAUSANNE, VEVEY

'Je suis le plus heureux des hommes! J'ai vu Coppet, Montfleury, Cologny, j'ai fait mon pèlerinage dans le parc de madame de Staël. . . . J'ai continué mon chemin par le plus charmant pays du monde, au bruit des eaux, en face des Alpes et du lac, . . . J'ai voulu loger à la *Clef*, où logea Rousseau; ce n'est plus qu'une maudite pinte avec l'enseigne ordinaire: Au bon Vin.'

SHARP, RICHARD. CHAMONIX

The 'Epistle to a friend at his villa' was written at Chamonix.

WILSON, DANIEL. SCHAFFHAUSEN, ZURICH, BASLE, MOUTIER, BIENNE, NEUCHÂTEL, ILE ST. PIERRE, BERNE, THUN, INTERLAKEN, LAUTERBRUNNEN, KLEINE SCHEIDEGG, GRINDELWALD, GROSSE SCHEIDEGG, MEIRINGEN, GRIMSEL PASS, FURKA PASS, ANDERMATT, ALTDORF, RIGI, LUCERNE, ZOFINGEN, BERNE, MORAT, LAUSANNE, GENEVA, CHAMONIX, TÊTE NOIRE PASS, MARTIGNY, GRAND ST. BERNARD, MARTIGNY, SION, BRIG, SIMPLON PASS, DOMODOSSOLA

The future Bishop of Calcutta visited Rousseau's house on the Ile St. Pierre:—'A book for entering the names of strangers is kept. I was determined to accompany my signature with some token of disagreement from the sentiments of this pernicious writer.' Yet when he saw Shelley's disagreement with some religious cant in the travellers' book at Chamonix, Wilson wrote: 'It is most painful for me to say, that one Englishman has for ever disgraced himself here by attaching to his name, in the strangers' book, an unblushing avowal of Atheism.'

1824

ANONYMOUS 8 C. JOUGNE, YVERDON, MOTIERS-TRAVERS, CREUX DU VAN, DENT DE VAULION, LAC DE JOUX, YVERDON, BERNE, HOFWYL, GENEVA

BROCKEDON, WILLIAM. GENEVA, CHAMONIX, COL DU BONHOMME, COL DE LA SEIGNE, COURMAYEUR, AOSTA, GRAND ST. BERNARD PASS, MARTIGNY, GENEVA

Brockedon was accompanied by the artist Clarkson Stanfield. At Aosta their bedroom door was twice mysteriously opened in the middle of the night, and Brockedon just stopped Stanfield from shooting at the intruder who was another tourist 'whose fears of Messieurs les Anglais kept him awake and restless, with the dread that his throat might be cut by *us* before the morning'.

CHATEAUBRIAND, FRANÇOIS RENÉ DE. NEUCHÂTEL

He joined his wife who had rented a house by the lake. 'La chaine des Alpes se déroulait nord et sud à une grande distance devant nous; nous étions adossés contre le Jura dont les flancs noircis de pins montaient à pic sur nos têtes. Le lac était désert, . . . Quand je montais au sommet du Jura, j'apercevais le lac de Bienne aux brises et aux flots de qui J.-J. Rousseau doit une de ses plus heureuses inspirations.'

HOGG, JOHN. GENEVA, LAUSANNE, NEUCHÂTEL, BIENNE, SOLEURE, AARAU, BADEN, SCHAFFHAUSEN, CONSTANCE, ZURICH, ALBIS, LUCERNE, RIGI, FLUELEN, ANDERMATT, FLUELEN, ALPNACHSTAD, LUNGERN, BRUNIG PASS, MEIRINGEN, HANDECK, GROSSE SCHEIDEGG, GRINDELWALD, KLEINE SCHEIDEGG, LAUTERBRUNNEN, INTERLAKEN, THUN, BERNE, FRIBOURG,

BULLE, VEVEY, BEX, MARTIGNY, TÊTE NOIRE PASS, CHAMONIX, COL DU BONHOMME, COL DE LA SEIGNE, COURMAYEUR, AOSTA, GRAND ST. BERNARD PASS, MARTIGNY, SION, BRIG, SIMPLON PASS, DOMODOSSOLA

'I must say that I felt great regret on quitting that beautiful and pastoral district of Switzerland—a country which, I may safely state, for its extent cannot yield to any in the world, especially in the old world, in interest and in varied and stupendous scenes, that present themselves on all sides to the traveller. The kindness and simplicity too of the inhabitants I always found added much to the delights of their country.'

LAMARTINE, ALPHONSE DE. GENEVA, SCHINZNACH, ZURICH, LUCERNE

LEWIS, SIR GEORGE CORNEWALL. BERNE, LAUSANNE, GENEVA, CHAMONIX, LAUSANNE

'There is a steam boat of ten-horse power that performs its journey from here to Geneva, thirty-six miles in six hours, set up by a Mr. Church, an American; the engineer used to work in the Liverpool packets. The Geneva people have just launched an opposition boat of greater power.'

RAOUL-ROCHETTE, DÉSIRÉ. PORRENTRUY, DELÉMONT, MOUTIER, BIENNE, ILE ST. PIERRE, MOUTIER, BASLE, BRUGG, LUCERNE, STANS, ENGELBERG, SURENEN PASS, ALTDORF, KLAUSEN PASS, LINTHAL, GLARUS, PRAGEL PASS, SCHWYZ

RICKMAN, E. S. GENEVA, CHAMONIX, TÊTE NOIRE PASS, MARTIGNY, SION, BRIG, SIMPLON PASS, DOMODOSSOLA, MILAN, FORMAZZA, GRIES PASS, OBERGESTELEN, GRIMSEL PASS, MEIRINGEN, BRUNIG PASS, LUCERNE, RIGI, SARNEN, BRUNIG PASS, BRIENZ, INTERLAKEN, THUN, BERNE, LAUSANNE, GENEVA

'At the hotel in this elevated region [Simplon], I encountered the late Edmund Kean and a lady, returning from Venice, and had an agreeable five minutes' chat while his carriage was waiting. . . . He had visited Switzerland before, and stood, therefore, somewhat higher in my estimation, from his avowed admiration of its varied and sublime scenery.'

SMITH, JOHN. GENEVA, CHAMONIX, COL DE BALME, MARTIGNY, LAUSANNE, GENEVA

'The captain of the vessel (the Guillaume Tell), a respectably behaved Englishman named Errington, told me that his engineer was English and the engine too. . . . The engineer of the boat (an old English man of war's man named Parry) . . . told me that an opposition boat was at work against them and that she yesterday made the tour of the lake.

She has an English engine (it was made up at Paris) which is worked by Englishmen. . . . Our honest tar is a little out of humour with his fare here. He came from Bourdeaux hither expecting (as the name of Geneva indicates to an Englishman) the finest gin. He came and found none.'

SNOECK, C. A. BASLE, BRUGG, BADEN, SCHAFFHAUSEN, WINTERTHUR, ZURICH, ALBIS, ZUG, RIGI, LUCERNE, ENTLIBUCH, LANGNAU, BERNE, THUN, OBERHOFEN, INTERLAKEN, LAUTERBRUNNEN, KLEINE SCHEIDEGG, GRINDELWALD, GROSSE SCHEIDEGG, MEIRINGEN, GRIMSEL PASS, FURKA PASS, HOSPENTHAL, ST. GOTTHARD PASS, AIROLO, AL ACQUA, SAN GIACOMO PASS, TOSA FALLS, FOPIANO, CREVOLA, SIMPLON PASS, BRIG, SION, MARTIGNY, VEVEY, LAUSANNE, GENEVA

THOMSON, WILLIAM. GENEVA, LAUSANNE, MARTIGNY, SION, BRIG, SIMPLON PASS, DOMODOSSOLA

UWINS, THOMAS. GENEVA, CHAMONIX, MARTIGNY, GENEVA
'In the mountains, Uwins, while trotting on his mule, sported an ample cloak lined with scarlet, and as the wind blew it about, the red made a great show; he having besides somewhat of a clerical air, the peasantry met him with genuflexions.'

VILLENEUVE, M. DE. GENEVA, CHAMONIX, GENEVA, LAUSANNE
A journey to Chamonix where he conversed with Jacques Balmat.

1825

ANONYMOUS 8 B. SCHAFFHAUSEN, ZURICH, ZUG, RIGI, SCHWYZ, LUCERNE, FLUELEN, ANDERMATT, FLUELEN, BUOCHS, STANS, SARNEN, BRUNIG PASS, BRIENZ, INTERLAKEN, THUN, BERNE, MORAT, MOUDON, VEVEY, LAUSANNE, GENEVA, CHAMONIX, GENEVA

'Is this Chamouni's valley of the wild
On which I gaze, from whence that glittering pile
Translucent as the stream is now beheld,
And which, upraised in mockery, seems to smile
Upon the summer's sun? Canst thou beguile
Our senses? Thou'rt not illusion's dream,
But the redundant offspring of the Alp,
Nursed in the lap of winter. . . .'

BROCKEDON, WILLIAM. CHATILLON, BREUIL, ST. THEODUL PASS, ZERMATT, VISP, SAAS, MONTE MORO PASS, MACUGNAGA, VOGOGNA, INTRA, LUVINO, LUGANO, PORLEZZA, MENAGGIO, CHIAVENNA, SPLÜGEN PASS, THUSIS, COIRE, WALLENSTADT, QUINTEN, RAGAZ, PFÄFERS, COIRE, THUSIS, SAN BERNARDINO PASS, MESOCCO, BELLINZONA, LOCARNO, BELLINZONA, AIROLO, ST. GOTTHARD PASS, ALTDORF, LUCERNE, BRUNIG PASS, MEIRIN-

GEN, GRIMSEL PASS, OBERGESTELEN, GRIES PASS, FORMAZZA, DOMODOSSOLA, SIMPLON PASS, BRIG, TURTMANN, SION, MARTIGNY, BEX, VEVEY, LAUSANNE NYON, ST. CERGUE

At Breuil the condition of the hut 'would have defied Hercules to sleep after his labours'. On his way over the St. Theodul pass he met three Englishmen (possibly Frank Walker among them) who were able then and there to supply him with some medicine of which he was in need.

CANDOLLE, AUGUSTIN PYRAME DE. GENEVA, NEUCHÂTEL, SOLEURE, ZOFINGEN, LUCERNE, SCHWYZ, ZUG, LUCERNE, SARNEN, BRUNIG PASS, BRIENZ, INTERLAKEN, ZWEISIMMEN, SAANEN, CHÂTEAU D'OEX, GENEVA

CLARK, EDMUND, & SHERWILL, MARKHAM. GENEVA, CHAMONIX, MONT BLANC

'On the evening before our departure, an English gentleman, full of the milk of human kindness, came to Captain Sherwill, saying, "So you are going upward, Sir?" "Think of it, Sir." "You'll be very cold." "So they say, Sir." "Wish I could be of any service!" "Sir, I thank you." "Afraid I can't: but stop! stay two seconds." The worthy gentleman vanished for an instant, and then re-appeared with a superb flannel night-cap. "There Sir", said he, holding up the night cap, with much benignity. "Take that, Sir; will be very serviceable, I assure you."'

COROT, CAMILLE. GENEVA, LAUSANNE, MARTIGNY

DOWNES, GEORGE. GENEVA, CHAMONIX, TÊTE NOIRE PASS, MARTIGNY, GENEVA, LAUSANNE, BERNE, THUN, INTERLAKEN, LAUTERBRUNNEN, KLEINE SCHEIDEGG, GRINDELWALD, INTERLAKEN, MEIRINGEN, BRUNIG PASS, LUCERNE, RIGI, ZURICH, RIGI, LUCERNE, ENTLIBUCH, BERNE, FRIBOURG, BULLE, GRUYÈRES, VEVEY, LAUSANNE, GENEVA, MARTIGNY, SION, BRIG, SIMPLON PASS, DOMODOSSOLA

Near Chamonix 'we beheld a description of animal rather frequent in these mountainous regions—not a chamois nor a lämmergeyer but —an Alpine dandy. He was fearfully rigged out for daring and desperate exploit, with belt, pole, and nicely embroidered jerkin—a costume admirably adapted for exciting female terror at the breakfast-table, and a reasonable apprehension that some formidable hillocks and rivulets would be encountered during the day, before the thing returned to preside over bread and butter at the vesper tea-table.'

HAZLITT, WILLIAM. DOMODOSSOLA, SIMPLON PASS, BRIG, SION, MARTIGNY, BEX, VEVEY, MARTIGNY, COL DE BALME, BASLE, CHAMONIX, GENEVA, LAUSANNE, VEVEY, YVERDON, NEUCHÂTEL, BIENNE, MOUTIER.

A literary pilgrimage to the scenes depicted by Rousseau whose friend Levade he met. In Sion Hazlitt asked whether there was any tradition of Rousseau having stayed; he was told 'that Monsieur Rousseau had never lived there, but that he had passed through about fourteen years before on his way to Italy, when he had only time to stop to take tea! Was this a mere stupid blunder, or one of the refractions of fame, founded on his mission as secretary to the Venetian ambassador a hundred years before?'

HOGG, THOMAS JEFFERSON. SCHAFFHAUSEN, ZURICH, RIGI, LUCERNE, ALTDORF, ST. GOTTHARD, WASSEN, SUSTEN PASS, GADMEN, MEIRINGEN, GROSSE SCHEIDEGG, GRINDELWALD, KLEINE SCHEIDEGG, LAUTERBRUNNEN, INTERLAKEN, THUN, BERNE, THUN, KANDERSTEG, GEMMI PASS, LEUK, SION, MARTIGNY, TÊTE NOIRE PASS, CHAMONIX, GENEVA, LAUSANNE, BEX, MARTIGNY, SION, BRIG, SIMPLON PASS, DOMODOSSOLA

'The Alps and glaciers exceed anything in sublimity that I co[d] possibly have imagined: I am never tired of looking at them.'

HUGO, VICTOR. GENEVA, CHAMONIX, TÊTE NOIRE PASS, MARTIGNY, BEX, GENEVA

'Les vallées des Alpes ont cela de remarquable, qu'elles sont en quelque sorte complètes. Chacune d'elles présente, souvent dans l'espace le plus borné, une espèce d'univers à part. Elles ont toutes leur aspect, leur forme, leur lumière, leurs bruits particuliers. On pourrait presque toujours résumer d'un mot l'effet général de leur physionomie. La vallée de Sallenches est un théâtre; la vallée de Servoz est un tombeau; la vallée de Chamonix est un temple.'

LA TROBE, CHARLES JAMES. NEUCHÂTEL, BERNE, THUN, STOCKHORN, INTERLAKEN, LAUTERBRUNNEN, KLEINE SCHEIDEGG, GRINDELWALD, GROSSE SCHEIDEGG, MEIRINGEN, GRIMSEL PASS, FURKA PASS, ANDERMATT, ALTDORF, RIGI, BRUNIG PASS, MEIRINGEN, GRIMSEL PASS, OBERGESTELEN, GRIES PASS, FORMAZZA, DOMODOSSOLA, SIMPLON PASS, BRIG, LEUK, GEMMI PASS, KANDERSTEG, ERLENBACH, STOCKHORN, ZWEISIMMEN, GSTAAD, GSTEIG, SANETSCH PASS, SION, MARTIGNY, LAUSANNE, NEUCHÂTEL

' I have seen a party of English arrive at a mountain cabaret at nightfall, when the host and his family would, in the usual course of things, have been thinking of their beds: they order dinner, and insist on having flesh, fish or fowl, foreign wines and liqueurs, just as though they were at the Star and Garter at Richmond; abuse the master and the domestics, dine at eight or nine, and sit over their cheer till past midnight.'

MARIE-AMÉLIE, QUEEN. ST. GENIS, VERSOIX, COPPET, GENEVA, NYON, LAUSANNE, BEX, MARTIGNY, SION, BRIG, SIMPLON PASS, DOMODOSSOLA, BAVENO, DOMODOSSOLA, SIMPLON PASS, BRIG, SION, MARTIGNY, EVIAN, THONON, GENEVA

'Nous sommes allés nous embarquer sur un bateau à vapeur nommé *le Léman.* C'était la première fois que je montais sur un bateau à vapeur et je n'étais pas trop rassurée. . . . Sur le bateau à vapeur, il faut faire attention à ne pas se mettre trop au milieu, afin d'éviter la chaleur de la machine qui est insupportable; quand le bateau est arrêté, le bruit causé par l'échappement de vapeur produit quelqu'inquiétude, mais sans motif sérieux.'

MEDWIN, THOMAS. GENEVA, CHAMONIX, VEVEY, BERNE, THUN, INTERLAKEN, GRINDELWALD

At Vevey Medwin called on Hazlitt who said: 'We passed some weeks at Brig, at the foot of the mountain; but I soon got sick of Alps and glaciers, and mean to make no excursions this summer. One range of alps is like another range of alps, one valley is like another valley; the eye can scarce distinguish the difference, so nearly alike are their features.'

MURRAY, JOHN. GENEVA, CHAMONIX, GENEVA, LAUSANNE, GENEVA, CHAMONIX, COL DE BALME, MARTIGNY, SION, BRIG, SIMPLON PASS, DOMODOSSOLA, MILAN, DOMODOSSOLA, SIMPLON PASS, BRIG, SION, MARTIGNY, GENEVA, NEUCHÂTEL, BERNE, THUN, INTERLAKEN, LAUTERBRUNNEN, GRINDELWALD, INTERLAKEN, MEIRINGEN, BRUNIG PASS, SARNEN, STANS, BECKENRIED, BRUNNEN, SCHWYZ, RIGI, ZURICH, BASLE

'We were not a little amused with a dandy, who somehow had got far out of his road, and wandered, not knowing whither he went. The cockney possessed all the inane folly of that listless tribe. Ennui had taken possession of his entire man, if indeed the term be not a misnomer. He bewailed his miserable lot—he seemed to have lost the log-book of his reckoning, and to be in a perfect maze. He thought he had certainly lost ten years of his (valuable) life by such an adventure, and doubtless, could he have procured Fortunatus's wishing cap, he would immediately have transported himself to Bond Street. He saw nothing in "Mount Blank", and wondered what others could see there to make such a fuss about.'

NODIER, CHARLES. GENEVA, CHAMONIX, TÊTE NOIRE PASS, MARTIGNY, GRAND ST. BERNARD, MARTIGNY, BEX, GENEVA

To pay for the journey which Victor Hugo and Nodier were proposing to make, Nodier had the idea of suggesting a book: 'Voyage poétique et pittoresque au Mont Blanc et à la Vallée de Chamonix', which they and Lamartine were to write, and Taylor was to illustrate. Nodier and Hugo each received 1,750 francs advance royalties, which just covered the cost of the journey. But the book was never written, for the publisher went bankrupt.

RAOUL-ROCHETTE, DÉSIRÉ. GESSENAY, GSTEIG, GENEVA, ST. GERVAIS, COL DU BONHOMME, COL DES FOURS, COL DE LA SEIGNE, COURMAYEUR, COL FERRET, COL DE FENÊTRE, GRAND ST. BERNARD, AOSTA

SHERER, COLONEL MOYLE. SCHAFFHAUSEN, ZURICH, ALBIS, ZUG, RIGI, LUCERNE, ALTDORF, ANDERMATT, FURKA PASS, HOSPENTHAL, ST. GOTTHARD PASS, BELLINZONA, LUGANO, PORLEZZA

'Dine where you will, some man has seen the Lake of Geneva and Montblanc; and you can ask no question about Switzerland at table, but some person is ready with a reply.' . . . 'The rules of travelling everywhere, but more especially in Switzerland, forbid either the joining or accosting others.'

STEVENSON, SETH WILLIAM. DOMODOSSOLA, SIMPLON PASS, BRIG, SION, MARTIGNY, TÊTE NOIRE PASS, CHAMONIX, COL DE BALME, MARTIGNY, LAUSANNE, GENEVA, YVERDON, PAYERNE, FRIBOURG, BERNE, THUN, INTERLAKEN, LAUTERBRUNNEN, GRINDELWALD, INTERLAKEN, MEIRINGEN, BRUNIG PASS, LUCERNE, RIGI, ZUG, ZURICH, SCHAFFHAUSEN

In the pass of the Tête Noire, Stevenson noted the inscription commemorating the purchase of a rock by Lord Porchester and Lady Georgina North. The French inscription was accompanied by a curious English version:

'Dunroc
Wheerever, wehatever fo see
Our hearts untervelted feundly turn to thee
Lady Georgina North, Lord Geutester
Un their returne from Italy, obteste May 10, 1821
These magnificent Reik end crested Chestever
Tablette commemorenti momenta pand' here,
bright, but soteling as the rep of the everes
Sun which gilded the branches of the surrounding trees.
And sure through many a varied scene
Un Kingne never came between.
May 10, 1821.
Farewell—A long farewell.'

TALLEYRAND, CHARLES MAURICE, PRINCE DE. GENEVA, COPPET

TRANT, CLARISSA. SCHAFFHAUSEN, ZURICH, WALLENSTADT, COIRE, THUSIS, SPLÜGEN PASS, CHIAVENNA

1826

ANONYMOUS 9. BASLE, SCHAFFHAUSEN, ST. GALL, APPENZELL, SCHWYZ, RIGI, ZURICH, LUCERNE, BRUNIG PASS, MEIRINGEN, GRIMSEL, MEIRINGEN, GROSSE SCHEIDEGG, GRINDELWALD

At the inn at Meiringen, a guest was drawing a cork with the corkscrew of his pocket-knife of which a blade was open. Another guest beseeched him to shut the blade, saying that he was reminded of a terrible occasion when a bridegroom, drawing a cork in this manner, plunged the blade straight into his bride's breast when the cork came out, and then, overcome with grief, into his own. One of the listeners to this tragic tale promptly fainted with horror, and the waiter said: 'That is very strange: very strange.' 'Why?' he was asked. 'Because the gentleman who has fainted is the executioner of Berne.'

BODDINGTON, MRS. (*c*). SCHAFFHAUSEN, BADEN, BERNE, THUN, INTERLAKEN, LAUTERBRUNNEN, GRINDELWALD, INTERLAKEN, BRIENZ, GRIMSEL, MEIRINGEN, INTERLAKEN, BERNE, EMMENTHAL, LUCERNE, ZUG, EINSIEDELN, GLARUS, WALLENSTADT, COIRE, THUSIS, SPLÜGEN PASS, CHIAVENNA, MILAN, DOMODOSSOLA, SIMPLON PASS, BRIG, SION, MARTIGNY, LAUSANNE, ORBE, VALLORBE

At the village of Splügen, with a prevision of winter sports seasons. 'The landlord expatiates on the winter gaieties of his village; fireside gossiping, I suppose, or wine bibbing, or perhaps sledge races, perhaps balls. Our question of, "Que faites vous ici l'hiver?" has often been answered by "nous avons de jolis bals", in worse places than Splügen.'

BONAPARTE, PRINCE LOUIS NAPOLEON. ARENENBERG, ARBON, RORSCHACH, FELDKIRCH, COIRE, THUSIS, SAN BERNARDINO PASS, MESOCCO, BELLINZONA, LUGANO

BONINGTON, RICHARD PARKES. GENEVA, ST. GINGOLPH, ST. MAURICE, MARTIGNY, SION, BRIG, SIMPLON PASS, DOMODOSSOLA

At Brig he and his companion Rivet hoped to rest after four days in a diligence. But they were roused at two in the morning to start their journey over the Simplon, owing to the danger from avalanches.

CARNE, JOHN. THUN, WIMMIS, INTERLAKEN, LAUTERBRUNNEN, THUN, WEISSENBURG, ZWEISIMMEN, SAANEN, ROUGEMONT, CHÂTEAU D'OEX, GRUYÈRES, ZWEISIMMEN, THUN, KANDERSTEG, GEMMI PASS, LEUK, SION, SANETSCH PASS, GSTEIG, ZWEISIMMEN, THUN, INTERLAKEN, LAUTERBRUNNEN, KLEINE SCHEIDEGG, GRINDELWALD, FAULHORN, GROSSE SCHEIDEGG, MEIRINGEN, GRIMSEL PASS, GLETSCH, MEIRINGEN, BRIENZ, INTERLAKEN, THUN, BERNE, THUN, FRUTIGEN, ZWEISIMMEN, SAANEN, MONTBOVON, BULLE, VEVEY, EVIAN, LAUSANNE, GENEVA, MARTIGNY, GRAND ST. BERNARD, MARTIGNY, VEVEY

'The hamlet of Lauterbrunnen was half buried in the snow, and part of the roof and the chimney of the auberge were seen mocking the traveller as he passed. We wished to have proceeded to the Schmadri bach, but it was impossible. . . .'

CARTER, N. H. DOMODOSSOLA, SIMPLON PASS, BRIG, TURTMANN, SION, MARTIGNY, EVIAN, GENEVA, VEVEY, LAUSANNE, GENEVA, ROLLE, ST. CERGUE

CHATEAUBRIAND, FRANÇOIS RENÉ DE. GENEVA, LAUSANNE

'Je commençai à Lausanne les "Remarques" sur le premier ouvrage de ma vie, "L'Essai sur les révolutions anciennes et modernes". Je voyais de mes fenêtres ces rochers de Meillerie: Rousseau, écrivais-je dans une de ces Remarques, n'est décidément au-dessus des auteurs de son temps que dans une soixantaine de lettres de la "Nouvelle Héloïse", dans quelques pages des ses "Rêveries" et de ses "Confessions".'

CUSTINE, DELPHINE, MARQUISE DE. GENEVA, LAUSANNE, BEX

Of his interview with Delphine at Geneva, Chateaubriand wrote:—'I have seen her who confronted the scaffold with such courage. Whiter than fate, dressed in black, her figure wasted by death, her head dressed in its own unique silken adornment, I have seen her smile at me with her pale lips and her fair teeth, when she left Secherons, near Geneva, to breathe her last at Bex, at the entrance to the Valais.'

DISRAELI, BENJAMIN. GENEVA, MARTIGNY, SION, BRIG, SIMPLON PASS, DOMODOSSOLA

'At the termination of the Jura ridge which bounds one side of the plain of Geneva, did I on Friday morning witness the most magnificent sight in the world—the whole range of the high Alps with Mont Blanc in the centre without a cloud; the effect was so miraculous that for a long time I did not perceive the lovely scene under me, the plain and city and lake of Geneva.' At Geneva Disraeli employed Byron's boatman, Maurice.

DUVILLARD, LOUIS. LAUSANNE, VILLENEUVE, BEX, MARTIGNY, SION, BRIG, SIMPLON PASS, DOMODOSSOLA

'Montreux qui est un charmant village dont les maisons sont un peu trop entassées. . . .'

ERSKINE, THOMAS. GENEVA, COPPET, MARTIGNY, SION, BRIG, SIMPLON PASS, DOMODOSSOLA

'Oh! it is a land of beauty, this—of beauty that thrills the heart. I can weep at will whilst I look at it—I have spent this day among the sanctities of nature—amongst glens and green glades, and water-falls and towering rocks, and autumnal colours, and fallen leaves and gushing springs. There is something delightful in coming upon a fine water-fall by surprise, as it were, unconducted to it even by a footpath, so that you may almost consider yourself as the discoverer of it.'

FORBES, JAMES DAVID. GENEVA, CHAMONIX

'I conversed with the memorable guide "Le Géant". I considered his information as peculiarly valuable, for when he and one or two others are dead, (and he is nearly 70), all living record of some of the most daring and interesting adventures that have ever been made will be gone. He was of the second party that ever reached the summit of the highest European Alp. . . .'

LA TROBE, CHARLES JAMES. NEUCHÂTEL, CHASSERAL, BERNE, THUN, DIEMTIGTHAL, GRIMMIAP, LENK, RAWYL PASS, SION, MARTIGNY, GRAND ST. BERNARD PASS, AOSTA, PETIT ST. BERNARD PASS, BOURG ST. MAURICE, COL DU BONHOMME, ST. GERVAIS, GENEVA, MONTREUX, COL DE JAMAN, CHÂTEAU D'OEX, ZWEISIMMEN, THUN, BERNE, NEUCHÂTEL, BERNE, THUN, INTERLAKEN, BRIENZ, BRUNIG PASS, SARNEN, STANS, BRUNNEN, SCHWYZ, EINSIEDELN, HERISAU, ALTSTÄTTEN, SARGANS, GLARUS, PRAGEL PASS, SCHWYZ, GERSAU, BUOCHS, SARNEN, BRUNIG PASS, MEIRINGEN, BRIENZ, INTERLAKEN, LEISSIGEN, AESCHI, WIMMIS, ERLENBACH, BERNE, NEUCHÂTEL

'I heard a poor gentleman, in a chamber boarded off from the one I had the honour to occupy, sigh and groan aloud, at intervals, from bed-time till about one o'clock; and if any doubts had possessed my mind, respecting the cause of his disquietude, it was effectually removed, when, just after the bell of the Jesuits' church had tolled one, his patience gave way, and I was electrified, by hearing a thundering imprecation in good English, followed by the pathetic complaint—"they bite like the Devil".'

NECKER, LOUIS ALBERT. GENEVA, CHAMONIX

SENNONES, VICOMTE DE. SARGANS, COIRE, THUSIS, ANDEER, AVERS CRESTA, THUSIS, TIEFENKASTEL, FILISUR, BERGÜN, ALBULA PASS, PONTE, ST. MORITZ, MALOJA PASS, CHIAVENNA, SPLÜGEN PASS, THUSIS, REICHENAU, DISENTIS, OBERALP PASS, ANDERMATT

STUDER, GOTTLIEB. BERNE, GRINDELWALD, FAULHORN, GROSSE SCHEIDEGG, MEIRINGEN, JOCH PASS, ENGELBERG, STANS

THOMSON, WILLIAM. LUGANO, BELLINZONA, AMBRI-PIOTTA, ST. GOTTHARD PASS, ALTDORF, LUCERNE, BASLE

TÖPFFER, RODOLPHE. GENEVA, BURGDORF, ZOFINGEN, LUCERNE, RIGI

In 1823 Töpffer started a school of his own at Geneva for boys of every nationality. Each summer the holidays took the form of a walking tour in the Alps, an account of which he wrote and illustrated.

TRANT, CLARISSA. GENEVA, YVERDON, NEUCHÂTEL, ILE ST. PIERRE, BIENNE, MOUTIER, BASLE

'A steamboat has just been established on the lake of Neuchâtel, and by a singular chance we were the first English who had hitherto embarked in her. The Mechanics are English and one of them was accompanied by his wife, a pretty simple little Manchester girl, for whom we succeeded in procuring a good situation in the vessel. It is very doubtful whether this steamboat will repay the expense of the undertaking as the poor people of Yverdun and Neufchâtel are very cautious of committing their precious selves to the discretion of fire and smoke.'

WALTER, WEEVER. BASLE, HAUENSTEIN, SOLEURE, BERNE, FRIBOURG, VEVEY, BEX, MARTIGNY, COL DE BALME, CHAMONIX, TÊTE NOIRE PASS, MARTIGNY, VEVEY, COL DE JAMAN, CHÂTEAU D'OEX, ROUGEMONT, GESSENAY, ZWEISIMMEN, SPIEZ, INTERLAKEN, LAUTERBRUNNEN, KLEINE SCHEIDEGG, GRINDELWALD, GROSSE SCHEIDEGG, MEIRINGEN, BRIENZ, INTERLAKEN, BOLTIGEN, JAUN PASS, BULLE, VEVEY, MARTIGNY, SION, BRIG, SIMPLON PASS, DOMODOSSOLA

Col de Balme:—'Taken all in all this is perhaps one of the finest views in Switzerland, yet there is something wanting: it is nature in its grandest form; but it is inanimate nature: not a living thing, not a human habitation is visible, with the exception of the distant village of Chamouni.'

WIELAND, COLONEL. BASLE, LES RANGIERS, MOUTIER, BIENNE, MORAT, BERNE, THUN, ZWEISIMMEN, SAANEN, CHÂTEAU D'OEX, GRUYÈRES, BULLE, PAYERNE, VUILLY, AARBERG, SOLEURE, WEISSENSTEIN, DELÉMONT, BASLE

1827

ANGELO, HENRY. DOMODOSSOLA, SIMPLON PASS, BRIG, SION, MARTIGNY, EVIAN, THONON, GENEVA

'As I stood alone, I was seized with an awful species of fear, and was so lost in veneration and amazement, that I might have tumbled headlong from where I stood.'

AULDJO, JOHN. GENEVA, CHAMONIX, MONT BLANC, GENEVA

'I had provided a bottle of champagne, being desirous to see how this wine would be affected by the rarity of the air. I also wished to drink to the prosperity of the inhabitants of the world beneath me; for I could believe that there were no human beings so elevated as we were at that moment. The wire being removed, and the string cut, the cork flew out to a great distance, but the noise could hardly be heard. The wine rolled out in the most luxuriant foam, frothing to the very last drop, and we all drank of it with zest; but not three minutes had elapsed when repentance and pain followed; for the rapid escape of the fixed air which it still contained produced a choking and stifling sensation.'

BALL, JOHN. GENEVA, CHAMONIX

'We reached the top of the Col de la Faucille just before sunset. The sky was almost cloudless. We all got out. I managed to get a little apart from the others, and remained fixed for almost half an hour. The light gradually stole upwards from the lake over the nearer mountains, and then over the Savoy Alps, and finally the peak of Mont Blanc alone remained illumined. One little cloud only hung just over the peak. As the peak also became dim, the cloud remained like a glory over its head. For long years that scene recurred constantly to my mind, whether asleep or awake, and perhaps nothing has had so great an influence on my entire life.'

BERTOLOTTI, DAVIDE. ANNEXY, BONNEVILLE, CHAMONIX, CLUSES, SAMOËNS, SIXT, ST. JEOIRE, THONON, EVIAN, GENEVA

'To go from Geneva to Chamonix, ascend Montenvers, step on to the Mer de Glace, visit the source of the Arveyron and the Glacier des Bois, and then to retrace one's steps to Geneva, used to be a journey of some magnitude. Now it is the tour of the timid Frenchman; a true Englishwoman would be ashamed to content herself with it. Frail English girls scale peaks on to which, once, love of knowledge was barely able to attract ardent naturalists.'

BRUNNER, SAMUEL. ZERMATT

CARNE, JOHN. VEVEY, MARTIGNY, SION, BRIG, SIMPLON PASS, DOMODOSSOLA—DOMODOSSOLA, SIMPLON PASS, BRIG, SION, MARTIGNY, CHAMONIX, GENEVA, LAUSANNE, BERNE, THUN, INTERLAKEN, BRIENZ, BRUNIG PASS, LUCERNE, FLUELEN, BRUNNEN, SCHWYZ, EINSIEDELN, LUCERNE, BASLE

'The mountains on the opposite side of the valley rose in pointed and fantastic shapes, that looked, as the flood of yellow light rolled on them, like the minarets and cupolas of a gigantic eastern temple, whose domes are a mass of shade. On the spotless sides and summits of Mont Blanc the light grew more deep and fiery towards its close, and several times, when its breast had become a vast and white wilderness, the purple hues returned with a still fiercer glow, as if revelling in their beautiful resting places.'

CUCHETAT, CHARLES. BASLE, SCHAFFHAUSEN, ZURICH, ALBIS, ZUG, RIGI, LUCERNE, FLUELEN, ALTDORF, ANDERMATT, FURKA PASS, GRIMSEL PASS, MEIRINGEN, BRIENZ, INTERLAKEN, LAUTERBRUNNEN, THUN, KANDERSTEG, GEMMI PASS, LEUK, SION, MARTIGNY, TÊTE NOIRE PASS, CHAMONIX, GENEVA

FELLOWS, SIR CHARLES, & HAWES, W. SCHAFFHAUSEN, ZURICH, SCHWYZ, RIGI, LUCERNE, FLUELEN, ST. GOTTHARD PASS, BELLINZONA, LOCARNO, BAVENO, DOMODOSSOLA, SIMPLON PASS, BRIG, LEUK,

GEMMI PASS, KANDERSTEG, HOHTHÜRLI PASS, KIENTHAL, INTERLAKEN, BRIENZ, INTERLAKEN, THUN, BERNE, FRIBOURG, LAUSANNE, VEVEY, BEX, MARTIGNY, TÊTE NOIRE PASS, CHAMONIX, MONT BLANC, GENEVA

GRAY, ROBERT. LAUSANNE, VEVEY, CHILLON, BERNE, SCHAFFHAUSEN, ZURICH, ZUG, RIGI, WEGGIS, FLUELEN, ANDERMATT, FURKA PASS, GRIMSEL PASS, MEIRINGEN, INTERLAKEN, THUN, FRIBOURG, LAUSANNE, CHAMONIX, MARTIGNY, GRAND ST. BERNARD PASS, AOSTA, COURMAYEUR, GRAND ST. BERNARD PASS, MARTIGNY, LAUSANNE

HUGI, FRANZ JOSEPH. SOLEURE, BERNE, THUN, INTERLAKEN, LAUTERBRUNNEN, MEIRINGEN, GRIMSEL PASS, UNTERAAR GLACIER

LA TROBE, CHARLES JAMES. NEUCHÂTEL, BERNE, THUN, ERLENBACH, BERNE, NEUCHÂTEL

'Still one tranquil day among the Alps! A clear cloudless, winter's day; the sun shining for a few hours with almost insufferable brightness upon the snows which now covered all objects, from the margin of the Simmen, to the far peaks of the Niesen and Bettfluh rising above their endless waste of frozen pastures, except where the pine forest and precipices afforded points for the eye to rest upon amidst the dazzling brilliance of the scene.' (February.)

LIDDIARD, WILLIAM. GENEVA, CHAMONIX, COL DE BALME, MARTIGNY, VEVEY, GENEVA, LAUSANNE, MORAT, BERNE, THUN, INTERLAKEN, LAUTERBRUNNEN, KLEINE SCHEIDEGG, GRINDELWALD, GROSSE SCHEIDEGG, MEIRINGEN, BRUNIG PASS, LUCERNE, RIGI, ALTDORF, ANDERMATT, ST. GOTTHARD, ALTDORF, BRUNNEN, SCHWYZ, EINSIEDELN, LUCERNE, WILLISAU, BERNE, MORAT, LAUSANNE, GENEVA

MICHAELIS, ERNST HANS. LIESTAL, BADEN, ZURICH, ZUG, RIGI, ALTDORF, HOSPENTHAL, FURKA PASS, GRIMSEL PASS, MEIRINGEN, GROSSE SCHEIDEGG, GRINDELWALD, INTERLAKEN, THUN

SINCLAIR, J. D. GENEVA, LAUSANNE, MARTIGNY, SION, BRIG, SIMPLON PASS, DOMODOSSOLA, LUGANO, PORLEZZA

STEIN, CHRISTIAN GOTTFRIED DANIEL. RORSCHACH, ST. GALL, WINTERTHUR, ZURICH, ALBIS, ZUG, SCHWYZ, BRUNNEN, ALTDORF, LUCERNE, SURSEE, HINDELBANK, BERNE, THUN, INTERLAKEN, LAUTERBRUNNEN, KLEINE SCHEIDEGG, GRINDELWALD, GROSSE SCHEIDEGG, MEIRINGEN, BRIENZ, INTERLAKEN, THUN, BERNE, MORAT, FRIBOURG, LAUSANNE, GENEVA, MARTIGNY, SION, MARTIGNY, BEX, VEVEY, ST. SAPHORIN, LAC DE JOUX, ORBE, YVERDON, NEUCHÂTEL, BIENNE, SOLEURE, ZOFINGEN, AARAU, BADEN, EGLISAU, CONSTANCE

'Everybody whose head and heart are in the right place makes a pilgrimage to the Bernese Oberland.'

STUDER, GOTTLIEB. BERNE, THUN, INTERLAKEN, LAUTERBRUNNEN, KLEINE SCHEIDEGG, GRINDELWALD, GROSSE SCHEIDEGG, MEIRINGEN, BRUNIG PASS, SACHSELN, MELCHTAL, JÜCHLI PASS, ENGELBERG, STANS

TWINING, RICHARD. LUCERNE, SUMISWALD, THUN, INTERLAKEN, GRINDELWALD, BERNE, LAUSANNE, GENEVA, CHAMONIX, TÊTE NOIRE PASS, MARTIGNY, SION, BRIG, SIMPLON PASS, DOMODOSSOLA

Sumiswald: 'Here we have a complete specimen of a Swiss inn. Nothing can be more clean, neat and comfortable. . . . The piano was by far the best we have met with since leaving England.'

VALÉRY, M. GENEVA, CHAMONIX, COL DE BALME, MARTIGNY, LAUSANNE, GENEVA, EVIAN, MARTIGNY, SION, BRIG, SIMPLON PASS, DOMODOSSOLA

WALTER, WEEVER. COMO, CHIAVENNA, SPLÜGEN PASS, THUSIS, COIRE, SARGANS, SENNWALD, ALTSTÄTTEN, RHEINECK, CONSTANCE, SCHAFFHAUSEN

WILKIE, SIR DAVID. GENEVA, CHAMONIX, GENEVA, MARTIGNY, GRAND ST. BERNARD, MARTIGNY, GENEVA

1828

BROWN, YEATS. LAUTERBRUNNEN, ROTHTAL

An attempt on the Jungfrau with Frederick Slade.

CARUS, C. G. DOMODOSSOLA, SIMPLON PASS, BRIG, SION, MARTIGNY, COL DE BALME, CHAMONIX, GENEVA, LAUSANNE, MORAT, BERNE, THUN, INTERLAKEN, LAUTERBRUNNEN, KLEINE SCHEIDEGG, GRINDELWALD, GROSSE SCHEIDEGG, MEIRINGEN, SUSTEN PASS, WASSEN, AMSTEG, ALTDORF, FLUELEN, WEGGIS, RIGI, ZUG, ZURICH, EGLISAU, SCHAFFHAUSEN

'I had to shut my eyes and return in thought to the wonderful view of that morning on the glacier des Bossons. Are not glaciers the originals of the transparent crystal fairy castles of which one reads with so much pleasure when a child?'

CHATEAUBRIAND, FRANÇOIS RENÉ DE. GENEVA, LAUSANNE, MARTIGNY, SION, BRIG, SIMPLON PASS, DOMODOSSOLA

'Les rochers, dont la base s'étendait noircie à mes pieds, resplendissaient de rose au haut de la montagne, frappés des rayons du soleil.'

COOPER, JAMES FENIMORE. LES VERRIÈRES, NEUCHÂTEL, BERNE, THUN, INTERLAKEN, LAUTERBRUNNEN, KLEINE SCHEIDEGG, GRINDELWALD, GROSSE SCHEIDEGG, MEIRINGEN, INTERLAKEN, BERNE, BADEN, SCHAFFHAUSEN, RORSCHACH, ALTSTÄTTEN, GAIS, ST. GALL, HERISAU, ZURICH,

ALBIS, ZUG, RIGI, LUCERNE, LANGNAU, BERNE, THUN, INTERLAKEN, BRIENZ, BRUNIG PASS, STANS, BRUNNEN, SCHWYZ, EINSIEDELN, GLARUS, WALLENSTADT, COIRE, DISENTIS, OBERALP PASS, ANDERMATT, FURKA PASS, GRIMSEL PASS, MEIRINGEN, INTERLAKEN, BERNE, MORAT, LAUSANNE, GENEVA, MARTIGNY, SION, BRIG, SIMPLON PASS, DOMODOSSOLA

At Thun the author of *The Last of the Mohicans* saw a friend of his, a captain in the Swiss army, marching at the head of his men, and, 'in obedience to an intimation that it would be permitted, I joined him in the march, in order to inquire after my family; and thus, you will see, I have had the honour of serving in the Swiss ranks'.

HOBHOUSE, JOHN CAM (LORD BROUGHTON). GENEVA, CLARENS, CHILLON, BEX, MARTIGNY, SION, LEUK, GEMMI PASS, KANDERSTEG, SPIEZ, INTERLAKEN, KANDERSTEG, GEMMI PASS, LEUK, BRIG, SIMPLON PASS, DOMODOSSOLA

'Drove over with Lord and Lady Tweeddale to the other side of the lake, and went by the back of the Villa Diodati, and found nothing changed but myself.' After this pilgrimage to the scene of 1816, he visited his sister Catherine Fane and her husband at Interlaken.

HUGI, FRANZ JOSEPH. SOLEURE, BERNE, THUN, INTERLAKEN, LAUTERBRUNNEN, KLEINE SCHEIDEGG, GRINDELWALD, GROSSE SCHEIDEGG, ROSENLAUI, URBACHSATTEL, MEIRINGEN, GRIMSEL PASS, OBERAARJOCH, HUGISATTEL, GRIMSEL PASS, OBERGESTELEN, VIESCH, MÄRJELENSEE, LAAX, BINN, ULRICHEN, NUFENEN PASS, AIROLO, ST. GOTTHARD PASS, WASSEN, SUSTEN PASS, MEIRINGEN, INTERLAKEN, BERNE, SOLEURE

Hugi's expedition to the Rothtal numbered forty persons, equipped with thermometers, barometers, instruments for boiling water, butter, oil and petrol, aërometers, chronometers, hygrometers, clinometers, crampons, sacs of wine and flasks of brandy, compasses, hooks, grapples, wire, rope, a travelling medicine-chest, plasters, eye-salve, lead ointment, foot ointment, and bootblacking. In spite of all this, however, he was not successful in his attempt to climb the Jungfrau.

MALMESBURY, EARL OF. BASLE, GENEVA, MARTIGNY, SION, BRIG, SIMPLON PASS, DOMODOSSOLA

Geneva: 'The luxurious hotels of later times were not thought of, and the best, but a very old-fashioned one the "Balances", received us. It is the same in which Casanova's romance with his Henriette took place, and they showed the pane of glass, which he mentions, on which he had cut her name with his ring.'

MAUDE, THOMAS. GENEVA, VILLENEUVE, CLARENS, GENEVA, CHAMONIX, GRAND ST. BERNARD, LUCERNE, RIGI, ZURICH, SCHAFFHAUSEN

'The blowing of the trumpet summoned, at a moment, nearly thirty ladies and gentlemen from their slumbers to the chilling top of the mount. Out of every window and door of the well-filled little auberge you saw, at the same instant, numerous fair and manly figures egressing—half clad, and shivering in the morning air, yet fearful of losing any part of the grand solar exhibition. Dutch, Swiss, French, Prussian, and English, came jumping out (as if they were *possessed*),—half asleep and bewildered.'

MICHAELIS, ERNST HANS. SCHAFFHAUSEN, AARAU, SOLEURE, BERNE, CHÂTEAU D'OEX, COL DES MOSSES, AIGLE, BEX, PAS DE CHEVILLE, SION, RIDDES, PIERRE À VOIR, CHABLE, COL DU CRET, EVOLENA, SION, SIERRE, ST. LUC, PAS DU BŒUF, TURTMANN, VISP, ZERMATT, ALLALIN PASS, SAAS, VISP, LEUK, SION, MARTIGNY, VEVEY, MORAT, BASLE

ROGER, ALEXANDRE SALOMON. NYON, LEUKERBAD, SION, MARTIGNY, TÊTE NOIRE PASS, VALLORCINE

ROHRDORF, CASPAR. BERNE, THUN, INTERLAKEN, GRINDELWALD, MÖNCHJOCH, JUNGFRAUJOCH

Rohrdorf got no farther than the Jungfraujoch, but after he had gone to Berne intending to return and make another attempt on the Jungfrau, his guides, without waiting for him, succeeded in making the third ascent of the mountain.

SAUVAN, M. GENEVA, MARTIGNY, SION, VISP, ZERMATT, STALDEN, SAAS, MONTE MORO, VISP, BRIG, FURKA PASS.

'Les étrangers aiment mieux admirer les grands spectacles de la nature dans l'oberland Bernois ou dans la vallée de Chamouni; on peut y pénétrer sans peine, et l'on y trouve toutes ces aisances de la vie qui acquièrent encore là un nouveau prix par le contraste. Au Mont-Rosa, au contraire, tout est difficultés, tout est privations. Les pentes sont roides, on y manque de sentiers tracés, et vers la fin d'une journée qui fut marquée par des fatigues et des périls, on ne rencontre, pour se reposer que des misérables chalets ouverts à tous les vents.'

TÖPFFER, RODOLPHE. GENEVA, COL D'ANTERNE, CHAMONIX

'In the course of an ascent it often happens that the elbow of the path one is on disappears from view before one is able to see the zigzag on which the path will continue. There comes a point where the path resembles a plank; sheer in front, sheer behind, and sheer on the right or the left; the vision becomes fascinated, imagination runs riot, and giddiness comes. If it is only momentary, all is well. But if it grows, then the heart thumps, the head goes round, the legs shake, and, incapable of moving forwards or backwards, of sitting down or standing up, the most self-assured grenadier in the world is changed into a lump from which is heard: "come and get me out; come very quickly and get me out." . . . Parents, encourage your sons to climb trees. . . .'

1829

AGASSIZ, L. VALLORBE, LAUSANNE, GENEVA, VEVEY, COL DE JAMAN, CHÂTEAU D'OEX, SAANEN, ZWEISIMMEN, INTERLAKEN, LAUTERBRUNNEN, GRINDELWALD, GROSSE SCHEIDEGG, MEIRINGEN, BRUNIG PASS, LUCERNE, RIGI, ALTDORF, ANDERMATT, FURKA PASS, OBERGESTELEN, BRIG, SION, MARTIGNY, LAUSANNE, FRIBOURG, BERNE, AARBURG, ZURICH, SCHAFFHAUSEN, AARAU, SOLEURE, BIENNE, ILE ST. PIERRE, NEUCHÂTEL, LA CHAUX DE FONDS, LE LOCLE, MOTIERS-TRAVERS, STE. CROIX, VALLORBE, LAUSANNE, GENEVA, CHAMONIX, COL DE BALME, MARTIGNY, GRAND ST. BERNARD, MARTIGNY, BEX, LAUSANNE

The Spanish proverb may be paraphrased: 'He who has not seen Switzerland has seen nothing!'

ARNOLD, THOMAS. ST. CERGUE

'How completely is the Jura like Cithaeron, with its napai and leimones, and all that scenery which Euripides has given to the life in the Bacchae. Immediately beyond the post-house at St. Cergues, the view opens,—one that I never saw surpassed, nor can I ever.'

BRUNNER, SAMUEL. BERNE, THUN, KANDERSTEG, LÖTSCHEN PASS, FERDEN, VISP, SAAS, MONTE MORO PASS, MACUGNAGA, FORMAZZA, GRIES PASS, OBERGESTELEN, GRIMSEL PASS, MEIRINGEN, INTERLAKEN, THUN, BERNE

BUNBURY, SIR HENRY EDWARD. GENEVA, LAUSANNE, BERNE, THUN, INTERLAKEN, LAUTERBRUNNEN, KLEINE SCHEIDEGG, GRINDELWALD, GROSSE SCHEIDEGG, MEIRINGEN, COIRE, THUSIS, SPLÜGEN PASS, CHIAVENNA, DOMODOSSOLA, SIMPLON PASS, BRIG, ZURICH

COBBETT, JAMES P. DOMODOSSOLA, SIMPLON PASS, BRIG, SION, MARTIGNY, GRAND ST. BERNARD, MARTIGNY, LAUSANNE, GENEVA

FÉE, A. L. A. GENEVA, CHAMONIX, COL DE BALME, MARTIGNY, LAUSANNE, FRIBOURG, BERNE, NEUCHÂTEL, ILE ST. PIERRE, NEUVEVILLE, NEUCHÂTEL, LA CHAUX DE FONDS, LE LOCLE, LES BRENETS

At the Hotel at Chamonix, two Englishmen had summoned the Chief guide to complain of the conduct of their guide who had refused to take them to the Jardin. He was Jacques Balmat.

HOUGHTON, RICHARD MONCKTON MILNES, LORD. CHAMONIX, INTERLAKEN

'Within the Switzer's varied land,
When Summer chases high the snow,
You'll meet with many a youthful band
Of strangers wande'ring to and fro: . . .'

HUGI, FRANZ JOSEPH. SOLEURE, BERNE, THUN, INTERLAKEN, LAUTERBRUNNEN, PETERSGRAT, KIPPEL, LÖTSCHENLÜCKE PASS, MÄRJELENSEE, VIESCH, ULRICHEN, ULRICHERJOCH PASS, GRIMSEL, OBERAARJOCH PASS, FINSTERAARHORN, GRIMSEL, MEIRINGEN, BRUNIG PASS, STANS, RIGI, LUCERNE, PILATUS, ENTLIBUCH, BERNE, SOLEURE

Hugi's guides Leuthold and Währen made the first ascent of the Finsteraarhorn, while Hugi himself reached a point a couple of hundred feet below.

JOHNSON, JAMES. GENEVA, LAUSANNE, MARTIGNY, SION, BRIG, SIMPLON PASS, DOMODOSSOLA

'Let no one expect that the scenery of Switzerland or of Italy can confer anything like lasting pleasure, without a regular avocation or pursuit. On the contrary, the stronger the impression made by these or any other countries at first—and the more sensibly their beauties are felt—the sooner will the excitement and gratification be over—and the more irksome will be the satiety which must inevitably ensue.'

ROGER, ALEXANDRE SALOMON. NYON, EVIAN, DENT D'OCHE, LEYSIN, COL DES MOSSES, CHÂTEAU D'OEX, MOLÉSON, VEVEY, NYON

WILLIAMS, CHARLES, J. B. ST. CERGUE, NYON, VEVEY, MARTIGNY, COL DE BALME, CHAMONIX, TÊTE NOIRE PASS, MARTIGNY, VEVEY, LAUSANNE

1830

BODDINGTON, MRS. LES VERRIÈRES, NEUCHÂTEL, BERNE, THUN, INTERLAKEN, GRINDELWALD, MEIRINGEN, GRIMSEL PASS, FURKA PASS, ANDERMATT, ALTDORF, BUOCHS, SARNEN, BRUNIG PASS, MEIRINGEN, INTERLAKEN, THUN, BERNE, ST. URBAN, LUCERNE, RIGI, LUCERNE, ZOFINGEN, AARBURG, BASLE

CANDOLLE, AUGUSTIN PYRAME DE. GENEVA, BERNE, AARAU, SCHINZNACH, ZURICH, WINTERTHUR, ST. GALL, TROGEN, GAIS, ST. GALL, UZNACH, RAPPERSWIL, EINSIEDELN, SCHWYZ, ALTDORF, ZUG, LUCERNE, LANGNAU, BERNE, GENEVA

Lady Stamford Raffles accompanied de Candolle on part of this tour. At Einsiedeln she played the organ and the people who filled the church, not suspecting that the organist was a heretic, promptly started to pray.

ENGELHARDT, CHRISTIAN MORITZ. BERNE, THUN, INTERLAKEN, MEIRINGEN, GRIMSEL PASS, FURKA PASS, ANDERMATT, ALTDORF, RIGI, LUCERNE, ZURICH, SCHAFFHAUSEN

GREVILLE, CHARLES C. F. DOMODOSSOLA, SIMPLON PASS, BRIG, SION, MARTIGNY, EVIAN, GENEVA

HUGI, FRANZ JOSEPH. SOLEURE, BERNE, THUN, INTERLAKEN, GRINDELWALD, MEIRINGEN, GRIMSEL PASS, UNTERAAR GLACIER

INGLIS, H. D. BASLE, ZURICH, ZUG, EINSIEDELN, GLARUS, WALLENSTADT, COIRE, FILISUR, BERGÜN, ALBULA PASS, PONTE, SCHULS, MARTINSBRUCK, PONTE, ALBULA PASS, FILISUR, COIRE, DISENTIS, OBERALP PASS, ANDERMATT, ALTDORF, LUCERNE, BERNE, THUN, INTERLAKEN, LAUTERBRUNNEN, KLEINE SCHEIDEGG, GRINDELWALD, INTERLAKEN, ZWEISIMMEN, SAANEN, CHÂTEAU D'OEX, COL DE JAMAN, VEVEY, GENEVA

LA TROBE, CHARLES JAMES. ERLENBACH, INTERLAKEN, BRIENZ, BRUNIG PASS, SARNEN, GERSAU, SCHWYZ, PRAGEL PASS, GLARUS, WALLENSTADT, COIRE, LENZERHEIDE, TIEFENKASTEL, JULIER PASS, ST. MORITZ, SCHULS, MARTINSBRUCK—STELVIO PASS, UMBRAIL PASS, STA. MARIA, OFEN PASS, ZERNEZ, ZUOZ, PONTE, ALBULA PASS, ALVANEU, LENZERHEIDE, COIRE, DISENTIS, OBERALP PASS, ANDERMATT, WASSEN, SUSTEN PASS, MEIRINGEN, INTERLAKEN, ERLENBACH

At Zuoz, Latrobe had to spend the night in a room with a man and his wife. 'Kept awake, my unwonted position condemned me to be witness to such constant snarling, grunting, and snorting, on the part of the man;—and sighing, wheezing, complaining, and general uneasiness, on the part of the woman, as alternately excited my smiles, wrath, and commiseration.'

MANZONI, GIULIETTA. SAN BERNARDINO, SAN BERNARDINO PASS, SPLÜGEN, ANDEER, SAN BERNARDINO, ST. MORITZ

MICHELET, JULES. DOMODOSSOLA, SIMPLON PASS, BRIG, SION, MARTIGNY, LAUSANNE, VALLORBE

'En montant au-dessus du village de Simplon, nature nue et plus hostile — neige rare, neige fréquente — montagne blanche avec des griffes noires au pied — l'hospice — les nouvelles galeries (de neige bleue) sous le glacier, l'avalanche passe par dessus, inscription sépulcrale — *nous restâmes ici ensevelis 40 jours* — précipice de six mille pieds — Brieg au bas.'

These notes formed the raw material for the book which Michelet eventually wrote: *La Montagne*.

MINTO, LORD. CHAMONIX, MONT BUET, MARTIGNY, SION, VISP, ZERMATT, SAAS, VISP, MARTIGNY

Of the priest's house at Zermatt, Lord Minto wrote: 'The dirt, too, was quite dry and of very old standing, so as to have become very little offensive.'

MONTBEL, COMTE DE. LES VERRIÈRES, NEUCHÂTEL, YVERDON, LAUSANNE, MORAT, BERNE, FRIBOURG, BERNE, LENZBURG, BADEN, ZURICH, WINTERTHUR, CONSTANCE

ROGER, ALEXANDRE SALOMON. NYON, LEUKERBAD, VISP, ZERMATT

Zermatt, 'durant le séjour que j'avais fait dans la chambre du chapelain, j'avais eu le temps de m'apercevoir qu'elle renfermait un genre de population fort incommode pour les personnes à peau délicate. . . . Les draps avaient servi à vingt voyageurs avant moi.'

ROSCOE, THOMAS (*c*). GENEVA, LAUSANNE, MARTIGNY, SION, BRIG, SIMPLON PASS, DOMODOSSOLA

TÖPFFER, RODOLPHE. GENEVA, MARTIGNY, TÊTE NOIRE PASS, CHAMONIX, SERVOZ, COL D'ANTERNE, SIXT, GENEVA

Crossing the Col d'Anterne, Töpffer had his adventure with the haughty 'Milord' and his daughter Clara, who, disdainful of their guide and of Töpffer at Servoz before starting, soon found themselves in trouble and forced to eat humble pie.

TRENCH, FRANCIS. CHIAVENNA, SPLÜGEN PASS, THUSIS, COIRE, ZURICH, BASLE

TRENCH, R. DOMODOSSOLA, SIMPLON PASS, BRIG, SION, MARTIGNY, VEVEY, LAUSANNE, GENEVA, LAUSANNE, VALLORBE

WILBRAHAM, EDWARD BOOTLE. GENEVA, CHAMONIX, MONT BLANC, GENEVA

'I should most earnestly advise no one to attempt the ascent of Mont Blanc; for though I found myself amply repaid by my success for all fatigue and troubles, the chances are very great indeed against any one having again a journey so prosperous in weather and every other respect as mine was.'

1831

CHATEAUBRIAND, FRANÇOIS RENÉ DE. GENEVA

'Du lieu où je vous écris, monsieur, j'aperçois la maison de campagne qu'habita Lord Byron, et les toits du château de Mme. de Staël. Où est le barde de *Childe Harold*? Où est l'auteur de *Corinne*? Ma trop longue vie ressemble à ces voies romaines bordées de monuments funèbres.'

HAKE, GORDON. GENEVA, LAUSANNE, CHILLON, MARTIGNY, SION, BRIG, SIMPLON PASS, DOMODOSSOLA

'Before I went to Italy I could not write; after I had crossed the Simplon I could: the wonders I saw wholly revolutionized my soul. There was height above height of snow that disregarded the sun; or, if it yielded to its insinuations, it was only to drip, into bayonets of ice. There were cataracts that had so far to fall, that the eyes reached the bottom of the gulph first, and seemed only overtaken by the waters with which they started.'

HUGI, FRANZ JOSEPH. SOLEURE, BERNE, THUN, INTERLAKEN, MEIRINGEN, GAULI PASS, UNTERAAR GLACIER, GRIMSEL PASS, FURKA PASS, ANDERMATT, ALTDORF, LUCERNE, SOLEURE

MENDELSSOHN-BARTHOLDY, FELIX. DOMODOSSOLA, SIMPLON PASS, BRIG, SION, MARTIGNY, COL DE BALME, CHAMONIX, MARTIGNY, VEVEY, COL DE JAMAN, CHÂTEAU D'OEX, SAANEN, ZWEISIMMEN, INTERLAKEN, LAUTERBRUNNEN, KLEINE SCHEIDEGG, GRINDELWALD, FAULHORN, GROSSE SCHEIDEGG, MEIRINGEN, GRIMSEL PASS, FURKA PASS, ANDERMATT, ALTDORF, LUCERNE, BRUNIG PASS, MEIRINGEN, JOCH PASS, ENGELBERG, LUCERNE, RIGI, EINSIEDELN, WALLENSTADT, ALTSTÄTTEN, TROGEN, ST. GALL

'People had tried to persuade me that the gigantic forms of the Swiss Alps that have haunted me from my childhood had been exaggerated in my imagination, and that after all a snowy mountain was not in reality so grand as I thought. I almost dreaded being undeceived, but at first sight of the foreground of the Alps from the lake of Como veiled in clouds, with here and there a surface of bright snow, sharp black points rearing their heads, and sinking precipitously into the lake, the hills as they rose first scattered over with trees and villages, then covered with moss, and then bleak and desolate, full of snowy clefts,—I felt just as I formerly did, and saw that I had exaggerated nothing.'
During this journey, Mendelssohn worked at his 'Italian' and 'Scottish' symphonies, and the 'Hebrides' overture.

MORSE, SAMUEL B. F. DOMODOSSOLA, SIMPLON PASS, BRIG, MARTIGNY, GENEVA, LUCERNE, RIGI, ZURICH, SCHAFFHAUSEN

Morse, of the telegraph and Morse code, wrote on the Rigi after seeing the sunrise, 'I had found too little comfort in the wretched thing that had been provided for me in the shape of a bed to desire to return thither, and I also felt too strongly the emotions which the scene I had just witnessed had excited, to wish for their dissipation in troubled dreams.'

ROGER, ALEXANDRE SALOMON. NYON, LEUKERBAD, BRIG, OBERGESTELEN, FURKA PASS, ANDERMATT, ST. GOTTHARD PASS, AIROLO, AL ACQUA, SAN GIACOMO PASS, TOSA FALLS, GRIES PASS, ULRICHEN, BRIG, LEUKERBAD, BRIG, SIMPLON PASS, DOMODOSSOLA, MACUGNAGA, MONTE MORO PASS, SAAS, VISP, MARTIGNY, NYON

1832

ANONYMOUS 9 A. LAUSANNE, LUCERNE, WERDENBERG, RAGAZ, PFÄFERS, MAIENFELD, FELDKIRCH, RAGAZ, WALLENSTADT, BLUDENZ, INNSBRUCK, MERANO, MALS, RESCHEN, SCHEIDECK, LANDECK, ARLBERG, FELDKIRCH, RAGAZ, COIRE, THUSIS, ANDEER, SAN BERNARDINO PAS, MESOCCO, BELLINZONA, LOCARNO, LUGANO, COMO

BALZAC, HONORÉ DE. GENEVA

Balzac had just broken with Mme de Castries.

BÖRNE, LUDWIG. SCHAFFHAUSEN, ZURICH, AARAU, LUCERNE, STANS, ALTDORF, BRUNNEN, SCHWYZ, ZUG, LUCERNE

'The country round Lucerne is like a warehouse of nature in which a hundred beautiful spots lie stacked, awaiting buyers.'

CHATEAUBRIAND, FRANÇOIS RENÉ DE. BASLE, LUCERNE, ALTDORF, ST. GOTTHARD PASS, BELLINZONA, LUGANO, ST. GOTTHARD PASS, ALTDORF, LUCERNE, ZURICH, CONSTANCE, ARENENBERG, ZURICH, LUCERNE, ST. URBAN, BERNE, LAUSANNE, GENEVA.

'Au surplus, j'ai beau me battre les flancs pour arriver à l'exaltation alpine des écrivains de montagne, j'y perds ma peine. Au physique, cet air vierge et balsamique qui doit ranimer mes forces, raréfier mon sang, désenfumer ma tête fatiguée, me donner une faim insatiable, un repos sans rêves, ne produit point sur moi ces effets. Je ne respire pas mieux, mon sang ne circule pas plus vite, ma tête n'est pas moins lourde au ciel des Alpes qu'à Paris. . . . Si les montagnes de nos climats peuvent justifier les éloges de leurs admirateurs, ce n'est que quand elles sont enveloppées dans la nuit dont elles épaississent le chaos.'
During this journey Chateaubriand met Alexandre Dumas at Lucerne, Mme Récamier at Constance and Geneva, and called on Queen Hortense and Louis Napoleon at Arenenberg.

COOPER, JAMES FENIMORE. SCHAFFHAUSEN, ZURICH, EINSIEDELN, SCHWYZ, LUCERNE, BRUNIG PASS, MEIRINGEN, INTERLAKEN, LAUTERBRUNNEN, GRINDELWALD, THUN, BERNE, MORAT, VEVEY, MARTIGNY, GRAND ST. BERNARD, MARTIGNY, GENEVA

DUMAS, ALEXANDRE. GENEVA, CHILLON, BEX, MARTIGNY, COL DE BALME, CHAMONIX, TÊTE NOIRE PASS, MARTIGNY, GRAND ST. BERNARD PASS, AOSTA, PETIT ST. BERNARD PASS, BOURG ST. MAURICE, AIX LES BAINS, GENEVA, YVERDON, GRANDSON, MORAT, BERNE, THUN, INTERLAKEN, LAUTERBRUNNEN, KLEINE SCHEIDEGG, GRINDELWALD, FAULHORN, GROSSE SCHEIDEGG, MEIRINGEN, INTERLAKEN, KANDERSTEG, GEMMI PASS, LEUK, BRIG, FURKA PASS, ANDERMATT, ALTDORF, LUCERNE, RIGI, SARNEN, LUCERNE, ZURICH, GLARUS, LINTHAL, KISTEN PASS, ILANZ, COIRE, PFÄFERS,

ALTSTÄTTEN, APPENZELL, CONSTANCE, ARENENBERG, SCHAFFHAUSEN, BADEN, AARAU, SOLEURE, WEISSENSTEIN, BIENNE, ILE ST. PIERRE, YVERDON, GENEVA, MARTIGNY, SION, BRIG, SIMPLON PASS, DOMODOSSOLA

It has been said of the 'Impressions de voyage', in which Dumas described his battle with the guides on the Faulhorn and with the river at Rosenlaui, his fears of cannibalism at Obergestelen, his bear steak at Martigny, his meetings with Chateaubriand and Queen Hortense, and his drive with a drunken coachman over the Great St. Bernard, that it is his best work.

DYKE, THOMAS. BASLE, BRUGG, BADEN, ZURICH, ZUG, RIGI, LUCERNE, ENTLIBUCH, LANGNAU, BERNE, THUN, INTERLAKEN, LAUTERBRUNNEN, BRIENZ, BRUNIG PASS, SARNEN, STANS, ENGELBERG, JOCH PASS, MEIRINGEN, GROSSE SCHEIDEGG, GRINDELWALD, INTERLAKEN, THUN, BERNE, MORAT, LAUSANNE, GENEVA

'Would that I had been born a mountaineer, to have held intercourse with the fairies, and to have looked forth every morning of my life upon the majesty of the wonderful "Sons of Earth". And the earth has reason to be proud of such sons as the Swiss mountains. If a man be disappointed at the apparent elevation of the Alps, let him ascend their lower basements, and enter into their rocky wonders, peering down into their tremendous abysses, or gazing up to the abodes of the chamois and eagle; then, if he come down and still complain of their not answering his previous expectations, he had better return home as quickly as he can, go to bed, and *enjoy* himself there for a fortnight.'

ENGELHARDT, CHRISTIAN MORITZ. BASLE, BERNE, THUN, INTERLAKEN, GRINDELWALD, FAULHORN, GIESSBACH, MEIRINGEN, GRIMSEL PASS, FURKA PASS, ANDERMATT, OBERALP PASS, DISENTIS, BONADUZ, THUSIS, HINTERRHEIN, SPLÜGEN PASS, CHIAVENNA, MILAN, DOMODOSSOLA, SIMPLON PASS, BRIG, SION, MARTIGNY, CHAMONIX, GENEVA, NEUCHÂTEL, BIENNE, BASLE

FEARNSIDE, W. G. (*c*). BASLE, SCHAFFHAUSEN, CONSTANCE, ROR-SCHACH, COIRE, DISENTIS, LUKMANIER PASS, OLIVONE, BELLINZONA, MESOCCO, SAN BERNARDINO PASS, THUSIS, REICHENAU

'We had the pleasure, a short time ago, of conversing with the good and learned Placidus, who resides in a village not far from the abbey [of Disentis], and, although bent under a heavy burden of years and infirmity, still exhibits some gleams of that mental fire by which he was once animated.'

FORBES, JAMES DAVID. GENEVA, CHAMONIX, COL DU BONHOMME, COL DES FOURS, COL DE LA SEIGNE, COURMAYEUR, AOSTA, GRAND ST. BER-NARD PASS, MARTIGNY, GENEVA

On the Mer de Glace, Forbes saw fragments of the ladder that de

Saussure had left on the Col du Géant in 1788. Forbes calculated from the position of this ladder that the glacier had moved nearly 300 feet a year.

HUGI, FRANZ JOSEPH. SOLEURE, BERNE, THUN, INTERLAKEN, GRINDELWALD, FAULHORN

A visit to the glaciers in early January to study the conversion of snow into ice. Hugi also spent three days in the newly built hut on the Faulhorn.

LYELL, SIR CHARLES. SCHAFFHAUSEN, BERNE, THUN, INTERLAKEN, SUMISWALD, BERNE, GURNIGEL, FRIBOURG, VEVEY, BEX, MARTIGNY, SION, BRIG, SIMPLON PASS, DOMODOSSOLA

MALMESBURY, EARL OF. GENEVA

Geneva: 'One evening we took a sailing boat and went upon the lake. The halyard slipped out of the block, and my brother's swarming up the mast capsized the boat. Lady Fitzharris, with the most wonderful coolness, turned to me, both of us being in the water, saying, "Don't be afraid: I won't lay hold of you, but tell me what to do.' My brother, who had got entangled under the sail, came up and by putting her hands on our shoulders we kept her up for a quarter of an hour, till a watchmaker who was rowing his wife, took her in.'

NECKER, LOUIS ALBERT. GENEVA, INTERLAKEN, BRIG

A journey with J. D. Forbes during which Necker observed and studied the 'optical phenomenon when the direct rays of the sun are concealed by a line of forest fringing some rising ground between the spectator and the sun. The outlines of the trees, and even their entire stems, are then seen to shine with a white light of dazzling brilliancy, resembling frosted silver.'

PONSONBY, JOHN VISCOUNT. THUN

Lord Ponsonby found Colonel Knechtenhofer's house 'Bellevue' so pleasant that he suggested its conversion into an hotel. Knechtenhofer fell in with the suggestion and thereby started Thun as a tourist centre with its celebrated 'Hotel Bellevue'.

RITCHIE, LEITCH (*c*). ST. CERGUE, NYON, GENEVA, LAUSANNE, MARTIGNY, SION, BRIG, SIMPLON PASS, DOMODOSSOLA

ROGER, ALEXANDRE SALOMON. NYON, LEUKERBAD, BRIG, FURKA PASS, ANDERMATT, OBERALP PASS, DISENTIS, REICHENAU, FILISUR, ALBULA PASS, ST. MORITZ, JULIER PASS, TIEFENKASTEL, REICHENAU, DISENTIS, OBERALP PASS, ANDERMATT, FURKA PASS, BRIG

TÖPFFER, RODOLPHE. GENEVA, ANNECY, BOURG ST. MAURICE, PETIT ST. BERNARD PASS, AOSTA, GRAND ST. BERNARD PASS, MARTIGNY, SION,

LEUK, GEMMI PASS, KANDERSTEG, MÜLLINEN, INTERLAKEN, MEIRINGEN, GROSSE SCHEIDEGG, GRINDELWALD, KLEINE SCHEIDEGG, LAUTERBRUNNEN, INTERLAKEN, THUN, BERNE, FRIBOURG, LAUSANNE, GENEVA

'At Müllinen Töpffer sent out from the inn to the local shop for some snuff. A sternutatory powder was brought to him of such an appearance and colour that a committee was appointed ad hoc to investigate it. Some of its members emitted the opinion that it was spruce sawdust; others considered it to be ferruginous schist, while others again were of the view that its basis rested on a bucolic and bovine composition. Meanwhile the coffee was brought in. It was green. The committee got busy again and was on the point of coming to bovine conclusions . . .'

ZELLER, CONRAD. SION, EVOLENA, COL DU ZATÉ, VAL MOIRY, GRIMENTZ, ZINAL, SIERRE

In the Val d'Anniviers Zeller met some boys with garlands of flowers in their hats. This showed that they had been to mass, which, when they were up on the alp, they did only once a summer, when their friends gave them flowers.

1833

ANDERSEN, HANS CHRISTIAN. GENEVA, LAUSANNE, VEVEY, CHILLON, LE LOCLE, BRIG, SIMPLON PASS, DOMODOSSOLA

The author of the *Fairy Tales* stayed for some time at Le Locle and described the scenery and recollections of his stay in his novel *O.T.* While there he finished his poem 'Agnete and the Merman'. The Alps he referred to as 'The Earth's huge folded wings . . . What if she lifted them, I thought, and spread abroad her mighty pinions with their variegated tapestry of black forest, wild waterfall, and swimming cloud.'

ANONYMOUS 9 A. DOMODOSSOLA, SIMPLON PASS, BRIG, SIMPLON PASS, DOMODOSSOLA

BALZAC, HONORÉ DE. NEUCHÂTEL, BIENNE, MOTIERS-TRAVERS, GENEVA

'J'ai rapporté de Suisse l'idée d'un beau livre, ma foi!' This was to be *Seraphita.*
'Jamais je n'ai vu de plus ravissants pays que ceux que j'ai admirés; le Val-de-Travers semble fait pour deux amants.'
Balzac went to Neuchâtel from Besançon to see Mme Hanska, and it was also to visit her that he went to Geneva later in the year. There, he finished the third dizain of the *Contes Drolatiques.*

BATEMAN, MRS. SCHAFFHAUSEN, ZURICH, ZUG, LUCERNE, BRUNIG PASS, MEIRINGEN, INTERLAKEN, GRINDELWALD, LAUTERBRUNNEN, THUN, BERNE, LAUSANNE, GENEVA, CHAMONIX, COL DE BALME, MARTIGNY, VEVEY, LAUSANNE, MORAT, BERNE, SOLEURE, BASLE

'Its proximity to Mont Blanc and the Mer de Glace will always make Chamouny interesting in the highest degree; but the valley itself is far surpassed in beauty by that of Sarnen: the climate of the latter too, is infinitely preferable: . . . I had no notion that the ascent of Mont Blanc was so difficult as it is here described to be and that it is so seldom attempted.'

BÖRNE, LUDWIG. BERNE, LAUSANNE, GENEVA, MONTREUX.

'I would not care to travel as people do in Switzerland. To chase from one place to another, for weeks and months, to enjoy nothing thoroughly but only to taste, is that not foolish? If a mountain or a valley pleases you, why go away to another valley, another mountain, merely to be able to say at home that you have been there?'

CANDOLLE, AUGUSTIN PYRAME DE. GENEVA, OUCHY, LAUSANNE, MOUDON, BERNE, LUCERNE, SCHWYZ, ALTDORF, ST. GOTTHARD PASS, FAIDO, BELLINZONA, LUGANO, COMO, CHIAVENNA, SPLÜGEN PASS, THUSIS, COIRE, PFÄFERS, WESEN, GLARUS, RAPPERSWIL, ZUG, LUCERNE, GENEVA

CHATEAUBRIAND, FRANÇOIS RENÉ DE. GENEVA, BEX, MARTIGNY, SION, BRIG, SIMPLON PASS, DOMODOSSOLA

Simplon:—'Un certain jeu de lumière et d'ombre en accroissait la magie. On était caressé d'un petit souffle que notre ancienne langue appelait *l'aure*, sorte d'avant-brise du matin, baignée et parfumée dans la rosée.'

DODD, — . SCHAFFHAUSEN, ZURICH, LUCERNE, RIGI, BRUNNEN, FLUELEN, ALTDORF, ANDERMATT, ST. GOTTHARD PASS, AIROLO, BELLINZONA, LOCARNO, BAVENO, DOMODOSSOLA, SIMPLON PASS, BRIG, OBERGESTELEN, GRIMSEL PASS, MEIRINGEN, GROSSE SCHEIDEGG, GRINDELWALD, KLEINE SCHEIDEGG, LAUTERBRUNNEN, INTERLAKEN, THUN, BERNE, MORAT, LAUSANNE, VILLENEUVE, BEX, MARTIGNY, GRAND ST. BERNARD PASS, AOSTA, COURMAYEUR, COL DE LA SEIGNE, COL DES FOURS, COL DU BONHOMME, CHAMONIX, GENEVA

'I shall never look upon the like again, nor will time ever efface that scene from my memory. It struck me that it was not possible for mortal man to experience more happiness than I then enjoyed. The Garden is said to be between nine and ten thousand feet above the level of the sea; and, to borrow a quaint expression of John Galt's, I may safely say that in body and spirit I was never so near heaven before.'

EMERSON, RALPH WALDO. DOMODOSSOLA, SIMPLON PASS, BRIG, SION, MARTIGNY, GENEVA

'To oblige my companions, and protesting all the way upon the unworthiness of his memory, I went to Ferney.'

HEER, OSWALD. ANDERMATT, ST. GOTTHARD PASS, BELLINZONA, MESOCCO, SAN BERNARDINO PASS, HINTERRHEIN, AVERS CRESTA, STALLERBERG PASS, BIVIO, JULIER PASS, ST. MORITZ, BERNINA PASS

KNIGHTON, SIR WILLIAM. BASLE, BERNE, LAUSANNE, GENEVA

LYTTON, EDWARD BULWER, LORD. GENEVA, COPPET, CLARENS, EVIAN, MEILLERIE, VILLENEUVE, MARTIGNY

'There are some places in the world, which imaginative persons, who contract a sympathy with Genius, feel it almost a duty to visit. Not to perform such pilgrimages seems a neglect of one of the objects of life. . . . Of these none are more sacred than "Leman with its crystal face".'

PIXÉRÉCOURT, GILBERT DE. BASLE, SOLEURE, WEISSENSTEIN, VEVEY, GENEVA, CHAMONIX

'J'ai consigné les deux lignes suivantes sur le registre ouvert aux voyageurs dans le pavillon de la Flégère, à Chamouny: Le 17 août 1833, grâce à la magnésie anglaise calcinée, un goutteux invétéré a pu monter à pied jusqu'à la croix de la Flégère en deux heures et demie.'

ROGER, ALEXANDRE SALOMON. NYON, MARTIGNY, GRAND ST. BERNARD PASS, AOSTA, CHATILLON, BREUIL, ST. THEODUL PASS, ZERMATT, STALDEN, SAAS, VISP, SION, MARTIGNY, NYON

RUSKIN, JOHN. SCHAFFHAUSEN, COIRE, THUSIS, SPLÜGEN PASS, CHIAVENNA, MILAN, AOSTA, GRAND ST. BERNARD PASS, MARTIGNY, VEVEY, BERNE, THUN, INTERLAKEN, LUCERNE, ZURICH, BADEN, BASLE, GENEVA, CHAMONIX

'It was again fortunate that we took the grandest pass into Italy—that the first ravine of the main Alps I saw was the Via Mala.'
On the way to Basle the Ruskins ran into the civil war then raging between Basle-City and Basle-Country. As a result of this journey Ruskin wrote 'Facts and considerations on the strata of Mont Blanc, and on some instances of twisted strata observable in Switzerland'.

STANHOPE, PHILIP HENRY, EARL. SCHAFFHAUSEN, CONSTANCE, WINTERTHUR, ZURICH, ZUG, SCHWYZ, BRUNNEN, FLUELEN, ANDERMATT, HOSPENTHAL, ALTDORF, BRUNNEN, LUCERNE, BRAMEGG, ENTLIBUCH, LANGNAU, THUN, INTERLAKEN, LAUTERBRUNNEN, GRINDELWALD, INTERLAKEN,

BRIENZ, MEIRINGEN, INTERLAKEN, THUN, BERNE, MURGENTHAL, BADEN, ZURICH, CONSTANCE, RORSCHACH, RHEINECK, RAGAZ, COIRE, THUSIS, SPLÜGEN PASS, CHIAVENNA

M. Lamy, the artist who kept a print-shop at Berne, told Lord Stanhope that he had been in the habit of accompanying English travellers in the Alps to make sketches for them at 4*s.* 6*d.* a day. He had accompanied Byron in the Oberland, but that worthy Lord had attempted to employ his services to seduce a Swiss girl.

TÖPFFER, RODOLPHE. GENEVA, MARTIGNY, GRAND ST. BERNARD PASS, AOSTA, MILAN, DOMODOSSOLA, SIMPLON PASS, BRIG, SION, MARTIGNY, GENEVA

'What does one look for on a journey? Pleasure. Now, ten minutes' halt on the march are worth more than an hour at the inn; twenty minutes' more than two hours, and so on. Therefore, if you do not halt, you only get to the inn ten minutes earlier, and those ten minutes get lost without profit in the hour which you spend there.'

VIRIDET, MARC. ZERMATT, SAAS, ROSSBODEN PASS, SIMPLON

Viridet's is the first recorded visit to an inn at Saas, Moritz Zurbrücken's 'Sonne'.

WALSH, COMTE THEOBALD (*c*). ANDERMATT, OBERALP PASS, DISENTIS, ILANZ, PEIDEN, VALS, VALSERBERG PASS, HINTERRHEIN, THUSIS, COIRE, SARGANS, ST. GALL, APPENZELL, LICHTENSTEIG, GLARUS, LINTHAL, KLAUSEN PASS, ALTDORF

Peiden: 'L'hôte me mena dans une des chambres les plus décentes; en passant l'inspection du lit, je lui fis observer que les draps n'étaient pas propres, "impossible! s'écria-t-il d'un air d'assurance, on n'y a encore couché qu'une seule fois."'

WILDER, F. (*c*). BASLE, BADEN, ZURICH, RAPPERSWIL, GLARUS, LINTHAL, WESEN, WALLENSTADT, COIRE, THUSIS, SPLÜGEN, COIRE, WESEN, ZUG, RIGI, LUCERNE, THUN, INTERLAKEN, GRINDELWALD, LAUTERBRUNNEN, INTERLAKEN, THUN, BERNE, FRIBOURG, VEVEY, LAUSANNE, GENEVA, CHAMONIX, COL DE BALME, MARTIGNY, SION, BRIG, SIMPLON PASS, DOMODOSSOLA

1834

ANONYMOUS 9 E. BASLE, BALSTHAL, SOLEURE, BERNE, THUN, INTERLAKEN, LAUTERBRUNNEN, KLEINE SCHEIDEGG, GRINDELWALD, GROSSE SCHEIDEGG, MEIRINGEN, BRUNIG PASS, LUNGERN, LUCERNE, ZURICH, HORGEN, ZUG, RIGI, BRUNNEN, FLUELEN, ALTDORF, ANDERMATT, ST. GOTTHARD PASS, BELLINZONA, MAGADINO, BAVENO, DOMODOSSOLA, SIMPLON PASS, BRIG, SION, MARTIGNY, COL DE BALME, CHAMONIX, GENEVA

BARRY, MARTIN. GRINDELWALD, FAULHORN, MARTIGNY, COL DE BALME, CHAMONIX, MONT BLANC, NEUCHÂTEL, BASLE

'I have stood upon the high altar of the Faulhorn. There, at earliest dawn, with the still loftier summits of the other Bernese Alps, mailed with ice, in line immediately before me, watched,—until the highest peak of all caught the sun's rays, and shone in the twilight as a point of gold; this standing for a while alone; and then another, and another mountain-top was gilded, until there was a chain of brightness; then a wall, with pyramids, of rosy light; lastly, the great source of light rose, beaming the refulgence of the morning.'

CHARPENTIER, JEAN DE. BEX, MEIRINGEN, BRUNIG PASS, LUCERNE

COROT, CAMILLE. DOMODOSSOLA, SIMPLON PASS, BRIG, SION, MARTIGNY, GENEVA

FRIPP, GEORGE A. SCHAFFHAUSEN, ZURICH, WALLENSTADT, COIRE, THUSIS, SPLÜGEN PASS, CHIAVENNA, MILAN

GROTE, GEORGE. GENEVA, CHAMONIX, COL DE BALME, MARTIGNY, GENEVA, LAUSANNE, BERNE, THUN

HARE, MARIA. MILAN, BELLINZONA, ST. GOTTHARD PASS, ALTDORF, FLUELEN, ZURICH

'The sublimity and grandeur of the mountain scenery, though lifting one up indeed above this world, was lifting one up to a God of power and majesty, not of love, and gave me a deep and painfully oppressive feeling.'

HAUSSEZ, BARON LEMERCHER D' (*c*). ANNECY, BONNEVILLE, CHAMONIX

'Afin d'échapper aux reproches de ces gens qui affectent de louer à outrance ce que les autres n'ont pas vu, je ne voulus pas m'éloigner de la Savoie, sans avoir visité la vallée tant célébrée de Chamouny. C'est une excursion obligée pour tout voyageur qui va en Italie.'

HAYWARD, ABRAHAM. ZURICH, WALLENSTADT, COIRE, THUSIS, SPLÜGEN PASS, CHIAVENNA, MILAN, DOMODOSSOLA, SIMPLON PASS, BRIG, SION, MARTIGNY, GENEVA, CHAMONIX, GENEVA, LAUSANNE, BERNE, BASLE

'I merely mention my trip with — to Chamouni for the sake of mentioning a singular encounter on the way. At St. Martin, where all regular travelling terminates, we found Sir John Bailey, the ex-judge, who at the age of seventy-two, had just been up the mountain in a car. He seemed delighted with everything.'

HEER, OSWALD. MATT, ELM, PANIXER PASS, ILANZ, VALS, VALSERBERG PASS, SPLÜGEN PASS, CHIAVENNA, MALOJA PASS, PONTRESINA, CAMPOVASTO, FUORCLA LAVIRUM, LIVIGNO, SAN GIACOMO DI FRAELE, STA. MARIA, SCARL PASS, FETAN, SÜS, SCALETTA PASS, DAVOS

JOHNSON, JAMES. SCHAFFHAUSEN, ZURICH, WALLENSTADT, RAGAZ, PFÄFERS

'In the enjoyment of Swiss or Alpine scenery, everything depends on the state of the atmosphere, and on that of our health and spirits at the time. Hence it is that one person is delighted with a prospect which another passes without pleasure or surprise at all.'

MACGREGOR, JOHN. BASLE, BADEN, SCHAFFHAUSEN, CONSTANCE, ST. GALL, APPENZELL, ALTSTÄTTEN, SARGANS, RAGAZ, PFÄFERS, COIRE, FLIMS, SEGNES PASS, ELM, GLARUS, ZURICH, ALBIS, ZUG, SCHWYZ, BRUNNEN, ALTDORF, ANDERMATT, ALTDORF, LUCERNE, PILATUS, ENTLIBUCH, THUN, INTERLAKEN, LAUTERBRUNNEN, GRINDELWALD, GROSSE SCHEIDEGG, MEIRINGEN, INTERLAKEN, THUN, BERNE, MORAT, NEUCHÂTEL, YVERDON, LAUSANNE, BEX, EVIAN, GENEVA, CHAMONIX, GENEVA

'The iron-built steam-boat which traverses the lake of Neuchâtel, . . . an iron vessel propelled by steam, floating between the Alps and the Jura! What a triumph in the progress of human invention!—and what next? Steam carriages rolling over the Simplon and the St. Gothard,—not impossible nor unlikely. This is a graceful and swift vessel . . .'

MAYR, JOHANN HEINRICH. ST. GALL, COIRE, LENZERHEIDE, FILISUR, BERGÜN, ALBULA PASS, ST. MORITZ

The first winter visitor to the Engadine.

MAZZINI, GIUSEPPE. GENEVA, LAUSANNE, BERNE, BIENNE, GRENCHEN

MUSSET, ALFRED DE. DOMODOSSOLA, SIMPLON PASS, BRIG, SION, MARTIGNY, GENEVA

'Quand tu passeras le Simplon, pense à moi, George; c'était la première fois que les spectres éternels des Alpes se levaient devant moi, dans leur forme et dans leur calme. J'étais seul dans le cabriolet, je ne sais comment rendre ce que j'ai éprouvé. Il me semblait que ces géants me parlaient de toutes les grandeurs sorties de la main de Dieu.' This journey, away from George Sand, was reflected in de Musset's *Souvenirs des Alpes*.

REY, W. MÜNSTER, ULRICHEN, NUFENEN PASS, AL ACQUA, AIROLO, ST. GOTTHARD PASS, HOSPENTHAL, ANDERMATT, OBERALP PASS, ALP TIARMS, CALMOT, ANDERMATT, REALP, FURKA PASS, GLETSCH, SAASBERG

ROGER, ALEXANDRE SALOMON. NYON, SCHINZNACH, EINSIEDELN, SCHWYZ, LUCERNE, SOLEURE, MORAT, NYON

SAND, GEORGE. DOMODOSSOLA, SIMPLON PASS, BRIG, SION, MARTIGNY, COL DE BALME, CHAMONIX, MARTIGNY, LAUSANNE, GENEVA

'George Sand était en costume d'homme. A dos de mulet, nous avons franchi le Col de Balme et nous nous sommes transportés à Chamounix, où le jour suivant nous avons entrepris à pied l'ascension du mont Blanc avec une longue caravane d'Anglais, de Français, d'Allemands et d'Américains. Arrivés à la Mer de Glace . . .'

TILLY, COMTE HENRI DE. CHAMONIX, MONT BLANC, GENEVA

The first Frenchman to ascend Mont Blanc.

WILKLEY, EDWARD. DOMODOSSOLA, SIMPLON PASS, BRIG, SION, MARTIGNY, LAUSANNE, GENEVA, CHAMONIX, GENEVA, LAUSANNE, VEVEY, BULLE, GRUYÈRES, FRIBOURG, BERNE, THUN, INTERLAKEN, LAUTERBRUNNEN, KLEINE SCHEIDEGG, GRINDELWALD, GROSSE SCHEIDEGG, MEIRINGEN, BRUNIG PASS, SARNEN, ALPNACH, WEGGIS, RIGI, LUCERNE, ZUG, ZURICH, SCHAFFHAUSEN, BASLE

Two days after Wilkley's visit to Chamonix, 'a French gentleman and his two daughters were attacked by a robber on the Col de Balme. He fired a pistol at them, but missed. . . .' As for himself, the *Guillaume Tell* on which Wilkley sailed from Geneva to Lausanne caught fire.

WILLIS, N. P. DOMODOSSOLA, SIMPLON PASS, BRIG, SION, MARTIGNY, ST. GINGOLPH, EVIAN, GENEVA, LAUSANNE, GENEVA

'The world has a great many sweet spots in it, and I have found many a one which would make fitting scenery for the brightest act of life's changeful drama—but here is one, where it seems to me as difficult not to feel genial and kindly, as for Taglioni to keep from floating away like a smoke-curl when she is dancing in La Bayadere.'

1835

ANONYMOUS 9 B. SCHAFFHAUSEN, CONSTANCE, WINTERTHUR, ZURICH, EINSIEDELN, ZUG, RIGI, LUCERNE, FLUELEN, ALTDORF, ANDERMATT, FURKA PASS, GRIMSEL PASS, MEIRINGEN, GROSSE SCHEIDEGG, GRINDELWALD, KLEINE SCHEIDEGG, LAUTERBRUNNEN, INTERLAKEN, THUN, ZWEISIMMEN, SAANEN, GRUYÈRES, VEVEY, GENEVA, CHAMONIX, TÊTE NOIRE PASS, MARTIGNY, GRAND ST. BERNARD, MARTIGNY, SION, LEUK, GEMMI PASS, KANDERSTEG, INTERLAKEN, BRIENZ, BRUNIG PASS, SARNEN, LUCERNE, ALBIS, ZURICH, BADEN, AARAU, SOLEURE, WEISSENSTEIN, BERNE, BIENNE, ILE ST. PIERRE, NEUCHÂTEL, MORAT, FRIBOURG, YVERDON, LAUSANNE, GENEVA

CALAME, ALEXANDRE. GENEVA, LAUSANNE, BERNE, THUN, INTERLAKEN, LAUTERBRUNNEN, KLEINE SCHEIDEGG, GRINDELWALD, GROSSE SCHEIDEGG, MEIRINGEN, HANDECK, BRIENZ, INTERLAKEN, THUN, BERNE, LAUSANNE, GENEVA

Lady Osborne, who had admired the young artist's work, commissioned him to paint a picture of the Handeck falls. He accordingly went and spent some time there in this and subsequent years, under primitive conditions.

In 1838 he painted the 'Orage à la Handeck' which immediately established his reputation as an alpine painter.

DINO, DUCHESSE DE. CONSTANCE, ST. GALL, HEINRICHSBAD, UZNACH, ZUG, LUCERNE, LANGNAU, BERNE, FRIBOURG, LAUSANNE, VEVEY, BEX, EVIAN, GENEVA, NYON, ST. CERGUE

ENGELHARDT, CHRISTIAN MORITZ. BASLE, MOUTIER, BERNE, LAUSANNE, BEX, MARTIGNY, SION, VISP, ZERMATT, STALDEN, SAAS, MONTE MORO PASS, MACUGNAGA, BAVENO, LUINO, LUGANO, PORLEZZA, MENAGGIO, CHIAVENNA, SPLÜGEN PASS, THUSIS, COIRE, ZURICH

On the way to Saas, his guide, like Sherasmin in *Oberon*, said that time lay heavily upon him if they advanced in silence: 'Engelhardt should speak to him.'

FARADAY, MICHAEL. GENEVA, CHAMONIX, TÊTE NOIRE PASS, MARTIGNY, VEVEY, FRIBOURG, BERNE

'We are almost surfeited with magnificent scenery, and for myself I would rather not see it with an exhausted appetite. The weather has been most delightful, and everything in our favour, so that the scenery has been in the most beautiful condition. Mont Blanc, above all, is wonderful, and I could not but feel at it what I have often felt before, that painting is far behind poetry in cases of high expression, of which this is one. No artist should try to paint Mont Blanc; it is utterly out of his reach.'

FORBES, EDWARD. GENEVA, MARTIGNY, SION, LEUK, GEMMI PASS, KANDERSTEG, INTERLAKEN, GRINDELWALD, LAUTERBRUNNEN, INTERLAKEN, THUN, BERNE, INTERLAKEN, FAULHORN, BERNE, AARAU, BASLE

HAUSSEZ, BARON LEMERCHIER D' (*c*). GENEVA, VEVEY, BULLE, GRUYÈRES, CHÂTEAU D'OEX, ZWEISIMMEN, THUN, INTERLAKEN, BRIENZ, BRUNIG PASS, LUCERNE, ZUG, ZURICH, BADEN, BERNE, FRIBOURG, LAUSANNE, GENEVA, EVIAN, MARTIGNY, GRAND ST. BERNARD, MARTIGNY, SION, BRIG, SIMPLON PASS, DOMODOSSOLA, MILAN, MAGADINO, BELLINZONA, MESOCCO, SAN BERNARDINO PASS, THUSIS, COIRE, SARGANS, ALTSTÄTTEN, APPENZELL, ST. GALL, SCHAFFHAUSEN, BASLE, NEUCHÂTEL, YVERDON, GENEVA

'On ne visite guère la Suisse que pour changer de place, pour voir ce que l'on ne trouve pas habituellement autour de soi, pour avoir dans la mémoire des noms de lieux qui ne sont pas dans celle de tout le monde. On ne la visite enfin que par ton, par désoeuvrement, par orgueil; rarement par un véritable sentiment de curiosité. Au retour, on exagère aux autres et à soi-même les jouissances que l'on a éprouvées, afin de ne pas rester au-dessous de l'admiration de ceux qui ont précédé, afin d'en exciter à son tour, afin de se procurer une compensation aux fatigues et un complément au plaisir du voyage. Mais au fond, on est las de la course, et on ne l'achève que pour ne pas revenir sur ses pas.'

HEER, OSWALD. MATT, ELM, PANIXER PASS, BRIGELS, SOMVIX, GREINA PASS, SCARADRA ALP, SORREDA PASS, ZERVREILA, PLATTENSCHLUCHT PASS, ZAPPORT, SPLÜGEN PASS, PASSO DI SURETTA, AVERS CRESTA, STALLERBERG PASS, BIVIO, JULIER PASS, CAMPOVASTO, PIZ LAVIRUM, LIVIGNO, OFEN PASS, ZERNEZ, PIZ LANGUARD, LAVIN, SAMNAUN, PONTRESINA, PIZ PALÜ

HIESTAND, HENRY. SCHAFFHAUSEN, ZURICH, BASLE

HOLMES, OLIVER WENDELL. GENEVA, MARTIGNY, GRAND ST. BERNARD, LUCERNE, RIGI, SCHAFFHAUSEN, COIRE, THUSIS, SPLÜGEN PASS, CHIAVENNA

'The majesty and beauty of the scenery of Switzerland, as you know, have made it a thoroughfare of travelling Europe, and especially of the English, who swarm in it to the most outrageous extent. And yet so vast and so varied, so savage in some regions and so lovely in others, is the country we have been through, that the steamboats on the lakes, and the great hotels and splendid roads which one meets with from time to time, leave too slight traces on the face of Nature to take away the sense of freshness and wildness that characterise it.'

LYELL, SIR CHARLES. PORRENTRUY, NEUCHÂTEL, BERNE, THUN, INTERLAKEN, LAUTERBRUNNEN, MEIRINGEN, URBACHTAL, BRUNIG PASS, LUCERNE

O'CONNOR, MATTHEW. BASLE, BADEN, ZURICH, EINSIEDELN, WESEN, WALLENSTADT, COIRE, THUSIS, SAN BERNARDINO PASS, MESOCCO, BELLINZONA, LOCARNO, AIROLO, ST. GOTTHARD PASS, ALTDORF, BRUNNEN, SCHWYZ, ZUG, ZURICH, BASLE

'We took up our quarters at Clonach, a village of scattered houses, with orchards and chestnut trees intervening between them. It resembled a German canton in the days of Tacitus.'

ROBY, JOHN. SCHAFFHAUSEN, ZURICH, RIGI, LUCERNE, LANGNAU, BERNE, THUN, INTERLAKEN, GRINDELWALD, LAUTERBRUNNEN, THUN, BERNE, LAUSANNE, GENEVA, CHAMONIX, TÊTE NOIRE PASS, MARTIGNY, SION, BRIG, SIMPLON PASS, DOMODOSSOLA

'Mont Blanc! I started to the window, and the hoary monarch of the mountains was in full view! His white brow glittering with the frost of primeval ages. So had he shone, over those dark mountains, upon that vast lake, four thousand years. . . .'

ROCCA, GENERAL HENRI DELLA. COURMAYEUR, COL DE LA SEIGNE, COL DES FOURS, COL DU BONHOMME, ST. GERVAIS, CHAMONIX, TÊTE NOIRE PASS, TRIENT, ORSIÈRES, COL FERRET, COURMAYEUR

This tour of Mont Blanc was made for a bet, in thirty-six hours continuous walking, with one hour's rest.

ROGER, ALEXANDRE SALOMON. NYON, FRIBOURG, BERNE, SCHINZNACH, ZURICH, GLARUS, LINTHAL, KLAUSEN PASS, ALTDORF, BECKENRIED, ENGELBERG, LUCERNE, SCHINZNACH, BERNE, NYON, ST. MAURICE, DENT DE MORCLES, MARTIGNY, ORSIÈRES, VAL FERRET, COL DE FENÊTRE, GRAND ST. BERNARD, MARTIGNY, NYON

RUSKIN, JOHN. GENEVA, CHAMONIX, MARTIGNY, GRAND ST. BERNARD PASS, AOSTA, COURMAYEUR, GRAND ST. BERNARD PASS, MARTIGNY, LAUSANNE, YVERDON, NEUCHÂTEL, BASLE, SCHAFFHAUSEN, CONSTANCE, ZURICH, ZUG, SCHWYZ, BRUNNEN, ALTDORF, ANDERMATT, ST. GOTTHARD, ALTDORF, RIGI, SARNEN, BRUNIG PASS, MEIRINGEN, GRIMSEL, MEIRINGEN, GROSSE SCHEIDEGG, GRINDELWALD, KLEINE SCHEIDEGG, LAUTERBRUNNEN, INTERLAKEN, THUN, BERNE, FRIBOURG, LAUSANNE, BERNE, BADEN, WINTERTHUR, ST. GALL, FELDKIRCH

'The Col de la Faucille, on that day of 1835, opened to me in distinct vision the Holy Land of my future work and true home in this world.'

SHUTTLEWORTH, R. J. BERNE, THUN, KANDERSTEG, GEMMI PASS, LEUK, VISP, ZERMATT, ALLALIN PASS, RANDA, VISP, BRIG, MÜNSTER, GRIMSEL PASS, MEIRINGEN, INTERLAKEN, THUN, BERNE

One member of the party nearly fell into a crevasse. 'Yet such is the indifference to danger in such situations, that his first exclamation on our handling him rather unceremoniously was "take care what you are about, you'll tear my trousers".'

STRUTT, MRS. ELIZABETH. LAUSANNE, VEVEY, CHATEL ST. DENIS, BULLE, GRUYÈRES, ROSSINIÈRE, SAANEN, ZWEISIMMEN, THUN, INTERLAKEN, GRINDELWALD, KLEINE SCHEIDEGG, LAUTERBRUNNEN, INTERLAKEN, SPIEZ, ZWEISIMMEN, VEVEY, MARTIGNY, SION, BRIG, ROSSINIÈRE, LA SARRAZ, ORBE, ROMAINMOTIER, LAUSANNE, GENEVA, NYON, ST. CERGUE, YVERDON, NEUCHÂTEL, MOUTIER, BASLE, SOLEURE, MORAT, FRIBOURG, VEVEY

The inn on the Kleine Scheidegg had just been built. '"Here," said mine host, as in four steps he visited the four departments of his at present only existing étage, "here, the salle à manger and four lodgers; below, the offices, and four more;" he paused, cast a wistful, calculating glance towards a kind of loft where he had lately mounted by the help of a short ladder, to search for some eggs—no—it was but a passing thought—"Eight persons, then, biens logés, bien nourris, and plenty of amusements."'

TÖPFFER, RODOLPHE. GENEVA, CHAMONIX, TÊTE NOIRE PASS, MARTIGNY, GENEVA, VEVEY, FRIBOURG, BERNE, THUN, INTERLAKEN, LAUTERBRUNNEN, KLEINE SCHEIDEGG, GRINDELWALD, INTERLAKEN, THUN, BERNE, LAUSANNE, GENEVA

The Hotel du Faucon at Fribourg is described as 'dark, mysterious, with tortuous creaking staircases, without any manager or management, and left to the care of some waiters who are either motionless or else prowl slowly about the dining room in slippers'.

1836

AGASSIZ, JEAN LOUIS RODOLPHE. NEUCHÂTEL, BEX

'Through the highly interesting works of Venetz and de Charpentier upon Glaciers, my attention was carried to these phenomena. In the autumn of 1836 I went to Bex, where I spent several months, and under the guidance of M. de Charpentier gradually learned to understand these remarkable phenomena.' Agassiz and his family stayed at La Sallaz where he also invited Karl Schimper to join him. There the notion of the Ice Age originated.

BALZAC, HONORÉ DE. DOMODOSSOLA, SIMPLON PASS, BRIG, SION, MARTIGNY, LAUSANNE, GENEVA

On this journey Balzac's companion was Mme Marbouty dressed in men's clothing and passing as his page.

BRECKINRIDGE, ROBERT J. SCHAFFHAUSEN, CONSTANCE, ZURICH, ZUG, LUCERNE, ENTLIBUCH, BERNE, FRIBOURG, PAYERNE, LAUSANNE, GENEVA

' . . . The sheet of still water, stretched like a beautiful bow at the base of the surrounding mountains. The largest and loveliest of the Swiss lakes—the loftiest and most majestic of all the mountains in the northern hemisphere, greeted us for the first time, almost at the same moment.'

BRUNNER, SAMUEL. BERNE, THUN, KANDERSTEG, GEMMI PASS, LEUKERBAD, VISP, ZERMATT

CUMMING, W. F. CONSTANCE, SCHAFFHAUSEN, ZURICH, AARAU, SOLEURE, WEISSENSTEIN, BERNE, THUN, INTERLAKEN, LAUTERBRUNNEN, KLEINE SCHEIDEGG, GRINDELWALD, FAULHORN, GROSSE SCHEIDEGG, ROSENLAUI, MEIRINGEN, BRIENZ, INTERLAKEN, THUN, BERNE, FRIBOURG, LAUSANNE, GENEVA

'There were a great many passengers on board. Amongst the number was one group that engrossed universal attention. It consisted of three persons; the gentleman is a celebrated German musician, of most eccentric appearance, with long fair hair hanging down over his shoulders, . . . One of his female companions was a woman of about forty, possessing the remains of considerable beauty. . . . But the figure that engrossed all eyes, was that of the other female, a young woman of twenty-two, with sallow complexion, and long black hair, hanging straight down over the back of her neck, and dressed in all respects as a man, . . . and though last, not least—*in wonder*—a cigar in her mouth!'

ENGELHARDT, CHRISTIAN MORITZ. BASLE, BERNE, THUN, KANDERSTEG, GEMMI PASS, LEUK, VISP, ZERMATT, STALDEN, SAAS FEE

At St. Niklaus the servant at the priest's house, unaccustomed to the luxuries of life, made a decoction of snuff for Engelhardt under the impression that it was coffee.

FISK, WILBUR. DOMODOSSOLA, SIMPLON PASS, BRIG, SION, MARTIGNY, BEX, VEVEY, LAUSANNE, NYON, GENEVA, LAUSANNE, FRIBOURG, BERNE, SOLEURE, BASLE

'The limpid mirror of the lake lay beneath us, and the Alps reared up their successive peaks and towering heights on the opposite side, until Mont Blanc himself, that three-headed monster, terminated the prospect, by basing himself on other mountains for his pedestal, and wreathing for himself a capital from the clouds of heaven.'

HALL, FANNY W. GENEVA, CHAMONIX, GENEVA, ROLLE, LAUSANNE, PAYERNE, BERNE, BIENNE, BASLE

'Having been reared in the cold climate of New England, I had, at an early age, acquired the somewhat *unfeminine* accomplishment of walking and sliding on the ice; and, though out of practice for many years, I found on this occasion the benefit of my early discipline.'

HUGI, FRANZ JOSEPH. SOLEURE, BERNE, THUN, INTERLAKEN, MEIRINGEN, GRIMSEL PASS, UNTERAAR GLACIER

LISZT, FRANZ. GENEVA, LUCERNE, WALLENSTADT, BEX, VEYRIER, MONNETIER, GENEVA, CHAMONIX, TÊTE NOIRE PASS, MARTIGNY, VEVEY, BULLE, FRIBOURG, LAUSANNE, GENEVA

Liszt and the comtesse d'Agoult had set up house in Geneva, whence they made many excursions. In her memoirs, she wrote: 'Deux mois passèrent de la sorte, au milieu des plus grands spectacles de la nature alpestre, . . . Personne ne savait notre nom dans les maisons isolées, dans les hameaux où nous nous arrêtions de préférence . . . Les bords du lac de Wallenstadt nous retinrent longtemps. Franz y composa, pour moi, une mélancolique harmonie, imitative du soupir des flots et de la cadence des avirons, que je n'ai jamais pu entendre sans pleurer.

Nous demeurâmes ensuite dans la vallée du Rhone, près de Bex, où nous fîmes lecture d'*Obermann* et de *Jocelyn*.' Liszt's compositions during this time were 'Au lac de Wallenstadt', 'Les cloches de Genève', 'La vallée d'Obermann', 'La chapelle de Guillaume Tell', and 'Fleurs mélodiques des Alpes'.

LONGFELLOW, HENRY WADSWORTH. CONSTANCE, SCHAFFHAUSEN, ZURICH, RIGI, ALTDORF, ANDERMATT, FURKA PASS, GRIMSEL PASS, MEIRINGEN, GIESSBACH, INTERLAKEN, LAUTERBRUNNEN, GRINDELWALD, THUN, BERNE, LAUSANNE, VEVEY, GENEVA, CHAMONIX, GENEVA, LAUSANNE, BERNE, THUN, INTERLAKEN, BRIENZ, BRUNIG PASS, LUCERNE, ZURICH, SCHAFFHAUSEN

From the Grimsel, Longfellow described the Rhone glacier as 'lying like a glove with its palm downward, and the fingers crooked and close, —a gauntlet of ice which centuries ago Winter threw down in defiance to the Sun'. Part of the scene of *Hyperion* is laid in Switzerland, as a result of this tour.

MARRYAT, CAPTAIN FREDERICK. BASLE, SOLEURE, BERNE, LAUSANNE, OUCHY, GENEVA, LAUSANNE

Marryat settled at 'Élysée' near Lausanne.

MEYER, CONRAD FERDINAND. ZURICH, GLARUS, STACHELBERG, LINTHAL, SANDALP, KLAUSEN PASS, ALTDORF, FLUELEN, RIGI, ZURICH

O'FLANAGAN, J. RODERICK. GENEVA, VILLENEUVE, VEVEY, LAUSANNE, GENEVA, CHAMONIX, TÊTE NOIRE PASS, MARTIGNY, GRAND ST. BERNARD PASS, AOSTA, GRAND ST. BERNARD PASS, MARTIGNY, SION, LEUK, GEMMI PASS, KANDERSTEG, THUN, BERNE, THUN, INTERLAKEN, LAUTERBRUNNEN, KLEINE SCHEIDEGG, GRINDELWALD, FAULHORN, GROSSE SCHEIDEGG, MEIRINGEN, GRIMSEL PASS, FURKA PASS, ANDERMATT, ALTDORF, FLUELEN, RIGI, ZUG, ZURICH, RICHTERSWIL, WESEN, RAGAZ, PFÄFERS, ALTSTÄTTEN, TROGEN, ST. GALL, CONSTANCE, SCHAFFHAUSEN, BASLE

'I prefer lakes to mountains, for after all, there is a great sameness in mountains; and what is more tiresome, it is either climb, climb, or descend, descend, till your very knees bend under you.'

PICTET, ADOLPHE. GENEVA, CHAMONIX, TÊTE NOIRE PASS, MARTIGNY, VEVEY, BULLE, FRIBOURG, LAUSANNE, GENEVA

At the Hotel de l'Union at Chamonix, Pictet's party included Liszt, the Comtesse d'Agoult, and George Sand.
'— Who are those people? dit à son voisin un gros Anglais qui occupait le bout de la table. — I don't know, lui répondit flegmatiquement le compatriote qu'il interrogeait.— Monsieur, qui sont ce peuple? reprit l'Anglais en se tournant de l'autre côté.'

SAND, GEORGE. GENEVA, CHAMONIX, TÊTE NOIRE PASS, MARTIGNY, VEVEY, BULLE, FRIBOURG, LAUSANNE, GENEVA

'Je me suis démandé, en regardant attentivement le crâne, la physionomie et l'attitude des cinquante Anglais des deux sexes qui chaque soir se renouvelaient autour de chaque table d'hôte de la Suisse, quel pouvait être le but de tant de pèlerinages lointains, périlleux et difficiles, et je crois avoir fini par le découvrir . . . Pour une Anglaise le vrai but de la vie est de réussir à traverser les régions les plus élevées et les plus orageuses sans avoir un cheveu dérangé à son chignon. . . . Pour un Anglais, c'est de rentrer dans sa patrie après avoir fait le tour du monde sans avoir sali ses gants ni troué ses bottes.'

STUDER, GOTTLIEB. BERNE, ZURICH, DAVOS, SCALETTA PASS, SCANFS, BEVERS, PIZ PADELLA, ST. MORITZ, JULIER PASS, BIVIO, STALLERBERG PASS, AVERS CRESTA, THUSIS, ILANZ, KISTEN PASS, LINTHAL, ALTDORF, SURENEN PASS, ENGELBERG, JOCH PASS, BAUMGARTENALP, HOHENSTOLLEN, BRIENZ, INTERLAKEN, THUN, BERNE

TICKNOR, GEORGE. GRINDELWALD, KLEINE SCHEIDEGG, LAUTERBRUNNEN, INTERLAKEN, THUN, BERNE, LAUSANNE, GENEVA, MARTIGNY, SION, BRIG, SIMPLON PASS, DOMODOSSOLA

'I think the Jungfrau, as seen from the high pass of the Wengern Alp, —where, in the solitudes of nature, you stand, as it were, in the immediate presence of one of the grandest and most glorious works of God, —produces more religious feelings and associations than anything I ever witnessed, which belonged to merely physical existence.'

TÖPFFER, RODOLPHE. GENEVA, MARTIGNY, SION, LEUKERBAD, GEMMI PASS, KANDERSTEG, INTERLAKEN, MEIRINGEN, GRIMSEL PASS, FURKA PASS, ANDERMATT, ALTDORF, BRUNNEN, SCHWYZ, EINSIEDELN, ZURICH, ZUG, LUCERNE, BERNE, LAUSANNE, GENEVA

'Our nephews, crowded into carriages slipping along on rails with the speed of lightning, will go from Geneva to lunch at Interlaken, to dine at Altdorf, and to sleep at Basle.' On the Grimsel pass Töpffer's party met Hugi who was on the way to his hut on the Unteraar glacier.

TURNER, JOSEPH MALLORD WILLIAM. LAUSANNE, GENEVA, CHAMONIX, MARTIGNY, GRAND ST. BERNARD PASS, AOSTA, COURMAYEUR

Turner's companion Munro said 'all along, wherever he could get a few minutes, he had his little sketch-book out, many being remarkable, but he seemed to tire at last and got careless and slovenly'.

1837

ALBERT, PRINCE CONSORT. BASLE, MOUTIER, BIENNE, ILE ST. PIERRE, ELFENAU, BERNE, THUN, INTERLAKEN, BRIENZ, BRUNIG PASS, ALPNACH, LUCERNE, RIGI, BRUNNEN, FLUELEN, ANDERMATT, FURKA PASS, GLETSCH, GRIMSEL PASS, MEIRINGEN, GROSSE SCHEIDEGG, FAULHORN, GRINDELWALD, KLEINE SCHEIDEGG, LAUTERBRUNNEN, INTERLAKEN, THUN, BERNE, ELFENAU, FRIBOURG, LAUSANNE, OUCHY, GENEVA, CHAMONIX, COL DE BALME, MARTIGNY, BEX, VERNEX, VEVEY, MARTIGNY, SION, BRIG, SIMPLON PASS, DOMODOSSOLA

The prince and his brother were travelling on the advice of the King of the Belgians, for rumour had already connected Albert's name with that of Victoria. He sent her a book containing views of all the places he visited except two: from the Rigi he sent her a pressed alpenrose, and from Ferney a scrap of Voltaire's handwriting.

ANONYMOUS 9 C (*c*). DOMODOSSOLA, SIMPLON PASS, BRIG, SION, MARTIGNY, BEX, VEVEY, LAUSANNE, GENEVA, CHAMONIX, GENEVA, LAUSANNE, MORAT, BERNE, THUN, INTERLAKEN, LAUTERBRUNNEN, THUN, BERNE, LANGENTHAL, ST. URBAN, LUCERNE, ZURICH, SCHAFFHAUSEN

Voltaire's gardener was still alive, to take tourists round Ferney.

ANONYMOUS 9 D (*c*). GENEVA, CHAMONIX, MARTIGNY, SION, BRIG, SIMPLON PASS, DOMODOSSOLA, MILAN, COMO, LUGANO, BELLINZONA, ST. GOTTHARD PASS, ALTDORF, FLUELEN, RIGI, LUCERNE, SARNEN, BRUNIG PASS, MEIRINGEN, ROSENLAUI, BRIENZ, INTERLAKEN, LAUTERBRUNNEN, KLEINE SCHEIDEGG, GRINDELWALD, INTERLAKEN, THUN, BERNE, SCHAFFHAUSEN

ATKINS, HENRY MARTIN. GENEVA, CHAMONIX, MONT BLANC, GENEVA

Accompanying Atkins's party was Michel Balmat's dog, the first to reach the summit of Mont Blanc.

BALZAC, HONORÉ DE. LES VERRIÈRES, NEUCHÂTEL, ILE ST. PIERRE, SION, BRIG, SIMPLON PASS, DOMODOSSOLA, COMO, BELLINZONA, ST. GOTTHARD PASS, ALTDORF, LUCERNE, BASLE

'Cependant j'avais fait un voyage horriblement beau; il est bon de l'avoir fait. Mais c'est comme notre déroute de Russie: heureux qui a vu la Bérésina et se trouve sur ses jambes, sain et sauf! J'ai passé le Saint-Gothard avec quinze pieds de neige sur les sentiers par lesquels je l'ai traversé, attendu que la route n'était même pas visible dans la personne des hauts piquets qui l'indiquent; que les ponts jetés sur les torrents ne se voyaient pas plus que les torrents eux-mêmes. J'ai monté le Saint-Gothard à une heure du matin, par une lune sublime;

j'y ai vu le lever du soleil dans les neiges. Il faut avoir vu cela dans sa vie.' The impressions gained on this journey served for his *Albert Savarin.*

BECHER, AUGUSTA. GENEVA, VEYRIER, SIERNE

'And then crossing the Jura—snow still lying, and through the snow the lovely purple crocus and blue gentian peeping out; and then, at a certain turn of the road I so well remember, mother set me facing—such a sight—and said, "what do you think that is?" I said, "the sea". But it was the Lake of Geneva, so lovely, to lie before my delighted eyes all that summer . . .'

BEDDOES, THOMAS LOVELL. ZURICH, GLARUS, LINTHAL, SANDALP, RIGI, GRINDELWALD, FAULHORN, MEIRINGEN, GRIMSEL PASS, SIEDELHORN

'These summer excursions among the vallies, the glaciers and the mighty eminences of this magnificent country are to me the most delightful of all relaxations, without w[h] I sh[d] be as dull and sour as the refuse whey, in w[h] no pig has dipped his snout . . .'

DRINKWATER, MISS. SCHAFFHAUSEN, ZURICH, RAPPERSWIL, SARGANS, PFÄFERS, COIRE, THUSIS, SAN BERNARDINO PASS, MESOCCO, BELLINZONA, MAGADINO, LOCARNO, AIROLO, ST. GOTTHARD PASS, ALTDORF, BRUNNEN, RIGI, LUCERNE, BRUNIG PASS, MEIRINGEN, GRIMSEL PASS, OBERGESTELEN, GRIMSEL PASS, MEIRINGEN, JOCH PASS, ENGELBERG, SURENEN PASS, ALTDORF, WASSEN, SUSTEN PASS, MEIRINGEN, GROSSE SCHEIDEGG, GRINDELWALD, FAULHORN, KLEINE SCHEIDEGG, LAUTERBRUNNEN, INTERLAKEN, KANDERSTEG, GEMMI PASS, LEUK, SION, SANETSCH PASS, GSTEIG, KRINNEN PASS, LAUENEN, TRÜTTLISBERG PASS, LENK, ZWEISIMMEN, THUN, BERNE, BASLE

ENGELHARDT, CHRISTIAN MORITZ. BASLE, BERNE, THUN, KANDERSTEG, GEMMI PASS, LEUK, SION, EVOLENA, AROLLA, COL DE TORRENT, VISSOIE, SIERRE, VISP, ZERMATT, VISP, BRIG, FURKA PASS, ANDERMATT, ALTDORF, BRUNNEN, ZUG

The priest at Evolena had a housekeeper who 'pretexed illness, would scarcely consent to give lodging at all, and when we spoke of wanting two beds, behaved out of malice and laziness like sourness personified. At length, however, a small silver coin glinting in her hand, her face cleared of its wrinkles and resumed its normal condition, which was not so bad. . . .'

GROTE, GEORGE. LES VERRIÈRES, NEUCHÂTEL, SOLEURE, BERNE, THUN, LUCERNE

'Mousing in the Buchhandlungen' is the great pastime, lugging away armfulls of stuff to cram the carriage withal, to the dismay of poor

"Henry", who is at his wits' end how to stow the same so as to leave room for "Mistress" to get in'.

HERBERT, HENRY. GENEVA, VILLENEUVE, VEVEY, LAUSANNE, YVERDON, VALLORBE, LAC DE JOUX, DENT DE VAULION

The unfortunate Herbert who was walking about the Jura alone, fell through the trap of a water tank and was drowned.

MURRAY, JOHN. NEUCHÂTEL, LUCERNE, RIGI, GENEVA

At Neuchâtel Murray called on Agassiz. 'He took me up the hill behind the town (a member of the Jura range) and gave me a very instructive lecture on the singular isolated blocks of granite which have been transported no one knows how from the Alps, and there is no rock of the same kind nearer than the Alps as the distance must be 150 miles.'

The year after this journey, the first edition of the *Handbook to Switzerland* appeared with, in the Introduction, the following lines: 'The passion for climbing mountains so ardent in a young traveller soon cools; and they who have surmounted the Righi, the Faulhorn, and the Dole, may fairly consider any further ascents a waste of time and labour.'

NECKER, LOUIS ALBERT. GENEVA, VISP, ZERMATT, SAAS, BRIG, OBERGESTELEN

SAINTE-BEUVE, C. A. DE. GENEVA, LAUSANNE, BERNE, THUN, INTERLAKEN, LAUTERBRUNNEN, KLEINE SCHEIDEGG, GRINDELWALD, INTERLAKEN, BRIENZ, BRUNIG PASS, LUCERNE, ALTDORF, BRUNNEN, SCHWYZ, LUCERNE, LANGNAU, BERNE, LAUSANNE, AIGLE, LAUSANNE

As a literary pilgrim to scenes associated with Byron, Rousseau, Voltaire, Sénancour and Chénier, Sainte-Beuve stayed at Aigle with Juste Olivier. There the idea was formed of his giving a course of lectures at Lausanne Academy, the result of which was his famous study of 'Port Royal', and his professorship at Lausanne.

STENDHAL. GENEVA, OUCHY, VEVEY, VILLENEUVE, ST. GINGOLPH, THONON, GENEVA

'Sur le bateau à vapeur, nous nous enivrons de limonade gazeuse; elle est excellente.'

TICKNOR, GEORGE. TRAFOI, STELVIO PASS, BORMIO, TIRANO, CHIAVENNA, SPLÜGEN PASS, THUSIS, COIRE, FELDKIRCH

TÖPFFER, RODOLPHE. GENEVA, TANNINGE, SIXT, COL D'ANTERNE, SERVOZ, ST. GERVAIS, COL DU BONHOMME, COL DE LA SEIGNE, COURMAYEUR,

AOSTA, MILAN, LUGANO, DOMODOSSOLA, SIMPLON PASS, BRIG, SION, MARTIGNY, GENEVA

The innkeeper at Verrès had been guide to Brockedon. At the moment of departure two of Töpffer's boys said to the innkeeper: 'Sir, you have behind your house a small garden. Now in this garden there are some excellent muscatelle grapes. We have assuredly eaten a few bunches—how much do we owe you?' The innkeeper laughed and fetched a ladder.

1838

ANGEVILLE, HENRIETTE D'. GENEVA, CHAMONIX, MONT BLANC

ANSTED, D. T. LAUSANNE, MEX, COSSONAY, COL DE MOLLENDRUZ, LAC DE JOUX, VALLORBE, JOUGNE, LES VERRIÈRES, LA BRÉVINE, LE LOCLE, LA CHAUX DE FONDS, ST. BRAIS, PORRENTRUY, DELÉMONT, MOUTIER, WEISSENSTEIN, SOLEURE, BIENNE, ILE ST. PIERRE, NEUVEVILLE, BIENNE, BERNE

Ansted attended the geological congress at Porrentruy where Agassiz expounded his theory of the Ice Age. The geologists then went on an excursion, but at Rousseau's house on the Ile St. Pierre, 'For want, I suppose, of out-of-door work, the society held a meeting in the bedroom of the Frenchman's idol, some of the members sitting on three chairs, with which the room was furnished, some on the table, others on the floor, and the rest, of whom I was one, on the very bed on which he had slept.'

ARRIVABENE, GIOVANNI. MAGADINO, LOCARNO, BELLINZONA, MESOCCO, SAN BERNARDINO PASS, THUSIS, COIRE

BUCKLAND, WILLIAM. NEUCHÂTEL, BERNE, THUN, INTERLAKEN, GRINDELWALD, ROSENLAUI

The future Dean of Westminster was studying glaciers, and while at first hostile to Agassiz's glacial theory, he soon afterwards accepted it.

CALLOW, WILLIAM. VALLORBE, LAUSANNE, VEVEY, VILLENEUVE, GENEVA, CHAMONIX, COL DU BONHOMME, COL DE LA SEIGNE, COURMAYEUR, AOSTA, GRAND ST. BERNARD PASS, MARTIGNY, SION, LEUK, GEMMI PASS, KANDERSTEG, THUN, INTERLAKEN, LAUTERBRUNNEN, KLEINE SCHEIDEGG, GRINDELWALD, GROSSE SCHEIDEGG, MEIRINGEN, GRIMSEL PASS, FURKA PASS, ANDERMATT, FLUELEN, LUCERNE, ZURICH, RAPPERSWIL, WESEN, RAGAZ, PFÄFFERS, RORSCHACH, SCHAFFHAUSEN

The distinguished water-colour painter was on a sketching tour with Forman. At Chamonix they visited the Jardin and Couvercle and 'the next day we went with guides up Mont Blanc'; how far does not appear.

DESOR, EDOUARD. NEUCHÂTEL, BERNE, THUN, INTERLAKEN, MEIRINGEN, GRIMSEL PASS, MEIRINGEN, INTERLAKEN, BERNE, NEUCHÂTEL, LAUSANNE, BEX, VERNAYAZ, COL DE SALVAN, CHAMONIX, COL DE BALME, MARTIGNY

This was the first of Agassiz's expeditions undertaken to find evidence in support of the theory of the Ice Age. It convinced Agassiz's party and eventually converted Dean Buckland.

EARLE, PLINY. GENEVA, LAUSANNE, MONTREUX, ST. MAURICE, MARTIGNY, SION, BRIG, SIMPLON PASS, DOMODOSSOLA

ENGELHARDT, CHRISTIAN MORITZ. BASLE, BERNE, THUN, KANDERSTEG, GEMMI PASS, LEUK, VISP, ZERMATT

Among the visitors to Zermatt this year were a M. Gillion from Paris, Professor Carl Brunner, and Lory the artist.

GÉRARD DE NERVAL. GENEVA, LAUSANNE, BERNE, ZURICH, CONSTANCE

'Mais où est le Mont Blanc? me disais-je le premier soir; j'ai suivi les bords du lac, j'ai fait le tour des remparts, n'osant demander à personne: où est donc le Mont Blanc? Et j'ai fini par l'admirer sous la forme d'un immense nuage blanc et rouge, qui réalisait le rêve de mon imagination. Malheureusement, pendant que je calculais en moi-même les dangers que pouvait présenter le projet d'aller planter tout en haut un drapeau tricolore, pendant qu'il me semblait voir circuler des ours noirs sur la neige immaculée de sa cime, voilà que ma montagne a manqué de base tout à coup; quant au véritable Mont Blanc, tu comprendras qu'ensuite il m'ait causé peu d'impression.'

GODEFFROY, C. SION, EVOLENA, AROLLA, COL DE COLLON, AOSTA, IVREA, MACUGNAGA

HERVEY, CHARLES. CONSTANCE, SCHAFFHAUSEN, COIRE, THUSIS, SPLÜGEN PASS, LUCERNE, RIGI, INTERLAKEN, LAUTERBRUNNEN, GRINDELWALD, BRIENZ, THUN, BERNE, GENEVA, CHILLON, BEX, MARTIGNY, SION, BRIG, SIMPLON PASS, DOMODOSSOLA

HOFFMANN, G. BASLE, LUCERNE, ISENTHAL, ALTDORF, AMSTEG, MADERANERTAL, CAVARDIRASLÜCKE PASS, DISENTIS, KRÜZLI PASS, MADERANERTAL, AMSTEG, ST. GOTTHARD, HOSPENTHAL, FURKA PASS, GRIMSEL PASS, MEIRINGEN, GROSSE SCHEIDEGG, GRINDELWALD, FAULHORN

LAMONT, MARTHA MACDONALD. ZURICH, LUCERNE, LANGNAU, BERNE, THUN, INTERLAKEN, GRINDELWALD, THUN, BERNE, LAUSANNE, GENEVA, CHAMONIX

'I was entranced by that lake of Thun. And our drive of two miles after we landed, through Unterseen to Interlaken, was lovely; yet I can scarcely say I was delighted by it; for then, after my feelings on the lake, I began to be oppressed with beauty, and to cry to Nature, "Hold, enough!".'

MEYER, CONRAD FERDINAND. ZURICH, RAPPERSWIL, WESEN, RAGAZ, COIRE, THUSIS, SPLÜGEN PASS, CHIAVENNA, MALOJA PASS, SILVAPLANA

MICHELET, JULES. BESANÇON, MORAT, BERNE, THUN, INTERLAKEN, GRINDELWALD, MEIRINGEN, BRUNIG PASS, LUCERNE, ALTDORF, ST. GOTTHARD PASS, BELLINZONA, LUGANO, COMO

'Ces premiers bonds du Tessin sont une belle chose. Il s'élance d'une arche de neige, non pas savonneux, comme la Reuss, mais pur, azuré. Il précipite ses belles et héroïques eaux à travers des roches polies, formant des chutes hardies, sans crainte, hésitation, avide de l'avenir — ô jeunesse, ô espérance.'

MUNDT, THEODOR. SCHAFFHAUSEN, ZURICH, LUCERNE, BERNE, LAUSANNE, GENEVA

'The mountains are the Gods and also the goblins of the land, and no wanderer through Switzerland can boast of avoiding their teasing and railing him.'

NIGHTINGALE, FLORENCE. GENEVA

Sismondi 'escorted the Nightingale party up the Salève. They made that not very formidable ascent first on donkeys and then "in a sledge covered with straw and drawn by four oxen".'

SMITH, ALBERT. ST. CERGUE, NYON, GENEVA, CHAMONIX, TÊTE NOIRE PASS, MARTIGNY, GRAND ST. BERNARD PASS, AOSTA

'The story that the Mer de Glace resembles the sea suddenly frozen in a storm is all nonsense. From Montanvert it looks rather like a magnified white ploughed field.'

SPINOLA, H. DE (*c*). BASLE, SCHAFFHAUSEN, CONSTANCE, RHEINECK, ST. GALL, APPENZELL, GAIS, WINTERTHUR, ZURICH, LUCERNE, SOLEURE, BERNE, MORAT, FRIBOURG, ILE ST. PIERRE, NEUCHÂTEL, YVERDON, LAUSANNE, VEVEY, GENEVA, CHAMONIX, MARTIGNY, GRAND ST. BERNARD

TÖPFFER, RODOLPHE. GENEVA, MARTIGNY, SION, BRIG, MÜNSTER, FURKA PASS, HOSPENTHAL, ST. GOTTHARD PASS, BELLINZONA, ROVEREDO, MESOCCO, SAN BERNARDINO PASS, THUSIS, COIRE, WALLENSTADT, GLARUS, PRAGEL PASS, SCHWYZ, LUCERNE, BRUNIG PASS, BRIENZ, INTERLAKEN, THUN, BERNE, LAUSANNE, GENEVA

The inn at Roveredo was unfinished. 'An amorphous juxtaposition of planks, benches, tables and apparatus, bearing sacks, paillasses, and rags. . . . As soon as touched they creak; as soon as rested upon they come apart; as soon as one has got to sleep the neighbouring scaffolding crashes to the floor . . . various utensils of all descriptions complete the furnishings while complicating the perils in case of disaster.'

VEUILLOT, LOUIS. GENEVA, LAUSANNE, FRIBOURG, GRUYÈRES, MOLÉSON, CHARMEY, VALSAINTE, COL DE CHÉSALETTE, SCHWARZSEE, FRIBOURG, BERNE, THUN, INTERLAKEN, LAUTERBRUNNEN, INTERLAKEN, BRIENZ, BRUNIG PASS, LUCERNE, SCHWYZ, EINSIEDELN, ZURICH, BASLE

Giessbach: 'Un Anglais s'y rendit accompagné d'une vache qu'il avait embarquée à Brientz, malgré mille difficultés, et que plusieurs guides menaient solennellement. Arrivé au pied de la cascade, il but un verre de lait chaud, puis revint, sans avoir un instant perdu son sangfroid et sa gravité.'

YOUNG, JULIAN CHARLES. GENEVA, LAUSANNE, BERNE, THUN, LUCERNE, ALTDORF, ANDERMATT, ST. GOTTHARD PASS, BELLINZONA, LOCARNO

'As to my luckless wife, I saw her whirled away in such giddy, reckless boisterous fashion,—her face towards me, the back of her head towards her horse's heels,—that I regarded her as irretrievably doomed to destruction. At one time I became so alarmed that I shouted to my driver to tell hers to slacken speed. The answer to my appeal was the thrust of a horse-pistol in my face—a plain intimation that I might expect its contents down my throat if I did not hold my jaw while careering through the most critical part of the Val Tremola.'

1839

ARNOLD, THOMAS. ST. CERGUE

'I am come out . . . to see the morning sun on Mont Blanc and on the Lake, and to look with more, I trust, than outward eyes on this glorious scene. It is overpowering, like all other intense beauty, if you dwell upon it.'

BRAY, MRS. A. E. SCHAFFHAUSEN, ZURICH, ZUG, LUCERNE, LANGNAU, BERNE, THUN, INTERLAKEN, LAUTERBRUNNEN, GRINDELWALD, INTERLAKEN, MEIRINGEN, INTERLAKEN, THUN, BERNE, FRIBOURG, LAUSANNE, GENEVA, CHAMONIX, GENEVA, NEUCHÂTEL, SOLEURE, BALSTHAL, BASLE

This was the first year of the steamer on the lake of Brienz. 'Our damsel at the inn had informed us it was the worst of all steamers. She told us, also, it was so badly managed, the sparks flew about so much from the engine, that the wife of the Lutheran minister, on returning to Brienz, had very lately her umbrella set on fire and burnt on board the boat . . . We soon found out that she had spoken the truth about the steamer; for I had a small hole in my parasol and another in my gown, and Mr. Bray had one also in the arm of his coat, all made by the red-hot flying sparks.'

BUNSEN, CHRISTIAN, BARON. LES VERRIÈRES, NEUCHÂTEL, BERNE, AARAU, BADEN, ZURICH, BERNE

DESBAROLLES, ADOLPHE. BASLE, ZURICH, EINSIEDELN, WALLENSTADT, COIRE, THUSIS, HINTERRHEIN, VALSERBERG PASS, VALS, ILANZ, DISENTIS, OBERALP PASS, ANDERMATT, FURKA PASS, GRIMSEL PASS, MEIRINGEN, GROSSE SCHEIDEGG, GRINDELWALD, KLEINE SCHEIDEGG, LAUTERBRUNNEN, INTERLAKEN, THUN, BERNE, NEUCHÂTEL

Desbarolles's tour, which lasted a month, cost 200 francs, including the coach fares from Paris to Switzerland and back again.

DESOR, EDOUARD. NEUCHÂTEL, BERNE, THUN, KANDERSTEG, GEMMI PASS, LEUK, VISP, ZERMATT, VISP, BRIG, MÖREL, BETTMERGRAT, VIESCH, OBERGESTELEN, GRIMSEL PASS, UNTERAAR GLACIER

'It is impossible, gentlemen; no one ever crosses the Weissthor except to go to Macugnaga on a pilgrimage, and you gentlemen are not making a pilgrimage.'

DE VERE, AUBREY. BRIENZ, INTERLAKEN, MEIRINGEN, HANDECK

At Handeck, de Vere met a man who regarded all praise of the Alps 'as a distinct aspersion on Ireland. "What can you compare here", he demanded, "with the mountains of the Wicklow?" "Perhaps", I replied, "one might name the mountains of the Mont Blanc range". "Oh!" he replied, "they are out of all reason! I am after walking along the Chamouni valley for three days, and I only saw four of those mountains! Sure in Wicklow I have counted as many as eight of them in three hours!".'

ENGELHARDT, CHRISTIAN MORITZ. BASLE, BERNE, THUN, KANDERSTEG, GEMMI PASS, LEUK, VISP, ZERMATT, VISP, BRIG, LEUK, GEMMI PASS, KANDERSTEG, THUN, BERNE, BASLE

On the way to Zermatt, Engelhardt learned of the opening of an inn there, and of the regulation removing from the priests their right to take in travellers. Engelhardt was so upset at this innovation that he was on the point of giving up his visit to Zermatt altogether, when it occurred to him that the regulation could not take away the priest's right to put up his friends in his own house.

FORBES, JAMES DAVID. CHAMONIX, COL DU BONHOMME, COL DE LA SEIGNE, COURMAYEUR

'The scenery was not less fine to me than I recollect at the commencement of my Alpine journeys, and at this I greatly rejoice.'

FRÖBEL, JULIUS. ZURICH, AARAU, BERNE, THUN, KANDERSTEG, GEMMI PASS, LEUK, SION, HÉRÉMENCE, COL DE RIEDMATTEN, AROLLA, EVOLENA, COL DE BRÉONNA, VAL MOIRY, AYER, PAS DE FORCLETTA, TURTMANN, SION, MARTIGNY, LAUSANNE, BERNE, ZURICH

In the Val d'Hérens Fröbel was shown the hiding-place used by the young men during the French occupation of the Valais in order to avoid conscription in Napoleon's army. They were supplied with food by their girl-friends who carried it up to them in their mountain fastness. Fröbel's informant continues: 'Le résultat en fut de petits garçons.'

FRY, ELISABETH. GENEVA, LAUSANNE, FRIBOURG, BERNE, THUN, INTERLAKEN, GRINDELWALD, BÖNIGEN, BRIENZ, THUN, BERNE, LUCERNE, ZURICH

. . .'Switzerland is certainly a wonderful country and very attractive, but I think no more so than the Pyrenees. Sweet as it is, the flats of East and West Ham look to *us* sweeter . . . I also hope our circulation of books and tracts has been useful, and the establishment of at least one library at Brienz, for the use of the labouring classes.'

GRANT, HARRY ALLEN. CHAMONIX

GRAY, ASA. CONSTANCE, ZURICH, HORGEN, ZUG, RIGI, WÄGGIS, STANS, ENGELBERG, JOCH PASS, MEIRINGEN, GROSSE SCHEIDEGG, GRINDELWALD, KLEINE SCHEIDEGG, LAUTERBRUNNEN, BÖNIGEN, GIESSBACH, BRIENZ, MEIRINGEN, GRIMSEL PASS, OBERGESTELEN, BRIG, SION, MARTIGNY, COL DE BALME, MARTIGNY, VILLENEUVE, GENEVA

'I entered the little valley of Engelberg, the most beautiful and picturesque I have seen, probably the finest in Switzerland. At least that of Meyringen and this of Grindelwald, where I am now writing, are not to be compared with it. I only wonder it is so little known. I think it not improbable that I am the first American that has visited it.'

HOLMES, MRS. DALKEITH. GENEVA, CHAMONIX, GENEVA, LAUSANNE, VEVEY, BULLE, FRIBOURG, BERNE, THUN, INTERLAKEN, LAUTERBRUNNEN, GRINDELWALD, THUN, ZWEISIMMEN, SAANEN, CHÂTEAU D'OEX, GRUYÈRES, VEVEY, MARTIGNY, SION, BRIG, SIMPLON PASS, DOMODOSSOLA

'An English gentleman visited Chillon with the intention of painting not only the dungeon, but Bonnivard! For this purpose he chose a gendarme of spare habit, having a long beard and a sallow face, chained him to the pillar, and commenced his work saying "vous bon Bonnivard" . . . One day unfortunately, a feeling of pity overcame his comrade in the courtyard above, and he descended to relieve him. . . . The newcomer was a healthy, very young man, stout and beardless . . . and the amateur, in despair, when the fat man assumed the chain, could only hold his first prisoner fast, stamp his foot and shake his head at the other, and repeat all the French he knew, "lui bon Bonnivard, rester. Vous aller, pas bon Bonnivard".'

HUGO, VICTOR. BASLE, ZURICH, SCHAFFHAUSEN, LUCERNE, RIGI, LUCERNE, LANGNAU, THUN, BERNE, FRIBOURG, BULLE, VEVEY, LAUSANNE, GENEVA

Rigi: 'En présence de ce spectacle inexprimable, on comprend les crétins dont pullulent la Suisse et la Savoie. Les Alpes font beaucoup d'idiots. Il n'est pas donné à toutes les intelligences de faire ménage avec de telles merveilles et de promener du matin au soir sans éblouissement et sans stupeur un rayon visuel terrestre de cinquante lieues.'

LAING, SAMUEL. BASLE, ZUG, LUCERNE, RIGI, BRIENZ, GRINDELWALD, MONTREUX, GENEVA

'We, the inhabitants of the parish of Montreux, are of unspeakable interest in the speculations of the enlightened prosers on political economy in the winter evening re-unions of Geneva and Lausanne. They demonstrate from our sage example, to a simpering circle of wives and daughters-in-law, the wisdom, duty, possibility, and utility of keeping the numbers of a community, be it a nation, parish, or family, in due Malthusian ratio to the means of living . . . It appears from the register of this our parish of Montreux that the proportion of births to the population is 1 to 46, while in the rest of Switzerland it is reckoned 1 to 27 or 28.'

MALKIN, A. T. LAUTERBRUNNEN, KLEINE SCHEIDEGG, GRINDELWALD, FAULHORN, LAUTERBRUNNEN, TSCHINGEL PASS, KANDERSTEG, SERVOZ, MONT BUET, CHAMONIX

On the Faulhorn 'the quarters are of course not of the best; however we got tolerable coffee, and good bread, butter, and milk. No fleas. Charges not out of the way, considering—15 francs for tea, breakfast, and lodging for two.' At Zermatt 'I made my tea in a shaving pot, and washed my hands in a slop basin, and, as in the days of the patriarchs, had a sheep killed for my refection.'

MARTINEAU, HARRIET. BASLE, JOUGNE, LAUSANNE, LUGANO, BELLINZONA, ST. GOTTHARD PASS, LUCERNE, BASLE

Near Jougne, Harriet Martineau visited Toussaint l'Ouverture's prison at the Fort de Joux 'and it was virtually decided that "the Hour and the Man" should be written.'

SAINTE-BEUVE, C. A. DE. GENEVA, LAUSANNE, AIGLE, TOUR D'AI, COMBALLAZ, LAUSANNE, EYSINS, LAUSANNE, VALLORBE

> 'Pardon, cher Olivier, si votre alpestre audace
> Jusqu'aux hardis sommets ne me décide pas;
> Si quelque chose en moi résiste et pèse en bas;
> Si, pour un seul ravin, tantôt j'ai crié grâce!'

SCHOTT, ALBERT. ZURICH, BERNE, THUN, KANDERSTEG, GEMMI PASS, LEUK, SION, MARTIGNY, GRAND ST. BERNARD PASS, AOSTA, PONT ST. MARTIN, ISSIME, GABI, GRESSONEY, COL D'OLEN, ALAGNA, BOCCHETTA DI ALAGNA PASS, RIMASCO, RIMA, COL DEL PICCOLO ALTARE, MACUGNAGA, PONTE GRANDE, BANNIO, DROCHETTA PASS, RIMELLA, VARALLO, ARONA, MAGADINO, BELLINZONA, MESOCCO, SAN BERNARDINO PASS, THUSIS, COIRE, WALLENSTADT, ZURICH

Macugnaga: 'The travellers' book which dates from 1825 shows the names of many Italians, and also of many Swiss who come from the Valais over the Monte Moro pass, few Frenchmen, scarcely any Germans, but of course Englishmen who are ubiquitous.'

SEDGWICK, MISS. BASLE, BIENNE, AARBERG, BERNE, LAUSANNE, GENEVA, CHAMONIX, GENEVA

'A cry went from mouth to mouth of "The Alps! The Alps! The Alps!" Our hearts and—yes, I will tell you the whole truth—our eyes were full; for how, but by knowing how we felt, can you estimate the sensations they are fitted to produce? We have read descriptions of them in manuscript and print, in prose and poetry; we know their measurement; we have seen sketches, and paintings, and models of them; and yet, I think, if we had looked into the planet Jupiter, we could scarcely have felt a stronger emotion of surprise. In truth, up, up, where they hung and shone, they seemed to belong to heaven rather than earth.'

STUDER, BERNHARD. BERNE, THUN, KANDERSTEG, GEMMI PASS, LEUK, VISP, ZERMATT, SAAS, MONTE MORO PASS, MACUGNAGA, TURLO PASS, ALAGNA, IVREA, AOSTA, COURMAYEUR, COL DE LA SEIGNE, COL DU BONHOMME, ST. GERVAIS, SIXT, EVIAN

As a result of this journey Studer became converted to the Glacial theory.

STUDER, GOTTLIEB. BERNE, THUN, INTERLAKEN, MEIRINGEN, MÜHLESTALDEN, TRIFTLIMMI PASS, GRIMSEL PASS, STRAHLEGG PASS, GRINDELWALD, INTERLAKEN, THUN, BERNE

'Recently an inflexible Englishman selected the Strahlegg for his honeymoon journey and crossed it successfully with his young and equally determined bride.'

TÖPFFER, RODOLPHE. GENEVA, MARTIGNY, GRAND ST. BERNARD PASS, AOSTA, MILAN, CHIAVENNA, SPLÜGEN PASS, THUSIS, REICHENAU, DISENTIS, OBERALP PASS, ANDERMATT, ALTDORF, LUCERNE

'Travels on foot, notwithstanding their risks and dangers, even without a Mentor, but undertaken with chosen Telemachi as rich in health as they are poor in wealth, are certainly one of the best ways of making education in one of its aspects virile, healthy, and invigorating.'

WHATELEY, RICHARD. BASLE, ZURICH, COIRE, THUSIS, SPLÜGEN PASS, CHIAVENNA

1840

AMIEL, HENRI-FRÉDÉRIC. GENEVA, NEUCHÂTEL, BIENNE, BERNE, THUN, INTERLAKEN, LAUTERBRUNNEN, KLEINE SCHEIDEGG, GRINDELWALD, GROSSE SCHEIDEGG, MEIRINGEN, BRUNIG PASS, LUCERNE, RIGI, ZOFINGEN, GENEVA

'Les sites gracieux, frais, solitaires, comme celui du Brünig, avec un sentier perdu dans les pentes de la montagne, dominé par les forêts, et dominant les prairies de la vallée, serpentant entre des roches mousseuses, dont les quartiers servent de chemin aux piétons et d'enclume aux fers de chevaux qui passent, c'est une des plus agréables choses qu'on puisse imaginer.'

ARNOLD, THOMAS. MILAN, BELLINZONA, ST. GOTTHARD PASS, AMSTEG, ALTDORF, LUCERNE

BARROW, JOHN. SCHAFFHAUSEN, ZURICH, WALLENSTADT, COIRE, THUSIS, SPLÜGEN PASS, CHIAVENNA

BUNSEN, CHRISTIAN, BARON & FRANCES, BARONESS. BERNE, LAUSANNE, COPPET, GENEVA, LAUSANNE, YVERDON, NEUCHÂTEL, AVENCHES, MORAT, BERNE

CALAME, ALEXANDRE. GENEVA, VISP, ZERMATT, STALDEN, SAAS, MONTE MORO PASS, MACUGNAGA, VENZONE

Calame had wished to stay for some time and paint at Macugnaga, but the 'insectes dévorants' drove him away, and it was from Venzone that he painted his famous 'Vue de la Vallée d'Anzasca'.

DESOR, EDOUARD. NEUCHÂTEL, BERNE, THUN, INTERLAKEN, MEIRINGEN, GRIMSEL PASS, UNTERAAR GLACIER, STRAHLEGG PASS, GRINDELWALD, GROSSE SCHEIDEGG, MEIRINGEN, GRIMSEL PASS, UNTERAAR GLACIER

This was the first year of the occupation by Agassiz and his party of the rock shelter on the Unteraar glacier, famous by the name of 'Hotel des Neuchatelois'.

ENGELHARDT, CHRISTIAN MORITZ. BASLE, BERNE, LEUKERBAD, VISP, SAAS FEE

MALKIN, A. T. VISP, ZERMATT, ST. THEODUL PASS, COL DES CIMES BLANCHES, ST. JACQUES D'AYAS, BETTA FURKA PASS, GRESSONEY, COL D'OLEN, ALAGNA, TURLO PASS, MACUGNAGA, MONTE MORO PASS, SAAS, VISP, SION, PAS DE CHEVILLE, BEX, MARTIGNY, SION, VISP, ZERMATT, VISP, BRIG, EGGISHORN, BRIG, KIPPEL, LÖTSCHEN PASS, KANDERSTEG

Malkin's is perhaps the earliest description of the Eggishorn: 'Altogether this is certainly one of the finest views that I have seen in Switzerland, and worthy of being more frequently visited.'

MAURICE, FREDERICK DENISON. LAUSANNE, BERNE, THUN, INTERLAKEN, LAUTERBRUNNEN, KLEINE SCHEIDEGG, GRINDELWALD, INTERLAKEN, THUN, BERNE, LUCERNE, ZURICH

MICKIEWICZ, ADAM. LAUSANNE, BERNE, INTERLAKEN, ZURICH

'Je préfère nos paysages Lithuaniens sur lesquels on peut s'étendre et dormir à ces mirages lointains qui fatiguent les yeux. . . .'

PICKERING, ANNA MARIA WILHELMINA. SCHAFFHAUSEN, ZURICH, ALBIS, LUCERNE, THUN, INTERLAKEN, GRINDELWALD, BASLE

'I did not pass a very comfortable night at l'Aigle Noire at Grindelwald, as we were at the foot of the Wetterhorn and its glaciers, and heard, alternately, the thunder roar, and the avalanches falling with almost incessant lightning, and a wind, which would have unroofed the houses, without the heavy stones, with which they are all protected. However, it was well worth a little nervousness to pass a night in such scenery.'

SHELLEY, MARY. SCHAFFHAUSEN, ZURICH, WALLENSTADT, COIRE, THUSIS, SPLÜGEN PASS, CHIAVENNA, MILAN, DOMODOSSOLA, SIMPLON PASS, BRIG, SION, MARTIGNY, VEVEY, GENEVA

'There was no horror; but there was grandeur. There was a majestic simplicity that inspired awe; the naked bones of a gigantic world were here: the elemental substance of fair mother Earth, an abode for mighty spirits who need not the ministrations of food and shelter that keep man alive, but whose vast shapes could only find, in these giant crags, a home proportionate to their power.'

STANLEY, ARTHUR PENRHYN. BASLE, BERNE, THUN, INTERLAKEN, LAUTERBRUNNEN, KLEINE SCHEIDEGG, GRINDELWALD, FAULHORN, LUCERNE, GENEVA, MARTIGNY, SION, BRIG, SIMPLON PASS, DOMODOSSOLA

'Do you ask my opinion of Switzerland? . . . in the investigation of the assertion that the Swiss mountains are beautiful; with a certain amount of clouds, a sunset, a cheerful companion, a contented stomach, I think it perfectly true; but with too many clouds, or none at all, with a glaring noonday sun, alone, or tearing up a hill after dinner, I think it perfectly false.'

STUDER, GOTTLIEB. BERNE, THUN, INTERLAKEN, LAUTERBRUNNEN, TSCHINGEL PASS, KANDERSTEG, THUN, BERNE

'Crossing the lake of Thun in favourable weather is beautiful beyond compare, and worthy of a journey in Elysium; around the blue basin with its ring of pleasant friendly villages, the Alps in their proudest form and magic variety rise up to the vault of heaven with glorious majesty.'

TÖPFFER, RODOLPHE. GENEVA, CHAMONIX, TÊTE NOIRE PASS, MARTIGNY, SION, LEUKERBAD, GEMMI PASS, KANDERSTEG, INTERLAKEN,

LAUTERBRUNNEN, KLEINE SCHEIDEGG, GRINDELWALD, GROSSE SCHEIDEGG, MEIRINGEN, BRUNIG PASS, LUCERNE, RIGI, ZUG, ZURICH, SOLEURE, BIENNE, LAUSANNE, GENEVA

'Everything is picturesque enough if the weather is fine, the route varied, the shade cool, the table well provided, and the beds passable. Shops are a distraction, shopkeepers amusing, and inns even on the Rigi are pleasant. . . . Walking, with its vicissitudes, adventures, and even its miseries, gives savour to everything. And if it is pleasurable on the plains, it has additional and quite different attractions in the mountains. . . . After these mountain wanderings, repose and the plains give pleasure, and one feels better able to consent to spend eleven months in them.'

TORR, T. S. GENEVA, MARTIGNY, SION, BRIG, SIMPLON PASS, DOMODOSSOLA

TURGENEV, IVAN. MAGADINO, BELLINZONA, AIROLO, ST. GOTTHARD PASS, ALTDORF, FLUELEN, LUCERNE, BASLE

'Le spectacle de la nature me causait des impressions très vives, mais je ne recherchai pas le moins du monde ce que l'on nomme communément ses beautés, les montagnes extraordinaires, les précipices, les chutes d'eau, je n'aimais point à être contraint d'admirer la nature, à me sentir troublé par elle.'

During his journey from Italy to Germany, Turgenev managed to lose an umbrella, a cloak, a box, a walking-stick, a lorgnon, a pillow, a penknife, a purse, three towels, two handkerchiefs, two shirts, and, for a time, his heart.

VERNON, WILLIAM WARREN. GENEVA, LAUSANNE, MARTIGNY, SION, BRIG, SIMPLON PASS, DOMODOSSOLA

'There were two steamers at that time plying on the lake, the *Helvétie* (English built) and the *Léman* (Swiss built) as to the respective merits of which we children were prepared to wage uncompromising war against the *Léman*. There was a very ancient tumble-down little steamer, called the *Winkelried*, moored off the Île Jean Jacques Rousseau, left there to rot away, having apparently been a dead failure from the first.'

1841

AMIEL, HENRI-FRÉDÉRIC. GENEVA, FILLINGE, FAUCIGNY

'La journée fut magnifique. Je m'accoudai sur un roc au bord de l'abîme et je contemplai ce paysage avec admiration. A ma gauche, la montagne descendait à pic dans le précipice, à ma droite s'enfuyaient des champs labourés, où tintaient les clochettes de quelques attelages. Je voyais le lac et Genève dans le lointain. Les monts déchiquetés de la

Savoie, le Bornand, les Brézons, couronnaient le paysage de leurs lignes bizarres. Le tout éclairé d'un jour si transparent, dans une atmosphère si tranquille, que c'était à se jeter à genoux.'

ANONYMOUS 10. ZURICH, ZUG, RIGI, LUCERNE, BRUNIG PASS, BRIENZ, INTERLAKEN, LAUTERBRUNNEN, KLEINE SCHEIDEGG, GRINDELWALD, GROSSE SCHEIDEGG, MEIRINGEN, GRIMSEL PASS, OBERGESTELEN, BRIG, SION, MARTIGNY, COL DE BALME, CHAMONIX

BARING-GOULD, SABINE. BASLE, BERNE, LUCERNE, RIGI, LUCERNE, THUN, BERNE, VEVEY

'It is singular the Swiss wood-carvers have not progressed in a century, but continue to cut the same uninteresting and inartistic salad-bowls and spoons, brackets, paper-cutters, chalets and little bears.'

BUNSEN, FRANCES, BARONESS. BERNE, LUCERNE, FLUELEN, ANDERMATT, FLUELEN, LUCERNE, BERNE, LAUSANNE, LAVEY

CHAMBERS, WILLIAM. BASLE, BADEN, ZURICH, ALBIS, ZUG, LUCERNE, LANGNAU, THUN, BERNE, MORAT, LAUSANNE, VEVEY, GENEVA, LAUSANNE, FRIBOURG, BERNE, NEUCHÂTEL, LES VERRIÈRES

CHORLEY, HENRY FOTHERGILL. CHIAVENNA, SPLÜGEN PASS, THUSIS, COIRE, ZURICH, BRUGG, BASLE

On his journey through Switzerland, Chorley had found a pipe with the portrait of Lady Blessington painted on the bowl.

. . . 'Then take, nor scorn this humble clay,
In vulgar guise a truth expressing,
That even in our ungrateful day,
Mankind, for all the cynics say,
Still knows the value of a blessing.'

CLARKE, ANDREW. DOMODOSSOLA, SIMPLON PASS, BRIG, SION, MARTIGNY, BEX, CHILLON, MONTREUX, LAUSANNE, NYON, GENEVA

'To visit Chillon, Clarens, and Lausanne, in one day, where the fancy of Byron and Rousseau delighted to ramble, is likely to recompense us for our uninviting route.'

DESOR, EDOUARD. NEUCHÂTEL, BERNE, THUN, INTERLAKEN, MEIRINGEN, GRIMSEL PASS, UNTERAAR GLACIER, MEIRINGEN, ROSENLAUI, MEIRINGEN, BERNE, NEUCHÂTEL, BERNE, MEIRINGEN, GRIMSEL PASS, UNTERAAR GLACIER, OBERGESTELEN, ULRICHEN, GRIES PASS, TOSA FALLS, ALBRUN PASS, BINN, OBERGESTELEN, GRIMSEL PASS, OBERAARJOCH, MÄRJELENSEE, JUNGFRAU, VIESCH, GRIMSEL PASS, UNTERAAR GLACIER

Two English peers, mistaking the Hotel des Neuchatelois for a real inn, tried to stay and use it as a hunting-box. On the other

'This is certainly one of the finest views that I have seen in Switzerland, and worthy of being more frequently visited'

(*Swiss Federal Railways*)

A. T. MALKIN, 1840; Eggishorn

'The people seem to treat their horses, cattle, &c. kindly, and the animals, consequently, seem to have more intelligence, . . . for if anything occurs, they look on as with considerable interest'

(*Paul Popper*) MICHAEL FARADAY, 1841

hand, Lord Enniskillen, J. D. Forbes, and Mr. Heath were welcomed as guests. The party also saw Mr. and Mrs. Cowan on their way over the Strahlegg pass from Grindelwald to the Grimsel, Mrs. Cowan in a sedan chair.

DONIZETTI, GAETANO. BASLE, LUCERNE, FLUELEN, ST. GOTTHARD PASS, AIROLO, BELLINZONA, MILAN

During his stay in Switzerland the previous year, Donizetti had composed his opera *Rita.* This year he started composing *Linda di Chamounix* on Rossi's poem, but it is not clear that he ever went there.

ENGELHARDT, CHRISTIAN MORITZ. BASLE, LEUKERBAD, VISP, SAAS FEE, STALDEN, ZERMATT

FARADAY, MICHAEL. BASLE, MOUTIER, BIENNE, BERNE, THUN, KANDERSTEG, GEMMI PASS, LEUKERBAD, GEMMI PASS, KANDERSTEG, THUN, INTERLAKEN, LAUTERBRUNNEN, KLEINE SCHEIDEGG, GRINDELWALD, INTERLAKEN, MEIRINGEN, GRIMSEL PASS, FURKA PASS, ANDERMATT, ALTDORF, LUCERNE, ZUG, ZURICH, SCHAFFHAUSEN, BASLE

On the Kleine Scheidegg Faraday says of the alphorn, 'by dexterous blowing, the lad could bring out the harmonic notes of two or even three octaves, and so made his rough instrument discourse excellent music. It was rich, and full, and very pleasant, filling these immense spaces with sound. A wall of rock a good way off returned a fine echo, the time being such that five or six notes were given back to us after the horn was silent; and as different parts of the precipice returned the sound at different times, very beautiful combinations of the notes took place—the distant faint echo of the echo lingering beautifully on the ear at last. He then gave us a bang with an iron cannon, but that was not so good.'

At the Grimsel Faraday met Forbes.

FORBES, JAMES DAVID. COURMAYEUR, COL FERRET, MARTIGNY, SION, BRIG, OBERGESTELEN, GRIMSEL PASS, UNTERAAR GLACIER, OBERAARJOCH, MÄRJELENSEE, JUNGFRAU, VIESCH, BRIG, VISP, SAAS FEE, STALDEN, ZERMATT, VISP, SION, MARTIGNY, SALVAN, LAUSANNE, NEUCHÂTEL, BERNE, BASLE

This was the year of Forbes's stay with Agassiz at the 'Hotel des Neuchatelois' on the Unteraar glacier, and of his, the first British, ascent of the Jungfrau.

LAMARTINE, ALPHONSE DE. GENEVA, VILLENEUVE, BEX, ST. MAURICE, LAVEY, VEVEY, THUN, INTERLAKEN, BERNE, FRIBOURG, LAUSANNE, EVIAN, GENEVA

The poem 'Ressouvenir du Lac Léman' was the result of this journey.

MARTINS, CHARLES. GRINDELWALD, FAULHORN

Two months on the Faulhorn making scientific observations.

RUSKIN, JOHN. GENEVA, LAUSANNE, NEUCHÂTEL, TAVANNES, BASLE

'The sun is setting on Lake Leman, and I am sitting at my own room window, watching the opposite outline. The snow on the high point, fresh, is dazzlingly bright, but only there; it shades softly down on the red crags. I dim my eye—it glows like a moonrise in the grey sky. I cannot write for looking at it. Brighter yet! now it is running to the left, glowing on the pastures and pines. Oh, beautiful! The hills are all becoming misty fire, and all is grey beneath them and above. Yet redder! The middle bit is all snow; it is bursting into conflagration, over purple shades. Now the light has left the bases, but it is far along to the left on the broad field of snow—less and less—but redder and redder. Oh, glorious! It is going fast; only the middle peak has it still,—fading fast, fading—gone. All is cold but the sky, whose spray clouds are red above, and a soft clear twilight still far down the lake with the Voirons and Salève against it. When shall I—Nay, now there is a faint red glow again on the snowfields to the left. It must have been a cloud which took it off before. When shall I see the sun, set again on Lake Leman, and who will be with me—or who not! All is cold now.'

STUDER, GOTTLIEB. BERNE, THUN, INTERLAKEN, GRINDELWALD, SCHWARZHORN, ROSENLAUI, MEIRINGEN, GADMEN, STEIN, SUSTENHORN, MÜHLESTALDEN, STEINLIMMI PASS, STEINHAUSHORN, GUTTANNEN, GRIMSEL PASS

TALFOURD, THOMAS NOON. GENEVA, CHAMONIX, TÊTE NOIRE PASS, MARTIGNY, SION, LEUKERBAD, GEMMI PASS, KANDERSTEG, INTERLAKEN, LAUTERBRUNNEN, KLEINE SCHEIDEGG, GRINDELWALD, THUN, BERNE, BASLE

Lauterbrunnen: 'On the left, a pile of brown gigantic rocks uprose—say rather one rock, for there was perfect unity of style in mighty irregularities—which seemed like a huge exaggeration of an old English mansion of the age of Henry the Seventh—with pinnacles—clustered chimneys—gable ends—vast porches—fretted, broken stories—niches for great statues—an entire picture—which might be one of Cattermole's illustrations of Dickens expanded into giant form and petrified!'

TÖPFFER, RODOLPHE. GENEVA, EVIAN, VILLENEUVE, GENEVA, AIGLE, COL DES MOSSES, CHÂTEAU D'OEX, SAANEN, ZWEISIMMEN, INTERLAKEN, MEIRINGEN, GRIMSEL PASS, FURKA PASS, ANDERMATT, OBERALP PASS, DISENTIS, COIRE, LENZERHEIDE, TIEFENKASTEL, JULIER PASS, ST. MORITZ, PONTRESINA, BERNINA PASS, TIRANO, BORMIO, STELVIO PASS, VENICE, MILAN, DOMODOSSOLA, SIMPLON PASS, BRIG, SION, MARTIGNY, GENEVA

On the Grimsel pass Töpffer's party met Forbes and Agassiz, but missed Faraday by one day. St. Moritz is described as 'a little town composed of stables and billiard-saloons where bearded bath-guests pass their time; one of those places that owe to the transient presence of invalids a little false vivacity, much cigar smoke, and a grotesque mixture of busy peasants, idle gentry, tipplers, makers of cheese, and of cannons at billiards.'

TURNER, JOSEPH MALLORD WILLIAM. LUCERNE, CONSTANCE, ZURICH, ALTDORF, ST. GOTTHARD PASS, BELLINZONA, CHIAVENNA, SPLÜGEN PASS, THUSIS

During this journey Turner worked at his *Lucerne and Berne* sketch-book. On his return he worked up four sketches: *The Pass of the Splügen, Mont Righi, morning, Mont Righi, evening,* and *Lake Lucerne from above Brunnen.*

VIGNET, LOUIS. GENEVA, CHAMONIX, COL DU BONHOMME, COL DE LA SEIGNE, COURMAYEUR, COL FERRET, COL DE FENÊTRE, GRAND ST. BERNARD PASS, MARTIGNY, LAUSANNE, GENEVA

'Déjà, l'an 1841 régnant par la grâce de Dieu, le Prieuré de Chamonix, — je veux le redire encore, au risque d'entendre mes lectrices me traiter de radoteur, — le Prieuré prenait les allures d'une capitale microscopique. La civilisation s'y installait en conquérante. En trois mois de représentation le théâtre ne désemplissait pas.'

VOGT, CARL. BERNE, THUN, INTERLAKEN, ISELTWALD, FAULHORN, GROSSE SCHEIDEGG, ROSENLAUI, MEIRINGEN, GRIMSEL PASS, UNTERAAR GLACIER, MEIRINGEN, INTERLAKEN, ST. BEATENBERG, THUN, BERNE

Among the visitors to the Grimsel hospice were 'some Englishmen who did not quite know how to sit down to table as they had not been introduced and therefore did not know who had the best claims to precedence'; also an English lady blue-stocking, and a Scotsman of the 44th Regiment, who had come straight all the way to consult Agassiz on a fossil shark's tooth that he had found in the London Clay.

YATES, MRS. ASHTON. BASLE, ZURICH, ZUG, LUCERNE, LANGNAU, THUN, INTERLAKEN, LAUTERBRUNNEN, GRINDELWALD, GROSSE SCHEIDEGG, MEIRINGEN, INTERLAKEN, THUN, BERNE, FRIBOURG, MORAT, LAUSANNE, GENEVA, CHAMONIX, TÊTE NOIRE PASS, MARTIGNY, SION, BRIG, SIMPLON PASS, DOMODOSSOLA

'The captain [of the steamer on the lake of Brienz], a very fine-looking young man, spoke German so fluently, that I took him for a Swiss. On hearing us talking English, he accosted me in that language, and after a little conversation he said, "it is most surprising that the English should come in such numbers to this country, when the scenery in Scotland is so much more beautiful . . ." I listened without being convinced—however, I respected his nationality, and wishing to change the subject to one equally gratifying to his *amor patriae* on which we might agree, I asked him if he was not proud of Sir Walter Scott: he answered very coolly, "He was my uncle".'

1842

COROT, CAMILLE. GENEVA, MORNEX, MONTREUX, FRIBOURG, GRUYÈRES, THUN, INTERLAKEN

While Corot was carousing one night in Montreux with his young brother artists the fire alarm was given, whereupon all flew to the fire engine and rushed it through the night in pouring rain to Vevey. Corot kept his place in the team as far as Vevey where he had to give up through exhaustion.

DESOR, EDOUARD. NEUCHÂTEL, BERNE, THUN, INTERLAKEN, MEIRINGEN, GRIMSEL PASS, UNTERAAR GLACIER, LAUTERBRUNNEN

The 'Hotel des Neuchatelois' was this year replaced by a large tent known as the 'Ark'. One Sunday, the workmen who had assisted in sinking shafts and doing other work on the glacier for the scientists came with their wives and families, and dancing went on all night in the 'Ark', to the music of a fiddle and dulcimer. This is probably the only example of a ball held on a glacier.

DURBIN, JOHN P. GENEVA, CHAMONIX, COL DE BALME, MARTIGNY, GRAND ST. BERNARD, MARTIGNY, VILLENEUVE, GENEVA, NYON, LAUSANNE, PAYERNE, FRIBOURG, BERNE, LANGNAU, LUCERNE, ZUG, ZURICH, BASLE

'An old gardener of M. Voltaire still lives on the premises—a pleasant, garrulous old man, who has many stories to tell of his celebrated master.'

ENGELHARDT, CHRISTIAN MORITZ. BASLE, LEUKERBAD, VISP, SAAS FEE

FORBES, JAMES DAVID. BERNE, LAUSANNE, BEX, GENEVA, CHAMONIX, COL DU BONHOMME, COL DE LA SEIGNE, COURMAYEUR, COL DU GÉANT, CHAMONIX, TÊTE NOIRE PASS, MARTIGNY, GRAND ST. BERNARD, SEMBRANCHER, CHERMONTANE, COL DE FENÊTRE DE BALME, VALPELLINE, PRARAYÉ, COL DE COLLON, AROLLA, EVOLENA, COL D'HÉRENS, ZERMATT, ST. THEODUL PASS, BREUIL, COL DE PORTOLA, AYAS, COL DE RANZOLA, GRESSONEY, COL D'OLEN, ALAGNA, TURLO PASS, MACUGNAGA, MONTE MORO PASS, SAAS, STALDEN, VISP, SION, MARTIGNY, CHAMONIX, GENEVA, BERNE, BASLE

'We knew too well what accommodation might be expected even in the capital of a remote Vallaisan valley to anticipate any luxuries at Evolena. Indeed, Mr. Studer had already been there the previous year, and having lodged with the Curé, forewarned me that our accommodation would not be splendid. A change had, however, occurred in the establishment of the "Pfarrhaus" since 1841, by the introduction of the Curé's sister, who usually lived at Sion, a person of ungovernable temper and rude manners, who seemed to find pleasure in the arrival of strangers only as fresh subjects whereon to vent her spleen. . . .'

GODWIN, MRS. C. G. SCHAFFHAUSEN, ZURICH, ALBIS, ZUG, LUCERNE, ENTLIBUCH, THUN, INTERLAKEN, LAUTERBRUNNEN, GRINDELWALD, THUN, BERNE, FRIBOURG, BULLE, VEVEY, GENEVA, ROLLE, NEUCHÂTEL, SOLEURE, BASLE

GOODWIN, HARVEY. GRIMSEL PASS, UNTERAAR GLACIER, CHAMONIX

MENDELSSOHN-BARTHOLDY, FELIX. INTERLAKEN, LAUTERBRUNNEN, GRINDELWALD, FAULHORN, MEIRINGEN, GRIMSEL PASS, FURKA PASS, ANDERMATT, ALTDORF, SURENEN PASS, ENGELBERG, LUCERNE, ZURICH

'When I see this country with my wife, I have quite a different impression from the previous times; then I wished forthwith to climb every crested mountain, and to run into every meadow; this time, on the contrary, I should like to stay everywhere, and to remain for months in one spot.'

ROSTAN, J. L. LAUSANNE, AIGLE, ORMONT-DESSUS

The Methodist missionary had to contend with grievous discouragements. 'The views spread by the Plymouth Brethren sapped the very foundations of all evangelical activity. . . .' There was also opposition from the Darbyists: 'The Irvingites also have their disciples. The Lardonists who have essayed to walk on the waters of the lake, also have their adherents.'

RUSKIN, JOHN. GENEVA, CHAMONIX, GENEVA

'Chamouni is such a place! There is no sky like its sky . . . There is no air like its air. Coming down from Chamouni into the lower world is like coming out of open morning air into an ale-house parlour where people have been sleeping and smoking with the door shut all night.'

SHERMAN, MRS. FELDKIRCH, RAGAZ, PFÄFERS, COIRE, THUSIS, SAN BERNARDINO PASS, MESOCCO, BELLINZONA, AIROLO, ST. GOTTHARD PASS, ANDERMATT, FLUELEN, LUCERNE, RIGI, SARNEN, BRUNIG PASS, MEIRINGEN, GRIMSEL, MEIRINGEN, GROSSE SCHEIDEGG, GRINDELWALD, KLEINE SCHEIDEGG, LAUTERBRUNNEN, INTERLAKEN, THUN, BERNE, FRIBOURG, VEVEY, MARTIGNY, TÊTE NOIRE PASS, CHAMONIX, GENEVA, LAUSANNE, YVERDON, NEUCHÂTEL, BIENNE, MOUTIER, BASLE

'Neither Byron's pen nor Claude's pencil could give an adequate idea of the awful grandeur of this sublime scene—glaciers spread at your feet, covering a surface of many miles—peaks of mountains, sparkling with eternal snows [the Finster-Aarhorn, the Schreckhorn, and others], towering above in their purity and might—shivered rocks, which the avalanches have rent and broken, presenting their rugged sides, and threatening to overwhelm you—roaring torrents, pouring down from the icy caverns with foaming fury—give an impression of the power which creates these wonders which can never be effaced. We seem to see in them the awful God; but how refreshing it is to believe

"This awful God is ours . . .".'

STUDER, GOTTLIEB. BERNE, THUN, INTERLAKEN, MEIRINGEN, GRIMSEL PASS, OBERGESTELEN, VIESCH, JUNGFRAU, EGGISHORN, OBERAARJOCH, GRIMSEL PASS, GUTTANNEN, MÄHRENHORN, SÄTTELI PASS, ENGSTLENALP, JOCH PASS, TITLIS, MEIRINGEN, INTERLAKEN, THUN, BERNE

'The hour that I spent on the summit of the Jungfrau was among the finest in my life, and the magnificent impression which it left on my mind was so vivid that long afterwards images of that day frequently formed the subject of my dreams.'

TALFOURD, THOMAS NOON. SCHAFFHAUSEN, ZURICH, WALLENSTADT, COIRE, THUSIS, SPLÜGEN PASS, CHIAVENNA, COMO, LUGANO, BELLINZONA, ST. GOTTHARD PASS, ALTDORF, LUCERNE, LANGNAU, BERNE, MOUTIER, BASLE

'There is also this remarkable beauty of the St. Gotthard pass—more remarkable in recollection than in enjoyment—that it consists simply of the courses of two rivers: the Reuss leads you into Switzerland, the Ticino to Italy; and every picture of grandeur or beauty by the way has its own river for its "secret remembrancer". Who amidst such aspiring labour or such headlong pressure could wish for a happier artificial memory than is supplied by the courses of these rivers?'

TÖPFFER, RODOLPHE. GENEVA, MARTIGNY, COL DE BALME, CHAMONIX, COL DU BONHOMME, COL DE LA SEIGNE, COURMAYEUR, COL FERRET, MARTIGNY, SION, EVOLENA, SION, VISP, ZERMATT, VISP, BRIG, OBERGESTELEN, GRIMSEL PASS, MEIRINGEN, INTERLAKEN, THUN, BERNE, LAUSANNE, GENEVA

The steamer on the lake of Brienz shipped a lot of English ladies at Giessbach, and, to make room for these on deck, the hatch leading down to the saloon and other apartments was covered over and chairs placed thereon. Presently, a tourist rushed up, very intent on descending the stairs. He was promptly seized by the crew and pushed over the railings and in through a porthole to the deck that he so urgently desired to visit.

TURNER, JOSEPH MALLORD WILLIAM. LUCERNE, ZURICH, ZUG, ALTDORF, ST. GOTTHARD PASS, BELLINZONA

The sketches made during this journey served for the water-colour pictures of *Goldau*, *St. Gotthard* (or *Faido*), *Kussnacht*, *Zug*, and *Zurich*.

WEITBRECHT, JOHN JAMES. BASLE, BERNE, GURNIGEL, INTERLAKEN, MEIRINGEN, GRIMSEL PASS, LAUSANNE, BERNE, ZURICH

1843

ARGYLL, GEORGE DOUGLAS, DUKE OF. COMO, LUGANO, MAGADINO, LOCARNO, DOMODOSSOLA, SIMPLON PASS, BRIG, SION, MARTIGNY, LAUSANNE, GENEVA, CHAMONIX, GENEVA, LAUSANNE, YVERDON, SCHAFFHAUSEN

The geologist statesman duke had taken a new double-barrel Purdey with him, and hearing that there was a Tiro Fédérale at Locarno, decided to go and try his luck: 'but I had no chance with them'.

BAKUNIN, MICHAEL. ZURICH, NYON, ILE ST. PIERRE, BERNE, THUN, INTERLAKEN

Bakunin and his friends ran out of money during their tour of the Bernese Oberland, and it is a measure of Bakunin's powers of persuasion that he was able to borrow a hundred francs from his mountain guide.

CLOUGH, ARTHUR HUGH. DOMODOSSOLA, SIMPLON PASS, BRIG, OBERGESTELEN, GRIMSEL PASS, MEIRINGEN, GRINDELWALD, FAULHORN, INTERLAKEN, THUN, BERNE, BASLE

'Have you the Giesbach seen? a Fall
In Switzerland you say, that's all;
That, and an inn from which proceeds
A path that to the Faulhorn leads.' . . .

COTTA, BERNHARD. BASLE, MOUTIER, BIENNE, NEUCHÂTEL, GENEVA, CHAMONIX, TÊTE NOIRE PASS, MARTIGNY, VEVEY, BULLE, FRIBOURG, BERNE, THUN, INTERLAKEN, LAUTERBRUNNEN, KLEINE SCHEIDEGG, GRINDELWALD, FAULHORN, GROSSE SCHEIDEGG, MEIRINGEN, ALTDORF, ST. GOTTHARD PASS, BELLINZONA

DESOR, EDOUARD. NEUCHÂTEL, BERNE, THUN, INTERLAKEN, MEIRINGEN, GRIMSEL PASS, UNTERAAR GLACIER, MEIRINGEN, GROSSE SCHEIDEGG, GRINDELWALD, FAULHORN

For this year's scientific observations on the Unteraar glacier, the 'Hotel des Neuchatelois' and the 'Ark' were replaced by a building on dry land by the side of the glacier, known as the 'Pavillon'.

DE VERE, AUBREY. BASLE, LUCERNE, FLUELEN, HOSPENTHAL, ST. GOTTHARD PASS, BELLINZONA, LUGANO, SAN SALVATORE, PORLEZZA, MENAGGIO, COMO

De Vere was accompanied by Sir Henry Taylor who did not appreciate the Alps, for, 'after a long silence he looked up and said, "I pray to Heaven I may never see mountains *of this sort* again" '.

FORBES, JAMES DAVID. BEX, MARTIGNY, COL DE BALME, CHAMONIX, TÊTE NOIRE PASS, MARTIGNY, SION, LEUK, GEMMI PASS,

KANDERSTEG, INTERLAKEN, GRINDELWALD, FAULHORN, GROSSE SCHEIDEGG, MEIRINGEN, INTERLAKEN, THUN, BERNE, ZURICH

On the Mer de Glace 'I found a piece of wood which on examination appeared to have once formed part of a ladder, a very stout one, as it had holes for the insertion of the rungs. This may probably have been a portion of de Saussure's ladder, much chafed by the glacier. It was almost at the same spot that I found similar fragments in 1832.'

GOBAT, SAMUEL. BERNE, ALBISBRUNN, SOLEURE, WEISSENSTEIN

HEUGH, HUGH. BASLE, MOUTIER, BERNE, NEUCHÂTEL, LAUSANNE, GENEVA, CHAMONIX, GENEVA

'This land of Alp and lake is, indeed, a mountain temple reared for the human mind on the dull unvaried plains of Europe, to which men of every country resort, from an irresistible impulse to feel intensely, at least once in their lives, the majesty of nature . . . Sinai and Horeb have associations infinitely more instructive and sacred; but I question whether that solemn vale on which the tribes stood, and over which the precipices of Horeb impended, had anything physical, more majestic, awful and sublime, than the breast of Mont Blanc, his hoary head, and his countless pinnacles far above the eagle's flight, than the awful rocks that environ the Mer de Glace, than the assemblage of grandeur in the valley of Chamouni.'

LIDDELL, HENRY GEORGE. THUN, INTERLAKEN, GRINDELWALD, FAULHORN

MALKIN, A. T. GRINDELWALD, STRAHLEGG PASS, GRIMSEL PASS, CHAMONIX, COL DU BONHOMME, BOURG ST. MAURICE, COL DE GALEZE, AOSTA, PRARAYÉ, COL DE COLLON, AROLLA, EVOLENA, COL D'HÉRENS, ZERMATT, ST. NIKLAUS, JUNG PASS, TURTMANN

'The view from the Col d'Hérens is indescribable. I believe the reason why it is said that people never see anything from the top of Mont Blanc is that they can give no clear account of it, combined perhaps with a certain indistinctness from the rarity of the air. There is an immensity in the High Alps, when seen from these elevations, which the mind can hardly take in; and after using all your eyes for half an hour you find on the descent that you have but a hazy recollection, and wonder what you were doing on the top not to know more about it.'

MICHELET, JULES. GENEVA, LAUSANNE

Michelet was engaged on the volume on Louis XI of his history of France.

OLIVIER, JUSTE. LAUSANNE, MARTIGNY, VISP, ZERMATT

Zermatt: 'De l'agneau rôti, du poulet, des pommes de terre, des œufs, du riz frit; au dessert, du fromage et de l'amande huileuse et parfumée du pin-arole; enfin du vin muscat blanc cacheté comme au temps d'Horace avec de la cire: en voilà bien assez pour ne pas périr de faim et ne périr que d'attente et d'ennui. . . .'

STUDER, GOTTLIEB. BERNE, THUN, INTERLAKEN, LAUTERBRUNNEN, MÜRREN, SCHILTHORN

At Mürren 'the inhabitants of the village, and particularly the female part of the population, crowded with eager curiosity round the uncommon spectacle of arriving visitors. But these, seizing the opportunity of combining a short rest with some refreshment, selected the nicest from among the group of maidens, and exacted as the price of curiosity—a kiss? no; a large jug of steaming coffee!'

TALFOURD, THOMAS NOON. BASLE, MOUTIER, BIENNE, BERNE, FRIBOURG, VEVEY, GENEVA, CHAMONIX, COL DE BALME, MARTIGNY, VEVEY, BULLE, CHÂTEAU D'OEX, SAANEN, ZWEISIMMEN, THUN, EMMENTHAL, LUCERNE, ZUG, ZURICH, BASLE

Talfourd made an attempt on Mont Blanc with Mr. Bosworth who, at the Grands Mulets, 'early in the afternoon, put up an awning against the rock, and supported it by poles, under which he proposed to sleep and to include us;—which seemed to justify me in applying to our position the words of the fated Richard:—

"Here pitch our tent; even here in Bosworth field—
Up with my tent; here will I lie to-night;
But where to-morrow?—Well, all's one for that;
Up with the tent".'

TURNER, JOSEPH MALLORD WILLIAM. LUCERNE, GOLDAU, ALTDORF, ST. GOTTHARD PASS

'An intimate friend, while travelling in the Jura, says Mr. Lovell Reeve, came to an inn where Turner had only just before entered his name in the visiting-book. Anxious to be sure of his identity, and to be in pursuit of him, he inquired of his host what sort of man his visitor was. "A rough, clumsy man", was the reply; "and you may know him by his always having a pencil in his hand." '

1844

ANONYMOUS 10 C. GENEVA, CHAMONIX, TÊTE NOIRE PASS, MARTIGNY, GRAND ST. BERNARD, MARTIGNY, SION, LEUK, GEMMI PASS, KANDERSTEG, INTERLAKEN, MEIRINGEN, GRIMSEL PASS, FURKA PASS, ANDERMATT, FLUELEN, LUCERNE, RIGI, ARTH, ZURICH, BERNE, FRIBOURG, VEVEY, LAUSANNE, GENEVA

ARGYLL, GEORGE DOUGLAS, DUKE OF. CHIAVENNA, SPLÜGEN PASS, THUSIS, COIRE, WALLENSTADT, ZURICH, BASLE

'No part even of happy Switzerland struck me as happier than all the slopes and valleys which collectively are known as the Rheinwald.'

BOUGY, ALFRED DE. VALLORBE, ORBE, LAUSANNE, GENEVA, EVIAN, ST. GINGOLPH, LAUSANNE

Bougy relates the story of an Englishman who made the tour of the Lake of Geneva on a charabanc, a vehicle on which the traveller always sat facing sideways. But as he travelled with his back to the Lake all the time, he never saw it. And when he returned to England he could not understand what people were talking about when they mentioned it.

BUCKINGHAM, JAMES SILK. SCHAFFHAUSEN, ZURICH, ZUG, LUCERNE, LANGNAU, BERNE, THUN, INTERLAKEN, LAUTERBRUNNEN, KLEINE SCHEIDEGG, GRINDELWALD, THUN, BERNE, VEVEY, GENEVA, MARTIGNY, GENEVA, CHAMONIX, GENEVA, LAUSANNE, YVERDON, NEUCHÂTEL, BIENNE, MOUTIER, BASLE

CAIRNS, JOHN. COMO, LUGANO, LUINO, BAVENO, DOMODOSSOLA, SIMPLON PASS, BRIG, MARTIGNY, CHAMONIX, GENEVA, LAUSANNE, MORAT, BERNE, THUN, INTERLAKEN, LAUTERBRUNNEN, RIGI, LUCERNE, BASLE

'Mounting in face of the dazzling snows and stupendous height of the Jungfrau, I sat down in the clear morning sun, in solitude broken only by the bells of the cattle and the solemn thunder of the descending avalanches, and, gazing full upon the majestic peaks around, read some chapters of the New Testament and worshipped the God of salvation in this glorious and awful temple of nature.'

DENMAN, GEORGE. MILAN, BELLINZONA, ST. GOTTHARD PASS, ALTDORF, FLUELEN, LUCERNE, BASLE

Crossing the lake of Lucerne 'one Italian advocate gave us infinite amusement by what we considered his unreasonable fears of shipwreck. The same gentleman had exhibited great terror in the descent from the St. Gotthard pass, and I am sorry to remember that we maliciously increased his terror, for whenever he shouted out of the window to the postillion, who was rattling down the zig-zags at marvellous speed, "Per carita, etc. etc.," and the postillion, who spoke German, wished to know what the gentleman said, we answered in bad German, "He says that it is not fast enough".'

DESOR, EDOUARD. NEUCHÂTEL, BERNE, THUN, INTERLAKEN, MEIRINGEN, GRIMSEL PASS, UNTERAAR GLACIER, OBERGESTELEN, MÜNSTER, BLINDENTAL, KUMMEN FURKE PASS, RAPPENTAL, BINN, RITTER PASS, VEGLIA, PASSO DI VALTENDRA, PASSO DI BUSCAGNA, DEVERO, SOLECCHIO, TOSA FALLS, SAN GIACOMO PASS, AL ACQUA, NUFENEN PASS, OBERGESTELEN, GRIMSEL PASS, UNTERAAR GLACIER, WETTERHORN

One night in the 'Pavillon' when the wind was blowing very hard, Desor overheard a dialogue between two guides. 'Hans, listen.' 'Yes, what is it?' 'I think that the wind is going to blow us away.' 'I think so too. What shall we do?' 'We must wake the masters.' 'No, I don't think so. It will be time enough when the roof has gone.' 'You are right; we must wait and let them sleep peacefully.'

DICKENS, CHARLES. DOMODOSSOLA, SIMPLON PASS, BRIG, SION, MARTIGNY, LAUSANNE, FRIBOURG, BASLE

'We began the ascent of the Simplon that same night. . . . Most favourable state of circumstances for journeying up that tremendous pass! The brightest moon I ever saw, all night, and daybreak on the summit. The glory of which, making great wastes of snow a rosy red, exceeds all telling. We sledged through the snow on the summit for two hours or so.... The cold in Switzerland, since, has been something quite indescribable. My eyes are tingling to-night as one may suppose cymbals to tingle when they have been lustily played. It is positive pain to me to write. . . .'

DUPIN, J. P. GENEVA, VILLENEUVE, LAVEY, MARTIGNY, SION, VISP, ZERMATT, VISP, MARTIGNY, MONTREUX, GENEVA

Dr. Dupin was accompanied by Abraham Emmanuel Thomas, the botanist of Bex.

FORBES, JAMES DAVID. LUGANO, BELLINZONA, BAVENO, DOMODOSSOLA, SIMPLON PASS, BRIG, VIESCH, EGGISHORN, BRIG, GENEVA, CHAMONIX

'I feel more and more that I owe my life to the Alps. I had a threatening of illness in the north of Italy, which left me, not ill indeed, but in a state which admitted of no exertion with pleasure, as you may judge when I tell you that I went up Monte S. Salvatore at Lugano one morning, and was so exhausted that I could hardly reach the top, and had to rest a whole day after it. The Simplon quite altered matters.'

HOFFMANN, GEORG. AMSTEG, MADERANERTAL, KLEINE WINDGÄLLE

MARTINS, CHARLES. GENEVA, CHAMONIX, MONT BLANC

MASSIE, J. W. BASLE, MOUTIER, BIENNE, BERNE, MORAT, FRIBOURG, NEUCHÂTEL, YVERDON, LAUSANNE, GENEVA

Under the heading 'moral grandeur preferred', Massie resisted the temptation to see Chamonix—'this gigantic altar to nature's God, which was raised by God's own hand' and, instead, made for the scenes of Luther's labours.

PARKER, THEODORE. BASLE, BERNE, LAUSANNE, GENEVA, ZURICH, SCHAFFHAUSEN

PARKMAN, FRANCIS. CHIAVENNA, SPLÜGEN PASS, FERRERA, ANDEER, THUSIS, COIRE

'I spent the day yesterday in the valley of Ferrera, one of the wildest and loneliest in the Alps, and accessible only by a bad foot-path. . . . I never knew a place so haunted by "those airy tongues that syllable men's names".... I never left any place with more regret than these mountains.'

ROGET, PETER MARK. BASLE, MOUTIER, TAVANNES, BIENNE, AARBERG, BERNE, FRIBOURG, CHATEL ST. DENIS, VEVEY, GENEVA, CHAMONIX, TÊTE NOIRE PASS, MARTIGNY, LIDDES, MARTIGNY, SION, LEUK, GEMMI PASS, KANDERSTEG, INTERLAKEN, GRINDELWALD, MEIRINGEN, BRUNIG PASS, LUCERNE, ALTDORF, ST. GOTTHARD PASS, FAIDO, BELLINZONA, MAGADINO, MILAN, COMO, CHIAVENNA, SPLÜGEN PASS, THUSIS, COIRE, ZURICH, SCHAFFHAUSEN, BASLE

Chamonix: 'The influx of travellers was so great that all the hotels were soon completely filled, and many were obliged to put up with makeshift accommodation, such as whole families sleeping in one room, straw supplying the place of beds, and eight persons were reported to have slept upon a billiard table.'

RUSKIN, JOHN. GENEVA, CHAMONIX, GENEVA, MARTIGNY, SION, BRIG, SIMPLON PASS, DOMODOSSOLA, SIMPLON PASS, BRIG, VISP, ZERMATT, VISP, BELALP, BRIG, MARTIGNY, CHAMONIX, MONT BUET, SIXT, VEVEY, GENEVA

At Simplon, Ruskin met J. D. Forbes and became his firm supporter in Forbes's later controversy with Tyndall. Ruskin's is the first recorded visit to Belalp.

SNOW, ROBERT. DOMODOSSOLA, SIMPLON PASS, BRIG, SION, MARTIGNY, CHAMONIX, GENEVA, CHAMONIX, COL DU GÉANT, COURMAYEUR, COL DE LA SEIGNE, COL DU BONHOMME, ST. GERVAIS, GENEVA

'Ye travellers all in realms remote,
Give ear unto the doleful note
Of one who sings the Table d'Hote.
Curst Table d'Hote! In blank despair
You sit, and sit, until your chair
Seems stuffed with nettles (I've no patience
With these reunions of nations)
Awaiting after long inaction,
Repletion without satisfaction;
Till like Iulus, you feel able
To masticate the very table.
And when you're served, the soup is cold;
The wine is hot; the poultry old;
Nay, whatso'er the meat you're picking,
One truth is clear—it is no chicken . . .'

TURNER, JOSEPH MALLORD WILLIAM. LUCERNE, THUN, INTERLAKEN, GRINDELWALD

Switzerland was 'a cauldron of squabbling, political or religious. . . . The rains came on early and I could not cross the Alps—twice I tried was sent back, with a wet jacket and worn out boots.'

VERNON, WILLIAM WARREN. CHIAVENNA, SPLÜGEN PASS, THUSIS, COIRE, ZURICH, BERNE, LAUSANNE, BERNE, BASLE

In this year Vernon's father, Lord Vernon, won second prize in the Tir Fédéral at Basle. As Swiss citizenship was obligatory for competitors, the Canton of Geneva obliged by conferring its citizenship on him for the purpose.

VIGNET, LOUIS. BERNE, THUN, INTERLAKEN, LAUTERBRUNNEN, KLEINE SCHEIDEGG, GRINDELWALD, INTERLAKEN, THUN

'Assez fréquemment la Yungfrau se fait tirer l'oreille. Si vous n'avez le loisir d'attendre la fin de ses caprices ni le commencement de ses avalanches, vite un artilleur du crû, posté là, vous guettant, accourt son petit canon sous le bras. Il le pose à terre, le charge, l'amorce et le braque contre la montagne revêche.... Feu! le coup part, l'avalanche aussi, détaché bon gré mal gré par l'ébranlement de l'air. Le tour est joué. Prix fixe: un franc. Si même s'établit la concurrence qui est l'âme du commerce, on peut se procurer pour soixante-quinze centimes des avalanches très confortables et très réussies.'

WESTON, G. F. CONSTANCE, SCHAFFHAUSEN, ZURICH, HORGEN, ZUG, RIGI, LUCERNE, FLUELEN, ANDERMATT, HOSPENTHAL, FURKA PASS, GRIMSEL PASS, MEIRINGEN, GROSSE SCHEIDEGG, GRINDELWALD, KLEINE SCHEIDEGG, LAUTERBRUNNEN, INTERLAKEN, THUN, BERNE, SOLEURE, BASLE, MOUTIER, BIENNE, NEUCHÂTEL, YVERDON, LAUSANNE, GENEVA, CHAMONIX, COL DU BONHOMME, COL DE LA SEIGNE, COURMAYEUR, AOSTA, GRAND ST. BERNARD, AOSTA

'One may form an idea of the mountains and lakes of Switzerland by magnifying Primrose Hill and the Serpentine respectively, but a glacier is without a type in our country.'

1845

AGASSIZ, JEAN LOUIS RODOLPHE. NEUCHÂTEL, BERNE, THUN, INTERLAKEN, MEIRINGEN, GRIMSEL PASS, UNTERAAR GLACIER, LAUTERAARSATTEL, WETTERHORN (HASLE JUNGFRAU)

With Vogt and Bovet, Agassiz made the second tourist's ascent of the Hasle Jungfrau peak of the Wetterhorn, the third ascent in all. The first was made in the previous year by Desor's guides Jaun and Bannholzer. This was Agassiz's last season in the Alps.

ALEXANDER, WILLIAM LINDSAY. BASLE, MOUTIER, BIENNE, NEUCHÂTEL, LAUSANNE, GENEVA, CHAMONIX, GENEVA, LAUSANNE, BERNE, THUN, INTERLAKEN, LAUTERBRUNNEN, KLEINE SCHEIDEGG, GRINDELWALD, INTERLAKEN, THUN, BERNE, BASLE

BALL, JOHN. NEUCHÂTEL, CHAUMONT, LAUSANNE, BEX, MARTIGNY, SION, VISP, ZERMATT, ST. NIKLAUS, JUNG PASS, MEIDEN PASS, ST. LUC, SIERRE, VISP, ZERMATT, SCHWARZTHOR PASS, ST. JACQUES D'AYAS, BETTA FURKA PASS, GRESSONEY

'Received in succession the visit of many of the village notabilities. A quite unusual depth of excitement was apparent, but it was only just before I started that I learned the real cause of the interest that had been shown in the success of my project. It was not any abstract interest in geographical science, nor a desire to enter into closer relations with the German population of Gressonay, nor yet the notion that Tourists might be attracted to their valley by a new and interesting pass: the practical mind of Zermatt had detected in the new route a grand opportunity for carrying on free Trade with Piedmont uninterrupted by the douaniers of His Sardinian Majesty.'

BERTHOUD, FRITZ. NEUCHÂTEL, BERNE, THUN, INTERLAKEN, BRIENZ, BRUNIG PASS, SARNEN, STANS, BECKENRIED, FLUELEN, ALTDORF, ANDERMATT, HOSPENTHAL, FURKA PASS, GRIMSEL PASS, MEIRINGEN, BRIENZ, INTERLAKEN, BERNE, NEUCHÂTEL

CHEEVER, GEORGE BARRELL (*c*). GENEVA, CHAMONIX, TÊTE NOIRE PASS, MARTIGNY, GRAND ST. BERNARD PASS, AOSTA, COURMAYEUR, COL DE LA SEIGNE, COL DU BONHOMME, CHAMONIX, GENEVA, MARTIGNY, SION, LEUK, GEMMI PASS, KANDERSTEG, INTERLAKEN, LAUTERBRUNNEN, KLEINE SCHEIDEGG, GRINDELWALD, GROSSE SCHEIDEGG, MEIRINGEN, GRIMSEL PASS, FURKA PASS, ANDERMATT, ALTDORF, LUCERNE, RIGI, EINSIEDELN, ZURICH, COIRE, THUSIS, SPLÜGEN PASS, CHIAVENNA

'It was an if an angel had flown round the horizon of mountain ranges, and lighted up each of their white pyramidal points in succession, like a row of gigantic lamps burning with rosy fires. Just so the sun suddenly tipped the highest points and lines of the snowy outline, and then, descending lower on the body of the mountains, it was as if an invisible Omnipotent had taken them, and dipped the whole range in a glowing pink. . . . The vision was so radiant, so full of sudden, vast, and unimaginable beauty and splendour, that methinks a phalanx of the Sons of God, who might have been passing at that moment, could not have helped stopping and shouting for joy.'

COSTELLO, LOUISA STUART. MENAGGIO, PORLEZZA, LUGANO, LOCARNO, COMO—RAGAZ, PFÄFERS, WALLENSTADT

DICKENS, CHARLES. BELLINZONA, ST. GOTTHARD PASS, ALTDORF, LUCERNE

'We came over the St. Gothard, which has been open only eight days. The road is cut through the snow, and the carriage winds along a narrow path between two massive snow walls, twenty feet high or more. Vast plains of snow range up the mountain-sides above the road, itself seven thousand feet above the sea; and tremendous waterfalls, hewing out arches for themselves in the vast drifts, go thundering down from precipices into deep chasms, here and there and everywhere; the blue water tearing through the white snow with an awful beauty that is most sublime. . . . Oh God! what a beautiful country it is.'

FLAUBERT, GUSTAVE. DOMODOSSOLA, SIMPLON PASS, BRIG, SION, MARTIGNY, CHILLON, COPPET, GENEVA

Of the descent from the Simplon pass Flaubert wrote: 'C'est en commençant à descendre que la vue devient magnifique: la vallée part de dessous vos pieds et ouvre son angle immense vers l'horizon, portant sur ses flancs ses pins et ses neiges. — Indescriptible! il faut rêver et se souvenir.'

HEADLEY, J. T. DOMODOSSOLA, SIMPLON PASS, BRIG, SION, MARTIGNY, COL DE BALME, CHAMONIX, TÊTE NOIRE PASS, MARTIGNY, GENEVA, LAUSANNE, FRIBOURG, BERNE, THUN, INTERLAKEN, LAUTERBRUNNEN, KLEINE SCHEIDEGG, GRINDELWALD, GROSSE SCHEIDEGG, MEIRINGEN, BRUNIG PASS, LUCERNE, RIGI, ZUG, ZURICH, BRUGG, BASLE

'There they stood, a mass of rose-coloured snow mountains, towering away in the heavens: they had suddenly lost their massive strength and weight, and light as frost work, and apparently transparent as a rose-tinted shell, they seemed the fit home of spiritual beings: and then what serenity and silence over them all. There was none of the life and motion of flashing sunbeams; none of the glitter of life itself on mountain summits, but a deep quiet, that seemed almost holy, resting there, as if that rose-tinted top was bathed in the mellow radiance that one might dream of as belonging to a sunset in heaven. My eye wandered down the now ethereal form of Mont Blanc till it rested on a wreath of fir trees, whose deep green contrasted strangely with that pure colour. I stood bewildered—it seemed a magic land; but the glorious vision like all beauty, was as transient as the hour that gave it birth. Fainter and fainter again grew the tints, till all passed away, and Mont Blanc stood white, and cold, and ghost-like against the evening sky.'

ROTH, GOTTFRIED. GRINDELWALD, WETTERHORN

The second ascent of the Hasle Jungfrau peak of the Wetterhorn; the first by a tourist (with F. Fankhauser), and the first from Grindelwald. The first ascent had been made from Rosenlaui by Desor's guides Bannholzer and Jaun in 1844.

RUSKIN, JOHN. MACUGNAGA, DOMODOSSOLA, FORMAZZA, SAN GIACOMO PASS, AIROLO, FAIDO, BELLINZONA, BAVENO, COMO, MILAN, DOMODOSSOLA, SIMPLON PASS, BRIG, SION, MARTIGNY, NYON, GENEVA

'Monte Rosa, occasionally seen at the extremity of the valley, is a mere white heap, with no more form in it than a haycock after a thunder-shower.'

SPEER, STANHOPE TEMPLEMAN. INTERLAKEN, GRINDELWALD, GROSSE SCHEIDEGG, MEIRINGEN, GRIMSEL PASS, UNTERAAR GLACIER, LAUTERAARSATTEL, WETTERHORN (MITTELHORN), ROSENLAUI, GROSSE SCHEIDEGG, GRINDELWALD, INTERLAKEN

The first ascent of the Mittelhorn peak of the Wetterhorn. 'Two days previous to our ascent some Swiss gentlemen, indignant at the idea of allowing "un Anglais" to be the first to scale their virgin peak, had, in company with three chamois hunters, made another attempt from Grindelwald. To our gratification it proved a failure.' The Swiss gentlemen were Fankhauser and Roth. They did not fail.

TAYLOR, BAYARD. SCHAFFHAUSEN, ZURICH, RAPPERSWIL, EINSIEDELN, SCHWYZ, BRUNNEN, ALTDORF, ST. GOTTHARD PASS, BELLINZONA, MAGADINO

'Milton is first fully appreciated when you look up from his page to the snowy ramparts of the Alps, which shut all out but the heaven of whose beauty he sang.'

1846

ALSOP, CHRISTINE MAJOLIER. GENEVA, LAUSANNE, AIGLE, VEVEY, BERNE, BASLE

At Aigle the populace attacked the prayer meeting which Mrs. Alsop and other Quakers were holding at the inn, and drenched the participants with a fire-engine as they went home.

ANDERSEN, HANS CHRISTIAN. GENEVA, VEVEY, FRIBOURG, BERNE, THUN, INTERLAKEN, LAUTERBRUNNEN, GRINDELWALD, BASLE

'I went immediately to Vevey; here, on the lake-side with Savoy's snow-covered mountains, it was a blessing to breathe and live.'

ARNOLD, MATTHEW. GENEVA, VEVEY, GLION

Arnold had visited George Sand at Nohant and made his way to Switzerland, his mind full of Sénancour's *Obermann*.

BALZAC, HONORÉ DE. DOMODOSSOLA, SIMPLON PASS, BRIG, SION, MARTIGNY, GENEVA

With Mme Hanska.

CLOUGH, ARTHUR HUGH. BASLE, LUCERNE, ALTDORF, ST. GOTTHARD PASS, BELLINZONA, MAGADINO, LUGANO

Clough was accompanied by his sister Anne.

CORSON, JOHN W. BASLE, LIESTAL, HAUENSTEIN, OLTEN, LUCERNE, RIGI, WÄGGIS, FLUELEN, WASSEN, SUSTEN PASS, MEIRINGEN, GROSSE

SCHEIDEGG, GRINDELWALD, KLEINE SCHEIDEGG, LAUTERBRUNNEN, INTERLAKEN, THUN, BERNE, NEUCHÂTEL, YVERDON, LAUSANNE, GENEVA, CHAMONIX, TÊTE NOIRE PASS, MARTIGNY, GRAND ST. BERNARD, MARTIGNY, LAUSANNE, GENEVA

DICKENS, CHARLES. BASLE, NEUCHÂTEL, LAUSANNE, MARTIGNY, COL DE BALME, CHAMONIX, TÊTE NOIRE PASS, MARTIGNY, GRAND ST. BERNARD PASS, MARTIGNY, LAUSANNE, GENEVA

Dickens settled at Lausanne at 'Rosemont', where he began to write *Dombey & Son*, and, soon afterwards, *The Battle of Life*.
'We went by a mountain pass not often crossed by ladies, called the Col de Balme, where your imagination may picture Kate and Georgy on mules *for ten hours at a stretch* riding up and down the most frightful precipices. We returned by the pass of the Tête Noire, which Talfourd knows, and which is of a different character, but astonishingly fine too. Mont Blanc, and the valley of Chamounix, and the Mer de Glace, and all the wonders of that most wonderful place, are above and beyond one's wildest expectations. I cannot imagine anything in nature more stupendous or sublime.'
The Great St. Bernard pass figured later in *Little Dorrit*.

FORBES, JAMES DAVID. ANNECY, CHAMONIX, COL DU BONHOMME, COL DE LA SEIGNE, COURMAYEUR, CHAMONIX, COL DE BALME, MARTIGNY, BEX, PAS DE CHEVILLE, SION, BRIG, OBERGESTELEN, GRIMSEL PASS, UNTERAAR GLACIER

KOHL, J. G. BASLE, BERNE, THUN, INTERLAKEN, GRINDELWALD, MEIRINGEN, BRUNIG PASS, STANS, BRIENZERROTHORN, INTERLAKEN, LAUTERBRUNNEN, MÜRREN

'The position of Mürren is really unique. Some forty households lie in a group without forming regular streets, on the bald mountain plateau. Surrounding it is a gigantic amphitheatre of peaks whose appearance defies anything that the pen can write about their magnificence and interest.'

LELAND, CHARLES GODFREY. DOMODOSSOLA, SIMPLON PASS, BRIG, SION, MARTIGNY, GENEVA, BERNE, BASLE—BASLE, LUCERNE, RIGI

MORGAN, JOHN MINTER. BASLE, SCHAFFHAUSEN, CONSTANCE, WINTERTHUR, ZURICH, BADEN, AARAU, LUCERNE, BERNE, FRIBOURG, NEUCHÂTEL, YVERDON, LAUSANNE, GENEVA, CHAMONIX, TÊTE NOIRE PASS, MARTIGNY, VEVEY, LAUSANNE, GENEVA, LAUSANNE, BERNE, ZURICH, ST. GALL, TROGEN—SCHAFFHAUSEN, ZURICH, BERNE, FRIBOURG, BULLE, VEVEY, LAUSANNE, GENEVA

Peddling his plan for the Self-supporting village in the hope of getting it adopted.

PESTALOZZI, MRS. CONRAD. LOCARNO, BELLINZONA, ST. GOTTHARD PASS, LUCERNE, LENZBURG, SCHINZNACH, HALLWIL, LENZBURG

READE, JOHN EDMUND (*c*). GENEVA, CHAMONIX, VEVEY, LAUSANNE, BERNE, THUN, INTERLAKEN, LAUTERBRUNNEN, MÜRREN, GRINDELWALD, MÄNNLICHEN, FAULHORN, LUCERNE, VEVEY, MARTIGNY, SION, BRIG, SIMPLON PASS, DOMODOSSOLA

'There is no village throughout all Oberland which can compare with Mürren for picturesque beauty, or for the wildness of its romantic situation. It is thrown among the very heart of the mountains, of which one counts the numerous summits; all turning, as if in reverence, to their queen, the Jungfrau.'

REY, W. GENEVA, MARTIGNY, SION, BRIG, FURKA PASS, ANDERMATT, OBERALP PASS, DISENTIS, COIRE, LENZERHEIDE, TIEFENKASTEL, JULIER PASS, ST. MORITZ, ZUOZ, PIZ D'EZEN, PONTRESINA, MUNT PERS, PIZ MORTEL, SASSAL MASONE, PONTE, ALBULA PASS, FILISUR, ALVANEU, TIEFENKASTEL, THUSIS, COIRE

'Voyageur prudent, apportez dans l'Engadine, en sus de votre pique, douze jours de vivres sur votre dos, au cas où il serait assez large pour être chargé à l'égal d'un légionnaire romain; ou bien munissez-vous d'un bagage plus maniable, d'une bonne ceinture plaquant sur l'estomac. Car, sachez-le, les rôtis sont de l'année précédente, les légumes et les fruits viennent du Tyrol quand ils viennent, la volaille peut arriver d'Italie par le courrier de Chiavenna, et si vous en désirez, donnez cinq jours pour écrire, aller et revenir, vous serez servi.'

RUSKIN, JOHN. VEVEY, GENEVA, CHAMONIX, GRINDELWALD, FAULHORN, LUCERNE

'It struck me suddenly how utterly different the impression of such a scene would be, if it were in a strange land, and in one without history; how dear to the feeling is the pine of Switzerland compared to that of Canada.'

SAFFORD, DANIEL. BASLE, DELÉMONT, BERNE, LAUSANNE, GENEVA, CHAMONIX, JARDIN, MARTIGNY, VILLENEUVE, GENEVA, NYON, ST. CERGUE

'We had a delightful view of Mont Blanc, and many other high peaks of the Alps. Long after the sun had passed from view, we could see his rays lingering upon these. Mont Blanc detained them longest. At length from perfect white it became tinged with pink, as it received the borrowed rays from the clouds above it. From a bright pink it became darker and darker, until it faded away from our view. The whole scene was splendid, and the close sombre and impressive. I could not but feel and say "Our God is a great God, above all gods".'

SELBORNE, ROUNDELL PALMER, LORD. BASLE, LUCERNE, FLUELEN, ALTDORF, ST. GOTTHARD PASS, BELLINZONA, LOCARNO

SHAFTESBURY, ANTHONY ASHLEY COOPER, EARL OF. BASLE, LUCERNE, INTERLAKEN, GRINDELWALD, THUN, BERNE

'Never was a river born so suddenly and so magnificently. It does not come creeping in a thread-like stream, from small and silent fountains, but gushes forth in full size, like Minerva from Jupiter's head, and rushing with thunder into an amphitheatre of mountains, escapes through the windings of the valley. On either side of these mighty pyramids of ice, stands an enormous mountain of naked granite, and behind them rise the lofty and terrible peaks of the Vischerhorn, covered with masses of everlasting snow. There they all stand in the stillest and most awful majesty, engaged, as it were, to watch the only thing that has sound and motion, the river, which issues from a beautiful archway, beautiful in the form and colour of the ice, at the foot of the glacier.'

TALFOURD, THOMAS NOON. DOMODOSSOLA, SIMPLON PASS, BRIG, SION, MARTIGNY, COL DE BALME, CHAMONIX, TÊTE NOIRE PASS, MARTIGNY, BEX, LAUSANNE, BIENNE, MOUTIER, BASLE

'From Vevey, a voiture conveyed us to Lausanne, where our friend and the world's favourite, Mr. Charles Dickens, expected us to visit him at a villa where he has resided for a few months.'

TENNYSON, ALFRED. BASLE, LUCERNE, WEGGIS, RIGI, SARNEN, LUNGERN, BRUNIG PASS, MEIRINGEN, GRINDELWALD, KLEINE SCHEIDEGG, LAUTERBRUNNEN, INTERLAKEN, THUN, BERNE, LAUSANNE, CHAMONIX

'Two other things in Switzerland I *did* see, the stateliest bits of land-skip I ever saw, one was a look down on the valley of Lauterbrunnen while we were descending from the Wengern Alp, the other a view of the Bernese Alps . . . I was satisfied with the size of crags, but mountains, great mountains disappointed me.'

WOLFF, PIERRE-ETIENNE. GENEVA, SAMOËNS, MEIRINGEN, GRIMSEL PASS, LAUTERAARSATTEL PASS, ROSENLAUI, GROSSE SCHEIDEGG, FAULHORN, GRINDELWALD, INTERLAKEN, ZWEISIMMEN, SAANEN, CHÂTEAU D'OEX, COL DES MOSSES, ORMONTS-DESSOUS, AIGLE, MONTHEY, GENEVA

1847

ASTLEY, SIR JOHN DUGDALE. LAUSANNE, CLARENS, BASSET, VEVEY

'The charms of those beautiful mountains were too much for me, and, instead of walking the flat road to Lausanne, I used to spend most of my time upon the summits of the lower range of mountains.'

CHORLEY, HENRY FOTHERGILL. INTERLAKEN

'The last day which they spent together at Ringgenberg, a hamlet on the lake of Brienz, in the little church of which Mendelssohn played the organ to him for nearly an hour, was thenceforth a sacred memory. . . .'

COLMAN, HENRY. BASLE, BERNE, HOFWYL, THUN, INTERLAKEN, LAUTERBRUNNEN, KLEINE SCHEIDEGG, GRINDELWALD, INTERLAKEN, THUN, BERNE, FRIBOURG, VEVEY, MARTIGNY, CHAMONIX, MARTIGNY, SION, BRIG, SIMPLON PASS, DOMODOSSOLA

DUFOUR, GENERAL GUILLAUME HENRI. BERNE, MORAT, COURTEPIN, GROLLEY, BELFAUX, FAOUG, BERNE, AARAU, MURI, SINS, LUCERNE, BERNE

General Dufour commanded the Federal troops in the civil war against the Confederate Cantons of the 'Sonderbund': Lucerne, Schwyz, Uri, Unterwalden Zug, Fribourg, and Valais. Hostilities started on 3 November and by 24 November all the refractory Cantons had surrendered. The casualties to the Federal troops were 74 killed and 377 wounded; those to the Confederates, 24 killed and 116 wounded.

FAYRER, SIR JOSEPH. BASLE, BERNE, ZURICH, RAGAZ, COIRE, THUSIS, SPLÜGEN PASS, CHIAVENNA

GROTE, GEORGE. GENEVA, LAUSANNE, BERNE, THUN, INTERLAKEN, BERNE, ZURICH, ST. GALL, TROGEN

Grote called on Mendelssohn at Interlaken. As a result of this journey Grote wrote his book on the political state of Switzerland.

HOFFMANN, GEORG. AMSTEG, MADERANERTAL, KRÜZLI PASS, OBERALPSTOCK

KOHL, J. G. LUCERNE, ALTDORF, AMSTEG, MADERANERTAL, ENGELBERG, SCHWYZ, EINSIEDELN, RIGI, LUCERNE, ENTLIBUCH, INTERLAKEN, ZURICH, APPENZELL, COIRE, THUSIS, SPLÜGEN PASS, CHIAVENNA, LUGANO, BELLINZONA, ST. GOTTHARD PASS, ANDERMATT, FURKA PASS, GRIMSEL PASS, MEIRINGEN, INTERLAKEN, THUN, FRIBOURG, VEVEY, MARTIGNY, TÊTE NOIRE PASS, CHAMONIX, GENEVA, LAUSANNE, NEUCHÂTEL, LA CHAUX DE FONDS, LE LOCLE, SOLEURE, BALSTHAL, BASLE

LEVER, CHARLES. BREGENZ, ZURICH, COIRE, THUSIS, SPLÜGEN PASS, CHIAVENNA, COMO

'The most enduring tastes a man can cultivate (avarice apart) are, I believe, the love of scenery and music. There I feel stronger than ever: the former has, perhaps from living a good deal alone, become a passion with me, and I am better pleased to have glens, glaciers, and cataracts than the fascinations of soirées.' The author of *Charles O'Malley* was now writing *The Knight of Gwynne*, and the experiences of his journey provided material for *The Dodd Family abroad.*

MANNING, HENRY EDWARD, CARDINAL. BASLE, LUCERNE, BASLE

'The opposite coast, a long low land rising to a gentle ridge, clothed with trees and verdure, houses and villages to the water's edge. Behind it the Rigi; sharp-pointed, irregular; the lower ranges covered with rich green; the upper wild, barren and bald. The sunset lit up the shore with a sort of glaring, homely, cheerful light. The mountain seemed to burn with a red heat. The whole, with all its outlines and tints, and lights and shadows, lay upon the lake. As the sun went down the lights went upwards, leaving range after range in a dark cold green on a black misty grey.'

MENDELSSOHN-BARTHOLDY, FELIX. ZURICH, THUN, INTERLAKEN

Mendelssohn had gone to Switzerland to recover from the blow of the death of his sister Fanny. At Interlaken he was visited by J. G. Kohl, H. F. Chorley, and George Grote.

MÜGGE, THEODORE. SCHAFFHAUSEN, ZURICH, LUCERNE, ENGELBERG, SURENEN PASS, ALTDORF, ANDERMATT, ALTDORF, BRUNNEN, SCHWYZ, EINSIEDELN, SCHWYZ, PRAGEL PASS, GLARUS, LINTHAL, SANDALP, GLARUS, WATTWIL, LICHTENSTEIG, HERISAU, ST. GALL, APPENZELL, COIRE, THUSIS, SAN BERNARDINO PASS, MESOCCO, BELLINZONA, ST. GOTTHARD PASS, ANDERMATT, FURKA PASS, GRIMSEL PASS, MEIRINGEN, INTERLAKEN, THUN, BERNE, THUN, KANDERSTEG, GEMMI PASS, LEUK, SION, MARTIGNY, GENEVA, LAUSANNE, FRIBOURG, BERNE, MORAT, NEUCHÂTEL, LA CHAUX DE FONDS, MOUTIER, BASLE

'Much will never be done with railroads in this country. Over the Alps they are not to be thought of; but even in the hilly foreland the difficulties would be too many and too great to allow of sufficient profit.' Actually, this was the very year of the opening of the first Swiss railway, from Zurich to Baden.

NOEL, BAPTIST W. GENEVA, CHAMONIX, GENEVA, LAUSANNE, BERNE, THUN, INTERLAKEN, LAUTERBRUNNEN, KLEINE SCHEIDEGG, GRINDELWALD, INTERLAKEN, MEIRINGEN, BRUNIG PASS, LUCERNE, RIGI, ZURICH, WALLENSTADT, COIRE, THUSIS, VIA MALA, COIRE, ZURICH, BASLE

'The only melancholy feature in our drive [from Lucerne to Zurich] was the sight of some small redoubts, at which about a dozen men were working, near a bridge over the Reuss at Gisikon; symptoms of an approaching civil war.' A few days after Noel had passed by this place it became the scene of stubborn fighting in the 'Sonderbund' war.

REYNOLDS, HENRY ROBERT. SCHAFFHAUSEN, ZURICH, RIGI, LUCERNE, INTERLAKEN, BERNE, VEVEY, LAUSANNE, GENEVA, CHAMONIX, GENEVA

'The whole glory of association that Byron and Rousseau have thrown over this spot [Vevey] started into recollection. There with the unutterable stillness, the vast expanse of waters, the deep blue heavens, the thoughts of home, the hopes of heaven, quite unmanned me.'

TRENCH, FRANCIS. BASLE, MOUTIER, BIENNE, NEUCHÂTEL, YVERDON, LAUSANNE, VEVEY, MONTREUX, MARTIGNY, COL DE BALME, CHAMONIX, COL DU BONHOMME, COL DE LA SEIGNE, COURMAYEUR, AOSTA, GRAND ST. BERNARD PASS, MARTIGNY, LAUSANNE, YVERDON, NEUCHÂTEL, BIENNE, SONCEBOS, BASLE

ULRICH, MELCHIOR. VISP, SAAS, ALLALIN PASS, TÄSCH

'As from early youth I took keen enjoyment from mountain tours, the Valais with its giants could not fail to exert its attraction upon me. In 1836 I had thought out a plan to get from the Simplon to the Great St. Bernard over all the glaciers at the heads of the valleys: a grandiose plan which I eventually had the good fortune to bring to fruition.'

1848

ALEARDI, ALEARDO. MILAN, BELLINZONA, ST. GOTTHARD PASS, ALTDORF, LUCERNE, BASLE

Crossing the St. Gotthard the Italian patriot met numbers of Poles on their way to fight for Italy.

ARNOLD, MATTHEW. GENEVA, VEVEY, COL DE JAMAN, CHÂTEAU D'OEX, SAANEN, ZWEISIMMEN, THUN, INTERLAKEN, GRINDELWALD, FAULHORN, INTERLAKEN, KANDERSTEG, GEMMI PASS, LEUK, BRIG, SIMPLON PASS, DOMODOSSOLA, SIMPLON PASS, BRIG, LEUK, GEMMI PASS, KANDERSTEG, THUN

'I love gossip and the small-wood of humanity generally among these raw mammoth-belched half-delightful objects the Swiss Alps.'

BUNBURY, SIR CHARLES JAMES FOX. GENEVA, CHAMONIX, GENEVA, LAUSANNE, BERNE, THUN, INTERLAKEN, BASLE

ENGELHARDT, CHRISTIAN MORITZ. BASLE, VEVEY, BEX, MARTIGNY, SION, VISP, SAAS FEE, STALDEN, ZERMATT

'At a short distance from Zermatt I met a distinguished-looking white-haired Englishman, and having seen his visiting card at St. Niklaus, I greeted him as Mr. Forbes the Edinburgh scientist and natural philosopher. But he answered that he was a doctor of medicine and unrelated to his namesake.' This meeting was providential, for Engelhardt's brother fell over the stairs of the hotel and Forbes was able to bandage and treat him.

FORBES, JOHN. BASLE, ZURICH, ZUG, RIGI, GOLDAU, ROTHENTURM, SCHINDELLEGI, RAPPERSWIL, WALLENSTADT, COIRE, THUSIS, VIA MALA, COIRE, WALLENSTADT, GLARUS, LINTHAL, KLAUSEN PASS, ALTDORF, LUCERNE, BRUNIG PASS, MEIRINGEN, GROSSE SCHEIDEGG, GRINDELWALD, KLEINE SCHEIDEGG, LAUTERBRUNNEN, INTERLAKEN, KANDERSTEG, GEMMI PASS, LEUK, VISP, ZERMATT, VISP, SION, MARTIGNY, GENEVA, CHAMONIX, COL DU BONHOMME, COL DES FOURS, COL DE LA SEIGNE, COURMAYEUR, AOSTA, GRAND ST. BERNARD PASS, MARTIGNY, COL DE BALME, CHAMONIX, GENEVA, LAUSANNE, YVERDON, NEUCHÂTEL, AARBERG, BIENNE, MOUTIER, BASLE

Forbes described Zermatt as 'a crowded assemblage of dark, dirty-looking wooden houses, with the usual exception of the church, which is neat, even handsome, both externally and internally. The inn is also of wood, but it is new and of considerable size, having a large eating room and half a dozen or more bedrooms on two floors.' . . . 'Taking the whole of the accommodations into account, the traveller may consider himself fortunate in being able to obtain them. . . .'

FRY, SIR EDWARD. GENEVA, CHAMONIX, MARTIGNY, GRAND ST. BERNARD, MARTIGNY, SION, BRIG, OBERGESTELEN, FURKA PASS, ANDERMATT

HOFFMANN, GEORG. AMSTEG, MADERANERTAL, KRÜZLISTOCK, GROSSE WINDGÄLLE

KIRKLAND, MRS. CHIAVENNA, SPLÜGEN PASS, THUSIS, COIRE, WALLENSTADT, ZURICH, ZUG, RIGI, LUCERNE, BRUNIG PASS, BRIENZ, INTERLAKEN, LAUTERBRUNNEN, INTERLAKEN, THUN, BERNE, FRIBOURG, BULLE, VEVEY, MARTIGNY, TÊTE NOIRE PASS, CHAMONIX, GENEVA, LAUSANNE, NEUCHÂTEL, BIENNE, BASLE

MAZZINI, GIUSEPPE. LUCERNE, ALTDORF, ST. GOTTHARD, BELLINZONA, LUGANO, CHIASSO, COMO, MILAN, LUGANO, ST. GOTTHARD PASS, ALTDORF, LUCERNE, SOLEURE, GRENCHEN

From Chiasso, Mazzini joined Garibaldi's column to fight the Austrians, and when it retreated he returned to Lugano. Crossing the St. Gotthard pass, he wrote to the Ashursts; 'I passed the St. Gotthard; there was danger but the scenery was sublime, divine. No-one who has not been there can know how much poetry there is to be found at the highest point of the road, on a little plain surrounded by the peaks of the Alps, in a perpetual silence that speaks to you of God. Agnosticism is impossible in the Alps.'

MURCHISON, SIR RODERICK. CHAMBÉRY, CHAMONIX, GENEVA, VEVEY, MARTIGNY, ORSIÈRES, COL FERRET, COURMAYEUR, AOSTA, GRAND ST. BERNARD PASS, MARTIGNY, VEVEY, SOLEURE, BERNE, THUN, INTERLAKEN, GRINDELWALD, MEIRINGEN, BRUNIG PASS, ALPNACHSTAD, PILATUS, SCHWYZ, EINSIEDELN, GLARUS, ELM, SEGNES PASS, RAGAZ, APPENZELL, BASLE

In spite of personal demonstrations by Charpentier, he refused to accept the former extension of the glaciers.

TROLLOPE, T. ADOLPHUS. BELLINZONA, MESOCCO, SAN BERNARDINO PASS, THUSIS, COIRE, ZURICH, BERNE, THUN, INTERLAKEN

'There has hardly, perhaps, as yet, elapsed time enough since Switzerland was to an Englishman even as Herne Bay or Brighton, for me to write of it as I might of Palmyra or Thebes. But really, things look as if such would ere long be the case. I seem to be travelling through a deserted country—so sad a "world too wide" for their shrunk customers are all the preparations and arrangements for tourists and pleasure-hunters. I feel tempted to exclaim with Alexander Selkirk—vel quasi—

I am monarch of all I survey;
My claims there is none to repel;
From Lake Leman to Zurich's fair sea
I am Lord of each boat and hotel.'

ULRICH, MELCHIOR. KANDERSTEG, GEMMI PASS, LEUK, VISP, SAAS, RIED PASS, ST. NIKLAUS, ZERMATT

1849

ARNOLD, MATTHEW. BASLE, BERNE, THUN, KANDERSTEG, GEMMI PASS, LEUKERBAD, GEMMI PASS, KANDERSTEG, THUN, BERNE, BASLE

'I am here in a curious and not altogether comfortable state: however to-morrow I carry my aching head to the mountains and to my cousin the Blumlisalp.

Fast, fast by my window
The rushing winds go
Towards the ice-cumbered gorges,
The vast fields of snow.
There the torrents drive upward
Their rock-strangled hum,
And the avalanch thunders
The hoarse torrent dumb.
I come, O ye mountains—
Ye torrents, I come.'

CLARKE, JAMES FREEMAN. SCHAFFHAUSEN, ZURICH, ALBIS, ZUG, RIGI, KÜSSNACHT, LUCERNE, FLUELEN, ANDERMATT, REALP, FURKA PASS,

GRIMSEL PASS, MEIRINGEN, GROSSE SCHEIDEGG, GRINDELWALD, KLEINE SCHEIDEGG, LAUTERBRUNNEN, INTERLAKEN, KANDERSTEG, GEMMI PASS, LEUK, SION, MARTIGNY, COL DE BALME, CHAMONIX, GENEVA, VEVEY, BULLE, FRIBOURG, BERNE, SOLEURE, BALSTHAL, WALDENBURG, BASLE

'On Lake Leman I grew more intimate with Rousseau; and on the Wengern Alp and the Rhine I understood Byron.... One thing which struck me frequently while among these mountains, was the remarkable way in which they separate one from all familiar thoughts and things. They put a great gulf between the mind and all its accustomed subjects of contemplation; and in this way give a sense of entire repose to the faculties.'

CLOUGH, ARTHUR HUGH. GENEVA, INTERLAKEN

In a letter to Matthew Arnold written from Rome during the siege, Clough expressed his yearning to be in Switzerland, 'reposing in the bosom of nature from the fatigues of art and the turmoil of war'.

COEURDEROY, ERNEST. ST. CERGUE, NYON, GENEVA, MARTIGNY, LUCERNE, GRINDELWALD, BERNE, LAUSANNE

'Le Waldstaetten, le beau bateau, s'éveille sur le lit moelleux des ondes. Sur ses flancs qui reluisent, il porte avec orgueil les devises des cantons unis. Fume, Waldstaetten, comme un étudiant de Heidelberg qui rêve gloire, quand la liberté lui monte au cerveau: ta noire fumée fait rire l'éclatant soleil.'

COTTA, BERNHARD. MARTINSBRUCK, FETAN, SÜS, ZERNEZ, ST. MORITZ, JULIER PASS, TIEFENKASTEL, LENZERHEIDE, COIRE, REICHENAU, DISENTIS, OBERALP PASS, ANDERMATT, FURKA PASS, GRIMSEL PASS, MEIRINGEN, INTERLAKEN, THUN, BERNE, LUCERNE, RIGI, ZURICH, SCHAFFHAUSEN, RORSCHACH

ELIOT, GEORGE. DOMODOSSOLA, SIMPLON PASS, BRIG, SION, MARTIGNY, CHAMONIX, GENEVA

'I am quite satisfied to be at Geneva instead of Paris; in fact, I am becoming passionately attached to the mountains, the lake, the streets, my own room, and, above all, the dear people with whom I live.' She stayed there for nine months.

ENGELHARDT, CHRISTIAN MORITZ. BASLE, VEVEY, BEX, SION, VISP, SAAS FEE, STALDEN, ZERMATT, VISP, BRIG, SIMPLON, BRIG, LEUKERBAD

'At the crowded dinner table at Zermatt, with its many English guests, ... my modesty as an author was subjected to severe strain. My works dealing with these regions were not unknown, and I was soon forced to own up to them. I spoke of the reference to my book in Professor James Forbes' Travels through the Pennine Alps, and of meeting his namesake Dr. John Forbes, in Zermatt the year before. The Englishmen became more and more excited, for the latter also had apparently referred to me. "How so?" I asked. He had recently published a book in which I am mentioned, and containing some of my pictures. One of the Englishmen rushed upstairs to fetch a copy. . . .'

GREISCHE, ANATOLE SCITIVAUX DE. ST. CERGUE, NYON, GENEVA, LAUSANNE, MARTIGNY, TÊTE NOIRE PASS, CHAMONIX, COL DU BONHOMME, COL DE LA SEIGNE, COURMAYEUR, AOSTA, GRAND ST. BERNARD PASS, MARTIGNY, VISP, LEUK, GEMMI PASS, KANDERSTEG, INTERLAKEN, LAUTERBRUNNEN, KLEINE SCHEIDEGG, GRINDELWALD, GROSSE SCHEIDEGG, MEIRINGEN, GRIMSEL PASS, FURKA PASS, ANDERMATT, OBERALP PASS, DISENTIS, COIRE, GLARUS, LINTHAL, KLAUSEN PASS, ALTDORF, LUCERNE, RIGI, ZUG, ZURICH, SCHAFFHAUSEN

Gletsch:—'Il y avait là égarée dans un pli des rochers, comme un grain de sable dans un sillon, une malheureuse petite auberge. Eh! bien, n'eut-on pas l'audace dans cet affreux trou de nous proposer du champagne? C'est une fille qui garde une robe de soie quand elle a mis sa dernière chemise au Mont-de-Piété.'

HERZEN, ALEXANDER. GENEVA, VISP, ST. NIKLAUS, ZERMATT, VISP, GENEVA

The Russian exile set out from Geneva with Georg Herwegh the German poet and revolutionary. At an inn near St. Niklaus, where the simple hostess looked after them to the best of her slender resources, Herzen asked how much they owed her. 'The hostess thought for a long time, went into the next room to study the matter, and at length decided to ask 5 francs, after stressing the dearness of prices and transport. "What," said Herzen, "does that include the horses' feed?" She misunderstood and quickly said "four francs will be sufficient".'

MARSHALL HALL, MRS. GRINDELWALD, MEIRINGEN, GRIMSEL PASS, OBERGESTELEN, VISP, ZERMATT

MAZZINI, GIUSEPPE. GENEVA, LAUSANNE

MEDICI, COLONEL GIACOMO. VARESE, SAN MAFFEO, LUGANO, BELLINZONA, SAN JORIO PASS, GRAVEDONA, MENAGGIO, PORLEZZA, CAVARNIA, SAN LUCIO, LUGANO

Medici held a command in Garibaldi's army in the campaign in Lombardy, alternately pouncing on the Austrians, being pressed back into Switzerland and interned, escaping, and starting again. At San Maffeo, he held out for four hours with 68 men against General Aspre's 5,000. Crowds of spectators came out on the neighbouring Swiss mountains to see the battle, after which Medici and his men slid off their rock into Swiss territory.

PARLATORE, FILIPPO. AOSTA, COURMAYEUR, COL DE LA SEIGNE, COL DES FOURS, COL DU BONHOMME, CHAMONIX, GENEVA, MARTIGNY, GRAND ST. BERNARD PASS, AOSTA

RUSKIN, JOHN. ST. CERGUE, NYON, GENEVA, VEVEY, CHAMONIX, MARTIGNY, VEVEY, GENEVA, CHAMONIX, COL DU BONHOMME, COL DE LA SEIGNE, COURMAYEUR, COL FERRET, ORSIÈRES, MARTIGNY, SION, VISP, ZERMATT, VISP, MARTIGNY, CHAMONIX, MARTIGNY, SION, LEUK, GEMMI, LEUK, MARTIGNY, GENEVA—GENEVA, CHAMONIX, GENEVA

Took 'The first sun-portrait ever taken of the Matterhorn (and as far as I know of any Swiss mountain whatever)'. He was collecting material for volume 4 of *Modern Painters*.

SCHURZ, CARL. BASLE, MOUTIER, MONTOZ, RENCHENETTE, DORNACH, ZURICH

The future United States Secretary of the Interior has just escaped from the siege of Rastatt.

SMITH, ALBERT. BASLE, BRUGG, BADEN, ZURICH, ALBIS, ZUG, RIGI, WEGGIS, LUCERNE, FLUELEN, AMSTEG, ANDERMATT, HOSPENTHAL, FURKA PASS, GRIMSEL PASS, MEIRINGEN, GROSSE SCHEIDEGG, GRINDELWALD, KLEINE SCHEIDEGG, LAUTERBRUNNEN, INTERLAKEN, THUN, BERNE, KANDERSTEG, GEMMI PASS, LEUK, SION, MARTIGNY, GRAND ST. BERNARD, MARTIGNY, VILLENEUVE, GENEVA, CHAMONIX, TÊTE NOIRE PASS, MARTIGNY, SION, BRIG, SIMPLON PASS, DOMODOSSOLA, VARALLO

TORR, T. S. INTERLAKEN, LAUTERBRUNNEN, KLEINE SCHEIDEGG, GRINDELWALD, FAULHORN

'You would be amused at seeing what monkies the fashionable gentlemen do make of themselves in dress: perhaps one dressed like a mountaineer, or William Tell, will wear white kid gloves, or thin patent boots, or some other incongruity equally ridiculous.'

TYNDALL, JOHN. BASLE, ZURICH, LACHEN, ZUG, RIGI, FLUELEN, ANDERMATT, FURKA PASS, OBERWALD, GRIMSEL PASS, MEIRINGEN, GROSSE SCHEIDEGG, GRINDELWALD, KLEINE SCHEIDEGG, LAUTERBRUNNEN, INTERLAKEN, THUN, BERNE, SOLEURE, BASLE

Tyndall had missed the way to the Grimsel from the Furka pass and gone on to Oberwald. From there he eventually found his way to the Grimsel. 'My remarks on this scramble would make a climber smile possibly with contempt for the man who could refer to such a thing as difficult. The language of my journal regarding it, however is, "By the Lord, I should not like to repeat this ascent".'

ULRICH, MELCHIOR. BRIG, MONTE LEONE, SIMPLON, ZWISCHBERGEN PASS, SAAS, ADLER PASS, ZERMATT, COL D'HÉRENS, EVOLENA, AROLLA, PAS DE CHÈVRES, COL DE SEILON, COL DU MONT ROUGE, CHERMONTANE

WAGNER, RICHARD. RORSCHACH, ZURICH, RAPPERSWIL, APPENZELL, RORSCHACH, ZURICH

'As on the last day of May, about six o'clock in the evening, I came to Zurich from Oberstrass, and saw for the first time the Alps of Glarus round the lake glowing in gorgeous sunshine, I decided at once, without however making a definite conscious resolution, that I would overcome all obstacles in the way of my settling there.'

1850

BALL, B. L. LEUKERBAD, TORRENTHORN

BULLARD, MRS. A. T. J. BASLE, BERNE, FRIBOURG, BULLE, VEVEY, GENEVA, CHAMONIX, TÊTE NOIRE PASS, MARTIGNY, SION, VISP, BRIG, SIMPLON PASS, DOMODOSSOLA

CALVERT, GEORGE H. THUN, INTERLAKEN, LAUTERBRUNNEN, KLEINE SCHEIDEGG, GRINDELWALD

'When the sun shines, travelling in Switzerland is a perpetual festival. Mother Earth holds here a jubilee. . . . At Grindelwald we visited one of the glaciers—a huge, creeping, Saurian monster, with its tail high up among the eternal snows, its body prostrate in a rocky gorge, and its head flattened upon the green valley, into which it was spouting turbid water.'

COLE, MRS. H. WARWICK. THUN, KANDERSTEG, GEMMI PASS, LEUK, VISP, ZERMATT, VISP, SION, MARTIGNY, GRAND ST. BERNARD PASS, AOSTA, COURMAYEUR

'We were fortunate enough to secure a bedroom in the little wooden inn belonging to the village doctor, Herr Lauber, which was then the only house for the reception of travellers in Zermatt. It was tolerably comfortable, but unfortunately the floors looked as if they had never been washed since the house was built.'

ENGELHARDT, CHRISTIAN MORITZ. BASLE, SION, VISP, SAAS FEE, VISP, LEUKERBAD

'At nightfall some foot travellers arrived at Zurbrücken's inn at Saas; an English family with only one pack horse. The father, elderly, bald, stout, well dressed and of ruddy countenance; the mother, ill with rheumatism and fatigue; the handsome daughter, bravely coping with the difficulties of life.' Next day, Sunday, 'in the evening he came into the parlour with his wife and daughter and gave a Christian homily to the numerous inhabitants who were present. His wife followed, and they then distributed New Testaments in an attractive small German edition. One inhabitant to whom I afterwards spoke was delighted with the gift and resolved to study the scriptures attentively.'

FORBES, JAMES DAVID. BASLE, BERNE, CHAMONIX, COL BLANC, FENÊTRE DE SALEINAZ, ORSIÈRES

'My heart remains where my body can never be. . . . My yearnings towards the Colinton banks, and towards the Swiss mountains, are much on a par with homesickness!'

GAUTIER, THÉOPHILE. GENEVA, LAUSANNE, MARTIGNY, SION, BRIG, SIMPLON PASS, DOMODOSSOLA

GRAY, ASA. BASLE, MOUTIER, BIENNE, NEUCHÂTEL, GENEVA, CHAMONIX, GENEVA, LAUSANNE, FRIBOURG, BERNE, THUN, INTERLAKEN, LAUTERBRUNNEN, KLEINE SCHEIDEGG, GRINDELWALD

PATTESON, JOHN COLERIDGE. CHAMONIX, GENEVA

SCHEFFEL, JOSEPH VIKTOR. SÄCKINGEN, LUCERNE, FLUELEN, ST. GOTTHARD PASS, AIROLO, ST. GOTTHARD PASS, ALTDORF, RIGI, LUCERNE, ZURICH

Rigi: 'Switzerland is truly a lovely land, but when a man is surrounded by grey misty infinity and the storm whistles through the clouds, Nature stops and drinking begins. Happy he who understands the science of drinking, for storm and weather cannot touch him. I sit with the inner contentment of Germanic composure before my glass, after having drunk as is due to the honourable neighbours, Pilatus and Glärnisch, as well as to the Schreck-, Wetter-, and Aarhorn system and the icy Jungfrau.'

TORR, JOHN. SCHAFFHAUSEN, ZURICH, LUCERNE, ESCHHOLZMATT, INTERLAKEN, LAUTERBRUNNEN, KLEINE SCHEIDEGG, INTERLAKEN, THUN, BERNE, SOLEURE, BASLE

'July 23. Lauterbrunnen, here I had the misfortune to fall over the Wengern Alp and break my leg, and was confined to my bed at this place 11 days and then at Interlaken till Sept. 21. Expenses at Hotels 730 francs, surgeon 330 do.—1060.'

TOWNSEND, GEORGE. CHIAVENNA, SPLÜGEN PASS, THUSIS, COIRE, WALLENSTADT, ZURICH, BASLE

ULRICH, MELCHIOR. KANDERSTEG, LÖTSCHEN PASS, KIPPEL, BRIG, SIMPLON PASS, MONTE LEONE, ALGABY, WEISSMIESSATTEL, ZWISCHBERGEN PASS, SAAS FEE, VISP, SION, MARTIGNY, LOURTIER, MARTIGNY, AIGLE, ORMONT-DESSUS, DIABLERETS, SANETSCH PASS, GSTEIG

At Saas 'since the previous year, a new inn, the Monte Rosa, has been established by Alois Zurbrücken. The pleasant rooms are comfortable, service is clean, food plentiful and the cost low.'

WAGNER, RICHARD. ZURICH, GENEVA, VILLENEUVE, MARTIGNY, SION, VISP, ZERMATT, VISP, THUN, ZURICH, RIGI, LUCERNE, ZURICH

From the Hotel Byron at Villeneuve, Wagner and his friend Ritter set out for Zermatt so that 'there, at the foot of the immense and wonderfully beautiful Matterhorn, we could at all events regard ourselves as shut off from the rest of the world'. But the visit was not a success. Meanwhile his wife had taken a house at Zurich-Enge, whence Wagner subsequently wrote, 'in the whole wide world I would not wish to live anywhere but here'.

WALLACE, HORACE BINNEY. BASLE, MOUTIER, BIENNE, BERNE, THUN, INTERLAKEN, LAUTERBRUNNEN, KLEINE SCHEIDEGG, GRINDELWALD, FAULHORN, GROSSE SCHEIDEGG, MEIRINGEN, GRIMSEL PASS, FURKA PASS, HOSPENTHAL, ST. GOTTHARD, ANDERMATT, ALTDORF, FLUELEN, LUCERNE, ARTH, RIGI, ZUG, ZURICH, SCHAFFHAUSEN, ZURICH, BERNE, LAUSANNE, GENEVA, CHAMONIX, GENEVA, CHILLON, MARTIGNY, SION, BRIG, SIMPLON PASS, DOMODOSSOLA

'Perhaps no intellectual emotion of our matured life comes upon us with so much novelty, and strength, and delight, as that shock of surprise and pleasure which we receive from the sight of the snowy pinnacles of the Alps, shooting up into the blue heaven, and standing together in silent mysterious vastness.'

WILLS, ALFRED. CHAMONIX, COL DU BONHOMME, COL DE LA SEIGNE, COURMAYEUR, AOSTA, GRAND ST. BERNARD PASS, MARTIGNY, VISP, ZERMATT, VISP, LEUK, GEMMI PASS, KANDERSTEG, INTERLAKEN, SCHYNIGE PLATTE

The first recorded ascent of the Schynige Platte by a visitor.

1851

CALAME, ALEXANDRE. GENEVA, LAUSANNE, BERNE, THUN, INTERLAKEN, MEIRINGEN, HANDECK

Handeck: 'J'ai été distrait, vers midi, par une caravane d'Anglais, dames, messieurs, jeunes filles, domestiques et femmes de chambre, qui sont arrivés au chalet dans l'accoutrement le plus godiche. Ils sont repartis, pour le Grimsel, une heure après, couverts de peaux de chèvre, qui à pied, qui en chaise ou à cheval: c'était vraiment très drôle. Mais ce qui ne l'était pas moins, c'était la mine du papa Sibach, qui mettait tout sens dessus dessous à leur intention et qui en a été quitte pour ses frais. Mes Anglais ont bu de l'eau fraiche et du lait, laissant là et champagne et côtelettes et omelettes. . . .'

DOBELL, SYDNEY. BASLE, BERNE, VEVEY, CHAMONIX, TÊTE NOIRE PASS, MARTIGNY

'Chamouni suited us both. I should like to live here for several months: its variety is inexhaustible. . . . Whatever else we may see I have no hope of surpassing this ideal of an alpine valley.' Dobell described it in *Balder*.

ENGELHARDT, CHRISTIAN MORITZ. BASLE, BERNE, VEVEY, MARTIGNY, SION, VISP, ZERMATT, VISP, LEUKERBAD

'I was greeted by name and received a friendly handshake from a boy who was acting as guide to an Englishman returning from Zermatt. On the tourist asking the boy who I was, he replied, "he is called simply the Father of the Valley, because tourists visit it so frequently since he published his book".'

GOBINEAU, COMTE ARTHUR DE. BASLE, ZURICH, ST. GALL, APPENZELL, TROGEN, ALTSTÄTTEN, COIRE, THUSIS, SPLÜGEN PASS, CHIAVENNA

'Je ne puis penser sans fureur que si ce Jacobin de Guillaume Tell ne s'était jamais disputé pour un mauvais chapeau avec cet autre imbécile de Gessler, je ne serais pas ici à m'ennuyer et à me rendre malade comme je fais.'

GREELEY, HORACE. COMO, LUGANO, BELLINZONA, AIROLO, ST. GOTTHARD PASS, ALTDORF, FLUELEN, LUCERNE, BASLE

HARRISON, FREDERIC. SCHAFFHAUSEN, ZURICH, ARTH, RIGI, ALTDORF, ANDERMATT, FURKA PASS, GRIMSEL PASS, MEIRINGEN, GROSSE SCHEIDEGG, FAULHORN, GRINDELWALD, INTERLAKEN, KANDERSTEG, GEMMI PASS, LEUK, VISP, ZERMATT, ST. THEODUL PASS, BREUIL, CHATILLON, AOSTA, COURMAYEUR, COL DE LA SEIGNE, COL DU BONHOMME, CHAMONIX, TÊTE NOIRE PASS, MARTIGNY, VEVEY, GENEVA

'Over the Furka I became half crazy, and left my party, which I only recovered on coming down from Faulhorn. . . . Walked to Zermatt. Met the second Sir Robert Peel, who wanted to turn us out of the public saloon—declined to move. . . . Old wooden hotel de Mont Rose (Seiler). In hotel with Mr. and Mrs. Robert Lowe (Lord Sherbrooke).'

PHILIPS, FRANCIS. OUCHY, VEVEY, MARTIGNY, TÊTE NOIRE PASS, CHAMONIX, MONT BLANC, GENSON, OUCHY

'A patriotic Englishman suddenly rushed into the middle of the road in front of us, and shouted in a loud voice, "three cheers for the travellers". He uttered an energetic "Hip! Hip!" and then suddenly stopped short, hearing no responsive echoes from the crowds, (who evidently thought that the worthy man was suffering under some temporary derangement).'

RUSKIN, JOHN. GENEVA, CHAMONIX, GENEVA, VEVEY, MARTIGNY, GRAND ST. BERNARD PASS, AOSTA

'The valley of Chamouni, another spot also unique in its way, is rapidly being turned into a kind of Cremorne Gardens; and I can foresee, within the perspective of but few years, the town of Lucerne consisting of a row of symmetrical hotels round the foot of the lake, its old bridges destroyed, an iron one built over the Reuss, and an acacia promenade carried along the lake shore, with a German band playing under a Chinese temple at the end of it, and the enlightened travellers, representatives of European civilisation, performing before the Alps, in each afternoon summer sunlight, in their modern manner, the Dance of Death.'

SCHEFFEL, JOSEPH VIKTOR. SÄCKINGEN, LUCERNE, FLUELEN, ALTDORF, ANDERMATT, OBERALP PASS, DISENTIS, COIRE, LENZERHEIDE, FILISUR, BERGÜN, ALBULA PASS, PONTRESINA

'At the "Adler" at Ponte resina, the visitors' book shows how seldom the marvels of these valleys and mountains receive the attention that they deserve. Here and there a stray tourist turns up—or that tireless migrant across hill and dale the Heidelberg student; the Englishman is very rare, and if a German coleopterist or botanist reaches thus far to botanise between rock and ice, the fact is noted in the local newspapers.'

SCHLAGINTWEIT, ADOLPH & HERMANN. ZURICH, ZUG, RIGI, LUCERNE, ENTLIBUCH, THUN, INTERLAKEN, GRINDELWALD, GROSSE SCHEIDEGG, MEIRINGEN, URBACHSATTEL PASS, GAULI PASS, GRIMSEL, OBERAARSATTEL PASS, VIESCH, BRIG, VISP, ZERMATT, MONTE ROSA, WEISSTHOR PASS, MACUGNAGA, TURLO PASS, ALAGNA, COL D'OLEN, GRESSONEY, COL D'ARANSOLE, BRUSSONE, COL DE JOUX, CHATILLON, AOSTA, COURMAYEUR, COL DE LA SEIGNE, LE CHAPIU, COL DU BONHOMME, CHAMONIX

SCHURZ, CARL. ZURICH, BERNE, THUN, INTERLAKEN, LAUTERBRUNNEN, KLEINE SCHEIDEGG, GRINDELWALD, FAULHORN, GROSSE SCHEIDEGG, MEIRINGEN, INTERLAKEN, THUN, BERNE

'Of all the wonderful views that I saw, the deepest impression was produced upon me, not by the vast panoramas, as from the top of the Faulhorn, where large groups and chains of the Alps are embraced in one gaze, but it was the single mountain peak reaching up into the blue sunny ether from a bank of clouds that separated it from the nether world, and standing there as something distinct and individual. It was the image of the eternally firm, the unchangeable, the certain, looking down as from a throne in serene sunlight upon the eternally unstable and untrustworthy.'

SEWELL, ELIZABETH MISSING. CONSTANCE, ZURICH, ALBIS, LUCERNE, RIGI, LUCERNE, LANGNAU, THUN, INTERLAKEN, GRINDELWALD, FAULHORN, MEIRINGEN, GRIMSEL PASS, OBERGESTELEN, BRIG, SION, MARTIGNY, LAUSANNE, GENEVA, CHAMONIX, TÊTE NOIRE PASS, MARTIGNY, SION, BRIG, SIMPLON PASS, DOMODOSSOLA, MILAN, TIRANO, BORMIO, STELVIO PASS, INNSBRUCK, VENICE, MILAN, CHIAVENNA, SPLÜGEN PASS, THUSIS, COIRE, ZURICH, BASLE

'I take it for granted you all understand that when I speak of a bed, it is almost always without curtains, and that carpets are things unheard of.'

SILLIMAN, BENJAMIN. COMO, VARESE, DOMODOSSOLA, SIMPLON PASS, BRIG, SION, MARTIGNY, BEX, EVIAN, GENEVA, CHAMONIX, GENEVA, LAUSANNE, YVERDON, STE. CROIX, CÔTE AUX FÉES, NEUCHÂTEL, BERNE, SOLEURE, BALSTHAL, LIESTAL, BASLE

'As we watched these snow-peaks, the evening red began to illuminate them, and one after another of the whole group blushed deeply at the parting glance of the god of day. Jungfrau, first on the left, showed her own pure white complexion; and gradually each successive peak and valley, even to the "bald, awful front" of Mont Blanc himself, lost the rosy hue. . . . With a pensive feeling of regret, we saw the dull gray of evening creeping over the scene, when suddenly, to our surprise, the auroral red reappeared upon the summit of Mont Blanc, and soon, one by one, each successive peak resumed the same lovely tint of rose. Charmed with the magic of this natural diorama, we waited with deep interest to witness the *second sunset,* and to puzzle our ingenuity for a satisfactory explanation of this remarkable phenomenon.'

SMITH, ALBERT. GENEVA, CHAMONIX, MONT BLANC

The provisions which Albert Smith's party took up Mont Blanc were as follows: 60 bottles of vin ordinaire, 6 of Bordeaux, 10 of St. George, 15 of St. Jean, 3 of cognac, 1 of syrup of raspberries, 6 of lemonade, 2 of champagne, 20 loaves of bread, 10 small cheeses, 6 packets of chocolate, 6 of sugar, 4 of prunes, 4 of raisins, 2 of salt, 4 wax candles, 6 lemons, 4 legs of mutton, 4 shoulders of mutton, 6 pieces of veal, 1 piece of beef, 11 large fowls, 35 small fowls.

TAPPAN, HENRY P. BASLE, MOUTIER, BIENNE, NEUCHÂTEL, YVERDON, LAUSANNE, GENEVA, MORAT, BERNE, THUN, INTERLAKEN, LAUTERBRUNNEN, GRINDELWALD, INTERLAKEN, THUN, LANGNAU, LUCERNE, ALBIS, ZURICH, BADEN, BASLE

'But there were the Alps! I repeated to myself: these are the Alps—the Alps! How wild were my emotions! I felt ready to leap from the vehicle, to clap my hands, and shout aloud, The Alps—The Alps! I realised that I was in Switzerland.'

THACKERAY, W. M. BASLE, BERNE, LUCERNE, FLUELEN, ST. GOTTHARD PASS, BELLINZONA, LOCARNO

'We had the most delightful ride yesterday from Basle, going through a country which I suppose prepares one for the spendider scenery of the Alps; kind good-natured little mountains, not too awful to look at, but encouraging in appearance, and leading us gradually up to the enormities which we are to contemplate in a day or two.'

WAGNER, RICHARD. ZURICH, ST. GALL, RORSCHACH, SÄNTIS, ZURICH, SCHWYZ, BRUNNEN, BECKENRIED, ENGELBERG, SURENEN PASS, ALTDORF, AMSTEG, MADERANERTAL, AMSTEG, ALTDORF, FLUELEN, ZURICH, ALBISBRUNN

It was while taking the waters at Albisbrunn that Wagner settled in his mind the complete plan for the Nibelung Ring.

WITMER, THEODORE B. (*c*). CHIAVENNA, SPLÜGEN PASS, THUSIS, REICHENAU, DISENTIS, OBERALP PASS, ANDERMATT, FURKA PASS, GRIMSEL PASS, MEIRINGEN, GROSSE SCHEIDEGG, GRINDELWALD, KLEINE SCHEIDEGG, LAUTERBRUNNEN, INTERLAKEN, KANDERSTEG, GEMMI PASS, LEUK, SION, MARTIGNY, COL DE BALME, CHAMONIX, GENEVA

'I am getting heartily tired of Switzerland. It is a tread-mill country—up hill all the time; with the same objects, under different names, staring you in the face.'

1852

ANDERSEN, HANS CHRISTIAN. COMO, LUGANO, BELLINZONA, ST. GOTTHARD PASS, ALTDORF, LUCERNE, SCHAFFHAUSEN

On one occasion 'Are you a Swiss?' I asked the driver. He answered 'Yes'. 'That cannot be true,' said I. 'I come from a long way off, from far up in the North, and there we have read of Switzerland and heard of William Tell, and the noble, brave Swiss people stand in high honor with us; and now! I come down here, so that I may tell people at home truly about these brave people, and then I take my seat in a carriage over there the other side of the square, show the address where I want to go,—it is only a few steps to drive, and I am carried all over the town on a half-hour tour. It is a cheat, and no Swiss will cheat. You are not a Swiss!' The man at this was quite abashed: he was a young fellow, and burst out, 'You shall not pay at all, or only pay what you please. The Swiss are brave folk.'

BROWNE, J. D. H. LUCERNE, CHAMONIX, MONT BLANC

BULWER, J. REDFORD. CHAMONIX, MONT BLANC, COL DU BONHOMME, COL DE LA SEIGNE, COURMAYEUR, AOSTA, CHATILLON, BREUIL, ST. THEODUL PASS, ZERMATT, WEISSTHOR PASS, MACUGNAGA

DRUMMOND, D. T. K. BASLE, MOUTIER, BERNE, THUN, INTERLAKEN, LAUTERBRUNNEN, THUN, ZWEISIMMEN, CHÂTEAU D'OEX, BULLE,

VEVEY, GENEVA, MARTIGNY, GRAND ST. BERNARD PASS, AOSTA, MILAN, COMO, MENAGGIO, PORLEZZA, LUGANO, BAVENO, MACUGNAGA, MONTE MORO PASS, MACUGNAGA, DOMODOSSOLA, SIMPLON PASS, BRIG, LEUK, GEMMI PASS, KANDERSTEG, THUN, LUCERNE, ALTDORF, ST. GOTTHARD PASS, BELLINZONA, LUGANO, MILAN, CHIAVENNA, SPLÜGEN PASS, THUSIS, COIRE, ZURICH, LUCERNE, THUN

DUFF, MOUNTSTUART E. GRANT. LAUTERBRUNNEN, KLEINE SCHEIDEGG, GRINDELWALD, MEIRINGEN, GRIMSEL, MEIRINGEN, INTERLAKEN, THUN, FRIBOURG, LAUSANNE, MARTIGNY, GRAND ST. BERNARD PASS, AOSTA, MILAN, COMO, LUGANO, MACUGNAGA, WEISSTHOR PASS, ZERMATT, VISP, LEUK, GEMMI PASS, KANDERSTEG, INTERLAKEN, THUN, BERNE, BIENNE, MOUTIER, BASLE

'Who can forget the start before the little hamlet is awake—the stars fading out one by one over Italy—the mighty peaks flushing in the growing day—then the blaze of sunlight as we emerge from the valley shadows, as the sound of the Alp horn comes up along the pastures to tell us that the world below is rising to its labour? Ere long we reach the snow-line, and see perhaps the chamois, which loves the debatable land between frost and flowers, playing above us till our constant advance makes it fear that harm is intended. Who can forget the hours of struggle over rock and snow-slope—hurrying here lest the avalanches should overwhelm us, there lying down exhausted, and careless, for the time, of avalanches and everything else? At last comes the joy of setting foot upon the topmost ridge, and looking down on another and different world. . . .'

FELTON, CORNELIUS CONWAY. CONSTANCE, ZURICH, ZUG, LUCERNE, RIGI, GOLDAU, FLUELEN, ALTDORF, ANDERMATT, HOSPENTHAL, FURKA PASS, GRIMSEL PASS, MEIRINGEN, BRIENZ, INTERLAKEN, THUN, BERNE, FRIBOURG, MORAT, NEUCHÂTEL, LAUSANNE, GENEVA, CHAMONIX, MARTIGNY, SION, BRIG, SIMPLON PASS, DOMODOSSOLA

'Though the memory of Agassiz freshly lives among these mountains and these realms of snow and ice, it is the memory of an illustrious but departed dynasty—a sort of Rhamses the Great, whose gigantic figure awes the existing race, but sways it no longer.'

FERGUSON, ROBERT. BASLE, ZURICH, GOLDAU, RIGI, LUCERNE, SCHWYZ, EINSIEDELN, RAPPERSWIL, LUCERNE, ENTLIBUCH, SCHLIERENBERG PASS, SARNEN, PILATUS, SCHWYZ, PRAGEL PASS, GLARUS, KLAUSEN PASS, ALTDORF, SURENEN PASS, ENGELBERG, JOCH PASS, MEIRINGEN, GROSSE SCHEIDEGG, GRINDELWALD, KLEINE SCHEIDEGG, LAUTERBRUNNEN, INTERLAKEN, KANDERSTEG, GEMMI PASS, LEUK, SION, MARTIGNY, CHAMONIX

'M. Bourrit relates finding here [Grindelwald] a burgher of Berne who had been banished to this Siberia of Switzerland on account of an affair of honour. A severe punishment it would be, no doubt, to spend a winter here. . . .'

RAMSAY, ANDREW CROMBIE. BASLE, ZURICH, LUCERNE, INTERLAKEN, MEIRINGEN, GRIMSEL PASS, OBERGESTELEN, BRIG, TURTMANN, SION, MARTIGNY, CHAMONIX, GENEVA

'Opened his eyes so wide that he feared they would never close again.'

RUSKIN, JOHN. COMO, LUGANO, BELLINZONA, AIROLO, ST. GOTTHARD PASS, FLUELEN, LUCERNE, BASLE

Airolo: 'I do not know when I have reached a more delightful place for a Sunday's rest. There is a new inn here, not a fashionable hotel, but small, clean and Swiss.'

RUSSELL, GEORGE. GENEVA, CHAMONIX, TÊTE NOIRE PASS, MARTIGNY

SCHEFFEL, JOSEPH VIKTOR. BASLE, BERNE, THUN, KANDERSTEG, GEMMI PASS, LEUK, BRIG, SIMPLON PASS, DOMODOSSOLA

It was after this journey that Scheffel wrote his *Trompeter von Säckingen*.

STUDER, GOTTLIEB. BERNE, SAANEN, LAUENEN, GELTEN PASS, SION, HÉRÉMENCE, COL DE SEILON, COL DU MONT ROUGE, CHANRION, COL DE CRÊTE SÈCHE, BIONNAZ, PRARAYÉ, COL DE COLLON, AROLLA, SION, SIERRE, ZINAL, SIERRE, VISP, ZERMATT, SCHWARZBERG-WEISSTHOR PASS, SAAS

ULRICH, MELCHIOR. LAUENEN, GELTENGRAT, SION, HÉRÉMENCE, COL DE SEILON, COL DU MONT ROUGE, CHANRION, COL DE CRÊTE SÈCHE, BIONNAZ, PRARAYÉ, COL DE COLLON, AROLLA, EVOLENA, SION, SIERRE, ZINAL, SIERRE, VISP, ZERMATT, SCHWARZBERG-WEISSTHOR PASS, SAAS

VIZETELLY, HENRY. INTERLAKEN, LAUTERBRUNNEN, WENGERNALP, LAUTERBRUNNEN, INTERLAKEN, GIESSBACH, MEIRINGEN, GRIMSEL PASS, FURKA PASS, ANDERMATT, OBERALP PASS, DISENTIS, ILANZ, REICHENAU, COIRE, FELDKIRCH

'I suggested producing an edition of *Hyperion*, with engravings of the different scenes in which the hero of the romance figures, from sketches to be made by Mr. Birket Foster on the spot.'

WAGNER, RICHARD. ZURICH, LUCERNE, BRUNIG PASS, MEIRINGEN, INTERLAKEN, LAUTERBRUNNEN, KLEINE SCHEIDEGG, GRINDELWALD, FAULHORN, GROSSE SCHEIDEGG, MEIRINGEN, GRIMSEL PASS, OBERGESTELEN, GRIES PASS, FORMAZZA, BAVENO, LOCARNO, BELLINZONA, LUGANO, DOMODOSSOLA, SIMPLON PASS, BRIG, SION, MARTIGNY, CHAMONIX, GENEVA, ZURICH, GLARUS, ZURICH

Staying at Fluntern, above Zurich, Wagner, who had finished writing the book of the *Rhinegold*, wrote that of the *Walkyries*.

WILLS, ALFRED. INTERLAKEN, LAUTERBRUNNEN, TSCHINGEL PASS, KANDERSTEG, GEMMI PASS, LEUK, BRIG, SIMPLON PASS, DOMODOSSOLA, MACUGNAGA, MONTO MORO PASS, SAAS FEE, ALLALIN PASS, ZERMATT, ST. THEODUL PASS, BREUIL, CHATILLON, AOSTA, GRAND ST. BERNARD PASS, MARTIGNY, COL DE BALME, CHAMONIX, GENEVA

'There is no inn I know, in which so great an improvement has taken place in a short time, as in the Hotel du Mont Rose [at Saas]. When I first went there, in 1852, the fleas were intolerable. Their size, and the fierceness of their appetite, exceeded anything of the kind I ever knew; and when a cold or wet day drove one near the fire, their attacks became unendurable; and there was nothing for it, but to retire, and have a grand hunt, when we always found.'

1853

CHAMIER, CAPTAIN. BASLE, MOUTIER, BERNE, THUN, INTERLAKEN, LAUTERBRUNNEN, KLEINE SCHEIDEGG, GRINDELWALD, INTERLAKEN, ZWEISIMMEN, SAANEN, CHÂTEAU D'OEX, VEVEY, BERNE, GENEVA, CHAMONIX, GENEVA, MARTIGNY, SION, BRIG, SIMPLON PASS, DOMODOSSOLA

'I hardly know any where a more pleasing walk than from St. Denis to Vevay. What an enchanting view! and what a burst of magnificence it is, as, rounding the various turns to diminish the descent, the eye first lights upon the lake of Geneva, when the snow-capped Dent de Midi, the beautiful and cultivated slopes, the deep ravines, and the elegant luxury, which seems everywhere, burst upon the eye. It must be a cold heart that does not beat quicker at this sight.'

DICKENS, CHARLES. BASLE, BERNE, LAUSANNE, GENEVA, CHAMONIX, TÊTE NOIRE PASS, MARTIGNY, SION, BRIG, SIMPLON PASS, DOMODOSSOLA

Dickens was with Wilkie Collins and Augustus Egg. At Chamonix, Hôtel de Londres, they ordered hot baths. 'Thereupon the keys of the bathrooms were found with immense difficulty, women ran backwards and forwards across the bridge, men bore in great quantities of wood, a horrible furnace was lighted, and a smoke was raised which filled the whole valley. This began at half-past three, and we congratulated each other on the distinction we should probably acquire by being the cause of the conflagration of the whole village. We sat by the fire until half-past five, and still no baths. . . . Ever since the smoke has poured forth in enormous volume, and the furnace has blazed, and the women have gone and come over the bridge, and piles of wood have been carried in; but we observe a general avoidance of us by the establishment which still looks like failure.'

It was on the Simplon that Dickens and Collins laid the scene of their *No thoroughfare*.

DORÉ, GUSTAVE. GENEVA, CHAMONIX

FOX, JOSEPH H. SCHAFFHAUSEN, ZURICH, ALBIS, ZUG, RIGI, FLUELEN, ALTDORF, KLAUSEN PASS, LINTHAL, GLARUS, WESEN, COIRE, THUSIS, SPLÜGEN PASS, CHIAVENNA, MILAN, MAGADINO, BELLINZONA, ST. GOTTHARD PASS, WASSEN, ANDERMATT, FURKA PASS, GRIMSEL PASS, MEIRINGEN, GROSSE SCHEIDEGG, GRINDELWALD, KLEINE SCHEIDEGG, LAUTERBRUNNEN, INTERLAKEN, THUN, BERNE, THUN, KANDERSTEG, GEMMI PASS, LEUK, VISP, ZERMATT, ST. THEODUL PASS, BREUIL, CHATILLON, AOSTA, GRAND ST. BERNARD PASS, MARTIGNY, LAUSANNE, NEUCHÂTEL, BASLE

GRANT, JAMES. BASLE, BADEN, ZURICH, HORGEN, ZUG, RIGI, LUCERNE, LUNGERN, BRUNIG PASS, MEIRINGEN, ROSENLAUI, GROSSE SCHEIDEGG, GRINDELWALD, INTERLAKEN, THUN, BERNE, VEVEY, MARTIGNY, TÊTE NOIRE PASS, CHAMONIX, GENEVA

'I wish that there were any means of ascertaining the number of persons who have caught colds, ending in consumption and death, through sleeping in damp sheets on the top of the Rigi.'

HUDSON, CHARLES. GENEVA, ST. GERVAIS, AIGUILLE DU GOUTER

LE VERT, OCTAVIA WALTON. GENEVA, LAUSANNE, VEVEY, MARTIGNY, SION, BRIG, SIMPLON PASS, DOMODOSSOLA

LISZT, FRANZ. BASLE, ZURICH, RICHTERSWIL, SCHWYZ, BRUNNEN, GRÜTLI, BRUNNEN, ZUG, ZURICH

An excursion with Wagner and Herwegh. 'C'est moi qui avais proposé cette excursion à trois, pour échapper d'abord aux visiteurs qui menacent de nous encombrer ici — et causer à poitrine ouverte, si l'occasion s'en trouvait, avec Wagner. J'avais aussi un besoin secret de me laisser gagner par une de ces grandes impressions que les grands sites me font — et me résignai à dépenser une centaine de francs à cette fin.'

MACAULAY, THOMAS BABINGTON. BASLE, BERNE, LAUSANNE, VEVEY, GENEVA

'I dare say you will despise me for saying that, on the whole, I expect more pleasure from the cathedrals of Cologne, and Strasburg, than from the Bernese Alps, or the Lake of Geneva.'

MACGREGOR, JOHN. BASLE, BADEN, ZURICH, SCHAFFHAUSEN, CONSTANCE, ZURICH, HORGEN, ZUG, RIGI, FLUELEN, HOSPENTHAL, ST. GOTTHARD, LA FIBBIA, HOSPENTHAL, FURKA PASS, GALENSTOCK, GRIMSEL, CHAMONIX, MONT BLANC, GRAND ST. BERNARD

'Seldom had there been so propitious an ascent, and with Mr. Albert Smith as chairman, the whole party sat down next day to an excellent dinner in the open air, with all the travellers then in Chamounix as admiring spectators of the very characteristic scene. The bridge was illuminated, the guns were fired at intervals, the Englishmen made speeches and the guides sang lugubrious songs.'

NORTHBROOK, FRANCIS THORNHILL BARING, LORD. GENEVA, CHAMONIX, MARTIGNY, GRAND ST. BERNARD PASS, AOSTA, COURMAYEUR, COL DE LA SEIGNE, BOURG ST. MAURICE, ANNECY, GENEVA, LAUSANNE, BERNE, THUN, INTERLAKEN, GRINDELWALD, FAULHORN, ANDERMATT, ALTDORF, LUCERNE, SCHAFFHAUSEN, ST. GALL, ZURICH, COIRE, THUSIS, SPLÜGEN PASS, CHIAVENNA

REYNOLDS, HENRY ROBERT. BASLE, ROSENLAUI, LUCERNE

'There it is! [Lake of Lucerne] glittering like the Sea of Glass before the Great White Throne.'

SHELLEY, FRANCES, LADY. CONSTANCE, SCHAFFHAUSEN, ZURICH, LUCERNE, BERNE, FRIBOURG, BULLE, VEVEY, OUCHY, GENEVA

'We arrived at Vevey in full view of a lovely sunset. . . . I turned from my window with regret; and entered the salon of the hotel, which, for that evening at least, extinguished every feeling of romance. A large lady from Boston was extended at full length on the only sofa in the room, and harangued in unmusical tones the other ladies present.'

SMITH, ALBERT. CHAMONIX

Smith spent a night in the newly erected hut at the Grands Mulets with nearly fifty other travellers, including Lord Killeen, Colonel de Bathe, Howard Russell, MacGregor, Fanshawe, Shuldham, and Burrows. 'We were all blocked together like the inmates of a slave-ship.'

SMITH, JOHN DENHAM. BASLE, ZURICH, ALBIS, LUCERNE, BERNE, VEVEY, GENEVA, CHAMONIX, GENEVA

'The Lake itself is of charming extent and variety. Nearing it, just as you descend the hill to Vevay, on the road from Berne, its azure expanse opened with great effect upon our view. On the opposite shore, the Alps seemed to meet us at our coming. All on a sudden they revealed themselves in a congregated body. They reminded us of a troop of maidens on a bridal morn; for the light fleecy clouds hung modestly and gracefully over their brows in veil-like beauty, disclosing only parts of their fine, yet gentle images of loveliness and splendour.'

SPENCER, HERBERT. BASLE, ZURICH, RIGI, FLUELEN, ANDERMATT, FURKA PASS, GRIMSEL PASS, MEIRINGEN, GROSSE SCHEIDEGG, GRINDELWALD, FAULHORN, KLEINE SCHEIDEGG, LAUTERBRUNNEN, INTERLAKEN,

THUN, KANDERSTEG, GEMMI PASS, LEUK, VISP, ZERMATT, VISP, SION, MARTIGNY, VEVEY, BASLE

'I was much disappointed from the absence of fine colouring. Grey and green and brown are the prevailing tints. In consequence of the clearness of the air there is very little atmospheric effect, and a general absence of those various tones which this gives. In this respect Switzerland is far inferior to Scotland. . . . On the whole, though Switzerland fully equalled my anticipations in respect of its grandeur, it did not do so in respect of its beauty.'

STOWE, HARRIET BEECHER. GENEVA, ST. CERGUE, GENEVA, CHAMONIX, TÊTE NOIRE PASS, MARTIGNY, GRAND ST. BERNARD, MARTIGNY, CHILLON, GENEVA, LAUSANNE, FRIBOURG, BERNE, THUN, INTERLAKEN, LAUTERBRUNNEN, KLEINE SCHEIDEGG, GRINDELWALD, GROSSE SCHEIDEGG, MEIRINGEN, INTERLAKEN, THUN, LANGNAU, LUCERNE, RIGI, BASLE

'It was touching to listen to the talk of these secluded mountaineers. The good hostess, even the servant maids, hung about H., expressing such tender interest for the slave. All had read Uncle Tom. And it had apparently been an era in their life's monotony, for they said, "O, madam, do write another! Remember, our winter nights here are very long!" '

THACKERAY, WILLIAM MAKEPEACE. VEVEY, GENEVA, LAUSANNE, VEVEY, BULLE, FRIBOURG, BERNE, ZURICH, BASLE

Thackeray had begun to write *The Newcomes*. At Vevey the story was getting on 'very pleasantly'. Very soon he wrote that he had spent 'as pleasant a fortnight as ever I have had in my life, plenty of work, play, health, money, good children. What could man ask for more?'

ULRICH, MELCHIOR. ZURICH, GLARUS, STACHELBERG, PANTENBRÜCKE, TÖDI

WAGNER, RICHARD. ZURICH, INTERLAKEN, ZURICH, RICHTERSWIL, SCHWYZ, BRUNNEN, GRÜTLI, ZUG, ZURICH, COIRE, TIEFENKASTEL, JULIER PASS, ST. MORITZ, PONTRESINA, COIRE, ZURICH, GENEVA, ANDERMATT, ZURICH, BASLE, ZURICH

Together with Liszt and Herwegh, Wagner visited the Grütli where they repeated the oath of brotherhood of the original founders of the Swiss Confederation.

WALLACE, ALFRED RUSSELL. GENEVA, CHAMONIX, TÊTE NOIRE PASS, MARTIGNY, SION, LEUK, GEMMI PASS, KANDERSTEG, THUN

'Although I enjoyed this my first visit to snowy mountains and glaciers, I had not at that time sufficient knowledge to fully appreciate them.'

WHITE, WALTER. BASLE, MOUTIER, BIENNE, BERNE, THUN, INTERLAKEN, LAUTERBRUNNEN, INTERLAKEN, KANDERSTEG, GEMMI PASS, LEUK, SION, MARTIGNY, GRAND ST. BERNARD PASS, AOSTA, COURMAYEUR, COL DE LA SEIGNE, COL DES FOURS, COL DU BONHOMME, CHAMONIX, GENEVA

'From Thun to the head of the lake is about ten miles. You land at Neuhaus, a place made up of a wooden wharf, a wooden hotel, and piles of firewood, and nothing else except the mob of touters, guides, porters, drivers, carriages, and miscellaneous people, that wait your disembarkation. The scene reminded me of Chertsey on a sham-fight day at the camp, so great was the clamour and confusion. There was a party of three Englishmen, who showed their want of self-reliance by hiring a guide there and then to take them to Chamonix; which was something like hiring a guide at Oxford to show you the way to Ben Nevis.'

WILLS, ALFRED. CHAMONIX, VISP, SAAS FEE, ADLER PASS, ZERMATT

'The Val d'Anniviers, which runs southwards from Sierre, and the parallel valley of Turtmann have probably never been explored by a single amateur, and, from what little I could learn of them, would appear to be still more barbarous than the neighbouring valleys of Herins and Heremence. . . . Balmat told me that he once had occasion to penetrate a few miles up the Val d'Anniviers many years ago, and found the natives living in a state of nudity and filth, almost too gross and disgusting to relate.'

YOUNG, JULIAN CHARLES. GENEVA, CHAMONIX, COL DU BONHOMME, COL DE LA SEIGNE, COURMAYEUR, AOSTA

1854

BLACKWELL, EARDLEY J. GRINDELWALD, GROSSE SCHEIDEGG, ROSENLAUI, WETTERHORN (HASLE JUNGFRAU), CHAMONIX, MONT BLANC

Mr. Heathman met Mr. Blackwell at Chamonix just before the latter's ascent of Mont Blanc. 'On parting with him for his ascent, I wished him success, and all the pleasure which he anticipated, although, said I, I confess, I do not know what that is. He replied he did not know either, except being an idle man he loved the excitement, and always felt a desire to accomplish what others had done before him.'

CALAME, ALEXANDRE. GENEVA, LAUSANNE, BERNE, THUN, INTERLAKEN, ISENFLUH, LAUTERBRUNNEN, ROSENLAUI

EASTLAKE, LADY ELISABETH. BASLE, LUCERNE, FLUELEN, ANDERMATT, ST. GOTTHARD PASS, BELLINZONA, LOCARNO, MILAN, CHIAVENNA, SPLÜGEN PASS, THUSIS, COIRE

Crossing the Splügen pass 'the conducteur swallowed an egg and some brandy to fortify himself, rubbed his hands, clapped me on the shoulder with a "Wie geht's, Madame?" '

FRASER, GENERAL SIR THOMAS. BERNE, ZURICH, LUCERNE, RIGI, BRUNIG PASS, BRIENZ, GRINDELWALD, LAUTERBRUNNEN, INTERLAKEN, THUN, BERNE, LAUSANNE, GENEVA

HALL, NEWMAN. CHAMONIX

'The first time I spent a Sunday at Chamonix, as there was no English church, I endeavoured, as always, to supply the gap. The landlord could not grant the use of a room in the hotel, because it would cost him his tenancy, under the law of a Roman Catholic government. So I proposed to hold evening worship under the trees, using the liturgy with free prayer and hymns. I was afterwards informed that some who were present petitioned, through our Government, that English visitors should be allowed freedom of worship. Permission was then given to build an English church. A few years after, I had the great pleasure of worshipping in the beautiful little church erected outside the village, and I thank God for allowing me, in however small a degree, to have been instrumental in its erection.'

HARE, AUGUSTUS J. C. GENEVA, CHAMONIX, COL DU BONHOMME, COL DE LA SEIGNE, COURMAYEUR, AOSTA, GRAND ST. BERNARD PASS, MARTIGNY, VEVEY, MARTIGNY, SION, VISP, ZERMATT, VISP, LEUK, GEMMI PASS, KANDERSTEG, THUN, LUCERNE, ALTDORF, ANDERMATT, ENGELBERG, SARNEN, BRUNIG PASS, MEIRINGEN, GROSSE SCHEIDEGG, GRINDELWALD, BASLE

Of Zermatt Hare wrote: 'It is a grand view but I could never care for it. . . . I am very glad to have seen it, but, if I can help it, nothing shall ever induce me to see it again.'

HARRISON, FREDERIC. GRINDELWALD, STRAHLEGG PASS, GRIMSEL, LÖTSCHENLÜCKE PASS, KIPPEL, LÖTSCHEN PASS, KANDERSTEG, HOHTHÜRLI PASS, SEFINENFURKE PASS, MÜRREN, LAUTERBRUNNEN

'We claimed to have "founded" Mürren as a station. The double Col from Kandersteg to Lauterbrunnen is a long day; and in 1853–4 at Mürren there was neither inn, nor hut, nor so much as a glass of milk to be got in the two or three poor chalets there. At Lauterbrunnen, Interlaken, and Thun we filled the hotel registers with vehement praise of the views and air of Mürren and rebukes to the indolence of tourists who neglected so magnificent a station. The next year if I remember, I found a small Gasthaus installed in the noble plateau. . . .'

HEATHMAN, W. G. LES VERRIÈRES, NEUCHÂTEL, ALBIS, BERNE, THUN, INTERLAKEN, LAUTERBRUNNEN, KLEINE SCHEIDEGG, GRINDELWALD, FAULHORN, GROSSE SCHEIDEGG, MEIRINGEN, INTERLAKEN, ZWEISIMMEN, SAANEN, CHÂTEAU D'OEX, COL DES MOSSES, AIGLE, VEVEY, MARTIGNY,

COL DE BALME, CHAMONIX, TÊTE NOIRE PASS, MARTIGNY, SION, VISP, ZERMATT, VISP, BRIG, SIMPLON PASS, DOMODOSSOLA, LOCARNO, BELLINZONA, MESOCCO, SAN BERNARDINO PASS, THUSIS, COIRE, ZURICH, EINSIEDELN, SCHWYZ, RIGI, LUCERNE, BRUNIG PASS, BRIENZ, INTERLAKEN, THUN, FRIBOURG, BERNE, BIENNE, MOUTIER, BASLE

'It is really too bad to deter tourists, as books of travel sometimes do, by their narrations of all that is frightful, and I can only account for it on that principle of human nature which is apt to overrate its own hardihood. Tourists should remember that, however courageous they may appear to themselves in thus estimating their powers, they alarm and prevent others from treading the same paths. . . . Who, for instance, would have thought of riding to Zermatt, when one says, "the path in many places is carried along a deep slope, where a slip of a mule would hurry the unfortunate passenger to his certain destruction"?'

HINCHLIFF, T. W. ZURICH, RIGI, FLUELEN, ALTDORF, KLAUSEN PASS, LINTHAL, GLARUS, WESEN, COIRE, THUSIS, REICHENAU, DISENTIS, OBERALP PASS, ANDERMATT, FURKA PASS, GRIMSEL PASS, MEIRINGEN, GRINDELWALD, FAULHORN, GIESSBACH, INTERLAKEN, KANDERSTEG, GEMMI PASS, LEUK, VISP, ZERMATT, ST. THEODUL PASS, BREUIL, CHATILLON, AOSTA, COURMAYEUR, COL DE LA SEIGNE, COL DU BONHOMME, CHAMONIX

On the Faulhorn 'we were soon dressed and out of the house, watching the gradual approach of dawn, thoroughly absorbed in the first near view of the Oberland giants, which broke upon us unexpectedly after the intense obscurity of the evening before. "Look at the Wetterhorn!" cried some one, as its summit gleamed with the first rose of dawn: and in a few moments the double crest of the Schreckhorn followed its example; peak after peak seemed warmed with life, the Jungfrau blushed even more beautifully than her neighbours, and soon from the Wetterhorn in the East to the Wildstrubel in the West, a long row of fires glowed upon mighty altars, truly worthy of the gods.'

HORT, F. J. A. GENEVA, CHAMONIX, COL DU BONHOMME, COL DE LA SEIGNE, COURMAYEUR, COL FERRET, COL DE FENÊTRE, GRAND ST. BERNARD PASS, MARTIGNY, SION, VISP, ZERMATT, STALDEN, SAAS, VISP, LEUK, GEMMI PASS, KANDERSTEG, THUN, BERNE, THUN, INTERLAKEN, LAUTERBRUNNEN, KLEINE SCHEIDEGG, GRINDELWALD, FAULHORN, GROSSE SCHEIDEGG, MEIRINGEN, GRIMSEL PASS, FURKA PASS, ANDERMATT, ALTDORF, LUCERNE, RIGI, ZURICH, WALLENSTADT, RAGAZ, RORSCHACH, SCHAFFHAUSEN, MILAN, DOMODOSSOLA, SIMPLON PASS, BRIG, FERDEN, LÖTSCHEN PASS, KANDERSTEG

MARSH, GEORGE PERKINS. CHAMONIX, TÊTE NOIRE PASS, MARTIGNY, SION, LEUK, GEMMI PASS, KANDERSTEG, THUN, BERNE, BIENNE, MOUTIER, BASLE

ORSINI, FELICE. GENEVA, ZURICH, COIRE, ST. MORITZ, MALOJA, BERNINA PASS, CAVAGLIA, POSCHIAVO, BERNINA PASS, SAMADEN, ALBULA

PASS, BERGÜN, COIRE, ZURICH, LUCERNE, FLUELEN, ST. GOTTHARD PASS, BELLINZONA, MILAN

Together with Mazzini, Orsini was at St. Moritz to concert plans for operations against the Austrians in the Valtelline, over the Bernina and Muretto passes.

RAFFLES, W. WINTER. GENEVA, VILLENEUVE, MARTIGNY, SION, VISP, ZERMATT, COL D'HÉRENS, EVOLENA, AROLLA, COL DE COLLON, PRARAYÉ, AOSTA, COURMAYEUR, COL DE LA SEIGNE, COL DES FOURS, COL DU BONHOMME, CHAMONIX, MONT BLANC

By a primitive form of application of the principles of sonic radar, Raffles's guide framed his course over the glacier by shouting 'Mont Collon', and being guided by the echo.

RUSKIN, JOHN. GENEVA, VEVEY, FRIBOURG, CHÂTEAU D'OEX, ZWEISIMMEN. THUN, INTERLAKEN, LUCERNE, CHAMONIX, GENEVA, CHAMONIX, MARTIGNY, SION, MARTIGNY, GENEVA

'Every day here [Chamonix] I seem to see further into nature and into myself—and into futurity.'
At Sion Ruskin made the notes for the chapter on 'Mountain Gloom' in *Modern Painters*.

SCHEFFEL, JOSEPH VIKTOR. ST. GALL, SÄNTIS, WILDKIRCHLI

Scheffel was writing his *Ekkehard*, and visiting on the spot the scenes of his hero's life.

SHAND, ALEXANDER INNES (*c*). VISP, ZERMATT

STUDER, GOTTLIEB. LEUK, GEMMI PASS, GROSS RINDERHORN, KANDERSTEG

'I returned gratefully and joyously conscious of the fact that I had lived a day of earthly glory such as is seldom man's lot to enjoy, and is reserved only for those who are susceptible to the uplifting impressions of magnificent scenes of nature, and who are not afraid of providing themselves with this great pleasure at the cost of exertion and danger.'

TALBOT, ISRAEL TISDALE. CHAMONIX, MONT BLANC

VIGNOLES, CHARLES BLACKER. GENEVA, MORGES, LAUSANNE, YVERDON, PAYERNE, FRIBOURG, BERNE

Vignoles was appointed Engineer in Chief of the Western Railway of Switzerland. His son Henry, as Resident Engineer, constructed the line from Lausanne to Morges and Yverdon under his father's direction. 'One of the first wrought iron trellis bridges used in railway construction was erected on this railway near Morges. The natives nicknamed it the "toothpick" bridge, and predicted its speedy collapse; and when a locomotive was for the first time taken over it by Mr. Henry Vignoles, no one but the driver would go with him on the engine, whilst crowds were collected near to witness the expected fall of the bridge.'

WAGNER, RICHARD. ZURICH, MONTREUX, LAUSANNE, GENEVA, LUCERNE, SEELISBERG, ZURICH

Wagner was composing the *Walkyries.*

WILLS, ALFRED. CHAMONIX, VISP, SAAS FEE, VISP, LEUK, GEMMI PASS, KANDERSTEG, THUN, INTERLAKEN, GRINDELWALD, WETTERHORN

Wills's ascent of the Wetterhorn, although not the first, was the starting-point of the English offensive on the high peaks. It made an impression in Switzerland also, for Wills relates that he heard himself styled 'Der Wetterhorner Herr'.

1855

ANDERSEN, HANS CHRISTIAN. LUCERNE, BRUNNEN, ZURICH

At Brunnen 'The evening before the day I was to set out, there glided out in front of the hotel a boat with torches and music; it looked charming to us. All the guests at the hotel came out on the balcony.
"What does it mean?" I asked Agathe.
"It is a greeting for you," said she.
"O, don't fancy such a thing," I replied—"music on my account,"
"But it is", she replied.'

ANDERSON, EUSTACE. BASLE, BERNE, LAUSANNE, GENEVA, CHAMONIX, MONT BLANC, GENEVA

BLOOMFIELD, GEORGIANA, BARONESS. THUN, INTERLAKEN, KANDERSTEG

'We were reading together on the second floor of the great hotel at Thun, when suddenly the room began to shake and the windows rattle, as if a heavy dray cart was being driven under them. We rushed to the door which was locked. I wrenched it open and got out of the house; as we ran down the stairs they seemed to rock under us, like the companion ladder of a ship in a heavy swell; and when we got out we found all the inhabitants of the hotel looking pale with terror, standing out on the lawn, and we then realised that there had been a severe shock of an earthquake. . . . An old English lady was staying in the hotel at Thun the day of the earthquake, and we were greatly amused at hearing that she gave her servant strict orders to put her umbrella and galoshes ready next her bed-side every night, in case there should be another shock!'

COLEMAN, EDMUND THOMAS. CHAMONIX, MONT BLANC

'DORA D'ISTRIA', COUNTESS. CONSTANCE, SCHAFFHAUSEN, ZURICH, ZUG, RIGI, LUCERNE, BERNE, THUN, INTERLAKEN, GRINDELWALD, MÖNCH, BASLE

The Rumanian princess Kolzoff-Masalsky planted the banner of Wallachia on the Mönch, but Leslie Stephen said: 'though I should be sorry to be uncivil to a lady, I must confess that the account bears strong internal evidence of describing an ascent to a point which was not the top'. The Mönch was first ascended by Dr. Porges of Vienna in 1857.

EASTLAKE, LADY ELISABETH. RORSCHACH, GAIS, ALTSTÄTTEN, COIRE, THUSIS, SPLÜGEN PASS, CHIAVENNA

'Gais is noted for its goats' whey, which professes to cure weak lungs, delicate throats, etc., and the air itself is famed for salubrity. Surrounded as we are with meadows like green velvet, over which rise Alps of considerable grandeur, I can believe in any good results. We do nothing but congratulate ourselves on our good fortune in coming to this place.'

ENGELHARDT, CHRISTIAN MORITZ. ZERMATT

EWING, ALEXANDER. BASLE, BERNE, VEVEY

HAWTREY, STEPHEN. VEVEY, MARTIGNY, COL DE BALME, CHAMONIX, MARTIGNY, SION, VISP, ZERMATT, CIMA DI JAZZI, STALDEN, SAAS, MONTE MORO PASS, MACUGNAGA, VARALLO, ORTA, AOSTA, GRAND ST. BERNARD PASS, MARTIGNY, LUCERNE, RIGI

'While I am writing this, imagine the changes creeping on, a deeper tint of rose, getting more and more beautiful till the moment of dissolution, and looking round on the whole horizon, there was a succession of tints, from gold through rosier and paler tints of rose to violet, and at last to softest green. Now one part died, then another, then another. Now the head of Mont Blanc alone is rosy. Now, even that has changed, and the whole mountain is dead.'

HEARD, GEORGE W. GENEVA, CHAMONIX

'There was a French gentleman at Chamouni, who was engaged in some scientific investigations among the mountains, who has been very kind to us before we started, and gave us several little things. We invited him also [to dinner]. He came and we found him a very agreeable companion: to our surprise we learned afterwards that he was the Duke of Brabant' (Leopold II of Belgium).

HINCHLIFF, T. W. INTERLAKEN, LAUTERBRUNNEN, KLEINE SCHEIDEGG, GRINDELWALD, FAULHORN, GROSSE SCHEIDEGG, MEIRINGEN, GRIMSEL PASS, STRAHLEGG PASS, GRINDELWALD, INTERLAKEN, KANDERSTEG,

GEMMI PASS, LEUK, VISP, ZERMATT, ST. THEODUL PASS, BREUIL, CHATILLON, AOSTA, GRAND ST. BERNARD, COL DE FENÊTRE, COL FERRET, COURMAYEUR, COL DE LA SEIGNE, COL DU BONHOMME, CHAMONIX, MONT BUET, COL DE BALME, MARTIGNY, SION, RAWIL PASS, LENK, THUN, BERNE, BASLE

'In 1855 I met at the [Great St. Bernard] hospice a dentist who spoke French with a fine nasal Yankee twang. . . . He employed his leisure time in filling up little blue tickets with the name and address of his firm in Paris and New York, which I found he was in the habit of sticking on walls and window-sills in the hotels where he lodged . . . and I should hardly have been surprised at hearing that he had offered to pull out the monks' teeth, instead of rewarding their hospitality in the more customary manner.'

HUDSON, CHARLES. ZERMATT, MONTE ROSA, COURMAYEUR, COL DE LA SEIGNE, COL DU BONHOMME, ST. GERVAIS, MONT BLANC, CHAMONIX

. . .'A report, indeed, was getting rife that certain Englishmen had started two days before from St. Gervais, and had fixed upon the summit of Mont Blanc as the goal of their ambition. . . . However, no supposition could be more absurd than that a small party of Englishmen should have actually ascended from some other point,—that they should have overcome the difficulties of the route,—and finally, without guides, without a ladder, and without a knowledge of the path usually pursued, have arrived at Chamonix.'

KENNEDY, E. S. ZERMATT, EVOLENA, COL DU MONT ROUGE, CHANRION, COL DE FENÊTRE DE BALME, AOSTA, COURMAYEUR, COL DE LA SEIGNE, COL DU BONHOMME, ST. GERVAIS, MONT BLANC, CHAMONIX

KING, REV. S. W. MARTIGNY, GRAND ST. BERNARD PASS, ST. REMY, COL DE SERENA, COURMAYEUR, COL DE LA SEIGNE, BOURG ST. MAURICE, PETIT ST. BERNARD PASS, AOSTA, OLLOMONT, PRARAYÉ, COL DE VESSONEY, ST. BARTHELEMY, BREUIL, ST. THEODUL, CHATILLON, COL DE JOUX, BRUSSONE, AYAS, BETTA FURKA PASS, GRESSONEY, CHATILLON, BRUSSONE, COL DE RANZOLA, GRESSONEY, COL D'OLEN, ALAGNA, COL D'EGUA, MACUGNAGA, MONTE MORO, DOMODOSSOLA, FORMAZZA, GRIES PASS, ULRICHEN

MOTLEY, JOHN LOTHROP. VEVEY, BERNE, BASLE

The historian of the Dutch Republic 'left Vevey after more than a year's residence (very profitably employed for the children)'.

PACKE, CHARLES. VALLORBE, LAUSANNE, VEVEY, COL DE JAMAN, CHÂTEAU D'OEX, SAANEN, ZWEISIMMEN, THUN, BERNE, THUN, INTERLAKEN, LAUTERBRUNNEN, KLEINE SCHEIDEGG, GRINDELWALD, FAULHORN, GROSSE SCHEIDEGG, MEIRINGEN, GRIMSEL PASS, FURKA PASS, ANDERMATT, ALTDORF, LUCERNE, BRUNIG PASS, BRIENZ, INTERLAKEN, KANDERSTEG, GEMMI PASS, LEUK, SION, MARTIGNY, COL DE BALME, CHAMONIX, GENEVA

PUMPELLY, RAPHAEL. BASLE, LUCERNE, FLUELEN, ST. GOTTHARD, ANDERMATT, FURKA PASS, OBERGESTELEN, BRIG, LEUK, CHAMONIX

TUPPER, MARTIN. CONSTANCE, SCHAFFHAUSEN, ZURICH, ALBIS, LUCERNE, RIGI, ALTDORF, ST. GOTTHARD PASS, BELLINZONA, LUGANO, COMO, DOMODOSSOLA, SIMPLON PASS, BRIG, SION, MARTIGNY, LAUSANNE, GENEVA, CHAMONIX, GENEVA

VIGNET, LOUIS. MEIRINGEN, GRIMSEL PASS, OBERGESTELEN, VIESCH, EGGISHORN

Vignet and his friends were having a picnic lunch on the Eggishorn, together with two Englishmen, one of whom they had rescued from a precipice. The other Englishman 'se frappe le front coupable d'un oubli, et, lentement, du ton le plus britannique, avec la plus sérieuse allure,
— une nouvelle à moa . . . que voos ne savez pas . . .
— la nouvelle! la nouvelle!
— Sebastopol est pris!'

WEILENMANN, JOHANN JAKOB. ANDERMATT, FURKA PASS, BRIG, VISP, ZERMATT, MONTE ROSA

Among Weilenmann's companions on this second ascent of the highest summit of Monte Rosa were Henry William Watson and Francis Vaughan Hawkins.

1856

BONNEY, THOMAS GEORGE. BASLE, MOUTIER, BIENNE, YVERDON, LAUSANNE, GENEVA, CHAMONIX, TÊTE NOIRE PASS, MARTIGNY, GRAND ST. BERNARD, MARTIGNY, LAUSANNE, FRIBOURG, BERNE, BASLE

BREMER, FREDRIKA. BASLE, MOUTIER, BERNE, THUN, INTERLAKEN, LAUTERBRUNNEN, THUN, BERNE, LAUSANNE, GRUYÈRES, CHÂTEAU D'OEX, ROUGEMONT, COL DES MOSSES, COMBALLAZ, CHÂTEAU D'OEX, SAANEN, ZWEISIMMEN, INTERLAKEN, LAUTERBRUNNEN, MEIRINGEN, ROSENLAUI, GRIMSEL PASS, FURKA PASS, ANDERMATT, ALTDORF, SCHWYZ, LUCERNE, RIGI, STANS, SARNEN, LUCERNE, ALBIS, ZURICH, RAPPERSWIL, EINSIEDELN, ZURICH, BADEN, BRUGG, BASLE

BUNSEN, CHRISTIAN, BARON. BASLE, MOUTIER, BIENNE, YVERDON, LAUSANNE, COPPET, GENEVA, CHAMONIX, GENEVA, COPPET, VEVEY, BULLE, CHÂTEAU D'OEX, SAANEN, ZWEISIMMEN, INTERLAKEN, LUCERNE, RIGI, BASLE

BUTLER, HENRY MONTAGU. GENEVA, CHAMONIX, COL DU BONHOMME, COL DE LA SEIGNE, COURMAYEUR, AOSTA, CHATILLON, BREUIL, ST. THEODUL PASS, ZERMATT, MONTE ROSA

CATLOW, AGNES & MARIA. BASLE, MOUTIER, WEISSENSTEIN, SOLEURE, BERNE, LANGNAU, LUCERNE, ZUG, ALTDORF, ST. GOTTHARD PASS, BELLINZONA, ST. GOTTHARD PASS, AMSTEG, ALTDORF, STANS, BRUNIG PASS, BRIENZ, INTERLAKEN, GRINDELWALD, KLEINE SCHEIDEGG, LAUTERBRUNNEN, INTERLAKEN, ZWEISIMMEN, SAANEN, CHÂTEAU D'OEX, VEVEY, GENEVA, CHAMONIX

'If the good old times should ever come again, when human beings were transformed into rocks, streams, and rivers, and such were to be our fate, we should crave permission of the ruling powers to become those pretty streams the Black and White Lütschine.'

CLOWES, G. BASLE, LUCERNE, RIGI, FLUELEN, ALTDORF, ANDERMATT, FURKA PASS, GRIMSEL PASS, MEIRINGEN, INTERLAKEN, LAUTERBRUNNEN, KLEINE SCHEIDEGG, GRINDELWALD, FAULHORN, GROSSE SCHEIDEGG, MEIRINGEN, INTERLAKEN, KANDERSTEG, GEMMI PASS, LEUK, SION, MARTIGNY, COL DE BALME, CHAMONIX, GENEVA, VEVEY, MARTIGNY, SION, VISP, ZERMATT, VISP, BRIG, SIMPLON PASS, DOMODOSSOLA, CHIAVENNA, SPLÜGEN PASS, THUSIS, COIRE, RAGAZ, ZURICH, SCHAFFHAUSEN

COLE, MRS. H. WARWICK. ANDERMATT, ST. GOTTHARD PASS, AIROLO, AL ACQUA, SAN GIACOMO PASS, TOSA FALLS, GRIES PASS, ULRICHEN, VIESCH, EGGISHORN, BRIG, VISP, ZERMATT, STALDEN, SAAS, MONTE MORO PASS, MACUGNAGA

'On reaching the Hotel de la Jungfrau [Eggishorn], the landlord warmly welcomed us, conducted us to the best rooms in his then half-built inn, and made us as comfortable as he could. . . . In the evening the stove in the salle-à-manger smoked, a fault which has since been remedied; and therefore, as it was too cold to sit without a fire at so great an elevation, we went down into the guides' room below, which was equally large, and there the genial warmth of a wood fire was really quite enjoyable though, during the day, we had suffered so much from the heat. The landlord, guides, and porters played at cards at an adjoining table, and none seemed in the least degree disturbed by our presence, whilst we, equally at our ease, wrote letters; and then my companions in turn selected and read aloud some favourite sonnets from a pocket edition of Shakespeare.'

DARGAUD, J. M. BASLE, BIENNE, BERNE, THUN, INTERLAKEN, LAUTERBRUNNEN, INTERLAKEN, STOCKHORN, INTERLAKEN, BRIENZ, BRUNIG PASS, LUCERNE, RIGI, SARNEN, BRUNIG PASS, MEIRINGEN, GROSSE SCHEIDEGG, GRINDELWALD, INTERLAKEN, THUN, BERNE, LAUSANNE, VEVEY

'Il faudrait tout juger du haut des Alpes. De la cime de ces augustes monts, il ne reste debout que l'amour, l'amitié, la poésie, la philosophie et la théologie des esprits, non des textes.'

FAIRBANKS, HENRY. RIGI, FLUELEN, ANDERMATT, FURKA PASS, GRIMSEL PASS, MEIRINGEN, GROSSE SCHEIDEGG, GRINDELWALD, FAULHORN,

KLEINE SCHEIDEGG, LAUTERBRUNNEN, INTERLAKEN, KANDERSTEG, GEMMI PASS, LEUK, SION, MARTIGNY, COL DE BALME, CHAMONIX, MONT BLANC, GENEVA

FOX, JOSEPH H. GENEVA, CHAMONIX, COL DU GÉANT, COURMAYEUR, AOSTA, PRARAYÉ, COL DE COLLON, AROLLA, LES HAUDÈRES, COL D'HÉRENS, ZERMATT, ST. THEODUL PASS, COL DES CIMES BLANCHES, ST. JACQUES D'AYAS, BRUSSONE, COL DE RANZOLA, GRESSONEY, COL DE VAL DOBBIA, VARALLO, DOMODOSSOLA, SIMPLON PASS, BRIG, SION, MARTIGNY, TÊTE NOIRE PASS, CHAMONIX, COL DE BALME, MARTIGNY, LAUSANNE, YVERDON, BIENNE, BASLE

GUTHRIE, THOMAS. CHAMONIX, MARTIGNY, FRIBOURG, BERNE, THUN, INTERLAKEN, LAUTERBRUNNEN, KLEINE SCHEIDEGG, GRINDELWALD, INTERLAKEN, LUCERNE

'An early start for an expedition among the mountains found Dr. Guthrie the first of his party astir, and his buoyant glee on such occasions sometimes brought him into trouble. At Interlaken, with a long day over the Wengern Alp in view, we remember his thundering, before five o'clock of a brilliant summer morning, at the doors of his party, one after the other, along the corridor of the Hotel Bellevue. He was for the time manifestly oblivious that the said hotel was not his own dwelling-house—a fact which was recalled to mind by the sudden apparition from behind a door, of the white nightcap and black beard of an irascible little Frenchman, who, in loud and indignant tones, exclaimed, "Vat for you make dat great noise? it is much shame".'

HARE, LUCEBELLA. ST. GERVAIS, AIGUILLE DU GOUTER

HINCHLIFF, T. W. SCHAFFHAUSEN, ZURICH, RIGI, LUCERNE, ALTDORF, ANDERMATT, FURKA PASS, GRIMSEL PASS, MEIRINGEN, GROSSE SCHEIDEGG, GRINDELWALD, FAULHORN, KLEINE SCHEIDEGG, LAUTERBRUNNEN, INTERLAKEN, KANDERSTEG, GEMMI PASS, LEUK, VISP, ZERMATT, MONTE ROSA, STALDEN, SAAS, MONTE MORO PASS, MACUGNAGA, VARALLO, RIVA, COL DE VAL DOBBIA, GRESSONEY, COL DE RANZOLA, BRUSSONE, COL DE JOUX, CHATILLON, AOSTA, GRAND ST. BERNARD PASS, COL DE FENÊTRE, COL FERRET, COURMAYEUR, COL DE LA SEIGNE, COL DES FOURS, COL DU BONHOMME, CHAMONIX, TÊTE NOIRE PASS, MARTIGNY, VEVEY, BERNE, BASLE

On the Monte Moro 'we overtook a man walking leisurely along by himself. The wind was cold and severe, so we descended the south side a little way to get under the shelter of some lofty rocks, where we prepared for lunch, and invited the stranger to join us. To my great surprise, he declined, and passed on in the same quiet way as before, anxiously looking about him. In a quarter of an hour the mystery was solved by the appearance of several men who had followed us, each of them carrying a large bale of goods on his back, and steadily following the course over the snow taken by the first man. Our porter explained that this was a party of smugglers working their way over into Italy, the first man acting as a sort of pilot-fish to see whether the way was clear.'

HORT, F. J. A. LUCERNE, PILATUS, ENGSTLENALP, LAUTERBRUNNEN, KLEINE SCHEIDEGG, GRINDELWALD, STRAHLEGG PASS, GRIMSEL PASS, OBERGESTELEN, VIESCH, EGGISHORN, JUNGFRAU, BRIG, LEUK, GEMMI PASS, ALTELS, KANDERSTEG, LÄMMERNJOCH PASS, SIERRE, SION, MARTIGNY, COL DE BALME, CHAMONIX, GENEVA

'Our bed was hay, and one of the guides assured us that we need not be afraid of cold, *parce que les vaches sont en dessous, et vous en aurez la chaleur*. There were, in fact, not only *vaches* but *cochons*; but we should probably have got to sleep before midnight had it not been for one pertinacious *vache* who carried a bell, which she thought it necessary to ring in a vicious manner at intervals of a quarter of an hour.'

HUXLEY, THOMAS HENRY. INTERLAKEN, LAUTERBRUNNEN, KLEINE SCHEIDEGG, GRINDELWALD, MEIRINGEN, GRIMSEL PASS, OBERGESTELEN, BRIG, VISP, ZERMATT, VISP, LEUK, GEMMI PASS, KANDERSTEG, INTERLAKEN, BERNE

LEE, ROBERT. GENEVA, CHAMONIX, TÊTE NOIRE PASS, MARTIGNY, VEVEY, GENEVA, LAUSANNE, FRIBOURG, BERNE, THUN, INTERLAKEN, LAUTERBRUNNEN, KLEINE SCHEIDEGG, GRINDELWALD, GROSSE SCHEIDEGG, MEIRINGEN, BRUNIG PASS, SARNEN, WEGGIS, RIGI, LUCERNE, ZURICH, BASLE

LONGMAN, WILLIAM. SCHAFFHAUSEN, ZURICH, WALLENSTADT, COIRE, THUSIS, SPLÜGEN PASS, CHIAVENNA, MENAGGIO, PORLEZZA, LUGANO, LOCARNO, BELLINZONA, ST. GOTTHARD PASS, ANDERMATT, FURKA PASS, GRIMSEL PASS, MEIRINGEN, SUSTEN PASS, WASSEN, ALTDORF, LUCERNE, RIGI, ENGELBERG, JOCH PASS, MEIRINGEN, GRINDELWALD, KLEINE SCHEIDEGG, LAUTERBRUNNEN, TSCHINGEL PASS, KANDERSTEG, GEMMI PASS, LEUK, VISP, ZERMATT, ST. THEODUL PASS, BREUIL, CHATILLON, AOSTA, COURMAYEUR, COL DE LA SEIGNE, COL DES FOURS, COL DU BONHOMME, CHAMONIX, MONT BUET, TÊTE NOIRE PASS, MARTIGNY, GENEVA

'I was so charmed with the scenery, that I confess I was continually tormented with the idea that nothing to come could equal, or, at any rate, surpass it.'

MALKIN, A. T. VISP, ZERMATT, STALDEN, SAAS, VISP, SION, MARTIGNY, BEX, MARTIGNY, BOURG ST. PIERRE, MONT VELAN

At Saas Fee: 'there is not a lovelier spot in Switzerland—emerald meadows set in frosted silver; for the valley is almost encircled by a brilliant amphitheatre of glaciers descending from the Alphubel—and the Mischabelhörner.'

MATHEWS, WILLIAM. LAUSANNE, MONTHEY, CHAMPÉRY, DENT DU MIDI, SALANFE, CHAMONIX, TÊTE NOIRE PASS, MARTIGNY, CHABLE, COMBIN DE CORBASSIÈRE, CHERMONTANE, COL DU MONT ROUGE, PAS DE CHÈVRES, AROLLA, LES HAUDÈRES, COL D'HÉRENS, ZERMATT, MONTE ROSA, NEW WEISSTHOR PASS, MACUGNAGA, LUGANO

In a letter to Hort describing this tour, Mathews suggested the formation of an Alpine Club.

MICHELET, JULES. MONTREUX, LUCERNE

Michelet had become interested in insects, and found much material for his book *L'Insecte* in a little pinewood behind Seeburg, near Lucerne.

ROTH, ABRAHAM. BERNE, THUN, KANDERSTEG, TSCHINGEL PASS, LAUTERBRUNNEN, INTERLAKEN, THUN, BERNE

'My puritan republican countrymen are wont nowadays to shrug their shoulders when speaking of Interlaken, as if the presence of so many foreigners desecrated it, and the smart set there were insufferable. They say that the fragrance of the trees is swamped by the odour of Eau de Mille Fleurs and patchouli, and that the wasp-like waists of the ladies spoil one's taste for the Jungfrau.'

RUSKIN, JOHN. BASLE, MONTREUX, BERNE, THUN, INTERLAKEN, LAUTERBRUNNEN, THUN, BERNE, FRIBOURG, VEVEY, GENEVA, CHAMONIX, GENEVA, FRIBOURG, BULLE, GENEVA

'Something of the same temper which makes the English soldier do always all that is possible, and attempt more than is possible, joins its influence with that of mere avarice in tempting the English merchant into risks which he cannot justify, and efforts which he cannot sustain, and the same passion for adventure which our travellers gratify every summer on perilous snow-wreaths and cloud-encompassed precipices, surrounds with a romantic fascination the glittering of a hollow investment, and gilds the clouds that curl round gulfs of ruin.'

RUSSELL, LORD JOHN. BASLE, LUCERNE, BERNE, LAUSANNE, MARTIGNY, SION, BRIG, SIMPLON PASS, DOMODOSSOLA

STUDER, GOTTLIEB. AOSTA, GRAND ST. BERNARD PASS, MONT VELAN, BOURG ST. PIERRE, MARTIGNY, BEX, MONTHEY, CHAMPÉRY, DENT DU MIDI

TUCKETT, FRANCIS FOX. GENEVA, CHAMONIX, COL DU GÉANT, COURMAYEUR, AOSTA, BIONAZ, PRARAYÉ, COL DE COLLON, AROLLA, EVOLENA, COL D'HÉRENS, ZERMATT, ADLER PASS, SAAS, STALDEN, ZERMATT,

ST. THEODUL PASS, COL DES CIMES BLANCHES, ST. JACQUES D'AYAS, BRUSSONE, COL DE RANZOLA, GRESSONEY, COL DE VAL DOBBIA, RIVA, VARALLO

'At Evolena we had a long chat with a substantial-looking man who is going with two or three others to construct an inn, for the benefit of travellers, there being none at present, and we took down all the particulars, as it is desirable that the fact should be known.'

TYNDALL, JOHN. INTERLAKEN, LAUTERBRUNNEN, KLEINE SCHEIDEGG, GRINDELWALD, GROSSE SCHEIDEGG, MEIRINGEN, GRIMSEL PASS, UNTERAAR GLACIER, FURKA PASS, ANDERMATT, LANDECK

In after years T. H. Huxley wrote: 'Tyndall took up glacier work in consequence of a conversation at my table, and we went out to Switzerland together.'

WAGNER, RICHARD. ZURICH, SCHWYZ, BRUNNEN, GENEVA, MORNEX, ZURICH, RORSCHACH, ZURICH

From Mornex Wagner used to go up the Salève regularly. At first he always took a volume of Byron with him, but in full view of Mont Blanc it never got read. On his return to Zurich he set to work on *Siegfried* and was nearly maddened by the noise of a smithy outside his house, until the bangs suddenly suggested to him the motif of Siegfried's anger against Mime.

WITTE, KARL. PONTRESINA

In the following year Witte wrote that 'Pontresina swarmed with tourists. In the "Krone" at Gredig's, in the "Kreuz" at Christ's, there was frequently no accommodation to be had, and one was very content to secure a modest sleeping place with other room-mates. Meanwhile carpenters and joiners sawed, planed and hammered far into the night to increase the accommodation in Gredig's inn.'

1857

ALBERT EDWARD, PRINCE OF WALES. MARTIGNY, TÊTE NOIRE PASS, CHAMONIX, CONTAMINES, GRAND ST. BERNARD, GRINDELWALD, GROSSE SCHEIDEGG, MEIRINGEN

'The Royal Party, accompanied by Mr. Albert Smith, who is now at Chamounix, and had the honour of acting as guide on this occasion, visited the Cascade du Dard, and afterwards traversed the Glacier des Bossons.'

The Prince of Wales presented a piano to the hospice of the Great St. Bernard.

ANONYMOUS 10 A. GENEVA, LAUSANNE, BERNE, LANGNAU, WOHLHUSEN, MENZNAU, LUCERNE

ANONYMOUS 11. BASLE, BERNE, THUN, INTERLAKEN, BRIENZ, BRUNIG PASS, LUCERNE, ZURICH, SCHAFFHAUSEN, ZURICH, BRUGG, AARAU, BERNE, THUN, INTERLAKEN, GRINDELWALD, INTERLAKEN, WEISSENBURG, KANDERSTEG, LUCERNE, ALTDORF, ST. GOTTHARD PASS, BELLINZONA, LUGANO

'I have now to tell of some of the excursions which we made into other parts of Switzerland, returning always to Thun for the Sunday, that we might occupy our accustomed places in the little English Church.'

ARNOLD, MATTHEW. BASLE, LUCERNE, ENGELBERG, JOCH PASS, MEIRINGEN, GRIMSEL PASS, OBERGESTELEN, BRIG, VISP, ZERMATT

This was another literary pilgrimage 'for Obermann's sake'.

BINET-HENTSCH, J. L. SAMADEN, PONTRESINA, PIZ, LANGUARD, FUORCLA SURLEJ, ST. MORITZ

BLANC, CHARLES (*c*). BASLE, LUCERNE, FLUELEN, ANDERMATT, ST. GOTTHARD PASS, AIROLO, BELLINZONA, LUGANO, COMO

BREMER, FREDRIKA. LAUSANNE, GENEVA, NEUCHÂTEL, LA CHAUX DE FONDS, LE LOCLE, MOTIERS-TRAVERS, BIENNE, ILE ST. PIERRE, BERNE, FRIBOURG, MONTREUX, BEX, GENEVA, CHAMONIX, TÊTE NOIRE PASS, MARTIGNY, GRAND ST. BERNARD, MARTIGNY, GENEVA, MARTIGNY, SION, VISP, ZERMATT, VISP, BRIG, SIMPLON PASS, DOMODOSSOLA

' "Mont Cervin est tout découvert!" I hastened up, and assuredly there stood the defiant, ice-clad giant—or, more properly, giantess, for it is in the form of a woman, with an immense crinoline—in glittering splendour rearing her proud head towards the clear blue heavens.'

BUTLER, ARTHUR JOHN. BASLE, GENEVA, CHAMONIX, MARTIGNY, GRAND ST. BERNARD

BUTLER, SAMUEL. SIMPLON PASS, BRIG, LEUK, GEMMI PASS, KANDERSTEG, FRUTIGEN, INTERLAKEN, LAUTERBRUNNEN, KLEINE SCHEIDEGG, GRINDELWALD, MEIRINGEN, GRIMSEL PASS, FURKA PASS, HOSPENTHAL, FLUELEN, LUCERNE, OLTEN, HAUENSTEIN PASS, BASLE

Grimsel Pass—'here we met an old lady, in a blue ugly, with a pair of green spectacles, carried in a *chaise à porteur*; she had taken it into her head in her old age that she would like to see a little of the world, and here she was. We had seen her lady's maid at the hospice, concerning whom we were told that she was "*bien sage*", and did not scream at the precipices.'

CATLOW, AGNES & MARIA. LUGANO, BELLINZONA, ST. GOTTHARD PASS, ALTDORF, BRUNNEN, RIGI, ZUG, GLARUS, LINTHAL, GLARUS, ZURICH, SCHAFFHAUSEN, CONSTANCE, ST. GALL, COIRE, THUSIS, SAN BERNARDINO PASS, MESOCCO, BELLINZONA, MAGADINO, DOMODOSSOLA, MACUGNAGA

FORSTER, R. W. E. ZERMATT, MONTE ROSA, ALTDORF, KLAUSEN PASS, LINTHAL, STACHELBERG, STALDEN, ELM, SEGNES PASS, REICHENAU, KUNKELS PASS, VÄTTIS, RAGAZ

Referring to Louis Philippe's room in the school at Reichenau, 'one day when I happened to be there, a young man visited this room, and appeared to feel more than ordinary emotion at seeing it. He wrote in the strangers' book, "Louis Philippe d'Orleans",—it was the Comte de Paris, the grandson of its former occupant.'

HARCOURT, SIR WILLIAM. CHAMONIX, TÊTE NOIRE PASS, MARTIGNY, SION, VISP, ZERMATT, WEISSTHOR, MACUGNAGA, VARALLO, ALAGNA, COL D'OLEN, GRESSONEY

In an inn visitors' book the future Chancellor of the Exchequer gave a foretaste of his own activities: 'The landlord is very civil and very extortionate.'

HARE, AUGUSTUS J. C. FELDKIRCH, SARGANS, WALLENSTADT, WESEN, COIRE, THUSIS, SAN BERNARDINO PASS, MESOCCO, BELLINZONA, LOCARNO

HARE, MARIA. LUCERNE, ENGELBERG, LUNGERN, BRUNIG, LUCERNE

HAYDEN, JOHN. BASLE, ZURICH, RAGAZ, COIRE, THUSIS, SAN BERNARDINO PASS, MESOCCO, BELLINZONA, ST. GOTTHARD PASS, ANDERMATT, ALTDORF, FLUELEN, LUCERNE, SARNEN, BRUNIG PASS, MEIRINGEN, GROSSE SCHEIDEGG, GRINDELWALD, KLEINE SCHEIDEGG, LAUTERBRUNNEN, INTERLAKEN, KANDERSTEG, GEMMI PASS, LEUK, SION, MARTIGNY, COL DE BALME, CHAMONIX, GENEVA

HINCHLIFF, T. W. CHAMONIX, MONT BLANC, EVOLENA, COL D'HÉRENS, ZERMATT, VISP, BRIG, SIMPLON PASS, DOMODOSSOLA, MACUGNAGA, WEISSTHOR PASS, ZERMATT, TRIFT PASS, ZINAL, AYER, SIERRE, LENK, WILDSTRUBEL, TRÜTTLISBERG PASS, LAUENEN, KRINNEN PASS, GSTEIG, COL DE PILLON, LES DIABLERETS, COL DE LA CROIX, VILLARS, GSTEIG, OLDENHORN

'In one corner of the gloomy room was a bed, out of which the old lady had just tumbled, and which she informed us that she occupied in joint tenancy with her niece. In the middle of the floor was a small mattress, from which she had stirred up a young shepherd, who was rubbing his eyes at the unwonted disturbance; and in the opposite corner to her own was a tolerably large bed, which we soon found was the only accommodation for travellers in the village of Ayer.'

HUXLEY, THOMAS HENRY. CHAMONIX, COL DU BONHOMME, COL DE LA SEIGNE, COURMAYEUR, AOSTA, GRAND ST. BERNARD PASS, MARTIGNY, COL DE BALME, CHAMONIX, NEUCHÂTEL

At Chamonix Huxley started up Mont Blanc with Tyndall, but 'three days in Switzerland had not given me my Swiss legs, and consequently

I remained at the Grands Mulets all alone in my glory. . . . I was there on a pinnacle like St. Simon Stylites, and nearly as dirty as that worthy saint must have been, but without any of his other claims to angelic assistance, so that I really did not see, if they had fallen into a crevasse, how I was going to help them.'

LYELL, SIR CHARLES. BASLE, ZURICH, SOLEURE, BIENNE, NEUCHÂTEL, LAUSANNE, VEVEY, FRIBOURG, BERNE, AARAU, ZURICH, ST. GALL, TROGEN, ALTDORF, ANDERMATT, FURKA PASS, OBERGESTELEN, BRIG, VISP, ZERMATT, BRIG, SIMPLON PASS, DOMODOSSOLA

MATHEWS, WILLIAM. ENGELBERG, TITLIS, JOCH PASS, MEIRINGEN, GROSSE SCHEIDEGG, FAULHORN, GRINDELWALD, STRAHLEGG PASS, GRIMSEL PASS, OBERGESTELEN, VIESCH, EGGISHORN, FINSTERAARHORN, BRIG, SION, RIDDES, COL DES ETABLONS, CHABLE, GRAND COMBIN, ORSIÈRES, COL DE BALME, CHAMONIX, COL D'ANTERNE, SIXT, GENEVA

'To those who feel wearied—as who does not at times—with the ceaseless mill-work of England in the nineteenth century, there is no medicine so soothing both to mind and body as Alpine travel, affording as it does interesting observation and healthy enjoyment for the present, and pleasant memories for the time to come.'

MÉRIMÉE, PROSPER. GENEVA, CHAMONIX, CHILLON, LAUSANNE

'La Suisse est toujours un admirable pays, mais on voyage maintenant trop facilement, et tant de gens s'en mêlent qu'il faut se battre tous les soirs pour avoir un lit.'

MEYER, CONRAD FERDINAND. ZURICH, STANS, ENGELBERG, TITLIS, LUCERNE

During this holiday Meyer began to draft his poem *Engelberg*.

QUINET, EDGAR. BASLE, SCHWEIZERHALLE, LUCERNE, RIGI, ALTDORF, ST. GOTTHARD PASS, MADERANERTAL, FLUELEN, BECKENRIED, ENGELBERG, LUCERNE, BERNE, THUN, INTERLAKEN, MEIRINGEN, GROSSE SCHEIDEGG, GRINDELWALD, KLEINE SCHEIDEGG, LAUTERBRUNNEN, INTERLAKEN, BRIENZ, BRUNIG PASS, LUCERNE, ALBIS, ZURICH, BASLE

'De tant de vallées que nous avons visitées en Suisse, nulle ne nous a laissé de si doux souvenirs que Lauterbrunnen; tout est là: le rustique et le sublime, le terrible dans les sommets, le champêtre dans le vallon. . . . Oui, nos yeux ont vu en trois jours tout ce que la nature renferme de grandeur: l'Oberland est le joyau de la Suisse, la Suisse le joyau de l'Europe.' This journey supplied much of the background of *Merlin l'Enchanteur*.

RICHARDSON, JOHN WIGHAM. ROMANSHORN, ZURICH, ZUG, RIGI, ALTDORF, ANDERMATT, FURKA PASS, GRIMSEL PASS, MEIRINGEN, INTERLAKEN, LAUTERBRUNNEN, INTERLAKEN, KANDERSTEG, GEMMI PASS, LEUK, SION, MARTIGNY, TÊTE NOIRE PASS, CHAMONIX, GENEVA, CHILLON, BASLE

SELBORNE, ROUNDELL PALMER, LORD. GENEVA, CHAMONIX, MARTIGNY, SION, VISP, ZERMATT, VISP, BRIG, SIMPLON PASS, DOMODOSSOLA, MILAN, COMO, MENAGGIO, PORLEZZA, LUGANO, BELLINZONA, ST. GOTTHARD PASS, ALTDORF, LUCERNE, BRUNIG PASS, MEIRINGEN, GROSSE SCHEIDEGG, GRINDELWALD, FAULHORN, INTERLAKEN, THUN, BERNE

'It was while we were walking over the Great Scheidegg on a brilliant autumn day from Reichenbach to Rosenlaui, that I first saw the Prince of Wales. I remember well that we met him coming from the opposite direction with his tutor Mr. Gibbs, just after we had been decorating our hats with the beautiful Gentiana asclepiadea.'

STANDEN, R. S. CHIAVENNA, SPLÜGEN PASS, THUSIS, COIRE, RAGAZ, PFÄFERS, RORSCHACH

STEPHEN, LESLIE. COURMAYEUR, AOSTA, GRAND ST. BERNARD PASS, MARTIGNY, COL DE BALME, CHAMONIX, GENEVA

'When long ago the Alps cast their spell upon me, it was woven in a great degree by the eloquence of *Modern Painters*. I hoped to share Ruskin's ecstasies in a reverent worship of Mont Blanc and the Matterhorn.'

STUDER, GOTTLIEB. BERNE, ZURICH, LINTHAL, STACHELBERG, SANDALP, CATSCHARAULS PASS, TRUNS, VERSAM, HEINZENBERG, THUSIS, SCHYN PASS, TIEFENKASTEL, FILISUR, ALBULA PASS, PONTE, PONTRESINA, PIZ LANGUARD, DIAVOLEZZA, BERNINA PASS, POSCHIAVO, ROVANO PASS, LANZADA, SONDRIO

Studer visited the artist Georgi in his hut by the Morteratsch glacier, and learned from him of the existence of the Diavolezza lake which at the time was known only to five men.

SUMNER, CHARLES. BASLE, BERNE, THUN, INTERLAKEN, BRIENZ, BRUNIG PASS, LUCERNE, FLUELEN, ANDERMATT, HOSPENTHAL, ST. GOTTHARD PASS, BELLINZONA, MAGADINO, TURIN, AOSTA, GRAND ST. BERNARD PASS, MARTIGNY, TÊTE NOIRE PASS, CHAMONIX, GENEVA, LAUSANNE, NEUCHÂTEL, BASLE

TOLSTOI, LEO. GENEVA, CLARENS, COL DE JAMAN, CHÂTEAU D'OEX, ZWEISIMMEN, THUN, INTERLAKEN, GRINDELWALD, GROSSE SCHEIDEGG, MEIRINGEN, INTERLAKEN, THUN, BERNE, FRIBOURG, VEVEY, GENEVA, TURIN, GRESSONEY-LA-TRINITÉ, COL DE RANZOLA, BRUSSONE, COL DE JOUX, CHATILLON, AOSTA, GRAND ST. BERNARD PASS, MARTIGNY, VEVEY, GENEVA, YVERDON, BERNE, LUCERNE, RIGI, ZUG, ZURICH, SCHAFFHAUSEN

At Lucerne there occurred the incident that led to his writing *Lucerne*. 'A tiny man singing Tyrolese songs to a guitar splendidly. I gave him something and invited him to sing in front of the Schweizerhof,—they gave him nothing! He went away shamefacedly muttering something and the crowd laughing at him. Before that, the crowd and the visitors on the hotel balcony had thronged together listening in silence. I overtook him and invited him to the Schweizerhof to have a drink. We were shown into another room. The singer is vulgar but pathetic. We drank. The waiter laughed and the hall-porter sat down. This upset me, I scolded them and grew terribly excited. . . .'

TROWER, FRED, JR. DOMODOSSOLA, SIMPLON PASS, BRIG, SION, MARTIGNY, VEVEY, BEX, MARTIGNY, TÊTE NOIRE PASS, CHAMONIX, COL DE BALME, MARTIGNY, BEX, VEVEY

TYNDALL, JOHN. GENEVA, CHAMONIX, MONT BLANC

This was the first season of Tyndall's systematic observations on the Mer de Glace. The hotel on the Montenvers was too noisy: 'for the sake of quiet, therefore, I had my bed placed in the *château* next door, —a little octagonal building erected by some kind and sentimental Frenchman, and dedicated "à la Nature".' This was the pavilion erected by Bourrit in 1795.

WAGNER, RICHARD. ZURICH

Otto Wesendonk gave the Wagners a house to live in, near his own. It was there that on Good Friday Wagner conceived the idea of *Parsifal*. He was, however, still working at *Siegfried*, and it was from the song of the birds in the forests of the Sihl valley that he derived the inspiration for the Forest music in that opera.

WEILENMANN, J. J. ST. GALL, PONTRESINA, DIAVOLEZZA, COMO, CHIASSO, BALERNA, SCUDELATTE, MONTE GENEROSO, CAMPIONE, MORCOTE, FIGINO, CARABBIA, SAN SALVATORE, LUGANO, OLIVONE, PREDASCA, PASSO CRISTALLINA, LUKMANIER PASS

'Tourists have not yet taken possession of Monte Generoso, for the guide books say little about it, and only few people trust themselves to see anything except through them.'

WILLS, ALFRED. CHAMONIX, MONT BUET, SIXT, CHAMONIX, FENÊTRE DE SALEINAZ, ORSIÈRES, GRAND ST. BERNARD PASS, AOSTA, COURMAYEUR, COL DU GÉANT, CHAMONIX, MONT BLANC, SIXT

Wills negotiated for the purchase of a plot of land at Sixt on which to build a house. But Monsieur le Curé did not like the idea. He had visions of a 'Protestant propaganda', cattle straying over the Englishman's land would be impounded; 'besides it was all nonsense about his wanting to build a place for autumn recreation; would he be likely to come a thousand miles from home for such a purpose? The fact was, he had found the vein of gold ore Jaques Balmat had failed to discover; and their forests—the pride and wealth of the valley—would be destroyed to find fuel for his smelting furnaces—or if not that, he wanted to build an hotel or some similar abomination.'

'From the terrace of the church there is such a gorgeous view that I was more than rewarded for my excursion to Morcote'

(*Swiss Federal Railways*)

J. J. WEILENMANN, 1857

'At four in the morning we were roused by the alphorn—I jumped up, saw it was raining, and returned to bed to try and sleep; but the droll call went droning through my head, and out of it has arisen a very lusty melody which the herdsman now blows to signal Isolde's ship'

(*Paul Popper*

WAGNER, 1859; Rigi

1858

ARNOLD, MATTHEW. GENEVA, VEVEY, BEX, PAS DE CHEVILLE, SION, VISP, ZERMATT, ST. THEODUL PASS, BREUIL, CHATILLON, AOSTA, GRAND ST. BERNARD PASS, MARTIGNY, GENEVA

ARUNDELL, ISABEL (LADY BURTON). GENEVA, CHAMONIX, COL DE BALME, MARTIGNY, VEVEY, GENEVA, LAUSANNE

'Chamounix is the second thing that has never disappointed me.... I lit my cigarette, and went a little ahead of my party. There are sacred moments and heavenly scenes I cannot share with the common herd.'

BARNARD, GEORGE (*c*). GENEVA, VILLENEUVE, CHILLON, MARTIGNY, SION, VISP, ZERMATT, STALDEN, SAAS FEE, MONTE MORO PASS, MACUGNAGA, PONTE GRANDE, ORTA, VARALLO, ALAGNA, COL D'OLEN, GRESSONEY, COL DE RANZOLA, BRUSSON, COL DE JOUX, CHATILLON, BREUIL, CHATILLON, AOSTA, GRAND ST. BERNARD PASS, MARTIGNY, SIXT, GENEVA

'There are subjects enough in Switzerland, and most magnificent ones, as every one knows; but beautiful pictures of the Alps are exceedingly rare, whereas Holland, one of the least picturesque of countries, has furnished materials for a countless number of fine works of art. It is pictorial effect that is wanting. Forms, of course, we all ought to draw correctly; but more than this is necessary, more even than the common light and shade belonging to each object; we must learn to place the objects, or the whole subject, before the spectator, with an adjustment of light and shade and colour that shall be true, and at the same time pleasing.'

BARRINGTON, CHARLES. GRINDELWALD, STRAHLEGG PASS, JUNGFRAU, GRINDELWALD, KLEINE SCHEIDEGG, EIGER

A newcomer to Switzerland without any previous alpine experience, Barrington made light of his passage of the Strahlegg and his ascent of the Jungfrau, on his return to Grindelwald. When it was then suggested that he should try the Eiger or the Matterhorn, he replied 'all right' and led his guides up the Eiger. This was its first ascent. As he was running short of money he left the Matterhorn alone and went home. He never visited Switzerland again.

BLUNT, WILFRID SCAWEN. ZERMATT, MONTE ROSA, COURMAYEUR, COL DU GÉANT, CHAMONIX, LAUSANNE

Blunt was nearly killed by an avalanche of stones, which event gave him a courage that was 'a revelation of the possibilities of manly action in the world which never left me afterwards; and I think my physical cowardice thus easily overcome has been in part the reason of what moral courage I have had at my command in later years. If the tremendous powers of nature, I reasoned with myself, can be thus met and conquered, why should I be afraid of men.' By way of proof of this proposition, 'not long after his accident he was the only one of a party of English boys at cricket near Lausanne to stand his ground against the irate Swiss owner of the meadow they were trampling down'.

BONNEY, THOMAS GEORGE. ZURICH, RIGI, LUCERNE, ALTDORF, ANDERMATT, FURKA PASS, GRIMSEL PASS, STRAHLEGG PASS, GRINDELWALD, FAULHORN, INTERLAKEN, MEIRINGEN, GRIMSEL PASS, OBERGESTELEN, EGGISHORN, BRIG, VISP, ZERMATT, NEW WEISSTHOR PASS, MACUGNAGA, MILAN, DOMODOSSOLA, SIMPLON PASS, BRIG, MARTIGNY

BROOKE, STOPFORD. OUCHY, BEX, MARTIGNY, CHAMONIX

'Byron wrote the *Prisoner of Chillon* in the Inn we are staying at, Hotel de l'Ancre; and it is a fit place for a poet. The scenery is not too grand to strip a writer of his self-consciousness, and is noble and tender enough to wake up all poetic power and delicacy.'

CAVOUR, CAMILLO. BASLE, ZURICH, ST. GALL, COIRE, THUSIS, SAN BERNARDINO PASS, MESOCCO, BELLINZONA, LOCARNO

Cavour had come to Coire to meet the promoters of the scheme for a railway and tunnel by the route of the Lukmanier pass. He had hoped to meet Thomas Brassey and to go over the proposed line of the railway with him, but Brassey could not come; a landslide blocked the Lukmanier pass so that Cavour had to go by another route, and the scheme never materialized.

COLE, MRS. H. WARWICK. GRINDELWALD, MEIRINGEN, GRIMSEL PASS, OBERGESTELEN, VIESCH, EGGISHORN, BRIG, SIMPLON PASS, DOMODOSSOLA, MACUGNAGA, COL DE BARANCA, VARALLO, ALAGNA, COL D'OLEN, GRESSONEY, COL DE RANZOLA, BRUSSONE, COL DE JOUX, CHATILLON, AOSTA, CHATILLON, VAL TOURNANCHE

'Of course every lady engaged on an Alpine journey will wear a broad-brimmed hat, which will relieve her from the incumbrance of a parasol. She should also have a dress of some light woollen material, such as carmelite or alpaca, which, in case of bad weather, does not look utterly forlorn when it has once been wetted and dried. Small rings should be sewn inside the seams of the dress, and a cord passed through them, the ends of which should be knotted together in such a way that the whole dress may be drawn up at a moment's notice to the requisite height. If the dress is too long, it catches the stones, especially when coming down hill, and sends them rolling on those below. I have heard more than one gentleman complain of painful blows suffered from such accidents. A lady's dress is inconvenient for mountain-travelling, even under the most careful management, and therefore every device which may render it less so should be adopted.'

COLEMAN, EDMUND THOMAS. ST. GERVAIS, BOSSES DU DROMADAIRE, CHAMONIX, COL DU BONHOMME, COL DE LA SEIGNE, COMBAL, COL DE MIAGE, ST. GERVAIS

DUCOMMUN, JULES-CÉSAR. GENEVA, ST. GERVAIS, DOME DU GOUTER, ST. GERVAIS, GENEVA

FAYRER, SIR JOSEPH. BASLE, BERNE, THUN, INTERLAKEN, GIESSBACH, MEIRINGEN, GRIMSEL PASS, SIEDELHORN, OBERGESTELEN, VIESCH, BRIG, VISP, ZERMATT, VISP, SION, MARTIGNY, BEX, VILLENEUVE, GENEVA

MARCET, WILLIAM. ST. MORITZ

'It occurred to me to try how long I could remain in the water; after about twenty-five minutes, commencing to feel uncomfortable, I got out of the bath, but was so intoxicated and tottering from the effects of the carbonic acid, that I could hardly dress. I rushed out into the fresh air, but just able to stand.'

MÉRIMÉE, PROSPER. LUCERNE, RIGI, GLETSCH, GRIMSEL PASS, MEIRINGEN, INTERLAKEN, THUN, BERNE, ZURICH

MEYER, CONRAD FERDINAND. MAGADINO, BELLINZONA, ST. GOTTHARD PASS, ALTDORF, LUCERNE, RIGI, ZUG, ZURICH, AARAU, ZOFINGEN, LUCERNE, ENGELBERG, JOCH PASS, ENGSTLENALP

PRESTWICH, SIR JOSEPH. BASLE, NEUCHÂTEL, MOTIERS-TRAVERS, BASLE, LAUSANNE, BEX, GRYON, ANZEINDAZ, CHAMONIX

QUINET, EDGAR. SCHAFFHAUSEN, WINTERTHUR, ST. GALL, APPENZELL, WEISSBAD, ST. GALL, WATTWIL, UZNACH, WESEN, GLARUS, LINTHAL, GLARUS, ZURICH, EGGBÜHL, BIENNE, ILE ST. PIERRE, NEUCHÂTEL, YVERDON, LAUSANNE, EVIAN, AMPHION, MONTREUX, VEYTAUX

Ile St. Pierre: 'Une parole a immortalisé ce coin de terre. Que serait-ce de plus, si une bataille y eût décidé du monde? Ainsi une pensée, une image, un accent, un certain rythme suffisent?'

RAMSAY, ANDREW CROMBIE. ZURICH, LUCERNE, BRUNIG PASS, MEIRINGEN, GROSSE SCHEIDEGG, GRINDELWALD, STRAHLEGG PASS, GRIMSEL PASS, OBERGESTELEN, VIESCH, EGGISHORN, BRIG, VISP, ZERMATT, VISP, SION, MARTIGNY, BEX, MONTHEY, GENEVA

RIVINGTON, ALEXANDER. BASLE, LUCERNE, RIGI, FLUELEN, HOSPENTHAL, ST. GOTTHARD PASS, BELLINZONA, LOCARNO, LUGANO, BAVENO, MACUGNAGA, MONTE MORO PASS, SAAS, STALDEN, ZERMATT, VISP, MARTIGNY, TÊTE NOIRE PASS, CHAMONIX, GENEVA

'I reached Stalden, and lay outside the churchyard there for some time enjoying the scenery, when I saw somebody with a hatchet walking down the valley in the direction of Visp: I trudged after him, and when I overtook him found it was Professor T-[ynda]-ll.'

ROTH, ABRAHAM. BERNE, THUN, INTERLAKEN, MEIRINGEN, STEIN, SUSTENHORN, GADMEN, TRIFT PASS, GRIMSEL PASS, MEIRINGEN, INTERLAKEN, THUN, BERNE

RUSKIN, JOHN. BASLE, RHEINFELDEN, BREMGARTEN, ZUG, BRUNNEN, FLUELEN, ST. GOTTHARD PASS, BELLINZONA, LOCARNO, TURIN, ANNECY, BONNEVILLE, CHAMONIX, GENEVA

'I was thinking, as I walked here yesterday, why it was that I am so especially fond of Switzerland, as distinguished from other countries; and I find the reason to be that I am so peculiarly sociable (provided only that people don't talk to me). In all other countries the masses of the people are collected in cities, . . . but in Switzerland the mass of the people is dispersed through the whole country.'

STEPHEN, LESLIE. ZURICH, GLARUS, LINTHAL, KLAUSEN PASS, ALTDORF, AMSTEG, BRISTENSTOCK, WASSEN, SUSTEN PASS, GADMEN, INNERTKIRCHEN, GRIMSEL PASS, OBERAARJOCH PASS, EGGISHORN, BRIG, VISP, ZERMATT, MONTE ROSA, ADLER PASS, SAAS, ZWISCHBERGEN PASS, SIMPLON, ISELLE, BACENO, GEISSPFAD PASS, BINN, VIESCH, EGGISHORN, BRIG, LEUK, GEMMI PASS, WILDSTRUBEL, LENK, HAHNENMOOS PASS, ADELBODEN, KANDERSTEG, HOHTHÜRLI PASS, SEFINENFURKE PASS, LAUTERBRUNNEN, GRINDELWALD, STRAHLEGG PASS, GRIMSEL PASS, GALENSTOCK

STUDER, GOTTLIEB. BERNE, ZWEISIMMEN, SAANEN, LAUENEN, GELTEN PASS, ARBAZ, SION, NENDAZ, MONT GELÉ, LOURTIER, GRAND COMBIN, MARTIGNY, BEX, CHAMPÉRY, DENT DU MIDI, COL DE SALANFE, ST. MAURICE, BEX

SUMNER, CHARLES. GENEVA, LAUSANNE, VEVEY, SOLEURE, BERNE, ZURICH, SCHAFFHAUSEN, CONSTANCE, RAGAZ, COIRE, THUSIS, SPLÜGEN PASS, CHIAVENNA

TYNDALL, JOHN. ZURICH, LUCERNE, BRUNIG PASS, MEIRINGEN, GROSSE SCHEIDEGG, GRINDELWALD, STRAHLEGG PASS, GRIMSEL PASS, OBERGESTELEN, VIESCH, EGGISHORN, FINSTERAARHORN, BRIG, VISP, ZERMATT, MONTE ROSA, STALDEN, SAAS FEE, VISP, SION, MARTIGNY, TÊTE NOIRE PASS, CHAMONIX, MONT BLANC

'I was anxious to quit Saas early next morning, but the curé expressed so strong a wish to show us what he called a terrible hole which he had himself discovered, that I consented to accompany him. We were joined by his assistant and the priest from Fee. . . . It was the very type of the robber den; and when I remarked this, it was at once proposed to sing a verse from Schiller's play. The young clergyman had a powerful voice—he led and we all chimed in . . . Herr Imseng wore his black coat; the others had taken theirs off, but they wore their clerical hats, black breeches and stockings. We formed a singular group.'

VERNON, WILLIAM WARREN. GENEVA, VEVEY, BEX, MARTIGNY, GRAND ST. BERNARD, TÊTE NOIRE PASS, CHAMONIX, GENEVA, VEVEY, ROCHERS DE NAYE, INTERLAKEN, GRINDELWALD, FAULHORN, VEVEY, GENEVA—GENEVA, BEX, MARTIGNY, SION, BRIG, SIMPLON PASS, DOMODOSSOLA

WAGNER, RICHARD. ZURICH, BRESTENBERG, HALLWIL, LUCERNE, ZURICH, GENEVA, LAUSANNE, MARTIGNY, SION, BRIG, SIMPLON PASS, DOMODOSSOLA

The relations between Wagner and Matilde Wesendonk made it impossible for things to continue as they were, and Wagner departed for Venice: his work on *The Ring* was interrupted for *Tristan and Isolde.*

WEILENMANN, J. J. ST. GALL, REMUS, LAVIN, PIZ LINARD, BERNE, ZWEISIMMEN, SAANEN, LAUENEN, GELTEN PASS, ARBUZ, SION, NENDAZ, MONT GELÉ, LOURTIER, GRAND COMBIN, LUGANO, BISSONE, ROVIO, MONTE GENEROSO, SCUDELATTE, ROVENNA, CERNOBBIO

WILLS, ALFRED. SIXT, MONT BUET, CHAMONIX, MONT BLANC, COL DU TOUR, MARTIGNY, SION, EVOLENA, COL D'HÉRENS, ZERMATT, VISP, SION, PAS DE CHEVILLE, BEX, CHAMPÉRY, COL DE COUX, COL DE GOLEZE, SIXT

'We had been led to suppose that we should find capital quarters at Evolena. A new hotel, it was said, was just finished, which would offer excellent accommodation to the wayfarer. . . . After a great deal of difficulty, the landlord was hunted up, but he said he had nothing ready and did not "receive" at present, though next season he would have twenty beds disposable. . . . We persuaded him to do his best for us, and a couple of beds were soon rigged up and looked comfortable enough. But we wanted something besides beds . . . Our host manifested a lordly indifference to our wants, shrugged his shoulders, and said he did not know what the village could furnish except black bread and the salted mutton of last year.'

1859

ADAMS, HENRY. ZURICH, THUN, VEVEY, CHAMONIX, MARTIGNY, BRIG, OBERGESTELEN, FURKA PASS, ANDERMATT, ST. GOTTHARD PASS, BELLINZONA, MILAN, CHIAVENNA, SPLÜGEN PASS, THUSIS, COIRE

ARNOLD, MATTHEW. BASLE, BERNE, LAUSANNE, GENEVA, MARTIGNY, CHAMONIX, GENEVA, LAUSANNE

BARNARD, GEORGE (*c*). LUCERNE, BRUNNEN, SCHWYZ, PRAGEL PASS, GLARUS, LINTHAL, SANDALP, KLAUSEN PASS, ALTDORF, WASSEN, SUSTEN PASS, MEIRINGEN, GROSSE SCHEIDEGG, GRINDELWALD, KLEINE

SCHEIDEGG, LAUTERBRUNNEN, MÜRREN, INTERLAKEN, KANDERSTEG, GEMMI PASS, LEUK, VIESCH, EGGISHORN

'From Mürren most delightful excursions can be made to the top of the Schilthorn, and also the extremity of the valley of Lauterbrunnen, a wild and secluded spot, perhaps containing more beauty than any other that I know.'

BONNEY, THOMAS GEORGE. BERNE, THUN, KANDERSTEG, GEMMI PASS, LEUK, VISP, ZERMATT, MONTE ROSA, MARTIGNY, MONTHEY

CAVOUR, CAMILLO. DOMODOSSOLA, SIMPLON PASS, BRIG, SION, MARTIGNY, HERMANCE, PRESSINGE, GENEVA, CHAMONIX, GENEVA

'Je m'étais acheminé vers la Suisse, cet hôpital des blessés politiques, mais l'annonce du Congrès de Zurich pouvant donner à mon projet une couleur suspecte, je me rabattrai sur la Savoie, et j'irai m'établir au pied du Mont Blanc, pour y oublier au milieu des merveilles de la nature les misères des affaires menées par les hommes.'

CIVIALE, AIMÉ. INTERLAKEN, LAUTERBRUNNEN, KLEINE SCHEIDEGG, GRINDELWALD, FAULHORN, GROSSE SCHEIDEGG, MEIRINGEN, GRIMSEL PASS, SIEDELHORN

ELIOT, GEORGE. LUCERNE

'Lucerne would be a strange region to me but for Calame's pictures. Through them I have a vision of it, but of course when I see it 'twill be another Luzern.' She was there for a week, 'glad to make a home at the charming Schweizerhof on the banks of the Lake . . . in quiet chat with the Congreves . . .'.

FELLENBERG, EDMUND VON. BERNE, THUN, INTERLAKEN, LAUTERBRUNNEN, MÜRREN, SEFINENFURKE PASS, KIENTHAL, HOHTHÜRLI PASS, KANDERSTEG, THUN, BERNE

FOX, JOSEPH H. INTERLAKEN, LAUTERBRUNNEN, MÜRREN, GRINDELWALD, STRAHLEGG PASS, GRIMSEL PASS, OBERGESTELEN, EGGISHORN, BRIG, VISP, ZERMATT, BREITHORN, MONTE ROSA, TRIFTJOCH PASS, ZINAL, BELLA TOLA PASS, TURTMANN, SION, MARTIGNY, ORSIÈRES, COL DU TOUR, CHAMONIX, GENEVA

'Imagine being the only English guest on the 29th July at one of the two hotels then open at Zermatt!' . . . 'At Zinal we found a little Inn which had just been opened, and at which I was the first English guest.'

FRESHFIELD, MRS. HENRY. THUN, INTERLAKEN, LAUTERBRUNNEN, MÜRREN, KLEINE SCHEIDEGG, GRINDELWALD, GROSSE SCHEIDEGG, MEIRINGEN, JOCH PASS, ENGELBERG, SURENEN PASS, ALTDORF, ANDERMATT, FURKA PASS, OBERGESTELEN, GRIES PASS, TOSA FALLS, DEVERIO, ALBRUN PASS, BINN, BRIG, SION, RAWYL PASS, LENK, TRÜTTLISBERG

PASS, LAUENEN, KRINNEN PASS, GSTEIG, COL DE PILLON, AIGLE, MARTIGNY, TÊTE NOIRE PASS, CHAMONIX

'An inn was built at the Alpine village of Mürren; and when we arrived at Thun, early in August 1859, we learnt that it was just completed. . . . We found a most attentive host, and had our choice of rooms, for the house was empty when we arrived. All looked clean and comfortable.'

GOUGH, JOHN B. GENEVA, CHAMONIX, TÊTE NOIRE PASS, MARTIGNY, VEVEY, BASLE

GÜSSFELDT, PAUL. VEVEY, CHAMPÉRY, DENT DU MIDI

'One fine morning all the guests at a hotel on the lake of Geneva facing the Dent du Midi were arguing whether the mountain had ever been climbed or was indeed climbable. I knew nothing about it, but when one of the guests laid a bet, I took it up and promised to climb the mountain. I succeeded and won my bet, but I also won much more, a passionate desire to do more and greater things. So the Dent du Midi, a mountain of about the height of Piz Languard, sealed my alpine career.'

HUDSON, CHARLES. CHAMONIX, BOSSES DU DROMADAIRE, MONT BLANC, SIXT

'To the Editor of the Times. Sir,—Although you pronounced Mont Blanc a "nuisance" and declared that nothing new could be said on the subject, you may not be unwilling to introduce a short notice of an ascent made last week, inasmuch as the summit was reached by a route hitherto generally supposed impracticable.'

KOSSUTH, LOUIS. VEVEY

After the tragedy of Villafranca the Hungarian patriot wrote 'with a bleeding heart I returned to England, after having sought consolation for some weeks with my wife and sons in the Alps of Savoy and Switzerland'.

MATHEWS, WILLIAM. LAUTERBRUNNEN, EIGERJOCH PASS, EGGISHORN, LÖTSCHENLÜCKE PASS, RIED, PETERSGRAT, KANDERSTEG, GEMMI PASS, LEUK, SIERRE, ZINAL, COL DURAND, ZERMATT, LYSJOCH PASS, GRESSONEY, COL DE RANZOLA, BRUSSONE, COL DE JOUX, CHATILLON, AOSTA, COURMAYEUR, COL DU GÉANT, CHAMONIX, MONT BLANC

'About the time of this excursion, the Rev. S. W. King and Mrs. King were enjoying the hospitality of the Baron Peccoz at his hunting chalet at Salzen near to the Lys glacier, where Delapierre brought them tidings of the fact that two Englishmen had reached Gressoney from the Riffel, by way of the snow plateau between Monte Rosa and the Lyskamm. At this absurd announcement, the Baron burst into a hearty fit of laughter, evidently relishing the joke that Delapierre had been made the victim of a hoax. Vain were the assurances of Mr. King that English gentlemen always spoke the truth.'

MEYER, CONRAD FERDINAND. ENGSTLENALP, JOCH PASS, TITLIS

PARKER, THEODORE. GENEVA, LAUSANNE, MONTREUX, NEUCHÂTEL, COMBE VARIN

Staying with Desor at Combe Varin, the American divine wrote his last tract 'A Bumble Bee's Thoughts on the Place and Purpose of Creation', which formed part of an album to which all Desor's learned guests (among whom was the physiologist Moleschott) contributed articles.

PRENTISS, ELIZABETH. VEVEY, CHAMONIX, VEVEY

The author of *Stepping Heavenward* wrote 'Our trip to Chamouni was very pleasant and did me a deal of good. If I could have kept on the mule-riding and mountain-viewing a few weeks I should have got quite built up. . . . Our landlord, called Monday to see if I would sell him my sewing-machine, as his wife was crazy to have one.'

RUSKIN, JOHN. CONSTANCE, SCHAFFHAUSEN, BADEN, BERNE, THUN, INTERLAKEN, THUN, BERNE, NEUCHÂTEL, LAUSANNE, GENEVA, CHAMONIX, GENEVA, LAUSANNE, NEUCHÂTEL, BIENNE, BASLE

Ruskin was at work on the last volume of *Modern Painters* in which he wrote:—'It is a great weakness, not to say worse than weakness, on the part of travellers, to extol chiefly what they think fewest people have seen or can see. I have climbed much, and wandered much, in the heart of the High Alps; but I have never yet seen anything which equalled the view from the cabin of the Montanvert.'

STEPHEN, LESLIE. KANDERSTEG, TSCHINGEL PASS, LAUTERBRUNNEN, GRINDELWALD, KLEINE SCHEIDEGG, EIGERJOCH PASS, EGGISHORN, LÖTSCHENLÜCKE PASS, RIED, PETERSGRAT, KANDERSTEG, LÖTSCHEN PASS, KIPPEL, BIETSCHHORN, LÖTSCHENLÜCKE PASS, EGGISHORN, BELALP, BRIG, VISP, SAAS, WEISSMIES, ZERMATT, DOM, RIMPFISCHHORN, ST. THEODUL PASS, BREUIL, CHATILLON, AOSTA, GRAND ST. BERNARD PASS, MARTIGNY, TÊTE NOIRE PASS, CHAMONIX

At Kippel 'after whittling at certain dried bits of stick, which are the prevailing substitutes for meat in those parts, accompanied by loaves whose consistency suggested that a Kippel father of a family would be doing a really humane action in giving his children stones for bread, we washed down our meal with draughts of vinegar'.

STRONG, AUGUST H. ZERMATT, ST. THEODUL PASS, CHATILLON, AOSTA, GRAND ST. BERNARD

'Quite a number of young Englishmen, members of the Alpine Club of London, were at our hotel. . . . They are a set of Englishmen so peculiar as to be well worth knowing. . . . They are full of talk, always in the best of humor, at home in a discussion of a point in the classics, or in the small talk of the drawing room, finished ladies' men, and yet, unlike most Englishmen, extremely removed from anything like the over-refinement of the exquisite. As hearty, kind, frank, modest, clear-spoken fellows as you ever saw.'

STUDER, GOTTLIEB. BERNE, THUN, INTERLAKEN, GRINDELWALD, LAUTERAARJOCH, GRIMSEL PASS, AVERS CRESTA, DUANA PASS, VICO-SOPRANO, MALOJA PASS, ST. MORITZ, PONTRESINA, PIZ LANGUARD, BERNINA PASS, POSCHIAVO

TECK, MARY ADELAIDE, DUCHESS OF. ROMANSHORN, ZURICH, ALBIS, ZUG, LUCERNE, AARBURG, BERNE, THUN, INTERLAKEN, GRINDELWALD, LAUTERBRUNNEN, WENGEN, INTERLAKEN, THUN, BERNE, FRIBOURG, LAUSANNE, GENEVA

THACKERAY, WILLIAM MAKEPEACE. COMO, CHIAVENNA, SPLÜGEN PASS, THUSIS, COIRE

At Coire Thackeray wrote the first of the *Roundabout Papers*: 'On a lazy idle boy'. 'There was a sweet pretty river walk we used to take in the evening, and mark the mountains round glooming with a deeper purple; the shades creeping up the golden walls.'

TUCKETT, FRANCIS FOX. GRINDELWALD, GROSSE SCHEIDEGG, MEIRINGEN, GRIMSEL PASS, OBERGESTELEN, EGGISHORN, ALETSCHHORN, LÖTSCHENLÜCKE PASS, KIPPEL, VISP, ZERMATT, BREITHORN, ST. THEODUL PASS, BREUIL, CHATILLON, AOSTA, GRAND ST. BERNARD PASS, ORSIÈRES, COL DU TOUR, CHAMONIX, MONT BUET, SIXT, COL DE SAGEROUX, CHAMPÉRY, LAUSANNE, GENEVA

'I had no time to describe the beauties of the Aeggishorn . . . the hotel is excellent and the landlord still better, he has lived for some months with John Birkbeck at Settle, speaks English, and is extremely attentive and obliging; you can live en pension at from three to five francs a day, and from what I saw of M. Wellig I am quite sure one would be liberally treated. He opened the hotel on purpose for me, and when after spending two or three days there, I asked for the bill, he positively refused to make any charge whatever, on the ground that everything was uncomfortable and no great variety of eatables forthcoming, though in reality I had found myself very well off.'

TYNDALL, JOHN. GENEVA, CHAMONIX

On Christmas day Chamonix was a little 'city of the dead'. There was no living thing in the streets, and neither sound nor light in the houses.

WAGNER, RICHARD. COMO, LUGANO, BELLINZONA, ST. GOTTHARD PASS, ALTDORF, LUCERNE, RIGI, ZURICH

At the Schweizerhof at Lucerne, Wagner continued to work at *Tristan and Isolde*. 'The last act promises famously; I drew profit for it even from my excursion up the Rigi. At four in the morning we were roused by the alphorn—I jumped up, saw it was raining, and returned to bed to try and sleep; but the droll call went droning through my head, and out of it has arisen a very lusty melody which the herdsman now blows to signal Isolde's ship, making a surprisingly merry and naive effect.'

WEILENMANN, JOHANN JAKOB. ST. GALL, SILS, PIZ CORVATSCH, PIZ TREMOGGIA, PIZ DELLA MARGNA, THUSIS, SPLÜGEN, NUFENEN, RHEINWALDHORN, GUFERHORN, FANELLAHORN, KIRCHALPHORN, NUFENEN, LAUTERBRUNNEN, TSCHINGEL PASS, PETERSGRAT, PLATTEN, LÖTSCHENLÜCKE, VIESCH, BRIG, SIMPLON, MONTE LEONE, BRIG, TURTMANN, COL DE TRACUIT, ZINAL, TRIFT PASS, ZERMATT, COL D'HÉRENS, LES HAUDÈRES, AROLLA, COL DE COLLON, PRARAYÉ, COL DE VALCOURNERA, BREUIL, ST. THEODUL PASS, ZERMATT, BOUVERET

1860

ALARÇON, PEDRO ANTONIO DE. GENEVA, CHAMONIX, TÊTE NOIRE PASS, MARTIGNY, SION, BRIG, SIMPLON PASS, DOMODOSSOLA

ANDERSEN, HANS CHRISTIAN. LA CHAUX DE FONDS, LE LOCLE, STE. CROIX, YVERDON, GENEVA, BASLE

'I was pleased at the wealth of my mother tongue, which is so supple and musical when it is spoken as it should be spoken. In Le Locle, on the Jura heights it was that I made this discovery. Jules Jurgensen's translation of the *Marsh King's Daughter*, and a few more of my Wonder Stories was issued with the imprint of Joel Cherbuliez in Geneva.'

ANONYMOUS 10 B. BASLE, SOLEURE, WEISSENSTEIN, LUCERNE, SARNEN, BRUNIG PASS, BRIENZ, INTERLAKEN, LAUTERBRUNNEN, GRINDELWALD, INTERLAKEN, THUN, BERNE, FRIBOURG, BULLE, VEVEY, GENEVA, CHAMONIX, GENEVA

BENEDICT, ERASTUS C. (*c*). ROMANSHORN, ZURICH, BADEN, BERNE, LAUSANNE, GENEVA, CHAMONIX, GENEVA, VEVEY, LAUSANNE, NEUCHÂTEL, SONCEBOZ, MOUTIER, BASLE

BONNEY, THOMAS GEORGE. CHATILLON, BREUIL, ST. THEODUL PASS, ZERMATT, MONTE ROSA, COL DE ZINAL, ZINAL, TRIFTJOCH PASS, ZERMATT, ADLER PASS, SAAS, MONTE MORO PASS, MACUGNAGA, PESTARENA, BINN, PREMIA, DISENTIS, GLARUS

Zinal: 'Found a newly-constructed "log-hut", with two little bedrooms, sweet with fresh pine-wood, no bigger than an ordinary ship's cabin, and a small salle à manger in which was a bed to hold a couple.'

BULLAR, WILLIAM. MENAGGIO, PORLEZZA, LUGANO, BELLINZONA, ST. GOTTHARD PASS, ALTDORF, LUCERNE, BASLE

'The dining hour amongst travellers being a little uncertain, preparations are, I suppose, made to meet these uncertainties. And, of course, when the host's dinner is hot, it is painful to him to see those whom he regards as his own customers drive on to a dinner further off. A party who preceded us were undergoing one of the experiments which they sometimes try with success as a means of delay. One of the carriage wheels was taken off, under the plea that something was wrong.'

CIVIALE, AIMÉ. GRINDELWALD, BERNE, GENEVA, CHAMONIX, TÊTE NOIRE PASS, TRIENT

DUFF, MOUNTSTUART E. GRANT. GENEVA, LAUSANNE, BERNE, ZURICH

ELIOT, GEORGE. CHIAVENNA, SPLÜGEN PASS, THUSIS, COIRE, ZURICH, BERNE, LAUSANNE, GENEVA

At Splügen 'in the evening we enjoyed a walk between the mountains, whose lower sides down to the torrent bed were set with tall dark pines. But the climax of grand—nay terrible—scenery came the next day as we traversed the Via Mala.'

FOX, JOSEPH H. BASLE, LUCERNE, ALTDORF, KLAUSEN PASS, LINTHAL, GLARUS, WESEN, WALLENSTADT, COIRE, THUSIS, SPLÜGEN PASS, CHIAVENNA, DOMODOSSOLA, SIMPLON PASS, BRIG, VISP, ZERMATT

FRESHFIELD, MRS. HENRY. GENEVA, SIXT, COL DE GOLEZE, COL DE COUX, CHAMPÉRY, MARTIGNY, GRAND ST. BERNARD PASS, AOSTA, CHATILLON, BREUIL, ST. THEODUL PASS, ZERMATT, STALDEN, SAAS, MONTE MORO PASS, MACUGNAGA, COL DI BARRANCA, VARALLO

GOULD, EMILY BLISS. BASLE, SCHAFFHAUSEN, ZURICH, CONSTANCE, RORSCHACH, SARGANS, COIRE, THUSIS, SPLÜGEN, THUSIS, COIRE, RAGAZ, PFÄFERS, COIRE, DISENTIS, OBERALP PASS, ANDERMATT, ALTDORF, LUCERNE, BRUNIG PASS, MEIRINGEN, GROSSE SCHEIDEGG, GRINDELWALD, INTERLAKEN, VISP, ZERMATT, VISP, MARTIGNY, CHAMONIX, GENEVA

'How gloriously the gorges opened new gates to admit more distant views! The chalets looked like squirrels climbing a tree, as they showed far up the mountain sides.'

HORT, F. J. A. LES AVANTS, BEX, VILLARS, MARTIGNY, SION, VISP, ZERMATT, ST. THEODUL PASS, BREUIL, CHATILLON, DOMODOSSOLA, FORMAZZA, GRIES PASS, ULRICHEN, VIESCH, EGGISHORN

JACOMB, FREDERICK WILLIAM. SAAS, ALLALINHORN, ZERMATT, COL D'HÉRENS, EVOLENA, COL DE TORRENT, COL DE SOREBOIS, ZINAL, TRIFTJOCH PASS, ZERMATT, ST. THEODUL PASS, BREUIL, COL DE VAL COURNERA, PRARAYÉ, COL DE VALPELLINE, ZERMATT

NAPOLEON III. ANNECY, THONON, SALLANCHES, CHAMONIX, BONNEVILLE, CHAMBÉRY

NORTH, MARIANNE. ZURICH, RAGAZ, PFÄFERS, GLARUS, LUCERNE, ENGELBERG, JOCH PASS, MEIRINGEN, GROSSE SCHEIDEGG, GRINDELWALD, KLEINE SCHEIDEGG, LAUTERBRUNNEN, INTERLAKEN, THUN, BERNE, FRIBOURG, MARTIGNY, SION, VISP, ZERMATT, STALDEN, SAAS, MONTE MORO PASS, MACUGNAGA, BAVENO, LUGANO, LUINO, VARALLO

'We fell in with the Francis Galtons at Meiringen and walked with them to Rosenlaui. . . . At Interlaken we fell in with Blumenbach and his cousin, and had much music on a bad piano. . . . Mr. George Meredith and Mr. Lionel Robinson were our fellow-prisoners at Macugnaga.'

OWEN, SIR RICHARD. VISP, ZERMATT, CIMA DI JAZZI, ST. THEODUL PASS, BREUIL

The great anatomist ascended the Cima di Jazzi with Mr. Hinchliff and Mr. and Mrs. H. W. Cole. 'Only once I felt the nausea described by many who toil up declivities in much rarified air. I stopped, held down my head, and then proceeding by slow steps, directing volition strongly into the leg muscles, and it soon went off. I kept the same position, and only became aware of the near termination of the climb by hearing a "Hurrah! Bravo Professor!" '

RIVINGTON, ALEXANDER. BASLE, ZURICH, RAGAZ, COIRE, THUSIS, SPLÜGEN PASS, CHIAVENNA

ROTH, ABRAHAM. BERNE, THUN, INTERLAKEN, MEIRINGEN, ROSENLAUI, WETTERHORN

RUSKIN, JOHN. GENEVA, CHAMONIX, LAUSANNE, FRIBOURG, NEUCHÂTEL, BASLE, LAUFENBURG, GENEVA

'I got a bound copy of the fifth volume of *Modern Painters* at St. Martin's in the summer of 1860, and in the valley of Chamouni I gave up my art-work and wrote this little book.' It was *Unto this Last.*

SCHEFFEL, JOSEPH VIKTOR. ZURICH, MEIRINGEN, ROSENLAUI, GRINDELWALD, FAULHORN, KLEINE SCHEIDEGG, LAUTERBRUNNEN, LUCERNE, SEELISBERG

SCHÖNBEIN, CHRISTIAN FRIEDRICH. BASLE, LUCERNE, RIGI

There was such a storm on the Rigi that the great chemist and discoverer of ozone wrote: 'Although I was in the centre of an ozone factory, it was too much of a good thing.' He was accompanied by Wilhelm Eisenlohr.

STEPHEN, LESLIE. GRINDELWALD, WETTERHORN, INTERLAKEN, KANDERSTEG, GEMMI PASS, LEUK, VISP, ZERMATT, SCHWARZBERG-WEISSTHOR PASS, SAAS, ALLALINHORN, ZERMATT, METTELHORN, ALPHUBELHORN, MONTE ROSA, VISP, JUNGFRAU, OBERAARJOCH, OBERAARHORN, INTERLAKEN, KANDERSTEG, BLUMLISALP

'We slept at the little chalet above the exquisite Oeschinen lake—a lake, so far as I know, of a beauty quite unrivalled in any of the high alpine districts.'

STILLMAN, W. J. GENEVA, CHAMONIX, LAUSANNE, FRIBOURG, NEUCHÂTEL, BASLE, LAUFENBURG, GENEVA, ST. MARTIN

'When the first sublime and overpowering impression of Chamonix and the majesty and gloom of its narrow valley wore off, it began to oppress me, and long before we got away I felt as if we were in a huge grave.'

TAYLOR, MEADOWS. CHIAVENNA, SPLÜGEN PASS, THUSIS, COIRE

THIOLY, F. GENEVA, MARTIGNY, SION, VISP, ZERMATT, MONTE ROSA

TUCKETT, FRANCIS FOX. ZURICH, WALLENSTADT, COIRE, THUSIS, SPLÜGEN PASS, CHIAVENNA, MILAN, DOMODOSSOLA, SIMPLON PASS, BRIG, VISP, ZERMATT, COL D'HÉRENS, EVOLENA, COL DE TORRENT, COL DE SOREBOIS, ZINAL, COL DURAND, ZERMATT, VISP, VIESCH, EGGISHORN, FINSTERAARHORN, BRIG, SION, MARTIGNY, TÊTE NOIRE PASS, CHAMONIX, MARTIGNY, GENEVA

TYNDALL, JOHN. THUN, INTERLAKEN, GRINDELWALD, FAULHORN, LAUTERBRUNNEN, LAWINENTOR PASS, EGGISHORN, BRIG, VISP, ZERMATT, ST. THEODUL PASS, BREUIL, CHATILLON, AOSTA, COURMAYEUR, COL DE LA SEIGNE, COL DU BONHOMME, CHAMONIX

'I may be permitted to refer to the question of diet at the higher Alpine hotels. If the authorities of the Alpine Club could be induced to take up this question, they might confer an inestimable benefit upon climbers. Through lack of wholesome nutriment, the noblest stations in the Alps are sometimes converted into dens of dyspepsia.'

URLIN, RICHARD DENNY. BASLE, LUCERNE, BRUNIG PASS, MEIRINGEN, INTERLAKEN, THUN, KANDERSTEG, GEMMI PASS, LEUK, SION, MARTIGNY, GENEVA, CHAMONIX

WHYMPER, EDWARD. KANDERSTEG, GEMMI PASS, LEUK, VISP, SAAS, STALDEN, ZERMATT, VISP, VIESCH, EGGISHORN, OBERGESTELEN, GRIMSEL PASS, MEIRINGEN, INTERLAKEN, LAUTERBRUNNEN, MÜRREN, INTERLAKEN, KIENTHAL, THUN, BERNE, NEUCHÂTEL, MORAT, FRIBOURG,

MARTIGNY, GRAND ST. BERNARD PASS, AOSTA, BIONAZ, COL DE VAL COURNERA, BREUIL, CHATILLON, AOSTA, COURMAYEUR, COL FERRET, ORSIÈRES, MARTIGNY, TÊTE NOIRE PASS, CHAMONIX, GENEVA

'I do not believe in the pretty views in which Switzerland is represented in the conventional manner. Everything here is *fine*, but I have not seen any *pretty* views. . . .'

WIGRAM, WOOLMORE. EGGISHORN, FINSTERAARHORN, BRIG, SION, MARTIGNY, CHAMONIX, GENEVA

WILLIAMS, CHARLES J. B. (*c*). INTERLAKEN, LAUTERBRUNNEN, MÜRREN, KLEINE SCHEIDEGG, GRINDELWALD, GROSSE SCHEIDEGG, MEIRINGEN, GRIMSEL PASS, OBERGESTELEN, BRIG, LEUK, GEMMI PASS, KANDERSTEG

1861

ABADIE, LOUIS D'. GENEVA, LAUSANNE, MOUDON, PAYERNE, FRIBOURG, BERNE, THUN, INTERLAKEN, LAUTERBRUNNEN, GRINDELWALD, BRIENZ, BRUNIG PASS, LUCERNE, ZURICH, BADEN, MELLINGEN, MURGENTHAL, BERNE, FRIBOURG, BULLE, VEVEY, GENEVA

ANDERSEN, HANS CHRISTIAN. DOMODOSSOLA, SIMPLON PASS, BRIG, SION, MARTIGNY, MONTREUX, LAUSANNE, LUCERNE, BRUNNEN, SCHWYZ, EINSIEDELN

'Our stay in Switzerland was longest at Montreux. Here was wrought my Wonder Story *The Ice Maiden*. The sad accident that befell the young bridal pair on their honey-moon, when they visited the little island by Villeneuve, and the bridegroom was drowned, I took for the fact that should be the basis of a story in which I would show the Swiss nature as it had lain in my thought after many visits to that glorious land.'

ANONYMOUS II A. GENEVA, LA DOLE, VILLENEUVE, LAUSANNE, GENEVA, CHAMONIX, TÊTE NOIRE PASS, MARTIGNY, SION, LEUKERBAD, TORRENTHORN, BRIG, SIMPLON PASS, DOMODOSSOLA, MILAN, CHIAVENNA, SPLÜGEN PASS, THUSIS, COIRE, WALLENSTADT, ZURICH, ZUG, RIGI, LUCERNE, FLUELEN, ANDERMATT, HOSPENTHAL, FURKA PASS, GRIMSEL PASS, MEIRINGEN, INTERLAKEN, LAUTERBRUNNEN, KLEINE SCHEIDEGG, GRINDELWALD, INTERLAKEN, THUN, BERNE, NEUCHÂTEL, GENEVA

Geneva: 'This afternoon somebody had my seat at the English Church, as, indeed, happens every week. I take it pretty good-naturedly, although turned out twice myself when comfortably seated in Sir Robert P——'s.'

BONNEY, THOMAS GEORGE. BERNE, THUN, KANDERSTEG, GEMMI PASS, LEUK, VISP, ZERMATT, ST. THEODUL PASS, BREUIL, CHATILLON, AOSTA, COURMAYEUR, CHIAVENNA, SPLÜGEN PASS, THUSIS, COIRE

BROWNE, G. F. NYON, ARZIER, LONGIROD, MARCHISY

BUXTON, SIR T. FOWELL. GENEVA, SIXT, MONT BUET, MARTIGNY, CHABLE, CHERMONTANE, COL DE CHERMONTANE, AROLLA, COL DE COLLON, PRARAYÉ, COL DE VALPELLINE, ZERMATT

At Chermontane 'The *bergers* kept up to a late hour, singing a wild sort of song, the burden of which was the might and the glory of the great Napoleon. It was strange, as we lay in that desolate cabin, with the sky above scarcely hidden by the stony roof, to find that the storms of European politics of half a century ago left their echoes still reverberating in that distant valley.'

CIVIALE, AIMÉ. VISP, ZERMATT, ST. THEODUL PASS, BREUIL, CHATILLON, AOSTA, COURMAYEUR, COL FERRET, ORSIÈRES, MARTIGNY

CLOUGH, ARTHUR HUGH. LES VERRIÈRES, NEUCHÂTEL, MARTIGNY, SION, BRIG, SIMPLON PASS, DOMODOSSOLA

DUFF, MOUNTSTUART E. GRANT. GENEVA, NEUCHÂTEL, ZURICH

FORSTER, R. W. E. BRUNNEN, SONNENBERG, ISENTHAL, URIROTSTOCK, ENGELBERG, JOCH PASS, ENGSTLENALP, SÄTTELI PASS, GADMEN, STEIN, MÜHLESTALDEN, TRIFTLIMMI PASS, GRIMSEL

FRESHFIELD, MRS. HENRY. LUCERNE, FLUELEN, ALTDORF, KLAUSEN PASS, LINTHAL, GLARUS, ELM, SEGNES PASS, REICHENAU, THUSIS, TIEFENKASTEL, FILISUR, BERGÜN, ALBULA PASS, PONTRESINA, ST. MORITZ, MALOJA, MURETTO PASS, CHIESA, PASSO CANCIANO, POSCHIAVO, FORCOLA DI LIVIGNO, LIVIGNO, CASANNA PASS, SCANFS, ZERNEZ, SÜS, FLUELA PASS, DAVOS, KLOSTERS, LANDQUART, WALLENSTADT, ZURICH

'Pontresina possesses the highest position, and the most central situation for the various excursions which we contemplated; we therefore decided to make it our head-quarters if the hotel promised tolerable comfort. To ascertain this my son walked up with Couttet late in the afternoon and returned with a satisfactory report.'

GODKIN, EDWIN LAWRENCE. GENEVA, MARTIGNY, SION, BRIG, BELALP

'While at Brig the innkeeper urged their going up to the Bel-Alp, where a new hotel was then just opened', of which Godkin and his wife were the first guests.

GUTHRIE, THOMAS. GENEVA, MARTIGNY, SION, VISP, ZERMATT, VISP, GENEVA

On his return to Edinburgh the Moderator of the Free Church of Scotland would ask his acquaintances, 'Have you seen Switzerland?' and when the reply was in the negative, 'then save up as much money', he would add, 'as will take you there. You will get a new revelation of the Creator's glory. I say to everybody, see the Alps before you die.'

HARDY, J. F. DAVOS, GRIALETSCH PASS, FLUELA-SCHWARZHORN, ZERNEZ, PONTRESINA, PIZ BERNINA, SAAS, ALPHUBELJOCH PASS, ZERMATT, LYSKAMM, ZERMATT, COL DE VALPELLINE, PRARAYÉ, COL D'OREN, CHERMONTANE, COL DE SONADON, BOURG ST. PIERRE, CHAMONIX, MONT BLANC, MONT BUET, SIXT, GENEVA

HORT, F. J. A. BASLE, ZURICH, COIRE, PONTRESINA, BERNINA PASS, TIRANO, BORMIO, STA. CATARINA

JACOMB, FREDERICK WILLIAM. MARTIGNY, BOURG ST. PIERRE, COL DU SONADON, OLLOMONT, MONT GELÉ, COL DE FAUDERY, AOSTA, CHATILLON, COL DE JOUX, BRUSSONE, COL DE RANZOLA, GRESSONEY, FELIKJOCH PASS, CASTOR, ZERMATT, ST. THEODUL PASS, BREUIL, CHATILLON, ST. GERVAIS, MONT BLANC, CHAMONIX, MONT BUET, SIXT, GENEVA

KENNEDY, E. S. DAVOS, GRIALETSCH PASS, FLUELA-SCHWARZHORN, ZERNEZ, PONTRESINA, PIZ BERNINA

'Herr Saratz, the President of the Republic of the Ober-Engadin, and his brother greeted us, one on each side of the carriage, and presenting us each with a bouquet of fresh flowers, congratulated us upon being the first strangers who had made the ascent of Pizzo Bernina. . . . As we neared the village of Pontresina the carriage stopped before a huge bonfire, and the band played "God save the Queen".'

LEAR, EDWARD. COURMAYEUR, AOSTA, GRAND ST. BERNARD PASS, MARTIGNY, VEVEY, GENEVA, CHAMONIX

Vevey 'is Paradise, and I don't see how the people there can have the impudence to suppose that they can go to Heaven after death'.

MEREDITH, GEORGE. BASLE, ZURICH, ROMANSHORN

'My first sight of the Alps has raised odd feelings. Here at last seems something more than earth, and visible, if not tangible. They have the whiteness, the silence, the beauty and mystery of thoughts seldom unveiled within us, but which conquer Earth when once they are.'

MILMAN, ARTHUR. PONTRESINA, FUORCLA CHAPÜTSCHIN, FUORCLA FEX-SCERSCEN, CHIESA, PASSO CANCIANO, POSCHIAVO, BERNINA PASS, PONTRESINA

PRESTON-THOMAS, HERBERT. GENEVA, CHAMONIX, COURMAYEUR, AOSTA, CHATILLON, ST. THEODUL PASS, ZERMATT, VISP, OBERGESTELEN, GRIMSEL PASS, MEIRINGEN, INTERLAKEN, GRINDELWALD, LUCERNE, BASLE

RAMSAY, ANDREW CROMBIE. BERNE, THUN, INTERLAKEN, MEIRINGEN, GRIMSEL PASS, OBERGESTELEN, OBERAARJOCH PASS, EGGISHORN, VIESCH, BRIG, VISP, ZERMATT, LYSKAMM, ST. THEODUL PASS, BREUIL, CHATILLON, IVREA, MILAN, COMO, LUGANO, BELLINZONA, MESOCCO, SAN BERNARDINO PASS, THUSIS, COIRE, WALLENSTADT, GLARUS, ELM, RICHETLI PASS, STACHELBERG, GLARUS, ZURICH

'Thun—the most lovely spot in the universe.'

RIVINGTON, ALEXANDER. BASLE, OLTEN, BERNE, THUN, KANDERSTEG, GEMMI PASS, LEUK, VISP, ZERMATT, MONTE ROSA, ST. THEODUL PASS, CHATILLON, AOSTA, COURMAYEUR, COL DU GÉANT, CHAMONIX, COL DE BALME, MARTIGNY, LAUSANNE, GENEVA

ROTH, ABRAHAM. BERNE, THUN, INTERLAKEN, BRIENZ, MEIRINGEN, GRIMSEL PASS, OBERAARJOCH, ROTHORNSATTEL, FINSTERAARHORN, VIESCH

RUSKIN, JOHN. GENEVA, BONNEVILLE, GENEVA, LUCERNE, ALTDORF, LUCERNE, BASLE

From Lucerne Ruskin wrote 'I never saw anything so entirely and solemnly *divine* as the calm winter days are here. . . . I never saw such things—didn't know what winter was made or meant for, before.'

SCHÖNBEIN, CHRISTIAN FRIEDRICH. BASLE, LUCERNE, SEELISBERG, NEUCHÂTEL, COMBE VARIN

SENIOR, NASSAU WILLIAM. GENEVA, LAUSANNE

STEPHEN, LESLIE. CHAMONIX, ST. GERVAIS, BOSSES DU DROMADAIRE, MONT BLANC, EVOLENA, COL D'HÉRENS, ZERMATT, NEW WEISSTHOR PASS, MACUGNAGA, SAAS, RIED PASS, ZERMATT, LYSJOCH PASS, BETTLINER PASS, SCHWARZTHOR PASS, ZERMATT, FINSTERAARHORN, GRINDELWALD, SCHRECKHORN

'Neither Chamouni nor Zermatt, in my opinion, is equal in grandeur and originality of design to the Bernese Oberland. No earthly object that I have seen approaches in grandeur to the stupendous mountain wall whose battlements overhang in mid-air the villages of Lauterbrunnen and Grindelwald; the lower hills that rise beneath it, like the long Atlantic rollers beaten back from the granite cliffs on our western coast, are a most effective contrast to its stern magnificence.'

STUDER, GOTTLIEB. ZUOZ, SAMADEN, JULIER PASS, TIEFENKASTEL, PARPAN PASS, COIRE, ZURICH, BERNE

SYMONDS, JOHN ADDINGTON. GENEVA, CHAMONIX, TÊTE NOIRE PASS, MARTIGNY, SION, BRIG, SIMPLON PASS, DOMODOSSOLA, LUGANO, BELLINZONA, ST. GOTTHARD PASS, ALTDORF, LUCERNE

'Standing in the middle of the Mer de Glace we saw Tacul before us, and on either hand the gorges of the Jardin and the Col du Géant, deep in untrampled snow and blazing in the sunlight. The sky above was like melted sapphire, deep and clear and gorgeous, and against it stood the innumerable red pikes of the Moine, the Géant, the Flambeau, Charmoz and Dru. I now felt that I had seen the Alps. All my dreams were realised, nor could there be anything more sublime.'

TUCKETT, FRANCIS FOX. GRINDELWALD, INTERLAKEN, KANDERSTEG, GEMMI PASS, LEUK, VISP, SAAS, ALPHUBEL PASS, ZERMATT, LYSJOCH PASS, GRESSONEY, COL DE VAL DOBBIA, ALAGNA, COL DE MOUD, RIMA, RIMASCO, COL D'EGUA, MACUGNAGA, OLD WEISSTHOR PASS, ZERMATT, COL DE VALPELLINE, PRARAYÉ, COL DE LA REUSE DE L'AROLLA, CHANRION, COL DE FENÊTRE DE BALME, AOSTA, GRAN PARADISO, COURMAYEUR, COL DU MONT TENDRE, CHAMONIX, ST. GERVAIS, BOSSES DU DROMADAIRE, MONT BLANC

TYNDALL, JOHN. BASLE, THUN, INTERLAKEN, MEIRINGEN, GAULI PASS, GRIMSEL PASS, OBERGESTELEN, EGGISHORN, BELALP, BRIG, VISP, RANDA, WEISSHORN, ZERMATT, SAAS, MONTE MORO PASS, MACUGNAGA, OLD WEISSTHOR PASS, ZERMATT

The first ascent of the Weisshorn.

WINKWORTH, STEPHEN. BERNE, THUN, KANDERSTEG, GEMMI PASS, LEUK, VISP, SAAS, ADLER PASS, ZERMATT, ST. THEODUL PASS, BREUIL, CHATILLON, AOSTA, COURMAYEUR, COL DU GÉANT, CHAMONIX, COL DE L'ARGENTIÈRE, LA FOULY, ORSIÈRES, COL DE BALME, CHAMONIX, MONT BLANC

1862

ALFORD, HENRY. BASLE, MOUTIER, WEISSENSTEIN, SOLEURE, BERNE, FRIBOURG, THUN, INTERLAKEN, LAUTERBRUNNEN, KLEINE SCHEIDEGG, GRINDELWALD, FAULHORN, GROSSE SCHEIDEGG, MEIRINGEN, BRUNIG PASS, SARNEN, LUCERNE, RIGI, ZURICH, ROMANSHORN

The Dean of Canterbury spent a week-end on the Faulhorn. '. . . A glorious sunset lifted up the mist, the colours changing from pale gold to deep gold, then to copper; then fading away to that queer corpse-like hue which succeeds the loss of the sun. . . . Service in our room with two Englishmen, members of the Alpine Club. Afternoon walked out on the zigzags and gathered flowers. . . .'

ANDERSEN, HANS CHRISTIAN. LUCERNE, BRUNNEN, SARNEN, BRUNIG PASS, BRIENZ, GIESSBACH, GRINDELWALD, INTERLAKEN, THUN, BERNE, MONTREUX

'A poem askest thou? I've none to give,
Else would I send my very best.
Here in Montreux the laurel grows but poems—none;
The last was Byron's—Byron's on Chillon.
Nature herself is here the poem,
And in my heart she rhymes anew.'

ANONYMOUS 11 B. BASLE, ZURICH, RAPPERSWIL, WESEN, WALLENSTADT, RAGAZ, COIRE, THUSIS, SPLÜGEN PASS, CHIAVENNA, COMO, MILAN, DOMODOSSOLA, SIMPLON PASS, BRIG, SION, MARTIGNY, TÊTE NOIRE PASS, CHAMONIX, GENEVA

BARROW, JOHN. CHAMONIX, COL DU GÉANT, COURMAYEUR, AOSTA, CHATILLON, BREUIL, ST. THEODUL PASS, ZERMATT, MONTE ROSA, VISP, SION

BURNE-JONES, EDWARD. BASLE, LUCERNE, FLUELEN, ST. GOTTHARD PASS, BELLINZONA, LUGANO, COMO

Burne-Jones's wife wrote referring to their stay at Fluelen, 'I have a vision of us three [herself, Burne-Jones and Ruskin] sitting together that evening, in a room with an exquisitely clean bare-boarded floor, and Mr. Ruskin reading Keats to us'.

CHEVALIER, CASIMIR ('DUVERNEY, JACQUES'). BASLE, SCHAFFHAUSEN, ST. GALL, ZURICH, EINSIEDELN, ZUG, LUCERNE, RIGI, FLUELEN, ALTDORF, ST. GOTTHARD PASS, BELLINZONA, MAGADINO, MILAN, DOMODOSSOLA, SIMPLON PASS, BRIG, LEUK, GEMMI PASS, KANDERSTEG, INTERLAKEN, LAUTERBRUNNEN, KLEINE SCHEIDEGG, GRINDELWALD, INTERLAKEN, THUN, BERNE, MORAT, LAUSANNE, GENEVA, CHAMONIX, TÊTE NOIRE PASS, MARTIGNY, BEX, GENEVA

CIVIALE, AIMÉ. EGGISHORN, BRIG, VISP, SAAS, SION, PIERRE À VOIR, MARTIGNY, BOUVERET

DESBAROLLES, ADOLPHE (*c*). BASLE, OLTEN, BERNE, THUN, INTERLAKEN, LAUTERBRUNNEN, BRIENZ, MEIRINGEN, ROSENLAUI, BRUNIG PASS, LUCERNE, ZURICH, RIGI, BRUNNEN, ALTDORF, ANDERMATT, FURKA PASS, GRIMSEL PASS, MEIRINGEN, INTERLAKEN, THUN, KANDERSTEG, GEMMI PASS, LEUK, BRIG, SIMPLON PASS, DOMODOSSOLA, CENTOVALLI, LOCARNO

Three francs fifty a day was Desbarolles's maximum expenditure.

HAMERTON, PHILIP GILBERT. LES VERRIÈRES, NEUCHÂTEL, GENEVA, LAUSANNE, BERNE, LUCERNE, BASLE

HORT, F. J. A. MÜRREN, ENGSTLENALP

Mürren: 'I am in luck at present as to people. Besides the old folk, another couple have turned up. At first I looked at them only with curiosity, and we wondered who they could be. . . . Today, at dinner they had a budget of letters, from which I found it was Dr. & Mrs. Acland of Oxford.'

HUXLEY, THOMAS HENRY. GRINDELWALD, FAULHORN, GROSSE SCHEIDEGG, MEIRINGEN, GRIMSEL PASS, OBERGESTELEN, EGGISHORN

JONES, REV. HARRY. BASLE, LUCERNE, RIGI, ALTDORF, ANDERMATT, FURKA PASS, GRIMSEL PASS, MEIRINGEN, GROSSE SCHEIDEGG, GRINDELWALD, KLEINE SCHEIDEGG, LAUTERBRUNNEN, MÜRREN, INTERLAKEN, THUN, BERNE, THUN, KANDERSTEG, GEMMI PASS, LEUK, VISP, ZERMATT, ST. THEODUL PASS, BREUIL, CHATILLON, AOSTA, COURMAYEUR, COL DE LA SEIGNE, COL DES FOURS, COL DU BONHOMME, CHAMONIX, GENEVA, VEVEY, AIGLE, LES ORMONTS

KEMBLE, FANNY. ZERMATT, VISP, BASLE, MOUTIER, SOLEURE, LUCERNE, RIGI, THUN, INTERLAKEN, LAUTERBRUNNEN, GRINDELWALD

Henry James wrote of Fanny Kemble: 'The Alpine guides loved her—she knew them all, and those for whom her name offered difficulties identified her charmingly as "la dame qui va chantant par les montagnes". She had sung, over hill and dale, all her days (music was in her blood), but those who had not been with her in Switzerland while she was still alert never knew what admirable nonsense she could talk, nor with what originality and gaiety she could invite the spirit of mirth, flinging herself, in the joy of high places, on the pianos of mountain inns, joking, punning, botanizing, encouraging the lowly and abasing the proud . . . Punctually on the first of June, every year, she went to Switzerland . . . for years she walked and climbed, and when she could no longer climb she rode. When she could no longer ride she was carried.'

KENNEDY, THOMAS S. SION, VISP, ZERMATT

This, presumably the first winter visit to Zermatt, was in January. 'The village presented a scene of almost utter desolation. . . . Not a person was in the streets, hardly a light in the houses, and the two inns were barred up and forsaken.'

LAVELEYE, ÉMILE DE. FORMAZZA, GRIES PASS, ULRICHEN, BRIG, VISP, ZERMATT, ST. THEODUL PASS, COL DES CIMES BLANCHES, ST. JACQUES D'AYAS, BETTA FURKA PASS, GRESSONEY, COL D'OLEN, ALAGNA, TURLO PASS, MACUGNAGA, MONTE MORO PASS, SAAS, VISP

LIEBIG, JUSTUS VON. ROMANSHORN, ZURICH, NEUCHÂTEL, COMBE VARIN, MONTREUX

RAMSAY, ANDREW CROMBIE. GENEVA, BEX, MONTHEY, COL DE PILLON, GSTEIG, SANETSCH PASS, SION, BRIG, BELALP, EGGISHORN, BRIG, TURTMANN

This year Ramsay produced his theory on the action of the ice of glaciers in the formation of lake basins.

RIVINGTON, ALEXANDER. BASLE, ZURICH, HORGEN, ZUG, BRUNNEN, FLUELEN, HERGISWIL, PILATUS, LUCERNE, ENGELBERG, TITLIS, SURENEN PASS, ALTDORF, ANDERMATT, FURKA PASS, GRIMSEL PASS, MEIRINGEN, GROSSE SCHEIDEGG, GRINDELWALD, KLEINE SCHEIDEGG, LAUTERBRUNNEN, MÜRREN, INTERLAKEN, THUN, BERNE, LAUSANNE, GENEVA

ROTH, ABRAHAM. BERNE, THUN, KANDERSTEG, DOLDENHORN, WEISSE FRAU, HOHTHÜRLI PASS, KIENTHAL, INTERLAKEN

'Such perhaps was the aspect of the chaotic earth, when the Creator issued His mighty decree: "Be created"—then vanished the waters and the mists, from the mire rose mountain and valley, from field and meadow sprang the verdant crop, the loftiest mountains donned their glittering glacier garb, whilst the genial sun illumined their crests with imperishable glory. So on this day shone the mightiest of the Alps, from the Finsteraarhorn to Mont Blanc, in the glory of the midday sun, high, high, like ourselves. . . .'

RUSKIN, JOHN. BASLE, LUCERNE, FLUELEN, ST. GOTTHARD PASS, BELLINZONA, LUGANO, MILAN, BAVENO, DOMODOSSOLA, SIMPLON PASS, BRIG, SION, MARTIGNY, GENEVA, MORNEX, BONNEVILLE, GENEVA—GENEVA, MORNEX

Ruskin met Sir John Nasmyth at Lucerne and went to Italy with Burne Jones and his wife. He took a cottage at Mornex and wrote *Munera pulveris*. The house, which subsequently became the Hotel et Pension des Glycines, was where Richard Wagner stayed.

SCHEFFEL, JOSEPH VIKTOR. DAVOS, SCALETTA PASS, ZERNEZ, SCHULS, TARASP, VULPERA, PONTRESINA

'From the hunting grounds of Davos, where the townhall is decorated with the masks of bears and wolves in place of corbels, I climbed over the bleakest of all Alpine passes, the 8,000-feet high Scaletta, strewn with the remains of avalanche-killed pack animals, covered with mist, and threatened by ice-fields.' It was during this journey that Scheffel was inspired to write his poem *Frau Aventiure*.

STEPHEN, LESLIE. ENGELBERG, JOCH PASS, MEIRINGEN, GRINDELWALD, KLEINE SCHEIDEGG, JUNGFRAUJOCH, VIESCHERJOCH, EGGISHORN, VISP, ZERMATT, WEISSHORN, LUGANO, CHIESA, MONTE DELLA DISGRAZIA

'Surely the Wengern Alp must be precisely the loveliest place in this world. To hurry past it, and listen to the roar of the avalanches, is a very unsatisfactory mode of enjoyment; it reminds one too much of letting off crackers in a cathedral. The mountains seem to be accomplices of the people who charge 50 centimes for an echo. But it does one's moral nature good to linger there at sunset or in the early morning, when tourists have ceased from travelling and the jaded cockney may enjoy a kind of spiritual bath in the soothing calmness of the scenery.'

STUDER, GOTTLIEB. SILVAPLANA, PONTRESINA, PIZ LANGUARD, FUORCLA DA FEX, SILS-MARIA, ST. MORITZ, JULIER PASS, TIEFENKASTEL, PARPAN PASS, COIRE, ZURICH, BERNE

SYMONDS, JOHN ADDINGTON. DOMODOSSOLA, SIMPLON PASS, BRIG, VISP, SION, MARTIGNY, LAUSANNE

'Art and man I always like better than Nature cold and simple. I feel at home in a town because men are everywhere the same, and *homo sum*, etc. . . . Scenery, when invested with association, becomes an object of passionate attachment to us, but I feel an alien among woods and lakes and mountains until that glow of sentiment has been thrown over them.'

TAYLOR, ISAAC. PONTRESINA, MALOJA PASS, CASTELMUR

TYNDALL, JOHN. GRINDELWALD, GROSSE SCHEIDEGG, MEIRINGEN, GRIMSEL PASS, EGGISHORN, BRIG, VISP, ZERMATT, MATTERJOCH PASS, BREUIL, PIC TYNDALL, COL DES CIMES BLANCHES, AYAS, GRESSONEY, ALAGNA, MACUGNAGA, MONTE MORO PASS, SAAS, ALPHUBELJOCH PASS, ZERMATT

'Committed thus and in other ways to the Matterhorn, the condition of my mind regarding it might be fitly compared to one of those uncheerful tenements often seen in the neighbourhood of London, where an adventurous contractor has laid the foundations, run up the walls, fixed the rafters, but stopped short, through bankruptcy, without completing the roof. As long as the Matterhorn remained unscaled, my Alpine life could hardly be said to be covered in.'

WHYMPER, EDWARD. ZERMATT, ST. THEODUL PASS, BREUIL, MONTE ROSA

This was the year of Whymper's fall on the Matterhorn. 'I was perfectly conscious of what was happening, and felt each blow; but, like a patient under chloroform, experienced no pain. Each blow was, naturally, more severe than that which preceded it, and I distinctly remember thinking, "well, if the next is harder still, that will be the end".'

WIGRAM, WOOLMORE. GRINDELWALD, STRAHLEGG PASS, GRIMSEL PASS, OBERGESTELEN, VIESCH, EGGISHORN, ALETSCHHORN, BRIG, VISP,

ZERMATT, COL D'HÉRENS, EVOLENA, DENT BLANCHE, COL D'HÉRENS, ZERMATT, COURMAYEUR, COL DU GÉANT, CHAMONIX, MONT BLANC

'In all mountain scenery there is no effect so impressive as the appearance of a great peak unexpectedly. . . . Such a view never loses its power, and is never forgotten. At one moment there was before the eyes nothing but a blank wall of rock or of snow, or a curtain of dull mist; the next you stand face to face with one of the grandest objects of nature; it is, apparently, close to you, even above you; and as the gaze wanders upwards, over ice and crag and snow, to the culminating summit, you believe almost that the majestic form has just risen to its place, and that it is aware of your presence.'

WILLIAMS, CHARLES J. B. LANDQUART, KLOSTERS, DAVOS, FILISUR, BERGÜN, ALBULA PASS, PONTRESINA, ST. MORITZ, MALOJA PASS, CHIAVENNA

'As there was no inducement to make excursions into snow and cloud (except for a few minutes, to keep ourselves warm), the disappointed travellers were shut up, miserable enough, in the *salle à manger*. An attempt was made to light the stove; but it ended in smoke, of which we had already too much from the unrestrained devotees of the pernicious weed. Then provisions ran short, and the viands of the *table d'hôte* were little more than *bouilli et compote de pruneaux*. So, feeling somewhat in danger of double starvation, and not being disposed to prolong this experiment of hybernation in a summer month, we ordered a carriage. . . .' So much for Pontresina.

WORDSWORTH, CHRISTOPHER. BASLE, LUCERNE, FLUELEN, ST. GOTTHARD PASS, AIROLO, FAIDO, BELLINZONA, MAGADINO

'It resembles the pass of Tempe, . . .'

1863

AEBY, CHRISTOPH. BERNE, THUN, INTERLAKEN, GRINDELWALD, WETTERHORN, LAUTERAARSATTEL, UNTERAAR GLACIER, EWIGSCHNEEHORN, URNENALP, WETTERLIMMI PASS, ROSENLAUI

ASTLEY, SIR JOHN DUGDALE. GENEVA, CHAMONIX, TÊTE NOIRE PASS, MARTIGNY, VEVEY, MARTIGNY, SION, LEUKERBAD, GEMMI PASS, KANDERSTEG, INTERLAKEN, BRUNIG PASS, LUCERNE, BASLE

BROWNE, G. F. NYON, ARZIER, ORMONT DESSUS, COL DE PILLON, OLDENHORN

BROWNING, OSCAR. CHAMONIX, ST. MORITZ, PONTRESINA, DIAVOLEZZA, MALOJA PASS, CHIAVENNA

BUXTON, EDWARD NORTH. PONTRESINA, PIZ SELLA, PIZ PALÜ

CIVIALE, AIMÉ. LUCERNE, FLUELEN, ALTDORF, ANDERMATT, ST. GOTTHARD, OBERALP PASS, DISENTIS, PIZ MURAUN, REICHENAU, THUSIS, TIEFENKASTEL, JULIER PASS, ST. MORITZ, PONTRESINA

FERGUSON, FERGUS. LES VERRIÈRES, NEUCHÂTEL, BERNE, THUN, INTERLAKEN, LAUTERBRUNNEN, WENGERNALP, INTERLAKEN, BERNE, FRIBOURG, LAUSANNE, GENEVA

'I saw groups of people gazing intently at some apparently distant object. On joining them, what did I see? The Bernese Alps! Their misty covering had vanished! There they stood, for the first time revealed to my delighted eyes; but throughout untold, uncounted ages they had lifted up these same bold and snow-covered peaks to the sky! . . . And meanwhile the Aar murmured at my feet, as if wishing to say—"These mountains are my cradle, yea, they are the mother of my stream; I'm glad you like them well".'

FORBES, MRS. E. A. BASLE, LUCERNE, RIGI, SARNEN, BRUNIG PASS, MEIRINGEN, ROSENLAUI, BRIENZ, INTERLAKEN, LAUTERBRUNNEN, INTERLAKEN, THUN, BERNE, LAUSANNE, GENEVA, CHAMONIX, TÊTE NOIRE PASS, MARTIGNY, SION, BRIG, SIMPLON PASS, DOMODOSSOLA

FOX, JOSEPH H. BORMIO, TIRANO, BERNINA PASS, PONTRESINA

FRESHFIELD, DOUGLAS W. ZERMATT, COURMAYEUR, COL DU GÉANT, CHAMONIX, MONT BLANC

HANNINGTON, JAMES. LUCERNE, INTERLAKEN, LAUTERBRUNNEN, KLEINE SCHEIDEGG, GRINDELWALD, GLETSCH, FURKA PASS, HOSPENTHAL, ST. GOTTHARD PASS, BELLINZONA, MILAN, DOMODOSSOLA, SIMPLON PASS, BRIG, MARTIGNY, CHAMONIX, GENEVA

HARDMAN, SIR WILLIAM. BASLE, BERNE, THUN, INTERLAKEN, GRINDELWALD, KLEINE SCHEIDEGG, LAUTERBRUNNEN, INTERLAKEN, THUN, ERLENBACH, ZWEISIMMEN, SAANEN, CHÂTEAU D'OEX, VEVEY, MARTIGNY, TÊTE NOIRE PASS, CHAMONIX, GENEVA, VEVEY, LAUSANNE, NEUCHÂTEL, LES VERRIÈRES

'Everybody bathes at Vevey. The entire population apparently spend a portion of their time in the Lake. On one occasion we passed close to a lady who was disporting herself a quarter of a mile from land without a particle of clothing on. . . .'

HARE, AUGUSTUS J. C. GENEVA, LAUSANNE, BERNE, THUN, INTERLAKEN, LAUTERBRUNNEN, GRINDELWALD

HARE, LUCY ANNE. BEX

'Bex is most delightful, and though hemmed in by high mountains, the rushing waters of the Avençon, fresh from the glacier, breathed coolness around. Our days glide by so peacefully, I never feel as if I wanted more than the few books I have. . . . With these mountains, this sky, and the pine-covered hills, one cannot feel alone. We are climbing the mountains, not going down.'

HARRISON, FREDERIC. ZERMATT, MONTE ROSA, CIMA DI JAZZI, WEISSTHOR PASS, MACUGNAGA

'We had not gone far when the young porter fell on me, and his eighteen stone knocked me off my feet; I fell on my companion; and all three on Lochmatter. In an instant the four of us were whirling down the ice precipice. I saw the spire of Macugnaga church between my feet, and felt that a few minutes more would take me for ever into the quiet graveyard.'

JONES, REV. HARRY. BASLE, OLTEN, BERNE, THUN, INTERLAKEN, BRIENZ, BRUNIG PASS, MEIRINGEN, JOCH PASS, MEIRINGEN, GRIMSEL PASS, OBERGESTELEN, VIESCH, EGGISHORN, BRIG, BELALP, BRIG, SIMPLON PASS, DOMODOSSOLA, LUGANO, ORTA, MACUGNAGA, MONTE MORO PASS, SAAS, VISP, SION, MARTIGNY, BEX, CHAMPÉRY, VEVEY, NEUCHÂTEL

'These table d'hôte dinners in the mountain inns are often very entertaining. The natural reserve of Englishmen gives way when you dine together in your shooting-jackets and slippers at some high and lonely spot. We had very merry meals at the Aeggishorn. There were about a dozen of us, though the house will contain many more, and among them one with a laugh so dancing and contagious, that he alone had need to be touched in order to set the table in good humour with itself. We talked about a Swiss Alpine Club, which it seems is more or less of a failure.'

LOWDER, CHARLES. CHAMONIX, TÊTE NOIRE PASS, MARTIGNY, SIERRE, ST. LUC, BELLA TOLA, PAS DU BOEUF, TURTMANN, AUGSTBORD PASS, ST. NIKLAUS, ZERMATT, VISP, BRIG, VIESCH, EGGISHORN, OBERWALD, GLETSCH, GRIMSEL PASS, MEIRINGEN, BRIENZ, INTERLAKEN

MARTINS, CHARLES. COIRE, TIEFENKASTEL, JULIER PASS, ST. MORITZ, SAMADEN, PONTRESINA, MALOJA PASS, CHIAVENNA, LUGANO

MEREDITH, GEORGE. DOMODOSSOLA, SIMPLON PASS, BRIG, SION, MARTIGNY, GENEVA

'Carry your fevers to the Alps, you of minds diseased; not to sit down in sight of them ruminating, for bodily ease and comfort will trick the soul and set you measuring our lean humanity against yonder sublime and infinite; but mount, rack the limbs, wrestle it out among the peaks; taste danger, sweat, earn rest: learn to discover ungrudgingly that haggard fatigue is the fair vision you have run to earth, and that rest is your uttermost reward.'

MUSAFIR, CAPTAIN. SCHAFFHAUSEN, LUCERNE, ENGELBERG, JOCH PASS, ENGSTLENALP, TITLIS, MEIRINGEN, BRIENZ, INTERLAKEN, LAUTERBRUNNEN, KLEINE SCHEIDEGG, GRINDELWALD, GROSSE SCHEIDEGG, MEIRINGEN, BRUNIG PASS, LUCERNE, ALTDORF, AMSTEG, MADERANERTAL, ANDERMATT, HOSPENTHAL

RAMBERT, EUGÈNE. ZURICH, GLARUS, LINTHAL, MUTTENSEE, SANDALP, CLARIDENSTOCK, LINTHAL

'Le soleil se levait justement; il se levait au dessous de nous, et ses rayons obliques rasaient la surface montante des neiges. Toutes les aspérités de la glace étincelaient. Mille cristaux suspendus dans les airs voltigeaient, comme de petites étoiles mobiles, dans une lumière adorable. Ce n'était ni du rose ni du violet; mais une teinte plus brillante que le violet, plus tendre que le rose, une sorte de lumière idéale comme on ne la conçoit qu'au haut des airs, et dont les neiges les plus pures ne semblent pas dignes d'être touchées.'

RIVINGTON, ALEXANDER. GENEVA, CHAMONIX, TÊTE NOIRE PASS, FINHAUT, VERNAYAZ, SION, SIERRE, ZINAL, TRIFTJOCH, ZERMATT, VISP, SION, OUCHY, FRIBOURG, BERNE, BASLE

RUSKIN, JOHN. MORNEX, CHAMONIX, GENEVA—GENEVA, BONNEVILLE, CHAMONIX, GENEVA, BADEN, SCHAFFHAUSEN, ZURICH, BASLE

Ruskin wanted to build a chalet above Bonneville; Rossetti was to design the decorations and Burne-Jones to paint the walls. But the Commune of Bonneville, thinking that he must have found a gold mine or coal bed since otherwise nobody would want to buy a barren rock, demanded an exorbitant price, and the project was dropped.

STUDER, GOTTLIEB. KANDERSTEG, LÖTSCHEN PASS, KIPPEL, BEICH PASS, BELALP, VISP, SAAS, MONTE MORO PASS, MACUGNAGA, VOGOGNA, BELLINZONA, CAMOGHE, MENAGGIO, COLICO, MORBEGNO, FORCELLA DI SAN MARTINO, VICOSOPRANO, MALOJA PASS, PONTRESINA, PIZ OT, PIZ MORTERATSCH, ALBULA PASS, FILISUR, PARPAN, STÄTZERHORN, TOMILS, DISENTIS, BRUNNI PASS, AMSTEG, FLUELEN, BECKENRIED, ENGELBERG, SCHLOSSBERG, JOCH PASS, MEIRINGEN, INTERLAKEN, THUN, BERNE

SYMONDS, JOHN ADDINGTON. BASLE, LUCERNE, SEELISBERG, ENGELBERG, JOCH PASS, MEIRINGEN, INTERLAKEN, LAUTERBRUNNEN, MÜRREN, ZURICH, UETLIBERG, THUN, LAUTERBRUNNEN, MÜRREN, WINTERTHUR, SCHAFFHAUSEN, CONSTANCE

'In those days there was only one little wooden inn at Mürren, the Silberhorn, kept by Herr Sterchi and his family. Life was very primitive, few people staying in the house beside ourselves; troops of tourists coming up from Interlaken to lunch, and going noisily away again. The George de Bunsens were our companions for some time, and while they were still there an English family arrived. I can remember looking out of Cecil's window and spying their advent one bright afternoon in early August. It annoyed us to think that the hotel would now be fuller. They were Mr. Frederick North, M.P. for Hastings, and his two daughters,' one of whom was to become Symonds's wife.

TUCKETT, FRANCIS FOX. BORMIO, TIRANO, BERNINA PASS, PONTRESINA, ST. MORITZ, JULIER PASS, TIEFENKASTEL, COIRE, WALLENSTADT, ZURICH, NEUCHÂTEL

TYNDALL, JOHN. MEIRINGEN, GADMEN, STEIN, GRIMSEL PASS, OBERAARJOCH PASS, EGGISHORN, JUNGFRAU

WEILENMANN, JOHANN JAKOB. ST. GALL, FINSTERAARHORN, VIESCH, BINN, ZINAL, LO BESSO, COL DURAND, ZERMATT, VISP

WHYMPER, EDWARD. CHATILLON, BREUIL, BREUILJOCH PASS, ZERMATT, COL DE VALPELLINE, PRARAYÉ, COL DE VALCOURNERA, BREUIL

WIGRAM, WOOLMORE. GRINDELWALD

WILBERFORCE, SAMUEL. ZERMATT, INTERLAKEN, LAUTERBRUNNEN, MÜRREN

'As we neared the top, the mist which had veiled the Jungfrau suddenly opened and we saw high in heaven the Silberhorn, and then the top. Just such a sight of glory as made my blessed wife in 1828 seize my hand and say, "Can that be earth?" A very happy day in the heights.'

1864

ALSTON, ALFRED HENRY. ZURICH, RIGI, FLUELEN, AMSTEG, ANDERMATT, OBERALP PASS, SEDRUN, DISENTIS, ILANZ, THUSIS, HINTERRHEIN, VALSERBERG PASS, VALS, VRIN, DIESRUT PASS, GREINA PASS, OLIVONE, BIASCA, AIROLO, ST. GOTTHARD PASS, HOSPENTHAL, FURKA PASS, VIESCH, EGGISHORN, BRIG, VISP, ZERMATT, MONTE ROSA, ST. THEODUL PASS, BREUIL, CHATILLON, AOSTA, COURMAYEUR, COL DU GÉANT, CHAMONIX, MONT BLANC, GENEVA

'The Matterhorn. Magnificent rock, with his broad breast fronting you, his back and loins covered with pure snow, and a glacier issuing from between his outstretched paws. There he reposes, standing out clear against the sky, like a colossal sphinx, calmly looking down on the world. . . . I have seen the glories of the Indies, the bright calm beauty of inland China, the blue skies and rich landscapes of Italy, the purple hills and ruined temples of Greece, the virgin forests and park-like lands of Tartary, the wild grandeurs of iceberg and glacier in Arctic seas, but Switzerland—three or four days' journey from our own doors—outstrips them all in those features which each alike possess and wherein mutual comparison is possible.'

ARNOLD, HOWARD PAYSON (*c*). LUCERNE, RIGI, FLUELEN, ALTDORF, ST. GOTTHARD PASS, BELLINZONA, LOCARNO

'Far off in long procession extend the Jungfrau and her attendant mountains, like a train of white-robed vestal virgins. But now the sun salutes their snow-covered foreheads, and as his first ardent rays strike them, like the angel, they answer

"with a blush, that grows
celestial rosy red, love's proper hue".

And now the sun strides high in the East, like a god going forth to battle; the clouds fall back at his approach, and exultant cheerful voices and clapping hands welcome the approach of the spirit of light.'

BONNEY, THOMAS GEORGE. GENEVA, THONON, MORZINE, COL DE JOUPLANE, SIXT, COL D'ANTERNE, MONT BUET, CHAMONIX, COL DU GÉANT, COURMAYEUR

Bonney passed through Morzine just after the military had 'put down' an epidemic of insanity. 'The scene in church at a confirmation by the Bishop of Annecy is described as follows by an eye-witness: "the church became a perfect hell. Nothing was heard but cries, blows, oaths, and blasphemies. . . . The victims of the disease, about a hundred in number, seemed to fall into simultaneous convulsions without any previous warning. . . . The greater number were young girls and women from fifteen to thirty years old." The government now decided to try strong measures. A troop of sixty soldiers was sent there.'

BROWNE, G. F. NYON, ARZIER, LA GENOLLIÈRE, NEUCHÂTEL, BERNE, THUN, SCHAFLOCH, GENEVA, BONNEVILLE, REPOSOIR, CHAMONIX, MONT BLANC, BEX, ANZEINDAZ, DIABLERETS

'We found a considerable crowd gathered round some object at the wooden cross in the little village, as Chamonix then was. The object proved to be the shrunken and contorted leg and foot of a man, which had come out that day at the foot of the glacier des Bossons. This was one of the relics of the party of Dr. Hamel.'

COOK, THOMAS. GENEVA, CHAMONIX, MARTIGNY, SION, LEUK, GEMMI PASS, KANDERSTEG, INTERLAKEN, BRIENZ, BRUNIG PASS, SARNEN, LUCERNE, BERNE, NEUCHÂTEL, LAUSANNE

This was the first of the conducted tours to Switzerland by Mr. Cook.

DEHANSY, CHARLES (*c*). GENEVA, LAUSANNE, BERNE, THUN, INTERLAKEN, BRIENZ, BRUNIG PASS, LUCERNE, RIGI, ALTDORF, ANDERMATT, FURKA PASS, GRIMSEL PASS, MEIRINGEN, GROSSE SCHEIDEGG, GRINDELWALD, KLEINE SCHEIDEGG, LAUTERBRUNNEN, INTERLAKEN, KANDERSTEG, GEMMI PASS, LEUK, SION, PAS DE CHEVILLE, BEX, MARTIGNY, COL DE BALME, CHAMONIX, ANNECY

EASTLAKE, LADY ELISABETH. GENEVA, OUCHY, LAUSANNE, BERNE, SCHAFFHAUSEN, RORSCHACH, COIRE, THUSIS, SPLÜGEN PASS, CHIAVENNA

'Ouchy . . . Little Prince Arthur arrived here the day before yesterday . . . the little fellow is an indefatigable pedestrian, and had been up to the "Grands Mulets" of Mont Blanc—a walk of thirteen hours.'

ELLIOTT, HENRY VENN. LAUSANNE, GEMMI PASS, RIGI, LUCERNE

EWING, ALEXANDER. BASLE, BERNE, VEVEY, MARTIGNY, SION

FRESHFIELD, DOUGLAS. GENEVA, THONON, BIOT, COL DE CHÉSERY, PORTE DU SOLEIL, CHAMPÉRY, COL DE SUSANFE, COL D'EMANEY, COL D'EMOUSSONS, CHAMONIX, COL DE BALME, CHAMPEX, BOURG ST. PIERRE, COL DU SONADON, CHERMONTANE, COL D'OREN, PRARAYÉ, COL DE VALPELLINE, ZERMATT, MONTE ROSA, ALPHUBELJOCH PASS, SAAS, ZWISCHBERGEN PASS, GONDO, PREMIA, FORMAZZA, BOCHETTA DI VAL MAGGIA, BIGNASCO, FUSIO, PASSO DI VESPERO, AIROLO, PIORA, PASSO DI COLOMBE, OLIVONE, SCARADRA PASS, ZERVREILA, PIZ VALRHEIN, SPLÜGEN, AVERS, MADRISER PASS, BONDO, PASSO DI FERRO, MASINO, MONTE SISSONE, MALOJA, ST. MORITZ, PONTRESINA, SELLA PASS, FELLARIA, PIZ PALÜ, BERNINA PASS, VAL VIOLA PASS, BORMIO

'At Fusio the inn was kept by a worthy couple whose puckered faces recalled some portrait of an early German master. But they were as lively as they were old, and no emergency, not even the arrival of three hungry Englishmen, found them without resources. On the occasion in question they boldly proceeded to sacrilege on our behalf. The village knew that the curé was going to have a fowl for dinner; the good dame hurried off to the parsonage, and like David robbed the tables of the priest.'

GASKELL, MRS. ELISABETH. PONTRESINA

Marianne North relates that Mrs. Gaskell took a room outside the village so as to be able to work in peace at *Wives and Daughters*, much of which was written at Pontresina, at the Steinbock hotel.

GIRDLESTONE, A. G. BASLE, LAUSANNE, BERNE, THUN, INTERLAKEN, GRINDELWALD, STRAHLEGG PASS, GRIMSEL, ENGELBERG, SILVRETTA, MACUGNAGA, WEISSTHOR PASS, ZERMATT

'The author has passed a portion of every long vacation since his university matriculation in Switzerland; and many an undergraduate might do well in spending in like manner part of his time in reading for the "schools" at some elevated mountain inn, such as the Engstlen Alp, Stein Alp, or Mürren; but mostly seeking for a stock of health which should enable him to dispense with vacation for the rest of the year.'

GROVE, SIR GEORGE. BASLE, LUCERNE, ALTDORF, ANDERMATT, ST. GOTTHARD PASS, FAIDO, BRIG, SION, MARTIGNY, CHAMONIX, GENEVA, LAUSANNE, BERNE, THUN, INTERLAKEN, BASLE

Referring to the waterfall opposite Faido, Grove wrote: 'The water enters sideways behind a great screen of rock, so that nothing is seen but a mass of white foam, innocent and joyous, tumbling in like a *baby*. This at once opens out into a wide clear basin without a ripple on the surface, and with the clear candid transparent look of *youth*. To this succeeds a rough hurrying portion over stones between rocks—full of noise and clamour, like the turmoil and strife and business of *mature manhood*, and from this it lastly sweeps down into its grave below the bridge like the exit of *age*.'

GUILLAUME, DR. NEUCHÂTEL, VALLANGIN, LES HAUTS GENEVEYS, TÊTE DE RANG, LA SAGNE, LES PONTS, LA JOUX, LA BRÉVINE, BÉMONT, ST. SULPICE, FLEURIER, MOTIERS, COMBE VARIN, LA TOURNE, NEUCHÂTEL

A school holiday and a visit to Edouard Desor at Combe Varin where the great scientist showed the students the tree under which Theodore Parker meditated over his work on the origin of religions, the grass on which Schönbein worked out his theory of ozone, the marsh where Charles Martins made his observations on the radiation of the earth, and the heap of timber on which Liebig sat when he explained the coming world-famine of manure.

HARDMAN, SIR WILLIAM. BASLE, LUCERNE, PILATUS, ALTDORF, ANDERMATT, OBERALP PASS, DISENTIS, COIRE, THUSIS, TIEFENKASTEL, JULIER PASS, ST. MORITZ, PONTRESINA, MALOJA PASS, CHIAVENNA, COMO, MILAN, TURIN, AOSTA, GRAND ST. BERNARD PASS, MARTIGNY, SION, VISP, BRIG, EGGISHORN, OBERGESTELEN, GRIMSEL PASS, MEIRINGEN, INTERLAKEN, BERNE

HARRISON, FREDERIC. CHAMONIX, MONT BLANC, ZERMATT, ADLER PASS, SAAS, ALPHUBELJOCH PASS, ZERMATT, VISP, BRIG, VIESCH, EGGISHORN, LAUSANNE, OUCHY

'To know, to feel, to understand the Alps is to know, to feel, to understand humanity. Poets, romancers, dramatists, moralists, historians, theologians, artists—all combine to give a special halo of charm to the Alps and the Alpine world at large.'

JONES, REV. HARRY. SCHAFFHAUSEN, CONSTANCE, RORSCHACH, COIRE, THUSIS, VIA MALA, THUSIS, TIEFENKASTEL, JULIER PASS, ST. MORITZ, PONTRESINA, JULIER PASS, TIEFENKASTEL, LENZERHEIDE, COIRE

Jones heard from Tyndall an account of his accident on Piz Morteratsch, and was one of the party which went out on the glacier 17 days after the accident to look for, and found, Tyndall's watch.

'The exquisite Oeschinen lake—a lake, so far as I know, of a beauty quite unrivalled in any of the high alpine districts'

(*Paul Popper*) LESLIE STEPHEN, 1860; Kandersteg

'I had formed high expectations of the scenery of the Val d'Anniviers, and the reality far exceeded my ideal'

(*Swiss Federal Railways*) A. W. MOORE, 1864; Zinal

LOWDER, CHARLES. LUCERNE, SEELISBERG, RIGI, MARTIGNY, COL DE BALME, CHAMONIX, ST. GERVAIS, SERVOZ, SIXT, MAGLAN, ST. GERVAIS, COURMAYEUR, AOSTA, CHATILLON, BREUIL, ST. THEODUL PASS, ZERMATT, NEW WEISSTHOR PASS, MACUGNAGA, STRESA, BELLINZONA, ST. GOTTHARD PASS, ALTDORF, LUCERNE, BASLE

McTEAR, ROBERT. GENEVA, LAUSANNE, BERNE, LUCERNE, RIGI, FLUELEN, ALTDORF, ST. GOTTHARD PASS, BELLINZONA, LUGANO, COMO

At Fluelen, McTear joined a 'Cook's lot' of 70 who for their passage of the St. Gotthard employed 9 diligences, 432 horses besides bullocks which assisted at some of the heavier stages, and 108 men.

MOORE, A. W. BOURG ST. MAURICE, COL DU BONHOMME, PAVILLON BELLEVUE, MONT BLANC, CHAMONIX, COL DU CHARDONNET, ORSIÈRES, MARTIGNY, SION, SIERRE, GRIMENTZ, COL DE BRÉONNA, EVOLENA, COL D'HÉRENS, ZERMATT, RANDA, BIESJOCH PASS, GRUBEN, ZMEIDEN PASS, ZINAL, MOMING PASS, ZERMATT, VISP, BRIG, BELALP, ALETSCHHORN, BEICH PASS, GUGGISTAFFEL, WETTERLÜCKE PASS, LAUTERBRUNNEN, GRINDELWALD, EIGER, WETTERHORN

'I had formed high expectations of the scenery of the Val d'Anniviers, and the reality far exceeded my ideal. Nothing is wanting to complete the effect, and rocks, woods, and water combine to form a perfect picture.'

MOULE, HENRY CARR GLYN. BASLE, ZURICH, LUCERNE, ANDERMATT, HANDECK, BRIENZ

MUSAFIR, CAPTAIN. BORMIO, TIRANO, BERNINA PASS, PONTRESINA, SAMADEN, ST. MORITZ, JULIER PASS, TIEFENKASTEL, COIRE, ZURICH, BASLE

NORTH, MARIANNE. RAGAZ, PFÄFERS, COIRE, TIEFENKASTEL, JULIER PASS, ST. MORITZ, PONTRESINA

'Settled ourselves in that paradise of Alpine climbers the Old Crown Inn. In those primitive days it was nearly all built of wood (as was the Chalet Inn at Mürren), and as the majority of its frequenters delighted in getting up in the very smallest hours of the morning, putting on heavily-nailed boots, and shouting at one another from room to room, it could not be called quiet quarters.'

PRESTON-THOMAS, HERBERT. OBERGESTELEN, GRIMSEL PASS, OBERAARJOCH PASS, FINSTERAARHORN, BELALP, BRIG, VISP, ZERMATT, MONTE ROSA, SCHWARZBERG-WEISSTHOR PASS, SAAS

'. . . From the Rhone valley to the Grimsel Hospice; and as I made a short cut by the shore of the usually frozen lake I became aware of the descent of a human body, head first, from a slab of rock above to the chilly water below. Its owner afterwards became the bishop of an English diocese, but at that period he had unfortunately not attained to the dignity of an apron; and when he rose to the surface after his header, he displayed an anxiety to know whether I was the first of a party likely to cut off his retreat to his clothes.' This was John Gott, afterwards bishop of Truro.

RACOWITZA, HELENE VON. GENEVA, BERNE, WABERN, LUCERNE, RIGI, WEGGIS, LUCERNE, WABERN, GENEVA, BEX, GENEVA

While descending from the Rigi to Weggis, Helene von Dönniges decided to become engaged to Ferdinand Lassalle, the friend of Karl Marx and founder of the German Workers' Party. This decision was to lead to Helene being smuggled over by night to Bex by her infuriated family, and to Lassalle's death in duel with Yanko von Racowitza who was to become Helene's husband.

ROSSETTI, WILLIAM. CHIAVENNA, SPLÜGEN PASS, THUSIS, COIRE, ZURICH, BASLE

SCHEFFEL, JOSEPH VIKTOR. RORSCHACH, COIRE, THUSIS, SAN BERNARDINO PASS, MESOCCO, BELLINZONA, LOCARNO, LUCERNE, BRESTENBERG

Author of *Ekkehard* and of the *Trompeter von Säckingen*, Scheffel contributed much to the spread of the reputation in Germany of the Grisons as a travel ground. The expression 'Engadina, Terra Fina' was the prefix that Scheffel set at the head of his poem *Die Alpenstrasse*, referring to the Bernina.

SMITH, WILLIAM. LES VERRIÈRES, NEUCHÂTEL, YVERDON, LAUSANNE, MARTIGNY, TÊTE NOIRE PASS, CHAMONIX, GENEVA, LAUSANNE, FRIBOURG, BERNE, OLTEN, LUCERNE, WEGGIS, RIGI, LUCERNE, SARNEN, BRUNIG PASS, BRIENZ, INTERLAKEN, SCHERZLIGEN, BERNE, LAUSANNE, GENEVA

At Ouchy: 'At one end of the table sat the "Napoleon of Excursions" Mr. Cook, having by his side his wife and daughter. Our manager was a perfect Job in the matter of patience, otherwise the incessant inquiries addressed to him, many of them needless, would have induced him to have marked out a track for himself.'

STEPHEN, LESLIE. ALTDORF, KLAUSEN PASS, KAMMLILÜCKE PASS, MADERANERTAL, AMSTEG, GÖSCHENEN, WINTERLÜCKE PASS, GRIMSEL PASS, STRAHLEGG PASS, GRINDELWALD, EIGER, LAUTERBRUNNEN, JUNGFRAU, EGGISHORN, ALETSCHHORN, BRIG, VISP, SAAS, ALPHUBELJOCH PASS, ZERMATT, LYSKAMM, TRIFTJOCH PASS, ZINAL, ROTHORN, MARTIGNY, ORSIÈRES, COL D'ARGENTIÈRE, CHAMONIX, MONT BLANC

'I may remark that Swiss enterprise has begun to penetrate these retired valleys. It is a mystery of difficult solution, how the spiders which live in certain retired and, as we would think, flyless corners of ancient libraries, preserve their existence; but it is still harder to discover how innkeepers in these rarely trodden valleys derive sufficient supplies from the mere waifs and strays that are thrown, as it were, from the main body of tourists. However that may be, a certain M. Epinay maintains a hospitable inn at Zinal.' While waiting there for the weather to clear, Stephen and his friends played cricket in the village street, and the first ball was sent crashing through the window of the chapel.

SYMONDS, JOHN ADDINGTON. PONTRESINA

On the bridge below Pontresina, Symonds became engaged to Catherine North, and they exchanged engagement rings on the top of Piz Languard.

TUCKETT, FRANCIS FOX. THUN, INTERLAKEN, LAUTERBRUNNEN, MÜRREN, TSCHINGEL PASS, PETERSGRAT, BLATTEN, BEICH PASS, BELALP, EGGISHORN, GROSS FIESCHERHORN, GRINDELWALD, GROSSE SCHEIDEGG, MEIRINGEN, JOCH PASS, ENGELBERG, GRASSEN PASS, WASSEN, ALTDORF, LUCERNE, ALTDORF, AMSTEG, MADERANERTAL, CLARIDEN PASS, STACHELBERG, PORTA DA SPESCHA, DISENTIS, REICHENAU, THUSIS, TIEFENKASTEL, FILISUR, BERGÜN, ESCHIA PASS, PIZ KESCH, PONTRESINA, SELLA PASS, MARINELLI PASS, PASSO DI VERONA, POSCHIAVO, BORMIO, ORTLER, RESCHEN-SCHEIDECK PASS, MARTINSBRUCK, SCHULS, PONTRESINA, MALOJA PASS, VICOSOPRANO, ZOCCA PASS, PASSO DEL MONTE SISSONE, MALOJA, SAMADEN, ZERNEZ, SÜS, FLUELA PASS, DAVOS, KLOSTERS, LANDQUART, RORSCHACH, SÄNTIS, APPENZELL, ZURICH

TUCKETT, LUCY. BERNE, THUN, INTERLAKEN, LAUTERBRUNNEN, MÜRREN, KLEINE SCHEIDEGG, GRINDELWALD, GROSSE SCHEIDEGG, MEIRINGEN, JOCH PASS, ENGELBERG, LUCERNE, ALTDORF, KLAUSEN PASS, LINTHAL, GLARUS, WALLENSTADT, COIRE, TIEFENKASTEL, FILISUR, BERGÜN, ALBULA PASS, PONTRESINA, BERNINA PASS, TIRANO, BORMIO, STELVIO PASS, STA. MARIA, OFEN PASS, ZERNEZ, PONTRESINA, ST. MORITZ, SAMADEN, ZERNEZ, SÜS, FLUELA PASS, DAVOS, KLOSTERS, LANDQUART, ZURICH

Lucy Tuckett's party included Miss Burgess, Mrs. Hustler, William Waterhouse, W. Fowler, Edward North Buxton, Mrs. Emily North Buxton, her sister Miss Digby, H. E. Buxton, and, intermittently, Lucy Tuckett's brother Francis Fox Tuckett. One of Lucy Tuckett's sketches of adventures at Pontresina is understood to represent the betrothal of Catherine North to John Addington Symonds.

TYNDALL, JOHN. THUSIS, VIA MALA, THUSIS, TIEFENKASTEL, JULIER PASS, ST. MORITZ, PONTRESINA, MORTERATSCH

'The patients at St. Moritz put me in mind of that Eastern prince whose physician induced him to kick a football under the impression that it contained a charm. The sagacious doctor knew that faith has a dynamic power unpossessed by knowledge. Through the agency of this power he stirred the prince to action, caused him to take wholesome exercise, and thus cured him of his ailments. At St. Moritz the water is probably the football.'

URQUHART, DAVID. GENEVA, ST. GERVAIS, CHAMONIX

It was in this year that Urquhart built the 'Chalet des Mélèzes'. 'The children brought up in the chalet, and as much at home on the mountains as young goats, used to watch with wicked glee the toil-worn and perspiring appearance of portly bishops and high-heeled French ladies as they emerged from the pine woods below the chalet on a visit to their father.' One of these children, Francis Fortescue Urquhart ('Sligger'), converted the chalet into nothing less than an institution for the benefit of his undergraduates.

VIGNET, LOUIS. STELVIO PASS, BORMIO, TIRANO, BERNINA PASS, PONTRESINA, MALOJA PASS, CHIAVENNA, SPLÜGEN PASS, THUSIS, COIRE

'Pontrésina! quatre syllabes se combinant en une note d'harmonie. J'ai vécu là quelques unes des heures bénies de mon existence. Chamonix, Zermatt, Interlaken sont les ancêtres, les doyens de Pontrésina. Laissez-aller! la fillette, la Benjamine, nous la voyons grandir et réclamer sa légitime.'

WAGNER, RICHARD. RORSCHACH, ZURICH, MARIAFELD

'Let me create more works like those which I conceived in that serene and glorious Switzerland, with my eyes on the beautiful gold-crowned mountains: they are masterpieces and nowhere else could I have conceived them.'

WEILENMANN, JOHANN JAKOB. ST. GALL, GALTÜR, VERMUNT PASS, GUARDA, PONTRESINA

WHYMPER, EDWARD. CHAMONIX, COL DE TRIOLET, MONT DOLENT, COURMAYEUR, AIGUILLE DE TRÉLATÈTE, COL DE LA SEIGNE, COL DU MONT TENDRE, CHAMONIX, COL DE BALME, MARTIGNY, SION, SIERRE, ZINAL, MOMING PASS, ZERMATT

At Zinal he watched the making of cheese, which involved blowing into the tub and from time to time taking puffs of tobacco from a very foul pipe.

1865

ACLAND, SIR HENRY. ENGELBERG

Acland was accompanied by Dean Liddell who, as soon as they had settled in at Engelberg, slipped on a moss-covered stone and broke his leg. Acland found himself in medical attention on his friend.

ALCOTT, LOUISA MAY. BASLE, BERNE, FRIBOURG, VEVEY, GENEVA

Staying at the same Pension (Victoria) at Vevey, was a Pole, Ladislas Wisinewski, who became the original of 'Laurie' in Louisa May Alcott's *Little Women*.

ARNOLD, MATTHEW. CHIAVENNA, SPLÜGEN PASS, THUSIS, COIRE, ZURICH, BERNE, LAUSANNE, GENEVA, LUCERNE, ZURICH, BASLE

BONNEY, THOMAS GEORGE. CHAMONIX, MONT BUET, BEX, COL DE LA CROIX, LES ORMONTS DESSUS, COL DES ANDERETS, LENK, AMMERTENSATTEL, ENGSTLIGENALP, KINDBETTLIHORN PASS, GEMMI

BOYD, A. K. H. (*c*). LUCERNE, SARNEN, BRUNIG PASS, MEIRINGEN, GROSSE SCHEIDEGG, GRINDELWALD

'The remembrance of foreign travel is pleasanter than the travel itself. For in remembrance there are none of the hosts that are dispelled by copious camphor: no wear of the muscles, nor of the lungs and heart: no eyes blinded with the sunshine on the snow; no parched throat and leathery tongue; no old goat's flesh disguised as chamois venison. The little drawbacks are forgot; but the absence of care and labour, the blue sky and the bright sun, glacier and cataract, and the snowy Alps remain.'

BRAHMS, JOHANNES. BASLE, ZURICH, WINTERTHUR

Brahms gave his first solo recital in Basle. Altogether, 'Switzerland was the guardian angel of his music, covering him with her shield and defending him with her spear when he was attacked'.

BUNSEN, FRANCES, BARONESS. BASLE, VEVEY, BLONAY

BUXTON, EDWARD NORTH. CHAMONIX, AIGUILLE DE BIONNASSAY

CIVIALE, AIMÉ. HINTERRHEIN, KIRCHALPHORN, ST. MORITZ, PONTRESINA, BERNINA PASS, TIRANO, BORMIO, UMBRAIL PASS, STA. MARIA, OFEN PASS, ZERNEZ, SÜS

FRESHFIELD, DOUGLAS. SONDRIO, CHIAREGGIO, PASSO DI MELLO, MASINO, PASSO DI BONDO, CHIAVENNA

GEORGE, H. B. GRINDELWALD, WETTERHORN, KLEINE SCHEIDEGG, JUNGFRAU, MÖNCHJOCH, GRINDELWALD, LAUTERAARJOCH PASS, GRIMSEL PASS, OBERGESTELEN, VIESCH, EGGISHORN, BELALP, BRIG, LEUK, GEMMI PASS, KANDERSTEG, TSCHINGEL PASS, LAUTERBRUNNEN

'An English lady may not unfrequently be seen trudging up to the Bell Alp, or up the long hot valley which leads to the Grimsel. She arrives thoroughly tired, and no wonder: she finds herself unfit to join in the excursions of her companions for two or three days. . . . These pleasures are lost to her by disregarding the golden rule for ladies travelling in the Alps—never walk when you can ride.'

GIRDLESTONE, A. G. VERNAYAZ, TÊTE NOIRE PASS, MONT BUET, CHAMONIX, COL DU GÉANT, COURMAYEUR, AOSTA, CHATILLON, BREUIL,

ST. THEODUL PASS, ZERMATT, MONTE ROSA, VISP, VIESCH, EGGISHORN, OBERGESTELEN, GRIMSEL PASS, MEIRINGEN, ENGSTLENALP, JOCH PASS, ENGELBERG, SURENEN PASS, ALTDORF, AMSTEG, MADERANERTAL, BRUNNI PASS, DISENTIS, PONTRESINA, FUORCLA SELLA, SONDRIO

GUILLAUME, DR. NEUCHÂTEL, GRANDSON, YVERDON, ESTAVAYER, PAYERNE, AVENCHES, MORAT, NEUCHÂTEL

GÜSSFELDT, PAUL. PONTRESINA, PIZ LANGUARD, PIZ ZUPO, ZERMATT, ST. THEODUL PASS, BREUIL

HALL, NEWMAN. ZERMATT

'I first met Professor Tyndall coming down from Zermatt carrying his ice-axe and a big coil of rope. He was looking sad. He had been spending several days searching for the bodies of those mountaineers who had just perished by the breaking of their rope, when near the summit of the Matterhorn. He told me that the mother of Lord Douglas had a morbid idea that her son was still alive on the rocks. He knew this to be impossible, but to calm her mind he had gone to Geneva and purchased 3,000 feet of rope, by which to be suspended so that he could with his eye sweep the precipice.'

HESSE, PRINCESS ALICE, GRAND DUCHESS OF. BASLE, LUCERNE, RIGI, BUOCHS, ENGELBERG, JOCH PASS, MEIRINGEN, BRIENZ

HORT, F. J. A. LUCERNE, PILATUS, ENGSTLENALP, EGGISHORN, VISP, ZERMATT

JEVONS, W. STANLEY. BASLE, LUCERNE, RIGI, ALPNACH, BRUNIG PASS, BRIENZ, INTERLAKEN, GRINDELWALD, KLEINE SCHEIDEGG, LAUTERBRUNNEN, MÜRREN, INTERLAKEN, THUN, BERNE, FRIBOURG, LAUSANNE

LANÇON, XAVIER. GENEVA, FRIBOURG, BERNE, THUN, INTERLAKEN, LAUTERBRUNNEN, INTERLAKEN, MEIRINGEN, BRUNIG PASS, STANS, BRUNNEN, FLUELEN, ALTDORF, LUCERNE, AARBURG, NEUCHÂTEL, LAUSANNE, ST. CERGUE, GENEVA

In conversation with a native of Sion, Lançon asked whether all was well in his canton:—'Oh oui! répondit-il, surtout depuis l'évènement providentiel . . . je veux dire la catastrophe épouvantable qui est arrivée dans la vallée de Zermatt. Vous savez que quatre Anglais, dont un Lord, ont fait un saut de 4000 pieds en descendant du Matterhorn.' —'Eh bien?'—'Eh bien! Toute l'Angleterre qui voyage voulut visiter le lieu funeste. Nos hotels ne suffisent pas.'

LIDDELL, A. G. C. VEVEY, CHAMONIX, GENEVA

LYELL, SIR CHARLES. SION, EVOLENA, VISP, STALDEN, VIESCH, EGGISHORN

'... Our Alpine tour answered very well. The weather upon the whole favourable and I accomplished the only two geological points I was bent on clearing up.' These were the composition of the earth-pyramids of Useigne and Stalden, and the aptness of the Marjelensee to explain the 'parallel roads of Glenroy'.

MACGREGOR, JOHN. CONSTANCE, SCHAFFHAUSEN, ZURICH, ZUG, LUCERNE, BREMGARTEN, COBLENZ, LAUFENBURG, RHEINFELDEN, BASLE

'A thousand miles in the Rob Roy canoe on twenty rivers and lakes in Europe.'

MAGEE, WILLIAM CONNOR. LUCERNE, BRUNIG PASS, BRIENZ, INTERLAKEN, GRINDELWALD, THUN, BERNE, VEVEY, ST. GINGOLPH, GENEVA

McCORMICK, JOSEPH. GRINDELWALD, INTERLAKEN, THUN, BERNE, LAUSANNE, MARTIGNY, CHAMONIX, MARTIGNY, GRINDELWALD, VISP, ZERMATT

A friend of Hudson, McCormick was one of the party that went out and found his body. No sooner had that been done than the body was found of another friend, Mr. Wilson, who had fallen off the Riffelhorn. Altogether, six violent deaths occurred during his stay at Zermatt which he was thankful to bring to a close.

MICHELET, JULES. ST. GERVAIS, CHAMONIX

'Entre les belles choses de ce monde deux sont accomplies, sans pair. Au lac de Genève, le *beau*, la noble et grande harmonie. Le *sublime* au lac de Lucerne.'

MOORE, A. W. STACHELBERG, TÖDI, DISENTIS, LUKMANIER PASS, CAMADRA PASS, OLIVONE, RHEINWALDHORN, VAL MALVAGLIA, ZAPPORT PASS, HINTERRHEIN, AVERS CRESTA, FORCELLINA PASS, LUNGHIN PASS, MALOJA, PONTRESINA, PIZ ROSEG, MALOJA PASS, CHIAVENNA, MILAN, ALAGNA, SESIAJOCH PASS, ZERMATT, COL D'HÉRENS, COL DE BERTOL, AROLLA, PIGNE D'AROLLA, COL DE SERPENTINE, CHANRION, COL DE FENÊTRE DE BALME, AOSTA, COURMAYEUR, MONT BLANC, CHAMONIX, MARTIGNY, SION, SIERRE, KIPPEL, BEICHFLUH, BELALP, MÖNCHJOCH PASS, GRINDELWALD

These were the first ascents of Piz Roseg, the Obergabelhorn, and of Mont Blanc from the Brenva, and the first crossings of the Camadra, Zapport, and Bertol passes.

NORTH, MARIANNE. LUCERNE, BRUNNEN, SCHWYZ, MUOTTA, PRAGEL PASS, VORAUEN, GLARUS, LINTHAL, WALLENSTADT, SARGANS, FELDKIRCH

ROSSETTI, CHRISTINA. BASLE, LUCERNE, FLUELEN, ALTDORF, ANDERMATT, ST. GOTTHARD PASS, BELLINZONA, LUGANO, COMO, CHIAVENNA, SPLÜGEN PASS, THUSIS, COIRE, WINTERTHUR, SCHAFFHAUSEN

'The mountains in their overwhelming might
Moved me to sadness when I saw them first,
And afterwards they moved me to delight;
Struck harmonies from silent chords which burst
Out into song, a song by memory nursed;
For ever unrenewed by touch or sight
Sleeps the keen magic of each day or night,
In pleasure and in wonder then immersed.
All Switzerland behind us on the ascent,
All Italy before us, we plunged down
St. Gothard, garden of forget-me-not:
Yet why should such a flower choose such a spot?
Could we forget that way which once we went
Though not one flower had bloomed to weave its crown.'

RUMBOLD, SIR HORACE. BERNE, LAUSANNE, GENEVA, CHAMONIX, TÊTE NOIRE PASS, MARTIGNY, OUCHY, LAUSANNE, BERNE

As British Minister at Berne, Rumbold superintended the erection of a cross on the spot where Mrs. Arbuthnot, on her honeymoon, had been struck by lightning at the foot of the Schilthorn above Mürren.

SPURGEON, CHARLES HADDON. BRIG, BELALP, EGGISHORN, OBERGESTELEN, GRIMSEL PASS, MEIRINGEN, GRINDELWALD, KLEINE SCHEIDEGG, LAUTERBRUNNEN

'The day in which I saw most of Creation's Grandeur was spent upon the Wengern Alp. My heart was near her God.'

TUCKETT, FRANCIS FOX. TIRANO, BERNINA PASS, PONTRESINA, PASSO DI VERONA, PASSO DI CAMPOLUGNO, CHIAREGGIO, PASSO DI MELLO, MASINO, PASSO DI BONDO, CHIAVENNA, SPLÜGEN PASS, THUSIS, REICHENAU, TRUNS, PIZ URLAUN, SANDALP PASS, STACHELBERG, GLARUS, ZURICH

TUCKETT, LUCY. PORLEZZA, LUGANO, BELLINZONA, AIROLO, ST. GOTTHARD PASS, ALTDORF, LUCERNE, ENGELBERG, BASLE

TYNDALL, JOHN. GLARUS, LINTHAL, KLAUSEN PASS, ALTDORF, WASSEN, SUSTEN PASS, MEIRINGEN, LAUTERBRUNNEN, MÜRREN, KANDERSTEG, GEMMI PASS, LEUK, VISP, ZERMATT, GENEVA

While crossing the Susten pass, Tyndall was asked by a guide if he knew Professor Tyndall, for 'he had been killed upon the Matterhorn'. When he had learned of the disaster to Whymper's party, Tyndall borrowed 3,000 feet of rope to be let down from the Matterhorn to scour the track along which the victims had fallen, in the hope of finding the body of Lord Francis Douglas. But as G. F. Browne relates 'the Syndic of Zermatt fortunately found out what was going on, and sent him and his ropes away; they had had plenty of Englishmen killed there; they did not want any more'.

WATSON, PHILIPPA H. MEIRINGEN

'While we were on the way to Meyringen a sad accident occurred on the Matterhorn, July 14th, when Mr. Whymper's companions—Mr. Hudson, a young Hadow and Lord Francis Douglas were killed. We were greatly shocked and impressed, for Mr. Hudson had been at our hotel, and had asked me to play the harmonium at the Sunday services only a few days previously.'

WEILENMANN, JOHANN JAKOB. ST. GALL, GALTÜR, PIZ BUIN, LAVIN, ZERNEZ, PONTRESINA, CRASTAGÜZZA, TRAFOI, MARTINSBRUCK, FIMBER PASS, ISCHGL, COIRE, MARTIGNY, CHABLE, CHERMONTANE, RUINETTE, FIONNAY, COL DE SEVREU, ROSABLANCHE, LIAPPEY, COL DE RIEDMATTEN, AROLLA, EVOLENA, COL DE LA MEINA, LIAPPEY, MONT BLANC DE SEILON, COL DE RIEDMATTEN, AROLLA, EVOLENA

WHYMPER, EDWARD. LAUTERBRUNNEN, TSCHINGEL PASS, PETERSGRAT, KIPPEL, TURTMANN, ZMEIDEN PASS, FORCLETTA PASS, ZINAL, GRAND CORNIER, DENT BLANCHE, AROLLA, COL D'HÉRENS, ZERMATT, ST. THEODUL PASS, BREUIL, CHATILLON, AOSTA, COURMAYEUR, CHAMONIX, AIGUILLE VERTE, COL DE TALÈFRE, AOSTA, COL DE FENÊTRE DE BALME, CHERMONTANE, RUINETTE, COL D'OREN, PRARAYÉ, COL DE VALCOURNERA, BREUIL, ST. THEODUL PASS, ZERMATT, MATTERHORN

At Zermatt, the Matterhorn catastrophe.

1866

ARNOLD, HOWARD PAYSON. LUCERNE, FLUELEN, ANDERMATT, FURKA PASS, GLETSCH, ROSENLAUI, GRINDELWALD, INTERLAKEN, ZERMATT, MARTIGNY, COL DE BALME, CHAMONIX, MONT BLANC

BACHELIN, A. NEUCHÂTEL, NOIRAIGUE, CREUX DU VAN

An excursion by schoolgirls, the boys' excursion having been cancelled owing to the Austro-Prussian war.

BRADBURY, JOHN. BASLE, SCHAFFHAUSEN, ZURICH, RAGAZ, COIRE, THUSIS, SPLÜGEN PASS, CHIAVENNA—MAGADINO, BELLINZONA, ST. GOTTHARD PASS, FLUELEN, LUCERNE, BERNE, NEUCHÂTEL, LES VERRIÈRES

BRAHMS, JOHANNES. WINTERTHUR, ZURICH, FLUNTERN, BERNE, THUN, INTERLAKEN, GRINDELWALD, LAUTERBRUNNEN, MÜRREN, LUCERNE,

SEELISBERG, ZUG, ZURICH, SCHAFFHAUSEN, WINTERTHUR, ZURICH, AARAU, BASLE

At a house in Fluntern above Zurich, with a wide and magnificent view over the lake, the mountains and the glaciers, Brahms composed his *Requiem*. His journey through the northern towns was a concert tour with Joachim.

BROOKS, PHILLIPS. BASLE, GENEVA, CHAMONIX, MACUGNAGA, DOMODOSSOLA, SIMPLON PASS, BRIG, LEUK, GEMMI PASS, KANDERSTEG, THUN, INTERLAKEN, LAUTERBRUNNEN, KLEINE SCHEIDEGG, GRINDELWALD, GROSSE SCHEIDEGG, MEIRINGEN, GIESSBACH, BRUNIG PASS, LUCERNE, RIGI, ALTDORF, ANDERMATT, ST. GOTTHARD PASS, BELLINZONA, LOCARNO, ARONA, LUGANO, COMO, CHIAVENNA, MALOJA PASS, ST. MORITZ, PONTRESINA, SILVAPLANA, JULIER PASS, TIEFENKASTEL, THUSIS, ANDEER, COIRE, ZURICH, CONSTANCE

'It has all been splendid. The beauty of Switzerland is, that it has no dull places, and one is never tired, only sometimes bewildered a little with its endless attractions.'

BROWNE, G. F. GENEVA, NYON, ARZIER, ST. GEORGES, BIÈRE

An excursion in January to see some of the ice-caves, which contained less ice than in July. This may have been due to the removal of ice for the restaurants of Geneva and Lausanne.

CIVIALE, AIMÉ. ST. LUC, BELLA TOLA, MARTIGNY, MAUVOISIN, COL DE FENÊTRE DE BALME, AOSTA

'Saint-Luc est un petit village d'aspect misérable, construit sur une pente très forte, dans lequel on trouve une grande maison très hospitalière, l'hotel de la Bella Tola, offrant une bonne installation; l'hotelier est très prévenant et d'un rare désintéressement. J'ai rencontré dans cet hotel deux Anglais très aimables; ils etaient sourds et muets.'

DARLEY, FELIX O. C. GENEVA, CHAMONIX, TÊTE NOIRE PASS, VERNAYAZ, VEVEY, MARTIGNY, SION, VISP, ZERMATT, VISP, BRIG, GLETSCH, GRIMSEL PASS, MEIRINGEN, RAGAZ, COIRE

FRESHFIELD, DOUGLAS. PONTRESINA, ALBULA PASS, BERGÜN, TINZENHORN, MÜHLEN, JULIER PASS, ST. MORITZ, MALOJA, ZUOZ, SONDRIO, MASINO, LANDQUART, KLOSTERS, VERSTANKLA PASS, ARDETZ, TARASP, ZERNEZ, PASSO DEL DIAVEL, LIVIGNO, VAL VIOLA, BORMIO

'If St. Moritz is, as Mr. Stephen thinks, the limbo of Switzerland set apart for the world—that is, for kings, millionaires and people who travel with couriers—Tarasp is its purgatory, providentially created for the class whom the flesh has rendered unfit for such Alpine paradises as Grindelwald, or even Pontresina.'

GIRDLESTONE, A. G. LAUSANNE, BEX, COL DE PILLON, GSTEIG, KRINNEN PASS, LAUENEN, TRÜTTLISBERG PASS, LENK, HAHNENMOOS PASS, ADELBODEN, BONDERKRINDEN PASS, KANDERSTEG, LÖTSCHEN PASS, KIPPEL, LÖTSCHENLÜCKE PASS, EGGISHORN, BELALP, BRIG, SIMPLON PASS, DOMODOSSOLA

Girdlestone and his companion had lost their way: 'I was becoming very anxious on his account, for the cold which invigorated me was clearly doing him harm; so I asked him to join me in silent prayer for guidance, and within five minutes afterwards we took a direction which proved to be the right one.'

HARRISON, FREDERIC. PONTRESINA, BELLAVISTA PASS, PIZ PALÜ, SELLA PASS, PONTRESINA

MEYER, CONRAD FERDINAND. ZURICH, RAPPERSWIL, UZNACH, COIRE, LENZERHEIDE, TIEFENKASTEL, MÜHLEN, JULIER PASS, SILVAPLANA, MALOJA PASS, SOGLIO, SILVAPLANA, SAMADEN, ZUOZ, ZERNEZ, TARASP, PONTRESINA, BERNINA PASS, LE PRESE, TIRANO, BORMIO, SONDRIO, BELLAGIO, MENAGGIO, PORLEZZA, LUGANO, BELLINZONA, MESOCCO, SAN BERNARDINO PASS, THUSIS, COIRE, ZURICH

MOORE, A. W. INTERLAKEN, GRINDELWALD, FINSTERAARJOCH PASS, STRAHLECK PASS, GRINDELWALD, FAULHORN

The first tour in the high Alps in winter (December).

PEABODY, ANDREW P. BASLE, LUCERNE, RIGI, FLUELEN, ALTDORF, ST. GOTTHARD PASS, HOSPENTHAL, FURKA PASS, GRIMSEL PASS, MEIRINGEN, GIESSBACH, INTERLAKEN, LAUTERBRUNNEN, KLEINE SCHEIDEGG, GRINDELWALD, INTERLAKEN, THUN, BERNE, LAUSANNE, GENEVA, LAUSANNE, MARTIGNY, SAXON, MARTIGNY, CHAMONIX, MARTIGNY, SION, BRIG, SIMPLON PASS, DOMODOSSOLA, LUINO, LUGANO, BELLAGIO

'I crossed the Wengern Alp, which, on its ascent and from its summit, brought me face to face with the Jungfrau. It was, indeed, a most solemn interview. . . . In its vastness, and its intense whiteness and brilliancy, it made me think continually of the "great white throne" in the Apocalypse.'

PRESTON-THOMAS, HERBERT. PONTRESINA, BERNINA PASS, VAL VIOLA PASS, CORNO DI DOSDÉ, CORNO DI CAMPO, CORNO DI LAGO, SPALMO

'I cannot help regretting the cosy little room at the "Krone", where Liszt's most brilliant pupil used to discourse to us the loveliest music as we sat in the twilight, letting the strains of the Moonlight Sonata fall softly on our ears while we watched the swaying pines and the white torrent, and the huge glacier flashing like silver armour on the breast of the giant opposite.'

RUSKIN, JOHN. LES VERRIÈRES, NEUCHÂTEL, BERNE, THUN, INTERLAKEN, GIESSBACH, LAUTERBRUNNEN, MEIRINGEN, LUCERNE, BADEN, SCHAFFHAUSEN, BADEN, BRUNNEN, LUCERNE, BERNE, VEVEY, GENEVA

Interlaken was 'all dust, misery and Casino, . . . the hills more and more divine'. Ruskin was travelling with Sir Walter and Lady Trevelyan; Lady Trevelyan died at Neuchâtel on this journey.

STEPHEN, LESLIE. KANDERSTEG, BALMHORN, TSCHINGEL PASS, LAUTERBRUNNEN, GRINDELWALD, MÖNCH, BRIG, VISP, ZERMATT, WEISSTHOR PASS, MACUGNAGA, SAAS, FLETSCHHORN, ZERMATT

'I went to Zermatt—the trysting-place—alone. I heard of their approach and walked down the valley to meet them. One of my sacred places ever afterwards was a point where the road winds round a little bluff near Täsch. Thence I descried the party arriving on mules. . . .' One of the 'party' was Thackeray's daughter, and in the following year she became Stephen's wife. Among Stephen's other companions was Oliver Wendell Holmes junr., with whom he climbed the Balmhorn and the Mönch.

SYMONDS, JOHN ADDINGTON. MACUGNAGA, IVREA, AOSTA, COURMAYEUR, AOSTA, GRAND ST. BERNARD PASS, MARTIGNY, LAUSANNE, BERNE, THUN, INTERLAKEN, LAUTERBRUNNEN, MÜRREN, BERNE, NEUCHÂTEL

'. . . I would not take Rome, Florence, and Naples in exchange for the chalets of Mürren.'

THIOLY, F. GENEVA, BOUVERET, MARTIGNY, SION, SIERRE, ZINAL, TRIFTJOCH PASS, ZERMATT

TUCKETT, FRANCIS FOX. BORMIO, TIRANO, SONDRIO, CHIESA, CRASTAGÜZZA SATTEL, PIZ BERNINA, PONTRESINA, JULIER PASS, TIEFENKASTEL, COIRE, ZURICH

It was Tuckett's habit to entertain the inhabitants of mountain villages with exhibitions of conjuring. 'As soon as the table was cleared a little entertainment was improvised for our worthy hosts and their family, in the shape of sundry simple conjuring tricks, winding up with a display of "drawing-room lightning", and magnesium wire, a small store of which portable articles can highly be recommended to mountaineers, as an unfailing means of making themselves agreeable to the simple Alpine folk.'

TYNDALL, JOHN. ENGSTLENALP, JOCH PASS, TITLIS, MEIRINGEN, GROSSE SCHEIDEGG, GRINDELWALD, FAULHORN, LAUTERBRUNNEN, TSCHINGEL PASS, PETERSGRAT, BLATTEN, LÖTSCHENLÜCKE PASS, EGGISHORN, BELALP, BRIG, SIMPLON PASS, DOMODOSSOLA, LUGANO, PORLEZZA, MENAGGIO, COMO, MILAN, MACUGNAGA, MONTE MORO PASS, SAAS, VISP, BRIG, BELALP

WAGNER, RICHARD. GENEVA, LUCERNE, TRIBSCHEN

Once again Wagner was a fugitive. At Geneva he took a house called 'Les Artichauts' where he again took up his scores of *Siegfried* and the *Mastersingers*. Minna had died, and, with Liszt's daughter, Cosima von Bülow, Wagner went to live at Tribschen where they were to live for six years.

WEILENMANN, JOHANN JAKOB. MARTIGNY, CHABLE, MAUVOISIN, CHERMONTANE, COL DE CRÊTE SÈCHE, COL DE LA CIARDONNET, BEC D'EPICOUN, CHANRION, POINTE D'OTEMMA

WHYMPER, EDWARD. ZERMATT, COL DE VALPELLINE, PRARAYÉ, ZERMATT

1867

AMIEL, HENRI-FRÉDÉRIC. GENEVA, SOLEURE, WEISSENSTEIN

'Vue merveilleuse, aveuglante de beauté! Au-dessus d'une mer de lait, inondée de lumière matinale, et dont les vagues houleuses viennent battre au pied des escarpements boisés du Weissenstein, plane à des hauteurs sublimes la ronde infinie des Alpes. Le côté oriental de l'horizon est noyé dans les splendeurs des brumes remontantes, mais à partir du Tödi toute la chaine flotte, pure et claire, entre la plaine neigeuse et le ciel d'un bleu pâle. L'assemblée des géants tient son concile au-dessus des vallées et des lacs que submergent les vapeurs.'

BAKUNIN, MICHAEL. GENEVA, VEVEY, CLARENS

At the Congress at Geneva of the League of Peace and Freedom, Bakunin was embraced by Garibaldi. Then Bakunin went to live with Zhukovsky at Clarens and became a neighbour of Princess Obolensky and Mroczkowski.

BATTERSEA, CONSTANCE. LUCERNE, RIGI

BELLOWS, HENRY W. LANDECK, RESCHEN-SCHEIDECK, MALS, TRAFOI, STELVIO PASS, BORMIO, TIRANO, BERNINA PASS, PONTRESINA, ST. MORITZ, JULIER PASS, TIEFENKASTEL, PARPAN PASS, COIRE, RAGAZ, PFÄFERS, WALLENSTADT, ZURICH, LUCERNE, FLUELEN, ALTDORF, WEGGIS, RIGI, LUCERNE, BRUNIG PASS, MEIRINGEN, INTERLAKEN, LAUTERBRUNNEN, KLEINE SCHEIDEGG, GRINDELWALD, INTERLAKEN, THUN, BERNE, FRIBOURG, VEVEY, GENEVA, CHAMONIX, COL DE BALME, MARTIGNY, SION, VISP, ZERMATT, VISP, SION, MARTIGNY, LAUSANNE, GENEVA, BASLE

'As the sun suddenly shot his first rays from the upper limb, the range of the Jungfrau melted into a delicate yellow, and deepening in tone, soon glowed with golden hues. The lower ranges caught up the theme, and soon a chorus of praise, all in tones of light, resounded from the mountain-tops, inaudibly singing Milton's sublime hymn, "Hail, holy light! offspring of heaven, first-born of the eternal", &c. as the sun *swiftly* rose, for he comes rejoicing like a strong man to run a race.'

BONNEY, THOMAS GEORGE. COIRE, FILISUR, ALBULA PASS, PONTRESINA, ST. MORITZ, BERNINA PASS, VAL VIOLA PASS, BORMIO, STELVIO PASS

BROWNING, OSCAR. PONTRESINA

'The only manner by which I could obtain sufficient nourishment was by attending two tables d'hôte, one after the other.'

DOSTOYEVSKY, FEODOR. BASLE, GENEVA

Anna Dostoyevsky wrote:—'To-day I saw, for the first time, mountains wrapped in a cloud, the clouds literally clinging to them. It is a curious sight, for the summits of the mountains are clear, and only their sides all cloudy. For the first time, too, I caught sight of the Swiss mountains, and real Swiss houses, little tiny affairs, quite unlike anything else.'
While in Geneva, Dostoyevsky wrote *The Idiot.*

FORNEY, JOHN W. BERNE, LUCERNE, ZURICH, BERNE, THUN, INTERLAKEN, GIESSBACH, BERNE, LAUSANNE, VEVEY, CHILLON, GENEVA

GARIBALDI, GIUSEPPE. DOMODOSSOLA, SIMPLON PASS, BRIG, SION, MARTIGNY, VILLENEUVE, LAUSANNE, GENEVA

'I not only admire mountains, but I love them as the welcome sentinels which the eye of the sailor often looks upon for whole days with passionate affection, and the sight of which fills his heart with joy.'

GIRDLESTONE, A. G. LAUSANNE, MARTIGNY, SION, LEUK, GEMMI PASS, KANDERSTEG, TSCHINGEL PASS, LAUTERBRUNNEN, GRINDELWALD, WETTERHORN, GRIMSEL PASS, EGGISHORN, HOSPENTHAL, ST. GOTTHARD PASS, BELLINZONA, SAN JORIO PASS, GRAVEDONA, CHIAVENNA, MALOJA PASS, PONTRESINA, ZERNEZ, SARSURA PASS, DAVOS, STRELA PASS, COIRE, GLARUS, LINTHAL, CLARIDEN PASS, MADERANERTAL, AMSTEG, WASSEN, SUSTEN PASS, STEINLIMMI PASS, GRIMSEL PASS, STRAHLEGG PASS, GRINDELWALD

GUILD, CURTIS. BASLE, ZURICH, RAPPERSWIL, ZUG, RIGI, KÜSSNACHT, LUCERNE, FLUELEN, ALTDORF, ANDERMATT, HOSPENTHAL, FLUELEN, LUCERNE, SARNEN, BRUNIG PASS, BRIENZ, INTERLAKEN, LAUTERBRUNNEN, KLEINE SCHEIDEGG, GRINDELWALD, INTERLAKEN, THUN, BERNE, FRIBOURG, LAUSANNE, VEVEY, VILLENEUVE, GENEVA, CHAMONIX,

TÊTE NOIRE PASS, MARTIGNY, SION, BRIG, SIMPLON PASS, DOMODOSSOLA, MILAN, CHIAVENNA, SPLÜGEN PASS, ANDEER, THUSIS, COIRE, PFÄFERS, SARGANS, SCHAFFHAUSEN

On the lake of Zurich 'we found our steamer was a mail-boat, and at the station, instead of the usual official in waiting, the sole occupant of the little pier was a huge Newfoundland dog who seized the little mail-pouch, holding perhaps a couple of quarts, that was tossed ashore, and galloped off with it at full speed for the village, half a mile distant, to the infinite amusement of the spectators. He was the regular mail-carrier, performing the service twice a day of bringing down the mail-pouch, which he deposited on the pier on the arrival of the boat, and carrying back the one which was left by it.'

HAESELER, CHARLES H. ZURICH, HORGEN, ZUG, RIGI, LUCERNE, FLUELEN, ALTDORF, ANDERMATT, ST. GOTTHARD, HOSPENTHAL, FLUELEN, LUCERNE, BERNE, THUN, INTERLAKEN, GRINDELWALD, INTERLAKEN, GIESSBACH, THUN, BERNE, LAUSANNE, GENEVA, CHAMONIX, TÊTE NOIRE PASS, MARTIGNY, VILLENEUVE, GENEVA, NEUCHÂTEL, ZURICH, SCHAFFHAUSEN

HARDWICK, CHARLES. COMO, LUGANO, BELLINZONA, ST. GOTTHARD PASS, ALTDORF, LUCERNE, RIGI, BASLE

HESSE, PRINCESS ALICE, GRAND DUCHESS OF. ZURICH, WALLENSTADT, COIRE, TIEFENKASTEL, JULIER PASS, ST. MORITZ, PONTRESINA, PIZ LANGUARD, HEUTAL, FIENO PASS, LIVIGNO, STRETTA PASS, BORMIO, STELVIO PASS, STA. MARIA, OFEN PASS, ZERNEZ, ST. MORITZ, COIRE

'The view over the valley and lakes of the Engadine, is beyond description beautiful.' Among the guests at St. Moritz were the Duchesse d'Aumale, the Parises, the Nemours, and Count and Countess Gleichen.

HORT, F. J. A. ANDERMATT, FURKA PASS, GLETSCH

At Gletsch Hort busied himself with his section on the Gnostics and the Greek Fathers for the Dictionary of Christian Antiquities.

HUNTER, SIR WILLIAM WILSON. NEUCHÂTEL, GENEVA, MARTIGNY, SION, BRIG, SIMPLON PASS, DOMODOSSOLA

HUTTON, R. H. BASLE, SCHAFFHAUSEN, RORSCHACH, ARLBERG, NAUDERS, MARTINSBRUCK, SCHULS, ZERNEZ, PONTRESINA, ALBULA PASS, FILISUR, DAVOS, KLOSTERS, LANDQUART, COIRE, WALLENSTADT, RAPPERSWIL, HORGEN, ZUG, RIGI, LUCERNE, BRUNIG PASS, MEIRINGEN, GROSSE SCHEIDEGG, GRINDELWALD, INTERLAKEN, THUN, BERNE

'. . . Anything more like the ideal "Happy Valley" I never saw. . . . We were rather roughly received, though. The people at the inn seemed to dislike us as foreigners, and the good old Swiss clergyman dragged us into his sermon rather pointedly on the Sunday, when impressing brotherly feeling on his people. . . . Davos is a primitive watering-place, frequented almost solely by Swiss.'

MEYER, CONRAD FERDINAND. SILVAPLANA, PONTRESINA, THUSIS, ZURICH

Meyer was going over the ground of the exploits of Jürg Jenatsch for the historical novel that he was about to write.

MICHELET, JULES. GENEVA, BEX, ZURICH, COIRE, TIEFENKASTEL, JULIER PASS, ST. MORITZ, PONTRESINA, MALOJA PASS, CHIAVENNA, SPLÜGEN PASS, THUSIS, COIRE

'Entre tous les chemins, je préfère les grandes voies historiques où l'humanité a passé.'

RAMBERT, EUGÈNE. BEX, LES PLANS

RUMBOLD, SIR HORACE. BERNE, THUN, INTERLAKEN, GIESSBACH, GRINDELWALD, THUN, BERNE, LUCERNE, FLUELEN, HOSPENTHAL, ST. GOTTHARD PASS, BELLINZONA, LUGANO, BELLINZONA, MESOCCO, SAN BERNARDINO PASS, THUSIS, COIRE, ZURICH, BERNE

'The aspect of all the country round Berne in its fullest winter garb was strikingly beautiful. This induced us to plan a sort of Arctic journey into the heart of the Oberland, which had never, so far as I know, been attempted before. The inns at Interlaken and the other places we wished to see being closed at this time of year, we had to give previous notice of our intended visit. . . . I believe that our small party may claim to have been the first explorers of these higher regions at such an unusual time of year.'

RUSSELL-KILLOUGH, COUNT HENRY. GENEVA, CHAMONIX, MONT BLANC, ZERMATT, BREITHORN, ADLER PASS, SAAS

SHALER, NATHANIEL. MONTREUX, CHAMONIX, LE LOCLE, GRINDELWALD, BRIG, VISP, ZERMATT

'Exhilarated by the pure air, for a while the body was indifferent to time and space and the feet carelessly trod the way to the great and mystic Matterhorn. But the east gradually brightened and the sun sent its hot rays down through the thick branches across the road that till then had been dark and cool. And at last, as the day progressed, the usual feud between body and soul, which for a time had been suspended, set in, and hunger and fatigue became the imperious facts in all nature.' Then the American geologist would exclaim 'Oh! I would swap the Alps for a gallon of buttermilk and a pone of Margaret's cron bread.'

STEPHEN, LESLIE. GRINDELWALD, MARTIGNY, SION, SIERRE, ZINAL, VISP, ZERMATT, BRIG, SIMPLON PASS, DOMODOSSOLA, CHIAVENNA, MALOJA PASS, COIRE

'I was married on June 19, and to avoid all folly of breakfasts, &c., we got it done at 8 a.m. . . . We went to Switzerland and visited my dear old mountains. . . .'

SYMONDS, JOHN ADDINGTON. GLION

'We spent a very happy month.' 'W. J. Courthope joined us . . . I cannot remember when we had more fun and amusement together.'

TOUSEY, SINCLAIR. GENEVA, CHAMONIX, TÊTE NOIRE PASS, MARTIGNY, LAUSANNE, BERNE, THUN, INTERLAKEN, LAUTERBRUNNEN, KLEINE SCHEIDEGG, GRINDELWALD, INTERLAKEN, THUN, BERNE, BASLE

'Of course I had, like hosts of other victims at Interlaken, to "do" the Wengern Alp.'

TUCKETT, FRANCIS FOX. STELVIO PASS, BORMIO, TIRANO, SONDRIO, CHIESA, MONTE DELLA DISGRAZIA, MASINO, VARENNA, MENAGGIO, LUGANO, LUINO, BAVENO, OMEGNA, PONTE GRANDE, MACUGNAGA, MONTE MORO PASS, SCHWARZBERG-WEISSTHOR PASS, ZERMATT, MONTE ROSA, VISP, MARTIGNY, LAUSANNE, GENEVA

'To Ponte Grande in the Val Anzasca, which we reached about 11 p.m., after a somewhat difficult but amusing descent through the chestnut woods, where, finding fireflies a rather inefficient mode of illumination, we had at length to light two of my candles (for chalet use) and march in solemn procession like evildoers performing nocturnal penance.'

TYNDALL, JOHN. GRINDELWALD, KLEINE SCHEIDEGG, EIGER, LAUTERBRUNNEN, TSCHINGEL PASS, PETERSGRAT, BLATTEN, BEICH PASS, BELALP, BRIG, VISP, ZERMATT, TRIFTJOCH PASS, ZINAL, COL DE SOREBOIS, COL DE TORRENT, EVOLENA, SION, VISP, ZERMATT

'It is not in the night nor in the day—it is not in any statical condition of the atmosphere—that the mountains look most sublime. It is during the few minutes of transition from twilight to full day through the splendours of the dawn.'

VIZARD, JOHN. LUGANO, MAGADINO, BELLINZONA, ST. GOTTHARD PASS, ALTDORF, LUCERNE, BRUNIG PASS, BRIENZ, INTERLAKEN, GRINDELWALD, LAUTERBRUNNEN, MÜRREN, INTERLAKEN, THUN, BERNE, BASLE, ZURICH, OLTEN, GENEVA, CHAMONIX

WALLACE, ALFRED RUSSEL. CHAMPÉRY, MARTIGNY, GRAND ST. BERNARD PASS, AOSTA, BECCA DI NONA, GRAND ST. BERNARD PASS, MARTIGNY, INTERLAKEN, GRINDELWALD, KLEINE SCHEIDEGG, LAUTERBRUNNEN

WEILENMANN, JOHANN JAKOB. ST. GALL, MARTIGNY, CHABLE, MAUVOISIN, TOUR DE BOUSSINE, COL DE SONADON, CHALET D'AMONT, COL DE MAISON BLANCHE, COL DE BOTZERESSE, MAUVOISIN, MONT PLEUREUR, COL DE VASEVAIE, LIAPPEY, SION

WILLIAMS, CHARLES J. B. (*c*). MACUGNAGA, MONTE MORO PASS, MATTMARK, SAAS

'I was thoroughly beaten before I got down to the desolate valley of Saas, where I was glad to go to bed at the first inn I came to, at the Matt-mark See, and required the clothes of three beds to make me warm.'

1868

AVEBURY, LORD. INTERLAKEN, LAUTERBRUNNEN, MÜRREN, KLEINE SCHEIDEGG, GRINDELWALD, LAUTERBRUNNEN, TSCHINGEL PASS, PETERSGRAT, RIED, LÖTSCHEN PASS, KANDERSTEG, THUN, BERNE

It is perhaps not without significance that it was Avebury, who knew the holiday land of Switzerland so well, who brought in the August Bank Holiday Act.

BAKUNIN, MICHAEL. BERNE, VEVEY, GENEVA, NEUCHÂTEL, LE LOCLE

During this journey, Bakunin founded the Alliance Internationale de la Démocratie Socialiste. The break between him and his anarchists on the one hand and Marx's Communists on the other took place at the Congress at Berne.

BONNEY, THOMAS GEORGE. ENGELBERG, SURENEN PASS, ALTDORF, MURG, WIDDERSTENFURKL, GLARUS, PRAGEL PASS, MUOTATAL, KATZENZEGEL PASS, SISIKON, ALTDORF, AMSTEG, MADERANERTAL, PLANURA PASS, THIERFEHD, RICHETLI PASS, ELM, SAUREN PASS, RAGAZ, COIRE, TIEFENKASTEL, JULIER PASS, ST. MORITZ, PONTRESINA

BRANDES, GEORGE. RAGAZ, PFÄFERS, LUCERNE, RIGI, INTERLAKEN, GRINDELWALD

'Switzerland added to my store of impressions with grand natural spectacles. I saw the Alps, and a thunderstorm in the Alps, passed starlit nights on the Swiss lakes, traced the courses of foaming mountain streams such as the Tamina at Pfäfers, ascended the Rigi at a silly forced march, and from the Kulm saw a procession of clouds that gripped my fancy like the procession of the Vanir in Northern Mythology. Many years afterwards I described it in the fourth volume of *Main Currents*.'

BROWN, JOHN. BASLE, GENEVA, VEVEY, CHÂTEL ST. DENIS, GRUYÈRES, SAANEN, ZWEISIMMEN, INTERLAKEN, GRINDELWALD, THUN, BERNE, LAUSANNE, GENEVA

'The rosy light of the sunset on the snowy Alps; it is quite wonderful; when every other mountain is lying in shadow they shine with a delicate rose splendour that is wonderfully lovely, and then when the sun sinks they get at once ghastly white like the dead.'

CONNAUGHT, ARTHUR, DUKE OF. BASLE, LUCERNE, BRUNIG PASS, MEIRINGEN, GAULI PASS, GRIMSEL PASS, OBERAARJOCH, EGGISHORN, BELALP, BRIG, VISP, ZERMATT, VISP, BRIG, SIMPLON PASS, DOMODOSSOLA, COMO, LUGANO, BELLINZONA, ST. GOTTHARD PASS, ALTDORF, LUCERNE

COOLIDGE, W. A. B. GRINDELWALD, WETTERHORN, BLÜMLISALPHORN, KANDERSTEG, GEMMI PASS, BALMHORN, ZAGEN PASS, LEUKERBAD, BRIG, BELALP, ALETSCHHORN, GROSS NESTHORN, MÖNCHJOCH PASS, GRINDELWALD

As a consolation for failure on the Eiger, Coolidge's guide Christian Almer made him a present of his dog Tschingel which became the most distinguished canine mountaineer.

DOSTOYEVSKY, FEODOR. GENEVA, VEVEY, MARTIGNY, SION, BRIG, SIMPLON PASS, DOMODOSSOLA

At Geneva Dostoyevsky's daughter Sonia died, which loss associated Switzerland with doom in his eyes. 'Vous connaissez le panorama du lac; à Vevey il est positivement mieux qu'à Montreux et Chillon qui sont à côté. Mais en dehors de ce panorama (et à vrai dire de quelques endroits, buts de promenade dans les montagnes, ce qu'il n'y avait pas à Genève) tout le reste est trop vilain, et nous avons peur de payer trop cher le panorama seul.'

DOWSING, WILLIAM. GENEVA, VEVEY, MARTIGNY, GRAND ST. BERNARD, MARTIGNY, TÊTE NOIRE PASS, CHAMONIX, GENEVA, LAUSANNE, FRIBOURG, BERNE, THUN, INTERLAKEN, LAUTERBRUNNEN, KLEINE SCHEIDEGG, GRINDELWALD, INTERLAKEN, BRIENZ, BRUNIG PASS, LUCERNE, BASLE

At the Hospice of the Great St. Bernard, Dowsing's attention was drawn to 'a beautiful pianoforte, by Broadwood, the gift of the Prince of Wales. It was alternately played by several ladies, and two gentlemen of our party, accompanied by the singing of hymns and selections of sacred and other music, which added very much to the enjoyment of all present.'

DUFF, MOUNTSTUART E. GRANT. ZURICH, ZUG, LUCERNE, SEMPACH, BERNE, LAUSANNE, GENEVA

ELLIOTT, JULIUS. SAAS, ALPHUBELJOCH PASS, ZERMATT, DOM, WEISSHORN, MATTERHORN

The first ascent of the Matterhorn from the Swiss side since the disaster of 1865.

GAUTIER, THÉOPHILE. GENEVA, CHAMONIX, TÊTE NOIRE PASS, MARTIGNY, BEX, CHAMPÉRY, MARTIGNY, SION, VISP, ZERMATT, VISP, BRIG, OBERGESTELEN, FURKA PASS, HOSPENTHAL

'Parfois le rideau de nuages se déchirait, et par la vaste ouverture, le vieux Mont Blanc apparaissait à son balcon, et comme roi des Alpes, saluait son peuple de montagnes d'une façon affable et majestueuse. Il daignait se laisser voir quelques minutes, puis il refermait le rideau. Ce mélange de nuages et de neige, ce chaos d'argent, ces vagues de lumière se brisant en écume de blancheur, ces phosphorescences diamantées voudraient, pour être exprimées, des mots qui manquent à la langue humaine et que trouverait le rêveur de l'Apocalypse dans l'extase de la vision; jamais plus radieux spectacle ne se déploya à nos yeux surpris, et nous eumes à ce moment la sensation complète du beau, du grand, du sublime. Les montagnes, comme les poètes, ont leur jour d'inspiration, et, ce soir-là, le Mont Blanc était en verve.'

GÜSSFELDT, PAUL. ZERMATT, MATTERHORN, OLD WEISSTHOR PASS, MACUGNAGA, MONTE MORO PASS, SAAS, ZERMATT, COL D'HÉRENS, EVOLENA, SION

HARRISON, FREDERIC. LUCERNE, ALTDORF, ST. GOTTHARD PASS, FAIDO, BELLINZONA, MAGADINO

'I hold, with Rousseau, Byron, and Ruskin, that the highest and deepest charm the Alps can give is found in their combination of glories, as often as not in their lakes, their wooded valleys, their upland pastures—nay, even in their villages and towns—with their long record of memorable things in literature, science, history and art.'

HOPKINS, GERARD MANLEY. GRINDELWALD, MEIRINGEN, GRIMSEL PASS, OBERGESTELEN, BRIG, VISP, ZERMATT, ST. THEODUL PASS, BREITHORN, BREUIL, CHATILLON, AOSTA, GRAND ST. BERNARD PASS, MARTIGNY, VEVEY, GENEVA

'... Not unapparent that the Matterhorn is like a Greek galley stranded, a reared-up rostrum—the sharp quains or arrêtes the gunwales, the deck of the forecastle looking upon Zermatt, the figure-head looking the other way, reaching up in the air, the cutwater and ram descending and abutting on a long reef, the gable-length of the mountain. . . . Up the Riffel, from which, the point of view somewhat changing, the Matterhorn looks like a sea-lion couchant or a sphinx, and again like the hooded-snake frontal worn by the Egyptian Kings.'

HUTTON, R. H. NEUCHÂTEL, BERNE, THUN, ZWEISIMMEN, SAANEN, CHÂTEAU D'OEX, COL DE JAMAN, VEVEY, CHAMPÉRY, COL DE COUX, COL DE GOLEZE, SIXT, COL D'ANTERNE, COL DE BRÉVENT, CHAMONIX

'A few steps downwards—we were still directly under the stately head of Jaman—and the most lovely landscape which either of us had ever beheld, I think, broke upon us: the fresh, still tender blue of the lake of Geneva shining in the morning sun, with soft, little islands of feathery-white mist strewn over its surface, as well as over the bright green alps sloping gently at our feet.'

KELSALL, THOMAS FORBES. BASLE, ZURICH, LUCERNE, GENEVA

Beddoes' literary executor was on a pilgrimage to the poet's haunts, paying homage also to those of Rousseau, Schiller, Shelley, and Byron.

LATROBE, JOHN HOYLEHURST BONEVAL. CHIAVENNA, SPLÜGEN PASS, THUSIS, COIRE, PFÄFERS, ZURICH, ZUG, LUCERNE, RIGI, FLUELEN, ANDERMATT, HOSPENTHAL, FURKA PASS, GRIMSEL PASS, MEIRINGEN, INTERLAKEN, LAUTERBRUNNEN, GRINDELWALD, INTERLAKEN, KANDERSTEG, GEMMI PASS, LEUK, SION, MARTIGNY, TÊTE NOIRE PASS, CHAMONIX, GENEVA, BERNE, BASLE

'The hotel of the Furca was taken possession of by the Queen of England and her suite not long after the writer's visit in 1868, and the common wayfarers were referred to a very modest shanty—it would be called in America—across the road.'

LOCKYER, SIR NORMAN. INTERLAKEN

LOWDER, CHARLES. LUCERNE, SEELISBERG, COIRE, THUSIS, SPLÜGEN PASS, CHIAVENNA, BELLAGIO, ST. MORITZ, PONTRESINA, BORMIO, STELVIO PASS.

PONSONBY, HENRY. LUCERNE, ENGELBERG, FLUELEN

'We went up to the other end of the lake and visited Tell's Chapel and then back only just in time for dinner. . . . Discourse at dinner about William Tell. "I'm sure", says the Queen, "if there is any doubt about his existence, Colonel Ponsonby don't believe in him." '

RAMBERT, EUGÈNE. ZURICH, RORSCHACH, RÜTI, BUCHS, RAGAZ

SYMONDS, JOHN ADDINGTON. MONTE GENEROSO, LUGANO, BELLINZONA, ST. GOTTHARD PASS, ALTDORF, LUCERNE, GRINDELWALD, LAUTERBRUNNEN, MÜRREN

'If you do walk in Switzerland and if you have not been here, pray make a point of seeing Mürren. I was six weeks in this inn five years ago, and many of the days were gilded.'

TEN HAMME, JOË DIERICX DE. BASLE, SCHAFFHAUSEN, ZURICH, ZUG, RIGI, WEGGIS, FLUELEN, ANDERMATT, FURKA PASS, GRIMSEL PASS, MEIRINGEN, INTERLAKEN, LAUTERBRUNNEN, WENGEN, INTERLAKEN, THUN, BERNE, BASLE

TYNDALL, JOHN. BRIENZ, GIESSBACH, INTERLAKEN, THUN, ZWEISIMMEN, LENK, TRÜTTLISBERG PASS, LAUENEN, KRINNEN PASS, GSTEIG, COL DE PILLON, AIGLE, MARTIGNY, GRAND ST. BERNARD PASS, AOSTA, CHATILLON, BREUIL, MATTERHORN, ZERMATT, SCHWARZBERG-WEISSTHOR PASS, MATTMARK, SAAS

Tyndall at last settled his account with the Matterhorn by traversing it from Breuil to Zermatt.

VICTORIA, QUEEN. LUCERNE, ENGELBERG, RIGI, PILATUS, FLUELEN, ALTDORF, ANDERMATT, FURKA PASS, LUCERNE

As Countess of Kent the Queen rented the Villa Pension Wallace at Lucerne. With Prince Arthur and Princess Louise the Queen went up Pilatus, 'escorted by her Highland attendants, who, if report speaks truth, have out-done the Swiss hillmen in mountain-walking'.

WILLIAMS, CHARLES J. B. (*c*). BERNE, THUN, INTERLAKEN, LAUTERBRUNNEN, GRINDELWALD, INTERLAKEN, MEIRINGEN, ROSENLAUI, GRIMSEL PASS, OBERGESTELEN, BRIG, SIMPLON PASS, DOMODOSSOLA

1869

BAKUNIN, MICHAEL. GENEVA, LE LOCLE, LA CHAUX DE FONDS, BASLE, GENEVA, BERNE, LUGANO, LOCARNO

At Le Locle, Bakunin addressed the local adherents of the International, and he attended the Congress of the International at Basle. He then intended to live at Lugano, but as that was already the headquarters of the Mazzinists, he settled at Locarno.

BUTLER, GEORGE. LUCERNE, PILATUS, RIGI, ALTDORF, ANDERMATT, FURKA PASS, GRIMSEL PASS, MEIRINGEN, INTERLAKEN, GRINDELWALD, FAULHORN, LAUTERBRUNNEN, MÜRREN, INTERLAKEN, THUN, BERNE, ROLLE, LA GORDANNE

'We did not stay long at Mürren as it was crowded to excess with English people, and there was hardly any accommodation. It is a strange mania I think which drives crowds of English people to any one place which happens to be the fashion for the time.'

BUTLER, SAMUEL. BASLE, LUCERNE, ALTDORF, ST. GOTTHARD PASS, BELLINZONA, LUGANO, COMO

'As much as possible I keep away from English-frequented hotels in Italy and Switzerland because I find that if I do not go to service on Sunday I am made uncomfortable. It is this bullying that I want to do away with.'

BYERS, S. H. M. ZURICH

'I was, in a way, representing my country in a republic five times as old as our own', wrote the United States' Consul. 'It was nearing sunset, when suddenly I happened to cast my eyes away from the people and the boats towards the upper end of the lake. "Look at the beautiful clouds," I exclaimed. My companion smiled. "They are not clouds," said he. "They are the Glarus Alps." It was the fairest sight I ever beheld in my life.'

COOLIDGE, W. A. B. MARTIGNY, TÊTE NOIRE PASS, CHAMONIX, MONT BLANC, DOME DE MIAGE, COL DE BERANGER, COL DU MONT TONDU, LES MOTTETS, COURMAYEUR, GRAND ST. BERNARD PASS, BOURG ST. PIERRE, GRAND COMBIN, ZERMATT, ST. THEODUL PASS, BREITHORN, MONTE ROSA, VISP, BRIG, BELALP

J. R. Green was at Belalp, and in his description of a mountaineer he wrote 'how many guides will he take, has he a dog . . .?' This was a reference to Tschingel, Coolidge's dog.

DUFF, MOUNTSTUART E. GRANT. GENEVA, TERRITET, GLION, LAUSANNE, THUN, GRINDELWALD, OLTEN

ELLIOTT, JULIUS. GRINDELWALD, SCHRECKHORN

'The air on the tops and slopes of the great snow mountains is to me more than anything the restorer of health and strength, the dispenser of enjoyment, the inspirer of hope. Their solitudes counteract the worries of incessant occupation in town life, their icy streams repair the shattered nerves, their glorious views minister ceaseless pleasures, and it is my own fault if their wondrous beauties do not raise my heart in deeper thankfulness, and truer affection, and more real comprehension to the great and loving Father whose hand is so visible everywhere.'
Elliott was killed on the Schreckhorn.

EVILL, WILLIAM. SCHAFFHAUSEN, COIRE, THUSIS, SPLÜGEN PASS, CHIAVENNA

'Mystic waterfalls of ice, frozen cascades held captive in mid-air, glistened and flashed and sparkled like jewels in the sunbeams; for already had Winter

"Torn the cataracts from the hills
And they clanked at his girdle like manacles".'

FOX, JOSEPH H. TIRANO, BERNINA PASS, PONTRESINA, PIZ CORVATSCH, ST. MORITZ, PIZ BERNINA, JULIER PASS, TIEFENKASTEL, REICHENAU, DISENTIS, OBERALP PASS, ANDERMATT, WASSEN, SUSTEN PASS, MEIRINGEN, JOCH PASS, TITLIS, ENGELBERG, LUCERNE

'We were joined by F. F. Tuckett and Eliot Howard, who had been in Styria. They brought with them green Styrian Rücksacks, and were the first to introduce them into Switzerland, where they gradually came into use, until they have now become universal. It is strange in looking back to remember how difficult it was at first to overcome the prejudice in favour of knapsacks.'

GAMBETTA, LÉON. VILLENEUVE, MONTREUX

'Je suis tout au fond du lac de Genève entre Villeneuve et Montreux, au pied des Alpes, dont je salue tous les matins les neiges éternelles, et quand le soleil les dore le soir de son dernier rayon, je me couche; je n'ai plus de montre, je suis brouillé avec les pendules, les Alpes avec le soleil pour cadran, voilà mon horloge.'

GIRDLESTONE, A. G. MARTIGNY, COL DU TOUR, CHAMONIX, MONT BLANC, COL DE TRÉLATÊTE, COURMAYEUR, AOSTA, CHATILLON, BREUIL, ST. THEODUL PASS, ZERMATT, ADLER PASS, SAAS, ALPHUBELJOCH PASS, ZERMATT, COL D'HÉRENS, EVOLENA

GRAY, ASA. RAGAZ, COIRE, PONTRESINA, VILLENEUVE, GENEVA, MARTIGNY, SION, SIERRE, VISP, ZERMATT, VISP, SION, MARTIGNY, VILLENEUVE, CHILLON, GENEVA, LAUSANNE, BERNE, THUN, INTERLAKEN, LAUTERBRUNNEN, MÜRREN, KLEINE SCHEIDEGG, GRINDELWALD, INTERLAKEN, THUN, BERNE, NEUCHÂTEL, LES VERRIÈRES

GREEN, JOHN RICHARD. LUCERNE, TREIB, BELALP

'What is it which makes men in Alpine travel-books write as men never write elsewhere? What is the origin of a style unique in literature, which misses both the sublime and the ridiculous, and constantly hops from tall-talk to a mirth feeble and inane?'

GÜSSFELDT, PAUL. PONTRESINA, MALOJA, MURETTO PASS, CHIAREGGIO, PASSO DI MELLO, MONTE DELLA DISGRAZIA, BAGNI DI MASINO, FORCELLA DI ZOCCA, CASACCIA, PONTRESINA, PIZ ROSEG, PIZ BERNINA

HAVERGAL, FRANCES RIDLEY. BASLE, SCHAFFHAUSEN, ZURICH, BERNE, THUN, INTERLAKEN, LAUTERBRUNNEN, MÜRREN, GRINDELWALD, INTERLAKEN, BRIENZ, BRUNIG PASS, LUCERNE, RIGI, LUCERNE, LANGNAU, BERNE, FRIBOURG, VEVEY, MARTIGNY, TÊTE NOIRE PASS, CHAMONIX, GENEVA, MORGES, NEUCHÂTEL, LES VERRIÈRES

'The sun had risen above the thick mist, and away in the south east were the weird giant outlines of the Bernese Oberland mountains bending towards the sun, as if they had been our mighty guardian spirits all night, and were resigning their charge ere they flew away into further light. The very mist was a folding of wings about their feet, and a veiling of what might be called angel brows, quiet and serene. It is no use laughing at "fancies"; wait till you have seen what we did from the roof of the Berner Hof.'

HOLL, FRANK. BASLE, LUCERNE, FLUELEN, ANDERMATT, ST. GOTTHARD PASS, BELLINZONA, LUGANO, COMO

JAVELLE, ÉMILE. VEVEY, MONTHEY, CHAMPÉRY, DENT DU MIDI

'Ne connaissez-vous pas sur les Alpes un lieu qui, sans être des plus admirables ou des plus vantés, dès la première fois vous frappa d'un charme secret, invincible, qui vous poursuit depuis dans bien des rêves: un lieu où il vous semble que vous passeriez le reste de vos jours sans désirer plus rien; un site qui toujours revient le premier à votre mémoire quand vous parlez des beautés des Alpes? Ce site, pour moi, c'est Bonnavaux.'

LAPORTE, ALBERT (*c*). GENEVA, CHAMONIX, TÊTE NOIRE PASS, MARTIGNY, GRAND ST. BERNARD PASS, AOSTA, COURMAYEUR, COL DE LA SEIGNE, COL DU BONHOMME, ST. GERVAIS, GENEVA, LAUSANNE, MORAT, BERNE, THUN, INTERLAKEN, LAUTERBRUNNEN, KLEINE SCHEIDEGG, GRINDELWALD, FAULHORN, GROSSE SCHEIDEGG, MEIRINGEN, INTERLAKEN, KANDERSTEG, GEMMI PASS, LEUK, VISP, ZERMATT, VISP, BRIG, OBERGESTELEN, FURKA PASS, ANDERMATT, ALTDORF, LUCERNE, RIGI, ZURICH, EINSIEDELN, WALLENSTADT, COIRE, THUSIS, VIA MALA, COIRE, ALTSTÄTTEN, APPENZELL, CONSTANCE, SCHAFFHAUSEN, BASLE

Grand St. Bernard: 'Ils entendirent des cris près du lac et y coururent. C'était un Anglais qui prenait un bain! Hâve de froid et grinçant de frisson il nageait comme un canard polaire, à travers les glaçons, en criant: "J'ai gagné mon pari".'

LEAF, WALTER. ST. MORITZ, PIZ CORVATSCH

'This little climb only whetted my appetite', a process which was helped on by Leaf's meeting Oscar Browning and Schütz Wilson.

MEYER, CONRAD FERDINAND. ZURICH, LUCERNE, PILATUS, FLUELEN, ALTDORF, ST. GOTTHARD PASS, ANDERMATT, OBERALP PASS, SEDRUN, DISENTIS, COIRE, ZURICH

'Our mountain quarters must be over 6,000 feet up, for I must be near the snow. The inn must have not more than four guest rooms, stairs without banisters, and service without waiters. It must smell of new hay.'

PATMORE, EMILY HONORIA. FRIBOURG, THUN, INTERLAKEN, LAUTERBRUNNEN, GRINDELWALD, LUCERNE, BASLE

ROOSEVELT, THEODORE. OUCHY, GENEVA, CHAMONIX

'I found several specimens to keep and we went on the great glacier called "Mother of Ice".'

RUSKIN, JOHN. LES VERRIÈRES, NEUCHÂTEL, VEVEY, MARTIGNY, SION, BRIG, SIMPLON PASS, DOMODOSSOLA, VENICE, MILAN, COMO, LUGANO,

BELLINZONA, ST. GOTTHARD PASS, HOSPENTHAL, ALTDORF, LUCERNE, BRUNIG PASS, BRIENZ, GIESSBACH, INTERLAKEN, THUN, BERNE, NEUCHÂTEL

Hospenthal:—'Here, in the old Inn you know so well, under the grassy hill you used to be so happy climbing in the morning, I got a letter from my cousin George telling me I am the first professor of art appointed at the English Universities.'

SCHREIBER, LADY CHARLOTTE. LES VERRIÈRES, NEUCHÂTEL, LAUSANNE, GENEVA, MARTIGNY, SION, SIERRE, BRIG, SIMPLON PASS, DOMODOSSOLA

Lausanne: 'have hopes from the curiosity shop'.
Geneva: 'all the shops very badly furnished in every way; no purchases'.
Brig: 'one antiquaire. . . .'

SIDGWICK, HENRY. MÜRREN

'The only thing of importance that I have to say about the Alps is that the view from Mürren is not only the sublimest thing I have ever seen in S., but I have seen nothing to compare with it in sublimity.'

STEPHEN, LESLIE. ST. MORITZ, BERNINA PASS, TIRANO, BORMIO, STA. CATARINA

Mrs. Stephen 'was ordered to take the baths at St. Moritz. . . . We found in one hotel a King, an imperial duchess, and some other equal swells. . . . We should have had to pay like princes and lodge like pigs. . . . I should rejoice if it could be made into the Norfolk Island of the Alps, and all kings, cockneys, persons travelling with couriers, Americans doing Europe against time, Cook's tourists and their like, commercial travellers, and especially that variety of English clergyman which travels in dazzling white ties and forces church services upon you by violence in remote country inns, could be confined within it to amuse or annoy each other.'

SYMONDS, JOHN ADDINGTON. MÜRREN, MEIRINGEN, GRIMSEL PASS, FURKA PASS, ANDERMATT, AMSTEG, MADERANERTAL, ALTDORF, FROHNALP, RIGI-SCHEIDECK, ENGELBERG

TEN HAMME, JOË DIERICX DE. BASLE, LUCERNE, LUNGERN, BRUNIG PASS, BRIENZ, INTERLAKEN, THUN, KANDERSTEG, GEMMI PASS, LEUK, SION, MARTIGNY, COL DE BALME, CHAMONIX, GENEVA, LAUSANNE, BERNE, BASLE

TENNYSON, ALFRED. SCHAFFHAUSEN, INTERLAKEN, LAUTERBRUNNEN, MÜRREN, KLEINE SCHEIDEGG, GRINDELWALD, GIESSBACH, BRIENZ, BRUNIG PASS, LUCERNE, BASLE

'Perhaps this earth and all that is on it—storms, mountains, cataracts, the sun and the skies—are the Almighty.'

TORR, CECIL. COIRE, THUSIS, SPLÜGEN PASS, CHIAVENNA, COMO, LUGANO, BELLINZONA, ST. GOTTHARD PASS, ALTDORF, FLUELEN, LUCERNE, BASLE

'The diligence had been attacked by brigands the night before in the narrow gorge below Airolo. It was twilight when we reached the gorge; and suddenly we heard men galloping towards us. My sister made up her mind at once that they were brigands; but they turned out to be an escort coming down to see us through, and they rode on with us, their carbines in their hands.'

TROLLOPE, THOMAS ADOLPHUS. LOCARNO, BELLINZONA, FAIDO, AIROLO, ST. GOTTHARD PASS, ANDERMATT, FLUELEN, LUCERNE, BASLE—SCHAFFHAUSEN, ZURICH, RAGAZ, PFÄFERS, COIRE, THUSIS, SPLÜGEN PASS, CHIAVENNA

Near Airolo Trollope's portmanteau was stolen from the diligence. The villagers turned out and caught the two thieves who had plunged into the river, each of them 'clad in three or four of my shirts and as many coats and waistcoats'.

TUCKETT, FRANCIS FOX. STELVIO PASS, BORMIO, TIRANO, BERNINA PASS, PONTRESINA, PIZ CORVATSCH, ST. MORITZ, PIZ BERNINA, JULIER PASS, TIEFENKASTEL, COIRE, THUSIS, HINTERRHEIN, LENTA PASS, VALS, ILANZ, DISENTIS, SANDALP PASS, LINTHAL, STACHELBERG, LUCERNE, PILATUS

TYNDALL, JOHN. GRINDELWALD, ZERMATT, BRIG, BELALP, ALETSCHHORN

'I know nothing which can compare in point of glory with these winter palaces of the mountaineer, under the opening illumination of the morning. And the best of it is, that no right of property in the scene could enhance its value.'

VAUGHAN, HERBERT, CARDINAL. LUCERNE, BASLE

'The lake very beautiful, the family very kind, but one's work is not here and every hour seems wasted when life is so short and there is so much to do in it.'

WARNER, CHARLES D. (*c*). BASLE, BERNE, THUN, FRIBOURG, GENEVA, CHAMONIX, TÊTE NOIRE PASS, MARTIGNY, SION, VISP, ZERMATT, VISP, LEUK, GEMMI PASS, KANDERSTEG, SPIEZ, ROMANSHORN

WATSON, PHILIPPA H. COMBALLAZ, VISP, ZERMATT, ST. THEODUL PASS, BREUIL, CHATILLON, AOSTA, GRAND ST. BERNARD PASS, MARTIGNY

WILLIAMS, CHARLES J. B. WESEN, GLARUS, COIRE, THUSIS, TIEFENKASTEL, JULIER PASS, ST. MORITZ, SAMADEN, PONTRESINA, BERNINA PASS, TIRANO, BORMIO

WILSON, H. SCHÜTZ. ZERMATT, DOM

YEO, J. BURNEY. COIRE, LENZERHEIDE, TIEFENKASTEL, JULIER PASS, ST. MORITZ, SCHULS, TARASP, SÜS, FLUELA PASS, DAVOS

'The village of St. Moritz is one of the dirtiest, the most untidy, the most irregularly and badly built in the whole valley; and I should say, from certain unsavoury smells which assail one in sundry quarters, very badly drained. . . . Davos is a dull, dreary, monotonous mountain valley, and an American who had spent a winter in the place assured me that, "to save his life, he would not pass another there".'

1870

ADAMS, HENRY. DOMODOSSOLA, SIMPLON PASS, BRIG, SION, MARTIGNY, OUCHY, GENEVA

'I have been so happy to get a few days in the wilderness where there was no society and nothing to think about, that I was very sorry to arrive here [Ouchy] where I am deep among Americans whom I least care to see.'

ALCOTT, LOUISA MAY. GENEVA, VEVEY, BEX, MARTIGNY, SION, BRIG, SIMPLON PASS, DOMODOSSOLA, LUINO, LUGANO, PORLEZZA, MENAGGIO

'The breaking out of this silly little war between France and Prussia . . . is sending troops of travellers to Switzerland for refuge; and all the large towns are brimful of people flying from Germany. It won't trouble us, for we have done France and don't mean to do Germany.'

AMIEL, HENRI-FRÉDÉRIC. GENEVA, BRIG, BELALP, ZURICH, BASLE

'Le panorama est d'une majesté grandiose. C'est la symphonie des montagnes, une cantate des Alpes au soleil. J'en suis ébloui et oppressé. Et ce qui domine, c'est la joie de pouvoir admirer, c'est à dire d'être redevenu contemplateur par le bien-être physique, de pouvoir sortir de moi et me donner aux choses, comme c'est le propre de mon état de santé. La gratitude se mêle à l'enthousiasme. Je reviens à moi-meme. Quelle bénédiction! Passé deux heures au pied du Sparrenhorn, dans un ravissement continu — Submergé de sensations. Regardé, senti, rêvé, pensé. . . .'

BAKUNIN, MICHAEL. LOCARNO, BELLINZONA, ST. GOTTHARD PASS, FLUELEN, LUCERNE, BERNE, NEUCHÂTEL, GENEVA—LOCARNO

Bakunin was on his way to Lyons where he hoped to start a revolution after the fall of Napoleon III. It was a failure and he returned to Locarno.

BONNEY, THOMAS GEORGE. BERNE, THUN, SCHAFLOCH, INTERLAKEN, LUCERNE, PILATUS

BRANDES, GEORGE. GENEVA, CHAMONIX, GENEVA, VEVEY, MONTREUX

'Mont Blanc suddenly appeared in its gleaming splendour, positively tiring and paining the eye. It was a new and strange feeling to be altogether hemmed in by mountains. It was oppressive to a plain-dweller to be shut in thus, and not to be able to get away from the immutable sheet of snow, with its jagged summits.'

BROOKS, PHILLIPS. GENEVA, CHAMONIX, COL DU BONHOMME, COL DE LA SEIGNE, COURMAYEUR, AOSTA, CHATILLON, BREUIL, ST. THEODUL PASS, ZERMATT, VISP, VIESCH, EGGISHORN, OBERGESTELEN, FURKA PASS, ANDERMATT, OBERALP PASS, DISENTIS, COIRE, PFÄFERS, RORSCHACH, NAUDERS, RESCHEN-SCHEIDECK PASS, TRAFOI, STELVIO PASS, BORMIO, TIRANO, BERNINA PASS, PONTRESINA, ALBULA PASS, FILISUR, COIRE, ZURICH, BERNE, LAUSANNE, GENEVA

BUNSEN, FRANCES, BARONESS. BASLE, CHÂTEAU D'OEX

'Most people agree in reckoning Château d'Oex "not desirable, except as a convenient centre for excursions"—which sounds just like what I don't like, and don't want. But, I find it a charming spot for staying at home, with the finest air blowing upon me, with only fields and woods and rocks and mountains to look at.'

COOLIDGE, W. A. B. COURMAYEUR, EVOLENA, DENT BLANCHE, ORMONTS-DESSUS, DIABLERETS, RANDA, BIESJOCH PASS, BRUNEGGHORN, TURTMANN

'Our guide, a purely local man, was rather at a loss on the crevassed and very steep glacier. Tschingel as usual went ahead, for she had a marvellous instinct for avoiding crevasses, smelling at doubtful spots to see if the snow bridges were strong enough to bear her, and seeming to know exactly when that was the case—possibly by means of the air coming through the snow.'

DENT, CLINTON, T. SAAS, ALPHUBELJOCH PASS, ZERMATT

At Saas, 'so pleased were the hotel authorities at the presence of a traveller that they exerted themselves to the utmost to entertain us well, and with remarkable results. I find a record of the dinner served. There were ten dishes in consecutive order, exclusive of what Americans call "fixings". As to the nature of nine it was difficult to speak with any degree of certainty, but the tenth was apparently a blackbird that had perished of starvation and whose attenuated form the chef had bulged out with extraneous matter.'

DUFF, MOUNTSTUART E. GRANT. GENEVA, MARTIGNY, SION, SIERRE, BRIG, VIESCH, EGGISHORN, OBERGESTELEN, FURKA PASS,

ANDERMATT, OBERALP PASS, DISENTIS, REICHENAU, THUSIS, SPLÜGEN PASS, CHIAVENNA, MALOJA PASS, SAMADEN, PONTRESINA

'To have moved so large a party [they were ten, among them Lubbock] at this season of the year in Switzerland would not usually have been an easy task, but the Franco-German War had emptied the hotels, and we had no trouble anywhere.'

HOWITT, MARY. BASLE, LUCERNE, GERSAU, BRUNNEN, RIGI, FLUELEN, BÜRGLEN, LUCERNE, ZURICH, RAGAZ, BELLAGIO

'Pension Agathe Aufdermauer, May 11, 1870. Yesterday we had an invasion of fresh inmates, but only for one night. It was Richard Wagner, the great composer, with a handsome young lady, legally or by courtesy his wife. She is Liszt's daughter.'

'My husband remarked to an artisan, who was seated under a tree, gazing down on the populous city and the lake [of Zurich], with its fringe of prosperous villages, "what a noble landscape! and how well, after the rain, the vines, corn, and potatoes look!" "Yes", replied the man, gloomily: "only there 's a war." '

HUTTON, R. H. BASLE, CONSTANCE, MERAN, STA. MARIA, OFEN PASS, ZERNEZ, ST. MORITZ, MALOJA PASS, CHIAVENNA, SPLÜGEN PASS, THUSIS, REICHENAU, DISENTIS, OBERALP PASS, ANDERMATT, FURKA PASS, OBERGESTELEN, BRIG, LEUK, GEMMI PASS, KANDERSTEG, THUN, BERNE

'At Bad St. Moritz we were more than welcome. The Queen of Wurtemberg, the Grand Duchess of Baden, and all their suites, had left within the last forty-eight hours, recalled by telegraph to Germany. The war had already made pacific vacancies in the crowded ranks of the St. Moritz bathers.'

JAVELLE, ÉMILE. VEVEY, EVIONNAZ, COL DE JORAT, DENT DU MIDI, VISP, ZERMATT, MATTERHORN

MEYER, CONRAD FERDINAND. PONTRESINA, SÜS, FLUELA PASS, DAVOS, KLOSTERS, LANDQUART, ZURICH

MOORE, A. W. GÖSCHENEN, UNTERWINTERJOCH PASS, GRIMSEL PASS, LAUTERAARSATTEL PASS, GRINDELWALD, LAUTERBRUNNEN, JUNGFRAU, EGGISHORN, LÖTSCHENLÜCKE PASS, FAFLERALP, BALTSCHIEDERJOCH PASS, VISP, ZERMATT, CIMA DI JAZZI, MONTE ROSA, CHAMONIX, AIGUILLE VERTE

NEWBERRY, JULIA. GENEVA, VEVEY, BEX

NORTH, MARIANNE. MONTE GENEROSO, BORMIO, STELVIO PASS, TRAFOI, ST. VALENTIN, SCHULS, SÜS, FLUELA PASS, DAVOS

RUSKIN, JOHN. GENEVA, VEVEY, MARTIGNY, SION, BRIG, SIMPLON PASS, DOMODOSSOLA, MILAN, COMO, BELLINZONA, AIROLO, ST. GOTTHARD

PASS, FLUELEN, SARNEN, BRUNIG PASS, BRIENZ, GIESSBACH, LAUTERBRUNNEN, THUN, BERNE, GENEVA

'I am examining the mountains with a view to my plan for the redemption of their barren slopes. There is just difficulty enough to make it a sublime piece of manual work.' In this year Ruskin seriously considered buying a house above Martigny.

STEPHEN, LESLIE. BERNE, THUN, INTERLAKEN, GRINDELWALD, VIESCHERJOCH PASS, EGGISHORN, VIESCH, VISP, ZERMATT, SAAS, VISP, RIED

At Saas Stephen and his friends 'got to playing "fly-loo" which means that everyone puts down a piece of sugar and a 10 centime piece before him, and the one on whose sugar the first fly settles, gets the money'.

SYMONDS, JOHN ADDINGTON. MONTE GENEROSO

Ill health: 'chest so weak', once more compelled Symonds to take a spring holiday in Switzerland. His wife's sister, Marianne North, joined the Symonds at Monte Generoso.

TROLLOPE, THOMAS ADOLPHUS. COMO, BELLINZONA, ST. GOTTHARD PASS, FLUELEN, LUCERNE, BASLE—BASLE, BERNE, KLEIN WABERN, FRIBOURG, THUN, INTERLAKEN, LAUTERBRUNNEN, GIESSBACH, BRIENZ, BRUNIG PASS, LUCERNE, BECKENRIED, FLUELEN, ST. GOTTHARD PASS, BELLINZONA, LUGANO, COMO

'During those weeks so fateful to Europe, and so quiet at little Thun dozing on its dozing life. . . .'

TYNDALL, JOHN. BELALP

'In 1870 I was again at the Bel Alp for several weeks, during which my interest was continually kept awake by telegrams from the seat of war; for the enterprising proprietors both at the Bel Alp and the Aeggishorn had run telegraphic wires from the valley of the Rhone up to their respective hotels.'

1871

ANONYMOUS 12. GENEVA, CHAMONIX, GENEVA, LAUSANNE, BERNE, THUN, INTERLAKEN, LAUTERBRUNNEN, GRINDELWALD, GROSSE SCHEIDEGG, MEIRINGEN, GRIMSEL PASS, FURKA PASS, ANDERMATT, ALTDORF, LUCERNE, BERNE, NEUCHÂTEL, LES VERRIÈRES

ARNOLD, MATTHEW. LES VERRIÈRES, NEUCHÂTEL, BERNE, THUN, INTERLAKEN, LAUTERBRUNNEN, KLEINE SCHEIDEGG, GRINDELWALD, MEIRINGEN, GRIMSEL PASS, OBERGESTELEN, BRIG, BELALP, LEUK, GEMMI PASS, KANDERSTEG, THUN, BERNE

'Crossing the Jura was delightful, and coming down the Val de Motiers Travers, where Rousseau lived for some time. I admire the

Jura more every time I see it, and all its streams are clear and beautiful—not like the snow water of the Alpine rivers.'

BROOKE, STOPFORD. OUCHY, VISP, ZERMATT

'An immense number of dull English are here, so dull that one asks what possible reason brought them to this place. They are varied by Alpine bores, the most fearful portions of the human race. Some are slow and solemn bores, others are jerky and good humoured, but all are loud and roar like bulls of Bashan. They defile the woods and degrade the mountains . . . Their talk was like their literature, if one may give that honoured name to the hotch potch of bad jokes and maimed descriptions, and overstated dangers and villainous English which fills the pages of Peaks, Passes, and Glaciers.'

BUTLER, SAMUEL. BASLE, LUCERNE, GERSAU, ALTDORF, ST. GOTTHARD PASS, BELLINZONA, MAGADINO, ARONA, VARALLO, BERGAMO, CHIAVENNA, SPLÜGEN PASS, THUSIS, COIRE

Butler had almost finished writing *Erewhon*. The going down into Erewhon is the descent through the valley of the Ticino from the St. Gotthard pass towards Bellinzona, and the view of the plains of Erewhon is that of Lombardy from the Sacro Monte at Varese.

COOLIDGE, W. A. B. GRINDELWALD, KLEINE SCHEIDEGG, EIGERJOCH PASS, METTENBERG, EIGER, JUNGFRAU, SAAS, ALPHUBELJOCH PASS, ZERMATT, TRIFTJOCH PASS, ZINAL, ZERMATT, VISP, BELALP, ZERMATT, MATTERHORN, BREUIL, ST. THEODUL PASS, ZERMATT, WEISSHORN, WANDFLUHJOCH PASS, DENT BLANCHE, VISP, RIED, BIETSCHHORN

Another great season for Tschingel. A mountaineer who was ascending the Jungfrau by the usual route 'later expressed to us his horrified amazement when he suddenly caught sight, on what were then supposed to be perpendicular cliffs, of a large party leisurely advancing—a number of guides and porters, a young man, a lady, and, to crown all, a dog trotting about'.

DENT, CLINTON T. SAAS, ZERMATT, MATTERHORN

'Is it always true that "a sorrow's crown of sorrow is remembering happier things"? Surely there is a keenness and a depth of pleasure to be found in recalling happiness, though it may never return in its old form; and the memory of pleasure just toned with a trace of sadness is one of the most profound emotions that can stir the human heart. Go on and climb the Alps ye that follow: nowhere else will you find the same pleasure.'

DUFF, MOUNTSTUART E. GRANT. LES VERRIÈRES, NEUCHÂTEL, LUCERNE, BRUNNEN, ALTDORF, ANDERMATT, FURKA PASS, OBERGESTELEN, BRIG, SIMPLON PASS, DOMODOSSOLA

FOX, JOSEPH H. GENEVA, SIXT, COL DE GOLEZE, COL DE COUX, CHAMPÉRY, DENT DU MIDI, MONTREUX, AIGLE, COL DE PILLON, GSTEIG, KRINNEN PASS, LAUENEN, TRÜTTLISBERG PASS, LENK, HAHNENMOOS PASS, ADELBODEN, ENGSTLIGENGRAT, GEMMI PASS, LEUK, BRIG, BELALP, BRIG, SION, MARTIGNY, THUN, INTERLAKEN, GRINDELWALD

GROVE, SIR GEORGE. LUCERNE, PILATUS, BRUNIG PASS, BRIENZ, INTERLAKEN, LAUTERBRUNNEN, MÜRREN

'I am not sure but when one is in these panic states one sees a great deal of beauty and gets a great deal of feeling out of scenes and things that would pass unnoticed in rude health . . . I wish I could describe the strange feeling that comes on me as I get higher and higher and more opposite the great mountains.'

HAVERGAL, FRANCES RIDLEY. BASLE, LUCERNE, ALTDORF, ANDERMATT, FURKA PASS, OBERGESTELEN, VIESCH, EGGISHORN, BELALP, BRIG, VISP, ZERMATT, ST. THEODUL PASS, BREUIL, CHATILLON, AOSTA, COURMAYEUR, COL DE LA SEIGNE, COL DU BONHOMME, CHAMONIX, COL DE BALME, MARTIGNY, LAUSANNE

'At our pet hotel at Zermatt we had hay duvets! of course too hot for July, but must be most comfortable in winter, and quite as much warmth as a good blanket . . . I shall try it myself for very poor people, if it comes a hard winter.' At Courmayeur the poor hymn-writer found 'the people here quite different from the Swiss, and not at all so ready to accept gospels'.

JAVELLE, ÉMILE. LAUSANNE, ZINAL, POINTE DE ZINAL, COL DURAND, ZERMATT, RANDA, WEISSHORN

JOWETT, BENJAMIN. GENEVA, MARTIGNY, SION, VISP, ZERMATT, VISP, BRIG, VIESCH, EGGISHORN, BRIG, SIMPLON PASS, DOMODOSSOLA, MILAN, TIRANO, LE PRESE, BERNINA PASS, PONTRESINA, THUSIS, COIRE

KEMBLE, FANNY (*c*). BRUNNEN, AXENSTEIN, TERRITET, BEX, MARTIGNY, SION, BRIG, SIMPLON PASS, DOMODOSSOLA

KNIGHTLEY OF FAWSLEY, LADY. BASLE, LUCERNE, FLUELEN, ANDERMATT, FURKA PASS, GRIMSEL PASS, MEIRINGEN, INTERLAKEN, GENEVA

'I don't think anybody ever had so much enjoyment crowded into one week as I have had in this last.'

MAZZINI, GIUSEPPE. LUCERNE, ALTDORF, ST. GOTTHARD PASS, AIROLO, BELLINZONA, LUGANO

From Lucerne to Airolo Mazzini had as his travelling companion Friedrich Nietzsche.

MERCIER, JEROME J. (*c*). LES VERRIÈRES, NEUCHÂTEL, BERNE, THUN, FRUTIGEN, ADELBODEN, HAHNENMOOS PASS, LENK, TRÜTTLISBERG PASS, LAUENEN, KRINNEN PASS, GSTEIG, COL DE PILLON, AIGLE, VEVEY, COL DE JAMAN, CHÂTEAU D'OEX, SAANEN, ZWEISIMMEN, THUN, INTERLAKEN, BRIENZ, LAUTERBRUNNEN, MÜRREN, KLEINE SCHEIDEGG, GRINDELWALD, GROSSE SCHEIDEGG, MEIRINGEN, GRIMSEL PASS, OBERGESTELEN, VIESCH, EGGISHORN, BRIG, VISP, ZERMATT, ST. THEODUL PASS, BREUIL, CHATILLON, COL DE JOUX, BRUSSONE, COL DE RANZOLA, GRESSONEY, COL DE VAL DOBBIA, ALAGNA, TURLO PASS, MACUGNAGA, MONTE MORO PASS, SAAS, VISP, SION, MARTIGNY, TÊTE NOIRE PASS, CHAMONIX, MARTIGNY, LAUSANNE, GENEVA

MEYER, CONRAD FERDINAND. DAVOS-WOLFGANG

'Here one can read only Homer and Shakespeare.'

NEWBERRY, JULIA. LUCERNE, ZURICH

'How I hate travelling in Europe, and above all travelling in Switzerland . . . It is absolutely necessary that we see the lake of Lucerne. Feeble protestations on my part.—Sister carries the day, and we *see* it.—See it with a ve(n)g(e)ance too.—It is roasting when we start, half way out a tremendous Alpine storm breaks over the lake.—The people on the narrow deck are packed like herrings in box, the only covering, an awning with oil cloth over it.—Down comes the rain, harder, heavier every minute. . . .'

NIETZSCHE, FRIEDRICH. BASLE, LUCERNE, ALTDORF, ST. GOTTHARD PASS, AIROLO, BELLINZONA, LUGANO, ST. GOTTHARD PASS, ALTDORF, TRIBSCHEN, LUCERNE, BASLE

From Lucerne to Airolo, Nietzsche had Mazzini as travelling companion. He finished his *Origin of Tragedy* at Lugano, and, on his return, saw Wagner at Tribschen.

PEAKE, ELIZABETH. BASLE, NEUCHÂTEL, YVERDON, LAUSANNE, GENEVA, CHAMONIX, GENEVA, VEVEY, BERNE, THUN, INTERLAKEN, GRINDELWALD, INTERLAKEN, BRIENZ, BRUNIG PASS, SARNEN, LUCERNE, FLUELEN, HOSPENTHAL, ST. GOTTHARD PASS, BELLINZONA, MAGADINO, MILAN, CHIAVENNA, SPLÜGEN PASS, THUSIS, COIRE, RORSCHACH

RENAN, ERNEST. PRANGINS, MARTIGNY, SION, BRIG, SIMPLON PASS, DOMODOSSOLA

STEPHEN, LESLIE. CHAMONIX, ST. GERVAIS, MONT MALLET

To Oliver Wendell Holmes junr.: 'You poor Yankees are to be pitied for many things, but for nothing so much as your distance from Switzerland.'

SYMONDS, JOHN ADDINGTON. CHAMONIX, MÜRREN, SCHYNIGE-PLATTE, INTERLAKEN, THUN, BERNE

It was during this journey that Symonds wrote *Love and Death* and *The Eiger and the Monk*. 'I used to write them in my head when walking over the glaciers or along the slopes and valleys of Mürren and the Schynige Platte.'

TOLLEMACHE, LIONEL. PONTRESINA, BERNINA HOSPICE

Tollemache relates the experience of Lady X. and her maid being shown into a room with three beds on arrival at the inn at Pontresina. After locking themselves in, they noticed a pair of trousers, and on asking whether they had the room to themselves, were told 'mais non, madame, pas tout à fait; le troisième lit est occupé depuis quelques jours par un monsieur; mais il est très tranquille.'

TUCKETT, FRANCIS FOX. GENEVA, SIXT, COL DE GOLEZE, COL DE COUX, CHAMPÉRY, AIGLE, COL DE PILLON, GSTEIG, KRINNEN PASS, LAUENEN, TRÜTTLISBERG PASS, LENK, HAHNENMOOS PASS, ADELBODEN, ENGSTLIGENGRAT, GEMMI PASS, LEUK, BRIG, BELALP, BRIG, MARTIGNY, LAUSANNE, BERNE, THUN, SCHAFLOCH, INTERLAKEN, MEIRINGEN, GROSSE SCHEIDEGG, GRINDELWALD, KLEINE SCHEIDEGG, LAUTERBRUNNEN, MÜRREN, INTERLAKEN

TYNDALL, JOHN. PONTRESINA

WEILENMANN, JOHANN JAKOB. ST. GALL, ISCHGL, FUTSCHÖL PASS, LAVIN, SÜS, PROMONTOGNO, BONDO, FORCELLA DI BOCCHETTA, SIVIGIA, PASSO DA TURBINESCA, BONDO

WILSON, H. SCHÜTZ. BASLE, INTERLAKEN, LAUTERBRUNNEN, KANDERSTEG, GEMMI PASS, LEUK, VIESCH, EGGISHORN, JUNGFRAU, VISP, ZERMATT, MONTE ROSA, ST. THEODUL PASS, BREUIL, CHATILLON, AOSTA, COURMAYEUR, COL DU GÉANT, CHAMONIX, MARTIGNY

1872

ADAMS, HENRY, AND MRS. MARIAN. BASLE, BERNE, GENEVA, BERNE, ZURICH, LINDAU—BERNE, LUCERNE, ALTDORF, ANDERMATT, ST. GOTTHARD PASS, FAIDO, BELLINZONA, LUGANO, CADENABBIA

'If Switzerland is to be every year more and more ravaged by tourists we shall have to flee to the Himalayas for novelty and quiet.'

BAKUNIN, MICHAEL. LOCARNO, BELLINZONA, ST. GOTTHARD PASS, LUCERNE, BASLE, ZURICH, BERNE, LA CHAUX DE FONDS, ST. IMIER, ZURICH, LOCARNO

Under Bakunin's leadership, the St. Imier Congress of the Democratic Socialist Alliance founded a sort of dissident International.

BUTLER, SAMUEL. BASLE, BERNE, THUN, INTERLAKEN, SCHYNIGE-PLATTE, LAUTERBRUNNEN, MÜRREN, KLEINE SCHEIDEGG, GRINDELWALD, INTERLAKEN, KANDERSTEG, GEMMI PASS, LEUK, VISP, SAAS, MONTE MORO PASS, MACUGNAGA, COL DI BARANCA, FOBELLO, ORTA, DOMODOSSOLA, SIMPLON PASS, BRIG, OBERGESTELEN, GRIMSEL PASS, MEIRINGEN, INTERLAKEN, BERNE

During this journey Butler was writing *The Fair Haven*. 'At this time I made it a rule to write a couple of pages of my book daily, and I generally wrote them while resting on a walk in the open air.'

BYERS, S. H. M. ZURICH, LUCERNE, RIGI, PILATUS

CONWAY, MARTIN. BASLE, BERNE, ZIMMERWALD, LUCERNE, RIGI-STAFFEL, AXENSTEIN, FROHNALPSTOCK, SCHWYZ, MYTHEN, ALTDORF, ANDERMATT, FURKA PASS, OBERGESTELEN, BRIG, VISP, ZERMATT, BREITHORN, VISP, SION, MARTIGNY, CHAMPÉRY, DENT DU MIDI, VEVEY

'It was not so much what I saw as the fact that I had climbed a real peak that kindled my enthusiastic joy. I knew now just what I wanted to do—to climb peak after peak, all the peaks in the Alps, all the mountains in the world. Every other occupation seemed trifling compared with that. I came down from the Mythen, like Moses from Sinai, bearing with me the law of my life.'

COOLIDGE, W. A. B. CHATILLON, BREUIL, ST. THEODUL PASS, ZERMATT, VISP, BRIG, BELALP, ALETSCHHORN, OBERAARJOCH PASS, GRIMSEL PASS, STRAHLEGG PASS, GRINDELWALD, SCHRECKHORN, KLEINE SCHEIDEGG, MÖNCH, JUNGFRAUJOCH PASS, KLEINE SCHEIDEGG, BELALP, GRÜNHORNLÜCKE PASS, FINSTERAARHORN, GROSSE FIESCHERHORN, AGASSIZJOCH PASS, FINSTERAARJOCH PASS, GRINDELWALD, WETTERHORN, ROSENLAUI, DOLDENHORN

This was Tschingel's greatest season. 'The clever dog often wept and howled when she was of opinion that we were in bad places.'

CRAWFORD, FRANCIS MARION. CHIAVENNA, MALOJA PASS, PONTRESINA, PIZ BERNINA

DENT, CLINTON T. CHAMONIX, MAUVOISIN, COL DU MONT ROUGE, PAS DE CHÈVRES, AROLLA, ZERMATT, ROTHORN

'Our trials were not over for the day when we reached the hotel. Two arch young things had prepared an ambuscade and surprised us successfully at the door of the hotel. Sweetly did they gush. "Oh! where had we been?" We said we had been up in the mountains, indicating the general line of locality with retrospective thumb. "Oh! wasn't it fearfully dangerous? Weren't we all tied tightly together?" (as if, on the principle of union being strength, we had been fastened up and bound like a bundle of quill pens). "Oh! hadn't we done something very wonderful?" . . . Happening to pass later on by the open door of the little salon, the following remark was overheard: "My dear, the conceit of these climbing objects is quite dreadful".'

FAWCETT, HENRY. ZERMATT, CIMA DI JAZZI

An ascent by a blind man.

FOX, JOSEPH H. DAVOS, KLOSTERS, PIZ BUIN, PONTRESINA, FUORCLA CHAPÜTSCHIN, PASSO TREMOGGIA, FORCELLA D'ENTOVA, CHIESA, TORRE, PASSO DI CORNA, ROSSA, PREDA, ROSSA, BOCHETTA DI REMOLUSSA, PIODA, MONTE SISSONE, MALOJA, PONTRESINA, PIZ ROSEG, LUCERNE

GAMBETTA, LÉON. CLARENS

'Nous jouissons doucement du plus admirable pays d'Europe, et je regrette seulement d'être forcé de rentrer trop tôt.'

GOS, ALBERT. GENEVA, BERNE, THUN, INTERLAKEN, MEIRINGEN, ROSENLAUI, INTERLAKEN, THUN, GENEVA, BERNE, THUN, INTERLAKEN, LAUTERBRUNNEN

'Des toits et un clocher pointèrent: Lauterbrunnen. A l'entrée du village, un joueur de cor des Alpes ajustait son bizarre instrument. De longues notes graves s'élevèrent, éveillant de multiples échos, et la cantate mélancolique monta se perdre vers les glaciers étincelants du Silberhorn. Ce fut mon baptême de la montagne; j'étais admis dans le sanctuaire des Alpes.'

GÜSSFELDT, PAUL. PONTRESINA, FUORCLA TSCHIERVA-SCERSCEN, SELLA PASS, PONTRESINA

HAGGARD, SIR H. RIDER. FLUELEN, ALTDORF, ANDERMATT, ST. GOTTHARD

'The pretty Swiss chambermaid, with whom we had made friends, took us to a mortuary near by and among a number of other such gruesome relics, showed us the skull of her own father, which she polished up affectionately with her apron. At the top of the pass we met my brother and my father who had accompanied him so far. The diligence drove off, we shouted our farewells, my father waving a tall white hat out of which, to the amazement of travellers, fell two towels and an assortment of cabbage leaves and other greenery. It was like a conjuring trick. I should explain that the day was hot, and my parent feared sunstroke.'

HORT, F. J. A. LUCERNE, FLUELEN, ALTDORF, AMSTEG

JAVELLE, ÉMILE. LAUSANNE, MARTIGNY, SION, SIERRE, ZINAL, MOMING PASS, ZERMATT, TRIFTJOCH PASS, ZINAL

'Little known as Zinal may be, it nevertheless boasts of an hotel; but happily it is still very primitive, as are also the good folk who conduct it. . . . There are two other travellers here—have I told you? I made their acquaintance at supper. One is an Englishman, Mr. T[uckett]; a fine man, as they all are, a member of the Alpine Club, a great climber of high summits. For the rest he is not eccentric, being neither haughty nor taciturn like so many of his countrymen, but on the contrary a pleasant talker.'

KLUCKER, CHRISTIAN. SAMADEN, PIZ TSCHIERVA

KROPOTKIN, PETER. ZURICH, GENEVA, NEUCHÂTEL, SONVILIER

MEYER, CONRAD FERDINAND. DAVOS-WOLFGANG

'I am now satisfied that I can see my way with *Jürg Jenatsch*, for I have mastered the dramatic structure and the characters of my material.'

MOORE, A. W. ALTDORF, AMSTEG, MADERANERTAL, OBERALPSTOCK, SEDRUN, OBERALP PASS, ANDERMATT, FURKA PASS, GRIMSEL PASS, STUDERHORN, EGGISHORN, BELALP, NESTHORN, VISP, SAAS, MISCHABELJOCH PASS, ZERMATT, COL D'HÉRENS, EVOLENA, SION, SANETSCH PASS, GSTEIG, KRINNEN PASS, LAUENEN, TRÜTTLISBERG PASS, LENK, WILDSTRUBEL, KANDERSTEG, GAMCHILÜCKE, KIENTHAL, SCHYNIGEPLATTE, GRINDELWALD, MÖNCH, ROSENHORN, MEIRINGEN

Moore dislocated his shoulder on the Weisshorn and returned to Zermatt: 'rumours having of course spread. Among the not very many tourists present—not including, as it happens, any mountaineers—the predominant feeling was certainly one of disappointment at the moderate extent of the disaster, as to which the wildest reports had been current, and I was regarded almost in the light of an impostor.'

NIETZSCHE, FRIEDRICH. BASLE, BADEN, ZURICH, WESEN, COIRE, PASSUG, THUSIS, SPLÜGEN PASS, CHIAVENNA, BERGAMO, CHIAVENNA, SPLÜGEN PASS, THUSIS, COIRE, RAGAZ, ZURICH, BASLE

'Splügen: Hotel Bodenhaus

. . . A wonderful rich loneliness, with magnificent roads on which I can wander for hours, sunk deep in thought, without falling over a precipice; and whenever I look around me there is something new and big to see. . . .'

RAMSAY, SIR JAMES. PONTRESINA, PIZ BERNINA, FUORCLA CHAPÜTSCHIN, PASSO TREMOGGIA, FORCELLA D'ENTOVA, CHIESA, TORRE, PASSO DI CORNA ROSSA, PREDA, ROSSA, BOCHETTA DI REMOLUSSA, PIODA, MONTE SISSONE, MALOJA, PONTRESINA, BERNINA PASS, LE PRESE, TIRANO

'Pleasant were the times at Pontresina in 1872; and pleasant was the company to be found at the Krone Hotel. Almost all the folk were English, but there was a German contingent in the house. We had not been at war with Germany in those days; but we differed from the

Germans, among other things, in the important question of the ventilation of the salle à manger. But our majority was overwhelming, and we could carry matters our own way. In fact, one evening I felt rather ashamed at finding the only real public room in the house usurped as a committee room, for the discussion of a matter concerning the English, and the English alone.'

RIMSKY KORSAKOW, NIKOLAY ANDREYEVICH. ZURICH, ZUG, RIGI, LUCERNE, FLUELEN, ANDERMATT, FURKA PASS, GRIMSEL PASS, MEIRINGEN, GROSSE SCHEIDEGG, GRINDELWALD, LAUTERBRUNNEN, INTERLAKEN, CHAMONIX, MARTIGNY, SION, BRIG, SIMPLON PASS, DOMODOSSOLA

RUSKIN, JOHN. DOMODOSSOLA, SIMPLON PASS, BRIG, SION, MARTIGNY, GENEVA

STEPHEN, LESLIE. ZERMATT, BIETSCHHORN

While walking in the Trift gorge with Sir George Trevelyan and Lord John Hervey, Stephen left the path and 'very soon it seemed to us that we were in difficulties'. It was this episode that suggested to Stephen the theme for his 'Bad Five Minutes'.

TROLLOPE, THOMAS ADOLPHUS. DOMODOSSOLA, SIMPLON PASS, BRIG, VISP, SIERRE, MARTIGNY, AIGLE, LES ORMONTS, VERS L'EGLISE, LA FORCLAZ, LE SEPEY, VERS L'EGLISE, VEVEY, GENEVA, NYON, LAUSANNE, AIGLE, VERS L'EGLISE, COL DES MOSSES, CHÂTEAU D'OEX, GSTAAD, GSTEIG, COL DE PILLON, VERS L'EGLISE, COL DES MOSSES, ROSSINIÈRE, MONTBOVON, COL DE JAMAN, VERNEX, AIGLE, VERS L'EGLISE, MARTIGNY, LEUK, GEMMI PASS, KANDERSTEG, FRUTIGEN, INTERLAKEN, LAUTERBRUNNEN, KLEINE SCHEIDEGG, GRINDELWALD, INTERLAKEN, THUN, ZWEISIMMEN, VEVEY

Les Ormonts: 'The district is a very lovely one; not after the fashion of the Bernese Oberland or the Vierwaldstättersee, or any of the regions which have been under the special patronage of the Alpine Club, but abounding in every beauty that rich pastures combined with plenty of wood and water, enclosed by mountains sufficiently high and sufficiently broken to delight the eye and tempt the humble valley climber, can produce by their most felicitous combinations.'

TUCKETT, FRANCIS FOX. BELLAGGIO, MONTE GENEROSO, LUGANO, BELLINZONA, OLIVONE, CAMADRA PASS, DISENTIS, OBERALP PASS, ANDERMATT, FURKA PASS, OBERGESTELEN, VIESCH, EGGISHORN, JUNGFRAU, KLEINE SCHEIDEGG, GRINDELWALD, INTERLAKEN, KANDERSTEG, GEMMI PASS, LEUK, SION, MARTIGNY, GRAND COMBIN, MAUVOISIN, COL DE SEILON, PAS DE CHÈVRES, AROLLA, EVOLENA, COL DU GRAND CORNIER, ZINAL, SIERRE, MARTIGNY, BERNE, LANGNAU, LUCERNE, ZURICH, LANDQUART, DAVOS, SCHIAHORN, PIZ BUIN, BLUDENZ, GLARUS, STACHELBERG, LINTHAL, TÖDI, GLARUS, ZURICH

TYNDALL, JOHN. CHAMONIX, BRIG, BELALP, EGGISHORN

URLIN, RICHARD DENNY. SILVAPLANA, SAMADEN, COIRE, RAGAZ, BERNE, THUN, INTERLAKEN, GRINDELWALD

VIGNET, LOUIS. GENEVA, LAUSANNE, BERNE, THUN, INTERLAKEN, LAUTERBRUNNEN, KLEINE SCHEIDEGG, GRINDELWALD, GROSSE SCHEIDEGG, MEIRINGEN, GRIMSEL PASS, OBERGESTELEN, BRIG

'Trente ans depuis mon voyage d'avant-garde. Les années s'envolent. Le glacier du Rhone est en retraite lui aussi. Le chalet a liquidé. Sur ses ruines trône un caravansérail galonné sur toutes les coutures. Le gaz y darde ses éclairs. A tous les étages des escouades de soubrettes endimanchées. On y sert des bains complets! Postes et Télégraphes.'

WEILENMANN, JOHANN JAKOB. ST. GALL, VISP, ZERMATT, VISP, LAUSANNE

WILSON, H. SCHÜTZ. LAUSANNE, MARTIGNY, BRIG, EGGISHORN, MÖNCHJOCH PASS, GRINDELWALD, WETTERHORN, ZERMATT, CHAMONIX, MONT BLANC

ZINCKE, F. BARHAM. LES VERRIÈRES, NEUCHÂTEL, LAUSANNE, MARTIGNY, SION, VISP, ZERMATT, SAAS, MONTE MORO PASS, MACUGNAGA, DOMODOSSOLA, SIMPLON PASS, BRIG, OBERGESTELEN, GRIMSEL PASS, MEIRINGEN, INTERLAKEN, LAUTERBRUNNEN, KLEINE SCHEIDEGG, GRINDELWALD, INTERLAKEN, KANDERSTEG, GEMMI PASS, LEUK, SION, MARTIGNY, VEVEY, BERNE, ZURICH

At Zermatt the Chaplain to Queen Victoria 'was requested to conduct Divine Service. The reading saloon was prepared for the purpose. I shortened the service by omitting the first lesson, the Te Deum, and the Litany. Before commencing I announced to the congregation that I should do this, giving as my reason that the room did not belong exclusively to us.'

1873

ANDERSEN, HANS CHRISTIAN. BERNE, VEVEY, GLION, BERNE, COIRE, THUSIS, SPLÜGEN PASS, CHIAVENNA, SAMADEN, PONTRESINA

Righi Vaudois: 'Everything is so beautiful. The snowy mountains rise aloft in the clear sunshine, there is a fragrance of grass and flowers, the beeches hang their fresh green fringed leaves over me in my wanderings, which, I must say, are not very far.'

BAKUNIN, MICHAEL. LOCARNO, BERNE, LOCARNO

BANCROFT, SQUIRE. BASLE, LUCERNE, RIGI, SARNEN, BRUNIG PASS, BRIENZ, INTERLAKEN, LAUTERBRUNNEN, INTERLAKEN, THUN, BERNE, LAUSANNE, MARTIGNY, GRAND ST. BERNARD, MARTIGNY, TÊTE NOIRE PASS, CHAMONIX

BONNEY, THOMAS GEORGE. FINSTERMÜNZ, SCHULS, ZERNEZ, PONTRESINA, FUORCLA SELLA-SCERSCEN, MALOJA PASS, CHIAVENNA, MILAN, ORTA, VOGOGNA, PONTE GRANDE, COL DI BARANCA, FOBELLO, VARALLO, ALAGNA, COL D'OLEN, GRESSONEY, BETTA FURKA, FIERI, SCHWARZTHOR PASS, ZERMATT, EVOLENA

'I believe that the streams from the Forno and Albigna glens formerly flowed into the Innthal, as those from the Fedoz and Fex still do, but that as the corrie at the head of the Maira gradually receded in a north-easterly direction, it interrupted and diverted, as its floor was on a lower level than theirs, first the torrent of the Albigna glen and then that from the Forno.'

CONRAD, JOSEPH. SCHAFFHAUSEN, ZURICH, LUCERNE, RIGI, FLUELEN, ANDERMATT, HOSPENTHAL, FURKA PASS, GRIMSEL PASS, MEIRINGEN

On the Furka pass an Englishman passed, the first real Englishman that the young Pole had seen. Conrad was arguing with his tutor, for he wanted to go to sea. His tutor was getting the better of the argument, when the passing 'unforgettable Englishman' tipped the scale. He smiled at Conrad; the tutor gave up the struggle. Conrad went to sea.

COURBET, GUSTAVE. LES VERRIÈRES, FLEURIER, LAUSANNE, VEVEY, BULLE, GRUYÈRES, GENEVA, NEUCHÂTEL, LA TOUR DE PEILZ

DENT, CLINTON T. CHAMONIX

' "Monsieur is going to the Jardin?" he remarked.
"No, Monsieur isn't." "Then beyond a doubt Monsieur will cross the Col du Géant?" he said, playing his trump card.
"No, Monsieur will not." "Pardon—where does Monsieur expect to go?" "On the present occasion we go to try the Aiguille du Dru".'

DURHAM, W. E. BASLE, LUCERNE, ALTDORF, AMSTEG, ANDERMATT, FURKA PASS, OBERGESTELEN, VIESCH, EGGISHORN, BRIG, VISP, ZERMATT, BREITHORN, ST. THEODUL PASS, BREUIL, CHATILLON, ORTA, LUGANO, COMO, CHIAVENNA, SPLÜGEN PASS, THUSIS, COIRE, SCHAFFHAUSEN

'I don't think I enjoyed the expedition. I was oppressed by the vastness of the whole thing. . . .'

FOX, JOSEPH H. DAVOS, FLUELA PASS, SÜS, LAVIN, PIZ LINARD, BERGÜN, PIZ KESCH, DAVOS, KLOSTERS, SILVRETTAHORN, SCHLAPPINER PASS, KLOSTERS, DAVOS, STRELA PASS, AROSA, MAIENFELDERFURKA PASS, DAVOS, TIEFENKASTEL, THUSIS, COIRE, ALTSTÄTTEN, GAIS, SÄNTIS

FRANKLAND, E. DAVOS

FULTON, CHARLES CARROLL. COMO, CHIAVENNA, SPLÜGEN PASS, THUSIS, COIRE, PFÄFERS, ZURICH, EINSIEDELN, LUCERNE, FLUELEN, VITZNAU, RIGI, BERNE, THUN, INTERLAKEN, LAUTERBRUNNEN, GIESSBACH, INTERLAKEN, THUN, BERNE, LAUSANNE, GENEVA

GOS, ALBERT. GENEVA, BERNE, THUN, FRUTIGEN, KANDERSTEG, OESCHINENALP

'Aux premiers jours de juillet, je fis mes bagages, malle, boite à couleurs, chevalet, toile, chassis, parasol, pliant et violon. Un bon ami m'accompagnait, et, bâton à la main, nous voilà partis, ivres de bonheur. Il n'y a aucune expression possible pour décrire l'état de grâce dans lequel je me trouvais. J'avais vingt et un ans; j'adorais la peinture et la musique; j'idolâtrais la montagne et d'aller au devant de l'inconnu resplendissant de beauté qui m'attendait, je me sentais des forces pour l'éternité. . . .'

GUILD, CURTIS. FINSTERMÜNZ, SCHULS, ZERNEZ, SAMADEN, ST. MORITZ, PONTRESINA, PONTE, ALBULA PASS, BERGÜN, FILISUR, TIEFENKASTEL, SCHYN PASS, THUSIS, COIRE

'. . . At Samaden, we enjoyed the unexpected pleasure of an interview with the Danish Author, Hans Christian Andersen. The good-natured fairy story-teller, who was then sojourning at the hotel, on hearing that two Americans that had read his books would like to see him, came to us with extended hands of welcome, though just returned from a fatiguing excursion to the Morteratsch glacier.'

HAVERGAL, FRANCES RIDLEY. NEUCHÂTEL, BERNE, LUCERNE, RIGI, SARNEN, BRUNIG PASS, BRIENZ, INTERLAKEN, SCHYNIGEPLATTE, GRINDELWALD, LAUTERBRUNNEN, MÜRREN, INTERLAKEN, THUN, BERNE, LAUSANNE, GENEVA, CHAMONIX, TÊTE NOIRE PASS, MARTIGNY, GENEVA

The railway up the Rigi was being completed by 'navvies'. 'I never was more sorry for not having brought more spiritual ammunition, for though I had tracts and "portions" for about forty, it was nothing like enough, and all would have accepted them had I had more.'

HORNBY, EMILY. ENGELBERG, TITLIS

HUGHES, HUGH PRICE. BASLE, LUCERNE, FLUELEN, ALTDORF, ANDERMATT, HOSPENTHAL, FURKA PASS, GRIMSEL PASS, MEIRINGEN, BRIENZ, MEIRINGEN, GROSSE SCHEIDEGG, GRINDELWALD, KLEINE SCHEIDEGG, LAUTERBRUNNEN, INTERLAKEN, THUN, KANDERSTEG, GEMMI PASS, LEUK, SION, MARTIGNY, COL DE BALME, CHAMONIX, GENEVA, LAUSANNE, GENEVA

JAVELLE, ÉMILE. LAUSANNE, ZINAL, ROTHHORN, ZERMATT

JEKYLL, GERTRUDE. LES AVANTS

Staying with the Blumenthals, 'beguiling the days with gardening, sketching, and walks among the flowery alpine pastures, and the nights with dramatic and musical pastimes. . . .'

KEMBLE, FANNY. EVOLENA, MACUGNAGA

'God knows how grateful I am for all I have enjoyed in this most wonderful and beautiful country.'

LOWELL, JAMES RUSSELL. BASLE, INTERLAKEN, LAUTERBRUNNEN, GENEVA, CHAMONIX, GENEVA, MARTIGNY, SION, BRIG, SIMPLON PASS, DOMODOSSOLA

'We have been through Switzerland, where I climbed some of the highest peaks with a spy-glass—a method I find very agreeable, and which spares honest sole-leathers. I am thinking of getting up an achromatic-telescope Alpine Club, to which none will be admitted till they have had two fits of gout, authenticated by a doctor's bill.'

MARRACKS R. (*c*). BASLE, OLTEN, LUCERNE, VITZNAU, RIGI, FLUELEN, LUCERNE, SARNEN, BRUNIG PASS, BRIENZ, INTERLAKEN, LAUTERBRUNNEN, GRINDELWALD, INTERLAKEN, THUN, BERNE, LAUSANNE, GENEVA, CHAMONIX, TÊTE NOIRE PASS, MARTIGNY, VILLENEUVE, LAUSANNE, VALORBE, JOUGNE

MEYER, CONRAD FERDINAND. ZURICH, COIRE, FLIMS, DISENTIS, SEDRUN, CHIAMUTT

At the source of the Rhine, Meyer's guide drew his attention to the echo and invited him to test it. With full voice Meyer shouted 'Bismarck!' A multiple echo answered from the depth, and the sound split on the rocks and repeated itself more and more distantly and faintly, until it became a timid inquiry. 'Pio Nono!' roared the guide with as much force as he could muster. 'Nono, nono?' came the answer, in tones more and more contemptuous, as if the Spirit of the Depths did not know this mortal name.

MONKSWELL, MARY, LADY. MEIRINGEN, ROSENLAUI, GROSSE SCHEIDEGG, GRINDELWALD, LAUTERBRUNNEN, MÜRREN, INTERLAKEN, KANDERSTEG, GEMMI PASS, LEUK, VISP, ZERMATT, ST. THEODUL PASS, CHATILLON, COURMAYEUR

Meiringen: 'We attended a grand exhibition of sketches by an artist (one Croft) up in his bedroom. It was a most impressive ceremony; Sir Henry Thompson, his daughter, Bob & I each collected our candles and marched upstairs with them till we looked like a religious procession.'

NIETZSCHE, FRIEDRICH. BASLE, COIRE, FLIMS

PRIME, SAMUEL IRENAEUS (*c*). GENEVA, LAUSANNE, FRIBOURG, BERNE, THUN, INTERLAKEN, MEIRINGEN, BRUNIG PASS, SARNEN, LUCERNE, FLUELEN, ALTDORF, ZURICH, RICHTERSWIL, EINSIEDELN, ZURICH, ST. GALL, TROGEN

RAMSAY, ANDREW CROMBIE. BASLE, LUCERNE, BRUNIG PASS, MEIRINGEN, GROSSE SCHEIDEGG, GRINDELWALD, KLEINE SCHEIDEGG, LAUTERBRUNNEN, INTERLAKEN, THUN, BERNE, BEX, BASLE

STEPHEN, LESLIE. CHAMONIX, COL DES HIRONDELLES, COURMAYEUR, EVIAN

SYMONDS, JOHN ADDINGTON. AOSTA

'After all, the Alps are the best. I say this deliberately, and I think I have a right to pronounce an opinion. If you do not yet know Switzerland, you have a joy to come which will last longer than anything which the Arts can give.'

TENNYSON, ALFRED. ST. MORITZ, PONTRESINA, MACUGNAGA, DOMODOSSOLA, SIMPLON PASS, BRIG, SIERRE, NEUCHÂTEL

'He has begun a poem, "The voice and the peak", describing the torrent in this valley,

Green-rushing from the rosy thorns of dawn.

The Val d'Anzasca is, he thinks, the grandest valley that he has seen in the Alps.'

WEILENMANN, JOHANN JAKOB. ST. GALL, VISP, ZERMATT, MATTERHORN, COL D'HÉRENS, ZERMATT, RANDA, WEISSHORN

WILSON, H. SCHÜTZ. GENEVA, MONTREUX, MARTIGNY, SION, SIERRE, LEUK, GEMMI PASS, BALMHORN, LEUK, VISP, ZERMATT, MONTREUX

Zermatt: 'there was the usual group of tourists in puggrees, looking like undertakers at the funeral of an infant, and suggesting Wimbledon and the row of targets which resemble a series of aces of clubs.'

ZINCKE, F. BARHAM. BASLE, BERNE, THUN, INTERLAKEN, MEIRINGEN, BRUNIG PASS, STANS, FLUELEN, ALTDORF, ST. GOTTHARD PASS, BELLINZONA, LUGANO, ST. GOTTHARD PASS, ALTDORF, SURENEN PASS, ENGELBERG, STANS, BRUNNEN, SCHWYZ, EINSIEDELN, GLARUS, PRAGEL PASS, SCHWYZ, RIGI, LUCERNE, BRUNIG PASS, MEIRINGEN, GRIMSEL PASS, OBERGESTELEN, VIESCH, EGGISHORN, BELALP, BRIG, SION, MARTIGNY, LAUSANNE, NEUCHÂTEL, LES VERRIÈRES

'I like staying nowhere, except at home. When I am travelling I like to be moving on. It was for that I left home. It seems to me insufferable to return in the evening to the place I left in the morning. The same distance in walking would have carried me to some new place: that is to say, I might have had something additional at the same cost of time and exertion. But there are many who, on this point, would not agree with me; and they, I think, might spend a week pleasantly at Riederalp.'

'Beguiling the days with gardening, sketching, and walks among the flowery alpine pastures'

(*Swiss Federal Railways*) GERTRUDE JEKYLL, 1873; Les Avants

'*So the Jungfrau* vis-à-vis-es *you frankly through the bright sweet intervening air. And then she has such moods; such unutterable smiles, such inscrutable sulks, such growls of rage suppressed, such thunder of avalanches, such crowns of stars*

(*Paul Popper*) THOMAS EDWARD BROWN, 1874

1874

BAKUNIN, MICHAEL. LOCARNO, BELLINZONA, MESOCCO, SAN BERNARDINO PASS, SPLÜGEN PASS, CHIAVENNA, BOLOGNA, CHIAVENNA, SPLÜGEN PASS, SIERRE, SAXON, NEUCHÂTEL, LUGANO

To reach Bologna in secret, Bakunin chose the route of the Splügen, at which village he wrote his *Mémoire Justificatif*.

BANCROFT, SQUIRE. LUCERNE, RIGI-KALTBAD, ALTDORF, ST. GOTTHARD PASS, BELLINZONA, LUGANO, PORLEZZA, MENAGGIO

BONNEY, THOMAS GEORGE. ST. LUC, ZERMATT, MATTERHORN, RIED PASS, SAAS, AROLLA, COL DE BRENEY, CHANRION

BRAHMS, JOHANNES. ZURICH, RÜSCHLIKON

In a house which he had espied from the lake and immediately decided that he wanted to live in, Brahms stayed at Rüschlikon. A number of songs were composed there, including Seven Songs for mixed choir op. 62, and Quartette for four solo voices and piano op. 64.

BROWN, THOMAS EDWARD. NEUCHÂTEL, BERNE, THUN, INTERLAKEN, LAUTERBRUNNEN, MÜRREN, CHAMONIX, GENEVA

'... So the Jungfrau *vis-a-vis*-es you frankly through the bright sweet intervening air. And then she has such moods; such unutterable smiles, such inscrutable sulks, such growls of rage suppressed, such thunder of avalanches, such crowns of stars. One evening our sunset was the real rose pink you have heard of so much. It fades, you know, into a deathlike chalk-white. That is the most *awful* thing. A sort of spasm seems to come over her face, and in an instant she is a corpse, rigid, and oh, so cold! Well, so she died, and you felt as if a great soul had ebbed away into the Heaven of heavens: and thankful, but very sad I went up to my room. I was reading by candle-light, for it gets dark immediately after sunset, when A. shrieked to me to come to the window. What a Resurrection—so gentle, so tender—like that sonnet of Milton's about his dead wife returning to vision! The moon had risen; and there was the Jungfrau.'

BUXTON, EDWARD NORTH. LIVIGNO

'My companion in 1874, who was rather inexperienced, was suffering from an ailment familiar to Alpine climbers fresh out from England.... Our remedies were not sufficiently potent, and prompt measures were necessary. . . . I sought the tonsured apothecary, who received me with delightful bonhomie in his den. . . . Seizing my hand the curé assured me that I need be in no further anxiety; that he had the very thing, a remedy that was *suro, suro*. . . . At 6 A.M. I think half the inhabitants of the valley had assembled outside. . . . Why should they not assemble to watch this contest between the priest and the devil? There was something like a cheer raised, when, at 6.30, I announced that the priest had exorcised the devil. . . .'

CARR, ALFRED. BASLE, LUCERNE, BRUNIG PASS, MEIRINGEN, GROSSE SCHEIDEGG, GRINDELWALD, ZÄSENBERG, LAUTERBRUNNEN, INTERLAKEN, KANDERSTEG, GEMMI PASS, LEUK, VISP, ZERMATT, CIMA DI JAZZI, VISP, SION, MARTIGNY, TÊTE NOIRE PASS, CHAMONIX, GENEVA

At Zermatt 'the first thing we did was to enquire for beds at the Hotel du Mont Rose, which turned out to be crowded, six beds having to be made up in the salon. We next tried the Hotel du Mont Cervin, with the same result, but the landlord very kindly offered to procure us beds at the Curé's chalet. When we got there, oh, such a place! The door was so narrow and low that it took some contriving to get into the house at all. It was a very low square room, on one side of which was a filthy-looking old woman standing over the fire frizzling something for the evening meal. Opposite this fireplace were two miserable-looking beds, nothing better than stretchers, these desirable-looking resting places were offered us for use during our stay at Zermatt, but you may be sure I declined their offer with many thanks and left this fever-suggesting hole to look for more comfortable quarters.'

COOLIDGE, W. A. B. CHAMONIX, TÊTE NOIRE PASS, MARTIGNY, LAUSANNE, BERNE, THUN, INTERLAKEN, LAUTERBRUNNEN, KLEINE SCHEIDEGG, GRINDELWALD, FAULHORN, WETTERHORN, MÖNCHJOCH PASS, JUNGFRAU

An excursion in January to the astonishment of the local population. 'The great inconvenience of winter travelling seems to me to consist in the total absence of water; we had to melt snow in order to make tea, soup, etc.'

FISKE, JOHN. GENEVA, LAUSANNE, FRIBOURG, BERNE, THUN, INTERLAKEN, GRINDELWALD, LAUTERBRUNNEN, INTERLAKEN, BRIENZ, BRUNIG PASS, LUCERNE, FLUELEN, ALTDORF, VITZNAU, RIGI, LUCERNE, BASLE

'But for sublimity, and beauty, and loveliness *combined*, I say that Switzerland is so far above all other countries, that there is no use in saying any more about it. To compare any other country with it is absurd. You must see it sometime.'

FRESHFIELD, DOUGLAS. FAIDO, VAL PRATO, BROGLIO, BIGNASCO, PASSO REDORTA, VAL VERZASCA, LOCARNO, CANNOBIA, STA. MARIA MAGGIORE

'Bignasco lives in my memory as one of the loveliest spots in the Italian Alps. Planted at the meeting-place of three valleys, the view up Val Bavona is only the fairest of the fair scenes which surround it.'

GONCOURT, EDMOND DE. LUCERNE, FLUELEN, ANDERMATT, FURKA PASS, GRIMSEL PASS, MEIRINGEN, GIESSBACH, ROMANSHORN, LINDAU, CONSTANCE, SCHAFFHAUSEN, BASLE

'Sur ces hauts sommets, le voyageur jouit de la pureté de l'air comme un gourmet d'eau jouit à Rome de la bonté de l'aqua felice . . . Décidément les voyages ne sont qu'une suite de petits supplices. On a tout le temps, trop chaud, trop froid, trop soif, trop faim, et tout le temps on est trop mal couché, trop mal nourri, pour beaucoup trop d'argent et de fatigue.'

GOS, ALBERT. GENEVA, VISP, ZERMATT, ST. NIKLAUS, EMD, TÖRBEL, ZAENECKEN, TURTMANN

'J'aime cette vallée comme on aime un vieil ami d'enfance. Ah! qu'elles sont fortes ces émotions, et neuves les sensations qu'on éprouve en allant avec passion à la decouverte, seul, très seul, muni de rares indications.'

GROVE, SIR GEORGE. CHAMONIX, BRIG, BELALP, OBERGESTELEN, FURKA PASS, ANDERMATT, ALTDORF, LUCERNE, BASLE

HAVERGAL, FRANCES RIDLEY. GRINDELWALD, FAULHORN, ORMONTS-DESSUS, COL DE PILLON, GSTEIG, SAANEN, CHÂTEAU D'OEX, COL DE JAMAN, MONTREUX

'Sunset on the Faulhorn! . . . Imagine yourself midway between heaven and earth; when the whole pageant, lasting nearly an hour was past, we sang "Abide with me".'

While at Ormonts-Dessus, Miss Havergal started writing *Little Pillows*.

JAVELLE, ÉMILE. VEVEY, ZERMATT, TIEFENMATTENJOCH, PRARAYÉ, DENT D'HÉRENS, BREUIL, MATTERHORN, ZERMATT

LOWDER, CHARLES. BERNE, THUN, INTERLAKEN, ST. MORITZ

NIETZSCHE, FRIEDRICH. BASLE, COIRE, FILISUR, BERGÜN, COIRE, RORSCHACH

PLUNKET, FREDERICA. THUN, INTERLAKEN, GRINDELWALD, LAUTERBRUNNEN, TSCHINGEL PASS, KANDERSTEG, INTERLAKEN, MEIRINGEN, JOCH PASS, ENGELBERG, LUCERNE, COIRE, THUSIS, TIEFENKASTEL, JULIER PASS, ST. MORITZ, PONTRESINA, BERNINA PASS, VAL VIOLA PASS, BORMIO

'A fortnight spent in the Engadine did not much alter the first impression it had made upon us. We still thought its scenery overpraised, and its climate unpleasant. The air there certainly is peculiarly light and bracing, but it is not very agreeable to be frozen every morning, baked at noon, and perished at night, nor to rise, as we did in the morning in August, and find a white world all around.'

PRITCHARD, H. BADEN (*c*). MENAGGIO, PORLEZZO, LUGANO, LUINO, DOMODOSSOLA, SIMPLON PASS, BRIG, SIERRE, SION, MARTIGNY, BOUVERET, GENEVA

RAMBERT, EUGÈNE. SCHWYZ, LUCERNE, LAUSANNE, MARTIGNY, SION, BRIG, OBERGESTELEN, FURKA PASS, ANDERMATT, ALTDORF, BRUNNEN, SCHWYZ

'Il y avait environ deux cents touristes sur le bateau qui m'a transporté à Lucerne, et je n'ai pas trouvé dans le nombre un seul Anglais, . . . il y a dix ans, sur deux cents touristes pris au hasard, au bord du lac des Quatre Cantons, on eût compté une centaine d'Anglais, au moins. Le public qu'attire la Suisse, particulièrement la Suisse centrale, a complètement changé. . . .'

RENAN, ERNEST. BRIENZ, AIROLO, BELLINZONA, LUGANO

'La Suisse m'a fait grand plaisir. Depuis la Norvège je n'avais pas vu quelque chose d'aussi grandiose ni d'aussi frais. Quelle verdure! Quelles eaux! Les lacs au fonds de profondes vallées sont sûrement une des plus belles choses de notre planète. Malheureusement les hôtels, les pensions gâtent bien tout cela. Dans vingt-cinq ans la région alpestre de la Suisse ne sera qu'un vaste hôtel garni.'

RICHARDSON, FANNY. GENEVA, CHAMONIX, MONT BLANC, TÊTE NOIRE PASS, CHATELARD, SALVAN, VERNAYAZ, MARTIGNY, GRAND ST. BERNARD, MARTIGNY, SION, EVOLENA, COL D'HÉRENS, ZERMATT, VISP, BRIG, SIMPLON PASS, DOMODOSSOLA, STRESA, LUINO, LUGANO, PORLEZZA, MENAGGIO, CHIAVENNA, MALOJA PASS, ST. MORITZ, PONTRESINA, DIAVOLEZZA, PONTE, ALBULA PASS, BERGÜN, PARPAN PASS, COIRE, ZURICH, BASLE

RITZ, CÉSAR. RIGI

Ritz was at this time head-waiter in the Rigi Kulm hotel. 'César loved to relate, with appropriate mimicry and hilarious laughter, the story of one morning when, in the midst of the sun's performance, a nasty wind came along and snatched the blanket from a dignified and whiskered Englishman. There he stood attired in his long woollen underwear! With a cry of horror he flung himself face downward in the snow, and he would not budge until someone had caught the errant blanket and wrapped him in it!

'It amused him also to describe one of the severe mountain storms that descended upon the exposed hotel with such ferocity that soon the corridors were full of night-capped gentlemen and ladies in curl-papers, who flung themselves upon their knees in anguish, praying heaven to spare them in its wrath. "It is the end of the world," they cried. The hotel, as a matter of fact, was struck, and the brand-new system of electric bells was completely out of order. General Moltke was one of the visitors that year. . . .'

RUSKIN, JOHN. GENEVA, CHAMONIX, ST. MARTIN, GENEVA

Ruskin returned to his favourite haunt to finish preparing his lectures on Mountain Form.

STEPHEN, LESLIE. COURMAYEUR, COL DU GÉANT, CHAMONIX

THOMPSON, SILVANUS P. BASLE, LAUFEN, MOUTIER, WEISSENSTEIN

'I took a final gaze upon those ethereal crests of unimaginable pearl, and turned to descend. . . . Well, one of the dreams of my life has been at last fulfilled. The snow peaks of the Alps are stamped into my mind for ever.'

TUCKETT, FRANCIS FOX. APPENZELL, SÄNTIS, WALLENSTADT, PFÄFERS, SARDONA PASS, ELM, GLARUS, EINSIEDELN, LUCERNE, ENGELBERG, JOCH PASS, ENGSTLENALP, SÄTTELI PASS, GADMEN, TRIFTLIMMI PASS, GLETSCH, BRIG, BELALP, BRIG, SIMPLON PASS, ISELLE, VEGLIA, PASSO DI VALTENDRA, PREMIA, TOSA FALLS, BOCHETTA DI VALMAGGIA, BIGNASCO, LOCARNO, MACUGNAGA, COL DELLE LOCCIE, LYSJOCH PASS, ZERMATT, LYSKAMM, ST. JACQUES D'AYAS, BRUSSONE, COL DE JOUX, CHATILLON, AOSTA, COURMAYEUR, PETIT ST. BERNARD PASS, BOURG ST. MAURICE

URLIN, RICHARD DENNY. BASLE, LUCERNE, FLUELEN, ANDERMATT, ST. GOTTHARD, HOSPENTHAL, FURKA PASS, OBERGESTELEN, VIESCH, EGGISHORN, BRIG, SIERRE, MARTIGNY, MONTREUX

WEILENMANN, JOHANN JAKOB. ST. GALL, SIERRE, KIPPEL, BIETSCHHORN, BEICH PASS, ALETSCHHORN, BELALP, BRIG, ZERMATT, ALPHUBELJOCH, SAAS

The hotel at Belalp was full of English. Weilenmann found himself roped in for an Anglican church service in the salon. He also met Miss Brevoort and her dog Tschingel 'in whom she had succeeded in awakening an aesthetic appreciation of mountain beauty'. There was also 'her nephew who accompanied her, basking in the glory of her sunshine, as mute as a fish and self-centred'. This was W. A. B. Coolidge.

WHYMPER, EDWARD. ZERMATT, MATTERHORN

Whymper's second ascent of the Matterhorn.

WILSON, H. SCHÜTZ. CHAMONIX, ZERMATT, SAAS, FLETSCHHORN

ZINCKE, F. BARHAM. INTERLAKEN, MEIRINGEN, SUSTEN PASS, WASSEN, ANDERMATT, OBERALP PASS, DISENTIS, COIRE, STRELA PASS, DAVOS, TIEFENKASTEL, THUSIS, ANDEER, AVERS CRESTA, FORCELLINA PASS, SEPTIMER PASS, CASACCIA, MALOJA PASS, ST. MORITZ, PONTRESINA,

HEUTAL, FIENO PASS, LIVIGNO, BORMIO, STELVIO PASS, TAUFERS, CRÜSCHETTA PASS, TARASP, SÜS, DAVOS, KLOSTERS, LANDQUART, COIRE, DISENTIS, LUKMANIER PASS, UOMO PASS, PIORA, AIROLO, CORNO PASS, GRIES PASS, ULRICHEN

'If these Prätigau peasants were transferred to this country, they could do in England what they do in the Prätigau. If 10,000 of our peasantry were transferred to the Prätigau, and put in possession of the existing houses, and of the land, and of every appliance needed for cultivating it, the only result would be universal starvation.'

1875

BANCROFT, SQUIRE. ZURICH, LUCERNE, RIGI-KALTBAD, SARNEN, BRUNIG PASS, BRIENZ, INTERLAKEN, LAUTERBRUNNEN, MÜRREN

At Lucerne, the Bancrofts saw the Duke of Connaught carrying his own luggage to his hotel.

BONNER, MISS. MARTIGNY, GRAND ST. BERNARD, MARTIGNY

'I then tried the piano which was presented by the Prince of Wales. The harmonium was given by the composer Blumenthal.'

BONNEY, THOMAS GEORGE. ZERMATT, CHANRION, COURMAYEUR, COL DE MIAGE, CHAMONIX

'Personally conducted parties, such as those organized by Cook and Lunn, were unknown half a century ago. I remember in 1875, seeing one gathered by the former walking into Chamonix. It was an irregular procession of incongruities, headed by an elderly clergyman in a top hat who "pegged" the footpath with his alpenstock at every step as if that were a ceremonial observance.'

BUTLER, JOSEPHINE. GENEVA, LAUSANNE, BERNE, NEUCHÂTEL, LA CHAUX DE FONDS

The ardent social reformer was visiting Switzerland in connexion with her work: 'How nobly dear little Switzerland has responded, has it not?'

COLLINGS, HENRY. LES VERRIÈRES, NEUCHÂTEL, CHAUMONT, BERNE, FRIBOURG, THUN, INTERLAKEN, LAUTERBRUNNEN, MÜRREN, INTERLAKEN, BRIENZ, BRUNIG PASS, LUCERNE, FLUELEN, VITZNAU, RIGI, GENEVA, CHAMONIX, MONT BLANC, TÊTE NOIRE PASS, MARTIGNY, GRAND ST. BERNARD, MARTIGNY, OUCHY

COOLIDGE, W. A. B. LAUTERBRUNNEN, KLEINE SCHEIDEGG, GRINDELWALD, KLEIN SCHRECKHORN, CHAMONIX, MONT BLANC, AIGUILLE VERTE, MONT BUET

HORNBY, EMILY. ZERMATT, MATTERHORN

HORT, F. J. A. PONTRESINA

ILLINGWORTH, JOHN RICHARDSON. ZERMATT

JAVELLE, ÉMILE. VEVEY, SALVAN, FENÊTRE DE SALEINAZ, CHAMPEX, ORSIÈRES, MARTIGNY, VERNAYAZ, SALVAN, AIGUILLE DU TOUR

LIÉGEARD, STEPHEN. COIRE, THUSIS, TIEFENKASTEL, JULIER PASS, ST. MORITZ, PONTRESINA, BERNINA PASS, TIRANO, BORMIO, STELVIO PASS, TRAFOI, MILAN, COMO, PORLEZZA, LUGANO, STRESA, LOCARNO, BELLINZONA, ST. GOTTHARD PASS, ALTDORF, LUCERNE

'Ponte Sarazino dont les transformations du langage ont fait Pontrésina. On va même jusqu'à vouloir retrouver encore la trace de ces envahisseurs sous le vocable d'une famille Saratz qui aurait, dit-on, du sang oriental dans les veines. L'un de ses membres exploite l'hotellerie de ce nom. Je ne sais s'il vous y traite en arabe, mais l'installation semble défier toute critique. Les Anglais après tout, pourraient seuls se plaindre, car ils se sont emparés de l'hotel Saratz, ainsi que de Malte et de Gibraltar: ils y ont fait escale et y tiennent garnison.'

LLOYD, FRANCIS. PONTRESINA, ST. MORITZ

Lloyd published the first English guide to 'Walks near Pontresina, not including long excursions or mountain ascents'.

MARCET, WILLIAM. GENEVA, YVOIRE, MARTIGNY, GRAND ST. BERNARD, MARTIGNY, VISP, ZERMATT, ST. THEODUL PASS, BREITHORN

MAXWELL, SIR HERBERT. BASLE, ZURICH, WALLENSTADT, COIRE, FILISUR, ALBULA PASS, PONTRESINA, MALOJA PASS, CHIAVENNA

RITCHIE, ANNE THACKERAY. INTERLAKEN, SCHYNIGEPLATTE, GRINDELWALD, ROSENLAUI, INTERLAKEN

'Interlaken. All Cambridge seems to be about. There is Henry Butcher sitting under a tree waiting for his luggage, in one of Leslie [Stephen]'s shirts. Mr. and Miss Browning were not at the station. Mr. Balfour is somewhere. We met Professor Tyndall, D.C.L., in the road, smilingly escorting some ladies of rank.'

STEPHEN, LESLIE. MURREN, GRINDELWALD, NÄSSIJOCH

'To me the Wengern Alp is a sacred place—the holy of holies in the mountain sanctuary, and the emotions produced when no desecrating influence is present and old memories rise up, softened by the sweet sadness of the scenery, belong to that innermost region of feeling which I would not, if I could, lay bare.'

STOCK, EUGENE. BERNE, THUN, INTERLAKEN, LUCERNE, FLUELEN, ALTDORF, ANDERMATT, FURKA PASS, GENEVA

SYMONDS, JOHN ADDINGTON. BRIG, BELALP, CHAMONIX

While at Chamonix Symonds was working at volume 2 of *The Renaissance in Italy.*

WILLS, MARY H. ZURICH, LUCERNE, RIGI, SARNEN, BRUNIG PASS, MEIRINGEN

WILSON, H. SCHÜTZ. GRINDELWALD, SCHRECKHORN

1876

BAKUNIN, MICHAEL. LUGANO, BELLINZINA, ST. GOTTHARD PASS, FLUELEN, LUCERNE, BERNE

At Berne, whither he had gone to see his friend Vogt, the great anarchist died.

BANCROFT, SQUIRE. ZURICH, RIGI-KALTBAD, ALTDORF, ANDERMATT, FURKA PASS, OBERGESTELEN, VIESCH, EGGISHORN, RIEDERALP, BELALP, BRIG

At the Rigi-Kaltbad, the Bancrofts found Palgrave Simpson, Arthur Cecil, and Clement Scott. Practical jokes were much to the fore, and one night while a dance was in progress, they drove some stray cows through the French windows in among the dancers. There was an old lady at the hotel whom, from her resemblance to him, they called 'Sir Julius Benedict'. Who should then turn up but Sir Julius himself, who greeted her, the first flame of his life.

BROOKE, STOPFORD. OUCHY, ST. MAURICE, ZERMATT

'The sun broke out and lit the head of the cone-shaped mountain that beyond the town fills up the end of the valley. We went into the old Abbey and heard the organ play the end of the service. Returning and going in the train one wild dream after another beset me and made my blood rush fast and warm. But as the rain fell on us it seemed to wipe them all out with a sponge. "Dreamer," it said to me, "why not try the possible, not the impossible?" And I answered, "I have always hated the possible all my life; I will hate it to the end".'

BROWNING, OSCAR. RIEDERALP

Browning presented the innkeeper at Riederalp with Voltaire's works in 100 volumes. Subsequently, one of Browning's pupils found that they had been buried, and had them dug up.

BUTLER, GEORGE. BERNE, THUN, INTERLAKEN, GRINDELWALD, INTERLAKEN, KANDERSTEG, GEMMI PASS, LEUK, VISP, ZERMATT

BUTLER, SAMUEL. LUCERNE, ALTDORF, ST. GOTTHARD PASS, FAIDO, BELLINZONA, LUGANO, MENDRISIO, LOCARNO, BIGNASCO, FUSIO, SASSELLO PASS, AIROLO, PIORA

Butler was writing *Life and Habit*. Referring to 'Grace! the old Pagan ideal whose charm even unlovely Paul could not withstand', he continues 'But the true grace, with her groves and high places, and troops of young men and maidens crowned with flowers, and singing of love and youth and wine—the true grace he drove out into the wilderness—high up, it may be, into Piora, and into such-like places. Happy they who harboured her in her ill report.'

CONWAY, MARTIN. PONTRESINA, FUORCLA PRIEVLUSA, PIZ PALÜ, PIZ ROSEG, PIZ BERNINA

'*On ne badine pas avec — la montagne.*'

COOLIDGE, W. A. B. CHAMONIX, ZERMATT, VISP, BRIG, BELALP, MADERANERTAL, PLANURA PASS, SANDALP, TÖDI, DISENTIS, COIRE, THUSIS, TIEFENKASTEL, JULIER PASS, ST. MORITZ, BERNINA PASS, TIRANO, APRICA PASS, EDOLO

COWELL, EDWARD BYLES. BASLE, BERNE, THUN, INTERLAKEN, LAUTERBRUNNEN, MÜRREN, LUCERNE, BASLE

DÉTRÉ, ERNEST. BASLE, SCHAFFHAUSEN, ZURICH, ZUG, LUCERNE, RIGI, SARNEN, BRUNIG PASS, MEIRINGEN, GROSSE SCHEIDEGG, GRINDELWALD, KLEINE SCHEIDEGG, LAUTERBRUNNEN, INTERLAKEN, THUN, BERNE, FRIBOURG, LAUSANNE, VEVEY, MARTIGNY, TÊTE NOIRE PASS, CHAMONIX, GENEVA

GAMBETTA, LÉON. CLARENS, MARTIGNY, SION, BRIG, SIMPLON

GOS, ALBERT. GENEVA, ZINAL

HAVERGAL, FRANCES RIDLEY. LAUSANNE, VERNAYAZ, FINHAUT, CHAMONIX, TÊTE NOIRE PASS, MARTIGNY, CHAMPEX, MARTIGNY, MONTHEY, CHAMPÉRY, MONTHEY, BERNE, THUN, INTERLAKEN, LAUTERBRUNNEN, ISENFLUH, WENGEN, INTERLAKEN, THUN, BERNE, BASLE

At Finhaut, Miss Havergal had been singing 'Only for Thee', and found that 'this gave immense satisfaction in our little pension'. So she set to and wrote 'Seulement pour Toi'. Later, in the diligence from Orsières to the Great St. Bernard the passengers started singing French songs. Miss Havergal then asked if they would join in singing a new song, 'Seulement pour Toi'. 'Finding the driver took up the chorus in bass, Frances went outside that he might see the words; and most heartily was it sung by all.'

HORNBY, EMILY. AROLLA, ZINAL, EGGISHORN, JUNGFRAU, FINSTERAARHORN, VIESCH, VISP, ZERMATT, DENT BLANCHE

'My eyes were very bad all day . . . sat in my room till dinner-time bathing them with milk, and last night, at the recommendation of my guide, went to bed with a piece of raw meat on each, like a prize-fighter, and it has certainly done them good.'

HORT, F. J. A. VISP, SAAS, MATTMARK

HUGHES, HUGH PRICE. ZERMATT, BREITHORN, WEISSTHOR, MACUGNAGA, ZERMATT, ENGELBERG, TITLIS, JOCH PASS, INNERTKIRCHEN, GRIMSEL PASS, OBERGESTELEN, VIESCH, EGGISHORN

'We had a kind of Church Congress on the Gorner Grat—one extreme Ritualist, a Broad Churchman, an Evangelical, and myself talked theology and became great friends. . . .'

JAVELLE, ÉMILE. VEVEY, COURMAYEUR, COL FERRET, TOUR NOIR, ZINAL

JOWETT, BENJAMIN. GENEVA, VEVEY, ST. MORITZ, LOCARNO, MACUGNAGA, MONTE MORO PASS, SAAS, ZERMATT, VISP, CHAMONIX, BASLE

KROPOTKIN, PETER. LA CHAUX DE FONDS, NEUCHÂTEL, BERNE, ST. IMIER

Kropotkin took part in a Red Flag demonstration in Berne.

MACDONALD, GREVILLE. RIEDERALP, ST. LUC

'As if inexorable Beauty and frozen Terror were almost too much for poor Londoners to bear, we had flowers in tenderest loveliness on every side; but the only one that lasted all the way up was the gentian, in divinely blue clusters in the snow itself, finer and larger as we ascended. Somehow they belonged to the Matterhorn, after all, and her grandeur to them . . . with the sky for us all. . . .'

MÜLLER, GEORGE. NEUCHÂTEL, BERNE, LUCERNE, RIGI, FLUELEN, ALTDORF, ANDERMATT, ST. GOTTHARD, ALTDORF, LUCERNE, ZURICH, ST. GALL, HEINRICHSBAD, HERISAU, HEIDEN, GLARUS, RAGAZ, TROGEN, HEIDEN, CONSTANCE, SCHAFFHAUSEN, BASLE

'These are no places, one would think, for infidels; for here, if *any*-where, the most careless even must be constrained to acknowledge that "the strength of the hills is His also".'

NIETZSCHE, FRIEDRICH. BASLE, MONTREUX, VEYTAUX, GENEVA, BEX

NOEL, RODEN. GENEVA, MEILLERIE, MACUGNAGA

QUEENSBERRY, JOHN SHOLTO DOUGLAS, MARQUIS OF. ZERMATT

RUSKIN, JOHN. GENEVA, MARTIGNY, SION, BRIG, SIMPLON PASS, DOMODOSSOLA

On the Simplon Ruskin wrote the Chapter of *Deucalion* entitled 'Thirty Years Since'.

STEPHEN, LESLIE. THUN, MEIRINGEN, GRIMSEL, GRINDELWALD, KLEINE SCHEIDEGG, LAUTERBRUNNEN, INTERLAKEN

'Scenery, even the wildest which is really enjoyable, derives half its charm from the occult sense of the human life and social forms moulded upon it.'
This was a journey in January.

SWEENEY, J. N. BASLE, LUCERNE, RIGI, SCHWYZ, EINSIEDELN, SCHWYZ, ALPNACH, BRÜNIG PASS, BRIENZ, INTERLAKEN, LAUTERBRUNNEN, INTERLAKEN, THUN, BERNE, NEUCHÂTEL

'It was up this mountain [Pilatus] 8,000 feet high, that our gracious Queen Victoria ascended in the summer of 1868. During my visit I was happy to tread in Her Majesty's footsteps, although I must confess that I did not succeed in mounting to the very top. But to do a little less than the Queen is not a dishonourable exploit.'

SYMONDS, JOHN ADDINGTON. MARTIGNY, TÊTE NOIRE PASS, CHAMONIX, SAAS, SIRWOLTEN PASS, SIMPLON PASS, BRIG, RIEDERALP

URLIN, RICHARD DENNY. LUCERNE, FLUELEN, ALTDORF, ST. GOTTHARD PASS, BELLINZONA, LUGANO, MILAN, GENEVA, LAUSANNE, MARTIGNY, TÊTE NOIRE PASS, CHAMONIX, GENEVA, LAUSANNE

WILSON, H. SCHÜTZ. ZERMATT, MATTERHORN

'Like Mary Queen of Scots, the Matterhorn, though irresistible in attraction, may yet be fatal to fascinated lovers.'

1877

ALLBUTT, SIR THOMAS CLIFFORD. BASLE, ZURICH, LANDQUART, KLOSTERS, DAVOS, PONTRESINA

'A well-known and most accomplished English writer said to me at Davos, "I was travelling, at Sir W. Jenner's advice, to Egypt. On my way I drifted here." This was John Addington Symonds, who was advised by Allbutt to stay at Davos.'

BANCROFT, SQUIRE. COIRE, FILISUR, ALBULA PASS, PONTRESINA, BERNINA PASS, TIRANO, BORMIO, STELVIO PASS

BROOKS, PHILLIPS. LUCERNE, BRUNIG PASS, BRIENZ, INTERLAKEN, GRINDELWALD, KLEINE SCHEIDEGG, LAUTERBRUNNEN, INTERLAKEN, THUN, VISP, ZERMATT, MARTIGNY, TÊTE NOIRE PASS, CHAMONIX

'The minister at Geneva wrote and wanted me to lay the corner stone of his new church, but I wrote him I could not, and he asked General Grant, which no doubt pleased him a great deal better.'

BROWNING, ROBERT. GENEVA, LA SAISIAZ

'. . . What will be the morning glory, when at dusk thus gleams the lake?
Light by light puts forth Geneva: what a land—and, of the land,
Can there be a lovelier station than this spot where now we stand? . . .'

BUTLER, JOSEPHINE. LUCERNE, ALTDORF, ANDERMATT, HOSPENTHAL, FURKA PASS, OBERGESTELEN, BRIG, SION, MARTIGNY, GENEVA

BUTLER, SAMUEL. MENDRISIO, MONTE BISBINO, BELLINZONA, FAIDO

Butler was writing *Life and Habit*.

CONWAY, MARTIN. ZERMATT, MONTE ROSA, ZINAL, AROLLA, PRARAYÉ, BREUIL, ST. THEODUL PASS, ZERMATT, ZINAL-ROTHORN, MATTERHORN, WEISSHORN, CHAMONIX

'Alone amid the high snows a man may abandon himself to the maddest frolic of delight. He may shout and sing and express his joy, and there will be none to call him mad or put him to shame. Rousseau-like, he may, if he pleases, lard the glacier with his tears. I had no call to weep nor often to shout, but I loved those lonely days high aloft. They were fraught with emotions long grown indistinct, but memory holds them embalmed in a fragrance none the less precious in that it escapes description.'

DORIGNY, CHARLES (*c*). BASLE, LUCERNE, RIGI, SARNEN, BRUNIG PASS, BRIENZ, INTERLAKEN, GRINDELWALD, INTERLAKEN, THUN, BERNE, FRIBOURG, LAUSANNE, GENEVA

GRANT, GENERAL ULYSSES S. BASLE, LUCERNE, INTERLAKEN, THUN, BERNE, GENEVA, CHAMONIX, MARTIGNY, SION, BRIG, SIMPLON PASS, DOMODOSSOLA, MILAN, CHIAVENNA, SPLÜGEN PASS, THUSIS, COIRE, RAGAZ, ZURICH, BASLE

After laying the corner-stone of the American Episcopalian Church at Geneva, the General said: 'I have never felt myself more happy than among this assembly of fellow republicans of America and Switzerland. I have long had a desire to visit the city where the Alabama claims were settled by arbitration without the effusion of blood, and where the principle of arbitration was established, which I hope will be resorted to by other nations and be the means of continuing peace to all mankind.' Mont Blanc was illuminated in honour of the General's visit.

GÜSSFELDT, PAUL. PONTRESINA, MONTE DI SCERSCEN, PONTE, PIZ KESCH

HERMAN, ANDRÉ. GENEVA, LAUSANNE, FRIBOURG, BERNE, LUCERNE, RIGI, SARNEN, BRUNIG PASS, BRIENZ, INTERLAKEN, LAUTERBRUNNEN, GRINDELWALD, FAULHORN, GROSSE SCHEIDEGG, MEIRINGEN, GRIMSEL PASS, FURKA PASS, HOSPENTHAL, ST. GOTTHARD PASS, AIROLO, BELLINZONA, LOCARNO, PALLANZA, DOMODOSSOLA, SIMPLON PASS, BRIG, SION, MARTIGNY

ILLINGWORTH, JOHN RICHARDSON. CHAMONIX, SION, EVOLENA, ZINAL, ZERMATT

'Absolutely and ideally jolly.'

KEMBLE, FANNY. STELVIO PASS, BORMIO, TIRANO, LE PRESE, BERNINA PASS, PONTRESINA, ST. MORITZ, JULIER PASS, TIEFENKASTEL, THUSIS, SPLÜGEN PASS, CHIAVENNA, MALOJA PASS, ST. MORITZ, SCHULS, TARASP, LANDECK, ARLBERG, FELDKIRCH, RAGAZ

At Thusis she met General Grant.

MAGGS, J. BASLE, SCHAFFHAUSEN, CONSTANCE, ZURICH, ZUG, LUCERNE, RIGI, FLUELEN, ANDERMATT, FURKA PASS, ANDERMATT, ALTDORF, LUCERNE, BRUNIG PASS, BRIENZ, GIESSBACH, INTERLAKEN, LAUTERBRUNNEN, GRINDELWALD, INTERLAKEN, THUN, BERNE, FRIBOURG, NEUCHÂTEL, LA CHAUX DE FONDS, FRIBOURG, LAUSANNE, VEVEY, MARTIGNY, TÊTE NOIRE PASS, CHAMONIX, GENEVA, LAUSANNE

'If distance lends enchantment to the view, it borrows from the size in return. Lay this original proverb well up in your minds, all ye who travel through Switzerland, for you will find such mighty mountains as Snowden and Ben-Nevis would look like dwarfs beside these giants of the Alps, and these giants of the Alps not looking so big as they really are, or as you expected to see them.'

MAUPASSANT, GUY DE. BASLE, BERNE, THUN, KANDERSTEG, GEMMI PASS, LEUKERBAD, SION, MARTIGNY, GENEVA

'C'est sauvage, mais très beau. Cette muraille de roches hautes de deux mille mètres, d'où glissent cent torrents pareils à des filets d'argent; ce bruit éternel de l'eau qui roule; ce village enseveli dans les Alpes d'où l'on voit, comme du fond d'un puits, le soleil lointain traverser le ciel; le glacier voisin, tout blanc dans l'échancrure de la montagne, et ce vallon plein de ruisseaux, plein d'arbres, plein de fraîcheur et de vie, qui descend vers le Rhône et laisse voir à l'horizon les cimes neigeuses du Piétmont: tout cela me séduit et m'enchante.' Maupassant's crossing of the Gemmi inspired his story *L'Auberge.*

NIETZSCHE, FRIEDRICH. RAGAZ, ZURICH, LUCERNE, BRUNIG PASS, MEIRINGEN, ROSENLAUI

RUSKIN, JOHN. DOMODOSSOLA, SIMPLON PASS, BRIG, SION, MARTIGNY, NYON

'Quite dazzling morning of old Alpine purity; sacredest light on soft pines, sacredest sound of birds and waters in the pure air, a turf of gentians on my window-sill, just opening to the sun. Yesterday up the valley that ends the gorge of Gondo, to its head; the wildest, far-away piece of lovely pastoral I remember.'

STEPHEN, LESLIE. INTERLAKEN, MEIRINGEN, GRIMSEL PASS, GALENSTOCK

'Had I the pen of Ruskin, I could not describe to you a tithe of the tender, melancholy, inspiring glories of the Alps in January.'

SYMONDS, JOHN ADDINGTON. BASLE, COIRE, LANDQUART, MEZZASELVA, KLOSTERS, DAVOS

TCHAIKOVSKY, PETER ILJITSCH. CLARENS

Tchaikovsky went to Clarens to recover from mental strain. He was able to resume work there and started *Eugene Onegin.* 'From my window I get a glorious view of the lake, the mountains of Savoy and the Dent du Midi. . . . But if you have ever had the experience, which perhaps no northerner can escape, of longing for wide open stretches, and uninterrupted horizon, and endless distance, a longing which at least with me sets in after a few days in the mountains, that is why in spite of the gorgeous beauty of this place, I should like to go to Italy.' At Clarens he stayed at the Villa Richelieu.

THOMPSON, SILVANUS P. BASLE, ZURICH, INTERLAKEN, LAUTERBRUNNEN, KLEINE SCHEIDEGG, GRINDELWALD, GROSSE SCHEIDEGG, MEIRINGEN, GRIMSEL PASS, OBERGESTELEN, VISP, ZERMATT, ST. THEODUL PASS, BREUIL

TYNDALL, JOHN. BELALP

In this year Tyndall built himself a house on Alp Lusgen near Belalp, whence the view of . . .

'Sky-touching Simplon pass—
Flanked by the Lion Mountain to the left,
While to the right the mighty Fletschorn lifts
A beetling brow, and spreads abroad its snows.
Dom, Cervin—Weisshorn of the dazzling dazzling crown—
Ye splendours of the Alps! Can earth elsewhere
Bring forth a rival? . . .'

WATERHOUSE, THEODORE. ST. MORITZ, PONTRESINA, BERNINA PASS, VAL VIOLA PASS, BORMIO

WILSON, CLAUDE. LEUK, GEMMI PASS, KANDERSTEG, TSCHINGEL PASS, MÜRREN, GRINDELWALD, WETTERHORN, ROSENLAUI, MEIRINGEN, ENGSTLENALP, AMSTEG, MADERANERTAL

WILSON, H. SCHÜTZ. ZERMATT

1878

ANONYMOUS 13 (*c*). BASLE, SCHAFFHAUSEN, ZURICH, WESEN, RAGAZ, PFÄFERS, COIRE, THUSIS, SPLÜGEN PASS, CHIAVENNA

BANCROFT, SQUIRE. RAGAZ, COIRE, THUSIS, TIEFENKASTEL, JULIER PASS, ST. MORITZ, PONTRESINA, JULIER PASS, TIEFENKASTEL, THUSIS, REICHENAU, DISENTIS, OBERALP PASS, ANDERMATT, ALTDORF, BRUNNEN, LUCERNE

At Pontresina the Bancrofts found Jenny Lind.
'For the benefit of the Verschönerungsverein! or paths and ways improvement society, . . . Mrs. Bancroft repeated her reading of the death of Jo from *Bleak House*; the result was very gratifying, and allows her to think in many a walk, as she treads the well-made paths, how much she helped to make them.'

BERNSTEIN, EDUARD. BASLE, OLTEN, LUCERNE, FLUELEN, ANDERMATT, ST. GOTTHARD PASS, BELLINZONA, LUGANO

'In a little place called Besso, in the upper part of Lugano, there stood in my time a one-storeyed house which the Italian Giuseppe Mazzini, the Hungarian Lajos Kossuth, the Pole Langiewicz, and the Russian Michael Bakunin had inhabited.'

BONNEY, THOMAS GEORGE. BELLINZONA, ST. GOTTHARD PASS, ALTDORF, LUCERNE

BROWNING, ROBERT. ZURICH, COIRE, THUSIS, SPLÜGEN PASS, CHIAVENNA

Browning and his sister stayed at the summit of the Splügen pass, taking long walks, and producing many of the poems of his *Dramatic Idylls.*

BURNE-JONES, EDWARD. GENEVA, CHAMONIX

Before starting, Burne-Jones wrote to his little girl, 'I have been in town to have my hair cut and my coat tried on, so that I may be respectable to walk among Halps with my daughter.' 'Halps' was a form introduced by Ruskin's valet who had once said, when his master was ill, that he hoped he would 'take pleasure in a Halp again'.

BUTLER, SAMUEL. FAIDO, BELLINZONA, VARESE, LOCARNO, BIGNASCO, FUSIO, CAMPOLUGNO PASS, FAIDO

'A man's holiday is his garden.'
It was in this year that Butler found the following notice in a Swiss hut: 'The care for the needy combustibles is absolutely the matter of the travellers, which must agree about it with the personal of the guides.'

CONWAY, MARTIN. TURTMANN, GRUBEN PASS, ZERMATT, TRIFTJOCH PASS, ZINAL, ROTHORN, ZERMATT, DOM

COOK, JOEL. BASLE, LUCERNE, RIGI, SARNEN, BRUNIG PASS, BRIENZ, GIESSBACH, INTERLAKEN, THUN, BERNE, FRIBOURG, LAUSANNE, GENEVA, CHAMONIX, TÊTE NOIRE PASS, MARTIGNY, LAUSANNE, GENEVA

DENT, CLINTON T. CHAMONIX, TÊTE NOIRE PASS, VERNAYAZ, MARTIGNY, VISP, BIETSCHHORN, RIED, GAMPEL, MARTIGNY, CHAMONIX, AIGUILLE DU DRU

GÜSSFELDT, PAUL. PONTRESINA, PIZZO BIANCO, BERNINASCHARTE, PIZ BERNINA

HALL, NEWMAN. CHAMONIX, COL DU BONHOMME, COL DE LA SEIGNE, COURMAYEUR, AOSTA, GRAND ST. BERNARD PASS, MARTIGNY

'It seemed as if the glory of God appeared on that mountain, as it did to Moses, but though awful, not terrible. The sky had been cloudless, but now there arose from the summit of the mountain a succession of fleecy domes—translucent, one above another, all radiant with rainbow splendour, blending together. Then the appearance of a majestic form bending over the mountain with extended wings iridescent—wrapped in a mantle with arms stretched out as in benediction—radiant with amber and azure and gold, burning with glory.'

HEWAT, KIRKWOOD. CHIAVENNA, SPLÜGEN PASS, THUSIS, COIRE, ZURICH, SCHAFFHAUSEN, CONSTANCE, ROMANSHORN, ZURICH, LUCERNE, FLUELEN, RIGI, LUCERNE, BERNE, LAUSANNE, GENEVA, CHAMONIX, MONT BLANC, COL DE BALME, MARTIGNY, LAUSANNE

HOLDEN, LUTHER L. GENEVA, LAUSANNE, FRIBOURG, BERNE, THUN, INTERLAKEN, LAUTERBRUNNEN, GRINDELWALD, INTERLAKEN, BRIENZ, BRUNIG PASS, SARNEN, LUCERNE, RIGI, BRUNNEN, LUCERNE, ZUG, ZURICH, SCHAFFHAUSEN, BASLE

ILLINGWORTH, JOHN RICHARDSON. ZINAL

JAVELLE, ÉMILE. VEVEY, ZINAL, LO BESSO, ZERMATT, UNTERGABELHORN, AROLLA, PIGNE D'AROLLA, SALVAN, TOUR SALLIÈRES

KEMBLE, FANNY. BRUNNEN

The Bancrofts met Fanny Kemble at Brunnen and wrote: 'no greater lover of the Alps has lived. Year after year, until old age has come, do the mountains draw her towards them, and many a sweet description of their beauties is to be found in her charming books.' It was of this period of her life that Henry James wrote: 'When her health ceased to permit the chaise-à-porteur it was as if the great warning had come. Then she moved and mounted only with wistful, with absolutely tearful eyes, sitting for hours on the balconies of high

'We left Chamouni once more for the nineteenth and, as it proved, for the last time to try the peak'

(*Paul Popper*) CLINTON DENT, 1878; Aiguille du Dru

'In no place where I ever camped out, have I felt so much at home, so tranquil in spirits, so sane and so contented, as I do here. It was a blessed wind, I think, which blew us hither'

JOHN ADDINGTON SYMONDS, 1878; Davos

perched hotels and gazing away at the paradise lost. She yielded the ground only inch by inch, but toward the end she had to accept the valleys almost altogether and to decline upon paltry compromises and Italian lakes.'

MACFARREN, WALTER. BASLE, NEUCHÂTEL, LAUSANNE, AIGLE, LES DIABLERETS, AIGLE, BERNE, THUN, INTERLAKEN, LAUTERBRUNNEN, MÜRREN, INTERLAKEN, BRUNIG PASS, LUCERNE

At Mürren MacFarren found Henry Montagu Butler and John Farmer. 'There was also present a certain lord of somewhat Calvinistic tendencies, and besides these, a number of young men of a Bohemian type; so that in making a tour of the balcony which surrounded the house, I could see in one apartment the High Church element reading, playing the piano, and conversing in a rational manner; in another, the noble Lord referred to and his sympathizing ladies and gentlemen all on their knees; in a third apartment, card-playing, smoking, and drinking, and other Bohemian-like amusements; and in a fourth, the younger gentlemen dancing with the waitresses to the music of a volunteer fiddler.'

MEYER, CONRAD FERDINAND. ZURICH, COIRE, SILVAPLANA, PONTRESINA

MÜLLER, GEORGE. NEUCHÂTEL, BERNE, THUN, INTERLAKEN, THUN, NEUCHÂTEL, LAUSANNE, VEVEY, BEX, AIGLE, MONTREUX, YVERDON, GENEVA

NIETZSCHE, FRIEDRICH. BASLE, GRINDELWALD, INTERLAKEN, BASLE

RIMBAUD, JEAN-ARTHUR. BASLE, LUCERNE, FLUELEN, ALTDORF, HOSPENTHAL, ST. GOTTHARD PASS, AIROLO, BELLINZONA, LUGANO, COMO

RUMBOLD, SIR HORACE. BERNE, THUN, INTERLAKEN, GRINDELWALD, MÄNNLICHEN, KLEINE SCHEIDEGG, LAUTERBRUNNEN, INTERLAKEN, THUN, BERNE, ST. MORITZ

'This and other excursions I made during the two summers I now spent in Switzerland fully confirmed me in my opinion that, for real majesty and beauty, the gigantic Andes, in all their rugged grandeur, cannot compare with the Swiss Alps.'

SYMONDS, JOHN ADDINGTON. DAVOS, FLUELA PASS, SÜS, SAMADEN, MALOJA PASS, CHIAVENNA, MONTE GENEROSO, DAVOS

'In no place where I ever camped out, have I felt so much at home, so tranquil in spirits, so sane and so contented, as I do here. It was a blessed wind, I think, which blew us hither.'

TCHAIKOVSKY, PETER ILJITSCH. GENEVA, CLARENS, LAUSANNE, ZURICH

Tchaikovsky was working at his Sonata in G major, Violin Concerto, and *Don Juan's Serenade*.

TWAIN, MARK. BASLE, LUCERNE, RIGI, SARNEN, BRUNIG PASS, BRIENZ, INTERLAKEN, KANDERSTEG, GEMMI PASS, LEUK, VISP, ZERMATT, VISP, SION, MARTIGNY, TÊTE NOIRE PASS, CHAMONIX, GENEVA

In a letter to Twichell ('Harris'), Clemens wrote: 'O Switzerland! The further it recedes into the enriching haze of time, the more intolerably delicious the charm of it and the cheer of it and the glory and majesty and solemnity and pathos of it grow . . . There are mountains and mountains and mountains in this world, but only these take you by the heartstrings. I wonder what the secret of it is. Well, time and time again it has seemed to me that I *must* drop everything and flee to Switzerland once more. It is a *longing*—a deep, strong, tugging *longing*—that is the word. We must go again, Joe.'

1879

BANCROFT, SQUIRE. PONTRESINA, ST. MORITZ

'At the Roseg Hotel, the friends we either found there, or who arrived soon afterwards, numbered Mr. and Mrs. Edmund Yates, Mr. (now Sir) Arthur Sullivan, Mr. Joseph Barnby, Mr. J. C. Parkinson, Mr. and Mrs. George Lewis, Mr. Otto Goldschmidt, Sir Daniel and Lady Lysons, Mr. Briton Riviere, Mr. Oscar Browning, Mr. Rudolph Lehmann, Mr. and Mrs. Meadows White, and Mr. Arthur Cecil. Does not the mere mention of these names bespeak a happy holiday?'

BLACKIE, JOHN STUART. LUINO, LUGANO, CHIAVENNA, SPLÜGEN PASS, THUSIS, COIRE, ST. GALL, CONSTANCE

'It was the most perfect drive that I ever made, and will leave a perfect pantheon of pictures in my mind. If I had yielded to timorous persuasions and returned by Turin and the Mont Cenis tunnel, I should have gone through life quite ashamed of myself, like a dog with tail not gallantly swirled up, but shamefully curled beneath its hurdies.'

BROWNING, OSCAR. PONTRESINA, SILS MARIA, MALOJA PASS, SOGLIO, CASACCIA, SEPTIMER PASS, BIVIO, JULIER PASS, ST. MORITZ, DAVOS, SCALETTA PASS, SCANFS, PONTRESINA, BERNINA PASS

BUTLER, SAMUEL. FAIDO, BELLINZONA, MESOCCO, VAL CALANCA, MENDRISIO, VARESE, VARALLO, FOBELLO, COL DE BARANCA, VOGOGNA, LOCARNO, BELLINZONA, BIASCA, LUKMANIER PASS, DISENTIS, COIRE, ZURICH, BASLE

Butler met Edward Lear at Varese, and he is 'the old English gentleman' of chapter 22 of *Alps and Sanctuaries* who, referring to a feast at Varese, said that 'he had seen one drunken man there—an Englishman—who kept abusing all he saw and crying out "Manchester 's the place for me".'

BYERS, S. H. M. ZURICH, RIGI, OBSTALDEN

CAPPER, SAMUEL JAMES. CONSTANCE, RORSCHACH, APPENZELL, ST. GALL, LANDQUART, SEEWIS, DAVOS, WIESEN, LENZERHEIDE, COIRE

'Once settled in our secluded retreat at Seewis, we were visited by many friends, one of whom tendered our host a note of the world-famous institution in Threadneedle Street in payment of his bill. With equal naiveté and trustfulness, he said the paper was unknown to him; but if I would say it was good, he would gladly take it. Of many strange experiences in my life, this of guaranteeing the stability of the Bank of England was, I think, the strangest.'

COOLIDGE, W. A. B. BASLE, BERNE, THUN, INTERLAKEN, GRINDELWALD, FAULHORN, MÄNNLICHEN, SCHRECKHORN

GÜSSFELDT, PAUL. ZERMATT, MONTE ROSA, BREITHORN, WEISSHORN, RIMPFISCHHORN, DENT BLANCHE, MATTERHORN, EGGISHORN, FINSTERAARHORN, JUNGFRAU, SILBERLÜCKE, KLEINE SCHEIDEGG, GRINDELWALD, PONTRESINA, SELLA PASS, MONTE DI SCERSCEN (WEISSKOPF)

'I thought of the fact that on this fine day many visitors would have been attracted to the Wengernalp to enjoy the thunder of the avalanches, and that I with my two companions were just at the right place at the right time to contribute to the spectacle.'

HALIFAX, CHARLES LINDLEY, VISCOUNT. DOMODOSSOLA, SIMPLON PASS, BRIG, SION, MARTIGNY, VEVEY, GENEVA

HARTE, BRET. BASLE, ZURICH, ZUG, RIGI, WESEN, ZURICH

To start with, Harte wrote 'I have tried, when my head or my stomach was not aching, to appreciate Swiss scenery. I am living in the hills overlooking lake Zurich—(whence the poem "By the margin of fair Zurich's waters") and I regret to say that the waters of Zurich are not "fair", and that the Californian mountains and coast ranges are vastly superior to these famous Alps—in every respect.'

JERSEY, COUNTESS OF. ZERMATT

'Somehow we conveyed these infants [her children] over glaciers and mountains to various places, including Zermatt. We contrived a sort of awning over a *chaise à porteurs* carried by guides—but they did a good bit of walking also.' Their ages were 6 and 3.

MEYER, CONRAD FERDINAND. ZURICH, COIRE, SILVAPLANA, ST. MORITZ, PONTRESINA

MUDDOCK, J. E. DAVOS

'By the merest chance made my way to Davos-Platz in Switzerland, and while there I became acquainted with John Addington Symonds. . . . Recognizing as I did the magnificent possibilities of this Alpine station, . . . I resolved to make it better known to my countrymen, as well as to render it more accessible, and to carry out certain improvements. I suggested drainage, a straightening of the river, an adequate water supply, and finally a railway . . . My suggestions met with ridicule.'

MUMMERY, A. F. PRARAYÉ, TIEFENMATTENJOCH PASS, ZERMATT, MISCHABELJOCH PASS, SAAS, LAQUINJOCH, FLETSCHHORN, SAAS, RIED PASS, ZERMATT, ZMUTTRIDGE-MATTERHORN, VISP, SION, MARTIGNY, CHAMONIX

'I am fain to confess a deplorable weakness in my character. No sooner have I ascended a peak than it becomes a friend, and delightful as it may be to seek "fresh woods and pastures new", in my heart of hearts I long for the slopes of which I know every wrinkle, and on which each crag awakens memories of mirth and laughter of the friends of long ago.'

NIETZSCHE, FRIEDRICH. BASLE, BERNE, ZURICH, DAVOS, WIESEN, ST. MORITZ, COIRE

STEPHEN, LESLIE. INTERLAKEN, GRINDELWALD, MEIRINGEN, GRIMSEL, MEIRINGEN, JOCH PASS, ENGELBERG, TITLIS

'I take an indefinable pleasure in seeing the old places, all asleep in the quiet snow.' An Interlaken newspaper mentioned that Stephen was proposing to make an expedition to the Grimsel in January. *The Times* picked up and published the news with the result that Stephen's family telegraphed to Interlaken imploring him 'not to attempt the perilous ascent of the Grimsel'.

SYMONDS, JOHN ADDINGTON. DAVOS, GENEVA, VEVEY, CHAMONIX, ARGENTIÈRE, DAVOS

TROLLOPE, THOMAS ADOLPHUS. BADEN, ZURICH, ZUG, RIGI-STAFFEL

Anthony Trollope came out to stay with his sick brother.

1880

ARNOLD, HOWARD PAYSON (*c*). PONTRESINA

'At Pontresina there were English and English. They exhibited every shade of religious complexion, from the shining lights who never failed to attend the morning service at seven throughout the week, to the latitudinarians who rarely were present on any day, but mostly chose to stay in their rooms, even on Sunday, and write letters, or read Colenso on the Pentateuch, "Literature and Dogma", or other wicked books. Midway between these two extremes came the great majority, the becomingly virtuous.'

ARNOLD, MATTHEW. PONTRESINA, MALOJA PASS, CHIAVENNA, COMO, LUGANO, LOCARNO, BELLINZONA, ST. GOTTHARD PASS, ALTDORF, LUCERNE, BASLE

'The valley I took led me to the Morteratsch glacier, which is perhaps the most beautiful thing here—a grand glacier folded in by the Bernina and his great compeers; lovely names they have, but you would not know them. But nowhere even in the Oberland have I seen a more beautiful line than they make; I lunched at the restaurant by the glacier and then wandered on by a path along the mountain side to a hut from which the ascent of the Bernina and the great peaks near him begins. I have seldom enjoyed anything more . . . . Mme Saratz knew my works perfectly well, and said she should give me the room she had given to Tennyson.'

BANCROFT, SQUIRE. PONTRESINA, ANDERMATT, ALTDORF, LUCERNE

BENSON, EDWARD FREDERICK AND EDWARD WHITE. BERNE, THUN, INTERLAKEN, LAUTERBRUNNEN, MÜRREN, GIMMELWALD

'My heart went out to the snow mountains, and has never yet come back. . . . We passed through Mürren on the way down, and there saw English people playing lawn-tennis on one of the hotel courts, and never shall I forget my father's upraised eyebrows and mouth of scorn as he said, "Fancy, playing lawn-tennis in sight of the Jungfrau".'

BONNEY, THOMAS GEORGE. COIRE, FILISUR, ALBULA PASS, PONTRESINA, BERNINA PASS, TIRANO

BROWNING, OSCAR. ZURICH, LUCERNE, LAUTERBRUNNEN, MÜRREN

BUTLER, SAMUEL. FAIDO, BELLINZONA, LOCARNO

During this stay at Faido, Butler corrected the proofs of *Unconscious Memory* and prepared sketches and notes for *Alps and Sanctuaries.*

CONWAY, MARTIN. ZERMATT

'Obscurities in descriptions of several ascents were cleared up by inspection of the ground during weeks spent at and about Zermatt in the summer of 1880. When I returned home my notes were in a sufficiently advanced condition to warrant publication. The little volume called "The Zermatt Pocket-Book" was thus prepared for the press.'

CUTLER, HARRIET OLIVE. BASLE, SEMPACH, LUCERNE, RIGI, FLUELEN, ALTDORF, LUCERNE, SARNEN, BRUNIG PASS, BRIENZ, GIESSBACH, MEIRINGEN, ROSENLAUI, GROSSE SCHEIDEGG, GRINDELWALD, KLEINE

SCHEIDEGG LAUTERBRUNNEN, MÜRREN, INTERLAKEN, THUN, BERNE, LAUSANNE, GENEVA, EVIAN, MARTIGNY, COL DE BALME, CHAMONIX, ST. GERVAIS, ANNECY

The echo of the alphorn 'is not Villon's echo:
"Echo parlant, quand bruyt on maine,
Dessus rivière ou sus estan,"
but a singing, tender, melodious, artistic echo. . . . Amphion's lyre set rocks in motion according to the Greeks. The alphorn does not set them in motion, but certainly fills them with emotion.'

FINSLER, GEORG. LUCERNE, FLUELEN, AMSTEG, BRISTEN, OBERALP-STOCK, SCHEERHORN

'I have often stood on such peaks and usually had the fortune of good weather, but a wonderful view thrills me so deeply every time that it is as if it were the first.'

FOX, JOSEPH H. LAUTERBRUNNEN, MÜRREN, KLEINE SCHEIDEGG, GRINDELWALD, MEIRINGEN, GRIMSEL PASS, OBERGESTELEN, BRIG, VISP, ZERMATT

'When crossing the Wengern Alp we met a blind man walking by the side of a guide who held his wrist. We afterwards heard that he was the celebrated Dr. Campbell, the head of the Institution for the blind at Norwood. Soon after we met him he made the ascent of Mont Blanc with the object of showing what a blind man can do.'

HALL, NEWMAN. LUGANO, LAUSANNE, CHAMONIX

'I conversed with Dr. Campbell, Principal of the College for the Blind. Though himself totally blind, he had climbed the Matterhorn with safety and delight. I asked him to explain the causes of his pleasure. "The bodily exercise, the mental excitement, the sense of difficulty overcome and danger escaped, the mental vision of what I knew was present. Besides, I saw more than my companions. A thick cloud concealed everything from them; but I had impressed it all on my brain in preparation, and I saw everything I expected to see".'

HOLLAND, MARY SIBYLLA. LAUSANNE, MONTREUX, VEYTAUX

LARDEN, WALTER. BASLE, LUCERNE, WÄGGIS, RIGI, PILATUS, ALTDORF, SURENEN PASS, ENGELBERG, JOCH PASS, MEIRINGEN, GROSSE SCHEIDEGG, FAULHORN, GRINDELWALD, KLEINE SCHEIDEGG, LAUTERBRUNNEN, GIMMELWALD, TSCHINGEL PASS, KANDERSTEG, GEMMI PASS, LEUK, BRIG, OBERGESTELEN, FURKA PASS, ANDERMATT, WASSEN, FLUELEN, WÄGGIS, LUCERNE, BASLE

LYTTELTON, EDWARD. PONTRESINA

Lyttelton was with J. E. C. Welldon, Alfred Cole, and E. W. Howson when they were all led up Piz Corvatsch by Charles Lacaita and narrowly escaped coming to grief.

MARCET, WILLIAM. GENEVA, YVOIRE, MARTIGNY, GRAND ST. BERNARD PASS, AOSTA, COURMAYEUR, COL DU GÉANT

MUMMERY, A. F. ZERMATT, COL DU LION, BREUIL, CHATILLON, AOSTA, COURMAYEUR, COL DU GÉANT, CHAMONIX, AIGUILLE DES CHARMOZ, COL DE BALME, MARTIGNY, SION, VISP

On the way up the Matterhorn, Mummery's guides lost their nerve completely at the sight of a light on the Gorner glacier, which they insisted was the ghost of a departed soul. The explanation was that a girls' school had been on the glacier and one girl had gone home before the others and unknown to them. Her absence from the party when discovered caused such alarm that the remainder returned to the glacier to look for her, presently becoming lost themselves. The sun set, and M. Seiler, becoming anxious, sent a guide to look for them with a lantern, and he 'spent the rest of the night in rescuing the disconsolate maidens from the various holes and chasms into which they had fallen'.

NAVEZ, LOUIS (*c*). BASLE, BERNE, THUN, INTERLAKEN, GRINDELWALD, FAULHORN, INTERLAKEN, THUN, BERNE, LAUSANNE, MARTIGNY, TÊTE NOIRE PASS, CHAMONIX, MARTIGNY, SION, VISP, ZERMATT, BREITHORN, CIMA DI JAZZI, COL D'HÉRENS, EVOLENA, SION, MONTREUX

'Evolena jouit d'une tranquillité profonde. A la place de ces bandes d'Anglais dégringolant comme des avalanches par tous les chemins descendant à Zermatt, on ne rencontre ici que des familles paysiblement couchées dans l'herbe et se livrant au doux plaisir de ne rien faire.'

SIDGWICK, HENRY. GRINDELWALD

'My wife and I are now taking a holiday for two or three weeks in about the only place in which I find it possible to take a complete holiday, i.e. close under snow mountains.'

STEVENSON, ROBERT LOUIS. DAVOS

'Figure me to yourself, I pray—
A man of my peculiar cut—
Apart from dancing and deray,
Into an Alpine valley shut;

Shut in a kind of damned Hotel,
Discountenanced by God and man;
The food?—Sir, you would do as well
To cram your belly full of bran.'

During his stay at Davos Stevenson corrected the proofs of *Virginibus Puerisque* and wrote his Essay on Pepys.

STOCK, EUGENE. ZURICH, ST. GALL, HEIDEN

'Going up the little mountain railway from Zurich to the Uetliberg I found myself sitting opposite the Lord Mayor of that year, Sir Francis Truscott, who was the printer of my Lessons and of the *Gleaner*. I was just greeting him when he whispered, "Don't betray me! I have just come from the Tyrol, and a friend touring there ahead of me told everybody the Lord Mayor was coming, and I have been charged double for everything".'

SYMONDS, JOHN ADDINGTON. DAVOS, KLOSTERS, LANDQUART, RAGAZ, MAIENFELD, COIRE, LENZERHEIDE, WIESEN, DAVOS

'There is a very interesting man come—Louis Stevenson.' Symonds's health now admitted of no doubt that 'nothing is left but to sit and moulder in the High Alps'. Accordingly he decided to build his own house at Davos. This was to be the Haus am Hof.

WOOLSON, CONSTANCE FENIMORE. COMO, LUGANO, BIASCA, ST. GOTTHARD PASS, FLUELEN, LUCERNE, BECKENRIED, INTERLAKEN, LAUTERBRUNNEN, MÜRREN, INTERLAKEN, THUN, BERNE, GENEVA, VEVEY, COPPET, GENEVA

'Were you in Lucerne? Did you not admire the Lion? I do, very much. . . .'

1881

BANCROFT, SQUIRE. COIRE, TIEFENKASTEL, JULIER PASS, ST. MORITZ, PONTRESINA, MALOJA PASS, PROMONTOGNO, CHIAVENNA, MENAGGIO, PORLEZZA, LUGANO, BELLINZONA, ST. GOTTHARD PASS, ALTDORF, LUCERNE

BONNEY, THOMAS GEORGE. SAAS, WEISSMIES, SIMPLON PASS, DOMODOSSOLA, BINN, EGGISHORN, JUNGFRAU, BELALP

BROWN, THOMAS EDWARD. MONTREUX, GLION, MARTIGNY, SION, EVOLENA, SION, BRIG, BELALP, LUCERNE

Belalp: 'This is the place! I have seen nothing to compare with it for a moment. It blends with all my humours, and mentally it makes me quite absolute. . . . Tyndall is here. . . .'

BUTLER, GEORGE. COIRE, FILISUR, ALBULA PASS, PONTRESINA, ST. MORITZ, JULIER PASS, TIEFENKASTEL, THUSIS, COIRE

CONWAY, MARTIN. VISP, STALDEN, BALFRINJOCH PASS, ZERMATT, WELLENKUPPE

DAUDET, ALPHONSE. BASLE, BERNE, THUN, INTERLAKEN, GRINDELWALD, LUCERNE, RIGI, FLUELEN

'. . . Ces horribles crevasses. . . . Si vous tombez dedans? Vous tombez sur la neige, monsieur Tartarin, et vous ne vous faites pas de mal: il y a toujours en bas, au fond, un portier, un chasseur, quelqu'un qui vous relève, vous brosse, vous secoue et gracieusement s'informe: "Monsieur n'a pas de bagages?" . . . L'entretien de ces crevasses est une des plus grosses dépenses de la compagnie.'

DUBOIS, ALBERT. LES VERRIÈRES, NEUCHÂTEL, LUCERNE, BRUNIG PASS, MEIRINGEN, GRIMSEL PASS, OBERGESTELEN, VIESCH, EGGISHORN, BRIG, VISP, ZERMATT, ST. THEODUL PASS, COL DES CIMES BLANCHES, FIERY, BETTA FURKA PASS, GRESSONEY LA TRINITÉ, COL D'OLEN, ALAGNA, FOBELLO, COL DI BARANCA, MACUGNAGA, DOMODOSSOLA, SIMPLON PASS, BRIG, SION, MARTIGNY, LAUSANNE, YVERDON, NEUCHÂTEL

Eggishorn:—'Dans la soirée, la scene devient amusante. Tout est transformé en chambres à coucher. On loge dans la salle à manger, au fumoir, au télégraphe. Un jeune anglais dort même dans une armoire. . . . La salle de lecture est encombrée de misses et de ladies qui n'ont pas l'air de vouloir céder la place. Nous avons soin de leur faire savoir que quatre gentlemen doivent occuper cette chambre. Voyant leur immobilité, nous tentons l'assaut de notre gite. Une première batterie composée de deux lits de camp est introduite dans la place. Personne ne bouge . . . expédition d'un troisième lit. Rien encore . . . un de nos amis simule bravement les préparatifs d'une toilette de nuit. Il eût fallu voir la garnison féminine fuir.'

GRAY, ASA. COMO, LUGANO, MILAN, DOMODOSSOLA, SIMPLON PASS, BRIG, SION, MARTIGNY, GENEVA

GÜSSFELDT, PAUL. BREUIL, COL DU LION, ZERMATT, TÄSCHHORN

HORNBY, EMILY. BREUIL, MATTERHORN, ZERMATT, ZINAL, RUITOR PASS, ZERMATT

HUGHES, HUGH PRICE. LAUSANNE, OUCHY, BOUVERET, VERNAYAZ, MARTIGNY, SION, EVOLENA, AROLLA, COURMAYEUR

JAVELLE, ÉMILE. VEVEY, ZINAL

JONES, C. A. BASLE, ZURICH, ZUG, RIGI, LUCERNE, BRUNIG PASS, BRIENZ, INTERLAKEN, LAUTERBRUNNEN, MÜRREN, GRINDELWALD, INTERLAKEN, THUN, BERNE, LAUSANNE, GENEVA, CHAMONIX, TÊTE NOIRE PASS, MARTIGNY, SION, VISP, ZERMATT, VISP, VIESCH, OBERGESTELEN, FURKA PASS, ANDERMATT, FLUELEN, LUCERNE, BASLE

Mürren: 'Just behind the hotel stands the pretty little English Church, designed by the great architect Street, who has so recently been taken from us. There is no other place of worship in the village, and the services are reverently conducted on Sundays and Holy Days during the summer months, and are a great comfort to those who take up their residence amongst the snow mountains for four or five weeks at a time.'

KENNEDY, BENJAMIN E. CHIAVENNA, SPLÜGEN PASS, THUSIS, COIRE, ZURICH, BASLE

KROPOTKIN, PETER. CLARENS, AIGLE, THONON

Kropotkin was expelled from Switzerland for his political activities at a moment when he and his wife were in the mountains above Aigle. While they were walking down to Aigle on their way out of the country, an English lady, sumptuously dressed, passed in a carriage and threw some religious tracts at them. Kropotkin picked them up, wrote on them the parable of the rich man and the Kingdom of Heaven and other quotations concerning Pharisees, and at Aigle, where the English lady was waiting in her carriage, he politely returned them to her.

LE MESURIER, W. H. LAUSANNE, MARTIGNY, COL DE BALME, CHAMONIX, MONT BLANC, GENEVA

LOCKE, DAVID R. GENEVA, CHILLON, MARTIGNY, TÊTE NOIRE PASS, CHAMONIX, GENEVA, LAUSANNE, FRIBOURG, BERNE, THUN, INTERLAKEN, BRIENZ, BRUNIG PASS, SARNEN, LUCERNE, RIGI, ZURICH, BASLE

'A Swiss horse would commit suicide were he taken to Illinois in winter or spring. It would pay America to imitate Switzerland in this particular.'

MUMMERY, A. F. COURMAYEUR, COL DU GÉANT, CHAMONIX, AIGUILLE VERTE, AIGUILLE DU GRÉPON

'The aesthetic value of an ascent generally varies with its difficulty. This, necessarily, leads us to the conclusion that the most difficult way up the most difficult peaks is always the right thing to attempt, whilst the easy slopes of ugly screes may with propriety be left to the scientist, with M. Janssen at their head. To those who, like myself, take a non-utilitarian view of the mountains, the great ridge of the Grépon may be safely recommended. . . .'

NAVEZ, LOUIS. DAVOS, LANDQUART, WALLENSTADT, ZURICH, ZUG, LUCERNE, FLUELEN, ANDERMATT, FLUELEN, BECKENRIED, STANS, BRUNIG PASS, BRIENZ, INTERLAKEN, THUN, BERNE, GENEVA, LAUSANNE, MONTREUX

NICOLL, LADY ROBERTSON. MÜRREN

'There was no railway then, only a mountain track up which we climbed, mules and donkeys carrying our luggage. Amongst our luggage was always at least one tin bath. . . . I remember the difficulty of strapping the tin bath on the mule's back.'

NIETZSCHE, FRIEDRICH. SILS MARIA

It was on a walk thither from Sils Maria, at a point near Surlej, that the notion of 'eternal recurrence' occurred to him.

RAMSAY, ANDREW CROMBIE. ST. MORITZ, MALOJA PASS, CHIAVENNA

ROGERS, CLARA KATHLEEN. LUCERNE, CHAMONIX, CHATELARD, SALVAN, VERNAYAZ, LAUSANNE

ROOSEVELT, THEODORE. ZERMATT, MATTERHORN

'A fairly hardy man, cautious but not cowardly, with good guides, has little to fear.'

SMILES, SAMUEL. PONTRESINA, BERNINA PASS, TIRANO, BORMIO, STELVIO PASS

Smiles was engaged in writing the autobiography of the inventor of the steam-hammer, Thomas Nasmyth.

STEPHEN, LESLIE. MÜRREN, DAVOS, FLUELA-SCHWARZHORN

STEVENSON, ROBERT LOUIS. DAVOS

'I am up here in a little chalet [am Stein], on the borders of a pine wood, overlooking a great part of the Davos Thal, a beautiful scene at night, with the moon upon the snowy mountains, and the lights warmly shining in the village. J. A. Symonds is next door to me, just at the foot of my Hill Difficulty (this you will please regard as the House Beautiful), and his society is my great stand-by.'
During this, Stevenson's last winter in Davos, he finished writing *Treasure Island*.

SYMONDS, JOHN ADDINGTON. DAVOS, MAIENFELDERFURKA PASS, AROSA, ALTEIN PASS, WIESEN, DAVOS

In January, Leslie Stephen visited Davos 'where there is now a colony of invalids. Amongst them is J. A. Symonds. I admire him for his energy in writing his books full of information in such a bookless wilderness.'

URLIN, RICHARD DENNY. BASLE, ZURICH, COIRE, SILVAPLANA, SILS, BERNE

WOOLSON, CONSTANCE FENIMORE. ENGELBERG

'. . . and altogether, it is very Alpine and delicious . . .'

1882

BANCROFT, SQUIRE. PONTRESINA

The English Church was opened by the Bishops of Bedford and Gloucester. Bancroft gave the bell and Mrs. Bancroft a window. A bench was erected in the woods by the villagers in honour of Mrs. Bancroft, and inscribed with her name. On the seat was written:

'If all the world 's a stage, as men repeat,
And all the men and women in it actors,
The more we owe to one who gives the seat,
And saves us all the greed of Swiss contractors.
And yet, ungrateful still, a fault I trace,
For Bancroft's not the name my faith was built on;
How gladly would I pay for any place,
If only I might sit by Marie Wilton.'

BOVET, ALBERT. AIROLO, PIORA, AL ACQUA, SAN GIACOMO PASS, TOSA FALLS, DOMODOSSOLA, MACUGNAGA, MONTE MORO PASS, SAAS-FEE

'Mais ce n'est pas tout que d'aimer la montagne — et la montagne, pour le Suisse, ce sont les Alpes — il faut la faire aimer.'

BROOKS, PHILLIPS. DOMODOSSOLA, SIMPLON PASS, BRIG, MARTIGNY, TÊTE NOIRE PASS, CHAMONIX, GENEVA

BUTLER, JOSEPHINE. ROLLE, LA GORDANNE, AIGLE, LES DIABLERETS, CHAMPÉRY

'Last evening was very beautiful. I sat alone for an hour under the large linden tree up above the vineyards, whence one sees the whole of the lake below. Mont Blanc rose, a mass of spotless snow, into a cloudless sky, and then majestically and slowly folded broader and broader shadows across his huge white shoulders as the sun lowered, and the portion of his snows which was still in the light became first golden and then ruby-coloured. Such a sight makes one think what must be the beauty of Him who creates, when His creation is so beautiful.'

COLLINGWOOD, W. GERSHOM. GENEVA, BONNEVILLE, CHAMONIX

'Is it not good to be here?—not uncompanioned, if we could call to share the scene, passionate and reverent, some true-lover of the mountains, like those hero-poets of the Greeks. Would they not dearly love this darling Ida of the Alps, the Parnassus of Savoy?'

CONWAY, MARTIN. GENEVA, MARTIGNY, SION, BRIG, BELALP, SIMPLON PASS, DOMODOSSOLA, MACUGNAGA, FILLAR PASS, ZERMATT,

ROTHORN, ST. THEODUL PASS, BREUIL, CHATILLON, AOSTA, COURMAYEUR

'What is a work of art but an incorporated emotion in flight from soul to soul? I have written above of the charm of solitude in the heart of the mountains, but visions of beauty die unless they are shared. Beauty perceived in common is the fertile union of souls.'

DEGAS, EDGAR. GENEVA, VEYRIER

'Hotel Beauséjour. Veyrier.

'. . . Il y a des voyageurs plus heureux que moi. Est-ce que je voyage moi, disait un chef de gare?'

D'INDY, VINCENT. LAUFENBURG, SCHINZNACH, AARAU

This journey led to the composition of a collection of piano waltzes (op. 17), *Helvetia.*

GÜSSFELDT, PAUL. ZERMATT, DOM, MATTERHORN

HAVERGAL, MARIA V. G. GENEVA, CHILLON, VERNAYAZ, FINHAUT, TÊTE NOIRE PASS, CHAMONIX, TÊTE NOIRE PASS, MARTIGNY, CHILLON, VEVEY, LAUSANNE, FRIBOURG, BERNE, THUN, INTERLAKEN, LAUTERBRUNNEN, WENGEN, INTERLAKEN, BRIENZ, BRUNIG PASS, LUCERNE, BERNE, LAUSANNE, GENEVA

Wengen: 'The walks in all directions reveal endless varieties of Swiss landscapes. The society there was extremely agreeable, and we enjoyed (what is rarely found) family worship every evening. . . . Soon after our evening meal was the time chosen, and afterwards nearly all united in amusing innocent games.'

HOLWORTHY, S. M. VALLORBE, LAUSANNE, CLARENS, AIGLE, BEX, CHIÈTRE, CHAMPÉRY, VERNAYAZ, FINHAUT, BEX, VILLARS, GENEVA

HORNBY, EMILY. ZERMATT, COL DE VALPELLINE, PRARAYÉ, COL DE LA REUSE DE L'AROLLA, CHANRION, COL DU SONADON, BOURG ST. PIERRE, ORSIÈRES, CHAMPEX, TÊTE NOIRE PASS, CHAMONIX

'Started over the Col de Champey, a green col, and I did enjoy it. It was such a relief to be on green after cold wet glaciers, and also, though very fine where we were, there were clouds on all the higher mountains, so I could enjoy myself with a clear conscience.'

JAVELLE, ÉMILE. VEVEY, SAAS FEE

KINGSFORD, ANNA MAY. LUCERNE, BERNE, LAUSANNE, MONTREUX, GENEVA

KLUCKER, CHRISTIAN. SILS, PIZ DELLA MARGNA, PIZ TREMOGGIA, PIZ BERNINA, PIZZO TORRONE

LARDEN, WALTER. BASLE, LUCERNE, MORSCHACH, RIEDERALP, BRIG, SION, AROLLA

Arolla:—'We got to the end of the world, and there saw an unfinished hotel sadly looking out on chaos. . . . We passed through a half-finished and most depressing passage . . . and found three sad visitors, one being Dr. Hort of Cambridge, eating marmot by the light (and smell) of one paraffin lamp. They told us that nineteen people had just left, having believed themselves to have been poisoned by verdigris.'

LAVELEYE, ÉMILE DE. BASLE, ZURICH, LUCERNE, ALTDORF, ST. GOTTHARD, AIROLO, BELLINZONA, LUGANO, COMO, GENEVA, NEUCHÂTEL

LEAR, EDWARD. MENDRISIO, MONTE GENEROSO

Monte Generoso: 'This place just now is not unlike the last Day, or universal judgment. Such heaps of unexpected persons keep turning up. Fanny Kemble, Mazzini's widow, Charles Acland M.P., all the Wells of Newstead, three nice Ladies Hamilton, Cross widower of George Eliot or Mrs. Lewes. I constantly expect to see the Sultan, Mrs. Gladstone, Sir Joshua Reynolds and the twelve apostles walk into the Hotel.'

MARCET, WILLIAM. BERNE, GURNIGEL, LUCERNE, ENGELBERG, ZURICH, LANDQUART, DAVOS, ZUOZ, ST. MORITZ, PONTRESINA

Marcet was at Pontresina when the English church was consecrated by the Bishop of Bedford. 'Between two and three hundred people join at table d'hote in the middle of the season at each of these hotels [Kronenhof and Roseg], and half at least are English. Dancing is one of the favourite evening amusements, but as the days are usually taken up with some excursion in the neighbourhood, many of the guests are glad to retire early. . . . Few of the visitors, however, are bent on hard climbing, and the proprietors of carriages and horses apparently fare infinitely better than the guides.'

NIETZSCHE, FRIEDRICH. LUCERNE, TRIBSCHEN, BASLE

PITMAN, MARIE J. (DEANE, MARJERY) (*c*). GENEVA, CHAMONIX

RUSKIN, JOHN. ST. CERGUE, NYON, GENEVA, SALLANCHES, GENEVA

'Mont Blanc entirely clear all the morning, fresh snow in perfect light on the Dorons, and the Varens a miracle of aerial majesty. I, happy in a more solemn way than of old, read a bit of Ezra and referred to Haggai ii, 9: "in this place will I give peace".'

'Snug little chalets, the peculiarly captivating cottage of Switzerland'

(*Swiss Federal Railways*) MARK TWAIN, 1878; Brienzwiler

'I wonder more than ever, why so few people seek the Engadine in winter'

(Amstutz) JOHN ADDINGTON SYMONDS, 1882; Samaden

SMYTH, DAME ETHEL. BERNE, THUN, INTERLAKEN, WILDERSWIL, SCHILTHORN, ALTDORF, ST. GOTTHARD PASS, BELLINZONA, MILAN

'On the top of that mountain I noticed what was so often to strike me afterwards, that in the joy of difficulties vanquished the mind of Faint-hearts is miraculously cleansed from all memory of these passing weaknesses.'

SYMONDS, JOHN ADDINGTON. DAVOS, FLUELA PASS, SÜS, SAMADEN, ST. MORITZ, PONTRESINA, BERNINA PASS, TIRANO, CHIAVENNA, SPLÜGEN PASS, THUSIS, DAVOS

'I wonder more than ever, why so few people seek the Engadine in winter.'

WIDMANN, J. V. BERNE, THUN, KANDERSTEG, GEMMI PASS, LEUK, SION, RAWYL PASS, LENK, BERNE

'Whoever descended from the Gemmi pass on July 20 to Leukerbad and took his mid-day meal at the "Maison Blanche" had his music for nothing. In the salon next to the dining room somebody thumped out with untiring energy the complete piano score of the "Mariage de Figaro". Guests came, sat, ate, drank and went, making way for others, but in the room next door the sound was without end. . . . What a curious privilege of music! Somebody takes his favourite composer with him on a tramp in the Alps and rams him down a hundred strange ears whether they like it or not. How we should open our eyes if anyone took his Goethe with him and suddenly started reading aloud.'

WISE, A. T. TUCKER. DAVOS, WIESEN

ZSIGMONDY, EMIL. CIERFS, SCARL PASS, SCHULS, LAVIN, PIZ LINARD, GUARDA, VERMUNT PASS, GALTÜR

1883

BANCROFT, SQUIRE. THUN, KANDERSTEG, GEMMI PASS, LEUK, VISP, ZERMATT

BITHRAY, EBENEZER (*c*). BASLE, LUCERNE, VITZNAU, RIGI, FLUELEN, ALTDORF, ST. GOTTHARD, BELLINZONA, LUGANO, COMO

'In death-like stillness, saw the morning sun literally tip the hill with gold. Away from the east, in a moment, a bright ray of light seemed to set on fire the snow-clad peaks, and they glittered like crystal in the early day; then, as it rose higher, the darkness seemed to nestle in the valleys and on the lake below, the mountain peaks standing out light in the midst of the darkness, and then when the sun was fully risen, the darkness was annihilated, and the whole scene was one of beauty indescribable.'

BONNEY, THOMAS GEORGE. MEIRINGEN, SUSTEN PASS, WASSEN, ST. GOTTHARD PASS, AIROLO, PIORA, TOSA FALLS, BINN, BELALP, KANDERSTEG

'I crossed from the Tosa Falls to the little village of Binn, which is now a rather favourite resort for lowland Swiss who cannot afford expensive pensions. There I spent the night in a small but thoroughly comfortable inn. It was spotlessly clean, looking like a new box, as well it might, for, as the landlord proved to me on a subsequent visit, I was the first person who slept there.'

BOOTH, CATHERINE. GENEVA, LAUSANNE, ROLLE, THONON, ANNEMASSE, SALÈVE, LAUSANNE, NEUCHÂTEL, LA PRISE, IMER

The leader of the Salvation Army in Switzerland was subjected to the most scandalous treatment by the police authorities in Geneva whence she was expelled, and in Neuchâtel where she was imprisoned and tried.

BROOKS, PHILLIPS. GENEVA, BERNE, THUN, INTERLAKEN, LAUTERBRUNNEN, MÜRREN, INTERLAKEN, BRIENZ, BRUNIG PASS, LUCERNE, ALTDORF, ST. GOTTHARD PASS, BELLINZONA, LUGANO, COMO

Mürren: 'I went to Church this morning in a little thing which the preacher declared to be the most splendidly situated church in Christendom, and I rather think he was right.'

BROWNING, ROBERT. GRESSONEY ST. JEAN

'Hotel Delapierre.

'We are in a beautiful place indeed, a paradise of coolness and quiet; just under Monte Rosa and its glaciers. . . . Six weeks in this delightful solitude, with one day only to prevent our leaving the house! On every other morning and afternoon we have walked right and left, never less and often more than five hours a day.'

BURNABY (MAIN, LEBLOND), MRS. CHAMONIX, AIGUILLE DU MIDI, COL DU CHARDONNET, ORSIÈRES, TÊTE NOIRE PASS, CHAMONIX, COL D'ARGENTIÈRE, LA FOULY, ORSIÈRES, TÊTE NOIRE PASS, CHAMONIX, GENEVA, MARTIGNY, GRAND ST. BERNARD PASS, AOSTA, CHATILLON, BREUIL, ST. THEODUL PASS, ZERMATT, VISP, MARTIGNY, EVIONNAZ, FINHAUT, SALVAN, CHAMONIX

BUTLER, GEORGE. NEUCHÂTEL, BIENNE, ILE ST. PIERRE, BERNE, THUN, INTERLAKEN, MEIRINGEN, ROSENLAUI, GROSSE SCHEIDEGG, GRINDELWALD, LAUTERBRUNNEN, MÜRREN, INTERLAKEN, THUN, BERNE

'Sir Robert Collier is there painting one of his great Royal Academy pictures of the Rosenlaui glacier.' At Mürren, Butler called on his brother Dr. Montagu Butler and saw 'the church which he got built there'.

COBDEN-SANDERSON, THOMAS JAMES. BASLE, BERNE, THUN, INTERLAKEN, LAUTERBRUNNEN, GIMMELWALD, MÜRREN, KLEINE SCHEIDEGG, GRINDELWALD, GROSSE SCHEIDEGG, MEIRINGEN, GRIMSEL PASS, OBERGESTELEN, VIESCH, EGGISHORN, BELALP, BRIG, SIMPLON PASS, DOMODOSSOLA

'I confess that I find staring at Nature, however beautiful it may be, results only in a sense of weariness and boredom. But make it a background of higher or even only of other thoughts; and how our impressions of it immediately change. All the day I have been bookless and thoughtless, and the Alps have not greatly interested me. But now tonight I open my book on *Reliure* and how the whole scene changes; immediately the Alps, the nearer heights of green, become vivid in my mind and interesting, and I see all I have seen today in another and more aerial light. . . . I am reading David's *Buddhism*, but the mountains come into my brain, and I must write of them.'

DAULLIA, ÉMILE. DELLE, SONCEBOZ, BIENNE, NEUCHÂTEL, BERNE, THUN, INTERLAKEN, BRIENZ, BRUNIG PASS, SARNEN, STANS, BECKENRIED, FLUELEN, ANDERMATT, FURKA PASS, VIESCH, EGGISHORN, RIEDERALP, BELALP, BRIG, GENEVA

GOSSE, EDMUND. VILLARS

'Most sad of mystics, see, I shut thy book,
And let mine eyes upon thy mountain rest;'

a reference to Sénancour's *Obermann*.

HORT, F. J. A. COIRE, TIEFENKASTEL, MÜHLEN, JULIER PASS, ST. MORITZ, PONTRESINA, BERNINA-HOSPICE

JOPLING, LOUISE. FLIMS, AXENSTEIN, LUGANO

'I had my sketching things with me, and I did many transcripts of the delightful views in the neighbourhood. Sir Robert Anstruther had with him his own horses, and his daughter and I rode about, much to the amazement of the peasantry, who, we heard, declared with awe that we had ridden our mounts all the way from England.'

KOTHARI, JEHANGIR H. GENEVA, CHAMONIX, TÊTE NOIRE PASS, MARTIGNY, LAUSANNE, BERNE, LUCERNE, ZURICH, WINTERTHUR, SCHAFFHAUSEN

Crossing the Mer de Glace, 'I was in a state of silent despair at having undertaken such a journey'.

LARDEN, WALTER. AROLLA, COL D'HÉRENS, ZERMATT, TRIFTJOCH PASS, ZINAL, COL DU GRAND CORNIER, AROLLA, COL DE COLLON, COL DE L'ÉVÊQUE, COL DE VUIGNETTE, AROLLA, SION, BERNE

Zinal:—'There was then one simple old-fashioned inn kept by Mme. Epiney. She asked but five francs for pension; and when some

English suggested an improvement or two, with a rise to six francs, she replied that she was a peasant woman and did not wish to be more; had no desire to be rich.'

NIETZSCHE, FRIEDRICH. SILS-MARIA

During this stay Nietzsche wrote the second part of *Thus spake Zarathustra.*

SMITH, GEORGE ADAM. LUCERNE, ZERMATT

STOCK, EUGENE. GENEVA, CHAMONIX, GRINDELWALD

SYMONDS, JOHN ADDINGTON. DAVOS, KLOSTERS, LANDQUART, COIRE, REICHENAU, DISENTIS, LUKMANIER PASS, OLIVONE, BIASCA, AIROLO, ST. GOTTHARD PASS, ANDERMATT, OBERALP PASS, DISENTIS, COIRE, DAVOS

TECK, MARY ADELAIDE, DUCHESS OF. ROMANSHORN, ZURICH, ZUG, LUCERNE, FLUELEN, GÖSCHENEN, ST. GOTTHARD PASS, BELLINZONA, LUGANO, COMO

THOMPSON, SILVANUS P. MEIRINGEN, GROSSE SCHEIDEGG, GRINDELWALD

WIDMANN, J. V. BERNE, GURNIGEL, GANTRISGRAT, WEISSENBURG, ZWEISIMMEN, SAANEN, GSTEIG, SANETSCH PASS, SION, EVOLENA, SION, BRIG, SIMPLON PASS, DOMODOSSOLA, COMO, CHIAVENNA, MALOJA PASS, ST. MORITZ, SCANFS, SCALETTA PASS, DAVOS, STRELA PASS, COIRE, DISENTIS, OBERALP PASS, ANDERMATT, ALTDORF, BRUNNEN

Evolena: 'Six Englishwomen are practising on the piano their church service for tomorrow—today is Saturday. Nothing is so appalling as when religion, which should blossom as a hidden flower within the quiet of a modest soul, takes on a form which imposes itself on society. And how utterly devoid of taste is this chant by the six untalented and completely unmusical Englishwomen! Frequently they sing on one and the same note twenty to thirty syllables which sound as if they were falling downstairs in an unseemly jumble and cascade of words, piling themselves up until, on the long-drawn-out final note, they find the mattress for their rest.'

WOOLSON, CONSTANCE FENIMORE. MILAN, BELLINZONA, ST. GOTTHARD PASS, FLUELEN, LUCERNE, ENGELBERG

'. . . the tunnel is well ventilated. . . .'

1884

BANCROFT, SQUIRE. COIRE, THUSIS, TIEFENKASTEL, JULIER PASS, ST. MORITZ

In winter, 'the life very much resembles that on shipboard—for, unlike the summer season, people do not now merely come and go—so in a short while everyone seems to know everybody else'.

BROWNING, ROBERT. ST. MORITZ

'Villa Berry.

'We have walked every day, morning and evening—afternoon, I should say—two or three hours each excursion the delicious mountain air surpassing any I was ever privileged to breathe. My sister is absolutely herself again, and something over.'

BRYCE, JAMES, VISCOUNT. AIROLO, ST. GOTTHARD PASS, ALTDORF, BÜRGLEN, KINZIG, KULM PASS, MUOTTA, PRAGEL PASS, GLARUS, ELM, PANIXER PASS, ILANZ

BUTLER, GEORGE. BERNE, THUN, ST. BEATENBERG, KANDERSTEG, GEMMI PASS, LEUK, VISP, ZERMATT, BASLE

BUTLER, HENRY MONTAGU. PONTRESINA

BUTLER, SAMUEL. POSCHIAVO, LE PRESE, BERNINA PASS, PONTRESINA, ST. MORITZ, MALOJA PASS, SOGLIO, PROMONTOGNO

Butler met Robert Browning at St. Moritz, and, at Promontogno the lady who kept sixteen parrots and who figures in his 'Ramblings in Cheapside'.

DAUDET, ALPHONSE. GENEVA, CHAMONIX, MONTREUX

'La Suisse en société, l'affermage des montagnes, les crevasses truquées. . . . alors, demanda Tartarin, très ému, la Jungfrau n'était pas préparée?' Most of *Tartarin* was written at Montreux.

DOUKHOVSKOY, BARBARA. LUCERNE, FLUELEN, RIGI, ALPNACH, BRUNIG PASS, BRIENZ, INTERLAKEN, GRINDELWALD, MONTREUX, MARTIGNY, TÊTE NOIRE PASS, CHAMONIX, GENEVA, LUCERNE, GÖSCHENEN, ANDERMATT, ST. GOTTHARD, GÖSCHENEN, COMO, MENAGGIO, PORLEZZA, LUGANO, COMO

'Here are the Alps towering in all their glory, their immense contours sharp and clear. . . . I am prepared to be delighted with everybody and everything.'

ELLERTON, JOHN. MONTREUX, VEYTAUX

'As for the walks, they are endless and ever fresh in deliciousness. Each day reveals some new vision of mountain glory, and the very road into Montreux is never twice alike. Moreover, there are charming groups of picturesque chalets, fountains, wood, and rock at every turn; but to say that is only to say that this is Switzerland.'

FOWLER, W. WARDE. LUCERNE, STANSSTAD, ENGELBERG, JOCH PASS, ENGSTLENALP, MEIRINGEN

'Switzerland is, in fact, an admirable centre for the study of migration; migration, that is, on a large scale, where the birds leave the country entirely, and also on that limited scale which we call in England "partial" migration. I believe that the Alps will some day win the attention of the ornithologists as being one of the best of all positions as a centre of observation.'

GREG, MRS. W. LES AVANTS, MONTE GENEROSO, PONTRESINA, DAVOS

GÜSSFELDT, PAUL. PONTRESINA, BERNINASCHARTE, PIZZO BIANCO

HALL, NEWMAN. PONTRESINA

'At the crag over the Morteratsch glacier from which my dear friend Charles Edward Reed fell and soared, July 29, 1884.

> . . . every spot on which a Christian dies,
> O'er whose long sleep heart-broken friends have wept,
> Becomes Heaven's portal. . . .'

HARE, AUGUSTUS J. C. BERNE, THUN, INTERLAKEN, LAUTERBRUNNEN, MÜRREN, ROSENLAUI

HOWARD, GENERAL OLIVER O. MILAN, BELLINZONA, ST. GOTTHARD PASS, ALTDORF, LUCERNE, BASLE

Bellinzona:—'We arrived at midnight and the hotels were closed and so we decided to stay in the depot, but the railroad agent said that he must close up that building and that we could not be allowed to remain in it, so we walked about the city for a while and when we were weary without asking permission crept into some cars that were waiting at the station, and slept there until the morning. . . .'

LARDEN, WALTER. ZINAL, TRIFTJOCH PASS, ZERMATT, COL DURAND, ZINAL, COL DE SOREBOIS, COL DE TORRENT, LES HAUDÈRES, AROLLA, PAS DE CHÈVRES, COL DE SEILON, COL DU MONT ROUGE, MAUVOISIN, MARTIGNY

'Arrived at Haudères very hungry and rather tired. There was no inn there then; but a native took us in to his house. We sat in a room of the real old Swiss type; sleeping bunks round it, and various wooden utensils hanging from the walls. The women sat at work; and both they and the man, who kept his hat on, stared at us with round-eyed curiosity as we ate. We had two bottles of curiously light-coloured wine, and unlimited bread, butter and cheese. The offer of five francs shocked them; they would hardly accept three francs. . . .'

MAIN, MRS. ELIZABETH (BURNABY, LeBLOND). ZERMATT, BIESHORN, RIED PASS, SAAS, WEISSMIES, RANDA, WEISSHORN, COIRE, TIEFENKASTEL, ST. MORITZ, PONTRESINA

'The troops of English who visit Pontresina in summer do not appear to have imparted much skill in their language to its inhabitants, judging by the wording of some of the notice-boards. We are informed when we enter some of the woods, that "in the months of July and August it will cuttered the wood in the forest. Because by the transport thereof stones are coming down, it is necessary to have care to it." "Dogs will by all means be chased from public rooms." "To prevent disagreeableness and reclamation for luncheon and diner table d'hote visitors are highly requested to be at the appointed tims." '

MEYER, CONRAD FERDINAND. ZURICH, GLARUS, KLÖNTHAL, RICHISAU

'For the first time for many years I have returned to the mountains, and with powerful effect. It was stupid of me to neglect this specific remedy.'

NIETZSCHE, FRIEDRICH. SILS-MARIA, ZURICH

PURTSCHELLER, LUDWIG. ZERMATT, MATTERHORN, BREUIL

SYMONDS, JOHN ADDINGTON. DAVOS, FLUELA-SCHWARZHORN, DAVOS, STRELA PASS, AROSA, KUPFENFLUH, DAVOS, KLOSTERS, SILVRETTA PASS, GUARDA, SÜS, FLUELA PASS, DAVOS

'By the time we stood upon the top [of the Schwarzhorn] at 3.45, Bernina, and Ortler, and Tödi were glowing with a faint half-conscious rose. And so the light stole gradually onward, fading the star and moon, disclosing all the hills of Switzerland and Tyrol, through that incalculably prolonged space of time which the sunrise always occupies. When I thought the sun must rise, there fell with bold impulsive sweep, from the zenith right into the cone of hidden fire, a white majestic meteor—a strange thrilling sight—as though some star had left her station, yearning to engulf herself in our terrestrial flame. At last a crest in Tyrol dazzled with true light; and in a few moments the whole of the Alp world was bathed in rosy golden day.'

TECK, MARY ADELAIDE, DUCHESS OF. MILAN, BELLINZONA, ST. GOTTHARD PASS, FLUELEN, SEELISBERG, RIGI, LUCERNE, ZUG, HORN

URLIN, RICHARD DENNY. BASLE, LUCERNE, BRUNNEN, ALTDORF, ST. GOTTHARD, BELLINZONA, COMO, CHIAVENNA, MALOJA PASS, SILS, PONTRESINA, DAVOS, KLOSTERS, LANDQUART

ZSIGMONDY, EMIL. MACUGNAGA, MONTE ROSA, ZERMATT, MATTERHORN, BREUIL, ST. THEODUL PASS, ZERMATT, ZINAL-ROTHORN, WEISSHORN, VISP, BIETSCHHORN, RIED

1885

BENSON, EDWARD WHITE. SION, VISP, ZERMATT, CIMA DI JAZZI

The Archbishop of Canterbury 'tried as far as possible to travel incognito, and was much vexed, I remember, at Visp at the evening table d'hote by a voluble clergyman who shouted to him as "Your Grace" down the length of a long table'.

BONNEY, THOMAS GEORGE. WASSEN, AMSTEG, MADERANERTAL, BRUNNI PASS, DISENTIS, LUKMANIER PASS, UOMO PASS, PIORA, OLIVONE, BELLINZONA, LUGANO, IVREA, AOSTA, GRAND ST. BERNARD PASS, MARTIGNY, CHAMPERY, SIXT

BOVET, ALBERT. NEUCHÂTEL, SION, EVOLENA, AROLLA, EVOLENA, COL DE TORRENT, ZINAL, ST. LUC, ZMEIDEN PASS, GRUBEN, TURTMANN, VISP, ZERMATT

'Quel spectacle imposant qu'une soirée passée à Zermatt, au sein de cette nature grandiose entourés de cette ceinture de montagnes, dont la moindre dentelure se découpe distinctement, au clair de la lune, ayant en face le géant noirâtre qui domine toute la scène, rafraîchis par l'haleine des glaciers, qui vous souffle la force et la vie, l'oreille bercée par les derniers tintements de la cloche argentine de la petite église, qui se prolongent et s'effacent comme une douce harmonie.'

BROOKS, PHILLIPS. BELLAGIO, ST. MORITZ, LUCERNE, INTERLAKEN, GRINDELWALD, KLEINE SCHEIDEGG, WENGERNALP, CHAMONIX

'You cannot think how splendid the great mountain was last night. The sky was perfectly clear and the moon was glorious, and the big round dome of snow shone like another world. The people stood and gazed at it and looked solemn. This morning it had changed, but was no less beautiful. It was like a great mass of silver. And so it stands there and changes from one sort of beauty for another, year after year, and age after age.'

BROWNING, ROBERT. GRESSONEY-ST.-JEAN

'We take our walks in the old way; two and a half hours before breakfast, three after it, in the most beautiful country I know.'

BUTLER, GEORGE. GENEVA, CHAMONIX, GRINDELWALD, INTERLAKEN, THUN, BERNE

BUTLER, SAMUEL. COIRE, THUSIS, SAN BERNARDINO PASS, SOAZZA, MESOCCO, BELLINZONA, VARALLO, VARESE

'I sat and wondered which of the Alpine passes Handel crossed when he went to Italy.'

FOX, JOSEPH H. LUCERNE, PILATUS, ALPNACH, MELCHTAL, STOREGG PASS, ENGELBERG, JOCH PASS, MEIRINGEN, GRIMSEL PASS, OBERAARJOCH PASS, EGGISHORN, FINSTERAARHORN, BELALP, ALETSCHHORN, BRIG, LEUK, GEMMI PASS, KANDERSTEG, INTERLAKEN, GRINDELWALD, WETTERHORN

GROVE, SIR GEORGE. LUCERNE, INTERLAKEN

GÜSSFELDT, PAUL. PONTRESINA, PIZ MORTERATSCH

HORNBY, EMILY. ZERMATT, COL DE VALPELLINE, COL DU MONT BRULÉ, AROLLA, COL DE SEILON, COL DU MONT ROUGE, MAUVOISIN, COL DES MAISONS BLANCHES, BOURG ST. PIERRE, ORSIÈRES, CHAMPEX, TÊTE NOIRE PASS, CHAMONIX

HORT, F. J. A. VISP, SAAS FEE

LARDEN, WALTER. BORMIO, VAL VIOLA PASS, LA RÖSA, BERNINA PASS, PONTRESINA, MALOJA PASS, CHIAVENNA, BELLAGIO, BAVENO, PESTARENA, MACUGNAGA, MONTE MORO PASS, SAAS, VISP, SION, AROLLA

MAIN, MRS. ELIZABETH. DAVOS, WIESEN

MEYER, CONRAD FERDINAND. ZURICH, COIRE, THUSIS, SPLÜGEN, LUGANO, ZURICH

'The valley is broad, the Hinterrhein flows through it, the sky is already southerly, the air fresh, but soft. . . . I have little wish to return home, for my old passion for the mountains has seized me.'

NIETZSCHE, FRIEDRICH. SILS-MARIA

PARKHURST, C. H. (*c*). GENEVA, VEVEY, VISP, ZERMATT, MONTE ROSA, MATTERHORN, WEISSHORN

PUPIN, MICHAEL. LUCERNE, WEGGIS, RIGI, PILATUS, ENGELBERG, TITLIS

SYMONDS, JOHN ADDINGTON. DAVOS, FLUELA PASS, SÜS, ZUOZ, PONTRESINA, BERNINA PASS, TIRANO, BORMIO, STELVIO PASS, STA MARIA, OFEN PASS, ZERNEZ, SÜS, FLUELA PASS, DAVOS

At Sta Maria, Symonds had great difficulty in dislodging the innkeeper's fowls, whose habit it was to roost beneath the bed he was occupying.

VAUGHAN, HERBERT, CARDINAL. LUCERNE, ENGELBERG, RIGI

'The people are good: but the externals of religion do not rejoice the eye and heart of a Catholic as they do in the Tyrol.'

WIDMANN, J. V. BERNE, SCHWARZENBURG, GUGGISBERG, SCHWARZSEE, CHARMEY, GRUYÈRES, CHÂTEAU D'OEX, GSTEIG, COL DE PILLON, LES DIABLERETS, COL DE LA CROIX, BEX, MARTIGNY, COL DE BALME, CHAMONIX, COL DU BONHOMME, COL DES FOURS, COL DE LA SEIGNE, COURMAYEUR, AOSTA, GRAND ST. BERNARD PASS, MARTIGNY, SION, LEUK, GEMMI PASS, KANDERSTEG, THUN, BERNE

Schwarzsee: 'The English men and women in the hotel reclined in virtuous boredom on sofas about the salon. Their presence conferred, however, the advantage that none of the other guests dared to touch the piano. A couple of individuals, it is true, hovered about the soundbox like fish at spawning time, but the solemn stares of the English on their sofas round the room were too much for them, and they suppressed their evil intentions.'

1886

BLUNT, WILFRID SCAWEN. GENEVA, CLARENS, MILAN

'To Switzerland, the land of lakes and snow,
And ancient freedom of ancestral type,
And modern innkeepers who cringe and bow,
And venal echoes, and Pans paid to pipe!
See I am come. . . .'

BRAHMS, JOHANNES. THUN, HOFSTETTEN, INTERLAKEN, LAUTERBRUNNEN, MÜRREN, INTERLAKEN, NIESEN

To be near his friend Widmann, Brahms spent the summer at Hofstetten where he completed the A-major 'Thunersonata' for piano and violin, and the C-minor trio.
'It is magnificent here. Incidentally, there are many beer gardens where the English do not penetrate; for my comfort that is no small matter.'
Brahms was dragged up the Niesen and wanted to spend the night on the summit; 'Poor fatty had nothing dry left with which to wipe the sweat off his face. He passed his umbrella continually over his cheeks', wrote his companion Thomsen.

BRIGG, M. A. BASLE, ZURICH, LUCERNE, RIGI, FLUELEN, ALTDORF, ANDERMATT, FURKA PASS, OBERGESTELEN, VIESCH, EGGISHORN, BRIG, VISP, ZERMATT, VISP, SION, MARTIGNY, LAUSANNE, GENEVA

BUTLER, GEORGE. MILAN, LUGANO, BELLINZONA, ST. GOTTHARD PASS, ALTDORF, LUCERNE, BASLE—BASLE, BERNE, THUN, INTERLAKEN, GRINDELWALD, THUN, BERNE, TERRITET

In 1883 it had occurred to Butler that 'a church was required at Grindelwald for the yearly increasing number of visitors who went there, and he set himself to promote the building of one'. In this year the church was consecrated by the Bishop of Ripon, its first chaplain being Canon Crowdy.

BUTLER, SAMUEL. LUCERNE, ALTDORF, ST. GOTTHARD PASS, FAIDO, PIORA, BELLINZONA, VARESE, MENDRISIO

'One day in the autumn of 1886 I walked up to Piora from Airolo, returning the same day. At Piora I met a very nice quiet man whose name I presently discovered, and who, I have since learned, is a well known and most liberal employer of labour somewhere in the north of England. He told me that he had been induced to visit Piora by a book which had made a great impression upon him. He could not recollect its title, but it had made a great impression on him; nor yet could he recollect the author's name, but the book had made a great impression on him; he could not remember even what else there was in the book; the only thing he knew was that it had made a great impression on him.'

CONWAY, MARTIN. BINN, CHERBADUNG, MONTE LEONE

DRUMMOND, HENRY. LUCERNE, AXENSTEIN, INTERLAKEN, VISP, ZERMATT, ST. THEODUL PASS, BREUIL, VAL TOURNANCHE

'There is but one spot in the world, and its name is Axenstein. In all my wanderings I never saw anything to approach the place from which I now scribble.'

FOWLER, W. WARDE. LUCERNE, BRUNIG PASS, MEIRINGEN, SUSTEN PASS, WASSEN, ANDERMATT, HOSPENTHAL, FURKA PASS, GRIMSEL PASS, MEIRINGEN

'The walk through the Gadmenthal up to the Susten pass was one to be remembered for beauty, though not ornithologically productive. The only curiosity that I saw was a Creeper running up a *house*; a very natural proceeding on the part of the bird, where the houses are of wood.'

GRÜN, CARL. SCHAFFHAUSEN, ZURICH, ZUG, RIGI, VITZNAU, LUCERNE, SARNEN, BRUNIG PASS, BRIENZ, INTERLAKEN, SPIEZ, KANDERSTEG, GEMMI PASS, LEUK, SION, MARTIGNY, COL DE BALME, CHAMONIX, TÊTE NOIRE PASS, MARTIGNY, VERNAYAZ, LAUSANNE, GENEVA, BERNE, BASLE

GÜSSFELDT, PAUL. ZERMATT, ST. THEODUL PASS, BREUIL, CHATILLON, AOSTA, COURMAYEUR, COL DE LA SEIGNE, COL DES FOURS, COL DU BONHOMME, COL DE VOZA, CHAMONIX, MONT BLANC, COL DU GÉANT, COURMAYEUR, ZERMATT, DENT D'HÉRENS, FELIKJOCH, GRESSONEY, LYSKAMM, CASTOR, SCHWARZTHOR PASS, ZERMATT

HUXLEY, THOMAS HENRY. SION, EVOLENA, AROLLA

'We saw at once that Evolena was a mistake for our purpose, and were confirmed in that opinion by a deluge of rain on Saturday. The hotel is down in a hole at the tail of a dirty Swiss village, and only redeemed by very good cooking. . . . Arolla suited us all to a T. and we are all in great force. As for me, I have not known of the existence of my liver, and except for the fact that I found fifteen or sixteen miles with a couple of thousand feet up and down quite enough, I could have deluded myself into the fond imagination that I was twenty years younger.'

KUGY, JULIUS. MACUGNAGA, MONTE ROSA, ZERMATT, MATTERHORN, ST. THEODUL PASS, BREUIL

'When I got back from the Matterhorn, I was asked by Güssfeldt, who was in Zermatt, how I found it. "Difficult," I said, without hesitation. "Thank God!" he exclaimed, "at last here's someone brave enough to call the Matterhorn difficult." '

LARDEN, WALTER. SAAS FEE, ADLER PASS, ZERMATT, STALDEN, SAAS, WEISSMIES, RIED PASS, RANDA, FEEJOCH PASS, SAAS, PORTIENGRAT

'At Saas Fee that summer there were no disagreeables, no cliques. The mountains and the love of the mountains seemed to dominate everything; and, for the purposes of expeditions, every one was assumed to know every one else. There were climbs in abundance, as serious work; and, as a relaxation for off days, there were glacier expeditions made perhaps in company with eighteen others or so, with exciting step-cutting. The latter excursions usually wound up with tea, and cream, and jam at Clara's restaurant on the moraine, high up between the two glaciers. In the evening we had good music (there were two excellent amateur violinists and several good vocalists), and once or twice Mr. Charles Dickens recited for us pieces out of his father's writings.'

MACQUOID, GILBERT S. BASLE, ZURICH, WESEN, LANDQUART, SEEWIS, KLOSTERS, DAVOS, WIESEN, LENZERHEIDE, COIRE, ZURICH

'Some of the villagers of Seewis are quaint. One day I met our old washerwoman, she stopped me, and carefully began to take a handkerchief from the top of her basket; some fine clove carnations lay exposed. I thought she meant me to have them, and I was stretching out my hand to take them when she gently but firmly drew the basket away and explained that she only offered them to me to smell, and that she did not intend to give them to me! It was evident that she thought she was giving me a great treat by allowing me to smell the flowers.'

MEYER, CONRAD FERDINAND. ZURICH, RHEINECK, WALZENHAUSEN, COIRE, PARPAN

Meyer was working at his *Temptation of Pescara*.

NIETZSCHE, FRIEDRICH. COIRE, SILS-MARIA

PALGRAVE, FRANCIS TURNER. VARALLO, FOBELLO, RIMELLA, ARONA, MENDRISIO, BELLINZONA, MESOCCO, BELLINZONA, ST. GOTTHARD PASS, ALTDORF, LUCERNE

'Drove up the San Bernardino valley. Saw the lofty fall of Buffalora: it was a sort of Spirit of the Waters. I had no notion that rock and mountain, stream and waterfall, could form a union so perfect and so ever-varying.'

SEGANTINI, GIOVANNI. TIRANO, BERNINA PASS, PONTRESINA, ST. MORITZ, JULIER PASS, SAVOGNIN

'I strove ever more after the heights. From the hills I went to the mountains, among the peasants, shepherds and dwellers in the High Alps, and up to their chalets and pastures. I studied the men, the animals, the country and the earth, in the innermost valleys of the Grisons, and settled in Savognin where I stayed for eight years. Many a summer have I spent in the high valleys, and winters in the chalets of those Alps. There it was that I turned my eyes particularly to the sun, by whose rays I lived, and which I wished to master. It was there that I studied nature in its most living form and brightest colours.'

SMYTH, DAME ETHEL. LUCERNE, ENGELBERG, JOCH PASS, MEIRINGEN, INTERLAKEN, WILDERSWIL

'Mercifully, mountaineering is a desperately expensive sport, for it is the only one for which I sometimes felt I might have neglected music and prepared for myself a life of remorse and misery.'

STORY, WILLIAM WETMORE. ST. MORITZ

The American sculptor built himself a house at St. Moritz, and Mrs. Story thus describes the laying of the foundation stone:—'We had asked everyone, and Italians, English and Americans crowded alike about us with warmest wishes and felicitations. Everyone admires the position. Papa had written a verse of dedication, which he read aloud, and a parchment was enclosed in a strong box in which, after the motto were inscribed the names of all present. This was placed by me in the hollow of the corner stone, and then by me plastered over. Then rose the singing voices of those who could sing (and even of some who couldn't) and the glorious old anthem "Praise God", etc. was re-echoed by the hills, . . . and then we had tea.'

SYMONDS, JOHN ADDINGTON. DAVOS, ST. MORITZ, MALOJA PASS, SOGLIO, CHIAVENNA, SPLÜGEN PASS, THUSIS, REICHENAU, COIRE, DAVOS, SERTIG PASS, BERGÜN, FILISUR, DAVOS

At Maloja 'we met no less than seventeen English acquaintances of all sorts and descriptions. But on Monday we broke away from these for a seven hours' walk up the sublime Murettothal and on the Forno glacier—really stupendous piece of high Italian, not Swiss, scenery. . . . A walk of about two hours' winding along the precipices above the [Maloja] pass, in spite of its hideous name, "Promenade des Artistes", is certainly one of the finest things in the Alpine region.'

TISSOT, VICTOR. BASLE, LUCERNE, ALTDORF, ST. GOTTHARD PASS, BELLINZONA, LUGANO, PORLEZZA, MENAGGIO, CHIAVENNA, MALOJA PASS, ST. MORITZ, PONTRESINA, ALBULA PASS, FILISUR, LENZERHEIDE, COIRE, REICHENAU, DISENTIS, OBERALP PASS, ANDERMATT, FURKA PASS, OBERGESTELEN, VIESCH, EGGISHORN, BELALP, BRIG, VISP, ZERMATT, VISP, GAMPEL, KIPPEL, SIERRE, VISSOYE, ZINAL, COL DE TORRENT, EVOLENA, SION, MARTIGNY, FINHAUT, VERNAYAZ, MONTREUX, COL DE JAMAN, GRUYÈRES

'Apart, shunning the crowd and the noise, I notice an old man stiff and erect, with the profile of a medallion, an aquiline nose, his forehead furrowed with wrinkles, thin lips, his chin cut in prominent angles, a martial gait under his surtout. It is Marshal von Moltke.' (St. Moritz.)

URLIN, RICHARD DENNY. LES VERRIÈRES, NEUCHÂTEL, LAUSANNE, MARTIGNY, SION, VISP, ZERMATT, VISP, MARTIGNY, VILLENEUVE, BASLE

WILKINSON, T. E. BASLE, BERNE, LAUSANNE, GENEVA, BERNE, THUN, INTERLAKEN, SCHYNIGEPLATTE, GRINDELWALD

'. . . All Switzerland is studded—mountains, lake-sides and valleys—with what I call my "button mushroom churches", for they spring up all over that country, and sometimes almost in a night!'

1887

BOVET, ALBERT (*c*). NEUCHÂTEL, AIROLO, PASSO NARET, FUSIO, BIGNASCO, CEVIO, LOCARNO, BIASCA, OLIVONE, LUKMANIER PASS, DISENTIS, REICHENAU

BRAHMS, JOHANNES. THUN, HOFSTETTEN, INTERLAKEN, LAUTERBRUNNEN, MÜRREN

While walking with Brahms from Mürren to Gimmelwald, Widmann referring to the giant mountains said: 'How impossible it is to fix this magnificence in the human mind and to reproduce it in poetry or in art.' Brahms answered: 'Everyone else who goes for a walk in the Alps with me usually says "that is just as in your third symphony", and so on. But not you. I like us.'
Yet, as Kalbeck says, 'The peaks of the Bernese Oberland rise before our eyes when we think of the A-flat Double Concerto for violin and cello.'

BROWNING, ROBERT. ST. MORITZ

'We are "snowed up" this morning; cannot leave our house to go to the hotel opposite, close by, where we get our meals! Such is Alpine treatment of travellers! Our amends is in the magnificence of the mountain, and its firs black against the universal white.'

BUTLER, GEORGE. BERNE, COMBALLAZ, LAUSANNE, VEVEY

BUTLER, SAMUEL. LUCERNE, ALTDORF, ST. GOTTHARD PASS, FAIDO, SASSELLO PASS, FUSIO, NARET PASS, BEDRETTO, FAIDO, BELLINZONA, VARALLO, ALAGNA, COL D'OLEN, GRESSONEY, ISSIME, AOSTA, MILAN, CHIAVENNA

CONWAY, MARTIN. BINN, OFENHORN, TOSA FALLS, BOCCHETTA DI VAL MAGGIA, VIGNASO

'Intoxicated with beauty, we arrived at Bignasco, prettiest village of all, with an inn at that time admirably kept.'

FINSLER, GEORG. BERNE, MEIRINGEN, GRIMSEL PASS, ULRICHEN, GRIES PASS, TOSA FALLS, SAN GIACOMO PASS, FONTANA, PIZZO CENTRALE

GÜSSFELDT, PAUL. ZERMATT, GABELHORN, MATTERHORN, FURGGENJOCH, ZERMATT, PONTRESINA, MONTE ROSSO DI SCERSCEN

HALL, NEWMAN. BELALP

The chaplain in charge requested Hall as a non-conformist not to attend communion, much to Tyndall's indignation. 'Some people,' said Tyndall, 'give me little credit for religious feeling. I assure you that when I walk here and gaze at these mountains, I am filled with adoration.'

HORT, F. J. A. GENEVA, CHAMONIX

'It was grievous work to be absent from England at the time of the Jubilee. . . . We three (Miss Blunt being with us) had our Jubilee services at the Montanvert, but there was no one else there to share them with.'

HUGHES, HUGH PRICE. CHAMONIX

Hughes and his wife had to wait on the Mer de Glace until their porter had found a guide to lead them across, as the usual track had become impassable. 'Our feelings can be imagined, but there was nothing else to be done! Fortunately, we had our rugs with us and, huddled up in these, we sat on the ice. It was soon quite dark and the stars shone out clear above us, making dimly visible the weird pinnacles surrounding us. Every now and again the ice gave an ominous crack and there was the horrid thought that possibly a crevasse might open out on the very spot on which we were sitting . . . I should think we sat there for nearly two hours.'

HUXLEY, THOMAS HENRY. LUCERNE, ALTDORF, AMSTEG, MADERANERTAL, ANDERMATT, FURKA PASS, OBERGESTELEN, BRIG, SION, EVOLENA, AROLLA, SION, MARTIGNY, MONTREUX, GLION

'We went to the Maderanerthal and stayed a week there. But I got no good out of it. It is charmingly pretty, but damp; and, moreover, the hotel was 50 per cent too full of people, mainly Deutschers, and we had to turn out into the open air after dinner because the salon and fumoir were full of beds.'

JONES, JOHN VIRIAMU. MÜRREN, MÖNCH, JUNGFRAU

KLUCKER, CHRISTIAN. SILS, PIZ CORVATSCH, CIMA DEL LARGO, MONTE SISSONE, MASINO, FORCELLA DI BONDO, PROMONTOGNO, SILS, MALOJA PASS, CHIAVENNA, LUGANO, VOGOGNA, MACUGNAGA, JÄGERHORN, ZERMATT, MATTERHORN, ROTHORN, VISP, RIED, PETERSGRAT, TSCHINGEL PASS, LAUTERBRUNNEN, INTERLAKEN, THUN

'I remarked that it might not have been amiss if our good Rubin had brought a lantern with him. This elicited from [Theodor] Curtius the laconic reply: "Not necessary. We can follow the scent of the man in front." Unfortunately he was right, for the odd and unpleasant odour that came from our leader was noticeable at a distance of ten paces and more. Such things are not restricted to Tibet, apparently.'

LARDEN, WALTER. GENEVA, CHAMONIX, COL DU GÉANT, COURMAYEUR, COL DE BELLE COMBE, GRAND ST. BERNARD PASS, BOURG ST. PIERRE, COL DES MAISONS BLANCHES, GRAND COMBIN, MAUVOISIN, COL DE MONT ROUGE, COL DE SEILON, AROLLA, DENT DES BOUQUETINS, MONT COLLON, COL DE MONT BRULÉ, COL DE VALPELLINE, ZERMATT, ADLER PASS, SAAS FEE

'One interesting feature of our stay at Arolla this time was the presence of Professor Huxley who was there with Mrs. Huxley, his daughter and son-in-law. He was so accessible to all, that two Swiss professors who were there could not believe, that he was really "the great Huxley"; for, said they, he talks to ordinary people just as if he were nobody.'

LEGGETT, BENJ. F. (*c*). ZURICH, ZUG, RIGI, LUCERNE, FLUELEN, ANDERMATT, FURKA PASS, GRIMSEL PASS, MEIRINGEN, INTERLAKEN, LAUTERBRUNNEN, KLEINE SCHEIDEGG, GRINDELWALD, INTERLAKEN, KANDERSTEG, GEMMI PASS, LEUK, VISP, ZERMATT, VISP, SION, MARTIGNY, COL DE BALME, CHAMONIX, TÊTE NOIRE PASS, MARTIGNY

LYTTELTON, EDWARD. SAAS FEE

Lyttelton was with J. E. C. Welldon and George Barnes:—'under his tutelage we learnt the lesson that at 12,000 feet of altitude the human frame is apt to clamour for sweets. There were ladies in our party,

Miss Oliphants from Datchet, but in regard to the craving for preserved apricots and peppermints, all supplied by Barnes, there was no distinction whatever between the sexes.'

MACQUOID, GILBERT S. BASLE, BERNE, THUN, KANDERSTEG, GEMMI PASS, LEUK, VISP, ZERMATT, VISP, BRIG, SIMPLON PASS, DOMODOSSOLA, LOCARNO, BELLINZONA, ST. GOTTHARD PASS, ALTDORF, LUCERNE, BERNE

MERIWETHER, LEE (*c*). DOMODOSSOLA, SIMPLON PASS, BRIG, SION, MARTIGNY, GENEVA, LAUSANNE, MARTIGNY, COL DE BALME, CHAMONIX, BERNE, THUN, INTERLAKEN, MEIRINGEN, GRIMSEL PASS, LUCERNE, ZURICH, SCHAFFHAUSEN

MEYER, CONRAD FERDINAND. ZURICH, MÜRREN

'. . . Do you know Mürren? Unforgettable. . . .'

MONK, JAMES A. GENEVA, LAUSANNE, MARTIGNY, GRAND ST. BERNARD, MARTIGNY, EVIAN, GENEVA

MONKSWELL, MARY, LADY. ROSENLAUI, BERNE, GLION

Glion:—'We immediately had a visit from Mr. Huxley.'

MUMMERY, A. F. ZERMATT, MATTERHORN, TÄSCHHORN

NIETZSCHE, FRIEDRICH. ZURICH, COIRE, SILS-MARIA

During this stay at Sils, Nietzsche wrote *Zur Genealogie der Moral*.

PURTSCHELLER, LUDWIG. KANDERSTEG, BALMHORN, ALTELS, BLÜMLISALPHORN, BELALP, ALETSCHHORN

SELBORNE, ROUNDELL PALMER, LORD. BELLAGIO, MONTE GENEROSO, BELLINZONA, AIROLO, PIORA

STEPHEN, LESLIE. MONTREUX, CLARENS, MARTIGNY, SION, VISP, ZERMATT

Overwork as Editor of the *Dictionary of National Biography* drove Stephen to the Alps where, at Zermatt in January, he and his friends had a hotel to themselves.

STOCK, EUGENE. VISP, ZERMATT, VISP, SIERRE, MARTIGNY, LAUSANNE

SYMONDS, JOHN ADDINGTON. DAVOS, THUSIS, SAN BERNARDINO PASS, MESOCCO, BELLINZONA, LOCARNO, BELLINZONA, ST. GOTTHARD PASS, ANDERMATT, OBERALP PASS, DISENTIS, COIRE, DAVOS, PISCHAHORN, VEREINA, KLOSTERS, DAVOS, THUSIS, ANDEER, AVERS CRESTA, DAVOS

While going up the Avers valley Symonds remarked: 'I have never seen anything in the way of high river scenery to equal this.'

TECK, MARY ADELAIDE, DUCHESS OF. COIRE, ALVANEU, FILISUR, ALBULA PASS, ST. MORITZ, MALOJA PASS, CHIAVENNA, CADENABBIA

'I do not know how ever I could have got through all the work of the past three months without St. Moritz's restoring power.' The 'work' was Queen Victoria's Golden Jubilee.

WIDMANN, J. V. BERNE, THUN, INTERLAKEN, LAUTERBRUNNEN, KLEINE SCHEIDEGG, GRINDELWALD, INTERLAKEN, BERNE

Widmann lost his dog by the side of the Grindelwald Eismeer, and it made its own way back to Berne, over the Kleine Scheidegg, Lauterbrunnen, and Thun.

WILKINSON, T. E. BASLE, ZURICH, BERNE, LAUSANNE

Zurich: 'I confirmed in the most hideous building on the Continent which calls itself the English Church. . . .'
Lausanne: 'I consecrated the very excellent church. . . .'

1888

BOVET, ALBERT. NEUCHÂTEL, LAUSANNE, MARTIGNY, CHAMPEX, ORSIÈRES, LOURTIER, MAUVOISIN, CHANRION, MARTIGNY, GAMPEL, KIPPEL, BRIG, VIESCH, BINN

'Les nobles paroles d'Eugène Rambert, à Thoune, reviennent involontairement en mémoire.
' "Voici ce que disent les montagnes: Au citoyen: si tu veux être libre, je suis ton rempart. Au chrétien: en haut ta confiance, élève-toi au-dessus de la poussière de ce monde. A la science: étudie-moi, sans te lasser jamais." '

BRAHMS, JOHANNES. THUN, HOFSTETTEN

BROWNING, OSCAR. COIRE, TIEFENKASTEL, JULIER PASS, ST. MORITZ, MALOJA

At the Maloja Hotel he found himself the recognized 'Hotel Boss'. 'It is a useful and indeed a necessary institution. He is a Master of Ceremonies like Beau Nash at Bath. His function is to keep people together, to preserve harmony, to keep up the standard of the hotel and to take care that no one is neglected or left out. . . . A Boss must have an anti-boss. This appeared in the shape of a lady whose activities soon became apparent. . . . Eventually I became tired of being a Boss and told Bancroft that he must take my place.'

BURTON, SIR RICHARD. MILAN, BELLINZONA, ST. GOTTHARD PASS, ALTDORF, LUCERNE, BERNE, LAUSANNE, AIGLE, ST. MAURICE, GENEVA

BUTLER, GEORGE. BERNE, THUN, INTERLAKEN, GRINDELWALD

BUTLER, HENRY MONTAGU. MÜRREN

'We are both perfectly well and perfectly happy. Every day makes me more thankful. We walk a great deal with lunch in my pocket, and also read a great deal of Greek together.'

COBDEN-SANDERSON, THOMAS JAMES. BELALP

'A great number of middle-aged and elderly ladies, and some young ones, a good many young men, and a great number of clergy including a bishop [Ellicott]. A sweet creature of a parson—young, shaved, and "high" I suppose—has just been in to inquire of me how I am. . . . I went on to the glacier to-day, and shouted for the joy of life.'

COOLIDGE, W. A. B. BERNE, THUN, INTERLAKEN, GRINDELWALD, FAULHORN, LAUTERBRUNNEN

A visit in January to Grindelwald where, to Coolidge's surprise, he found a large colony of English guests.

DOUGLAS, NORMAN. FINSTERMÜNZ, RESCHEN-SCHEIDECK PASS, TRAFOI, STELVIO PASS, BORMIO, TIRANO, CHIAVENNA, SPLÜGEN PASS, THUSIS, COIRE, RAGAZ, FELDKIRCH

DRUMMOND, HENRY. ENGELBERG, JOCH PASS, ENGSTLENALP, MEIRINGEN, GRIMSEL PASS, OBERGESTELEN, VIESCH, BRIG, SIMPLON PASS, DOMODOSSOLA, MILAN, BELLINZONA, ST. GOTTHARD PASS, ALTDORF, LUCERNE, ANDERMATT, VISP, ZERMATT

'I am lost in wonder all day long. Switzerland is the one place in the world which is never false to old impressions, which never betrays one by a shadow of disappointment, but grows in grandeur, with all one's faculties. I find this truer than ever this year, and I suppose this is my eighth or ninth time in it.'

HUXLEY, THOMAS HENRY. LUGANO, PORLEZZA, MENAGGIO, CHIAVENNA, MALOJA PASS, SILVAPLANA, JULIER PASS, TIEFENKASTEL, COIRE, RAGAZ, ZURICH

From Maloja Huxley wrote: 'In spite of all the bad weather we have had, I have nothing but praise for this place—the air is splendid, excellent walks for invalids, capital drainage, and the easiest to reach of all places 6,000 feet up.'

KLUCKER, CHRISTIAN. SILS, MALOJA PASS, PROMONTOGNO, SCIORA DI DENTRO, CHIAVENNA, MENAGGIO, LUGANO, FLUELEN, LUCERNE, BRUNIG PASS, BRIENZ, INTERLAKEN, GRINDELWALD, SCHRECKHORN, MITTELHORN

KUGY, JULIUS. COURMAYEUR, GRANDES JORASSES, ST. JACQUES D'AYAS, BETTA FURKA PASS, GRESSONEY, COL D'OLEN, ALAGNA, COL DELLE LOCCIE, MACUGNAGA

'Back to the east face of Monte Rosa. "Come here", said its glittering majesty. "I know of two things for you!" It was not the voice of the charmer, as other mountains can speak; it was the stern fearful voice of the Theban Sphinx, who slays those that cannot solve the riddle.'

LYTTELTON, EDWARD. ZERMATT

NIETZSCHE, FRIEDRICH. SILS-MARIA

PURTSCHELLER, LUDWIG. COURMAYEUR, COL DE LA PEULAZ, ORSIÈRES, SEMBRANCHER, MAUVOISIN, MONT BLANC DE SEILON, BEC D'EPICOUN

RUSKIN, JOHN. GENEVA, SALLANCHES, CHAMONIX, MARTIGNY, SION, BRIG, SIMPLON PASS, DOMODOSSOLA, THUN, MERLINGEN

On this, Ruskin's last visit to Switzerland, he wrote the penultimate chapter of *Praeterita*, and the 'Epilogue' to *Modern Painters* at Chamonix.
'The only days I can look back to as rightly and wisely spent, have been in sight of Mont Blanc, Monte Rosa, or the Jungfrau.'

STEPHEN, LESLIE. GRINDELWALD

'. . . Am said by affectionate people to be beginning to look fagged. This is only a kind fiction started to excuse a brief run to the Alps. That monomania still thrives, and I encourage it mildly, as it is becoming desirable to cling to one's youthful follies.'

WIDMANN, J. V. ZERMATT

At the 'Monte Rosa', Widmann found the blind Mr. 'Evertruth' whose decision to ascend the Matterhorn so as to go one better than the blind American who went up Mont Blanc, filled his wife and daughter with consternation. To start with, all went well because it rained every day. But to their horror, one day it turned out set fair and Mr. Evertruth ordered his guides to start at noon. The situation was saved by the suggestion of a young Englishman, Mr. Stone, that, like blind Gloucester in King Lear, Evertruth might be led about a harmless little side valley for appropriate times, precautions being taken against all possibilities of the illusion being shattered, such as, by meeting crowds of tourists, or a cow.

WILKINSON, T. E. MONTREUX, LES AVANTS, LAUSANNE, GENEVA, BERNE, THUN, INTERLAKEN, GRINDELWALD, LAUTERBRUNNEN, ISENFLUH

'There is a spot near Grindelwald which I greatly love; the ubiquitous Baedeker even does not draw attention to it, nor will I by mentioning its name and revealing its whereabouts. It is a walk of about an hour to a little grassy plateau between two waterfalls, with the grandest view to be obtained of Wetterhorn, Mönch, Eiger, and Jungfrau. I should like to build a chalet there.'

1889

BENSON, EDWARD FREDERICK AND EDWARD WHITE. ZERMATT, MATTERHORN, BREITHORN, ZINAL-ROTHORN

While E. F. Benson and his sister Mary Eleanor were disporting themselves on peaks, their father the Archbishop of Canterbury mused below at Zermatt: 'wonderfully soothing all the great sights are. They attempt nothing, they force nothing. There the peaks climb the sky and fence the world, and they fence you and bid you climb without a word to you, and their strong beauty puts all small thoughts to a quiet death, you feel as if you had passed something and were on the other side.'

BONNEY, THOMAS GEORGE. ANDERMATT, OBERALP PASS, DISENTIS, LUKMANIER PASS, UOMO PASS, PIORA, AIROLO, NUFENEN PASS, ULRICHEN, BINN, VISP, ZERMATT

BOVET, ALBERT. NEUCHÂTEL, ZURICH, WESEN, WÄGGITAL, SPEER, ZURICH, LUCERNE, BRUNIG PASS, MEIRINGEN, INTERLAKEN, LAUTERBRUNNEN, MÜRREN, SEFINENFURKE, KIENTHAL, REICHENBACH, INTERLAKEN

BURTON, SIR RICHARD. MONTREUX, ST. MAURICE, LAUSANNE, BERNE, LUCERNE, ALTDORF, ST. GOTTHARD PASS, BELLINZONA, MILAN

BUTLER, GEORGE. GENEVA, TERRITET, MONTREUX, LAUSANNE, VALLORBE

ELLACOMBE, HENRY NICHOLSON. LUCERNE, FLUELEN, HOSPENTHAL, FURKA PASS, OBERGESTELEN, BRIG, SION, MARTIGNY, FINHAUT

'I adopted a plan today for carrying my flowers as I collected them which I found most excellent. Tying the four corners of my handkerchief together with string, and then tying that to the head of my alpenstock, I had at once a light basket always open to take the flowers and carried at a most convenient point. I then understood the meaning of the bundles represented at the top of palmers' staves; it was the way they found most convenient to carry their little baggage, and the alpenstock is of course identical with the pilgrim's staff.'

FINSLER, GEORG. BERNE, THUN, INTERLAKEN, FAULHORN, GROSSE SCHEIDEGG, INNERTKIRCHEN, JOCH PASS, ENGELBERG, BRUNNEN, SCHWYZ, PRAGEL PASS, GLÄRNISCH, GLARUS, BUCHS, WILDHAUS, SÄNTIS, WEISSBAD

FLOWER, SIR WILLIAM HENRY. RIEDERALP, BELALP

FOX, JOSEPH H. TIRANO, BERNINA PASS, PONTRESINA, ALBULA PASS, FILISUR, COIRE

GODLEY, A. D. KIENTHAL, KANDERSTEG, MÄRWIGLÜCKE PASS, RIED, BIETSCHHORN, BEICH PASS, BELALP

'I recollected the perilous rock-and-glacier work which (according to Sir Walter Scott) menaces the incautious traveller on the route from Bale to Lucerne. (See *Anne of Geierstein*, chapters 1 and 2.)'

GÜSSFELDT, PAUL. ZERMATT, LYSKAMM

HALL, NEWMAN. ZERMATT

'I was seated near an athlete, whom I regarded as a distinguished member of the Alpine Club. Another mountaineer called him "Smith", and something was said about his being a Scotch parson. "May I ask if you are *Isaiah* Smith?"' It was George Adam Smith who had recently published a book on Isaiah.

HOGG, QUINTIN. BASLE, LUCERNE, ALTDORF, ANDERMATT, FURKA PASS, OBERGESTELEN, BRIG, VISP, ZERMATT, VISP, SION, MARTIGNY, LAUSANNE, BERNE

This was the first Polytechnic Continental holiday, conceived as an experiment to supplement school teaching in geography and history. The party consisted of sixty boys, three masters, and a doctor, lasted twenty-seven days, and cost £5. 19*s.* o*d.* per head.

HUXLEY, THOMAS HENRY. LUGANO, MONTE GENEROSO, MENAGGIO, CHIAVENNA, MALOJA

'I rejuvenate in Switzerland and senescate (if there is no such verb, there ought to be) in London.' Beside the lake of Sils a memorial has been erected to Huxley in the form of a block of granite, inscribed: 'In memory of the illustrious English writer and naturalist Thomas Henry Huxley, who spent many summers at the Kursaal, Maloja.'

JOHNSTON, SIR HARRY. BASLE, LUCERNE, ALTDORF, BELLINZONA, LOCARNO, BIGNASCO

On his journey out from England, Johnston kept on running into Douglas Freshfield who was travelling by the same train. At Bellinzona: ' "Where are you going?" each said to the other before we entered the Locarno train. "To a place you have never heard of", I said rather pompously, "to Bignasco. . . ." "Bignasco—never heard of it—?—!" gasped Freshfield. "Why, we *created* the place . . . I am part owner of the hotel".'

KUGY, JULIUS. COURMAYEUR, GLACIER DU DOME, DOME DU GOUTER, MONT BLANC, CHAMONIX, COL DU BONHOMME, COL DE LA SEIGNE, COURMAYEUR, GRAND ST. BERNARD PASS, MONT VELAN

LARDEN, WALTER. SION, EVOLENA, FERPECLE, COL DE BRICOLLA, COL DE L'ALLÉE, ZINAL, TRIFTJOCH PASS, ZERMATT, ALLALINJOCH PASS, SAAS, LES AVANTS, LAUSANNE, ZURICH, ROMANSHORN

'Is Ferpecle much altered now? I trust not. It was quite unique;

so small, so simple, and so friendly. A nice little girl of twelve (long since married and a mother) used to sit out on the big rock with me and chat away with perfect confidence and unreserve, and her small brother tried boulder-climbing with me. The house was like a toy chalet of wood, not a bit like an hotel. There was an outdoors douche house, and you turned the water on by placing sods in a runnel cut in the turf.'

MEYER, CONRAD FERDINAND. ZURICH, COIRE, THUSIS, SAN BERNARDINO PASS, SAN BERNARDINO

MONKSWELL, MARY, LADY. ROSENLAUI, BERNE

'A very much sunburnt middle-aged Englishman & 3 very striking-looking guides arrived about 4 o'c. from the top of the Wetterhorn . . . he turned out to be Mr Cross, who married George Eliot.'

PARRY, HUBERT. MENAGGIO, LUGANO, BERNE, MONTREUX

Parry was staying at the Blumenthal's chalet near Montreux.

PENNELL, JOSEPH. VISP, ZERMATT, RIMPFISCHHORN

RATTI, ACHILLE. MACUGNAGA, MONTE ROSA, ZUMSTEINSATTEL PASS, ZERMATT, MATTERHORN, ST. THEODUL PASS, BREUIL

This traverse of Monte Rosa by the future Pope Pius XI was the first by an Italian.

SMITH, LILIAN ADAM. LUCERNE, FLUELEN, ANDERMATT, FURKA PASS, BRIG, VISP, ZERMATT, VISP, GENEVA

Among the visitors whom Miss Buchanan met at the Riffel Alp were Dean Lefroy and Newman Hall, and George Adam Smith whom she married later in the year.

STEPHEN, LESLIE. DAVOS, GRINDELWALD

SYMONDS, JOHN ADDINGTON. DAVOS, FLUELA PASS, SÜS, ZUOZ, SAMADEN, ST. MORITZ, MALOJA PASS, CHIAVENNA, SONDRIO, APRICA PASS, VENICE, DAVOS, THUSIS, ANDEER, DAVOS

'Many as are the drawbacks of spending one's life at Davos, it has, aesthetically and sensually, the greatest pleasures which an epicure can hope for. All the Appenines, from Consuma to La Vernia, through Rieti, Aquila, Sulmona, Tivoli, have not a single line of beauty in them equal to what lies about us everywhere in this region. The beauty here, of line and profile, is so overwhelmingly rich, that artists cannot deal with it.'

TECK, MARY ADELAIDE, DUCHESS OF. COIRE, ALVANEU, FILISUR, ALBULA PASS, PONTE, ST. MORITZ

'What with one thing and another I was so utterly done up that a total change of scene, perfect rest, and bracing air were absolutely necessary for me, and all this I found at delightful St. Moritz, up in the Upper Engadine whence, after a month's stay, I returned a different being.'

WILKINSON, T. E. BASLE, BERNE, LAUSANNE, GENEVA, TERRITET, MARTIGNY, SION, VISP, ZERMATT

1890

BENSON, EDWARD FREDERICK AND EDWARD WHITE. RIEDER-FURKA, JUNGFRAU, EGGISHORN, BELALP

'My father had a larger supply of books than usual, for he was busy with his judgment in the Lincoln case.'

BROOKS, PHILLIPS. GENEVA, CHAMONIX, INTERLAKEN, GRINDELWALD, LUCERNE

BURTON, SIR RICHARD. FELDKIRCH, SARGANS, ZURICH, RAGAZ, LANDQUART, DAVOS, FLUELA PASS, SÜS, ZUOZ, ST. MORITZ, MALOJA PASS, CHIAVENNA, COMO

At Maloja they found Mr. and Mrs. Stanley, Dean Carington, Oscar Browning, Mr. Welldon, Sir John and Lady Hawkins, the Duchess of Leinster, Lady Maud Fitzgerald, Lord Elcho, Mrs. Main, Miss Oliphant, Mr. and Mrs. Bancroft, and Lord Dunraven.

BUTLER, SAMUEL. BASLE, LUCERNE, ALTDORF, ANDERMATT, FURKA PASS, OBERGESTELEN, BRIG, VISP, SAAS FEE, STALDEN, VISPERTERMINEN, VISP, BRIG, SIMPLON PASS, DOMODOSSOLA, VARALLO, BELLINZONA, FAIDO, ST. GOTTHARD PASS, ALTDORF, LUCERNE, BASLE

George Wherry relates: 'an impression of a stranger kneeling at a shrine often occurs to me. He was looking through the little grating of a chapel, one of the many that mark the stations on the high footpath to Saas Fee. At first I thought him to be a devoted penitent, until a nearer view proclaimed a shabby wanderer with a camera. We greeted one another politely enough to share the view of the coloured wooden figures of the sleeping disciples, and almost instantly I realized that the man was one of a thousand. . . . He proved to be Samuel Butler.'

CAMUS, THÉODORE. SAAS, ALPHUBELJOCH PASS, ZERMATT, WEISSHORN

CONWAY, MARTIN. CHAMONIX, MONT BLANC, CHAMPEX, BOURG ST. PIERRE, MONT VELAN, AOSTA, BY, COL VERT, CHERMONTANE, PRARAYÉ, COL DE CRÉTON, BREUIL, ST. THEODUL PASS, ZERMATT, VISP, BRIG, BERISAL, WASENHORN, VEGLIA

'An impression of a stranger kneeling at a shrine often occurs to me. He was looking through the little grating of a chapel, one of the many that mark the stations on the high footpath to Saas Fee. . . . He proved to be Samuel Butler'

(*Swiss Federal Railways*) GEORGE WHERRY, 1890; Saas

'Oh! I was glad to get back again to Loosern and Mount Palatious, I can tell you'

(Swiss Federal Railways) ALFRED CATHIE (servant to Samuel Butler), 1894

COOLIDGE, W. A. B. BASLE, BERNE, THUN, INTERLAKEN, GRINDELWALD, LAUTERBRUNNEN, CHAMPEX

A visit to Grindelwald in February, when an attempt to reach Mürren had to be given up owing to the softness of the snow.

FINSLER, GEORG. BERNE, THUN, INTERLAKEN, MÄNNLICHEN, GRINDELWALD, FAULHORN, ISELTWALD, INTERLAKEN, BERNE, BELLINZONA, PASSO DI JORIO, DONGO, CHIAVENNA, MALOJA PASS, PONTRESINA, PIZ LANGUARD, ST. MORITZ, JULIER PASS, MÜHLEN, TIEFENKASTEL, THUSIS, COIRE, BERNE, THUN, INTERLAKEN, GRINDELWALD

Finsler's second visit to Grindelwald was in December. 'Just as for many people there is a peculiar delight in visiting places at unusual times, such as going to a theatre in the day time, or through the quiet streets of a busy city by night, so a visit to high mountain regions in winter is a particular pleasure. . . . Except for ourselves there were only a few English people in the hotel, and more were to come after Christmas, for whom an ice-rink had already been prepared.'

FOX, JOSEPH H. TIRANO, BERNINA PASS, PONTRESINA, ZUOZ, SÜS, FLUELA PASS, DAVOS

GÜSSFELDT, PAUL. CHAMONIX, DENT DU GÉANT, COL DU GÉANT, COURMAYEUR

HORT, F. J. A. BERNE, THUN, KANDERSTEG, GEMMI PASS, LEUK, VISP, ZERMATT

LARDEN, WALTER. COIRE, LENZERHEIDE, TIEFENKASTEL, JULIER PASS, ST. MORITZ, PONTE, ALBULA PASS, FILISUR, COIRE

'Honestly, I should never now, recommend a winter in Switzerland to anyone who needed "picking up", unless he were strong enough to be out all day. St. Moritz in 1890 did me good every hour, indoors or out of doors; but it needs a lot of out of doors now to out-balance the effect of the heated hotels.'

LE BLOND, MRS. AUBREY (MRS. BURNABY, MRS. MAIN). ST. MORITZ

'Oscar Browning was staying at St. Moritz at the time and, knowing a certain little weakness of his, I had placed two comfortable basket chairs at the end of the tennis court with two large labels on them "Reserved for T. R. Hs." I also put a few smaller chairs next them. In one of those more modest chairs sat Oscar Browning for at least one hopeful hour, in fact till he discovered that our distinguished visitors had been installed for some time in the gallery above.'

MEYER, CONRAD FERDINAND. ZURICH, RIGI-SCHEIDEGG

NORMAN-NERUDA, L. PONTRESINA, MONTE SCERSCEN, PIZ ROSEG, PIZ BERNINA, DAVOS, KLOSTERS, GROSS SEEHORN, GROSS LITZNER, ZURICH, BERNE, LAUSANNE, VISP, ZERMATT, TRIFT PASS, ZINAL, WELLENKUPPE,

OBERGABELHORN, ZERMATT, LYSKAMM, DOM, DENT BLANCHE, JÄGERHORN, MACUGNAGA, CIMA DI JAZZI, ZERMATT

'Longer and longer fall the shadows, lower and lower sank the sun, gradually the deep rose-coloured flush of the snow-peaks became less intense, and faded away to make way for tenderer, fairy-like hues of a splendid after-glow, that mysterious rekindling of the glories of sunset, until at last even this last tinge of the sun's rays died away into grey twilight and the gloom of the night.'

OLIPHANT, MRS. M. O. W. DAVOS

'If you could imagine the unbroken expanses of snow, the dark pines, and the vulgar square dingy houses to be beautiful, it would be so.'

OMAN, SIR CHARLES. BELLINZONA

A spectator of the little attempt at revolution.

STANLEY, HENRY MORTON. MALOJA, CHIAVENNA

SYMONDS, JOHN ADDINGTON. DAVOS, FLUELA PASS, SÜS, SAMADEN, ST. MORITZ, MALOJA PASS, PLURS, CHIAVENNA, VENICE, DAVOS

TECK, MARY ADELAIDE, DUCHESS OF. ST. MORITZ, PONTRESINA, JULIER PASS, TIEFENKASTEL, COIRE, SARGANS

TOLLEMACHE, BEATRIX (*c*). ENGELBERG

URLIN, RICHARD DENNY. LUCERNE, ENGELBERG

WIDMANN, J. V. BERNE, THUN, ZWEISIMMEN, SAANEN, GSTEIG, SANETSCH PASS, SION, VISP, ZERMATT, VISP, BRIG, BELALP, OBERGESTELEN, GRIMSEL PASS, MEIRINGEN, GROSSE SCHEIDEGG, GRINDELWALD, INTERLAKEN, THUN, BERNE

'There are actually English women who find it cheaper to travel third class. . . . I don't object to the English provided that they don't make music. They didn't at Belalp; after a hard day's excursion, for example on the Sparrenhorn, they like to go to bed early. Of all the world's tourists, the English are the kindest to my little dog that accompanies me, and their love of animals is to me a very sympathetic trait in their national character. So I got on very well with the English at Belalp. But their nationality here is trumps, and one of them, Professor Tyndall, built himself a house here beside the inn many years ago, which he inhabited also this summer.'

WILKINSON, T. E. BASLE, LUCERNE, GÖSCHENEN, ANDERMATT, FURKA PASS, OBERGESTELEN, VIESCH, EGGISHORN, VIESCH, GRIMSEL PASS, MEIRINGEN

Grimsel: 'The intensely savage solitude, surrounded then and almost always with eternal snow, and lofty peaks, is most impressive. "Stand and look well at this", I said to the young friend I was with; "you will see nothing finer in all Switzerland".'

1891

ANDRÉ, AUGUSTE. LAUSANNE, VISP, ZERMATT, ADLER PASS, SAAS, CHABLE, MARTIGNY, SION, MORGINS, LAUSANNE, STE CROIX, CRÊT-JUNOD

'Efforce-toi, semble dire la montagne; car il n'y a pas de progrès sans effort. Patiente, car il faut lutter longtemps avant d'atteindre le but. Sois calme, car après l'orage vient le soleil qui réchauffe et réjouit. Vois, rongée par la pluie, la neige, la glace et les vents, je reste debout depuis des siècles, permanent appel à l'endurance, à la fermeté. Le secret du bonheur n'est pas de se jeter au-devant des orages ou de les fuir lâchement, mais de les supporter avec vaillance, sachant que s'ils dévastent parfois, ils servent à purifier aussi et font paraitre plus précieux le calme et la fraicheur qui leur succèdent.'

BENSON, EDWARD FREDERICK AND EDWARD WHITE. COIRE, PONTRESINA, PIZ PALÜ

While E. F. Benson and his brother Hugh had 'a most horrible experience' on Piz Palü, which fortunately turned out well, the Archbishop wrote in his diary: 'The region is too divided into infinite beautiful interests to fasten on and to hold one as the Riffel does with one over-mastering spell. It will not be so well remembered. But the beauties *are* infinite.'

BONNEY, THOMAS GEORGE. MEIRINGEN, GRIMSEL PASS, OBERGESTELEN, ULRICHEN, NUFENENSTOCK, SAAS, WEISSMIES

BUTLER, SAMUEL. BASLE, LUCERNE, SEELISBERG, ALTDORF, ST. GOTTHARD PASS, BELLINZONA, COMO, CHIAVENNA, TIRANO, BORMIO, EDOLO, APRICA PASS, SONDRIO, COLICO, VARESE, ARONA, VARALLO

'It was during the few days that I was at Chiavenna (at the Hotel Grotta Crimée) that I hit upon the feminine authorship of the Odyssey.' 'The walls of the house are painted in fresco, with a check pattern like the late Lord Brougham's trousers, and there are also pictures. One represents Mendelssohn. He is not called Mendelssohn, but I know him by his legs. He is in the costume of a dandy of some five-and-forty years ago, is smoking a cigar and appears to be making an offer of marriage to his cook.'

CÉZANNE, PAUL. NEUCHÂTEL, BERNE, FRIBOURG, VEVEY, LAUSANNE, GENEVA

Cézanne was not enamoured of the five months of table d'hôte that he spent in Switzerland. At the Hôtel du Soleil at Neuchâtel he painted and left behind two unfinished canvases, Bords du Lac de Neuchâtel, and Vallée de l'Areuse. They were found and painted over by another artist.

DUFF, MOUNTSTUART E. GRANT. BASLE, MOUTIER, BIENNE, LAUSANNE, VALLORBE

FINSLER, GEORG. BERNE, SCHÜPFHEIM, FLÜHELI, SATTELPASS, GISWIL, SACHSELN, FRUTT, ENGSTLENALP, INNERTKIRCHEN, GRIMSEL PASS, VIESCH, EGGISHORN, RIEDERALP, BRIG, KIPPEL, LÖTSCHEN PASS, KANDERSTEG, THUN, BERNE, THUN, INTERLAKEN, LAUTERBRUNNEN, KLEINE SCHEIDEGG, GRINDELWALD, GROSSE SCHEIDEGG, ROSENLAUI

FOX, JOSEPH H. BERNE, THUN, ST. BEATENBERG, INTERLAKEN, GRINDELWALD, LAUTERBRUNNEN, MÜRREN

GODLEY, A. D. ZINAL, TRIFTJOCH PASS, ZERMATT, JUNG PASS, MEIDEN PASS, ZINAL

Referring to the tourist, Godley wrote: 'Even when he only makes what I have heard a guide describe—in reference to the chief seats at feasts gradually attained by length of stay in hotels—as la grande ascension de la table d'hôte—even then he may be imbibing that enthusiasm for mountains, that animus ascendendi which is the sign of the true mountaineer; which will, one hopes, still send some Englishmen to the Alps when climbing as a fashion has passed into the limbo of forgotten pastimes.'

GROVE, SIR GEORGE. LAUSANNE, MARTIGNY, SION, VISP, ZERMATT

GÜSSFELDT, PAUL. COURMAYEUR, GRANDES JORASSES, COURMAYEUR, GLACIER DU MONT BLANC, MONT BLANC, GLACIER DU DOME, COURMAYEUR

HALL, NEWMAN. ZERMATT

HORSLEY, JOHN WILLIAM. MEIRINGEN

'For the first time, officiating as chaplain. . . . One evening there trudged into the hotel garden a party of unmistakable London lads, clerks and shopmen mainly, weary somewhat with the long walk from the Furka Pass, by the Grimsel Hospice and the Handegg Falls. They were from the Regent Street Polytechnic, and when I found that a fortnight in Switzerland had cost each under eight pounds, I first marvelled at what cooperation and contrivance and contracts could effect; and then, turning my thoughts to grimy Woolwich, I began to wonder whether "Woolwich on the Alps" was an impossibility.'

LARDEN, WALTER. MEIRINGEN, GADMEN, STEIN, ADELBODEN, BINN, BRIG, SION, MARTIGNY, CHABLE, CHANRION

MONKSWELL, MARY, LADY. ST. GERVAIS, CLUSES, SAMOENS, SIXT, ST. GERVAIS, NEUCHÂTEL, MORAT

A stay at the Chalet des Rochers and visits to Urquhart's Chalet des Mélèzes and to Sir Alfred Wills' Eagle's Nest.

MONTAGUE, CHARLES EDWARD. CHAMONIX, AIGUILLE DU MOINE

'I watch the sunshine stepping down the mountain that it climbed last night; and a mist forms from the Arve as it grows warmer, and goes uphill to meet the sunlight. Then the two hazes—of light and of water —make all that was clear ten minutes ago as pensive as a Corot; and I go through the joint mystery of them to Montanvert by the meadow path.'

NORMAN-NERUDA, L. ZERMATT, POINTE DE ZINAL, COL DURAND, ZINAL, SIERRE, VISP, ZERMATT, ST. THEODUL PASS, BREUIL

'Every conceivable means of whiling away the time had been tried and found wanting. The hotel had been climbed over and over again by every route and variant, with and without the aid of a rope, and a series of trials of strength between the various members of one particularly merry party had caused the officious interference of an English clergyman, who professed to be much shocked at the noise and loud laughter, "on a Sunday too", and especially that English ladies would join in such unseemly behaviour.'

RIMSKY KORSAKOW, NIKOLAY ANDREYEVICH. LUCERNE, SONNENBERG, ENGELBERG, ALTDORF, ANDERMATT, ST. GOTTHARD PASS, BELLINZONA, LUGANO

SMITH, GEORGE ADAM. ZERMATT, LAUSANNE

The Adam Smiths were travelling with a chameleon. 'At Zermatt Mr. Lascelles, the very tall science master at Harrow, put him upon a tartan plaid and the poor creature was very puzzled and finally turned a sort of dull grey. . . .' But at the Hotel Gibbon at Lausanne they lost their chameleon.

STANLEY, HENRY MORTON. MÜRREN

STEPHEN, LESLIE. ENGELBERG

URLIN, RICHARD DENNY. LAC DE JOUX, VALLORBE, ORBE, LAUSANNE

WHERRY, GEORGE. GENEVA, BOUVERET, MARTIGNY, GRAND ST. BERNARD PASS, AOSTA, CHATILLON, BREUIL, ST. THEODUL PASS, ZERMATT, MISCHABELJOCH PASS, SAAS FEE, ZERMATT, VISP, BRIG, RIEDERFURKA, BRIG, MARTIGNY, GENEVA

At the Täsch Alp hut 'my first experience here occurred of a real lady climber in action; she had sent on her guide and secured a room to herself, rather hard upon the unfortunate male, as the dens of the wooden cabin contain each two or three beds. . . . On this point I feel very strongly, that a lady should behave on such occasions exactly as if the cabin were a railway cabin.'

WILKINSON, T. E. BASLE, LANDQUART, DAVOS, LAUSANNE, BURIER, VEVEY, GENEVA

'I stayed with Mrs. John Addington Symonds, the learned author himself being in Italy. . . . In a snowstorm on 22 May, I confirmed the consumptive patients in the beautiful little church, which, to the great comfort of the invalids, has been built here. Davos is a sad place.'

1892

BROOKS, PHILLIPS. LANDECK, SCHULS, ZERNEZ, ZUOZ, ST. MORITZ, MALOJA PASS, CHIAVENNA, CADENABBIA, MONTE GENEROSO, LUGANO, BELLINZONA, ST. GOTTHARD PASS, ALTDORF, LUCERNE, BRUNIG PASS, BRIENZ, INTERLAKEN, GRINDELWALD, LAUTERBRUNNEN, INTERLAKEN, THUN, BERNE, MARTIGNY, TÊTE NOIRE PASS, CHAMONIX, GENEVA

'It was burnt down on Thursday, the Bear Hotel, the photographer's shop, and pretty nearly the whole village, a hundred houses in all destroyed, and ever so many wretched peasants thrown out into the cold world. It is quite awful.'

CAMUS, THÉODORE. CHAMONIX, AIGUILLE DE CHARMOZ, DENT DU GÉANT, LEYSIN

'Depuis 6 heures du matin il neige, il neige sans interruption et les flocons s'entassent autour de nous avec un accompagnement ravissant de tempête hurlante. De toute la journée on n'a rien vu, si ce n'est les tourbillons blancs qui tournoient de bas en haut et de l'est à l'ouest. Mais voilà que les vallées se montrent par dessous les nuages de neige. Le front aux vitres, je les regarde. . . .'

FINSLER, GEORG. BERNE, THUN, INTERLAKEN, GRINDELWALD, SCHWARZHORN, FAULHORN, SCHYNIGE PLATTE, INTERLAKEN, BERNE

FOX, JOSEPH H. GENEVA, CHAMONIX, MARTIGNY, GRAND ST. BERNARD PASS, AOSTA, COURMAYEUR, BAVENO, MACUGNAGA, DOMODOSSOLA, SIMPLON PASS, BRIG, SION, MARTIGNY

GODKIN, EDWIN LAWRENCE. BRIG, BELALP

'Tyndall was not far away. Mr Godkin visited him and heard him gird at the English clergy who frequented the Bel Alp.'

GRIBBLE, FRANCIS. AROLLA, SION, MONTREUX

On the Lower Arolla glacier, Gribble was held up by an armed brigand and robbed of his watch and money. But, as he said, 'I have, in the long run, made more money out of my brigand than my brigand extracted from me.'

GÜSSFELDT, PAUL. COURMAYEUR, GLACIER DE LA BRENVA, MONT BLANC, ST. GERVAIS

HORSLEY, JOHN WILLIAM. BASLE, LUCERNE, BRUNIG PASS, MEIRINGEN

'Personally conducting a party of fifty-one, mainly from Woolwich and Plumstead, of all ages and of both sexes; and this had developed each year until I had to limit my party to one hundred and forty, which was the accommodation of the dining room at the hotel.'

HORT, F. J. A. BERNE, FRIBOURG, LAUSANNE, MARTIGNY, SION, VISP, SAAS FEE

Hort was present at the consecration of the English church at Saas Fee by Bishop Marsden.

HUGHES, HUGH PRICE. GRINDELWALD

Hughes was attending the first of Henry Lunn's Reunion Conferences. 'The pill of ecclesiastical discussion was to be embedded in the jam of mountain excursions.'

KUGY, JULIUS. MONTE DELLA DISGRAZIA, CHIESA, CRASTAGÜZZA, PONTRESINA, PIZ BERNINA, ANDERMATT, FURKA PASS, GRIMSEL PASS, FINSTERAARHORN, GRÜNHORNLÜCKE, JUNGFRAU, MONCHJÖCH, GRINDELWALD.

'Great clouds of smoke were rising from the Grindelwald valley. I thought it must be a forest fire, while Kaufmann took it for dust from paths and moraines. When we reached the Bäregg, we saw what it was: Grindelwald was on fire! . . . Houses, hotels, railway station, wagons, haysheds, fences, cornfields, telegraph-poles, all were ablaze; . . . Kaufmann saw his house threatened, but still standing. His money was inside. We raced down, but by the time we were below, his house was a smouldering ruin. He took his place calmly at the fire-hose, while Bonetti and I laboured the whole afternoon, and throughout the night till next dawn, in the water-chain. British ladies stood side by side with the native inhabitants, passing the buckets. Purtscheller and Blodig had bravely rescued a piano and an omnibus, but these two valuable articles each started a fire to themselves later on. . . .'

LUNN, ARNOLD. GRINDELWALD

'I can still shut my eyes and see the Eiger snows blood-red in the glare reflected from the flames which consumed the greater part of Grindelwald.'

LUNN, SIR HENRY. GRINDELWALD

This was the first of the Reunion Conferences, which Lunn convened. One of its members reminded the meeting that 'in the early part of the fifteenth century, Nicholas of Basle, the great "friend of God",

from the Oberland, brought his followers . . . and these "friends of God" met together in their second and last conference at Grindelwald wondering who could help them to reform a wicked world.'
Lunn's conferences failed to reunite the churches, but they led him to turn his business sense and organizing ability to introducing people to the Alps in winter, and were therefore indirectly instrumental in furthering the development of winter sports.

MARSH, HERBERT. ZERMATT, ST. THEODUL PASS, BREUIL, FURGGJOCH PASS, ZERMATT, VISP, SIERRE, ZINAL, COL DE BOURDON, COL DE ZATÉ, EVOLENA, COL DE ZARMINE, AROLLA, COL DE BERTOL, BRICOLLA, COL DU GRAND CORNIER, ZINAL-ROTHORN, ZERMATT, MATTERHORN, ST. NIKLAUS, JUNG PASS, FORCLETTA PASS, ZINAL, MOMING PASS, ZERMATT, VISP, SIERRE, ZINAL, SIERRE, COL DE THIERRY, LENK, RAWYL PASS, SION, LEUKERBAD, BALMHORN, RIED, BEICH PASS, ALETSCHHORN, BELALP, SIERRE, RIED, BIETSCHHORN, LÖTSCHENLÜCKE PASS, EGGISHORN, BRIG, SIERRE

Belalp: 'At the hotel, which was almost quite empty, we made the late Professor Tyndall's acquaintance as he was holding a sort of little court in the hall before going up to his chalet for dinner.'

MUMMERY, A. F. CHAMONIX, AIGUILLE DES CHARMOZ, AIGUILLE DU GRÉPON

'The happy climber, like the aged Ulysses, is one who has "Drunk delight of battle with his peers", and this delight is only attainable by assaulting cliffs which tax to their utmost the powers of the mountaineers engaged.'

RONAT, G. (*c*). GENEVA, LAUSANNE, MONTREUX, SION, MONTHEY, TROISTORRENTS, EVIAN, THONON

VIRIEUX, EUGÈNE. GESSENAY, GSTEIG, SANETSCH PASS, SION, BRIG, VIESCH, EGGISHORN

'J'ai dit le cantique de l'oiseau dans la forêt, de la soldanelle et de la gentiane bleue — au premier rayon, la diane de l'Alpe d'Or — la fanfare glorieuse de midi — au crepuscule, l'angélus de toutes les cimes.'

WHERRY, GEORGE. BASLE, LUCERNE, BRUNIG PASS, MEIRINGEN, GRIMSEL PASS, OBERGESTELEN, BRIG, VISP, SAAS FEE, ZERMATT, TRIFTJOCH PASS, ZINAL, SIERRE, VIESCH, EGGISHORN, JUNGFRAU, LÖTSCHENLÜCKE PASS, RIED, SION, MARTIGNY, TÊTE NOIRE PASS, CHAMONIX, GENEVA

'The Grimsel Hospice is situated in the most savage rock scenery, and is not improved by containing a piano, electric bells, and a smart waiter in dress clothes.'

WIDMANN, J. V. BERNE, THUN, INTERLAKEN, MEIRINGEN, GRIMSEL PASS, FURKA PASS, HOSPENTHAL, ST. GOTTHARD PASS, AIROLO, NARET PASS, FUSIO, BIGNASCO, LOCARNO, ORTA

Sig. Dazio, the innkeeper at Fusio, had no sign or inscriptions on his walls, so that he could say to visitors, 'this is no inn and you need not expect to have any demands met other than those that I choose to grant'.

1893

BENSON, EDWARD WHITE. ZERMATT

'In spite of all civilising ideas I cannot but feel the railway up this valley a profanation. I only expected it to be a commonplacement.'

BONNEY, THOMAS GEORGE. HOSPENTHAL, ST. GOTTHARD PASS, FAIDO, BELLINZONA, MESOCCO, SAN BERNARDINO PASS, THUSIS, TIEFENKASTEL, ST. MORITZ, PONTRESINA, DAVOS

BOUHÉLIER, SAINT-GEORGES DE. BASLE, LUCERNE, FLUELEN, LUCERNE, BERNE, THUN, OBERHOFEN

'Cette Nature, où l'ai-je découverte sinon sur les rives boisées de l'Aare et dans les pinèdes embrunies qui avoisinent Oberhofen, en en couronnant les crêtes? Perdu au sein de ces belles solitudes, il se peut que j'y aie oublié le collège, mais j'y ai rencontré Dieu. Le "Naturisme" en est sorti, et la théorie des *grandeurs* de l'homme et celle de l'*héroisme quotidien* dont se sont inspirées plusieurs générations sans parfois s'en rendre compte. C'est en Suisse que j'en ai conçu le sentiment.'

CONAN DOYLE, SIR ARTHUR. LEUK, GEMMI PASS, KANDERSTEG, MEIRINGEN, DAVOS

The Reichenbach Falls suggested to Conan Doyle the solution which he adopted for finishing off Sherlock Holmes by making him fight Moriarty there.

COOLIDGE, W. A. B. FLIMS, ILANZ, VERSAM, SAFIEN-PLATZ, SAFIERBERG PASS, SPLÜGEN, WEISSHORN, ALPERSCHELLIHORN

DAVIES, SIR WALFORD. PORRENTRUY, LUCERNE, MORSCHACH, MYTHEN

DEGAS, EDGAR. INTERLAKEN

'Hotel Jungfrau. . . . Que d'Allemands ici, et des Français ridicules aussi. Si je ne me sentais pas être la simplicité même, . . . je craindrais pour mon effet.'

DUFF, MOUNTSTUART E. GRANT. VALLORBE, LAUSANNE, MONTREUX, GLION

ELLACOMBE, HENRY NICHOLSON. BERNE, THUN, ST. BEATENBERG, INTERLAKEN, GRINDELWALD, LAUTERBRUNNEN, MÜRREN

'I would far rather be a priest unto myself on one of the beautiful hill-sides than be condemned to one of the dreary Puritanical services in unworthy buildings which are so common throughout Switzerland, and advertised as "English Church service".'

FOX, JOSEPH H. GENEVA, CHAMONIX, MONT BUET, MARTIGNY, SION, VISP, SAAS, SCHWARZBERG-WEISSTHOR PASS, ZERMATT

GÜSSFELDT, PAUL. COURMAYEUR, AIGUILLE NOIRE DE PEUTERET, AIGUILLE BLANCHE DE PEUTERET, MONT BLANC DE COURMAYEUR, MONT BLANC, GLACIER DU DOME, COURMAYEUR

HUXLEY, THOMAS HENRY. MALOJA

Huxley was returning from a long walk and was hoping to slip unobtrusively away, 'but as he was descending the stairs, he met Her Royal Highness [the Duchess of Teck] coming up, and, seeing that she walked with difficulty, owing, I believe, to a weak knee, which troubled her, he at once offered his arm, and helped the princess to the room which had been prepared for tea.'

LARDEN, WALTER. BINN, ZERMATT, MONTE ROSA, MATTERHORN, MISCHABELJOCH PASS, SAAS FEE

LODGE, OLIVER. ZERMATT

'A search party came out of the hotel with lanterns and carrying chairs and went in search of us.'

MAARTENS, MAARTEN. LEYSIN, BEX, CHEXBRES, VEVEY

'Another slow, still snowstorm; February has been bad to us. You can hardly imagine what isolation it means. Day after day, from morning till night the thick white cloud shutting us in on all sides, pressed, almost tangibly, against the windows, and through its denseness the ceaseless soft fall of snow; inside the house silence, but for an occasional sound. . . .'

MARSH, HERBERT. TERRITET, AIGLE, COL DE PILLON, GSTEIG, SANETSCH PASS, SION, LEUK, GEMMI PASS, KANDERSTEG, DOLDENHORN, GEMMI PASS, LEUK, SION, MARTIGNY, CHAMONIX, AIGUILLE D'ARGENTIÈRE, TÊTE NOIRE PASS, MARTIGNY, SION, SIERRE, BRIG, BINN, VIESCH, EGGISHORN, FINSTERAARHORN, JUNGFRAU, BRIG, VISP, SAAS FEE, DOM, ZERMATT, SAAS, MONTE MORO PASS, MACUGNAGA, MONDELLI PASS, SAAS, PORTJENGRAT, LAQUINHORN, VISP, SION, AROLLA, DENT BLANCHE, COL DU GRAND CORNIER, ZINAL, SIERRE, VISP, ZERMATT, VISP, MARTIGNY, FIONNAY, CHANRION, RUINETTE, MARTIGNY, MONTREUX

MUMMERY, A. F. CHAMONIX, DENT DU REQUIN, AIGUILLE DU GRÉPON, AIGUILLE DU PLAN, TÊTE NOIRE PASS, MARTIGNY, SION, SIERRE, ZINAL

'Our critics, curiously enough, repeat in substance Mr. Ruskin's original taunt, that we regard the mountains as greased poles. I must confess that a natural and incurable denseness of understanding does not enable me to feel the sting of this taunt . . . I do not perceive the enormity or sin of climbing poles.'

MUNRO, HECTOR ('SAKI'). DAVOS

The Hotel des Iles collected money for entertainments, but never invited anyone from other hotels. So 'Saki' issued invitations to a party to be held on March 20 and sent them to all the other English hotels and to selected guests of the Kurhaus. The replies were to be sent to two men who, 'Saki' knew, had left the Hotel des Iles, so the letters would be forwarded. The day arrived, and the guests, and pandemonium. In the following winter the Hotel des Iles having learnt its lesson invited everybody to a concert. And nobody turned up.

NAEF, EDUARD. GLARUS, PRAGEL PASS, SCHWYZ

One of the earliest ski tours in Switzerland.

REY, GUIDO. VAL TOURNANCHE, MATTERHORN, HORNLI, FURGGENJOCH PASS, VAL TOURNANCHE

'Et pour peu que les nuages, courant à son entour secondent notre fantaisie par l'illusion d'optique, il nous semble que nous le voyons se mouvoir, incliner la tête comme de qui serait triste ou la redresser avec l'audace d'un Titan. . . . Je ne sais point de paroles assez puissantes pour décrire, à celui qui ne l'a pas vu, la magnificence du Rocher qui s'éléve à pic sur une hauteur de trois mille mêtres contre le ciel au fond de la vallée—figure changeante qui tour à tour attire et menace, et apparait parfois comme le produit angoissant d'un cataclysme et à d'autres fois comme une œuvre sereine et grande que la nature aurait donnée à l'homme pour l'ennoblissement de sa pensée.'

TECK, MARY ADELAIDE, DUCHESS OF. BASLE, ZURICH, COIRE, THUSIS, TIEFENKASTEL, JULIER PASS, ST. MORITZ, MALOJA, PONTE, ALBULA PASS, FILISUR, ALVANEU, TIEFENKASTEL, THUSIS, COIRE

The Duchess drove to Maloja with Dr. Welldon to see the recently excavated glacier-mills which, in her honour, were named the 'Princess Mary Adelaide mills'.

WHERRY, GEORGE. KANDERSTEG, GEMMI PASS, LEUK, SIERRE, ZINAL, COL DURAND, ZERMATT, DENT BLANCHE, WEISSHORN, FURGGJOCH PASS, BREUIL, CHATILLON, AOSTA, COURMAYEUR, MONT BLANC, CHAMONIX, AIGUILLE VERTE, GENEVA, ZERMATT

WHYMPER, EDWARD. VISP, ZERMATT, AROLLA, COL DE COLLON, PRARAYÉ, AOSTA, COURMAYEUR, MONT BLANC

WILKINSON, T. E. BASLE, LAUSANNE, MONTREUX, GENEVA, MORNEX

1894

AMERY, L. S. BASLE, LUCERNE, STANSERHORN, WOLFENSCHIESSEN, VISP, ZERMATT, ROTHORN, WEISSHORN, DENT BLANCHE, MATTERHORN

'Among those in whom our fame kindled the flame of ambition—short-lived in this direction at least—was our old schoolfellow Winston Churchill, who, in spite of our efforts to dissuade him from what we urged was a long and tiresome trudge unworthy of his prowess, insisted on climbing Monte Rosa, because it was actually the highest mountain in Switzerland.'

BUTLER, SAMUEL. BASLE, LUCERNE, FLUELEN, ANDERMATT, FLUELEN, RIGI

Butler had with him his man Alfred who did not altogether relish Butler's interest in chapels. 'Oh! I was glad to get back again to Loosern and Mount Palatious, I can tell you.' Then, when Butler had taken him up the Rigi and shown him all the wonders of the Alps from the top, Alfred said 'and now if you please, Sir, I should like to lie down on the grass here and have a read of *Tit-Bits*'.

CONAN DOYLE, SIR ARTHUR. DAVOS, MAIENFELDERFURKA PASS, AROSA, DAVOS, MALOJA, DAVOS

Conan Doyle's ski tour to Arosa was undertaken on the anniversary of the first crossing of the Maienfelderfurka by the Brangers. At Davos, Conan Doyle laid out the golf links, and began writing the *Brigadier Gerard* series.

CONWAY, WILLIAM MARTIN. COURMAYEUR, MONT BLANC, CHAMONIX, MONT BUET, COL DU VIEUX EMOSSON, COL D'EMANEY, COL DE SALANFE, ST. MAURICE, BEX, ANZEINDAZ, DIABLERETS, SANETSCH PASS, WILDHORN, RAWYL PASS, WILDSTRUBEL, GEMMI PASS, LEUK, VISP, ZERMATT, MONTE ROSA, VISP, RIED, LÖTSCHENLÜCKE PASS, JUNGFRAU, OBERAARJOCH PASS, GRIMSEL PASS, GALENSTOCK, GÖSCHENEN, AMSTEG, MADERANERTAL, GURKHA PASS, SANDALP PASS, THIERFEHD, HAUSSTOCK, ELM, SARDONA PASS, VÄTTIS, RAGAZ, LANDQUART, SEEWIS, SCESAPLANA, SCHRUNS, VERMUNT PASS, ARDETZ, SCHULS, NAUDERS

COOK, THEODORE ANDREA. ST. MORITZ

Describing the Cresta run and its history, Cook says of the stone pillars on the Julier pass: 'Surely they marked the starting-point of one of the longest toboggan runs before or since; and I cannot resist believing that the great commander, fertile in resources, there first showed his troops the way to use their shields and spears as instruments of locomotion.'

FOX, JOSEPH H. GENEVA, CHAMONIX, ZERMATT

GIDE, ANDRÉ. LAUSANNE, NEUCHÂTEL, LA BRÉVINE

At La Brévine Gide wrote *Paludes*, and afterwards laid the scene of his *Symphonie Pastorale.*

HALL, NEWMAN. ZERMATT

'Mountain beauty does not consist in magnitude, but in form. Magnitude causes wonder and awe, but form inspires admiration and delight. The forms of some of our hills are as beautiful as some of those of Switzerland, and often more so. Certainly the view is more varied. We may travel far before the Matterhorn is out of sight. I have gazed at it day by day till I have felt overawed by its unchanging outlines and terribleness.'

JOHNSTON, SIR HARRY. LINTHAL, GLARUS, WALLENSTADT, COIRE, ST. MORITZ, DOMODOSSOLA, SIMPLON PASS, BRIG, SION, MARTIGNY, LAUSANNE

'A driving tour which commenced at Coire in the Engadine. In a thoroughly comfortable kind of brake drawn by two and sometimes four horses, and driven by one of the nicest types of Swiss coachmen I have ever met, we seemed to drive through Paradise.'

LARDEN, WALTER. LAUSANNE, MARTIGNY, LEUK, GEMMI PASS, KANDERSTEG, BLÜMLISALP, BALMHORN, LÖTSCHEN PASS, RIED, BEICH PASS, ALETSCHHORN, BELALP, JUNGFRAU, FINSTERAARHORN

'We ascended the Aletsch glacier; and as we neared the hut which is built on the rocks at the base of the Kamm, at a height of 9,400 feet above the sea, I saw a turbaned head up above, and guessed at once that I had struck Sir Martin Conway doing "The Alps from End to End". And so it was. There I found him, with the two little Gurkhas.'

LODGE, ELEANOR C. BERNE, THUN, INTERLAKEN, LAUTERBRUNNEN, WENGEN, KLEINE SCHEIDEGG, INTERLAKEN, SPIEZ

Miss Lodge's companion, Miss Wordsworth 'was not a very good walker, her idea being to run uphill as fast as one could and then rest exhausted till the next spurt'.

MUMMERY, A. F. CHAMONIX, COL DES COURTES, COURMAYEUR, CHAMONIX, AIGUILLE VERTE, ZERMATT, ZMUTT RIDGE, MATTERHORN

PUMPELLY, RAPHAEL. COMO, LUCERNE, GRINDELWALD

PUPIN, MICHAEL. WALLENSTADT, FURKA PASS

While crossing the Furka pass, the Serbian shepherd turned American scientist hit upon the solution of the application of Lagrange's principle of dynamics to the passage of an electric current through a conductor.

RACOWITZA, HELENE VON. WENGERNALP

'I could not sleep because the full moon, in magical beauty in the heavens, threw an almost uncanny rosy light on the mountain kings Eiger, Mönch, and Jungfrau, so that the eternal snow glistened like gold dust. Again and again this glory of God drew me to the window. In the immense stillness of the loneliness of the mountains, the thundering of the avalanches, that crashed from time to time from the opposite heights, was the only earthly sound. It was as if one heard the breath of God.'

STEPHEN, LESLIE. CHAMONIX

TECK, MARY ADELAIDE, DUCHESS OF. ST. MORITZ, PONTRESINA

THOMPSON, SILVANUS P. ZERMATT, VISP, OBERGESTELEN, FURKA PASS, ANDERMATT

WHYMPER, EDWARD. CHAMONIX, COL DU BONHOMME, COL DE LA SEIGNE, COURMAYEUR, COL DU GÉANT, CHAMONIX, COL DU CHARDONNET, COL DE LA FENÊTRE, COL DU TOUR, CHAMONIX, MONT BLANC, MARTIGNY, SIERRE, ZINAL, TRIFTJOCH PASS, ZERMATT, GRINDELWALD, GENEVA

WILKINSON, T. E. SCHAFFHAUSEN, ZURICH, NEUCHÂTEL, LAUSANNE, TERRITET, CAUX

1895

BONNEY, THOMAS GEORGE. BERNE, THUN, KANDERSTEG, GEMMI PASS, LEUK, SIERRE, ZINAL, SIERRE, BRIG, OBERGESTELEN, GRIMSEL PASS, MEIRINGEN

'In old times one seldom returned home from the Alps without some addition to the number of one's friends; but now the average traveller is unattractive, and a crowded *salle à manger* especially with the much-vaunted separate tables, gives no opportunity for getting so far as acquaintance.'

BUTLER, SAMUEL. BASLE, LUCERNE, ALTDORF, WASSEN, HOSPENTHAL, ST. GOTTHARD PASS, BELLINZONA

'At Wassen we stayed at the Hotel des Alpes, where they had specially good Chianti this year; I suppose we must have drunk it all—at all events it was never so good in the following years. We used to take a bottle with us up the side valley to Meien, where we sketched all day, meeting for luncheon at the fountain in the village.'

CONAN DOYLE, SIR ARTHUR. DAVOS, CAUX

At Caux, Conan Doyle finished the first *Brigadier Gerard* series and began to write *Rodney Stone*.

FOX, JOSEPH H. GENEVA, CHAMONIX, COL DU CHARDONNET, FENÊTRE DE SALEINAZ, COL DU TOUR, CHAMONIX

'Now that my ice axe and rope have done their work and are hung up on the wall, I love to dwell on the past with all its delightful memories.'

HARTE, BRET. BASLE, NEUCHÂTEL, LAUSANNE, VEVEY, GLION, GENEVA, LAUSANNE, BERNE

'The dear old Sierras, after all, are infinitely finer with their freshness, their beauty, their absolute and wholesome rudeness and sincerity, and I never knew before how I really loved them, and how they have taken such a hold on my life; here everything is grand and spectacular —but in the very heart of the wilderness there is a suspicion of drains and the smell of French cooking comes in at your window, with the breath of the pines.'

LARDEN, WALTER. BINN, KRIEGALP PASS, DEVERO, SCATTAMINOJA PASS, TOSA FALLS, HOHSAND PASS, BINN, VIESCH, MÖNCH, JUNGFRAU, CHAMONIX, AIGUILLE DES CHARMOZ, AIGUILLE DU GÉANT, COURMAYEUR, MONT BLANC, CHAMONIX, AIGUILLE DE BLAITIÈRE

LODGE, OLIVER (*c*). OUCHY, MARTIGNY, SIERRE, ST. LUC, CHANDOLIN

RIVETT-CARNAC, J. H. WILDECK, GRINDELWALD

Rivett-Carnac had bought the castle of Wildeck but spent the winter at Grindelwald for seven seasons.

WALLACE, ALFRED RUSSEL. LUCERNE, STANS, STANSERHORN, FLUELEN, ANDERMATT, FURKA PASS, GRIMSEL PASS, MEIRINGEN, INTERLAKEN, LAUTERBRUNNEN, WENGERNALP

'So dreadfully persecuted by swarms of blood-sucking flies, which filled the air and covered us in thousands, piercing through our thin clothing, that we returned home some days earlier than we had intended.'

WHERRY, GEORGE. KANDERSTEG, PETERSGRAT, RIED, BIETSCHHORN, VISP, ZERMATT, MONTE ROSA, CHAMONIX

WHYMPER, EDWARD. ZERMATT, BREUILJOCH PASS, MATTERHORN, STALDEN, VISP

WIDMANN, J. V. BERNE, THUN, INTERLAKEN, LAUTERBRUNNEN, KLEINE SCHEIDEGG, GRINDELWALD, INTERLAKEN, BRIENZ, ROTHORN, INTERLAKEN, THUN, BERNE

WILKINSON, T. E. MILAN, LUGANO, LOCARNO, BELLINZONA, FLUELEN, ZURICH, BERNE, THUN, BERNE, LAUSANNE, GENEVA

1896

BONNEY, THOMAS GEORGE. THUSIS, SPLÜGEN, SAN BERNARDINO PASS, MESOCCO, LUKMANIER PASS, ST. GOTTHARD PASS, ALTDORF, LUCERNE

BUTLER, SAMUEL. LUCERNE, ALTDORF, ST. GOTTHARD PASS, BELLINZONA, LUGANO, LUINO, LOCARNO, BELLINZONA, ST. GOTTHARD PASS, ALTDORF, LUCERNE, BÜRGENSTOCK, BASLE

COOLIDGE, W. A. B. INTERLAKEN, HABKERN, CHUMELI PASS, MERLIGEN

FLOWER, SIR WILLIAM HENRY. KÜBLIS, ST. ANTÖNIEN

LARDEN, WALTER. LEUK, GEMMI PASS, KANDERSTEG, BLÜMLISALPHORN, PETERSGRAT, RIED, BEICH PASS, BELALP, VIESCH, BINN, BRIG, VISP, STALDEN, ZERMATT, ALPHUBELJOCH PASS, SAAS FEE, RIED PASS, ZERMATT, ROTHORN, ZINAL

'While I was at Kandersteg climbing with Abraham Müller I noticed one day a sort of pedlar bearing a wooden box on his back. I asked Abraham who and what the man was. He told me that he was an Italian scorpion-seller.' The purpose of buying scorpions is to prepare scorpion-oil for use in case of insect-bites.

MOULTON, LOUISE CHANDLER (*c*). LUCERNE, RIGI, BRUNIG PASS, BRIENZ, INTERLAKEN, THUN, BERNE, GENEVA, CHAMONIX, TÊTE NOIRE PASS, MARTIGNY, CHILLON, GENEVA

SMITH, J. MANTON. LUCERNE, STANS, STANSERHORN, RIGI, PILATUS, ALTDORF, ANDERMATT, LUCERNE, BRUNIG PASS, MEIRINGEN, INTERLAKEN, GRINDELWALD, FAULHORN, KLEINE SCHEIDEGG, LAUTERBRUNNEN, INTERLAKEN, THUN, BERNE, VISP, ZERMATT, GENEVA, BASLE

On the top of Pilatus: 'I struck up the Doxology to the tune of the Old Hundredth, and before we had finished that short verse of praise, the mist rolled up like a curtain, and for two or three minutes we got a glorious view of the snow mountains beyond. "Eh!" said our friend, "isn't it grand, it 's worth all the visit from England to see this sight!" "Well, friend", said I, "we have acknowledged the Lord, and he has been pleased to honour us for it." "Eh, me!" said the man, "let us sing again"; and, with my small pocket cornet, I struck up "Diadem".'

TECK, MARY ADELAIDE, DUCHESS OF. ST. MORITZ

WHERRY, GEORGE. BERNE, THUN, KANDERSTEG, GEMMI PASS, LEUK, SIERRE, MONTANA, SION, AROLLA, COL DE COLLON, BIONAZ, AOSTA

YOUNG, GEOFFREY WINTHROP. ZINAL

'On solitary scrambles over the Bella Tola, round the back of the Diablons, and over into the wild and then seldom visited Turtmannthal, with senses sharpened by watchful solitude, I slowly amassed experience. The sight of the perpetual semicircle of the great Pennine peaks, rounding off the valley, made me familiar with the shapes of glacier and of great snow ridge; and incidentally developed a passion for the glorious skylines of the Weisshorn and the Matterhorn which no number of ascents upon those two mountains, each in their own way supreme, has ever served to satisfy.'

1897

BONNEY, THOMAS GEORGE. AIROLO, PIORA, MEIRINGEN

BUTLER, ARTHUR JOHN. KLOSTERS, FLUCHTHORN

'Look at the opening of *Paradiso* xi, and you will see how one feels on a mountain-side on a fine morning.'

BUTLER, SAMUEL. BELLINZONA, ST. GOTTHARD PASS, WASSEN

Butler was starting to write his *Shakespeare's Sonnets Reconsidered.*

COBDEN-SANDERSON, THOMAS JAMES. BASLE, LAUSANNE, AIGLE, MORCLES, BALLAIGUES, BERNE, NYON, ST. CERGUE, MOREZ, ST. CLAUDE, COL DE LA FAUCILLE, LAC DE JOUX, VALLORBE

'May they all under a Swiss sky, in fresh Swiss air, grow well and strong, and lay up memories for times to come.'

COOLIDGE, W. A. B. ST. BEATENBERG, GEMMENALPHORN, HABKERN, KEMMERIBODEN, HOHGANT, INNERE GUMM PASS, EBLIGEN, BRIENZ

A visit to the region 'behind Interlaken'.

COULTON, G. G. LAUSANNE, MARTIGNY, COL DE BALME, TRIENT, MARTIGNY, LAUSANNE

'. . . At the little village of Trient. The big summer hotel there was in its natural winter state: no guests but the family and servants hibernating. . . . With them were the travelling cobbler and the travelling tailor, welcomed during the dead months to repair the ravages of summer wear. . . . Presently they started the subject of the Diamond Jubilee due in that year, 1897. It was pleasant to find how genuinely they were interested. . . . We were all hibernating in the same hole and talking as from man to man; seldom in my life have I had a more enjoyable evening than this.'

ELLACOMBE, HENRY NICHOLSON. LUCERNE, GÖSCHENEN, ST. GOTTHARD PASS, AIROLO, PIORA, BELLINZONA, LUGANO, MENDRISIO, MONTE GENEROSO, ARONA, ORTA, DOMODOSSOLA, SIMPLON PASS, BRIG, MARTIGNY, GENEVA

'If any readers of *The Guardian* are in search of a place in Switzerland where they will find quiet and rest in the midst of beautiful scenery and abundance of flowers I would recommend them to go to Piora.'

HALL, NEWMAN. ZERMATT

HARDY, THOMAS. LES VERRIÈRES, NEUCHÂTEL, BERNE, THUN, INTERLAKEN, GRINDELWALD, KLEINE SCHEIDEGG, LAUTERBRUNNEN, INTERLAKEN, THUN, BERNE, LAUSANNE, MARTIGNY, SION, VISP, ZERMATT, VISP, MARTIGNY, GENEVA

The Times's account of the celebration of Queen Victoria's Diamond Jubilee reached Hardy's hands while he was in the Oberland, 'and he took it out and read it in the snowy presence of the maiden-monarch that dominated the whole place'. At Lausanne he wrote his poem of that name on the anniversary of Gibbon's completion of his great work. At Zermatt he wrote his sonnet 'To the Matterhorn', and took part in the search for the body of an Englishman who had been lost.

LARDEN, WALTER. AROLLA, MONT COLLON, MAUVOISIN, GRAND COMBIN, BOURG ST. PIERRE, ORSIÈRES, LA FOULY, COL D'ARGENTIÈRE, CHAMONIX

LE BLOND, MRS. AUBREY. ST. MORITZ, MALOJA PASS, PROMONTOGNO, SOGLIO, SILS, ST. MORITZ

'The hotel keepers of St. Moritz were anxious to have a picture painted by Segantini for the Paris Exhibition of 1900.... They wished him to paint the view from the Schafberg.' Mrs. Le Blond accompanied the deputation to Segantini, who accepted the task and died on the Schafberg in 1899 while engaged in painting his picture.

LOHMÜLLER, WILHELM. MEIRINGEN, GUTTANNEN, GRIMSEL PASS, OBERAARJOCH PASS, GRÜNHORNLÜCKE PASS, BELALP, BRIG

The first ski traverse of the Bernese Oberland.

PADEREWSKY, IGNACY JAN. MORGES

To a friend who stood admiring Mont Blanc from the terrace of his house, 'Paderewsky shook his head. "Yes, that 's fine . . . for Sunday", he agreed. "But come over here", and he led his companion over to the left-hand corner of the terrace. There they looked down on an inlet of the Lake, a quiet arm of still water that resembled a little river in the midst of green pastures, the bluish foothills of the Jura descending to it in gentle slopes. The picture was intimate, harmonious, reminiscent of Poland in its soft and mellow appeal. Paderewsky stood silent contemplating the homelike loveliness of the pastoral scene.'

SMYTH, DAME ETHEL. RIVA, ALAGNA, COL D'OLEN, RIVA, SIGNALKUPPE, ZERMATT

Describing the sanitary arrangements at the Regina Margherita hut, 'what if a gale of one hundred miles an hour is raging? a gale in which not even a guide could stand without holding on to something, and which would blow you like a leaf right across to the Matterhorn? Explaining this, my two guides firmly gripped me and conducted me to the balcony, bidding me hold on to the rail with one hand, to the iron handle on the wall with the other, *and on no account to let go. . . .*'

TWAIN, MARK. LUCERNE, WEGGIS

'Weggis. Villa Bühlegg.
I would as soon spend my life in Weggis as anywhere in the geography.'

WHERRY, GEORGE. AROLLA, SION, SIERRE, VISP, ZERMATT

'The hotel at Arolla was now a hospital; besides the halt and maimed already mentioned, there was a lad in bed rather seriously ill, and others with minor maladies. A damaged doctor, I went my round each morning and evening as if at regular work, for I could not, even if fit to climb, have left my patients for any long expedition.'

WILKINSON, T. E. GENEVA, LAUSANNE, TERRITET, ZURICH, FELDKIRCH

1898

CHRISTEN, RODOLPHE. NOVARA, BELLINZONA, OSOGNA, AIROLO, ST. GOTTHARD PASS, ANDERMATT, ALTDORF, LUCERNE, SUMISWALD, BERNE, NEUCHÂTEL, LA CHAUX DE FONDS, ST. IMIER, SUMISWALD, ST. IMIER, LE LOCLE, MORTEAU

'The woods near the village [Sumiswald] are still, a restfulness full of mystery and peace, those columns high to the sky, with a roof of white snows, bring back to me the forest of colonnades of St. Paul, near Rome which I described to you, and the mysterious darkness of Notre Dame de Paris. But here it is all the work of the Almighty, not a trace of the work of men. The twittering of birds is the music of this temple.'

COBDEN-SANDERSON, THOMAS JAMES. VEVEY, ST. LÉGIER, MARTIGNY, VISP, SAAS FEE, VEVEY, BRIG, BELALP, VEVEY

'. . . Before me is a little plateau of deep green grass, flower-beds and fruit trees, and then, sheer below and far away, the Lake of Geneva, like a lower sky bounded by the aerial hills.'

DURHAM, W. E. MONTREUX, MARTIGNY, SION, BRIG, SIMPLON PASS, DOMODOSSOLA, LUGANO, BELLAGGIO, CHIAVENNA, MALOJA PASS, ST. MORITZ, PONTRESINA, PIZ BERNINA, ALBULA PASS, FILISUR, COIRE

ELIZABETH, EMPRESS OF AUSTRIA. TERRITET, CAUX, GENEVA

The Empress was murdered while waiting at Geneva for the steamer to return to Territet.

ELLACOMBE, HENRY NICHOLSON. ANNECY, CHAMONIX, TÊTE NOIRE PASS, FINHAUT, VERNAYAZ, MARTIGNY, SION, BRIG, SIMPLON PASS, DOMODOSSOLA, ORTA, TOSA FALLS, SAN GIACOMO PASS, AIROLO, PIORA, ST. GOTTHARD PASS, GÖSCHENEN

'FIELD, MICHAEL' (KATHERINE BRADLEY & EDITH COOPER). VISP, ZERMATT

'The day is golden: on top of the Riffel the sun shines through the trees till they are apparitions of light. . . .' Edith's father had left his hotel and never returned, and it was some time before his body was found, as a result of a search which Whymper had been active in initiating.

FOX, JOSEPH H. CHAMONIX, COL DE BALME, MARTIGNY, GRAND ST. BERNARD PASS, AOSTA, PETIT ST. BERNARD PASS, BOURG ST. MAURICE, ALBERTVILLE, MÉGÈVE, CHAMONIX

LARDEN, WALTER. BINN, BERISAL, SIMPLON, BRIG, VISP, ZERMATT, COL D'HÉRENS, AROLLA, PAS DE CHÈVRES, CHANRION, OTEMMA GLACIER, AROLLA

'I have never felt the peace and beauty of Arolla more strongly than I did when I saw it next . . . through the open window there breathed the pure air of the mountain pine-wood; above the sunlit trees the Pigne lifted its summit to the sky. Not a sound but the distant voice of the stream. No hotels, no clatter of mules, no smells of the crowded village. It was perfect.'

PARKER, JOSEPH. GENEVA, CHAMONIX

'Roamed about at pleasure, surveying again and again the wonders by which they were surrounded, and never grew weary of looking from their hotel windows at the monarch of mountains, Mont Blanc, with its silent fields of ice and snow. Dr. Parker spent some time in literary work, while Mrs. Parker walked, sketched and explored: heaven was in their hearts and about them.'

PURTSCHELLER, LUDWIG. CONCORDIA, FIESCHERHORN, GRÜNHORN, GLETSCHERHORN

SENNETT, A. R. LES VERRIÈRES, NEUCHÂTEL, MORAT, AVENCHES, FRIBOURG, BERNE

'What Ruskin said of the scenery on the road to Bern—some thirty years ago—is equally true of it to-day. Its "mountain spirit throwing into it a continual succession of slope and dale", being interpreted into cyclist language, means that it is somewhat hilly, but not tediously so.'

VIRIEUX, EUGÈNE. MORZINE, COL DE GOLÈZE, SAMOËNS, SIXT, SAMOËNS, COL DE GOLÈZE, COL DE COUX, CHAMPÉRY

WHERRY, GEORGE. MARTIGNY, FIONNAY, BEC D'EPICOUN, BIONAZ, MONT FAUDERY, CHANRION, SAAS

WILKINSON, T. E. BASLE, ZURICH, NEUCHÂTEL, GENEVA, LAUSANNE, CLARENS, TERRITET, VEVEY, THUN

YOUNG, GEOFFREY WINTHROP. FINSTERAARHORN, GRINDELWALD, LAUTERBRUNNEN, ROTHTAL, JUNGFRAU, BELALP, WITWE, GRAF, DAME ALYS, GROSS FUSSHORN

'We shared then a passion for poetical quotation; and to our preoccupation before dawn with Shelley's remarks about nature, I can alone attribute the melancholy fact that we found ourselves, with full daylight, ascending the south summit of that treacherous peak the Trugberg, in the cheerful belief that it was our Mecca, the Mönch.'

1899

BUTLER, SAMUEL. BASLE, LUCERNE, FLUELEN, WASSEN

On the steamer to Fluelen, 'Dr. Mandell Creighton (Bishop of London) was on board with his family. The bishop took us away from the others into a corner of the deck and made Butler talk.'

COOLIDGE, W. A. B. BRIENZ, BRIENZERROTHORN, SÖRENBERG, SCHÜPFHEIM, LANGNAU, TRÜBSCHACHEN, NAPF, LUCERNE, WIGGEN, MARBACH, SCHANGNAU, KEMMERIBODEN, SCHANGNAU, GRUNENBERG PASS, HABKERN, INTERLAKEN

DURHAM, W. E. PONTRESINA

ELLACOMBE, HENRY NICHOLSON. GENEVA, VEVEY, MARTIGNY, SION, BRIG, BELALP, BELLINZONA, MESOCCO, SAN BERNARDINO PASS, THUSIS, COIRE, CONSTANCE

'It has not been the less of a success because it has taught me rather sharply that I am too old to take a Swiss trip for walks and climbs. If I am spared to go again, I must go to one place and stay there and admire mountains from a distance without attempting difficult walks. Even if I am limited to that I may well be content and thankful.'

FOX, JOSEPH H. SAAS FEE, ZINAL, COL DE TORRENT, EVOLENA, AROLLA, PAS DE CHÈVRES, COL DU MONT ROUGE, MAUVOISIN, MARTIGNY

'In looking back I am more than ever convinced that for complete rest of mind and change of thought there is nothing to compare with a sojourn in the Alps.'

LARDEN, WALTER. LAUSANNE, LES AVANTS, KANDERSTEG, ANDERMATT, OBERALP PASS, DISENTIS, REICHENAU, THUSIS, ANDEER, AVERS

CRESTA, STALLERBERG PASS, BIVIO, JULIER PASS, SILS-MARIA, FUORCLA FEX-SCERSCEN, FUORCLA SELLA, FUORCLA SURLEJ, MONTE DELLA DISGRAZIA, PONTRESINA

'Of all places that I know, Sils Maria—unless it has changed—is the most perfect spot to make a long stay at, provided that one does not require to be within easy reach of many high climbs. . . . At Arolla and other high places you have (I must admit it) to make an effort if you are to get exercise; you must pound away up hill. But at Sils Maria you can walk, in delightful air, under fir-trees along the margin of the purest of mountain lakes.'

WILDE, OSCAR. GENEVA, GLAND

'. . . Mont Blanc: who at sunset flushes like a rose: with shame perhaps at the prevalence of tourists . . . but I don't like Switzerland: it has produced nothing but theologians and waiters.'

WILKINSON, T. E. BULLE, CHÂTEAU D'OEX, ROSSINIÈRE, LES MOSSES PASS, LE SÉPEY, LES DIABLERETS, AIGLE, TERRITET

YOUNG, GEOFFREY WINTHROP. BELALP, FUSSHORN, LONZAHORN, ZINAL, DENT BLANCHE, EVOLENA, SION, BELALP

'If five men on a long rope really allow themselves to become entangled, the result is insoluble in Euclidean space. The little lamps danced furiously round each other in the darkness, in a mazy fiendish cancan, to the accompaniment of three separate monotones of patois curses.'

1900

BONNEY, THOMAS GEORGE. AROLLA

BUTLER, SAMUEL. RIGI-SCHEIDECK, FLUELEN, WASSEN

A child struggling with the 'Preislied' in the Rigi-Scheidegg hotel was the starting point of Butler's view that 'in conveyancing the ultimately potent thing is not the deed but the invisible intention and desire of the parties to the deed'.

COOLIDGE, W. A. B. LUTHERNBAD

'The pension was really only 2½ francs including as much iron water from the neighbouring spring as one liked, and also *one* glass of wine a day.'

DÉROULÈDE, PAUL. LAUSANNE

DURHAM, W. E. MARTIGNY, SION, AROLLA, MONT COLLON, COL DE SEILON, MAUVOISIN, MARTIGNY, COL DE BALME, CHAMONIX, TÊTE NOIRE PASS, VERNAYAZ

'An old lady at Zermatt once asked why Mr. So-and-so always took two guides: "was he afraid of losing one of them?" '

FOX, JOSEPH H. MARTIGNY, SION, VISP, SAAS FEE, AROLLA

LARDEN, WALTER. MARTIGNY, GRAND ST. BERNARD PASS, AOSTA, GRAN PARADISO, BIONAZ, COL D'OREN, AROLLA, MONT BLANC DE SEILON, MAUVOISIN, MARTIGNY

'I trust that it is not a sign of a misanthropical disposition; but I confess that I like solitary and unconventional approaches to and departures from the mountains. The arrival alone, over some snow-covered Gemmi, allows the peace of the hills to descend upon one as one comes straight from the worries and anxieties of one's work in England; and a solitary departure over some pass permits the memories of the past summer to crystallise undisturbed.'

PICARD, EDMOND. ST. GERVAIS, DOME DU GOUTER, CHAMONIX

'Jamais, même en ballon, je ne fus si haut dans l'atmosphère, ni à ce point pris dans le détachement terrestre et dans la rêverie mystique de l'impalpable qui est en nous.'

RIMSKY KORSAKOW, NIKOLAY ANDREYEVICH. VITZNAU, LAUSANNE, GENEVA, CHAMONIX

'To gaze to our heart's content at Mont Blanc and walk among its foothills. . . .'

YOUNG, GEOFFREY WINTHROP. BELALP, FUSSHORN, HOHSTOCK, SAAS, ALPHUBELJOCH PASS, ZERMATT, FURGGJOCH PASS, BREUIL, COL DU LION, ZERMATT, RANDA, BIESJOCH, COL DE TRACUIT, ZINAL, YOUNG RIDGE, WEISSHORN

'The sunlit snow-spaces and their highland of jutting peaks, widening all ways to the circle of the horizon, looked to the eye the true surface of dignified earth. The remembered network of human activity, crowded and burrowing far down those insignificant creases of shadow, seemed to belong to the less real life of the two. . . .'

1901

BELL, GERTRUDE. GRINDELWALD, SCHRECKHORN, GROSSE SCHEIDEGG, ROSENLAUI, ENGELHÖRNER, INNERTKIRCHEN, GRINDELWALD

BELLOC, HILAIRE. DELLE, PORRENTRUY, STE URSANNE, MOUTIER, WEISSENSTEIN, SOLEURE, BURGDORF, LANGNAU, SCHANGNAU, WANNEN PASS, BRIENZ, GRIMSEL PASS, OBERGESTELEN, ULRICHEN, FURKA PASS, HOSPENTHAL, ST. GOTTHARD PASS, AIROLO, BELLINZONA, LUGANO, COMO

'Here were these magnificent creatures of God, I mean the Alps.'

BONNEY, THOMAS GEORGE. LES ORMONTS, LE SÉPEY, MARTIGNY, VISP, SAAS

BUTLER, SAMUEL. BASLE, LUCERNE, FLUELEN, WASSEN

During this, his last stay in Switzerland, Butler was engaged in 'editing his remains'.

COBDEN-SANDERSON, THOMAS JAMES. BELALP

DURHAM, W. E. AROLLA, DENT BLANCHE, EVOLENA, COL DE TORRENT, COL DE SOREBOIS, ZINAL, ROTHORN, ZERMATT, VISP, SIERRE

'Canon Girdlestone—pioneer of guideless climbing, but now more or less on the retired list—was there; what visitor at Arolla in the old days does not remember his tall spare figure, his breezy bonhomie, and his habit of emptying his afternoon bath out of his bedroom window, to the consternation of tea-drinkers on the gravel below?'

LARDEN, WALTER. VIESCH, BINN, KRIEGALP PASS, DEVERO, SCATTAMINOJO PASS, HAHNENJOCH PASS, TOSA FALLS, HOHSAND PASS, OFENHORN, BINN, VISP, RANDA, WEISSHORN, ZINAL-ROTHORN, ZINAL, EVOLENA, AROLLA, COL DE SEILON, MAUVOISIN, GRAND COMBIN, BOURG ST. PIERRE, ORSIÈRES, COL D'ARGENTIÈRE, CHAMONIX, AIGUILLE VERTE, PETIT DRU, LAUSANNE

'I reached the hotel much frayed and torn; especially there was lacking a most essential part of my knickers. All my luggage had long since (from Arolla) gone to Lausanne; so I was in a fix. I consulted the chambermaid. She had *green* tyrolese cloth only. "Impossible, Monsieur!" I explained. At last light dawned on her, and she cried—. But can I say it? Every one is shocked, and yet everyone laughs over it when they hear it privately. So I will venture. "Ah! je comprends, Monsieur! C'est seulement pour cacher la chemise!" Yes; that was my sole, my modest aim.'

MONKSWELL, MARY, LADY. ROSENLAUI, MEIRINGEN, ISELTWALD

'Miss Gertrude Bell, this truly wonderful woman, arrived from Grindelwald today with her two guides, Ulrich & Heinrich Fuhrer. Although she is to start at 4 a.m. tomorrow to climb in the Engelhörner, she played cricket with us this evening.'

MOSS, GERTRUDE E. MENAGGIO, PORLEZZA, LUGANO, BAVENO, LOCARNO, BELLINZONA, ST. GOTTHARD, LUCERNE, BASLE

'Lucerne was like a furnace. The Schweizerhof packed with people sitting out listening to a deafening band. . . .'

MOULE, HANDLEY CARR GLYN. ST. BEATENBERG

'To the Jungfrau
Oft as the Maiden Mount, sublime in her purity yonder,
Veiled in a glory of snow, musing I mark from below,
Not uprear'd from the valley, methinks was the radiant wonder;
Rather a hill of the sky silently sank from on high.'

WIDMANN, J. V. BERNE, FRAUENFELD, WIL, ALT ST. JOHANN, WILDHAUS, BUCHS, MAIENFELD, LANDQUART, DAVOS, SCALETTA PASS, SCANFS, BEVERS, SAMADEN, PONTRESINA, BERNINA PASS, POSCHIAVO, LE PRESE, TIRANO, COLICO, MENAGGIO, LUGANO, BELLINZONA, AIROLO, ST. GOTTHARD PASS, ANDERMATT, FLUELEN, LUCERNE, BRUNIG PASS, BRIENZ, INTERLAKEN, THUN, BERNE

'How powerfully the rocky mass of the Säntis towers above Alt St. Johann to the north east, its noble mountain-form increasing in impressiveness as one approaches Wildhaus. Can it be that this mountain spoke, as once Sinai to Moses, to the shepherd-boy of Wildhaus [Zwingli] who became the great reformer of Switzerland?'

WILKINSON, T. E. BASLE, ZURICH, DAVOS, BERNE, GENEVA, LAUSANNE, TERRITET

1902

BARKER, SIR HERBERT (*c*). ST. BEATENBERG

BELL, GERTRUDE. ROSENLAUI, WELLHORN, MEIRINGEN, GRIMSEL, FINSTERAARHORN, MEIRINGEN, ROSENLAUI

Gertrude Bell's great climb up the face of the Finsteraarhorn in a blizzard.

COBDEN-SANDERSON, THOMAS JAMES. BELALP

'Dear place amid the mountains, stars and the dawn, the mountain stream, the scents of the woods and of the thyme, the summer's heat, the distant snows, the clouds, the rain and the storm—nature's self, be with me still, when I am far away! Uphold, inspire!'

COOLIDGE, W. A. B. GLARUS, NÄFELS, OBERSEE

The kurhaus at Obersee was a 50 centime pension, this charge including room and bed but no linen or food.

COULTON, G. G. BASLE, OLTEN, BERNE, THUN, FRUTIGEN, ADELBODEN

'Not only the young, but the middle-aged like myself, and even the aged, accepted deliberately the role of Monks of Thelema, "fais ce que voudras".' This attitude on the part of these pioneers of winter sports led to serious trouble, for a fire that they lighted in a chalet on the Bonderspitze resulted in its being burnt down. 'Mr. Lunn, among other benevolent devices for our entertainment, had installed in the great dining-room a gramophone with an enormous and stentorian loud speaker. I will not here specify the exalted and dignified position, at home in England, of the gentleman who one evening crossed the crowded room and stuffed his woollen sweater into the throat of this boisterous foghorn.'

DICKINSON, GOLDSWORTHY LOWES. SCHULS, PIZ PISOC

'Though he deplored the ugliness of Switzerland, its lumpiness, spikiness, and woolliness, and often contrasted it with Italian grace, he could not forget the deep emotions and the radiant health vouchsafed there, nor the visions—oh that they were true!—when precipices and avalanches seemed to promise an ecstasy unattainable on earth.'

FOX, J. H. GRINDELWALD, MONTANA, SAAS FEE

HUGHES, HUGH PRICE. ADELBODEN, GRINDELWALD

'In expeditions his vitality would sometimes be such that elder ladies among his acquaintance who intended to walk a few yards with him and were therefore only thinly shod found themselves going the whole way, because he insisted that they should do so. He quoted, declaimed and cajoled, so that they arrived at their destination without experiencing any exhaustion.'

LARDEN, WALTER. VIESCH, EGGISHORN, BINN, KRIEGALP PASS, DEVERO, SCATTA-MINOJO PASS, TOSA FALLS, OFENHORN, BINN, BRIG, SION, AROLLA, MONT BLANC DE SEILON, COL DE BERTOL, COL D'HÉRENS, ZERMATT, ADLER PASS, EGGINERJOCH PASS, SAAS FEE, ALPHUBELJOCH PASS, ZERMATT, COL DE VALPELLINE, COL DU MONT BRULÉ, AROLLA, PAS DE CHÈVRES, COL DE SEILON, CHANRION, COL D'OTEMMA, AROLLA, SION, BRIG, OBERGESTELEN, GRIMSEL PASS, MEIRINGEN, FRUTT, ENGSTLENALP, TITLIS, NESSENTAL, THIERBERGLIMMI PASS, GÖSCHENEN, WASSEN, MEIEN, VORALPTAL, ERSTFELDERTAL, MEIEN, WASSENHORNJOCH PASS, TITLISJOCH PASS, ENGSTLENALP, INTERLAKEN, KANDERSTEG, BLÜMLISALPHORN, BALMHORN, BINN, RITTER PASS, VALTENDRA PASS, DEVERO, TOSA FALLS, HOHSANDHORN, BINN, SAFLISCH PASS, BERISAL, BRIG, MARTIGNY, CHAMÉPRY

'To the primitive little inn at Frutt, which is situated at a height of 6,160 feet above the sea in a treeless region rich in flowers. This seemed to be still a refuge for the Swiss, still uninvaded by the swarms of foreigners who take possession of their land in summer. All was simple, but all was good.'

LUNN, ARNOLD. ADELBODEN, ELSIGHORN, LAVEIGRAT, SCHWANDFEHLSPITZE

'That first season, Canon Savage, Percival Farrar, and a few others whose names I have forgotten, were almost the only visitors who ever attempted even the smallest tours on ski. . . . I came back from the Elsighorn, where I had scarcely skied for five minutes, drunk with the beauty of my first view from a winter summit.'

MONKSWELL, MARY, LADY. ROSENLAUI, ISELTWALD

'We had the great interest of seeing Gertrude Bell again. . . She certainly looks as if for once in her life she has had about enough.'

MUSSOLINI, BENITO. MILAN, CHIASSO, BELLINZONA, ST. GOTTHARD PASS, LUCERNE, YVERDON, ORBE, CHAVORNAY, LAUSANNE, OUCHY, MONTREUX, VEVEY, LAUSANNE

Orbe: 'I made one hundred and twenty one trips with a hand-barrow full of stones up to the second floor of a building in process of construction.'

'From ten until eleven, I stay in the public lavatory of Ouchy, from eleven to twelve, under an old barge.' Shortly after this, the socialist agitator was arrested in Lausanne for vagrancy.

RIVETT-CARNAC, J. H. CHÂTEAU D'OEX, ROUGEMONT

'The amusements are numerous and varied,—skating, lugeing, or "toboganning", and, what is now putting all other sports in the background, sheing or skeing, which is pronounced by those who are adept at both to be superior even to skating.'

SCHUSTER, CLAUD. MALOJA, PASSO LURANI, CIMA DI CASTELLO, MASINO, MONTE DELLA DISGRAZIA, CIMA DI ROSSO, FORNO, MALOJA

'There are moods in which one can only be satisfied with the gorgeous ostentation of the Gorner or the Mer de Glace, and the majesty of mountain form disclosed from topmost pinnacle to valley floor. In other manifestations of the mountain spirit you need a sense of separation from the murmur of the valley, and you may well be satisfied with the Forno.'

WIDMANN, J. V. BERNE, THUN, SPIEZ, FRUTIGEN, ADELBODEN, HAHNENMOOS PASS, LENK, ZWEISIMMEN, GSTAAD, LAUENEN, KRINNEN PASS, GSTEIG, COL DE PILLON, LES DIABLERETS, AIGLE, VEVEY, BERNE

At the inn at Gsteig a fat young Englishman suddenly pushed over the table a tract 'of female authorship, enjoining constant focusing of thoughts on Christ'. Later in the day, on the Col de Pillon, Widmann met the Englishman, who had covered himself with ink from his leaking fountain-pen. 'Have you any paper?' he asked. Widmann promptly felt in his pocket, pulled out a piece and offered it to him. 'No, no never!' gasped the Englishman. Widmann had unintentionally handed him his tract.

WILKINSON, T. E. LAUSANNE, TERRITET, VEVEY, CHÂTEAU D'OEX, GENEVA

'Drove to Château d'Oex, where I consecrated the new English Church.'

YOUNG, GEOFFREY WINTHROP. BELALP, ZENBACHHORN, GROSS NESTHORN

1903

COBDEN-SANDERSON, THOMAS JAMES. BELALP, RIEDER-FURKA

'I will reveal to you the purpose of my holidays—of my life of freedom upon the Alps. It is not to enjoy the air, to make pleasant excursions, to talk about the beauty of the weather, to admire the wonder of the view. I do all these things, but they are by the way, they are but a disguise in which I hide the higher purpose—which is to put my spirit into communion with that spirit of the larger aspects of the world, the sun's dawn and set, the night's silence and the day's, the persistent mountains' summits, unchanged amid our changes from year to year. . . .'

DURHAM, W. E. ZERMATT, ADLER PASS, SAAS FEE, WEISSMIES, FLETSCHHORN

'We came upon a party, consisting of two Frenchmen and two guides, who were almost hopelessly bogged. The heads only of the Frenchmen protruded from the snow, looking for all the world like two sad and despairing Alpine sphinxes.'

ELLACOMBE, HENRY NICHOLSON. BRIG, SIMPLON, ALGABY, ZWISCHBERGEN, MUSCERA PASS, PRESTINO, DOMODOSSOLA

'Such was our walk over the Muscera pass, and the reader may well ask what there was in it to distinguish it from other Swiss walks. There is this. In all my walks in search of flowers I have never and nowhere seen such a wealth of flowers as I saw there.'

FOX, J. H. GRINDELWALD, ROSENLAUI, KANDERSTEG

HAMILTON, CLAYTON. LOCARNO, BELLINZONA, ST. GOTTHARD PASS, AMSTEG, FLUELEN, LUCERNE, INTERLAKEN, LAUTERBRUNNEN, MÜRREN, LAUSANNE, VISP, ZERMATT

HOLMES, CHARLES JAMES. MEIRINGEN

'Coming to Meiringen I was thrilled to recognize there the scene of the drawing by J. R. Cozens, "A Valley with winding streams".'

LARDEN, WALTER. WASSEN, MEIEN, GÖSCHENERALP, UNTER-GLETSCHJOCH PASS, TIEFENBACH, WINTERLÜCKE PASS, GÖSCHENERALP, WASSEN, WASSENHORNJOCH PASS, ENGSTLENALP, ISENTHAL, URIROT-STOCK, ENGELBERG, WENDENJOCH PASS, WASSENHORNJOCH PASS, MEIEN, SUSTEN PASS, STEIN, WICHELPLANKSTOCK, WASSEN, OLIVONE, GARZURA PASS, PIZ SCHARBODEN, ZERVREILA, RHEINWALDHORN, FANELLA PASS, KIRCHALPLÜCKE PASS, SPLÜGEN, PIZ TAMBO, THUSIS, DAVOS

'. . . Though now middle-aged, I ventured to begin ski-ing. . . . Ski-ing at Davos I found myself among a new race of people. To them a mountain was a "thing to come down"; to me it still remained a "thing to go up". . . . Certainly it is a wonderful sport and the pleasures that it can give are perhaps, at the time, keener than any experienced in ordinary mountaineering. But I do not think that it can to at all the same degree fill the life, influence character, or cement friendships.'

MUSSOLINI, BENITO. LAUSANNE, NYON, BERNE, THUN, BERNE, LUCERNE, ST. GOTTHARD PASS, AIROLO, CHIASSO, CLARO, CRESCIANO, CASTIONE, BELLINZONA, LAUSANNE, FRIBOURG

For his part in fomenting the carpenters' strike at Berne, Mussolini was arrested and expelled from Switzerland in a vegetable truck; but he soon returned.

RAWNSLEY, CANON H. D. BERNE, THUN, ST. BEATENBERG, SPIEZ, KANDERSTEG, INTERLAKEN, LAUTERBRUNNEN, MÜRREN, MEIRINGEN, BRUNIG PASS, SARNEN, ALPNACH, VITZNAU, RIGI, BÜRGENSTOCK, ENGELBERG, LUCERNE

'The cuckoo calls, the woodpecker laughs, the red-start flickers, and the hostess of the Amisbühl is filling her garden-plot with heartsease full in flower; here is spring with summer full before us, and there is winter everlastingly. This is, I think, part of the reason that gives Amisbühl in May its magic.'

WILKINSON, T. E. BASLE, LAUSANNE, TERRITET, MARTIGNY, SION, SIERRE, BRIG, GLETSCH, FURKA PASS, ANDERMATT, GÖSCHENEN, FLUELEN, BRUNNEN, ZURICH

'. . . To Sierre, where I dedicated a very beautiful little chapel in the hotel grounds. Everything—marble, oak-work, stained glass by Clayton and Bell—good.'

1904

BELL, GERTRUDE. ZERMATT, BREUIL, MATTERHORN, ZERMATT

'Yes, as you say, why do people climb? I often wonder if one gets most pleasure out of the Alps this way. Some year I shall try the other and come and wander over grass passes and down exquisite Italian valleys and see how I like it.'

COBDEN-SANDERSON, THOMAS JAMES. PONTRESINA, ST. MORITZ

'I should like to found a league of silence—a society, the members of which should everyone be the sole and whole society, and whose rules should be, in the mountains, to say and reply to nothing—save cries of help in extremity. The silent obeisance of the head should be permitted, silent, solemn, dignified, on the mountain side or roads, but in all hotels or hostelries the silence of the visitors in one another's presence should be absolute.'

DURHAM, W. E. AOSTA, GRAND ST. BERNARD PASS, MARTIGNY, SION, EVOLENA, AROLLA, PAS DE CHÈVRES, MONT BLANC DE SEILLON, AROLLA, GRAND CORNIER, ZINAL, SIERRE

'. . . Arrived at Arolla in time for the morning service in the newly erected little English church. . . .'

FOX, J. H. MONTE GENEROSO, GRINDELWALD

LARDEN, WALTER. BINN, SION, AROLLA, COL DU MONT BRULÉ, COL DE VALPELLINE, ZERMATT, ADLER PASS, SAAS, ZWISCHBERGEN PASS, SIMPLON, MONTE LEONE

'On the way down, near Gondo, we saw wires overhead by which faggots of wood were shot down to the valley below. . . . Sparks are, I believe, often given out owing to the great friction; and it would be quite possible for a traveller who found himself after dark on the path of that lonely valley which we had just descended, to hear a hissing, ringing sound and see dimly a fiery dragon swooping down upon him.'

LENIN, VLADIMIR ILYICH. GENEVA, BERNE, MEIRINGEN

'It would be splendid if you could be clever enough to come over here for a week—not on business but simply for a rest and to meet me somewhere in the Alps.'

MUSSOLINI, BENITO. GENEVA, ZURICH, LAUSANNE, GENEVA, BELLINZONA, LAUSANNE, USTER, COIRE, ST. MARGRETEN

At Geneva, Mussolini was arrested for the third time in Switzerland, on this occasion for carrying a falsified passport.

WIDMANN, J. V. BERNE, ZURICH, COIRE, THUSIS, SAMADEN, ST. MORITZ, SILVAPLANA, MALOJA PASS, SOGLIO, CHIAVENNA, SPLÜGEN PASS, THUSIS

Referring to Nietzsche: 'Who knows but that his bitterest and most anti-human expression, that of the "Many too many", may not have been provoked by the sight of the tourists who in swarms overrun the Engadine every summer?'

YOUNG, GEOFFREY WINTHROP. EGGISHORN, STRAHLGRAT, KLEIN WANNEHORN, OBERGESTELEN, GRIMSEL PASS, ESCHERHORN, THIEREGGHORN

1905

BARKER, SIR HERBERT (*c*). VILLARS

'As we descended the slippery snow-covered foot-path, the almost vanished sun cast a blaze of fire-red luminance across the peaks of the *Dent du Midi*, touching them to incredible glory. My wife stood still for a moment and was mute. It was wonderful, almost awe-inspiring in its beauty. It has remained and will remain an ineffaceable memory.'

BOVIER, LÉON. DELLE, PORRENTRUY, COURRENDLIN, MOUTIER, BIENNE, NEUCHÂTEL, LES HAUTS GENEVEYS, TÊTE DE RANG, LA CHAUX DE

FONDS, MAISON-MONSIEUR, LES BRENETS, LA CHAUX DE FONDS, CHAMBRELIEN, CREUX DU VAN, NOIRAIGUE, NEUCHÂTEL, ESTAVAYER, FRIBOURG, BERNE, SOLEURE, WEISSENSTEIN, BALSTHAL, AARAU, LAURENZENBAD, ZURICH, SCHAFFHAUSEN, BASLE

COBDEN-SANDERSON, THOMAS JAMES. RIEDER-FURKA

'Amusement should *never*, even on a holiday, be made one's main occupation; it should be always subordinate to some great work always going on, and everywhere.'

COOLIDGE, W. A. B. ZUG, AEGERI, SCHWYZ, IBERGEREGG, EINSIEDELN, ETZEL, PFÄFFIKON, RAPPERSWIL, UZNACH, RICKEN PASS, WATTWIL, UNTERWASSER, NESSLAU, HEMBERG, URNÄSCH, APPENZELL, GAIS, ALTSTÄTTEN, ST. GALL, TROGEN, HEIDEN, RORSCHACH, CONSTANCE, STEIN, FRAUENFELD, WINTERTHUR, ZURICH, ALBIS, ZUG

DURHAM, W. E. BASLE, BERNE, INTERLAKEN, GRINDELWALD, WETTERHORN, EIGER, SCHRECKHORN, KLEINE SCHEIDEGG, JUNGFRAU, GRÜNHORNLÜCKE PASS, FINSTERAARHORN, STRAHLEGG PASS, GRINDELWALD, LAUTERBRUNNEN, BREITHORN, TSCHINGELHORN, PETERSGRAT, RIED, BIETSCHHORN, RARON, BRIG, BELALP, ALETSCHHORN, BRIG

'The surgeon from the Simplon tunnel works was summoned to Belalp, and stitched up my leg. . . .'

KUGY, JULIUS. COURMAYEUR, MACUGNAGA, NEW WEISSTOR PASS, ZERMATT, STRAHLHORN, RIMPFISCHHORN, ROTHORN, ZINAL

LAMPRELL, ERNEST E. BASLE, BERNE, THUN, KANDERSTEG, TSCHINGEL PASS, TSCHINGELHORN, PETERSGRAT, RIED, LÖTSCHENLÜCKE PASS, GRÜNHORNLÜCKE PASS, OBERAARJOCH PASS, GRIMSEL PASS, FURKA PASS, ANDERMATT, GÖSCHENEN, AMSTEG, BRISTEN, FLUELEN, LUCERNE, BASLE

A fortnight in Switzerland for five guineas.	£	*s.*	*d.*
Excursion ticket, Dover to Berne, Lucerne, or Zurich	2	2	10
Rail and boat in Switzerland		5	0
London to Dover return monthly ticket		10	0
Pension for 12 days	2	2	0
Expenses en route		5	2
	5	5	0

LARDEN, WALTER. AROLLA, COL D'HÉRENS, ZERMATT, RANDA, FESTIJOCH, DOM, DENT BLANCHE

ST. JOHN, SIR FREDERICK. BERNE, THUN, INTERLAKEN, KLEINE SCHEIDEGG

The British Minister to Switzerland was called upon to speak at the opening of the Jungfrau Railway. The beauties of the scene were hidden by pouring rain, and, more than dubious of the financial future of the undertaking, he likened the promoter of the railway to a young man wooing a beautiful damsel modestly hiding her charms behind a veil of tears. But what he really felt was 'I sincerely hope that this insensate scheme has since been abandoned, and that the process of vulgarising the "playground of Europe" has been arrested'.

YOUNG, GEOFFREY WINTHROP. CHAMONIX, AIGUILLE DE CHARMOZ, AIGUILLE DU GRÉPON, ZERMATT, WEISSHORN NORTH-EAST FACE, MATTERHORN FURGGEN RIDGE TO NORTH-EAST SHOULDER

'The Swiss valleys, like the Swiss people, are only discoverable in other than the summer months of tourist traffic. The Zermatt valley, as we may see it in August, has little charm of its own. I was puzzled, when at last I ventured to visit this innermost sanctuary sacred to the memory of the first mountaineering prophets, to account for their enthusiastic love of its dusty gorges, warm-smelly paths and sparse exhausted colours. Until, one winter, I rediscovered it.'

1906

AMERY, L. S. SION, AROLLA, AIGUILLES ROUGES, MONT BLANC DE SEILON, AROLLA, WANDFLUH, ZERMATT, ROTHORN, ZINAL, SIERRE

'The joys of such a climb [Aiguilles Rouges] are no more to be described in detail than the joys of a dance.'

DURHAM, W. E. SIERRE, VISSOYE, ZINAL, GRAND CORNIER, LO BESSO, COL DE TRACUIT, GRUBEN, COL DE FORCLETTA, ZINAL, ROTHORN, ZERMATT

'A party of Polytechnic tourists—young men from London—arrived in charge of a decrepit-looking guide, to spend the night at the hut. We were disposed to resent their intrusion, but soon felt ashamed of such feelings. They were courtesy itself and their delight in their superb surroundings was quite delightful to see. After dinner they sat outside on the rocks, and sang part-songs divinely. We retired early, and as I opened the window of the upstairs apartment, I heard one of them say, "Those gentlemen are starting very early; we must go up to bed now or else we shall disturb them".'

FOX, J. H. BALLAIGUES, CHAMONIX

HOLMES, D. T. GENEVA, LAUSANNE, VERNAYAZ, SALVAN, FINHAUT

'The dogma of the Total Depravity of man, on which Calvin laid such stress, cannot stand uncontradicted in view of the fact that a beautiful landscape has power to *evoke*, spontaneously, such noble thoughts and such hallowed aspirations. The Divinity which is *in* man is stirred to life when confronted by the divinity in nature. Hence, I say, that the best refutation of Calvin's doctrine is a ramble among the Alps or a boating excursion on the lake.'

KUGY, JULIUS. COURMAYEUR, COL DU GÉANT, AIGUILLE DU PLAN, MACUGNAGA, NORDEND, ZERMATT

LARDEN, WALTER. VIESCH, BINN, KRIEGALP PASS, DEVERO, SCATTAMINOJO PASS, HAHNENJOCH PASS, TOSA FALLS, HOHSANDHORN, BINN, VIESCH, EGGISHORN, MÖNCHJOCH PASS, EISMEER, KLEINE SCHEIDEGG, GRINDELWALD, WETTERHORN, SCHRECKHORN, FINSTERAARJOCH PASS, AGASSIZJOCH PASS, FINSTERAARHORN, GRÜNHORNLÜCKE PASS, LÖTSCHENLÜCKE PASS, RIED, BIETSCHHORN, RARON, VISP, ZERMATT, MATTERHORN, FURGGJOCH PASS, ZERMATT, LYSKAMM, OBERGABELHORN

'The Eiger glacier station soon came under our notice, and made us feel that the whole thing was a desecration. . . . Not only mountaineers, but all travellers of just taste, must surely feel that this railway is a desecration of nature; something like a merry-go-round in Westminster Abbey.'

RAVEL, MAURICE. GENEVA, HERMANCE

'Me voici donc, installé en Suisse mon vieux, et je ne regrette plus tant la mer. . . . J'attends un piano pour me remettre à la Cloche momentanément interrompue.'

WIDMANN, J. V. BERNE, THUSIS, ANDEER, SPLÜGEN

Before the monument to Thomas Allot Osborn, who died at Splügen in 1835 and was buried there, Widmann wrote a very touching soliloquy.

YOUNG, GEOFFREY WINTHROP. CHAMONIX, AIGUILLE DE CHARMOZ, AIGUILLE DU GRÉPON, AIGUILLE DE BLAITIÈRE, ZERMATT, TAESCHHORN SOUTH FACE, BREITHORN, WEISSHORN SOUTH FACE, DOM SOUTH FACE

'. . . Brought me across the path of that comet of the Alps, V. J. E. Ryan, and Josef and Franz Lochmatter. Into their tail—if they had one—little Josef Knubel and I were willingly swept, in somewhat irregular conjunction.'

1907

DURHAM, W. E. MARTIGNY, FIONNAY, MAUVOISIN, COMBIN DE CORBASSIÈRE, COL DES MAISONS BLANCHES, BOURG ST. PIERRE, MARTIGNY, SALVAN, DENT DU MIDI, CHAMONIX, AIGUILLE VERTE, AIGUILLE DE CHARMOZ, COL DU GÉANT, COURMAYEUR, COL DE LA TOUR RONDE, CHAMONIX

'As the light behind softens, and the rosy glow fades from the western sky, some wizard hand plays magic with the mountain [Dent du Midi]. It grows in height; its rocky horns become giant castles and cathedrals, set on high on some ethereal hill; blue mists float before them, changing into soft and pearly greys: all grows more indistinct, more fairy-like, till the vision fades in the darkness of the gathering night.'

ELLACOMBE, HENRY NICHOLSON. BASLE, LUCERNE, LUGANO, BELLINZONA, BIASCA, FAIDO, GÖSCHENEN

FOX, J. H. BALLAIGUES, MONTREUX, SAANEN, ZWEISIMMEN, INTERLAKEN, GRINDELWALD, ADELBODEN

LARDEN, WALTER. BINN, MARTIGNY, ORSIÈRES, VAL FERRET, COL D'ARGENTIÈRE, TOUR NOIRE, COL DES PLANARDS, BOURG ST. PIERRE, COL DE VALSOREY, OLLOMONT, COL DE MENEUVE, GRAND ST. BERNARD PASS, COL DE FENÊTRE, VAL FERRET, ORSIÈRES, CHAMPEX, AIGUILLE DU TOUR, GRANDE FOURCHE, CHAMPEX, PRAZ DE FORT, PETIT DARREI, PORTALET, CHAMPEX, BOURG ST. PIERRE, CHAMPEX, AIGUILLES DORÉES, COL D'ARPETTE, TRIENT, FINHAUT, CHAMPÉRY, MARTIGNY, SION, LEUK, GEMMI PASS, ROTHE KUMME, ADELBODEN, KANDERSTEG

MONKSWELL, MARY, LADY. MÜRREN, INTERLAKEN, ZWEISIMMEN, ROUGEMONT

A visit to Colonel Rivett-Carnac at Rougemont.

RECKITT, MAURICE B. GRINDELWALD

'A retired military man staying at Grindelwald induced me to share with him the expense of a guide up the Little Scheidegg. . . . and though there is nothing in the least difficult about either the climb or the run for competent skiers, I at any rate was very far from being such. . . . The military veteran was a good deal more tough, so it was arranged, quite reasonably, that he and the guide should leave me at the deserted little station of Alpiglen, under the rocks of the Eiger, and pick me up on the way down. . . . Hours passed in this solitude, but they did not reappear. . . . It then transpired that, with almost incredible irresponsibility, my companions, not finding my halting place to be on their direct route, had made no attempt to pick me up. They got into some trouble with the authorities of the Ski Club.'

THOMPSON, SILVANUS P. BRIENZ, AXALP

YOUNG, GEOFFREY WINTHROP. CHAMONIX, AIGUILLE DU PLAN, DENT DU REQUIN, L'ÉVÊQUE, AIGUILLE DU MIDI, ZERMATT, RIMPFISCHHORN, ROTHORN

1908

BENNETT, ARNOLD. VEVEY, GLION

'December 14. . . . Really the scene is enchantingly beautiful. We see Vevey as though from a balloon. At night its lights are fairy-like—I wish there was another word. Can't find one instantly.' During his stay he wrote *The Card*.

DESART, EARL OF (*c*). ST. MORITZ

'It's too rich and too black and too white, like living in a wedding cake. I should soon want some nice cheap plebeian mud.'

'Like living in a wedding cake'

(Amstutz) LORD DESART, 1908; St. Moritz

'In winter the Engadine hills grow into mighty mountains'

(*Swiss Federal Railways*)

CLAUD SCHUSTER, 1928; Maloja

HULL, EDWARD. GENEVA, CHAMONIX

The distinguished geologist wrote 'what was my amazement on seeing the renowned sea of ice under its present aspect as compared with its aspect when seen by me half a century previously! I could scarcely believe it to be the same glacier, so greatly had its mass shrunken.'

LUNN, ARNOLD. GRAND ST. BERNARD, MARTIGNY, SIERRE, MONTANA, WILDSTRUBEL, RAWYL PASS, LENK, TRÜTTLISBERG PASS, LAUENEN, KRINNEN PASS, GSTEIG, COL DE PILLON, LES DIABLERETS, COL DE LA CROIX, VILLARS

'Solitary climbing admits of no rational defence, nor need we seek to justify by reason the mystical value of moments which are the unique reward of the solitary climber, moments when the mountains throw off their reserve, and admit you to a communion denied to those who approach them fortified by the company of their kind. That brief half-hour on the Wildstrubel would have left a less enduring impression on my memory had I not been alone.' Lunn's companion on this pioneer ski-tour, Mr. Wybergh, had only been on ski three times, and stayed at the hut while Lunn ascended the Wildstrubel.

SALISBURY, F. S. BEX, GRYON, CHAMOSSAIRE, ANZEINDAZ, PONT DE NANT

'You must come here in the morning first and then again in the late evening when the stars are beginning to twinkle above the mountain tops, and the lamps of St. Maurice, Ollon, Aigle, and half a dozen other villages and hamlets answer them with sharp small points of light from the blackness of the gulf below. Then you realize, even more than in the daytime, the mighty presence of the mountains as they lift their shadowy peaks into the eternal silence.'

THOMPSON, SILVANUS P. BRIENZ, AXALP, MEIRINGEN, STEIN

1909

COBDEN-SANDERSON, THOMAS JAMES. RIEDER-FURKA

'. . . It is necessary that I should once more, in prelude, climb the heights, be alone, touch the primaeval in the world, Nature's simplest things. Before in the valley beauty was born, on the heights the sun touched the snow. I go to the heights.'

DURHAM, W. E. MARTIGNY, FIONNAY, MAUVOISIN, MONT PLEUREUR, AROLLA, COL DE CHERMONTANE, MAUVOISIN, COL DE PANOSSIÈRE, BOURG ST. PIERRE, CHANRION, COL DU MONT ROUGE, COL DE SEILON, AROLLA, COL D'HÉRENS, ZERMATT, OBERGABELHORN, TIEFENMATTENJOCH PASS, DENT D'HÉRENS, COL DE VALPELLINE, ZERMATT, ADLER PASS, STRAHLHORN, SAAS FEE, NADELHORN, SÜDLENZSPITZE, RANDA

LEFROY, WILLIAM. ZERMATT

Holy Trinity Riffel Alp. 1 Aug.
'My church was not as crowded as usual. The English are not here yet, but I preached my very heart out on "God is love". The attention was impressive and straining, and when the effort was over I was done.'
Eleven days later, the Dean of Norwich died at Riffel Alp.

LUNN, ARNOLD. ST. BEATENBERG, INTERLAKEN, KANDERSTEG, TSCHINGEL PASS, PETERSGRAT, KIPPEL, LÖTSCHENLÜCKE PASS, GRÜNHORNLÜCKE PASS, FINSTERAARHORN, OBERAARJOCH PASS, GRIMSEL PASS, MEIRINGEN, INTERLAKEN, ST. BEATENBERG—RIED, GAMPEL, MARTIGNY, CHAMPEX, BOURG ST. PIERRE, COL DE MEITEN, GRAND ST. BERNARD

'Since that January evening many years ago, I have explored every recess of that great region which I first saw from the Lötschenlücke, and when I revisit the pass the view is enriched by many memories. But it is not all gain. I see details which escaped me on my first visit, but perhaps I see too much. To climb is to exchange the rapture of first love and the adoration of the unknown for the companionable friendship founded on knowledge and understanding. Like Moses, the mountaineer can see the promised land but can never set foot in it, for the mountain that he climbs is not the mountain which he worships from afar. I shall never again see the uncharted unexplored snow-ways which I saw for the first and the last time from the enchanted window of the Lötschenlücke.'

MONRO, HAROLD (*c*). ST. CERGUE, NYON, GENEVA, LAUSANNE, VERNAYAZ, MARTIGNY, SION, BRIG, SIMPLON PASS, DOMODOSSOLA

'This fifth and last day in the Rhone Valley has in one way been most lovely of all, for the whole of it has been sacred to a certain mountain above Brigue at the valley's end. It is one of the peaks of Monte Leone: I do not wish to know the particular name. 'Tis as pure white as Mont Blanc, and far more gracious. In form it is like a strong god with arms outspread in benediction and it is altogether restful, in contrast to the peaks and galleries of the Bernese Alps. It has called and called to me: and I am coming.'

ROGET, F. F. ST. BEATENBERG, INTERLAKEN, KANDERSTEG, TSCHINGEL PASS, PETERSGRAT, KIPPEL, LÖTSCHENLÜCKE PASS, GRÜNHORNLÜCKE PASS, FINSTERAARHORN, OBERAARJOCH PASS, GRIMSEL PASS, MEIRINGEN, INTERLAKEN, ST. BEATENBERG

'This expedition, the first of its length at such altitudes at that time of year (January), was an Anglo-Swiss piece of work. It was performed in company with Arnold Lunn.'

YOUNG, GEOFFREY WINTHROP. BELALP, UNTERBACHHORN, GROSS NESTHORN SOUTH-EAST RIDGE, FINSTERAARHORN, JUNGFRAU,

CHAMONIX, AIGUILLE VERTE, AIGUILLE DU CHARDONNET, AIGUILLE DU GRÉPON, ZERMATT, WEISSHORN

'It was Giraldus Cambrensis who first remarked—"It is wonderful that when, after diligent search, all the stones have been removed from the mountains, and no more can be found, a few days after they reappear in greater quantities to those who seek them". Giraldus's experience of this discomfort will be confirmed by anyone who has slept out on a mountain side.'

1910

BENNETT, ARNOLD. LAUSANNE

'One of the most marvellous sunsets I ever saw tonight. The peaks of the Dent du Midi sticking alone out of cloud high up in the sky, like rosy teeth.' During his stay he wrote part of *Clayhanger*.

DURHAM, W. E. BASLE, ZURICH, COIRE, THUSIS, ANDEER, AVERS CRESTA, STALLERBERG PASS, BIVIO, JULIER PASS, SILVAPLANA, SILS-MARIA, FORNO, CASNILE PASS, VICOSOPRANO, MALOJA PASS, SILS, PONTRESINA, PIZ ROSEG, PIZ PALÜ, PIZ BERNINA, ST. MORITZ, SILS, PASSO TREMOGGIA, CHIESA, MONTE DELLA DISGRAZIA, LUGANO, BELLINZONA, GÖSCHENEN, ANDERMATT, HOSPENTHAL, FURKA PASS, GALENSTOCK, GRIMSEL PASS, MEIRINGEN, ROSENLAUI, DOSSENHORN, GROSSE SCHEIDEGG, GRINDELWALD, INTERLAKEN, MEIRINGEN, BRUNIG PASS, LUCERNE

LODGE, ELEANOR C. (*c*). LUCERNE, RIGI, BRUNIG PASS, MEIRINGEN, GRINDELWALD, LAUTERBRUNNEN, WENGEN, MEIRINGEN, GRIMSEL PASS, OBERGESTELEN, VISP, ZERMATT, VISP, BRIG, BELALP, LEUK, GEMMI PASS, KANDERSTEG, MONTREUX, OUCHY

'It was very hot, but despite that on the way down [the Rigi] Oliver took to his heels and began to run. I ran panting behind him thinking we must be late for the boat or that something odd had happened, but I could not catch him up to ask and we still ran on. All the people we passed stopped to stare, but still we ran faster and faster till we reached the bottom of the mountain. "What is it?" I panted. "Oh nothing. I just wanted to run", said Oliver.' But judging from Sir Oliver Lodge's version of this tour, his action was probably a protest at the prohibition of the use of railways which his sister imposed, and which he only survived by means of much 'surreptitious beer'.

POWYS, LLEWELYN. DAVOS

'. . . The great granite rocks that stand by the white splashing ice-cold stream as it dances down the Illyrian glen on its way to the Rhine. . . .'

ROGET, F. F. LES DIABLERETS, COL DE PILLON, GSTEIG, DIABLERETS, SANETSCH PASS, WILDHORN, RAWYL PASS, WILDSTRUBEL, LAMMERNJOCH PASS, GEMMI PASS, KANDERSTEG

STRAVINSKY, IVAN FEODOROWITCH. LAUSANNE, CLARENS

In the attic of his pension at Lausanne, Stravinsky began composing *Petrouschka* which he originally intended to be a concert piece. Diaghilew called on him and asked that it be made into a ballet.

THOMPSON, SILVANUS P. SAAS FEE, MONTE MORO PASS, MACUGNAGA

WICKHAM, EDWARD CHARLES. VEVEY, MARTIGNY, SION, VISP, ZERMATT, VISP, SIERRE

The Dean of Lincoln died at Sierre where he lies buried.

YOUNG, GEOFFREY WINTHROP. ZERMATT, DENT D'HÉRENS, TRIFTTHORN, ROTHORN, GABELJOCH

'It is said that few of us can dream colours; and perhaps that is why so many of us find the colourless chiaroscuro of high Alps the most suitable material for our mature day-dreaming. But all the more violently does our masterless collecting-agency of memory pounce upon and cling to the unexpected notes of colour or lighting which Nature may arbitrarily discover to us among our hills.'

1911

BONNEY, THOMAS GEORGE. BASLE, LUCERNE, FLUELEN, AIROLO, GRINDELWALD

COBDEN-SANDERSON, THOMAS JAMES. BRIG, RIEDERFURKA, BELALP, BRIG, LAUSANNE

'I live in these mountains with the sun and moon and stars and day and light, becoming ever more and more one with them, for ever more and more they fill my mind, and are myself.'

DURHAM, W. E. AOSTA, GRAND ST. BERNARD PASS, BOURG ST. PIERRE, GRAND COMBIN, FIONNAY, RUINETTE, MONT BLANC DE SEILON, PAS DE CHÈVRES, AROLLA, COL DE BERTOL, COL D'HÉRENS, ZERMATT, POLLUX, CASTOR, LYSKAMM, MATTERHORN, ALPHUBEL, SAAS FÉE

'. . . Slept at the Täschalp, where we met Mr. A. E. W. Mason and the Lochmatters. Mr. Mason had just arrived from England, and told me, on the authority of Mr. Lloyd George, how near we were at the moment to war with Germany.'

GRANDE, CONSTANCE. GRINDELWALD, SCHRECKHORN, KANDERSTEG

'What is the call of the Alps? It is the old question, never yet answered—in what does the fascination of climbing consist? Far from everyone is capable of feeling that fascination; and those who do feel it find a rare difficulty in expressing it in words. And the more keenly they feel it, the more does their difficulty increase. One writer alone seems to have been able to put into words the feeling of high solitary peaks—of the wilderness of mountains wherein there is no man—the nameless writer of the last chapters of the Book of Job.'

LAMBERT, LÉON. CHANRION, RUINETTE

'Quand plus tard sonnera pour moi l'heure des lointains souvenirs, quand touché par l'age je m'assiérai au foyer des choses les plus aimées pour en tisonner la cendre, lorsque lentement le cœur s'en ira gonflé toujours du regret des Monts, je prévois que c'est vers vous, ô cimes, qui vous élevez superbes et ardentes dans le ciel cérulé et infini, vers vous, plaines de neige éternelles, où chaque année pendant dix longs mois nul humain ne foule vos blancheurs, et où règne seul avec le vent qui beugle, l'angoissante solitude de la mort, le silence apeurant des antiques cités désertes, que se reporteront le plus complaisamment nos regards attendris.'

LENIN, VLADIMIR ILYICH. ZURICH, LUCERNE, PILATUS, GENEVA

To his mother Lenin wrote: 'I climbed Pilatus yesterday (2,122 metres). So far the weather is wonderful and I am having wonderful walks. . . .'

LUNN, ARNOLD. DENT BLANCHE, BOURG ST. PIERRE, GRAND COMBIN, LOURTIER

'The moment of arrival on the summit stands out—unique in my mountain memories. Nothing mattered now that I had finally routed the fears which had haunted me for two long years. I could still climb. . . .' It was but two years since Lunn's fall on Cader, and he still had an open wound and one leg two inches shorter than the other.

MALBY, REGINALD A. (*c*). BASLE, LUCERNE, BRUNIG PASS, MEIRINGEN, ROSENLAUI, BRIENZ, INTERLAKEN, THUN, MEIRINGEN

POWYS, LLEWELYN. AROSA, MAIENFELDERFURKA PASS, DAVOS

'. . . that intolerable *bubbling* sensation indicative of a haemorrhage. . . .'

ROGET, F. F. BOURG ST. PIERRE, COL DU SONADON, CHANRION, COL DE L'ÉVÊQUE, COL DE COLLON, COL DE BERTOL, DENT BLANCHE, COL D'HÉRENS, ZERMATT

'It has always been my fancy to unite in one sweep of vision the ocean and the mountains, the deepest with the highest. My Dent Blanche might be one of a school of whales stranded on high when the waters withdrew, and my harpoon was well placed, sticking in one of the vertebrae of her petrified spine.'

ROSE, F. HORACE. LES VERRIÈRES, NEUCHÂTEL, BERNE, THUN, INTERLAKEN, LAUTERBRUNNEN, KLEINE SCHEIDEGG, GRINDELWALD, INTERLAKEN, BRIENZ, BRUNIG PASS, LUCERNE, PILATUS, RIGI, FLUELEN, GÖSCHENEN, ANDERMATT, FURKA PASS, OBERGESTELEN, BRIG, VISP, ZERMATT, VISP, BRIG, SIMPLON PASS, DOMODOSSOLA

'How poor, how infinitesimal were such shabby apologies for mountains as we possess in South Africa! Before me was the blue lake and beyond it a belt of white, shimmering haze, breaking into shreds like carded wool. From this flimsy, unsubstantial base sprung up the monsters of the mountain world.'

SCHUSTER, CLAUD. LES ORMONTS, COL DE PILLON, DIABLERETS, SANETSCH PASS, WILDHORN, WILDSTRUBEL, GEMMI PASS, KANDERSTEG, LAUTERBRUNNEN, JUNGFRAU, GRINDELWALD, SCHRECKHORN, LAUTERBRUNNEN, BREITHORN, RIED, BIETSCHHORN

'If I were free to choose the best place from which to view these glories, I would take, rather than his [Leslie Stephen's] favourite Wengern Alp, the Upper Steinberg. Detailed comparison would force one to some show of depreciation of the former and between those heavenly courts who shall dare to sustain a preference?'

STRAVINSKY, IGOR. CLARENS

In a flat on the first floor of 'Les Tilleuls', Stravinsky composed *The Rite of Spring*, to the bewilderment of the other tenants.

THOMPSON, SILVANUS P. CHAMONIX

WIDMANN, J. V. BERNE, THUN, INTERLAKEN, MEIRINGEN, HANDECK

YOUNG, GEOFFREY WINTHROP. COURMAYEUR, BROUILLARD RIDGE, MONT BLANC, GRANDES JORASSES, CHAMONIX, MER DE GLACE, AIGUILLE DU GRÉPON

1912

DURHAM, W. E. SION, AROLLA, SION, MARTIGNY, GRAND ST. BERNARD PASS, AOSTA, GRAN PARADISO, GRIVOLA, COURMAYEUR, MONT BLANC, CHAMONIX, MARTIGNY, SION, SIERRE, MONTANA, WILDSTRUBEL, GEMMI PASS, BALMHORN, KANDERSTEG, BLÜMLISALPHORN, GSPALTENHORN, SEFINENFURKE PASS, MÜRREN, LAUTERBRUNNEN

'After dinner I saw Mrs. Simms directing a post-card to my wife. "What are you saying to her?" I asked. She passed the card across the table and I read, "We have just met your husband. I wish you could see his knickerbockers".'

GIDE, ANDRÉ. NEUCHÂTEL, ZURICH, ANDERMATT

'L'admiration de la montagne est une invention du protestantisme. . . . Si de l'arbre la montagne fait un sapin, on juge de ce qu'elle peut faire de l'homme. Esthétique et moralité de conifères.'

HAMILTON, HELEN (*c*). CHAMONIX, AIGUILLE DE CHARMOZ, TOUR NOIRE, AIGUILLE DU MIDI, AIGUILLE DU GRÉPON, DENT DU REQUIN, AIGUILLE VERTE, AIGUILLE D'ARGENTIÈRE, MONT BLANC

At the Vallot hut, 'one gentleman, arrayed in patent leather boots, white duck trousers, frock coat, gray suede gloves, and bowler hat, with a retinue of guides and a debilitated wife, declared he would go no farther. By way of emphasising his decision he banged the bowler on the snow with what little strength he had left. This action so infuriated his leading guide that he seized the offending object and, stamping heavily on it several times, flattened it out completely. This done, he swore by all his gods (only less politely) that go up Monsieur and Madame should to the very top. . . .'

LUNN, ARNOLD. MALOJA, FORNO, GRINDELWALD, KLEINE SCHEIDEGG, WENGEN, MÖNCH

'The Eiger chuckled. He had lured us on to the ice, and only one of us had crampons. Suddenly he released the full fury of his artillery. The lull which had tempted us was only a momentary pause. A gale leaped over the crest of the Eiger and the heavens were filled with fury; a stone whipped off the slope and whistled past like a shell, a flood of loose snow and ice poured down the rocks. "Take that!" screamed the wind, and out I went at full rope's length.'

MALBY, REGINALD A. GENEVA, SAMOËNS, SIXT, GENEVA, LAUSANNE, BEX, PONT DE NANT, MARTIGNY, SION, TURTMANN, GRUBEN, AUGSTBORD PASS, ST. NIKLAUS, ZERMATT, VISP, MARTIGNY, MONTREUX, GENEVA

YOUNG, GEOFFREY WINTHROP. GRINDELWALD, MÖNCH, ZERMATT, COL D'HÉRENS, LES HAUDÈRES, CHAMONIX, COL DU GÉANT, COURMAYEUR, POINTE ISOLÉE

'La pointe isolée, or l'Isolée—I gave it this name after a talk with Joseph Croux in which he had used the term descriptively—is a dark and stately pillar of rock, with a suggestion in its lines, as we see it from this side, of a human figure; a figure burdened with grief, but supporting its sorrow with tragic dignity and in solitude. I compared it once in thought to widowed Andromache upon the walls of Troy.'

1913

BAGGE, HENRY. GENEVA, EVIAN, OUCHY, LAUSANNE, YVERDON, ESTAVAYER, VEVEY, LAUSANNE, ROMONT, FRIBOURG, BERNE, NEUCHÂTEL, BIENNE, MORAT, BERNE, THUN, INTERLAKEN, LAUTERBRUNNEN, GRINDELWALD, INTERLAKEN, BRIENZ, BRUNIG PASS, LUCERNE, RIGI, ZURICH, SCHAFFHAUSEN, GENEVA, CHAMONIX, GENEVA

DURHAM, W. E. KANDERSTEG, GEMMI PASS, WILDSTRUBEL, RAWYL PASS, LENK, KANDERSTEG, GEMMI PASS, LEUK, VISP, ZERMATT, FEEJOCH PASS, SAAS FEE, ULRICHSHORN, BALFRIN, ST. NIKLAUS, ZERMATT, MONTE ROSA, TÄSCHHORN, COL D'HÉRENS, COL DES BOUQUETINS, COL DE COLLON, AROLLA

After passing the night lost in the snow and mist, 'Never shall I forget the surpassing beauty of that wondrous transformation scene—the white peaks silhouetted against the star-spangled sky, Mont Collon opposite glittering from summit to base in silver, the snowy glacier sweeping downwards below us, the very moraine and rocks around us clothed in purest white. It might have been a bridal of the Gods.'

FLECKER, JAMES ELROY. LEYSIN, GLION, SIERRE, MONTANA

Flecker was working as hard as his health would allow at *Hassan*. From Leysin ('a horrible town of disease') he wrote: '*Hassan* is finished, and gone to the typist, which is a great blessing.' Montana 'seems to be quite the place to come to—for health—but the desolation—the black fir-trees again and horrid snowy mountains are appalling after Glion'.

JOHNSTON, SIR HARRY. BERNE, GENEVA, LAUSANNE, LUCERNE, ZURICH, COIRE

LAWRENCE, DAVID HERBERT. CONSTANCE, SCHAFFHAUSEN, ZURICH, LUCERNE, FLUELEN, ALTDORF, ST. GOTTHARD PASS, BELLINZONA, LUGANO, COMO

'I walked all the way from Schaffhausen to Zurich, Lucerne, over the Gotthard to Airolo, Bellinzona, Lugano, Como. It was beautiful—Switzerland too touristy, however—spoilt. . . . So I walked across Switzerland—and am cured of that little country for ever. The only excitement in it is that you can throw a stone a frightfully long way down—that is forbidden by law. As for mountains,—if I stick my little finger over my head, I can see it shining against the sky and call it Monte Rosa. No, I can't do with mountains at close quarters—they are always in the way, and they are so stupid, never moving and never doing anything but obtrude themselves.'

RAVEL, MAURICE. CLARENS

Clarens was Ravel's father's birthplace, and there Ravel now collaborated with Stravinsky in the re-orchestration of Mussorgsky's *Khovantchina*.

STRAVINSKY, IGOR. CLARENS, LEYSIN

At his house at Clarens, 'Le Châtelard', Stravinsky composed his Japanese lyrics and, with Maurice Ravel, re-orchestrated Moussorgsky's *Khovantchina.* At Leysin he resumed work on *The Nightingale.*

THOMPSON, SILVANUS P. ZINAL, CHAMONIX

WHIDBORNE, GEORGE FERRIS. LAUSANNE, MONT PÈLERIN, MARTIGNY, FIONNAY, GRAND COMBIN, COL DE SONADON, CHANRION, COL DE MONT ROUGE, AROLLA

1914

COBDEN-SANDERSON, THOMAS JAMES. MONTANA, MONTREUX

A visit in January to the Châlet du Soleil, Countess Russell's house near Montana.

DURHAM, W. E. BEX, GRYON, DIABLERETS, SANETSCH PASS, SION, SANETSCH PASS, WILDHORN, RAWYL PASS, WILDSTRUBEL, GEMMI PASS, SCHWARZGRÄTLI, KANDERSTEG, TSCHINGEL PASS, BREITHORN, MÜRREN, ISENFLUH, LAUTERBRUNNEN, GRINDELWALD, GROSSE SCHEIDEGG, ROSENLAUI, ENGELHÖRNER, WETTERHORN, GRINDELWALD, LAUTERBRUNNEN, ROTHTAL, JUNGFRAU, ISENFLUH, SION, AROLLA, MONT COLLON, SION, MARTIGNY, LAUSANNE

FLECKER, JAMES ELROY. MONTANA, LOCARNO, DAVOS

Unable to endure Montana's 'eternal whitewash', very ill at Locarno, Flecker died at Davos on Jan. 3, 1915.

GRANDE, JULIAN. BERNE, ZERMATT

'. . . Attending an international gathering of mountaineers held in the Monte Rosa Hotel, to arrange for a memorial of Edward Whymper on the fiftieth anniversary of his ascent of the Matterhorn. Members of the Swiss, English, French, German, Austrian, and Italian Alpine Clubs sat at the "climbers' table", deciding with one accord to have a statue, representing the famous mountaineer as he was in 1865, erected at Zermatt to face the Matterhorn. . . . A week later the war began, and the memorial of Whymper has still to be erected.'

KELPER, D. DE (*c*). BASLE, LUCERNE, RIGI, BRUNNEN, ALPNACH, BRUNIG PASS, MEIRINGEN, INTERLAKEN, LAUTERBRUNNEN, GRINDELWALD, INTERLAKEN, THUN, BERNE, FRIBOURG, LAUSANNE, GENEVA

LUNN, ARNOLD. JUNGFRAUJOCH, FIESCHERHORN, EGGISHORN, VIESCH, VISP, ZERMATT, MONTE ROSA

RECKITT, MAURICE B. VILLARS

'Noel Curtis-Bennett . . . encouraged me to help him to put together what we called a revue. My principal job was to write a set of lyrics and officiate at the piano. Thus was born an enterprise which in post-war days became a more and more elaborate undertaking, and involved me as author, producer, pianist, and singer. . . . We could not start our rehearsing till one arrived in Villars, and we had but ten days or so for it, with nearly all the work sandwiched in between tea and dinner. . . . "Snow use", "The snow optimist", "The ski sheikh", "Palace in Wonderland", and all the rest of them, can linger only in the recollection of those who played in them, or, still more probably, in that of their author alone.'

STRAVINSKY, IGOR. SALVAN, CLARENS

At Salvan Stravinsky composed the *Songs of Pribaoutki*. At the Villa Pervenche at Clarens he started composing *Les Noces*.

YOUNG, GEOFFREY WINTHROP. BRIG, RIED, BIETSCHHORN, PETERSGRAT, GAMCHILÜCKE, GSPALTENHORN, BÜTTLASSEN, PETERSGRAT, BEICH PASS, BELALP, GAMCHILÜKE, GSPALTENHORN WEST RIDGE, SEFINENFURKE PASS, MÜRREN, JUNGFRAUJOCH, BELALP, ZERMATT, Z'MUTT RIDGE, MATTERHORN, CHAMONIX

After climbing the west ridge of the Gspaltenhorn, one of the last great unclimbed ridges in the Alps, 'we sun-basked voluptuously on the rocks, wholly abandoned to a tingling of apricot light without, while the slowly revolving rays of contentment, lassitude and rainbow-dreaming illuminated the past, the present, and the future for us within. They were hours of mere pleasure in being; such as leave no definite memory behind, and only survive in a heightening of our powers of appreciation, a deepening of our understanding of natural and human fellowship.'

1915

LENIN, VLADIMIR ILYICH. BERNE, ZIMMERWALD

At the Berne conference of the Bolsheviks the demand for a Third International was voiced. The Zimmerwald conference urged the workers of the world to refuse to fight in the war, much to Lenin's disgust since he saw that the war would, if it continued, provide the opportunity for revolution.

STRAVINSKY, IGOR. CHÂTEAU D'OEX, CLARENS, MORGES

Descending in the funicular from Glion, Stravinsky travelled with two drunks; one hiccoughed, the other kept on repeating a phrase at regular intervals. From this experience, Stravinsky derived one of the principal subjects for the feast in *Les Noces*. At Château d'Oex he began part of the composition of *Reynard*, which he continued at Morges at the Villa Rogivue. The French text for this was written by his friend C.-F. Ramuz.

TROTSKY, LEON. BERNE, ZIMMERWALD

'. . . Arranged to hold the meeting in a little village called Zimmerwald, high in the mountains. . . . The delegates, filling four stage coaches, set off for the mountains. . . . The hitherto unknown name of Zimmerwald was echoed throughout the world. This had a staggering effect on the hotel proprietor—The valiant Swiss told Grimm that he looked for a great increase in the value of his property and accordingly was ready to subscribe a certain sum to the funds of the Third International.'

1916

LENIN, VLADIMIR ILYICH. BERNE, THUN, KIENTHAL, ZURICH

In Zurich, after the Kienthal conference, Lenin wrote his pamphlet *Imperialism the Highest Stage of Capitalism.*

LUNN, ARNOLD. SIERRE, ZINAL, TRIFTJOCH PASS, ZERMATT

ROLLAND, ROMAIN. GENEVA, THUN, SIERRE

Au-dessus de la Mêlée was written at Geneva; *Les Précurseurs* at Sierre, where Romain Rolland was living when he learned that he had been awarded the Nobel Prize for literature.

TZARA, TRISTAN. ZURICH

Of the origin of Dadaism, Hans Arp wrote: 'I affirm that Tristan Tzara discovered the word *Dada* on the 8th of February 1916 at 6 o'clock in the evening. I was there with my twelve children when Tzara pronounced for the first time this word which aroused a legitimate enthusiasm in all of us. This took place at the Café de la Terrasse in Zurich and I had a roll of bread up my right nostril.'

1917

GIDE, ANDRÉ. GENEVA, BERNE, ENGELBERG, LUCERNE, SAAS FEE

'Quelle propreté partout. On n'ose pas jeter sa cigarette dans le lac. Pas de graffiti dans les urinoirs. . . .'

JOYCE, JAMES. ZURICH, LOCARNO

Joyce was writing *Ulysses*, which was typed in Zurich on a typewriter belonging to the Austro-Hungarian Relief Committee.

LUNN, ARNOLD. OBERAARJOCH PASS, GRIMSEL PASS, NÄGELISGRÄTLI, GALENSTOCK, GLETSCH, ZERMATT, DOM

' "Ah" said Knubel, "if all the journeys that I have ever made among the mountains were joined together they would reach to heaven." '

STRAVINSKY, IGOR. MORGES, AIGLE, LES DIABLERETS, MORGES

In a carpenter's shed at Diablerets into which he had introduced a piano, Stravinsky completed his Study for Pianola, and played it to Lord Berners. At the Maison Bornand at Morges he finished *Les Noces*, except for the orchestration which he started with the assistance of a piano, a harmonium, and several percussion instruments.

1918

LUNN, ARNOLD. MÜRREN, LAUTERBRUNNEN, KLEINE SCHEIDEGG, JUNGFRAUJOCH PASS, FIESCHERHORN, GRÜNHORNLÜCKE PASS, UNTERAARGLACIER, LAUTERAARSATTEL PASS, ROSENHORN, ROSENLAUI, MEIRINGEN, GRINDELWALD, SCHRECKHORN, WETTERHORN

'I have knocked about the mountains for many years, and they have given me unnumbered memories which are part and parcel of life's best things, and yet, somehow, all other hill memories seem dim beside the recollection of those four perfect days. All the conditions were just right—perfect companionship, perfect ski-ing, and perfect views.' The companions were British prisoners of war interned in Switzerland.

NIJINSKY, VASLAV. ST. MORITZ

'The young man, our stoker, made a few hesitating steps and quickly said, "Madame, forgive me; I may be wrong. We all love you both. You remember I told you that at home in my village at Sils-Maria as a child I used to do errands for Mr. Nietzsche? I carried his rucksack when he went to the Alps to work. Madame, he acted and looked just like Mr. Nijinsky does now. Please forgive me." '

STRAVINSKY, IGOR. MORGES

In collaboration with C.-F. Ramuz, Stravinsky wrote the *Soldier's Tale*, the scene of which is laid between Denges and Denezy.

1919

RILKE, RAINER MARIA. NYON, GENEVA, BERNE, ZURICH, COIRE, SOGLIO, MALOJA PASS, COIRE, ZURICH, LAUSANNE, BEGNINS SUR GLAND, NYON, ZURICH, ST. GALL, LUCERNE, BASLE, BERNE, WINTERTHUR, LOCARNO

'Mountains are from the start difficult for me to understand—I can see the Pyrenees, I have the most splendid recollections of the Atlas in North Africa, and when reading Tolstoy on the Caucasus I felt the indescribable thrill of their size. But these Swiss mountains? They nevertheless present something of an obstacle to me, they are so terribly numerous. Their shapes pile up on one another; I note with pleasure that here and there an outline stands out cleanly against the sky,—but I lack, how should I express it, the corresponding inner feeling which turns an impression into an experience.'

WINTER, J. B. SIERRE, MONTANA, SION, MARTIGNY, ST. GINGOLPH, EVIAN, THONON, ST. JEAN D'AILPH, COL DE GETS, BONNEVILLE

1920

ALLEN, PERCY STAFFORD. JOUGNE, VALLORBE, LAUSANNE, BASLE, PORRENTRUY

COBDEN-SANDERSON, THOMAS JAMES. CLARENS, MONTREUX, SIERRE, MONTANA

Cobden-Sanderson provided the motto on the porch of the Châlet du Soleil where he stayed with Lady Russell:

'On the heights
Love lives with Joy
Magnificent and Beautiful and Gay.'

LUNN, ARNOLD. ZERMATT, WEISSHORN, BIESJOCH PASS, BRUNEGGHORN, TURTMANN

'In the east the bar of the Oberland was silhouetted against a sky which was gradually growing lighter. The rich gloom of the valleys was pregnant with colour. The busy little skirmishers which go before the sun wove a web of light around the spurs and buttresses which fell from our feet to the ghostly gleam of the glacier below. The background of shadows was no longer flat and featureless, but showed up in relief, as rounded curves and convexities moulded themselves out of the darkness. Colour was at work, picking out in vivid green the May meadows which faced the east, annexing new territories conquered from the darkness, and mopping up the last dusky patches of the night. And then suddenly the sun leaped above the hills, and the bells in the long valley from Randa to St. Niklaus pealed out their salute to the oldest of the Gods.'

PILLEY, DOROTHY. CHAMONIX, AIGUILLE DU MOINE, AIGUILLE DU GRÉPON, DENT DU GÉANT, AIGUILLE DU DRU, COL DE BALME, MARTIGNY, CHAMPEX, PETIT CLOCHER DE PLANEREUSE

Descending from the Col de Balme, 'two sombre figures, the man in a dark blue suit, the woman ahead in black, were rushing with short determined dashes up the slope. Mind was dominating matter and in time they would infallibly arrive. We approached, and I perceived that the man was carrying a book as big as a family Bible under his arm. Something struck me as familiar about them in their earnestness. At closer range there was no mistaking Beatrice and Sydney Webb. . . .'

RILKE, RAINER MARIA. LOCARNO, PRATTELN, ZURICH, GENEVA, RAGAZ, ZURICH, GENEVA, MARTIGNY, SAXON, SION, SIERRE, GENEVA, BERG AM IRCHEL

'How beautiful the Valais is. . . . Among the valleys of Switzerland I have seen none as spacious: the Valais is a plain, wide between the mountains, and these are nothing but the background, not intruding with their mass, but of a softness of contour that at times produces the imaginary impression of mountains as seen in a reflection.'

SWINNERTON, FRANK. LAUSANNE, SIERRE, RANDOGNE, MONTANA

Swinnerton was on his way to stay with Lady Russell at the Châlet du Soleil. 'When, at Sierre, I tried to reach Randogne by funicular I found that I could travel only half the distance. However, as others intended to walk the rest of the way up the railway track, I decided to join them.' At the Châlet du Soleil he found Cobden-Sanderson and Festing Jones among others, and Augustine Birrell was expected when he left.

1921

BENEDICT, CLARE. BASLE, BADEN, BERNE, THUN, VEVEY, LAUSANNE, FRIBOURG, SOLEURE, LUCERNE, AXENSTEIN, RAGAZ, COIRE, WALLENSTADT, ST. GALL, CONSTANCE

CHAMBERLAIN, SIR AUSTEN. LES VERRIÈRES, NEUCHÂTEL, LAUSANNE, ST. MAURICE, GENEVA, ZURICH, RAPPERSWIL, ZUG, BRUNNEN, PILATUS, FLUELEN, ANDERMATT, HOSPENTHAL, FURKA PASS, GRIMSEL PASS, MEIRINGEN, ROSENLAUI, GRINDELWALD, KLEINE SCHEIDEGG, JUNGFRAUJOCH, INTERLAKEN, ADELBODEN, SPIEZ, ZWEISIMMEN, SAANEN, MONTREUX, BASLE, LUGANO

'. . . The mountains are clear of cloud and the lake is a brilliantly milky green, a fresh air comes in at my open window, to which the sun only gets round in the afternoon. Pilatus stands up sharp and clear against the blue sky at the head of the other arm of the lake opposite us and the bullfinches are playing about on the balcony outside. What more can one want?'

LUNN, ARNOLD. GAULIHÜTTE, WETTERLIMMI PASS, ROSENEGG, MITTELJOCH PASS, WETTERSATTEL PASS, MITTELHORN, WETTERHORN

'This zigzag tour in and out of the Wetterhorn passes is one of the most beautiful expeditions which I have ever done. The views were perfect, the ski-ing was perfect, and the tour was just about as much as one can comfortably manage in one day.'

MANSFIELD, KATHERINE. GENEVA, CLARENS, BAUGY, SIERRE, MONTANA

'Chalet des Sapins,
Montana.

'Heavily, more heavily than ever, falls the snow. It is hypnotizing. One looks, wonders vaguely how much has fallen and how much will fall and—looks again.'

OBERSON, GABRIEL. FRIBOURG, RIGGISBERG, THUN, INTERLAKEN, GRINDELWALD, GROSSE SCHEIDEGG, MEIRINGEN, GRIMSEL PASS, OBERGESTELEN, BRIG, LEUK, GEMMI PASS, KANDERSTEG, WIMMIS, RIGGISBERG, FRIBOURG

PILLEY, DOROTHY. VISP, SAAS FEE, PORTJENGRAT, ALPHUBELJOCH PASS, ZERMATT, ZMUTT-RIDGE, MATTERHORN, BREITHORN, VISP, SION, LES HAUDÈRES, FERPECLE, AROLLA, FERPECLE RIDGE, DENT BLANCHE, PETIT BOUQUETIN, SION

'The long tables of the "Mont Collon"; the stone stairs so steep after a "first day"; the crowded glass-walled verandah where one sits on cane chairs to gossip, to read detective novels, to play cards on wet days, with the feet against an electric heater; the miscellaneous rooms in which one interviews the guides over coffee and liqueurs; the salon which has the red plush chairs and sofa, and the regal gold-tasselled curtains and the piano, but in which one may not smoke—what is there in all these to hold the fancy?'

RILKE, RAINER MARIA. BERG AM IRCHEL, ZURICH, SOLOTHURN, ESTAVAYER, ETOY, SIERRE

'Chateau de Muzot sur Sierre.

'... Whenever I think of leaving Switzerland, the powerful attractiveness of this land rises up in an unexpected counter suggestion . . . just as a Rodin sculpture carries with it a spaciousness which it radiates around it, so to my eyes do the mountains and hills of the Valais; infinite space emanates from them and between them, so that this valley of the Rhône is anything but enclosed,—so very different from those valleys of the Grisons, often so picturesque but heavy on the mind.' It was here that the great German poet wrote his *Elegien*.

RÖNTGEN, WILHELM CONRAD. TIEFENKASTEL, LENZERHEIDE, PONTRESINA

'This is what I wanted to see once more in my life. This roaring stream is for me the symbol of potential power. . . . This morning we walked for quite a distance through the forest and along the roaring glacier water in the really very beautiful Rosegg valley. From time to time we had glorious views of the glacier far in the distance. We rested upon some benches which have supported many a good friend and my dear Bertha. Often I feel as if I were dreaming a happy dream. . . .' For forty years the discoverer of X-rays had taken his holidays at the Weisses Kreuz, Pontresina.

1922

ALLEN, PERCY STAFFORD. FELDKIRCH, THALWIL, ZURICH, BERNE, BIGLEN, BASLE

Biglen: 'a glorious view of the Bernese Oberland, from the Wetterhorn to the Jungfrau and Blumlisalp and beyond. By good fortune the weather was brilliant. Each morning we were out of bed by 5, to survey the sunrise, the snows turning from gray to pink and then gold, while a tiny old moon died away in the full light of day, as the sun's rays slowly struck down into the valley beneath us.'

HADOW, GRACE. RIED

'We climbed up about 3,000 ft. to one of those fascinating huts that has no guardian but is like a mixture of a fairy story and a doll's house.'

KER, WILLIAM PATON. VISP, STALDEN, SAAS, SIRWOLTEN PASS, SIMPLON PASS, BRIG, EGGISHORN, FINSTERAARHORN, EGGISHORN, BRIG, VISP, ZERMATT

'I did what no man has ever done—walked from the Eggishorn hotel down the Rhone valley through Brieg to Visp. I rested hours over breakfast at Moerell reading Dante, *Paradiso,* and some time at Brieg over tea: the last five miles into Visp in the cool of the evening. . . . William Wordsworth is everywhere—he and Jones on the Simplon must have seen the waterfall where Joseph and I descended to find the high road. Going down to Brieg we took a bit of the old road, same as 1790.'

OBERSON, GABRIEL. FRIBOURG, THUN, INTERLAKEN, MEIRINGEN, SUSTEN PASS, WASSEN, GÖSCHENEN, ANDERMATT, ST. GOTTHARD PASS, AIROLO, GÖSCHENEN, FLUELEN, LUCERNE, LANGNAU, BERNE, FRIBOURG

PILLEY, DOROTHY. CHAMONIX, TOUR RONDE, COURMAYEUR, MONT BLANC, CHAMONIX, AIGUILLE DE BLAITIÈRE, DENT DU REQUIN, MONT MALET, COURMAYEUR, AOSTA, GRAND ST. BERNARD PASS, ORSIÈRES, CHAMPEX, COL DES ECANDIES, FENÊTRE DES CHAMOIS, AIGUILLES DORÉES, AIGUILLE DU TOUR

At the Julien Dupuis Hut 'a movie party was in possession. . . . A scree slope just outside the hut was made the scene of most daring feats. Under the fire of a tilted camera on the hut roof, roped quartets in leather motor coats toiled and leaped and saved one another at the word of command. The chief energies of the outfit seemed indeed to be expended in shouting. They said it was the first picture to be taken in the Alps.'

SMYTHE, FRANK S. ZURICH, LINTHAL, SANDALP, TÖDI, PLANURA PASS, AMSTEG

'Like Father Placidus, I have a particular affection for the Tödi, for it was the first big mountain that I ever climbed. On this account I should be loth to visit it again lest, perchance, a more sophisticated worship should dim the memories of that early conquest.'

1923

ALLEN, PERCY STAFFORD. LE LOCLE, NEUCHÂTEL, BERNE, ESCHOLZMATT, LUCERNE, HERTENSTEIN, ZURICH, ZOFINGEN, BASLE

Pilatus 'one is prone to think hackneyed and inglorious, since the railway transported a hotel up there; and from Lucerne he doesn't present much of an outline. But from here [Hertenstein] his lines are splendid; and if he stood alone in a thirsty land, if we had him, for instance, in Oxfordshire, we should write poems about him all the time. An added attraction about him is that he was one of the first mountains ever climbed: his conquerors being two contemporaries of Erasmus.'

HADOW, GRACE. BERISAL, EVOLENA, AROLLA

'The great mountains begin to stand out against a pale sky and then the snow shows first dead white, then warmer, and then one peak becomes flame-colour; and one just holds one's breath and sees God walk in the Garden. It is like being blessed at the beginning of each day.'

JACKSON, EILEEN MONTAGUE. BASLE, COIRE, CHURWALDEN, TIEFENKASTEL, PONTRESINA, ST. MORITZ, PIZ LANGUARD, DIAVOLEZZA, DREI SCHWESTER, PIZ MORTERATSCH

'In the midst of all this display of art stood a fine carved bear, resting one paw on a glass decanter and offering liqueur glasses with the other to passers by.'

KER, WILLIAM PATON. MACUGNAGA

Of the Pizzo Bianco:—' "This is my mountain", he is reported to have said, only a little while before he sank down unconscious upon it.' He is buried at Macugnaga.

LUNN, ARNOLD. GRINDELWALD, LAUTERBRUNNEN, KLEINE SCHEIDEGG, EIGER

The first ski ascent of the Eiger.

'... Three tourists, by way of fortifying themselves against the ordeals of a night among the Alpine heights, had ordered a four-course dinner and two bottles of champagne. They washed down the champagne with comments on our putative rashness. "*Sehr gewagt*", murmured the fattest member of the party, "*sehr, sehr gewagt*" (very reckless). The charge of recklessness can be met with equanimity after a climb is safely over, but it has a remarkably depressing effect just as one is starting on a new and difficult expedition. . . . I could stand no more. Seizing an empty champagne bottle I remarked, "that is also *sehr gewagt*. More people die of over-eating and over-drinking than ever died on the mountains".'

OBERSON, GABRIEL. FRIBOURG, AIGLE, COL DE PILLON, DIABLERETS, SANETSCH PASS, GSTEIG, BULLE, FRIBOURG

PARKER, CORNELIA STRATTON. BERNE, THUN, INTERLAKEN, LAUTERBRUNNEN, JUNGFRAUJOCH, VIESCH, VISP, SAAS FEE, ALLALINHORN, ZERMATT, MATTERHORN, ST. NIKLAUS, AUGSTBORD PASS, GRUBEN, MEIDEN PASS, AYER, ZINAL, GRIMENTZ, COL DE TORRENT, EVOLENA, SION, GENEVA, AROSA

'But I'd made the top! We ate some good cookies and started back.'

PILLEY, DOROTHY. SIERRE, ZINAL, ROTHORN, ZERMATT, OBERGABELHORN, MONTE ROSA, LYSJOCH, LYSKAMM, FELIKJOCH, CASTOR, SCHWARZTHOR, ZERMATT, COL D'HÉRENS, LES HAUDÈRES, SION, BRIG, BELALP, ALETSCHHORN, MÖNCH, JUNGFRAUJOCH, JUNGFRAU, GRINDELWALD, SCHRECKHORN, STRAHLEGG PASS, GRIMSEL PASS, BRIG, KIPPEL, PETERSGRAT, BREITHORN, KANDERSTEG, VISP, ZERMATT, ST. THEODUL PASS, BREUIL, COL DE VAUFRÈDE, COL DE BELLATSA, PRARAYÉ, COL DE BERLON, CHANRION, MARTIGNY

'. . . We went up from the Concordia in the morning towards the Jungfraujoch. The restaurant there was an odd place, a cross between a cowshed and the Trocadero, with flavours of the Bakerloo Tube and the Caverns of Cheddar.'

WELZENBACH, WILLO. ZERMATT, ZMUTT-RIDGE, MATTERHORN, COL DU LION, COL DE TOURNANCHE, DENT D'HÉRENS, COL DE TIEFENMATTEN, ZERMATT

1924

ALLEN, PERCY STAFFORD. LES VERRIÈRES, NOIRAIGUE, GUNTEN, INTERLAKEN, SARNEN, MELCHTAL, LUCERNE, BRUNNEN, MORSCHACH, ZURICH, BRUGG, BASLE

Noiraigue:—'We are so much in love with this place that we find it difficult to go on. . . . Three out of our 4 days we have spent on the top of the green plateau behind the Creux du Van, 4,800 ft., enjoying the flowers and the sweet scents of thyme and mint and the splendid air: and today *the* view has come, all the Alps from the Oberland (dim) to Mont Blanc (brilliant) lined up before us.'

HADOW, GRACE. SIMPLON, SAAS FEE, FLETSCHHORN

'I have learned that to hang on the rope over a precipice makes me sympathise deeply with the martyrs who were sawn asunder. It hurts horribly—however it would hurt a great deal more without.'

LUNN, HENRY S. MÜRREN

At the Mürren Conference, Archbishop Söderblom preached, as he said, 'in this unrivalled cathedral, where we have come to praise God's sacred Name and to listen to His voice. This cathedral is orientated, though not west-east but north-south. Ice-capped peaks form the walls. The deep, green valley is the central alley, leading from the entrance gate up towards the choir. Grindelwald, Wengen on the one side, and Mürren, Gimmelwald on the other, form, as it were, the rows of benches. The rushing sounds of singing water from beneath Lauterbrunnen throughout the valley and the rolling echoes of thunder constitute the many-voiced organ. And in the shining white mystery of the Bernese Oberland in the south we imagine the altar, sometimes hidden, sometimes unveiled for awful adoration and worship.'

OBERSON, GABRIEL. FRIBOURG, CHAMPÉRY, SION, SANETSCH PASS, FRIBOURG, CHÂTEAU D'OEX, POINTE DE PARAY, GRANDVILLARD

PILLEY, DOROTHY. SION, LES HAUDÈRES, AROLLA, COL DE COLLON, PRARAYÉ, AROLLA, PAS DE CHÈVRES, COL DE LYREROSE, CHANRION, COL DE FENÊTRE DE BALME, BY, AOSTA, COGNE, GRIVOLA, GRAND ST. BERNARD PASS, MARTIGNY, SION, AROLLA, SION, LUGANO, MONTE GENEROSO, COMO, CHIAVENNA, MALOJA PASS, PASSO DI CASNILE, ALBIGNA, PASSO DI ZOCCA, BAGNI DI MASINO, SONDRIO, TIRANO, BORMIO, STELVIO PASS

Crossing the Col de Collon a skeleton was found, with a belt, square-toed shoes, and a purse which had contained Italian gold pieces of about 1780.

WELZENBACH, WILLO. ZERMATT, BREITHORN, OBERGABELHORN, SÜDLENZSPITZE, NADELHORN, HOHBERGHORN, WEISSTOR PASS, MACUGNAGA, MONTE ROSA, LOURTIER, GRAND COMBIN, COL DES VUIGNETTES, AROLLA

1925

HADOW, GRACE. SIMPLON, FLETSCHHORN, SAAS FEE, SÜDLENZSPITZE, NADELHORN

'We went up to the bivouac. It was like acting the sacrifice of Isaac. Dorsaz carrying a faggot on his back, the 14-year old Peter carrying blankets, and myself. Dorsaz sent me on ahead, and I shall never forget that walk with the mountains absolutely to oneself, and the purple evening light. We camped in a sheepfold under the rocks where Dorsaz lit a blazing fire, and Peter stirred the soup with a stick since we'd forgotten a spoon.'

JACKSON, EILEEN MONTAGUE. BASLE, MARTIGNY, TRIENT, AIGUILLE DU TOUR, MONT ARPILLE, CHAMONIX, MARTIGNY, VISP, ZERMATT, BREITHORN, WELLENKUPPE, MATTERHORN

Eileen's mother said that the Matterhorn was 'altogether too austere, too grand for me. It reminds me at the moment of a gaunt, cold, lonely old maid; but that beautiful fleecy cloud has the same softening effect that a chiffon scarf gives. I suppose', she went on—as if she were thinking aloud—'great heights must be lonely, and therefore, after all, it may be happier to mingle with the crowd.'

SCHUSTER, CLAUD. MÜRREN

'At about 9.30 one January night. The clear heavens were thick with stars. There was no wind or even motion in the air. Suddenly there came into vision a great light from the Eiger. It passed behind that mountain, and threw up in strong relief the long line from the summit of the Mönch. Beyond it, as I knew well, was the risen moon, and the stars in that quarter of the firmament paled their fires, "touched to death by diviner eyes". But to us it was as if we gazed from without at the very battlements of heaven, and as if, on the farther side, were its illumined courts.'

SMYTHE, FRANK S. GRINDELWALD, SCHRECKHORN

WELZENBACH, WILLO. COURMAYEUR, AIGUILLE BLANCHE DE PEUTERET, MONT BLANC DE COURMAYEUR, MONT BLANC, COURMAYEUR, ZERMATT, TAESCHHORN, LYSKAMM, DENT D'HÉRENS NORTH FACE

1926

ALLEN, PERCY STAFFORD. BASLE, LUCERNE, BRUNNEN, MORSCHACH, FLUELEN, ANDERMATT, OBERALP PASS, DISENTIS, COIRE, THUSIS, ANDEER, SPLÜGEN PASS, CHIAVENNA, BRESCIA, MILAN, DOMODOSSOLA, SIMPLON PASS, BRIG, SION, MARTIGNY, ST. MAURICE, LAUSANNE

'We set out along the road over the Splügen, by which Erasmus came back from Italy in 1509. . . . We walked up the Via Mala, and admired its terrific cliffs and wondered what Erasmus thought of them.'

BROWN, T. GRAHAM. GRINDELWALD, GRAND COMBIN, MONT VELAN, GRAND ST. BERNARD PASS, AOSTA, COURMAYEUR

'I examined the line of the old Brenva route carefully with my glass, and saw that the route did not go up so directly towards Mont Blanc as it had seemed to go in the first flush of disappointment. This meant that a more direct route might in fact be made, and this meant again that there was a proper Brenva face after all.'

HADOW, GRACE. DISENTIS, LUKMANIER PASS, AIROLO, ST. GOTTHARD PASS, HOSPENTHAL, FURKA PASS, BRIG, SAAS FEE

'Half way down the hill lies a little seventeenth century chapel. It has a porch as big as itself, white-washed, with white pillars and the arches a pale yellow. Today the pillars had garlands of green spruce and two little spruce trees guarded the entrance. There was something Greek about it and something very Swiss. . . .'

KLUCKER, CHRISTIAN. SILS

'Shall this incomparable pearl in the crown of lakes of our Swiss Alpine land be sacrificed for all future time to thoughtless speculation? . . . Are we free to dispose of a thing which, strictly speaking, belongs to a later generation, and has so high a value as our untouched Silsersee?'

MAN, HENRI DE. FLIMS

'Mon amour de la montagne était—et est encore—tel, qu'après quatre étés et trois hivers passés au même endroit, loin d'être blasé, j'étais encore plus sensible qu'auparavant aux beautés qui m'environnaient. Connaissant mieux le pays, les habitants y-compris, il avait pour moi plus de signification.'

WELZENBACH, WILLO. ZERMATT, BREITHORN, OBERGABELHORN SOUTH FACE, WEISSHORN, DOM, COURMAYEUR

1927

ALLEN, PERCY STAFFORD. BASLE, SOLEURE, WEISSENSTEIN, NEUCHÂTEL, NOIRAIGUE, COUVET, LES VERRIÈRES, BESANÇON, JOUGNE, VALLORBE, LAC DE JOUX, LAUSANNE, GENEVA

Lac de Joux: 'We went and saw and were conquered: and stayed 6 days, enjoying beautiful walks and views. From the crest of the ridge one could see the line of the Alps no great distance away; and the familiar but unfailingly beautiful sight of the dark pine tree-tops against the deep blue sky was a continual delight.'

BROWN, T. GRAHAM. ORSIÈRES, COL DU CHARDONNET, CHAMONIX, DENT DU REQUIN, COL DU GÉANT, COURMAYEUR, AIGUILLE DE TRELATÊTE, CHAMONIX, COL DU GÉANT, TORINO HUT, COL MOORE, SENTINELLE ROUGE, MONT BLANC

'The warm sun shone down the flank in our faces, turning the plates of wind-worn snow into silver, and there was great silence, so that everything seemed to be unsubstantiated, the climb not least. There had been a feeling of unreality in my old day-dream—as if fancy had outstripped probability or even possibility. Now, although the Brenva face had been won in fact, if not by the grand ridge of my hope, it was still dreamlike. The silence and the loneliness held me. There was none to share possession of the mountain at this hour of the day, and not the Brenva face alone, but also Mont Blanc itself, seemed to be peculiarly ours. Both were like intimate confidences to be enjoyed in the privacy of this splendid day.' Graham Brown was accompanied by Frank Smythe on this, the first ascent of the Brenva face of Mont Blanc.

HADOW, GRACE (*c*). AROLLA, DENT BLANCHE, ZERMATT

'The nice head waiter (who looked like an undergraduate) poured a cup of boiling tea over me, there were cries (not from me) of horror. When I had had my blouse washed and told him he need no longer worry as there wasn't a mark on it, he replied briefly but fervently, "Lob Gott". Fancy an English waiter saying "Praise God" when you told him he hadn't spoiled your blouse.'

LAUGHLIN, CLARA E. COMO, LUGANO, BELLINZONA, ST. GOTTHARD PASS, HOSPENTHAL, FURKA PASS, GLETSCH, ANDERMATT, ALTDORF, LUCERNE, RIGI, ZURICH, SCHAFFHAUSEN, LUCERNE, BRUNIG PASS, MEIRINGEN, INTERLAKEN, THUN, BERNE, MORAT, LAUSANNE, MARTIGNY, GRAND ST. BERNARD, MARTIGNY, VEVEY, GENEVA

'We didn't climb any mountains, except in automobiles: but we went up the Rigi in the cogwheel railway that is the oldest mountain railway in Switzerland.'

PILLEY, DOROTHY. SION, AROLLA, SION, RIED, PETERSGRAT, KANDERSTEG

'Most Alpine travellers find themselves drawn to the mountains by a two-fold pull—the impulse to go over new country and to revisit familiar scenes. And, after all the breaking of links which a long spell of travel imposes, the new scenes and new contacts and the strain of incessant novelty, to come back as it were to the best of one's past and fit into it again gives one a feeling of perpetuity.'

SMYTHE, FRANK S. CHAMONIX, AIGUILLE DU PLAN, COURMAYEUR, AIGUILLE BLANCHE DE PEUTERET, TOUR RONDE, COL MOORE, SENTINELLE ROUGE, MONT BLANC

'Bodily discomfort and a mental appreciation of mountain scenery may be incompatible, but the greatest gift of the hills are memories, and sitting in reminiscent mood by the fireside it is not the discomforts, the trials, and hardships of a mountain climb that one remembers, but the scenery through which one had moved, the joys that one has discovered, the laughter, freedom and good fellowship of mountaineering.'

WELZENBACH, WILLO. COURMAYEUR, GRANDES JORASSES, COL DU GÉANT, CHAMONIX

1928

ALLEN, PERCY STAFFORD. BASLE, OLTEN, LUCERNE, BRUNNEN, MORSCHACH, FLUELEN, ANDERMATT, FURKA PASS, BRIG, SION

BROWN, T. GRAHAM. KANDERSTEG, CHAMONIX, AIGUILLE DU GRÉPON, AIGUILLE VERTE, COL DU GÉANT, COURMAYEUR, ROUTE MAJOR, MONT BLANC DE COURMAYEUR, MONT BLANC, CHAMONIX, COL DU GÉANT, COURMAYEUR, ZERMATT, WEISSHORN

The second ascent of the Brenva face, the first by the Route Major. Graham Brown was accompanied by Frank Smythe.

HADOW, GRACE. SAMADEN, DISENTIS, LAUTERBRUNNEN, BREITHORN, PETERSGRAT, RIED, FINSTERAARHORN, GRIMSEL, KANDERSTEG, BALMHORN

LAWRENCE, DAVID HERBERT. LES DIABLERETS, GSTEIG

'Chalet Beau Site
Les Diablerets.

'. . . it is snowing again, a fine and crumbling snow. I must say, I don't like it. I am no snow-bird, I hate the stark and shroudy whiteness, white and black. It offends the painter in one—it is so uniform—only sometimes lovely contours, and pale blue gleams. But against life.'

PILLEY, DOROTHY. SION, AROLLA, DENT BLANCHE, COL D'HÉRENS, ZERMATT, RANDA, WEISSHORN, ZERMATT, ADLER PASS, SAAS FEE, FLETSCHHORN, SIMPLON PASS, BRIG, SION, MARTIGNY, GRAND ST. BERNARD, AOSTA, COURMAYEUR, MONT DOLENT, GRANDES JORASSES, ANNECY, ST. GERVAIS, GENEVA

' "All things considered", as Théophile Ribot remarked, "there is room to wonder whether there is not, in every *grande passion*, as much misery as joy." ' This was the first ascent of the Dent Blanche by the northern arête.

SCHUSTER, CLAUD. MALOJA

'All the affections and intimacies of a lifetime have never made me think the main Engadine valley beautiful in summer, until one comes to Maloja itself, to the surprise of the plunge to Italy and the enchantment of the secluded Ordlegna. But in winter the Engadine hills grow into mighty mountains. The empty slopes to Silvaplana reveal new outlines, and, at evening, glow with colour. The long line of lakes, smooth under their almost unbroken covering, has a soothing charm; Margna gleams and flushes; and, in the background, Badile and Cengallo, dashed with snow and shining with ice, put on an additional fantastic savagery.'

SMITH, GEORGE ADAM. CLARENS

'Looking at the peak of Jaman, George recalled his beloved Matthew Arnold, and he declaimed "Obermann" from beginning to end with all the memory and fervour of his youth.'

SMYTHE, FRANK S. CHAMONIX, SENTINELLE ROUGE, MONT BLANC DE COURMAYEUR, MONT BLANC, CHAMONIX

'If I live to be an old man, I shall sit by the fire and looking into the embers see two specks creeping up that vast mountainside, mere microcosms of flesh and blood on the frozen face of Eternity.' The other speck represents Professor Graham Brown.

1929

BROWN, T. GRAHAM. ZERMATT, TRIFTJOCH, TRIFTHORN, ROTHORN, COURMAYEUR, PIC MOORE, ZERMATT, ROTHORN, SCHALLIHORN

'It was Robert Louis Stevenson who wrote of walking tours: "He who is indeed of the brotherhood does not voyage in quest of the picturesque but of certain jolly humours—of the hope and spirit with which the march begins at morning, and the peace and spiritual repletion of the evening's rest". These words might have been written of mountaineering.'

SMITH, GEORGE ADAM. THUN, OBERHOFEN, VISP, ZERMATT

'Exactly forty years from the day that had given us to each other we were again at service in the little mountain chapel.' (RIFFELALP.)

SMITH, JANET ADAM. VISP, ZERMATT, RIMPFISCHHORN, ZNIEBELENHORN

'I looked up and saw the dawn on Monte Rosa:

> Night's candles are burnt out, and jocund day
> Stands tip-toe on the misty mountain-tops.

Here on the Alps I felt that same breathless catch at the heart, that same purity of joy, that I had sometimes known listening to Mozart, or looking at Piero's "Nativity" or Leonardo's "Virgin of the Rocks".'

SMYTHE, FRANK S. JUNGFRAUJOCH, EIGER

'Of the three peaks which overlook the Wengern Alp the Jungfrau is the most beautiful. Her long flowing glaciers, with their network of crevasses, suggest the robes of a Grecian maiden, whilst her dark precipices, friezed with gleaming ice, are symbolical of an unapproachable virginity. The Mönch is more staid: he suggests his name, and stands aloof from the affairs of life, his firm square summit in commune with the stars. And lastly, the "Ogre" springs from the pastures of Grindelwald and the Little Scheidegg in one tigerish sweep of rock and ice.' This was an attempt on the Eiger in January.

WELZENBACH, WILLO. CHAMONIX, LES COURTES, AIGUILLE VERTE, AIGUILLE DE BIONASSAY, GRINDELWALD, MITTELLEGI RIDGE, EIGER, SCHRECKHORN

1930

ALLEN, PERCY STAFFORD. ANNECY, COL DES ARAVIS, CHAMONIX, MARTIGNY, AIGLE, SPIEZ, BASLF

BROWN, T. GRAHAM. ZERMATT, WELLENKUPPE, OBERGABELHORN, DENT BLANCHE, PONTRESINA, PIZ BERNINA, PIZ SCERSCEN, CRASTAGÜZZA, PIZ ARGIENT, PIZ ZUPO, PIZ ROSEG, ZERMATT, TAESCHHORN, BREITHORN

'Even a bad season may give good and enjoyable climbing if you persevere against the weather. . . .'

CHAPMAN, F. SPENCER. DAVOS

Because a friend had been dared to do it but could not climb, Chapman scaled the statue of the naked man in the Kurpark and painted it red from head to foot. As his colour-scheme was criticized he went out the next night and painted it white. But this time he was caught, arrested, and fined £30.

LUNN, ARNOLD. ENGELBERG, JOCH PASS, MEIRINGEN, INTERLAKEN, LAUTERBRUNNEN, MÜRREN

'These Oberland peaks have a personality and a character that is all their own. The mountains of other ranges often suggest mass production in their wearisome repetition of ridge and spire and pyramid, but the Jungfrau, the Eiger and the Wetterhorn were made by hand, "God made them and broke the mould".'

WELZENBACH, WILLO. CHAMONIX, AIGUILLE DU GRÉPON, AIGUILLE DU CHARDONNET, AIGUILLE DE TALÈFRE, GRINDELWALD, GROSS FIESCHERHORN NORTH FACE

1931

BADEN POWELL, LORD. KANDERSTEG

'Up here among the Swiss mountains, in the green valley of Kandersteg, one is very remote from the fuss and hurry of the world. Yet, from where I sit in the flower-decked balcony of this chalet, I can see the flags of twenty two nations waving above the tents, and the camp fires of some three thousand young men gathered here.'

BROWN, T. GRAHAM. CHAMONIX, AIGUILLE DE CHARMOZ, AIGUILLE DU MIDI, TOUR RONDE, MONT MALLET, AIGUILLE DE ROCHEFORT, DENT DU GÉANT, BRENVA ROUTE, MONT BLANC

COPE, JOAN PENELOPE. BEX, VILLARS, VEVEY

'I was thrilled at the jagged snow-patched purple peaks that now came into view—the throthy gorges that rushed between rocks,—and through dark woods of ragged pines. I was even forced to confess to myself at the bottom of the proud little relentless heart of mine, that these grand sights quite surpassed my highest expectations. Of course when we arrived at the Hotel Anglais,—the usual travelling hitch and panic had to happen. . . .'

FAWCETT, DOUGLAS (*c*). ZERMATT, LYSKAMM, UNTERGABELHORN, OBERGABELHORN, VISP, SIERRE, MONTANA, LEUKERBAD, VISP, ZERMATT, MATTERHORN, VISP, BRIG, SIMPLON PASS, GONDO, BRIG, VISP, ZERMATT, VISP, MARTIGNY, CHAMPEX, VISP, ZERMATT, VISP, OBERWALD, GRIMSEL PASS, MEIRINGEN, INTERLAKEN, LAUTERBRUNNEN, MÜRREN

LUNN, ARNOLD. MÜRREN, LAUTERBRUNNEN, KLEINE SCHEIDEGG, GRINDELWALD, GROSSE SCHEIDEGG, MEIRINGEN, MÄGISALP, BRUNIG PASS, HERGISWIL, ENGELBERG, LUCERNE, BASLE

'Dante has summed up in three inimitable lines the character of a perfect ski duet . . . which may be rendered: "neither did our chat retard our pace, nor our speed spoil our discussion, but talking hard we went bravely on, like a ship driven by a fair wind".'

WELZENBACH, WILLO. GENEVA, CHAMONIX, AIGUILLE DE CHARMOZ NORTH FACE

1932

BROWN, T. GRAHAM. CHAMONIX, AIGUILLE DU MOINE, LES DROITES, AIGUILLE DU TACUL, COL DU GÉANT, COURMAYEUR, AIGUILLE BLANCHE DE PEUTERET, PIC ECCLES, MONT BROUILLARD, PEUTERET RIDGE, MONT BLANC, GRANDS MULETS, COL MAUDIT

ICHIKAWA, HARUKO. BASLE, GENEVA, BERNE, INTERLAKEN, LAUTERBRUNNEN, KLEINE SCHEIDEGG, JUNGFRAUJOCH, GRINDELWALD, INTERLAKEN, BRIENZ, LUCERNE, FLUELEN, ANDERMATT, FURKA PASS, OBERGESTELEN, BRIG, VISP, ZERMATT, VISP, MARTIGNY, CHAMONIX, GENEVA

'When I looked down from the square hole cut open in the stone wall upon the Aletsch glacier stretching below, all was white as far as the eye could reach. I felt as if I were peeping out from the window of an airship over the Milky Way in Heaven.' 'No! the Matterhorn is not a mountain. It is a large hatchet made of obsidian that cuts the blue sky.'

OBERSON, GABRIEL. FRIBOURG, MARTIGNY, ORSIÈRES, LA FOULY, TOUR NOIR, COL D'ARGENTIÈRE, CHAMONIX, AIGUILLE DU GRÉPON, MONT BLANC

'A la vitrine du kiosque, une vedette de cinéma évoque étrangement une femme aimée. Un monde de pensées très douces reprennent leur vol. Est-ce mollesse? Ou la montagne est-elle rudesse? L'un et l'autre, mais l'oisiveté ne me laisse pas le choix. Plutôt, ne pourrais-je pas dire que des liens subtils unissent tous les amours! La femme, cruelle par instant, m'enseignera à aimer la pierre, qui souvent m'effraie. Son image apparaîtra sur la cime altière et fera de ce paysage impassible une illustration du cœur. Si haut que je m'élève, la montagne gardera quelque chose d'humain. J'ai évolué, et jeté une nouvelle teinte sur d'antiques visions.'

WELZENBACH, WILLO. LAUTERBRUNNEN, GROSSHORN NORTH FACE, GSPALTENHORN NORTH-EAST FACE, GLETSCHERHORN NORTH-WEST FACE, JUNGFRAU, BREITHORN NORTH FACE

1933

BROWN, T. GRAHAM. ZERMATT, COURMAYEUR, MONT DOLENT, ROUTE MAJOR, COL MAJOR, SELLA HUT, AIGUILLE DE BIONNASSAY, DOME DU GOUTER, MONT BLANC, MONT MAUDIT, COL DU MIDI, COL DU GÉANT, COURMAYEUR, BROUILLARD RIDGE, MONT BLANC, COURMAYEUR, VIA DELLA PERA, MONT BLANC DE COURMAYEUR, MONT BLANC, DOME DU GOUTER, GLACIER DU DOME, COURMAYEUR

The triumphant completion of the Triptych of the Brenva face of Mont Blanc.

WELZENBACH, WILLO. CONSTANCE, ZURICH, LAUSANNE, MARTIGNY, CHAMONIX, AIGUILLE DE ROCHEFORT, GENEVA, MARTIGNY, BRIG, BELALP, NESTHORN NORTH FACE, OBERGESTELEN, GRIMSEL PASS, MEIRINGEN, BRUNIG PASS, LUCERNE, ZURICH, CONSTANCE

1934

SMITH, JANET ADAM. COURMAYEUR, AIGUILLE DE LA BRENVA, DENT DU GÉANT, AIGUILLE DU MIDI, CHAMONIX, AIGUILLE DU GRÉPON, DENT DU REQUIN, COL DU GÉANT, COURMAYEUR

'I knew the delicately balanced sensations of a start in the dark. One impulse draws you towards the climb, the top, the snow, the sun; another pulls you back, away from the cold and dark, into the fuggy warmth and lamplight of the hut. You shiver as you sling on your rucksack at the door of the hut, and the cold feeling in your stomach, the backward pull, does not quite leave you until you climb to the sunlight and are caught up into the full swing and beauty of the day.'

SMYTHE, FRANK S. BLUDENZ, FUORCLA DE CONFIN, KLOSTERS, DAVOS, PARSENN, LANGWIES, AROSA, WEISSHORN, TSCHIERTSCHEN, COIRE, WALLENSTADT, FLUMS, SPITZMEILEN PASS, ELM, RICHETLI PASS, LINTHAL, CLARIDEN PASS, MADERANERTAL, AMSTEG, GURTNELLEN, FELLILÜCKE PASS, OBERALP PASS, ANDERMATT, REALP, ROTONDO, LECKI PASS, FURKA PASS, OBERWALD, BRIG, KANDERSTEG, WILDSTRUBEL, KANDERSTEG, BONDERGRAT, ADELBODEN, HAHNENMOOS PASS, LENK, TRÜTTLISBERG PASS, LAUENEN, GSTAAD, CHÂTEAU D'OEX, MONTREUX

'There is no doubt that constant adherence to "Downhill only" ski-ing will produce a good ski-ing technique in the shortest possible time and that many fine racers have been produced thereby. But what a purgatory to undergo for anyone possessed of a grain of those qualities of pioneering and self-reliance which are reputed to be ingrained in our race. However, as previously suggested, ski-ing in other peoples' grooves is a useful discipline for commercial routine, and it produces a type without which the dictators of this world would have to go out of business.'

1935

OBERSON, GABRIEL. FRIBOURG, BERNE, BRIG, MÜNSTER, GALMIHÜTTE, GALMILÜCKE PASS, FINSTERAARHORNHÜTTE, GROSS WANNEHORN, GRÜNHORNLÜCKE PASS, LÖTSCHENLÜCKE PASS, GOPPENSTEIN

'Et quoi de plus agréable aussi que de glisser sur cette neige rugueuse du matin, dans une pente douce, avec un mouvement uniforme qui, par lui-même, postule devoir se prolonger très longtemps? On se trouve alors dans son élément. On fait du ski, bêtement si l'on veut, puisqu'on ne fait que marcher, mais enfin, on fait du ski. On est dans cette montagne attentive et intime, qui nous serre dans sa vaste solitude comme dans une caresse, qui nous livre à nos méditations et à nos contemplations comme un enfant qui va s'endormir le soir, dans son lit. Et n'est-ce pas des draps que cette vaste étendue blanche avec ses replis, ses creux sinueux et ses pentes uniformes qui déroutent l'optique?'

SMITH, JANET ADAM. COURMAYEUR, AOSTA, GRAND ST. BERNARD PASS, BOURG ST. PIERRE, COMBIN DE VALSOREY, CHANRION, COL DE L'ÉVÊQUE, COL DE BERTOL, COL D'HÉRENS, ZERMATT, MONTE ROSA, VISP, MARTIGNY, CHAMONIX, ST. GERVAIS, COL DE BÉRANGER, DOME DE MIAGE, AIGUILLE DE BIONNASSAY, DOME DU GOUTER, MONT BLANC, AIGUILLE DU GOUTER, ST. GERVAIS

'Here on this highest point of Monte Rosa, I found again that pure shock of joy that is one of the reasons why we climb, but that does not come on every mountain top; when the splendour of the scene and

'God made them and broke the mould'

(Swiss Federal Railways) ARNOLD LUNN, 1930; Interlaken

'On fait du ski, bêtement si l'on veut, puisqu'on ne fait que marcher, mais enfin, on fait du ski'

(*Paul Popper*)

GABRIEL OBERSON, 1935

the pleasure of the climb bring a sudden great sigh of elation, of fulfilment; when tears might come if it were not that they would complicate one's breathing. It is as impossible to recapture this fine shade of delight as it is to recapture those moments of illumination when we see the meaning and pattern of our lives; but we can remember that we have been blessed.'

1936

POWYS, LLEWELYN. LAUSANNE, LANDQUART, DAVOS

'They were really happy days and I do hope we manage to catch something of the spirit of the beautiful valley in our book' (*Swiss Essays*). Powys died at Davos in 1939.

SMITH, JANET ADAM. BREUIL, ST. THEODUL PASS, MATTERHORN, ZERMATT, ROTHORN, ZINAL, SIERRE, MARTIGNY, CHAMONIX

'I tried to realize where we were, not very successfully; our climb had been too natural, and the Matterhorn is a legend.'

1937

GRAVES, CHARLES. BASLE, BADEN, ZURICH, WALLENSTADT, RAGAZ, PFÄFERS, COIRE, LANDQUART, DAVOS, FLUELA PASS, SÜS, TARASP, ZERNEZ, ST. MORITZ, PONTRESINA, ALBULA PASS, FILISUR, TIEFENKASTEL, THUSIS, SAN BERNARDINO PASS, MESOCCO, BELLINZONA, LOCARNO, LUGANO, BELLINZONA, ST. GOTTHARD PASS, ANDERMATT, FLUELEN, LUCERNE, SARNEN, BRUNIG PASS, BRIENZ, INTERLAKEN, GRINDELWALD, KLEINE SCHEIDEGG, LAUTERBRUNNEN, INTERLAKEN, MEIRINGEN, GRIMSEL PASS, OBERGESTELEN, BRIG, VISP, ZERMATT, VISP, MARTIGNY, BEX, VILLARS, AIGLE, COL DE PILLON, GSTEIG, SAANEN, GRUYÈRES, BULLE, FRIBOURG, BERNE, MORAT, MOUDON, VEVEY, LAUSANNE, GENEVA

1938

SMITH, JANET ADAM. AOSTA, GRAND ST. BERNARD PASS, MARTIGNY, VISP, ZERMATT, VISP, VIESCH, EGGISHORN, FINSTERAARHORN, GRÜNHORN, JUNGFRAUJOCH, GRINDELWALD

'Sometimes, in the Alps, you walk on the top of the world, commanding vast prospects over far countries, using mountain ranges as your landmarks; and then, involved in the séracs of an ice-fall, or caught in mist, your world crumples and shrinks to five yards, in which each snow crystal claims your eye.'

YATES, ELIZABETH (*c*). MONTREUX, GSTAAD, LAUENEN, GIFFERHORN, RÜBLI, ZWEISIMMEN, LENK, WILDHORN

'Fingers of light pushed the night aside, making room for a flow of saffron which, pouring over the fleeing clouds, seemed to seize and lift them heavenward, shaking them into fragments, tinting each one with crimson and gold, then dispersing them over the world. When the drama of colour was at an end and the gates of night had opened wide, the sun flamed into the sky—but the broad high wall of the Kirchli screened it from them and only revealed the bars of light which proclaimed another day.'

1939

SMYTHE, FRANK S. CHAMONIX, TRELATÊTE, AIGUILLE DE BÉRANGER, COL DE MIAGE, AIGUILLE DE BIONASSAY, COL DE BIONASSAY, DOME DU GOUTER, MONT BLANC, COL DE LA BRENVA, COL DE LA FOURCHE, TORINO HUT, AIGUILLE DE ROCHEFORT, COL DU GÉANT, COURMAYEUR, COL DE FRESNAY, PIC ECCLES, COL ECCLES, MONT BLANC DE COURMAYEUR, MONT BLANC, CHAMONIX

'Ruskin was right when he wrote that the beauty of mountains is best appreciated from the valleys. He might have said that beauty is better appreciated through inaction than through action. The mountaineer who is interested in getting up and getting down a mountain as expeditiously as possible, and who in the matter of time and speed is concerned only with the competitive aspects of the sport, necessarily misses beauty. The true mountaineer, I affirm, that is the man who climbs mountains for spiritual as well as for physical reasons, is not concerned with haste except in the interests of safety, and likes to spend as many hours as possible on a mountain in order to contemplate the scenery.'

1940

LUNN, ARNOLD. MÜRREN, KLEINE SCHEIDEGG, INTERLAKEN

'The green meadows were powdered by snow-white blossom, but the scented manuscript of Spring and the chorus of mountain torrents in the fullness of their triumphant release from the prison of frost had lost their magic. I looked at the beloved Jungfrau showing through a dust of silver, and felt the stab of fear. If France collapsed, could England save Europe? And I knew that if Europe went down into the pit of Nazi slavery, and if Gauleiters were installed in Grindelwald and Mürren and Interlaken, May torrents might still make music for the Germans, but not for me.

Three parts of Spring's delightful things
—Aye and for me the fourth part too—

would perish if Switzerland died.'

1945

LUNN, ARNOLD. LES VERRIÈRES, NEUCHÂTEL, BERNE, INTERLAKEN, ZERMATT, GRINDELWALD, KLEINE SCHEIDEGG, MÜRREN, HERTENSTEIN, GENEVA, ZURICH, MEIRINGEN

'I hung out of the window awaiting the great moment—and then it came. My eyes sought the horizon. The Oberland was veiled in mist, but the long line of the limestone alps of Fribourg carried the eye southwards to the Dent du Midi, the last snow-covered peak which I saw in 1940, the first to welcome me back. . . .'

TOPOGRAPHICAL SECTION

Dates of visits of travellers to selected places

ADELBODEN

1740 Christen, W.
1777 Müller, J. von.
1858 Stephen, L.
1866 Girdlestone, A. G.
1871 Fox, J. H.
Mercier, J. J. (*c*).
Tuckett, F. F.
1891 Larden, W.
1902 Coulton, G. G.
Hughes, H. P.
Lunn, A.
Widmann, J. V.
1907 Fox, J. H.
Larden, W.
1921 Chamberlain, Sir A.
1934 Smythe, F. S.

ANNIVIERS, VAL D' (ZINAL)

1778 Bourrit, M. T.
1806 Thomas, L.
1812 Schiner, M. (*c*).
1813 Des Loges, C. (*c*).
1828 Michaelis, E. H.
1832 Zeller, C.
1837 Engelhardt, C. M.
1839 Fröbel, J.
1845 Ball, J.
1852 Studer, G.
Ulrich, M.
1857 Hinchliff, T. W.
1859 Fox, J. H.
Mathews, W.
Weilenmann, J. J.
1860 Bonney, T. G.
Jacomb, F. W.
Tuckett, F. F.
1863 Lowder, C.
Rivington, A.
Weilenmann, J. J.
1864 Moore, A. W.
Stephen, L.
Whymper, E.
1865 Whymper, E.
1866 Civiale, A.
Thioly, F.
1867 Stephen, L.
Tyndall, J.
1871 Coolidge, W. A. C.
1872 Javelle, E.
Tuckett, F. F.
1873 Javelle, E.
1874 Bonney, T. G.
1876 Gos, A.
Hornby, E.
Javelle, E.
Macdonald, G.
1877 Conway, M.
Illingworth, J. R.
1878 Illingworth, J. R.
Javelle, E.
1881 Hornby, E.
Javelle, E.
1883 Larden, W.
1884 Larden, W.
1885 Bovet, A.
1886 Tissot, V.
1889 Larden, W.
1890 Norman-Neruda, L.
1891 Godley, A. D.
Norman-Neruda, L.
1892 Marsh, G.
Wherry, G.

1893 Marsh, H.
Mummery, A. F.
Wherry, G.
1894 Whymper, E.
1895 Bonney, T. G.
Lodge, Sir O. (*c*).
1896 Larden, W.
Young, G. W.
1899 Fox, J. H.
Young, G. W.
1900 Young, G. W.
1901 Durham, W. E.
Larden, W.
1904 Durham, W. E.
1905 Kugy, J.
1906 Amery, L. S.
Durham, W. E.
1913 Thompson, S. P.
1916 Lunn, A.
1923 Parker, C. S.
Pilley, D.
1936 Smith, J. A.

AROSA

1806 Salis-Marschlins, K. U. von.
1873 Fox, J. H.
1881 Symonds, J. A.
1884 Symonds, J. A.
1894 Conan Doyle, Sir A.
1911 Powys, L.
1923 Parker, C. S.
1934 Smythe, F. S.

AVERS

1655 Hackaert, J.
1763 Dick, J.
1781 Hacquet, B.
1826 Sennones, Vicomte de.
1833 Heer, O.
1835 Heer, O.
1836 Studer, G.
1844 Parkmann, F.
1859 Studer, G.
1864 Freshfield, D.
1865 Moore, A. W.
1874 Zincke, F. B.
1887 Symonds, J. A.
1899 Larden, W.
1910 Durham, W. E.

BAGNES, VAL DE

1768 Thomas, A. (*c*).
1778 Bourrit, M. T.
1781 Saussure, H. B. de.
1813 Des Loges, C. (*c*).
1815 Charpentier, J. de.
1818 Bridel, P.
Lyell, Sir C.
Stanley, E.
1828 Michaelis, E. H.
1842 Forbes, J. D.
1849 Ulrich, M.
1850 Ulrich, M.
1852 Studer, G.
Ulrich, M.
1855 Kennedy, E. S.
1856 Mathews, W.
1857 Mathews, W.
1858 Studer, G.
Weilenmann, J. J.
1861 Buxton, Sir T. F.
Hardy, J. F.
Tuckett, F. F.
1864 Freshfield, D. W.
1865 Moore, A. W.
Weilenmann, J. J.
1866 Civiale, A.
Weilenmann, J. J.
1867 Weilenmann, J. J.
1872 Dent, C. T.
Tuckett, F. F.

1874 Bonney, T. G.
1875 Bonney, T. G.
1882 Hornby, E.
1884 Larden, W.
1885 Hornby, E.
1887 Larden, W.
1888 Bovet, A.
Purtscheller, L.
1890 Conway, M.
1891 Larden, W.
1893 Marsh, H.
1897 Larden, W.
1898 Larden, W.
1899 Fox, J. H.
1900 Durham, W. E.
Larden, W.
1901 Larden, W.
1902 Larden, W.
1907 Durham, W. E.
1909 Durham, W. E.
1911 Durham, W. E.
Lunn, A.
Roget, F. F.
1923 Pilley, D.
1924 Pilley, D.
Welzenbach, W.
1935 Smith, J. A.

BELALP

1844 Ruskin, J.
1859 Stephen, L.
1861 Godkin, E. L.
Tyndall, J.
1862 Ramsay, A. C.
1863 Jones, H.
1864 Morre, A. W.
Preston-Thomas, H.
Tuckett, F. F.
1865 George, H. B.
Moore, A. W.
Spurgeon, C. H.
1866 Girdlestone, A. G.
Tyndall, J.
1867 Tyndall, J.
1868 Connaught, Duke of.
Coolidge, W. A. B.
1869 Coolidge, W. A. B.
Green, J. R.
Tyndall, J.
1870 Amiel, H. F.
Tyndall, J.
1871 Arnold, M.
Coolidge, W. A. B.
Fox, J. H.
Havergal, F. R.
Tuckett, F. F.
1872 Coolidge, W. A. B.
Tyndall, J.
1873 Zincke, F. B.
1874 Grove, Sir G.
Tuckett, F. F.
Weilenmann, J. J.
1875 Symonds, J. A.
1876 Bancroft, S.
Coolidge, W. A. B.
1877 Tyndall, J.
1881 Bonney, T. G.
Brown, T. E.
1882 Conway, M.
1883 Bonney, T. G.
Cobden-Sanderson, T. J.
Daullia, E.
1885 Fox, J. H.
1886 Tissot, V.
1887 Hall, N.
Purtscheller, L.
1888 Cobden-Sanderson, T. J.
1889 Flower, Sir W. H.
Godley, A. D.
1890 Benson, E. F. & E. W.
Widmann, J. V.
1892 Godkin, E. L.
Marsh, H.
1894 Larden, W.
1897 Lohmüller, W.
1898 Cobden-Sanderson, T. J.
Young, G. W.
1899 Ellacombe, H. N.
Young, G. W.

1900 Young, G. W.
1901 Cobden-Sanderson, T. J.
1902 Cobden-Sanderson, T. J.
Young, G. W.
1903 Cobden-Sanderson, T. J.
1905 Durham, W. E.
1909 Young, G. W.
1910 Lodge, E. C. (*c*).
1911 Cobden-Sanderson, T. J.
1914 Young, G. W.
1923 Pilley, D.
1933 Welzenbach, W.

BINN

1803 Murith, L.
1812 Bernoulli, C.
1813 Rambuteau, C. P. de.
1828 Hugi, F. J.
1841 Desor, E.
1844 Desor, E.
1858 Stephen, L.
1859 Freshfield, Mrs. H.
1860 Bonney, T. G.
1863 Weilenmann, J. J.
1881 Bonney, T. G.
1883 Bonney, T. G.
1886 Conway, M.
1887 Conway, M.
1888 Bovet, A.
1889 Bonney, T. G.
1891 Larden, W.
1893 Larden, W.
1895 Larden, W.
1896 Larden, W.
1898 Larden, W.
1901 Larden, W.
1902 Larden, W.
1904 Larden, W.
1906 Larden, W.
1907 Larden, W.

CHAMONIX

1606 Sales, St. François de.
1669 Le Pays, R.
1690 Aranthon, J. d'.
1727 Sulzbach, Prince of.
1741 Pococke, R.
Stillingfleet, B.
Windham, W.
1742 Martel, P.
1750 Maugiron, Marquis de.
1754 De Luc, J. A.
1760 Saussure, H. B. de.
1761 Saussure, H. B. de.
1762 Rochefoucauld, Duc de la.
1764 Anonymous 2 c.
Saussure, H. B. de.
1765 Desmarest, N.
1766 Bourrit, M. T.
1767 Saussure, H. B. de.
1768 Derby, Countess of.
1769 Bourrit, M. T.
1770 Bourrit, M. T.
Pars, W.
1770 Saussure, H. B. de.
1771 Tremblaye, Ch. de la.
1772 Bordier, A. C.
Bourrit, M. T.
1773 Björnstahl, J. J.
Bourrit, M. T.
Hervey, W.
Moore, J.
1774 Bourrit, M. T.
Ferguson, A.
1775 Blaikie, W.
Bourrit, M. T.
Shuckburgh, Sir G.
1776 Bourrit, M. T.
Coxe, W.
Cozens, J. R.
Roque, M. de la.
Saussure, H. B. de.
1777 Bourrit, M. T.
1778 Pictet, M. A.
Saussure, H. B. de.
Studer, S. E.

1778 Vernet, J.
1779 Bourrit, M. T.
Goethe, J. W.
Martyn, T.
1780 Bourbonne, C. de.
Bourrit, M. T.
Brand, T.
1781 Garcin, J.-L.
La Borde, J. B. de.
Romilly, Sir S.
Saussure, H. B. de.
Towne, F.
1782 Bourrit, M. T.
1783 Beckford, W.
Berry, M.
Bourrit, M. T.
1784 Berry, M.
Bourrit, M. T.
Chenier, A.
La Roche, S. von.
Parsons, W.
Saussure, H. B. de.
Whalley, T. S.
1785 Bourrit, M. T.
Coxe, W.
Saussure, H. B. de.
1786 Bourrit, M. T.
Gersdorf, A. T. von.
Krock, A. H. von.
Pange, J. F. de.
Saussure, H. B. de.
Smith, J. W.
Stanley, Sir J. T.
1787 Beaufoy, M.
Bourrit, M. T.
Dzieduszycki, L. M.
Exchaquet, C. F.
Fontanes, J. A. L. de.
Frenilly, F. A. de.
Michaud, J.
Pennington, T.
Saussure, H. B. de.
Smith, J. E.
Steinbrenner, W. L.
Watkins, T.
Wyttenbach, J. S.
1788 Bourrit, M. T.
1788 Briche, Mme de la.
Cambry, J.
Florian, J. P. C. de.
Matthisson, F.
Meiners, C.
Saussure, H. B. de.
1789 Bourrit, M. T.
McTaggart, Mrs.
Rigby, E.
1790 Augerd, V.
Bourrit, M. T.
Grass, C.
Halem, G. A. von.
Hérault de Séchelles.
Serrant, M. de.
Wordsworth, W.
1791 Block, Baron von.
Bourrit, M. T.
Brun, Mme F.
Gray, R.
Holroyd, M. J.
Jacobi, G. A.
Owen, J.
Webster, Lady.
Wilkinson, J. L.
Wollaston, C. B.
1792 Bourrit, M. T.
Desnoues, A.
Glover, S. (*c*).
La Vallée, J.
Owen, J.
Reichard, H. A. O.
Whaley, T.
1793 Bourrit, M. T.
Dolomieu, D. de.
1794 Dolomieu, D. de.
1795 Bourrit, M. T.
Dolomieu, D. de.
Humboldt, A. von.
Lalande, J.
1797 Bourrit, M. T.
Chenedollé, C. de.
Dolomieu, D. de.
1798 Necker, L. A.
1799 Montgolfier E. A. de.
1800 Buch, L. von.
Cade, G.

1801 Bourrit, M. T.
Candolle, A. P. de.
Dolomieu, D. de.
Matthisson, F.
1802 Bourrit, M. T.
Lemaistre, J. G.
MacNevin, W. J.
Noel, G. T.
Philips, J. B.
Pollen, Col.
Reichard, H. A. O.
Turner, J. M. W.
1803 Bourrit, M. T.
Cazenove, H.
Necker, L. A.
Rumford, Count.
1804 Cazenove, H.
Contat, L.
Kinloch, F.
Schopenhauer, A. & J.
Witte, C.
1805 Bédoyère, H. de la.
Candolle, A. P. de.
Chateaubriand, F. R. de.
1806 Lejeune, Dr.
1807 Constant, R. de.
Irving, P.
Staël, Mme de.
Vigée-Lebrun, Mme.
1810 Benzenberg, J. F.
Ducrest, Mme.
Gottschalk, F.
Josephine, Empress.
Leschevin, P. X.
1811 Custine, A. de.
Reichard, H. A. O.
1812 Bourrit, M. T.
1813 Rambuteau, C. P. de.
1814 Bernard, R. B.
Brewster, Sir D.
Bridges, G. W.
Canning, S.
Caroline, Princess of Wales.
Holland, Sir H.
Marie Louise, Empress.
Milford, J.
Moulinié, C. E. F.
1814 Rogers, S.
Tisdall, J. T. T.
1815 Moulinié, C. E. F.
Romilly, Lady A.
Welden, L. von.
1816 Alison, Sir A.
Byron, Lord.
Clifford, Lady de.
Cockburn, J.
Hagen, F. H. von der.
Hobhouse, J. C.
Murchison, Sir R.
Playfair, J.
Polidori, J. W.
Sedgwick, A.
Shelley, F., Lady.
Shelley, P. B.
Sheppard, J.
Teignmouth, Lord.
Williams, H. W.
1817 Hog, R.
Moulinié, C. E. F.
Raffles, T.
Simond, L.
Southey, R.
Starke, M.
Ticknor, G.
Weston, S.
1818 Alison, Sir A.
Baillie, M.
Hall, B.
Lyell, Sir C.
Matthews, H.
Matzewski, Count.
1819 Anonymous 7.
Brydges, Sir E.
De La Beche, H. T.
Müller, W. L.
Rennie, Sir J.
Rensselaer, J. van.
Undrell, J.
1820 Ampère, J. J.
Bakewell, R.
Digby, K. H. (*c*).
Dornford, J.
Edgeworth, M.
Hamel, Dr.

1820 Montémont, A.
Mountain, A. S. H.
Robinson, H. C.
Wordsworth, D. & W.
1821 Bancroft, G.
Bessborough, Countess of.
Brockedon, W.
Raoul-Rochette, D.
Tennant, C.
1822 Clissold, F.
Duppa, R.
Gallatin, J.
Walsh, Comte T.
1823 Anonymous 8.
Anonymous 8 A.
Chapuys-Montlaville, L. A. de.
Forbes, M.
Jackson, H. H.
Johnson, J.
Sharp, R.
Wilson, D.
1824 Brockedon, W.
Hogg, J.
Lewis, Sir G. C.
Rickman, E. S.
Smith, J.
Uwins, T.
Villeneuve, M. de.
1825 Anonymous 8 B.
Clark, E.
Downes, G.
Hazlitt, W.
Hogg, T. J.
Hugo, V.
Medwin, T.
Murray, J.
Nodier, C.
Sherwill, M.
Stevenson, S. W.
1826 Forbes, J. D.
Necker, L. A.
Walter, W.
1827 Auldjo, J.
Ball, J.
Bertolotti, D.
Carne, J.
1827 Cuchetat, C.
Fellows, C.
Gray, R.
Hawes, W.
Liddiard, W.
Twining, R.
Valéry, M.
Wilkie, Sir D.
1828 Carus, C. G.
Maude, T.
Töpffer, R.
1829 Agassiz, L.
Fée, A. L. A.
Houghton, Lord.
Williams, C. J. B.
1830 Minto, Lord.
Töpffer, R.
Wilbraham, E. B.
1831 Mendelssohn-Bartholdy, F.
1832 Dumas, A.
Engelhardt, C. M.
Forbes, J. D.
1833 Bateman, Mrs.
Dodd, —.
Pixérécourt, G. de.
Ruskin, J.
Wilder, F. (*c*).
1834 Anonymous 9 E.
Barry, M.
Grote, G.
Haussez, Baron L. d'.
Hayward, A.
MacGregor, J.
Sand, G.
Tilly, Comte H. de.
Wilkley, E.
1835 Anonymous 9 B.
Faraday, M.
Roby, J.
Rocca, H. della.
Ruskin, J.
Töpffer, R.
1836 Hall, F. W.
Liszt, F.
Longfellow, H. W.
O'Flanagan, J. R.

1836 Pictet, A.
Sand, G.
Turner, J. M. W.
1837 Albert, Prince Consort.
Anonymous 9 C.
Anonymous 9 D. (*c*).
Atkins, H. M.
1838 Angeville, H. d'.
Callow, W.
Desor, E.
Lamont, M. M. (*c*).
Smith, A.
1839 Bray, Mrs.
Forbes, J. D.
Grant, H. A.
Holmes, Mrs. D.
Malkin, A. T.
Sedgwick, Miss.
1840 Töpffer, R.
1841 Anonymous 10.
Talfourd, T. N.
Vignet, L.
Yates, Mrs. A.
1842 Durbin, J. P.
Forbes, J. D.
Goodwin, H.
Ruskin, J.
Sherman, Mrs.
Töpffer, R.
1843 Argyll, Duke of.
Cotta, B.
Forbes, J. D.
Heugh, H.
Malkin, A. T.
Talfourd, T. N.
1844 Anonymous 10 C.
Buckingham, J. S.
Cairns, J.
Forbes, J. D.
Martins, C.
Roget, P. M.
Ruskin, J.
Snow, R.
Weston, G. F.
1845 Alexander, W.
Cheever, G. B.
Headley, J. T.
1846 Corson, J. W.
Dickens, C.
Forbes, J. D.
Morgan, J. M.
Reade, J. E. (*c*).
Safford, D.
Talfourd, T. N.
Tennyson, Lord A.
1847 Colman, H.
Kohl, J. G.
Noel, B.
Reynolds, H. R.
Trench, F.
1848 Bunbury, Sir C. J. F.
Forbes, J.
Fry, Sir E.
Kirkland, Mrs.
Murchison, Sir R.
1849 Clarke, J. F.
Eliot, G.
Greische, A. S. de.
Ruskin, J.
Smith, A.
1850 Bullard, A. T. J.
Forbes, J. D.
Gray, A.
Patteson, J. C.
Wallace, H. B.
Wills, A.
1851 Dobell, S.
Harrison, F.
Philips, F.
Ruskin, J.
Schlagintweit, A.
Sewell, E. M.
Silliman, B.
Smith, A.
Witmer, T. B. (*c*).
1852 Browne, J. D. H.
Bulwer, J. R.
Felton, C. C.
Ferguson, R.
Ramsay, A. C.
Russell, G.
Wagner, R.
Wills, A.
1853 Chamier, Capt.

1853 Dickens, C.
Doré, G.
Grant, J.
MacGregor, J.
Northbrook, Lord.
Smith, A.
Smith, J. D.
Stowe, H. B.
Wallace, A. R.
White, W.
Wills, A.
Young, J. C.
1854 Blackwell, E. J.
Hall, N.
Hare, A. J. C.
Heathman, W. G.
Hinchliff, T. W.
Hort, F. J. A.
Marsh, G. H.
Raffles, W. W.
Ruskin, J.
Talbot, I. T.
1855 Anderson, E.
Coleman, E. T.
Hawtrey, S.
Heard, G. W.
Hinchliff, T. W.
Hudson, C.
Kennedy, E. S.
Packe, C.
Pumpelly, R.
Tupper, M.
1856 Bonney, T. G.
Bunsen, C.
Butler, H. M.
Catlow, A.
Clowes, G.
Fairbanks, H.
Fox, J. H.
Guthrie, T.
Hinchliff, T. W.
Hort, F. J. A.
Lee, R.
Longman, W.
Mathews, W.
Ruskin, J.
Tuckett, F. F.
1857 Albert Edward, Prince of Wales.
Bremer, F.
Butler, A. J.
Harcourt, W.
Hayden, J.
Hinchliff, T. W.
Huxley, T. H.
Mathews, W.
Mérimée, P.
Richardson, J. W.
Selborne, Lord.
Stephen, L.
Sumner, C.
Trower, F.
Tyndall, J.
Wills, A.
1858 Arundell, I.
Blunt, W. S.
Brooke, S.
Coleman, E. T.
Ducommun, J. C.
Prestwich, Sir J.
Rivington, A.
Ruskin, J.
Tyndall, J.
Vernon, W. W.
1859 Adams, H.
Arnold, M.
Cavour, C.
Fox, J. H.
Gough, J. B.
Hudson, C.
Mathews, W.
Prentiss, E.
Ruskin, J.
Stephen, L.
Tuckett, F. F.
Tyndall, J.
1860 Alarçon, P. de.
Anonymous 10 B.
Benedict, E. C.
Civiale, A.
Gould, E. B.
Napoleon III.
Ruskin, J.
Stillman, W. J.

1860 Tuckett, F. F.
Tyndall, J.
Urlin, F. D.
Whymper, E.
Wigram, W.
1861 Anonymous 11 A.
Hardy, J. F.
Jacomb, F. W.
Lear, E.
Preston-Thomas, H.
Rivington, A.
Stephen, L.
Symonds, J. A.
Tuckett, F. F.
Winkworth, S.
1862 Anonymous 11 B.
Barrow, J.
Chevalier, C.
Jones, H.
Wigram, W.
1863 Astley, J. D.
Browning, O.
Forbes, Mrs. E. A.
Freshfield, D.
Hannington, J.
Hardman, Sir W.
Lowder, C.
Rivington, A.
Ruskin, J
1864 Alston, A. H.
Bonney, T. G.
Browne, G. F.
Cook, T.
Dehansy, C. (*c*).
Freshfield, D. W.
Grove, Sir G.
Harrison, F.
Lowder, C.
Moore, A. W.
Smith, W.
Stephen, L.
Urquhart, D.
Whymper, E.
1865 Bonney, T. G.
Buxton, E. N.
Girdlestone, A. G.
Liddell, A. G. C.
1865 McCormick, J.
Michelet, J.
Moore, A. W.
Rumbold, Sir H.
Whymper, E.
1866 Arnold, H. P.
Brooks, P.
Darley, F. O. C.
Peabody, A. P.
1867 Bellows, H. W.
Guild, C.
Haeseler, C. H.
Russell-Killough, H.
Shaler, N.
Tousey, S.
Vizard, J.
1868 Dowsing, W.
Gautier, T.
Hutton, R. H.
Latrobe, J. H. B.
1869 Coolidge, W. A. B.
Havergal, F. R.
Laporte, A. (*c*).
Roosevelt, T.
Ten Hamme, J. D. de.
Warner, C. D. (*c*).
1870 Brandes, G.
Brooks, P.
Moore, A. W.
1871 Anonymous 12.
Havergal, F. R.
Mercier, J. J. (*c*).
Peake, E.
Stephen, L.
Symonds, J. A.
Wilson, H. S.
1872 Dent, C. T.
Rimsky-Korsakow, N. A.
Tyndall, J.
Wilson, H. S.
1873 Bancroft, S.
Dent, C. T.
Havergal, F. R.
Hughes, H. P.
Lowell, J. R.
Marracks, R. (*c*).
Stephen, L.

1874 Brown, T. E.
Carr, A.
Coolidge, W. A. B.
Grove, Sir G.
Richardson, F.
Ruskin, J.
Stephen, L.
Wilson, H. S.
1875 Bonney, T. G.
Collings, H.
Coolidge, W. A. B.
Symonds, J. A.
1876 Coolidge, W. A. B.
Détré, E.
Havergal, F. R.
Jowett, B.
Symonds, J. A.
Urlin, R. D.
1877 Brooks, P.
Conway, M.
Illingworth, J. R.
Maggs, J.
1878 Burne-Jones, E.
Cook, J.
Dent, C. T.
Hall, N.
Hewat, K.
Twain, Mark.
1879 Symonds, J. A.
1880 Cutler, H. O.
Hall, N.
Mummery, A. F.
Navez, L. (*c*).
1881 Jones, C. A.
Le Mesurier, W. H.
Locke, D. R.
Mummery, A. F.
Rogers, C. K.
1882 Brooks, P.
Collingwood, W. G.
Havergal, M. V. G.
Hornby, E.
Pitman, M. J. (*c*).
1883 Burnaby (Main), Mrs.
Kothari, J. H.
Stock, E.
1884 Daudet, A.
1884 Doukhovskoy, B.
1885 Brooks, P.
Butler, G.
Hornby, E.
Widmann, J. V.
1886 Grün, C.
Güssfeldt, P.
1887 Hort, F. J. A.
Hughes, H. P.
Larden, W.
Leggett, B. F. (*c*).
Meriwether, L. (*c*).
1888 Ruskin, J.
1889 Kugy, J.
1890 Brooks, P.
Conway, M.
Güssfeldt, P.
1891 Montague, C. E.
1892 Brooks, P.
Camus, T.
Fox, F. J.
Mummery, A. F.
Wherry, G.
1893 Fox, J. H.
Marsh, H.
Mummery, A. F.
Wherry, G.
1894 Conway, M.
Fox, J. H.
Mummery, A. F.
Stephen, L.
Whymper, E.
1895 Fox, J. H.
Larden, W.
Wherry, G.
1896 Moulton, L. C. (*c*).
1897 Larden, W.
1898 Ellacombe, H. N.
Fox, J. H.
Parker, J.
1900 Durham, W. E.
Picard, E.
Rimsky Korsakow, A. N.
1901 Larden, W.
1905 Young, G. W.
1906 Fox, J. H.
Young, G. W.

1907 Durham, W. E.
Young, G. W.
1908 Hull, E.
1909 Young, G. W.
1911 Thompson, S. P.
Young, G. W.
1912 Durham, W. E.
Hamilton, H. (*c*).
Young, G. W.
1913 Bagge, H.
Thompson, S. P.
1914 Young, G. W.
1920 Pilley, D.
1922 Pilley, D.
1925 Jackson, E. M.
1927 Brown, T. G.
Smythe, F. S.
1927 Welzenbach, W.
1928 Brown, T. G.
Smythe, F. S.
1929 Welzenbach, W.
1930 Allen, P. S.
Welzenbach, W.
1931 Brown, G.
Welzenbach, W.
1932 Brown, T. G.
Ichikawa, H.
Oberson, G.
1933 Welzenbach, W.
1934 Smith, J. A.
1935 Smith, J. A.
1936 Smith, J. A.
1939 Smythe, F. S.

CHÂTEAU D'OEX (ROSSINIÈRE, ROUGEMONT)

1706 Bodmer, S.
1733 Haller, A. von.
1755 Sinner, E.
1775 Müller, J. von.
1777 Müller, J. von.
1778 Müller, J. von.
Randolph, —.
1779 Bonstetten, K. V. von.
Müller, J. von.
1780 Bridel, P.
1783 Saussure, H. B. de.
1784 Robert, F.
1792 Matthisson, F.
1794 Lascelles, R.
1796 Bridel, L.
1797 Bridel, P.
1799 Bridel, P.
1802 Turner, J. M. W.
1803 Buch, L. von.
1814 Tisdall, J. T. T.
1816 Byron, Lord.
Hobhouse, J. C.
Polidori, J. W.
1822 Walsh, Comte T.
1825 Candolle, A. P. de.
1826 Carne, J.
Latrobe, C. J.
1826 Walter, W.
Wieland, Col.
1828 Michaelis, E. H.
1829 Agassiz, L.
Roger, A. S.
1830 Inglis, H. D.
1831 Mendelssohn-Bartholdy, F.
1835 Haussez, Baron L. d'.
Strutt, Mrs. E.
1839 Holmes, Mrs. D.
1841 Töpffer, R.
1843 Talfourd, T. N.
1846 Wolff, P. E.
1848 Arnold, M.
1852 Drummond, D. T. K.
1854 Heathman, W. G.
Ruskin, J.
1855 Packe, C.
1856 Bremer, F.
Bunsen, C.
Catlow, A. & M.
1857 Tolstoi, L.
1863 Hardman, Sir W.
1868 Hutton, R. H.
1870 Bunsen, Baroness.
1871 Mercier, J. J. (*c*).
1872 Trollope, T. A.

1874 Havergal, F. R.
1885 Widmann, J. V.
1899 Wilkinson, T. E.
1902 Rivett-Carnac, J. H.
Wilkinson, T. E.
1907 Monkswell, M., Lady.
1915 Stravinsky, I.
1924 Oberson, G.
1934 Smythe, F. S.

DAVOS

1754 Walser, G.
1779 Coxe, W.
1790 Heigelin, J. F. (*c*).
1796 Bridel, L.
1806 Salis-Marschlins, K. U. von.
1821 Kasthofer, K.
1822 Kasthofer, K.
1834 Heer, O.
1836 Studer, G.
1861 Freshfield, Mrs. H.
Hardy, J. F.
Kennedy, E. S.
1862 Scheffel, J. V.
Williams, C. J. B.
1864 Tuckett, F. F.
Tuckett, L.
1867 Hutton, R. H.
1869 Yeo, J. B.
1870 Meyer, C. F.
North, M.
1871 Meyer, C. F.
1872 Fox, J. H.
Meyer, C. F.
Tuckett, F. F.
1873 Fox, J. H.
Frankland, E.
1874 Zincke, F. B.
1877 Allbut, Sir T. C.
Symonds, J. A.
1878 Symonds, J. A.
1879 Capper, S. J.
Muddock, J. E.
Nietzsche, F.
Symonds, J. A.
1880 Stevenson, R. L.
Symonds, J. A.
1881 Navez, L.
1881 Stephen, L.
Stevenson, R. L.
Symonds, J. A.
1882 Marcet, W.
Symonds, J. A.
Wise, A. T. T.
1883 Symonds, J. A.
1884 Greg, Mrs.
Symonds, J. A.
Urlin, R. D.
1885 Main, Mrs.
Symonds, J. A.
1886 MacQuoid, G. S.
Symonds, J. A.
1887 Symonds, J. A.
1889 Stephen, L.
Symonds, J. A.
1890 Burton, Sir R.
Fox, J. H.
Norman-Neruda, L.
Oliphant, Mrs.
Symonds, J. A.
1891 Wilkinson, T. E.
1893 Bonney, T. G.
Conan Doyle, A.
Munro, H. ('Saki').
1894 Conan Doyle, A.
1895 Conan Doyle, A.
1901 Widmann, J. V.
Wilkinson, T. E.
1903 Larden, W.
1910 Powys, L.
1911 Powys, L.
1914 Flecker, J. E.
1930 Chapman, F. S.
1934 Smythe, F. S.
1936 Powys, L.
1937 Graves, C.

EGGISHORN

1840 Malkin, A. T.
1842 Studer, G.
1844 Forbes, J. D.
1855 Vignet, L.
1856 Cole, Mrs. H. W.
Hort, F. J. A.
1857 Mathews, W.
1858 Bonney, T. G.
Cole, Mrs. H. W.
Ramsay, A. C.
Tyndall, J.
1859 Barnard, G. (*c*).
Fox, J. H.
Mathews, W.
Stephen, L.
Tuckett, F. F.
1860 Hort, F. J. A.
Tuckett, F. F.
Tyndall, J.
Whymper, E.
Wigram, W.
1861 Ramsay, A. C.
Tyndall, J.
1862 Civiale, A.
Huxley, T. H.
Ramsay, A. C.
Stephen, L.
Tyndall, J.
Wigram, W.
1863 Jones, H.
Lowder, C.
Tyndall, J.
1864 Alston, A. H.
Hardmann, Sir W.
Harrison, F.
Stephen, L.
Tuckett, F. F.
1865 George, H. B.
Girdlestone, A. G.
Hort, F. J. A.
Lyell, Sir C.
Spurgeon, C. H.
1866 Girdlestone, A. G.
Tyndall, J.
1867 Girdlestone, A. G.
1868 Connaught, Duke of.
1870 Brooks, P.
Duff, M. E. Grant.
Moore, A. W.
Stephen, L.
1871 Havergal, F. R.
Jowett, B.
Mercier, J. J. (*c*).
1872 Moore, A. W.
Tuckett, F. F.
Tyndall, J.
Wilson, H. S.
1873 Durham, W. E.
Zincke, F. B.
1874 Urlin, R. D.
1876 Bancroft, S.
Hughes, H. P.
1879 Güssfeldt, P.
1881 Bonney, T. G.
Dubois, A.
1883 Cobden-Sanderson, T. J.
Daullia, E.
1885 Fox, J. H.
1886 Brigg, M. A.
Tissot, V.
1890 Benson, E. W.
Wilkinson, T. E.
1891 Finsler, G.
1892 Marsh, H.
Virieux, E.
Wherry, G.
1893 Marsh, H.
1902 Larden, W.
1904 Young, G. W.
1906 Larden, W.
1914 Lunn, A.
1922 Ker, W. P.
1938 Smith, J. A.

EINSIEDELN

1494 Münzer, J.
1620 Burser, J. (*c*).
1665 Ray, J.
1683 Mabillon, J.
1705 Blainville, M. de.
1722 Saint-Maure, C. M. de.
1747 Stanhope, P.
1751 Anonymous 2 A.
1754 Anonymous 2 A.
1755 Gibbon, E.
1760 Casanova, J.
1763 Schinz, H. R.
1765 Pennant, T.
1775 Goethe, J. W.
Müller, J. von.
1776 Coxe, W.
Küttner, K. G.
1777 Besson, H.
Lenz, J. M. R.
Ramond de Carbonnières, L. E.
1778 Randolph, —.
1781 La Borde, J. B. de.
1782 Afsprung, J. M.
Meiners, C.
1784 Langle, Marquis de.
Mayer, C. J. de.
Robert, F.
Storr, G. K. C.
1786 Braunschweiger, N.
Whalley, T. S.
1787 Matthisson, F.
Steinbrenner, W. L.
1788 Cambry, J.
1789 Sabran, Comtesse de.
1790 Bridel, P.
Halem, G. A. von.
Wordsworth, W.
1791 Wollaston, C. B.
1792 Wynne, E.
1794 Bouterweck, F.
1795 Sabran, Comtesse de.
1796 Bridel, L.
1797 Enghien, Duc d'.
Goethe, J. W.
1801 Hölderlin, F.
1802 MacNevin, W. J.
1807 Schlegel, A. W.
1811 Custine, A. de.
1812 Wahlenberg, G.
1814 Tisdall, J. T. T.
1816 Cockburn, J.
1818 Simond, L.
Waring, S. M.
1820 Raoul-Rochette, D.
1823 Hirzel-Escher, H.
1826 Boddington, Mrs. (*c*).
1827 Carne, J.
Liddiard, W.
1828 Cooper, J. F.
1830 Candolle, A. P. de.
Inglis, H. D.
1831 Mendelssohn-Bartholdy, F.
1832 Cooper, J. F.
1834 Roger, A. S.
1835 Anonymous 9 B.
O'Connor, M.
1836 Töpffer, R.
1838 Veuillot, L.
1845 Cheever, G. B.
Taylor, B.
1847 Kohl, J. G.
Mügge, T.
1848 Murchison, Sir R.
1854 Heathman, W. G.
1856 Bremer, F.
1861 Andersen, H. C.
1862 Chevalier, C.
1869 Laporte, A. (*c*).
1873 Fulton, C. C.
Prime, S. I. (*c*).
Zincke, F. B.
1874 Tuckett, F. F.
1876 Sweeney, J. W.

ENGELBERG

1544 Stumpf, J.
1702 Scheuchzer, J. J.
1706 Scheuchzer, J. J.
1728 Haller, A. von.
1744 Waaser, J. E.
1752 Guettard, J. E. (*c*).
1753 Sinner, F.
1754 Anonymous 2 A.
1761 Gagnebin, A.
1767 Fuessli, J. C.
1776 Cozens, J. R.
1777 Besson, H.
Ramond de Carbonnières, L. E.
1778 Müller, J. von.
1782 Meiners, C.
1784 Chenier, A.
Saussure, H. B. de.
1785 Coxe, W.
Freygrabend, Dr.
1790 Sénancour, E. P. de.
1794 Lascelles, R.
Williams, H. M.
1795 Sabran, Comtesse de.
Sergent-Marceau, A.
1796 Bridel, L.
Tweddell, J.
1797 Enghien, Duc d'.
1811 Custine, A. de.
1812 Wahlenberg, G.
1814 Tisdall, J. T. T.
1820 Ampère, J. J.
Digby, K. H. (*c*).
Wordsworth, D. & W.
1822 Walsh, Comte T.
1824 Raoul-Rochette, D.
1826 Studer, G.
1827 Studer, G.
1831 Mendelssohn-Bartholdy, F.
1832 Dyke, T.
1835 Roger, A. S.
1836 Studer, G.
1837 Drinkwater, Miss.
1839 Gray, A.
1842 Mendelssohn-Bartholdy, F.
1847 Mügge, T.
1851 Wagner, R.
1852 Ferguson, R.
1854 Hare, A.
1856 Longman, W.
1857 Arnold, M.
Mathews, W.
Meyer, C. F.
Quinet, E.
1858 Meyer, C. F.
1859 Freshfield, Mrs. H.
1860 North, M.
1861 Forster, R. W. E.
1862 Rivington, A.
Stephen, L.
1863 Musafir, Capt.
Studer, G.
Symonds, J. A.
1864 Tuckett, F. F.
Tuckett, L.
1865 Acland, Sir H.
Girdlestone, A. G.
Hesse, Grand Duchess of.
Tuckett, L.
1868 Bonney, T. G.
Victoria, Queen.
1869 Fox, J. H.
1873 Hornby, E.
Zincke, F. B.
1874 Plunket, F.
Tuckett, F. F.
1876 Hughes, H. P.
1879 Stephen, L.
1880 Larden, W.
1881 Woolson, C. F.
1882 Marcet, W.
1883 Woolson, C. F.
1884 Fowler, W. W.
1885 Fox, J. H.
Pupin, M.
Vaughan, H.
1886 Smyth, E.

1888 Drummond, H.
1889 Finsler, G.
1890 Tollemache, B. (*c*).
Urlin, R. D.
1891 Rimsky Korsakow, A. N.
Stephen, L.
1903 Larden, W.
Rawnsley, H. D.
1917 Gide, A.
1930 Lunn, A.
1931 Lunn, A.

GRINDELWALD

1620 Hagenbach, J. J. (*c*).
1668 Muralt, J. von.
1690 Coxe, T.
1703 Hottinger, J. H.
1706 Bodmer, S.
1708 Burnet, W.
1709 Scheuchzer, J. J.
1723 Mann, Sir H.
1732 Haller, A. von.
1736 Haller, A. von.
1740 Christen, W.
1748 Altmann, J. G.
1756 Gruner, G. S.
1757 Wyss, R.
1758 Grimm, S. H.
1761 Gagnebin, A.
1763 Andreae, J. G.
1765 Pennant, T.
1766 Hirschfeld, C. C.
1770 Bourrit, M. T.
Pars, W.
Saussure, H. B. de.
1771 Pezay, M. de (*c*).
Tremblaye, Ch. de la.
Wyttenbach, J. S.
1774 De Luc, J. A.
1775 Blaikie, W.
1776 Coxe, W.
Cozens, J. R.
Wyttenbach, J. S.
1777 Besson, H.
Desjobert, L. C. F.
Lenz, J. M. R.
Querini, A.
Ramond de Carbonnières, L. E.
Saussure, H. B. de.
Volta, A.
1778 Bourrit, M. T.
Küttner, K. G.
Randolph, —.
Roque, M. de la.
1779 Goethe, J. W.
Martyn, T.
Studer, G. S.
1780 Heinse, J. J. W.
1781 La Borde, J. B. de.
Nicolai, F.
Storr, G. K. C.
1782 Meiners, C.
Paul, Czarevich.
1784 Guibert, Comte de.
Mayer, C. J. de.
Robert, F.
1785 Coxe, W.
1786 Braunschweiger, N.
Gerdsdorf, A. T. von.
Krock, A. H. von.
Ploucquet, W. G.
1787 Beaufoy, Mrs. M.
Frénilly, F. A. de.
Roland, Mme.
1788 Briche, Mme de la.
Cambry, J.
1789 Condé, Prince de.
Gauthier, Mme de.
Karamsin, N.
Spazier, K.
1790 Grass, C.
Halem, G. A. von.
Wordsworth, W.
1791 Brun, Mme F.
Jacobi, G. A.
Sneedorf, N.
Stollberg, F. N. von.
Wattenwyl, E. von.

1792 Escherny, F. L. d' (*c*).
Reichard, H. A. O.
Wyttenbach, J. S.
1793 Devonshire, Georgiana, Duchess of.
1794 Bouterweck, F.
Lascelles, R.
1795 Sabran, Comtesse de.
1796 Bridel, L.
Hegel, G. W. F.
Leslie, Sir J.
Wedgwood, T.
1797 Baggesen, J. I.
Chenedollé, C. de.
Enghien, Duc d'.
1798 Herbart, J. F.
1800 Bridel, L.
Meisner, F.
1801 Dolomieu, D. de.
Hölder, C. G. von.
1802 Lemaistre, J. G.
Turner, J. M. W.
1803 Rumford, Count.
1805 Yosy, A. (*c*).
1807 Schlegel, A. W.
Vigée-Lebrun, Mme.
1808 Gaudin, J. F. T.
1809 König, F. N.
Uklanski, K. T. von.
1810 Benzenberg, J. F.
1811 Weber, C. M. von.
1812 Chamisso, A. von.
Meyer, G.
Stapfer, P. A. (*c*).
1814 Frederick William III, King.
Genoude, E.
Wyss, J. R.
1815 Canning, S.
1816 Alison, Sir A.
Byron, Lord.
Cockburn, J.
Copplestone, E.
Hobhouse, J. C.
Langton, T.
Murchison, Sir R.
Polidori, J. W.
1816 Sedgwick, A.
Sheppard, J.
1817 Playfair, J.
Reichard, H. A. O.
Simond, L.
Southey, R.
Waring, S. M.
1818 Kent, Duke of.
Lyell, Sir C.
Matthews, H.
1819 Müller, W. L.
Raoul-Rochette, D.
Schultes, G. von.
1820 Bakewell, R.
Colston, M.
Digby, K. H.
Edgeworth, M.
Wordsworth, D. & W.
1821 Alison, Sir A.
1822 Duppa, R.
Mendelssohn-Bartholdy, F.
Walsh, Comte T.
1823 Chapuys Montlaville, L. A. de.
Forbes, M.
Johnson, J.
Wilson, D.
1824 Hogg, J.
Snoeck, C. A.
1825 Downes, G.
Hogg, T. J.
La Trobe, C. J.
Medwin, T.
Murray, J.
Stevenson, S. W.
1826 Anonymous 9.
Boddington, Mrs. (*c*).
Carne, J.
Studer, G.
Walter, W.
1827 Liddiard, W.
Michaelis, E. H.
Stein, C. G. D.
Studer, G.
Twining, R.
1828 Carus, C. G.
Cooper, J. F.

1828 Hugi, F. J.
Rohrdorf, C.
1829 Agassiz, L.
Bunbury, Sir H. E.
1830 Boddington, Mrs.
Hugi, F. J.
Inglis, H. D.
1831 Mendelssohn-Bartholdy, F.
1832 Cooper, J. F.
Dumas, A.
Dyke, T.
Engelhardt, C. M.
Hugi, F. J.
Töpffer, R.
1833 Bateman, Mrs.
Dodd, —.
Stanhope, Earl.
Wilder, F.
1834 Anonymous 9 E.
Barry, M.
MacGregor, J.
Wilkley, E.
1835 Anonymous 9 B.
Calame, A.
Forbes, E.
Roby, J.
Ruskin, J.
Strutt, E.
Töpffer, R.
1836 Cumming, W. F.
Longfellow, H. W.
O'Flanagan, J. R.
Ticknor, G.
1837 Albert, Prince Consort.
Anonymous 9 D. (*c*).
Beddoes, T. L.
Drinkwater, Miss.
1838 Buckland, W.
Callow, W.
Hervey, C.
Hoffmann, G.
Lamont, M. M. (*c*).
Michelet, J.
1839 Bray, Mrs.
Desbarolles, A. (*c*).
Fry, E.
Gray, A.
1839 Holmes, Mrs. D.
Laing, S.
Malkin, A. T.
Studer, G.
1840 Amiel, H. F.
Desor, E.
Maurice, F. D.
Pickering, A. M. W.
Stanley, A. P.
Töpffer, R.
1841 Anonymous 10.
Faraday, M.
Martins, C.
Studer, G.
Talfourd, T. N.
Vogt, C.
Yates, Mrs. A.
1842 Godwin, C. G.
Mendelssohn-Bartholdy, F.
Sherman, Mrs.
1843 Clough, A. H.
Cotta, B.
Desor, E.
Forbes, J. D.
Liddell, H. G.
Malkin, A. T.
1844 Buckingham, J. S.
Roget, P. M.
Turner, J. M. W.
Vignet, L.
Weston, G. F.
1845 Alexander, W.
Cheever, G. B.
Headley, J. T.
Roth, G.
Speer, S. T.
1846 Andersen, H. C.
Corson, J. W.
Kohl, J. G.
Reade, J. E. (*c*).
Ruskin, J.
Shaftesbury, Lord.
Tennyson, Lord.
Wolff, P. E.
1847 Colman, H.
Noel, B. W.
1848 Arnold, M.

1848 Forbes, J.
Murchison, Sir R.
1849 Clarke, J. F.
Coeurderoy, E.
Greische, A. S. de.
Marshall Hall, Mrs.
Smith, A.
Torr, T. S.
Tyndall, J.
1850 Calvert, G. H.
Gray, A.
Wallace, H. B.
1851 Harrison, F.
Schlagintweit, A.
Schurz, C.
Sewell, E. M.
Tappan, H. P.
Witmer, T. B. (*c*).
1852 Duff, M. E. Grant.
Ferguson, R.
Wagner, R.
1853 Chamier, Capt.
Fox, J. H.
Grant, J.
Northbrook, Lord.
Spencer, H.
Stowe, H. B.
1854 Blackwell, E. J.
Fraser, Sir T.
Hare, A. J. C.
Harrison, F.
Heathman, W. G.
Hinchliff, T. W.
Hort, F. J. A.
Wills, A.
1855 Hinchliff, T. W.
Packe, C.
1856 Catlow, A.
Clowes, G.
Fairbanks, H.
Guthrie, T.
Hinchliff, T. W.
Hort, F. J. A.
Huxley, T. H.
Lee, R.
Longman, W.
Tyndall, J.
1857 Albert Edward, Prince of Wales.
Anonymous 11.
Butler, S.
Hayden, J.
Mathews, W.
Quinet, E.
Selborne, Lord.
Tolstoi, L.
1858 Barrington, C.
Bonney, T. G.
Cole, Mrs. H. W.
Ramsay, A. C.
Stephen, L.
Tyndall, J.
Vernon, W. W.
1859 Barnard, G. (*c*).
Civiale, A.
Fox, J. H.
Freshfield, Mrs. H.
Stephen, L.
Studer, G.
Teck, Duchess of.
Tuckett, F. F.
1860 Anonymous 10 B.
Civiale, A.
Gould, E. B.
North, M.
Scheffel, J. V.
Stephen, L.
Tyndall, J.
Williams, C. J. B. (*c*).
1861 Abadie, L. d'.
Anonymous 11 A.
Preston-Thomas, H.
Stephen, L.
Tuckett, F. F.
1862 Alford, H.
Huxley, T. H.
Jones, H.
Kemble, F.
Rivington, A.
Stephen, L.
Tyndall, J.
Wigram, W.
1863 Aeby, C.
Hannington, J.

1863 Hardman, Sir W.
Hare, A. J. C.
Musafir, Capt.
Wigram, W.
1864 Dehansy, C. (*c*).
Girdlestone, A. G.
Moore, R. W.
Stephen, L.
Tuckett, F. F. & L.
1865 Boyd, A. K. H. (*c*).
George, H. B.
Jevons, W. S.
Magee, W. C.
McCormick, J.
Moore, A. W.
Spurgeon, C. H.
1866 Arnold, H. P.
Brahms, J.
Brooks, P.
Moore, A. W.
Peabody, A. P.
Stephen, L.
Tyndall, J.
1867 Bellows, H. W.
Girdlestone, A. G.
Guild, C.
Haeseler, C. H.
Hutton, R. H.
Rumbold, Sir H.
Shaler, N.
Stephen, L.
Tousey, S.
Tyndall, J.
Vizard, J.
Wallace, A. R.
1868 Avebury, Lord.
Brandes, G.
Brown, J.
Coolidge, W. A. B.
Dowsing, W.
Hopkins, G. M.
Latrobe, J. H. B.
Symonds, J. A.
Williams, C. J. B. (*c*).
1869 Butler, G.
Duff, M. E. Grant.
Elliott, J.
1869 Gray, A.
Havergal, F. R.
Laporte, A. (*c*).
Patmore, E. H.
Tennyson, Lord.
Tyndall, J.
1870 Moore, A. W.
Stephen, L.
1871 Anonymous 12.
Arnold, M.
Coolidge, W. A. B.
Fox, J. H.
Mercier, J. J. (*c*).
Peake, E.
Tuckett, F. F.
1872 Butler, S.
Coolidge, W. A. B.
Moore, A. W.
Rimsky Korsakov, N. A.
Trollope, T. A.
Tuckett, F. F.
Urlin, R. D.
Vignet, L.
Wilson, H. S.
Zincke, F. B.
1873 Havergal, F. R.
Hughes, H. P.
Marracks, R. (*c*).
Monkswell, Lady.
Ramsay, A. C.
1874 Carr, A.
Coolidge, W. A. B.
Fiske, J.
Havergal, F. R.
Plunket, F.
1875 Coolidge, W. A. B.
Ritchie, A. T.
Stephen, L.
Wilson, H. S.
1876 Butler, G.
Detré, E.
Stephen, L.
1877 Brooks, P.
Dorigny, C.
Herman, A.
Maggs, J.
Thompson, S. P.

1877 Wilson, C.
1878 Holden, L. C.
Nietzsche, F.
Rumbold, Sir H.
1879 Coolidge, W. A. B.
Güssfeldt, P.
Stephen, L.
1880 Cutler, H. O.
Fox, J. H.
Larden, W.
Navez, L. (*c*).
Sidgwick, H.
1881 Daudet, A.
Jones, C. A.
1883 Butler, G.
Cobden-Sanderson, T. J.
Stock, E.
Thompson, S. P.
1884 Doukhovskoy, B.
1885 Brooks, P.
Butler, G.
Fox, J. H.
1886 Butler, G.
Wilkinson, T. E.
1887 Leggett, B. F. (*c*).
Widmann, J. V.
1888 Butler, G.
Coolidge, W. A. B.
Klucker, C.
Stephen, L.
Wilkinson, T. E.
1889 Finsler, G.
Stephen, L.
1890 Brooks, P.
Coolidge, W. A. B.
Finsler, G.
Widmann, J. V.
1891 Finsler, G.
Fox, J. H.
1892 Brooks, G.
Finsler, G.
Hughes, H. P.
Kugy, J.
1892 Lunn, A.
Lunn, Sir H.
1893 Ellacombe, H. N.
1894 Pumpelly, R.
Whymper, E.
1895 Rivett-Carnac, J. H.
Widmann, J. V.
1896 Smith, J. M.
1897 Hardy, T.
1898 Young, G. W.
1901 Bell, G.
1902 Fox, J. H.
Hughes, H. P.
1903 Fox, J. H.
1904 Fox, J. H.
1905 Durham, W. E.
1906 Larden, W.
1907 Fox, J. H.
Reckitt, M. B.
1910 Durham, W. E.
Lodge, E. C. (*c*).
1911 Bonney, T. G.
Grande, C.
Rose, F. H.
Schuster, C.
1912 Lunn, A.
Young, G. W.
1913 Bagge, H.
1914 Durham, W. E.
Kelper, D. de. (*c*).
1918 Lunn, A.
1921 Chamberlain, Sir A.
Oberson, G.
1923 Lunn, A.
Pilley, D.
1925 Smythe, F. S.
1926 Brown, T. G.
1929 Welzenbach, W.
1930 Welzenbach, W.
1931 Lunn, A.
1937 Graves, C.
1938 Smith, J. A.
1945 Lunn, A.

HÉRENS, VAL D' (AROLLA, EVOLENA)

1768 Thomas, A. (*c*).
1790 Anonymous 5 A
1803 Hölder, G. S. von.
1806 Thomas, L.
1813 Des Loges, C. (*c*).
1828 Michaelis, E. H.
1832 Zeller, C.
1837 Engelhardt, C. M.
1838 Godeffroy, C.
1842 Forbes, J. D.
Töpffer, R.
1843 Malkin, A. T.
1849 Ulrich, M.
1852 Ulrich, M.
1854 Raffles, W. W.
1855 Kennedy, E. S.
1856 Fox, J. H.
Mathews, W.
Tuckett, F. F.
1858 Wills, A.
1859 Weilenmann, J. J.
1860 Jacomb, F. W.
Tuckett, F. F.
1861 Buxton, Sir T. F.
Stephen, L.
1862 Wigram, W.
1864 Moore, A. W.
1865 Lyell, Sir C.
Moore, A. W.
Weilenmann, J. J.
Whymper, E.
1867 Tyndall, J.
Weilenmann, J. J.
1868 Güssfeldt, P.
1869 Girdlestone, A. G.
1870 Coolidge, W. A. B.
1872 Dent, C. T.
1873 Bonney, T. G.
Kemble, F.
1874 Bonney, T. G.
Richardson, F.
1876 Hornby, E.
1877 Conway, M.
Illingworth, J. R.
1878 Javelle, E.
1880 Navez, L. (*c*).
1881 Brown, T. E.
Hughes, H. P.
1882 Larden, W.
1883 Larden, W.
Widmann, J. V.
1884 Larden, W.
1885 Bovet, A.
Hornby, E.
Larden, W.
1886 Huxley, T. H.
Tissot, V.
1887 Huxley, T. H.
Larden, W.
1889 Larden, W.
1892 Gribble, F.
Marsh, H.
1893 Marsh, H.
Whymper, E.
1896 Wherry, G.
1897 Larden, W.
Wherry, G.
1899 Fox, J. H.
Young, G. W.
1900 Bonney, T. G.
Durham, W. E.
Fox, J. H.
Larden, W.
1901 Durham, W. E.
Larden, W.
1902 Larden, W.
1904 Durham, W. E.
Larden, W.
1905 Larden, W.
1906 Amery, L. S.
1909 Durham, W. E.
1911 Durham, W. E.
1912 Durham, W. E.
1913 Durham, W. E.
1914 Durham, W. E.
1921 Pilley, D.
1923 Hadow, G.
Parker, O. S.

1923 Pilley, D.
1924 Pilley, D.
1927 Hadow, G. (*c*).
1927 Pilley, D.
1928 Pilley, D.

JOUX, LAC DE

1728 Haller, A. von.
1732 Haller, A. von.
1736 Seigneux de Correvon, G.
1755 Haller, A. von.
1769 Gorani, J.
1773 Brionne, Comtesse de.
Müller, J. von.
1774 De Luc, J. A.
1775 Blaikie, T.
1776 Coxe, W.
Cozens, J. R.
1778 Randolph, —.
1779 Goethe, J. W.
Gorani, J.
Saussure, H. B. de.
1781 Romilly, Sir S.
1784 Robert, F.
1787 Dzieduszycki, L. M.
1789 Davall, E.
Wyttenbach, J. S.
1794 Lascelles, R.
1803 Hölder, G. C. von.
1805 Candolle, A. P. de.
1814 Bernard, R. B.
1816 Langton, T.
1817 Simond, L.
1818 Waring, S. M.
1819 Moulinié, C. E. F.
1824 Anonymous 8 c.
1827 Stein, C. G. D.
1837 Herbert, H.
1838 Ansted, D. T.
1891 Urlin, R. D.
1897 Cobden-Sanderson, T. J.
1927 Allen, P. S.

LAUTERBRUNNEN

1620 Hagenbach, J. J. (*c*).
1732 Haller, A. von.
1736 Haller, A. von.
1740 Christen, W.
1742 Polier de Bottens.
1756 Gruner, G. S.
Haller, A. von.
1757 Wyss, R.
1758 Grimm, S. H.
1761 Gagnebin, A.
1763 Andreae, J. G.
1765 Pennant, T.
1766 Hirschfeld, C. C. L.
1770 Bourrit, M. T.
Pars, W.
1771 Pezay, M. de (*c*).
Wyttenbach, J. S.
1774 De Luc, J. A.
1776 Coxe, W.
Malesherbe, C. G. de L. de.
Wyttenbach, J. S.
1777 Besson, H.
Desjobert, J. C. F.
Querini, A.
Ramond de Carbonnières, L. E.
Saussure, H. B. de
Volta, A.
1778 Bourrit, M. T.
Küttner, K. G.
Randolph, —.
Roque, M. de la.
Vernet, J.
1779 Goethe, J. W.
Martyn, T.
Studer, G. S.
1780 Heinse, J. J. W.
1781 La Borde, J. B. de.
Storr, G. K. C.
1782 Meiners, C.
1784 Guibert, Comte de.
Mayer, C. J. de.

1784 Robert, F.
1785 Coxe, W.
1786 Braunschweiger, N.
Gersdorf, A. T. von.
Krock, A. H. von.
Ploucquet, W. G.
1787 Beaufoy, Mrs. M.
Frénilly, F. A. de.
Roland, Mme.
1788 Briche, Mme de la.
Cambry, J.
1789 Condé, Prince de.
Gauthier, Mme de.
Karamsin, N.
Spazier, K.
1790 Grass, C.
Halem, G. A. von.
Wordsworth, W.
1791 Block, Baron von.
Brun, Mme F.
Gray, R.
Jacobi, G. A.
Stollberg, F. L. von.
Wattenwyl, E. von.
Wyttenbach, J. S.
1792 Escherny, F. L. d' (*c*).
Reichard, H. A. O.
Wyttenbach, J. S.
1794 Bouterweck, F.
Lascelles, R.
1795 Sabran, Comtesse de.
1796 Bridel, L.
Hegel, G. W. F.
Wedgwood, T.
1797 Baggesen, J. I.
Chênedollé, C. de.
1798 Herbart, J. F.
1800 Meisner, F.
1801 Hölder, C. G. von.
1802 Lemaistre, J. G.
1804 Hegner, U.
1805 Yosy, A. (*c*).
1807 Schlegel, A. W.
Vigée-Lebrun, Mme.
1809 König, F. N.
Uklanski, K. T. von.
1810 Benzenberg, J. F.
1811 Custine, A. de.
Weber, C. M. von.
1812 Chamisso, A. von.
Stapfer, P. A. (*c*).
1814 Brewster, Sir D.
Frederick William III.
Genoude, E.
Marie-Louise, Empress.
Wyss, J. R.
1815 Canning, S.
1816 Alison, Sir A.
Byron, Lord.
Clifford, Lady de.
Cockburn, J.
Hobhouse, J. C.
Platen-Hallermünde, A. von.
Polidori, J. W.
Shelley, F., Lady.
Sheppard, J.
Spohr, L.
1817 Elliott, H.
Playfair, J.
Reichard, H. A. O.
Simond, L.
Waring, S. M.
1818 Kent, Duke of.
Lyell, Sir C.
Matthews, H.
1819 Müller, W. L.
Raoul-Rochette, D.
Schultes, G. von.
1820 Bakewell, R.
Colston, M.
Edgeworth, M.
Wordsworth, D. & W.
1821 Alison, Sir A.
Bancroft, G.
1822 Duppa, R.
Mendelssohn-Bartholdy, F.
Walsh, Comte T.
1823 Chapuys Montlaville, L. A. de.
Forbes, M.
Johnson, J.
Wilson, D.
1824 Hogg, J.

1824 Snoeck, C. A.
1825 Downes, G.
Hogg, T. J.
La Trobe, C. J.
Murray, J.
Stevenson, S. W.
1826 Boddington, Mrs.
Carne, J.
Walter, W.
1827 Cuchetat, C.
Hugi, F. J.
Liddiard, W.
Stein, C. G. D.
Studer, G.
1828 Brown, Y.
Carus, C. G.
Cooper, J. F.
Hugi, F. J.
1829 Agassiz, L.
Bunbury, Sir H.
Hugi, F. J.
1830 Inglis, H. D.
1831 Mendelssohn-Bartholdy, F.
1832 Cooper, J. F.
Dumas, A.
Dyke, T.
Töpffer, R.
1833 Bateman, Mrs.
Dodd, —.
Stanhope, Earl.
Wilder, F. (*c*).
1834 Anonymous 9 E.
MacGregor, J.
Wilkley, E.
1835 Anonymous 9 B.
Calame, A.
Forbes, E.
Lyell, Sir C.
Roby, J.
Ruskin, J.
Strutt, E.
Töpffer, R.
1836 Cumming, W. F.
Longfellow, H. W.
O'Flanagan, J. R.
Ticknor, G.
1837 Albert, Prince Consort.
1837 Anonymous 9 C (*c*).
Anonymous 9 D (*c*).
Drinkwater, Miss.
Sainte-Beuve, C.-A. de
1838 Callow, W.
Hervey, C.
Veuillot, L.
1839 Bray, Mrs.
Desbarolles, A. (*c*).
Gray, A.
Holmes, Mrs. D.
Malkin, A. T.
1840 Amiel, H. F.
Maurice, F. D.
Stanley, A. P.
Studer, G.
Töpffer, R.
1841 Anonymous 10.
Faraday, M.
Talfourd, T. N.
Yates, Mrs. A.
1842 Desor, E.
Godwin, G. C.
Mendelssohn-Bartholdy, F.
Sherman, Mrs.
1843 Cotta, B.
Studer, G.
1844 Buckingham, J. S.
Cairns, J.
Vignet, L.
Weston, G. F.
1845 Alexander, W.
Cheever, G. B.
Headley, J. T.
1846 Andersen, H. C.
Corson, J. W.
Kohl, J. G.
Reade, J. E. (*c*).
Tennyson, Lord.
1847 Colman, H.
Noel, B. W.
1848 Forbes, J.
Kirkland, Mrs.
1849 Clarke, J. F.
Greische, A. S. de.
Smith, A.
Torr, T. S.

1849 Tyndall, J.
1850 Calvert, G. H.
Gray, A.
Torr, J.
Wallace, H. B.
1851 Schurz, C.
Tappan, H. P.
Witmer, T. B. (*c*).
1852 Drummond, D. T. K.
Duff, M. E. Grant.
Ferguson, R.
Vizetelli, H.
Wagner, R.
Wills, A.
1853 Chamier, Capt.
Fox, J. H.
Spencer, H.
Stowe, H. B.
White, W.
1854 Calame, A.
Fraser, Sir T.
Harrison, F.
Heathman, W. G.
Hort, F. J. A.
1855 Hinchliff, T. W.
Packe, C.
1856 Bremer, F.
Catlow, A.
Clowes, G.
Dargaud, J. M.
Fairbanks, H.
Guthrie, T.
Hinchliff, T. W.
Hort, F. J. A.
Huxley, T. H.
Lee, R.
Longman, W.
Roth, R.
Ruskin, J.
Tyndall, J.
1857 Butler, S.
Hayden, J.
Quinet, E.
Richardson, J. W.
1858 Stephen, L.
1859 Barnard, G. (*c*).
Civiale, A.
1859 Fellenberg, E. von.
Fox, J. H.
Freshfield, Mrs. H.
Mathews, W.
Stephen, L.
Teck, Duchess of.
Weilenmann, J. J.
1860 Anonymous 10 B.
North, M.
Scheffel, J. V.
Tyndall, J.
Whymper, E.
Williams, C. J. B. (*c*).
1861 Abadie, L. d'.
Anonymous 11 A.
1862 Alford, H.
Chevalier, C.
Desbarolles, A.
Jones, H.
Kemble, F.
Rivington, A.
1863 Ferguson, F.
Forbes, E. A.
Hannington, J.
Hardman, Sir W.
Hare, A. J. C.
Musafir, Capt.
Symonds, J. A.
Wilberforce, S.
1864 Dehansy, C. (*c*).
Moore, A. W.
Stephen, L.
Tuckett, F. F.
Tuckett, L.
1865 George, H. B.
Jevons, W. S.
Lançon, X.
Spurgeon, C. H.
Tyndall, J.
Whymper, E.
1866 Brahms, J.
Brooks, P.
Peabody, A. P.
Ruskin, J.
Stephen, L.
Symonds, J. A.
Tyndall, J.

1867 Bellows, H. W.
Girdlestone, A. G.
Guild, C.
Tousey, S.
Tyndall, J.
Vizard, J.
Wallace, A. R.
1868 Avebury, Lord.
Dowsing, W.
Latrobe, J. H. B.
Symonds, J. A.
Ten Hamme, J. D. de.
Williams, C. J. B. (*c*).
1869 Butler, G.
Gray, A.
Havergal, F. R.
Laporte, A. (*c*).
Patmore, E. H.
Tennyson, Lord.
1870 Moore, A. W.
Ruskin, J.
Trollope, T. A.
1871 Anonymous 12.
Arnold, M.
Grove, Sir G.
Mercier, J. J. (*c*).
Tuckett, F. F.
Wilson, H. S.
1872 Butler, S.
Gos, A.
Rimsky Korsakow, N. A.
Trollope, T. A.
Vignet, L.
Zincke, F. B.
1873 Bancroft, S.
Fulton, C. C.
Havergal, F. R.
Hughes, H. P.
Lowell, J. R.
Marracks, R. (*c*).
Monkswell, Lady.
Ramsay, A. C.
1874 Brown, T. E.
Carr, A.
Coolidge, W. A. B.
Fiske, J.
Plunket, F.
1875 Bancroft, S.
Collings, H.
Coolidge, W. A. C.
1876 Cowell, E. B.
Détré, E.
Havergal, F. R.
Stephen, L.
Sweeney, J. N.
1877 Brooks, P.
Herman, A.
Maggs, J.
Thompson, S. P.
1878 Holden, L. C.
MacFarren, W.
Rumbold, Sir H.
1880 Benson, E. F. & E. W.
Browning, O.
Cutler, H. O.
Fox, J. H.
Larden, W.
Woolson, C. F.
1881 Jones, C. A.
1882 Havergal, M. V. G.
1883 Brooks, P.
Butler, G.
Cobden-Sanderson, T. J.
1884 Hare, A. J. C.
1886 Brahms, J.
1887 Brahms, J.
Klucker, C.
Leggett, B. F. (*c*).
Widmann, J. V.
1888 Coolidge, W. A. B.
Wilkinson, T. E.
1889 Bovet, A.
1890 Coolidge, W. A. B.
1891 Finsler, G.
Fox, J. H.
1892 Brooks, P.
1893 Ellacombe, H. N.
1894 Lodge, E. C.
1895 Wallace, A. R.
Widmann, J. V.
1896 Smith, J. M.
1897 Hardy, T.
1898 Young, G. W.
1903 Hamilton, C.

1903 Rawnsley, H. D.
1905 Durham, W. E.
1910 Lodge, E. C. (*c*).
1911 Rose, F.
Schuster, C.
1912 Durham, W. E.
1913 Bagge, H.
1914 Durham, W. E.
Kelper, D. de (*c*).
1918 Lunn, A.
1923 Lunn, A.
Parker, C. S.
1928 Hadow, G.
1930 Lunn, A.
1931 Lunn, A.
1932 Ichikawa, H.
Welzenbach, W.
1937 Graves, C.

LENK

1562 Platter, F.
1740 Christen, W.
1777 Müller, J. von.
1804 Bridel, P.
1812 Yosy, A.
1826 La Trobe, C. J.
1837 Drinkwater, Miss.
1855 Hinchliff, T. W.
1857 Hinchliff, T. W.
1858 Stephen, L.
1859 Freshfield, Mrs. H.
1865 Bonney, T. G.
1866 Girdlestone, A. G.
1868 Tyndall, J.
1871 Fox, J. H.
Mercier, J. J. (*c*).
Tuckett, F. F.
1872 Moore, A. W.
1882 Widmann, J. V.
1892 Marsh, H.
1902 Widmann, J. V.
1908 Lunn, A.
1913 Durham, W. E.
1934 Smythe, F. S.
1938 Yates, E. (*c*).

LÖTSCHEN VALLEY

1514 Platter, T.
1811 Meyer, J. R.
1829 Brunner, S.
Hugi, F. J.
1840 Malkin, A. T.
1850 Ulrich, M.
1854 Harrison, F.
Hort, F. J. A.
1859 Mathews, W.
Stephen, L.
Tuckett, F. F.
Weilenmann, J. J.
1863 Studer, G.
1864 Moore, A. W.
Tuckett, F. F.
1865 Moore, A. W.
Whymper, E.
1866 Girdlestone, A. G.
Tyndall, J.
1867 Tyndall, J.
1868 Avebury, Lord.
1870 Moore, A. W.
Stephen, L.
1871 Coolidge, W. A. B.
1874 Weilenmann, J. J.
1878 Dent, C. T.
1884 Zsigmondy, E.
1886 Tissot, V.
1887 Klucker, C.
1888 Bovet, A.
1889 Godley, A. D.
1891 Finsler, G.
1892 Marsh, H.
Wherry, G.
1894 Conway, M.
Larden, W.
1895 Wherry, G.
1896 Larden, W.

1905 Durham, W. E.
Lamprell, W. E. (*c*).
1906 Larden, W.
1909 Lunn, A.
Roget, F. F.
1911 Schuster, C.
1914 Young, G. W.
1922 Hadow, G.
1927 Pilley, D.
1928 Hadow, G.

LUGNEZ VALLEY (VALS, VRIN)

1726 Gesner, J.
1789 Placidus à Spescha.
1803 Buch, L. von.
1812 Escher, H. C.
1820 Placidus à Spescha.
1833 Walsh, Comte T. (*c*).
1834 Heer, O.
1835 Heer, O.
1839 Desbarolles, A.
1864 Alston, A. H.
1869 Tuckett, F. F.

MAGGIA, VAL (BIGNASCO, FUSIO)

1783 Saussure, H. B. de.
1795 Bonstetten, C. V. von.
1808 Gaudin, J. F. T.
1812 Escher, H. C.
1864 Freshfield, D.
1874 Freshfield, D.
Tuckett, F. F.
1876 Butler, S.
1878 Butler, S.
1887 Bovet, A.
Butler, S.
Conway, M.
1889 Johnston, Sir H.
1892 Widmann, J. V.

MÜRREN

1814 Wyss, J. R.
1843 Studer, G.
1846 Kohl, J. G.
Reade, J. F. (*c*).
1854 Harrison, F.
1859 Barnard, G. (*c*).
Fellenberg, E. von.
Fox, J. H.
Freshfield, Mrs. H.
1860 Whymper, E.
Williams, C. J. B. (*c*).
1862 Hort, F. J. A.
Jones, H.
Rivington, A.
1863 Symonds, J. A.
Wilberforce, S.
1864 Tuckett, F. F.
Tuckett, L.
1865 Jevons, W. S.
1866 Brahms, J.
Symonds, J. A.
1867 Vizard, J.
1868 Avebury, Lord.
Symonds, J. A.
1869 Butler, G.
Gray, A.
Havergal, F. R.
Sidgwick, H.
Symonds, J. A.
Tennyson, Lord.
1871 Grove, Sir G.
Mercier, J. J. (*c*).
Symonds, J. A.
Tuckett, F. F.
1873 Havergal, F. R.
1874 Brown, T. E.
1875 Bancroft, S.
Collings, H.
Stephen, L.
1876 Cowell, E. B.
1877 Wilson, C.
1878 MacFarren, W.

1880 Benson, E. F. & E. W.
Browning, O.
Cutler, H. O.
Fox, J. H.
Woolson, C. F.
1881 Jones, C. A.
Nicoll, Lady R.
Stephen, L.
1883 Brooks, P.
Butler, G.
Cobden-Sanderson, T. J.
1884 Hare, A. J. C.
1886 Brahms, J.
1887 Brahms, J.
Jones, J. V.
Meyer, C. F.
1888 Butler, H. M.
1889 Bovet, A.
1891 Fox, J. H.
Stanley, H. M.
1893 Ellacombe, H. N.
1903 Hamilton, C.
Rawnsley, H. D.
1907 Monkswell, Lady.
1912 Durham, W. E.
1914 Durham, W. E.
Young, G. W.
1918 Lunn, A.
1924 Lunn, Sir H.
1925 Schuster, C.
1930 Lunn, A.
1931 Fawcett, D. (*c*).
Lunn, A.
1940 Lunn, A.
1945 Lunn, A.

PONTRESINA

1549 Vergerio, P. P.
1556 Magny, O. de.
1656 Reresby, Sir J.
1786 Tscharner, J. B. von.
1790 Heigelin, J. F.
1812 Buch, L. von.
1834 Heer, O.
1835 Heer, O.
1841 Töpffer, R.
1846 Rey, W.
1851 Scheffel, J. V.
1853 Wagner, R.
1856 Witte, K.
1857 Binet-Hentsch, J. L.
Studer, G.
Weilenmann, J. J.
1859 Studer, G.
1861 Freshfield, Mrs. H.
Hardy, J. F.
Hort, F. J. A.
Kennedy, E. S.
Milman, A.
1863 Browning, O.
Buxton, E. N.
Civiale, A.
Fox, J. H.
1863 Martins, C.
Studer, G.
Tuckett, F. F.
1864 Freshfield, D.
Gaskell, Mrs.
Hardman, Sir W.
Jones, H.
Musafir, Capt.
North, M.
Symonds, J. A.
Tuckett, F. F.
Tuckett, L.
Tyndall, J.
Vignet, L.
Weilenmann, J. J.
1865 Civiale, A.
Girdlestone, A. G.
Güssfeldt, P.
Moore, A. W.
Tuckett, F. F.
Weilenmann, J. J.
1866 Brooks, P.
Harrison, F.
Meyer, C. F.
Preston-Thomas, H.
Tuckett, F. F.

1867 Bellows, H. W.
Bonney, T. G.
Browning, O.
Girdlestone, A. G.
Hesse, Grand Duchess of.
Hutton, R. H.
Meyer, C. F.
Michelet, J.
1868 Bonney, T. G.
Lowder, C.
1869 Fox, J. H.
Gray, A.
Güssfeldt, P.
Tuckett, F. F.
Williams, C. J. B.
1870 Brooks, P.
Duff, M. E. Grant.
Meyer, C. F.
1871 Jowett, B.
Tollemache, L.
Tyndall, J.
1872 Crawford, F. M.
Fox, J. H.
Güssfeldt, P.
Ramsay, Sir J.
1873 Andersen, H. C.
Bonney, T. G.
Guild, C.
Tennyson, Lord.
1874 Plunket, F.
Richardson, F.
Zincke, F. B.
1875 Hort, F. J. A.
Liégeard, S.
Lloyd, F.
Maxwell, Sir H.
1876 Conway, M.
1877 Allbutt, Sir T. C.
Bancroft, S.
Güssfeldt, P.
Kemble, F.
Waterhouse, T.
1878 Bancroft, S.
Güssfeldt, P.
Meyer, C. F.
1879 Bancroft, S.
Browning, O.
1879 Güssfeldt, P.
Meyer, C. F.
1880 Arnold, H. P. (*c*).
Arnold, M.
Bancroft, S.
Bonney, T. G.
Lyttelton, E.
1881 Bancroft, S.
Butler, G.
Smiles, S.
1882 Bancroft, S.
Marcet, W.
Symonds, J. A.
1883 Hort, F. J. A.
1884 Butler, H. M.
Butler, S.
Greg, Mrs. W.
Güssfeldt, P.
Hall, N.
Main, Mrs.
Urlin, R. D.
1885 Güssfeldt, P.
Larden, W.
Symonds, J. A.
1886 Segantini, G.
Tissot, V.
1887 Güssfeldt, P.
1889 Fox, J. H.
1890 Finsler, G.
Fox, J. H.
Norman-Neruda, L.
Teck, Duchess of.
1891 Benson, E. F. & E. W.
1892 Kugy, J.
1893 Bonney, T. G.
1894 Teck, Duchess of.
1898 Durham, W. E.
1899 Durham, W. E.
Larden, W.
1901 Widmann, J. V.
1904 Cobden-Sanderson, T. J.
1910 Durham, W. E.
1921 Röntgen, W. C.
1923 Jackson, E. M.
1930 Brown, T. G.
1937 Graves, C.

RIGI

1742 Sulzer, J. G.
1775 Goethe, J. W.
1780 Heinse, J. J. W.
1782 Afsprung, J. M.
Meister, L. (*c*).
1787 Frenilly, F. A. de.
1789 Grob, G. (*c*).
1795 Brun, Mme F.
1796 Bridel, L.
1801 Hölder, C. G. von.
1802 MacNevin, W. J.
1805 Reichard, H. A. O.
1807 Schlegel, A. W.
1811 Reichard, H. A. O.
Roger, A. S.
Weber, C. M. von.
1812 Wahlenberg, G.
1814 Marie Louise, Empress.
Tisdall, J. T. T.
1816 Alison, Sir A.
Langton, T.
Platen-Hallermünde, A. von.
Shelley, F., Lady.
1817 Elliott, H.
Hegner, U.
Playfair, J.
Simond, L.
Southey, R.
1818 Lyell, Sir C.
Matthews, H.
1819 Müller, W. L.
Raoul Rochette, D.
Schultes, G. von.
1820 Colston, M.
Coulmann, J. J.
Robinson, H. C.
Wordsworth, D. & W.
1821 Corrie, G. E.
Tennant, C.
1822 Duppa, R.
Walsh, Comte T.
1823 Wilson, D.
1824 Hogg, J.
1824 Rickman, E. S.
Snoeck, C. A.
1825 Anonymous 8 B.
Downes, G.
Hogg, T. F.
La Trobe, C. J.
Murray, J.
Sherer, M.
Stevenson, S. W.
1826 Anonymous 9.
Töpffer, R.
1827 Cuchetat, C.
Fellows, C.
Gray, R.
Hawes, W.
Liddiard, W.
Michaelis, E. H.
1828 Carus, C. G.
Cooper, J. F.
1829 Agassiz, L.
Hugi, F. J.
1830 Boddington, Mrs.
Engelhardt, C. M.
1831 Mendelssohn-Bartholdy, F.
Morse, S. F. B.
1832 Dumas, A.
Dyke, T.
1833 Dodd, —.
Wilder, F. (*c*).
1834 Anonymous 9 E.
Wilkley, E.
1835 Anonymous 9 B.
Holmes, O. W.
Roby, J.
Ruskin, J.
1836 Longfellow, H. W.
Meyer, C. F.
O'Flanagan, J. R.
1837 Albert, Prince Consort.
Anonymous 9 D (*c*).
Beddoes, T. L.
Drinkwater, Miss.
Murray, J.
1838 Hervey, C.

1839 Gray, A.
Hugo, V.
Laing, S.
1840 Amiel, H. F.
Töpffer, R.
1841 Anonymous 10.
Baring-Gould, S.
1842 Sherman, Mrs.
1844 Cairns, J.
Weston, G. F.
1845 Cheever, G. B.
Headley, J. T.
1846 Corson, J. W.
Leland, C. G.
Tennyson, Lord.
1847 Kohl, K. G.
Noel, B. W.
Reynolds, H. R.
1848 Forbes, J.
Kirkland, Mrs.
1849 Clarke, J. F.
Cotta, B.
Greische, A. S. de.
Smith, A.
Tyndall, J.
1850 Scheffel, J. V.
Wagner, R.
Wallace, H. B.
1851 Harrison, F.
Schlagintweit, A.
Sewell, E. M.
1852 Felton, C. C.
Ferguson, R.
1853 Fox, J. H.
Grant, J.
MacGregor, J.
Spencer, H.
Stowe, H. B.
1854 Fraser, Sir T.
Heathman, W. G.
Hinchliff, T. W.
Hort, F. J. A.
1855 Dora d'Istria, Countess.
Hawtrey, S.
Tupper, M.
1856 Bremer, F.
Clowes, G.
1856 Dargaud, J. M.
Fairbanks, H.
Hinchliff, T. W.
Lee, R.
Longman, W.
1857 Catlow, A.
Quinet, E.
Richardson, J. W.
Tolstoi, L.
1858 Bonney, T. G.
Mérimée, P.
Meyer, C. M.
Rivington, A.
1859 Wagner, R.
1860 Schönbein, C. F.
1861 Anonymous 11 A.
1862 Alford, H.
Chevalier, C.
Desbarolles, A.
Jones, H.
Kemble, F.
1863 Forbes, E. A.
1864 Alston, A. H.
Dehansy, C. (*c*).
Elliott, H.
Lowder, C.
McTear, R.
Racowitza, H. von.
Smith, W.
1865 Hesse, Grand Duchess of.
Jevons, W. S.
1866 Brooks, P.
Peabody, A. P.
1867 Battersea, C.
Bellows, H. W.
Guild, C.
Haeseler, C. H.
Hardwick, C.
Hutton, R. H.
1868 Brandes, G.
Latrobe, J. H. B.
Ten Hamme, J. D. de.
Victoria, Queen.
1869 Butler, G.
Havergal, F. R.
Laporte, A. (*c*).
Symonds, J. A.

1870 Howitt, M.
1872 Byers, S. H. M.
Conway, M.
Rimsky Korsakow, N. A.
1873 Bancroft, S.
Conrad, J.
Fulton, C. C.
Havergal, F. R.
Marracks, R. (*c*).
Zincke, F. B.
1874 Bancroft, S.
Fiske, J.
Ritz, C.
1875 Bancroft, S.
Collings, H.
Wills, M. H.
1876 Bancroft, S.
Détré, E.
Müller, G.
Sweeney, J. N.
1877 Dorigny, C. (*c*).
Herman, A.
Maggs, J.
1878 Cook, J.
Hewat, K.
1878 Holden, L. C.
Twain, Mark.
1879 Byers, S. H. M.
Harte, B.
Trollope, T. A.
1880 Cutler, H. O.
1881 Locke, D. R.
1883 Bithray, E. (*c*).
1884 Doukhovskoy, B.
1885 Pupin, M.
Vaughan, H.
1886 Brigg, M. A.
Grün, C.
1887 Leggett, B. F. (*c*).
1890 Meyer, C. F.
1894 Butler, S.
1896 Moulton, L. C. (*c*).
Smith, J. M.
1900 Butler, S.
1910 Lodge, E. C. (*c*).
1911 Rose, F. H.
1913 Bagge, H.
1914 Kelper, D. de (*c*).
1927 Laughlin, C. E.

SAAS

1768 Thomas, A. (*c*).
1795 Thomas, A.
1802 Buch, L. von.
1803 Murith, L.
1809 Gaudin, J. F. T.
1821 Charpentier, J. de.
1822 Hirzel Escher, H.
1825 Brockedon, W.
1828 Michaelis, E. H.
Sauvan, M.
1829 Brunner, S.
1830 Minto, Lord.
1831 Roger, A. S.
1833 Roger, A. S.
Viridet, M.
1835 Engelhardt, C. M.
1836 Engelhardt, C. M.
1837 Necker, L. A.
1839 Studer, B.
1840 Calame, A.
Engelhardt, C. M.
Malkin, A. T.
1841 Engelhardt, C. M.
Forbes, J. D.
1842 Engelhardt, C. M.
Forbes, J. D.
1847 Ulrich, M.
1848 Engelhardt, C. M.
Ulrich, M.
1849 Engelhardt, C. M.
Ulrich, M.
1850 Engelhardt, C. M.
Ulrich, M.
1852 Studer, G.
Ulrich, M.
Wills, A.
1853 Wills, A.
1854 Hort, F. J. A.

1854 Wills, A.
1855 Hawtrey, S.
1856 Cole, Mrs. H. W.
Hinchliff, T. W.
Malkin, A. T.
Tuckett, F. F.
1858 Barnard, G. (*c*).
Rivington, A.
Stephen, L.
Tyndall, J.
1859 Stephen, L.
1860 Bonney, T. G.
Freshfield, Mrs. H.
North, M.
Stephen, L.
1861 Hardy, J. F.
Stephen, L.
Tuckett, F. F.
Tyndall, J.
Winkworth, S.
1862 Civiale, A.
Laveleye, E. de.
Tyndall, J.
1863 Jones, H.
Studer, G.
1864 Freshfield, D.
Harrison, F.
Preston-Thomas, H.
Stephen, L.
1866 Stephen, L.
Tyndall, J.
1867 Russell-Killough, H.
Williams, C. J. B. (*c*).
1868 Elliott, J.
Tyndall, J.
1870 Dent, C. T.
Stephen, L.
1871 Coolidge, W. A. B.
Dent, C. T.
Mercier, J. J. (*c*).
1872 Butler, S.
Moore, A. W.
Zincke, F. B.
1874 Bonney, T. G.
Weilenmann, J. J.
1874 Wilson, H. S.
1876 Hort, F. J. A.
Jowett, B.
Symonds, J. A.
1882 Bovet, A.
Javelle, E.
1884 Main, Mrs.
1885 Hort, F. J. A.
Larden, W.
1886 Larden, W.
1887 Larden, W.
Lyttelton, E.
1889 Larden, W.
1890 Butler, S.
1891 André, A.
Bonney, T. G.
Wherry, G.
1892 Hort, F. J. A.
Wherry, G.
1893 Fox, J. H.
Larden, W.
Marsh, H.
1896 Larden, W.
1898 Cobden-Sanderson, T. J.
Wherry, G.
1899 Fox, J. H.
1900 Fox, J. H.
Young, G. W.
1901 Bonney, T. G.
1902 Fox, J. H.
Larden, W.
1903 Durham, W. E.
1904 Larden, W.
1909 Durham, W. E.
1910 Thompson, S. P.
1911 Durham, W. E.
1913 Durham, W. E.
1917 Gide, A.
1921 Pilley, D.
1922 Ker, W. P.
1923 Parker, C. S.
1924 Hadow, G.
1925 Hadow, G.
1926 Hadow, G.
1928 Pilley, D.

ST. MORITZ (AND SILS)

1535 Paracelsus.
1703 Scheuchzer, J. J.
1707 Scheuchzer, J. J.
1726 Gesner, J.
1750 Walser, G.
1774 Pilati di Tassullo, C. A.
1779 Coxe, W.
1781 Hacquet, B.
Pol, L.
1787 Frénilly, L. A. de.
1790 Heigelin, J. F. (*c*).
1796 Bridel, L.
1806 Meyer, D.
1812 Buch, L. von.
Gaudin, J. F. T.
1822 Kasthofer, K.
1826 Sennones, Vicomte de.
1830 La Trobe, C. J.
Manzoni, G.
1832 Roger, A. S.
1833 Heer, O.
1834 Mayr, J. H.
1836 Studer, G.
1838 Meyer, C. F.
1841 Töpffer, R.
1846 Rey, W.
1849 Cotta, B.
1853 Wagner, R.
1854 Orsini, F.
1857 Binet-Hentsch, J. L.
1858 Marcet, W.
1859 Studer, G.
Weilenmann, J. J.
1861 Freshfield, Mrs. H.
1862 Studer, G.
Williams, C. J. B.
1863 Browning, O.
Civiale, A.
Martins, C.
Tuckett, F. F.
1864 Freshfield, D.
Hardman, Sir W.
Jones, H.
Musafir, Capt.
North, M.
1864 Tuckett, F. F.
Tuckett, L.
Tyndall, J.
Vignet, L.
1865 Civiale, A.
1866 Brooks, P.
Freshfield, D.
Meyer, C. F.
1867 Bellows, H. W.
Bonney, T. G.
Hesse, Grand Duchess of.
Meyer, C. F.
Michelet, J.
1868 Bonney, T. G.
Lowder, C.
1869 Fox, J. H.
Leaf, W.
Stephen, L.
Tuckett, F. F.
Williams, C. J. B.
Yeo, J. B.
1870 Hutton, R. H.
1872 Urlin, R. D.
1873 Guild, C.
Tennyson, Lord.
1874 Lowder, C.
Plunket, F.
Richardson, F.
Zincke, F. B.
1875 Liégeard, S.
Lloyd, F.
1876 Coolidge, W. A. B.
Jowett, B.
1877 Kemble, F.
Waterhouse, T.
1878 Bancroft, S.
Meyer, C. F.
Rumbold, Sir H.
1879 Bancroft, S.
Browning, O.
Meyer, C. F.
Nietzsche, F.
1881 Bancroft, S.
Butler, G.
Ramsay, A. C.

1881 Urlin, R. D.
1882 Klucker, C.
1883 Hort, F. J. A.
Nietzsche, F.
Widmann, J. V.
1884 Bancroft, S.
Browning, R.
Butler, S.
Main, Mrs.
Nietzsche, F.
Urlin, R. D.
1885 Brooks, P.
Nietzsche, F.
1886 Nietzsche, F.
Segantini, G.
Story, W. W.
Tissot, V.
1887 Browning, R.
Klucker, C.
Nietzsche, F.
Teck, Duchess of.
1888 Browning, O.
Klucker, C.
1889 Symonds, J. A.
Teck, Duchess of.
1890 Burton, Sir R.
Finsler, G.
Larden, W.
Le Blond (Main), Mrs.
Symonds, J. A.
Teck, Duchess of.
1892 Brooks, P.
1893 Bonney, T. G.
Teck, Duchess of.
1894 Cook, T. A.
Johnston, Sir H.
1896 Teck, Duchess of.
1897 Le Blond (Main), Mrs.
1904 Cobden-Sanderson, T. J.
Widmann, J. V.
1910 Durham, W. E.
1918 Nijinsky, V.
1923 Jackson, E. M.
1926 Klucker, C.
1937 Graves, C.

SIXT

1765 De Luc, J. A.
1766 Saussure, H. B. de.
1770 De Luc, J. A.
1772 De Luc, J. A.
1775 Blaikie, W.
1794 Dolomieu, D. de.
1827 Bertolotti, D.
1830 Töpffer, R.
1837 Töpffer, R.
1839 Studer, B.
1844 Ruskin, J.
1857 Mathews, W.
Wills, A.
1858 Barnard, G. (*c*).
1858 Wills, A.
1859 Hudson, C.
1860 Freshfield, Mrs. H.
1861 Buxton, Sir T. F.
Hardy, J. F.
Jacomb, F. W.
1864 Bonney, T. G.
1868 Hutton, R. H.
1871 Fox, J. H.
Tuckett, F. F.
1885 Bonney, T. G.
1891 Monkswell, Lady.
1898 Virieux, E.

ZERMATT VALLEY

1524 Tschudi, A. (*c*).
1620 Burser, J. (*c*).
1765 Thomas, A. & P.
1766 Ricou, J. D.
1789 Saussure, H. B. de.
1792 Schleicher, J. C.
1795 Thomas, A.
1800 Cade, G.
1803 Murith, L.
Necker, L. A.

1809 Gaudin, J. F. T.
1813 Rambuteau, C. P. de.
1815 Charpentier, J. de.
1820 Gay, J.
1821 Welden, L. von.
1822 Hirzel-Escher, H.
1825 Brockedon, W.
1827 Brunner, S.
1828 Michaelis, E. H.
Sauvan, M.
1830 Minto, Lord.
Roger, A. S.
1833 Roger, A. S.
Viridet, M.
1835 Engelhardt, C. M.
Shuttleworth, R. J.
1836 Brunner, S.
Engelhardt, C. M.
1837 Engelhardt, C. M.
Necker, L. A.
1838 Engelhardt, C. M.
1839 Desor, E.
Engelhardt, C. M.
Studer, B.
1840 Calame, A.
Malkin, A. T.
1841 Engelhardt, C. M.
Forbes, J. D.
1842 Forbes, J. D.
Töpffer, R.
1843 Olivier, J.
1844 Dupin, J. P.
Ruskin, J.
1845 Ball, J.
1847 Ulrich, M.
1848 Engelhardt, C. M.
Forbes, J.
Ulrich, M.
1849 Engelhardt, C. M.
Herzen, A.
Marshall Hall, Mrs.
Ruskin, J.
Ulrich, M.
1850 Cole, Mrs. H. W.
Wagner, R.
Wills, A.
1851 Engelhardt, C. M.
1851 Harrison, F.
Schlagintweit, A.
1852 Bulwer, J. R.
Duff, M. E. Grant.
Studer, G.
Ulrich, M.
Wills, A.
1853 Fox, J. H.
Spencer, H.
Wills, A.
1854 Hare, A. J. C.
Heathman, W. G.
Hinchliff, T. W.
Hort, F. J. A.
Raffles, W. W.
Shand, A. (*c*).
1855 Engelhardt, C. M.
Hawtrey, S.
Hinchliff, T. W.
Hudson, C.
Kennedy, E. S.
Weilenmann, J. J.
1856 Butler, H. M.
Clowes, G.
Cole, Mrs. H. W.
Fox, J. H.
Hinchliff, T. W.
Huxley, H.
Longman, W.
Malkin, A. T.
Mathews, W.
Tuckett, F. F.
1857 Arnold, M.
Forster, R. W. E.
Harcourt, W.
Hinchliff, T. W.
Lyell, Sir C.
Selborne, Lord.
1858 Arnold, M.
Barnard, G. (*c*).
Blunt, W. S.
Bonney, T. G.
Fayrer, Sir J.
Ramsay, A. C.
Rivington, A.
Stephen, L.
Tyndall, J.

1858 Wills, A.
1859 Bonney, T. G.
Fox, J. H.
Mathews, W.
Stephen, L.
Tuckett, F. F.
Weilenmann, J. J.
1860 Bonney, T. G.
Fox, J. H.
Freshfield, Mrs. H.
Gould, E. B.
Hort, F. J. A.
Jacomb, F. W.
North, M.
Owen, Sir R.
Stephen, L.
Thioly, F.
Tuckett, F. F.
Whymper, E.
1861 Bonney, T. G.
Buxton, Sir T. F.
Civiale, A.
Guthrie, T.
Hardy, J. F.
Jacomb, F. W.
Preston-Thomas, H.
Ramsay, A. C.
Rivington, A.
Stephen, L.
Tuckett, F. F.
Tyndall, J.
Winkworth, S.
1862 Barrow, J.
Jones, H.
Kemble, F.
Kennedy, T. S.
Laveleye, E. de.
Stephen, L.
Whymper, E.
Wigram, W.
1863 Freshfield, D.
Harrison, F.
Lowder, C.
Rivington, A.
Weilenmann, J. J.
Whymper, E.
Wilberforce, S.
1864 Alston, A. H.
Freshfield, D.
Girdlestone, A. G.
Harrison, F.
Lowder, C.
Moore, A. W.
Preston-Thomas, H.
Stephen, L.
Whymper, E.
1865 Girdlestone, A. G.
Güssfeldt, P.
Hall, N.
Hort, F. J. A.
Lyell, Sir C.
McCormick, J.
Moore, A. W.
Tyndall, J.
Whymper, E.
1866 Arnold, H. P.
Darley, F. O. C.
Stephen, L.
Thioly, F.
Whymper, E.
1867 Bellows, H. W.
Russell-Killough, H.
Shaler, N.
Stephen, L.
Tuckett, F. F.
Tyndall, J.
1868 Connaught, Duke of.
Elliott, J.
Gautier, T.
Güssfeldt, P.
Hopkins, G. M.
Tyndall, J.
1869 Coolidge, W. A. B.
Girdlestone, A. G.
Gray, A.
Laporte, A. (*c*).
Tyndall, J.
Warner, C. D. (*c*).
Wilson, H. S.
1870 Brooks, P.
Coolidge, W. A. C.
Dent, C. T.
Javelle, E.
Moore, A. W.

1870 Stephen, L.
1871 Brooke, S.
Coolidge, W. A. C.
Dent, C. T.
Havergal, F. R.
Javelle, E.
Jowett, B.
Mercier, J. J. (*c*).
Wilson, H. S.
1872 Conway, M.
Coolidge, W. A. B.
Dent, C. T.
Fawcett, H.
Javelle, E.
Moore, A. W.
Stephen, L.
Weilenmann, J. J.
Wilson, H. S.
Zincke, F. B.
1873 Bonney, T. G.
Durham, W. E.
Javelle, E.
Monkswell, Lady.
Weilenmann, J. J.
Wilson, H. S.
1874 Bonney, T. G.
Carr, A.
Gos, A.
Javelle, E.
Richardson, F.
Tuckett, F. F.
Weilenmann, J. J.
Whymper, E.
Wilson, H. S.
1875 Bonney, T. G.
Hornby, E.
Illingworth, J. R.
Marcet, W.
1876 Brooke, S.
Butler, G.
Coolidge, W. A. B.
Hornby, E.
Jowett, B.
Queensberry, Lord.
Wilson, H. S.
1877 Brooks, P.
Conway, M.
1877 Illingworth, J. R.
Thompson, S. P.
Wilson, H. S.
1878 Conway, M.
Javelle, E.
Twain, Mark.
1879 Güssfeldt, P.
Jersey, Countess of.
Mummery, A. F.
1880 Conway, M.
Fox, J. H.
Mummery, A. F.
Navez, L. (*c*).
1881 Conway, M.
Dubois, A.
Güssfeldt, P.
Hornby, E.
Jones, C. A.
Roosevelt, T.
1882 Conway, M.
Güssfeldt, P.
Hornby, E.
1883 Bancroft, S.
Burnaby (Main), Mrs.
Larden, W.
Smith, G. A.
1884 Butler, G.
Larden, W.
Main, Mrs.
Purtscheller, L.
Zsigmondy, E.
1885 Benson, E. W.
Bovet, A.
Hornby, E.
Parkhurst, C. H. (*c*).
1886 Brigg, M. A.
Güssfeldt, P.
Kugy, J.
Larden, W.
Tissot, V.
Urlin, R. D.
1887 Güssfeldt, P.
Klucker, C.
Larden, W.
Leggett, B. F. (*c*).
MacQuoid, G. S.
Mummery, A. F.

1887 Stephen, L.
Stock, E.
1888 Lyttelton, E.
Widmann, J. V.
1889 Benson, E. F. & E. W.
Bonney, T. G.
Güssfeldt, P.
Hall, N.
Hogg, Q.
Larden, W.
Pennell, J.
Ratti, A.
Smith, L. A.
Wilkinson, T. E.
1890 Camus, T.
Conway, M.
Hort, F. J. A.
Norman-Neruda, L.
Widmann, J. V.
1891 André, A.
Godley, A. D.
Grove, Sir G.
Hall, N.
Norman-Neruda, L.
Smith, G. A.
Wherry, G.
1892 Marsh, H.
Wherry, G.
1893 Benson, E. W.
Fox, J. H.
Larden, W.
Lodge, Sir O.
Marsh, H.
Wherry, G.
Whymper, E.
1894 Amery, L. S.
Conway, M.
Fox, J. H.
Hall, N.
Mummery, A. F.
Thompson, S. P.
Whymper, E.
1895 Wherry, G.
Whymper, E.
1896 Larden, W.
Smith, J. M.
1897 Hall, N.
1897 Hardy, T.
Smyth, E.
Wherry, G.
1898 'Field, M.'
Larden, W.
1900 Young, G. W.
1901 Durham, W. E.
1902 Larden, W.
1903 Durham, W. E.
Hamilton, C.
1904 Bell, G.
Larden, W.
1905 Kugy, J.
Larden, W.
Young, G. W.
1906 Amery, L. S.
Durham, W. E.
Kugy, J.
Larden, W.
Young, G. W.
1907 Young, G. W.
1910 Lodge, E. C. (*c*).
Wickham, E. C.
Young, G. W.
1911 Durham, W. E.
Roget, F. F.
Rose, F. M.
1912 Malby, R. A.
Young, G. W.
1913 Durham, W. E.
1914 Grande, J.
Lunn, A.
Young, G. W.
1916 Lunn, A.
1917 Lunn, A.
1920 Lunn, A.
1921 Pilley, D.
1922 Ker, W. P.
1923 Parker, C. S.
Pilley, D.
Welzenbach, W.
1924 Welzenbach, W.
1925 Jackson, E. M.
Welzenbach, W.
1926 Welzenbach, W.
1927 Hadow, G. (*c*).
1928 Brown, T. G.

1928 Pilley, D.
1929 Brown, T. G.
Smith, G. A.
Smith, J. A.
1930 Brown, T. G.
1931 Fawcett, D. (*c*).
1932 Ichikawa, H.
1935 Smith, J. A.
1936 Smith, J. A.
1937 Graves, C.
1938 Smith, J. A.
1945 Lunn, A.

ALPHABETICAL SECTION

Names of travellers, with bibliographical references to their works, and the dates of their travels

ABADIE, L. D'. *Trente jours de voyage en Suisse*, Paris, s.d.; **1861.**

ACLAND, SIR HENRY. *A Memoir*, J. B. Atlay, London, 1903; **1865.**

ADAM OF USK. *Chronicon*, edited by E. M. Thompson, London, 1904; **1402.**

ADAMS, HENRY. *Letters*, London, 1930; **1859, 1870, 1872.**

ADAMS, MRS. MARIAN. *Letters of Mrs. Henry Adams*, edited by W. Thoron, London, 1937; **1872.**

ADDISON, JOSEPH. *Remarks on several parts of Italy etc.*, London, 1745; **1702.** *Letters of Joseph Addison*, edited by W. Graham, Oxford, 1941; **1702.**

AEBY, CHRISTOPH. *Das Hochgebirge von Grindelwald*, Coblenz, 1865; **1863.**

AFSPRUNG, JOHANN MICHAEL. *Reise durch einige Cantone der Eidgenossenschaft*, Leipzig, 1784; **1782.**

AGASSIZ, JEAN LOUIS RODOLPHE. *Life, Letters & Works*, J. Marcou, New York, 1896; **1836.** *United Services Journal*, 50, 1846; **1845.**

AGASSIZ, L. *A Journey to Switzerland*, London, 1833; **1829.**

AISSÉ, MLLE. *Lettres*, Paris, 1943; **1729.**

ALARÇON, PEDRO ANTONIO DE. *De Madrid a Napoles*, Madrid, 1886; **1860.**

ALBERT, PRINCE CONSORT. *The early years of the Prince Consort*, C. Grey, London, 1867; **1837.**

ALBERT DE STADE. 'Urkunden und Regesten zur Geschichte des St. Gotthardweges', H. von Liebenau. *Archiv für schweizerische Geschichte*, 19, p. 280, 1874; **1236.**

ALBERT EDWARD, PRINCE OF WALES. *The Boyhood of a Great King*, A. M. Broadley, London, 1906; **1857.**

ALCOTT, LOUISA MAY. *Her life, letters and journals*, edited by E. D. Cheney, London, 1889; **1865, 1870.**

ALEARDI, A. *Epistolario*, Verona, 1879; **1848.**

ALEXANDER, WILLIAM LINDSAY. *Switzerland and the Swiss churches*, Glasgow, 1846; **1845.**

ALFORD, H. *Life, journals & letters*, London, 1873; **1862.**

ALISON, SIR ARCHIBALD. *Some account of my life. An Autobiography*, Edinburgh, 1883; **1816, 1818, 1821.**

ALLBUTT, SIR THOMAS CLIFFORD. 'On Davos as a health resort', *The Lancet*, ii. 1877; **1877.**

ALLEN, P. S. *Letters*, Oxford, 1939; **1920, 1922, 1923, 1924, 1926, 1927, 1928, 1930.**

ALLSTON, WASHINGTON. *Life and Letters*, J. B. Flagg, London, 1893; **1804.**

ALSOP, C. M. *Memorials*, M. Braithwaite, London, 1881; **1846.**

ALSTON, ALFRED HENRY. *Ready, o ready*, London, 1873; **1864.**

ALTMANN, JOHANN GEORG. *Versuch einer historischen und physikalischen Beschreibung der Helvetischen Eisbergen*, Zurich, 1751; **1748.**

AMERY, LEOPOLD S. *Days of fresh air*, London, 1939; **1894, 1906.**

AMIEL, HENRI FRÉDÉRIC. *Fragment d'un journal intime*, Genève, 1922; **1867, 1870.** *La jeunesse d'H. F. Amiel*, B. Bouvier, Paris, 1935; **1840, 1841.**

AMPÈRE, JEAN-JACQUES. *Correspondance et Souvenirs*, Paris, s.d.; **1820.**

ANDERSEN, HANS CHRISTIAN. *The Story of My Life*, Boston, 1880; **1833, 1846, 1852, 1855, 1860, 1861, 1862.** *Biography*, R. Nisbet Bain, London, 1895; **1833, 1873.**

ANDERSON, EUSTACE. *Chamouni and Mont Blanc*, London, 1856; **1855.**

ANDRÉ, A. *Sur nos monts.* Genève, 1895; **1891.**

ANDREAE, JOHANN GERHARD. *Briefe aus der Schweiz nach Hannover geschrieben*, Zürich & Winterthur, 1776; **1763.**

ANGELO, H. *Reminiscences*, London, 1830; **1827.**

ANGEVILLE, HENRIETTE D'. 'Le carnet vert', V. Augerd, *Revue Alpine*, 6, 1900; **1838.**

ANONYMOUS 1. *Zeitschrift für Kulturgeschichte*, 4 Ser., 2, 272; **1492.**

ANONYMOUS 1 A. 'De Bienne à Genève à travers le Pays de Vaud', *Revue Historique Vaudoise*, 10, 1902; **1747.**

ANONYMOUS 2. *Voiage historique et politique de Suisse, d'Italie et d'Allemagne*, Francfort, 1736; **1720.**

ANONYMOUS 2 A. 'Zur schweizer Turistik im 18. Jahrhundert', A. Bruckner, *Die Alpen*, 7, 1931; **1751, 1754.**

ANONYMOUS 2 B. 'Zur schweizer Turistik im 18. Jahrhundert', A. Bruckner, *Die Alpen*, 7, 1931; **1754.**

ANONYMOUS 2 C. 'Premiers voyages à Chamouni', H. Ferrand, *Revue Alpine*, 18, 103, 1912; **1764.**

ANONYMOUS 3. 'Voyage en Suisse dont je dédie le récit à un personnage bizarre que je ne nomme pas', publié par C.-E. Engel, *Die Alpen*, 17, 1941; **1768.**

ANONYMOUS 4. *Excursions into Normandy and Brittany, up the Loire to Orleans, and Paris, from thence to Dijon, Besançon and Basle, through Switzerland, Geneva, and Lyons, to Paris, Calais and Dieppe*, London 1774; *circ.* **1774.**

ANONYMOUS 5. 'Anmerkungen auf einer Reise durch Savien und Rheinwald', *Der Sammler*, 5, 115, 1783; *c.* **1782.**

ANONYMOUS 5 A. In *La Suisse et ses amis*, C.-E. Engel, 196, Neuchâtel, 1943; **1790.**

ANONYMOUS 6. *A sketch of modern France in a series of letters to a lady of fashion. Written in the years 1796 and 1797 during a tour through France. By a Lady*, edited by E. L. Moody, London, 1798; **1796.**

ANONYMOUS 7. *Quinze jours en Suisse. Promenades d'un jeune peintre français dans les Cantons du midi*, Paris, 1822; **1819.**

ANONYMOUS 7 A. *Mementoes historical and classical, of a tour through parts of France, Switzerland, and Italy*, London, 1824; **1821.**

ANONYMOUS 7 B. *Journal of a Tour in France, Switzerland, and Lombardy, . . .*, Brentford & London, 1821; **1818.**

ANONYMOUS 8. *A tour to Great St. Bernard, and round Mont Blanc*, London, 1827; **1823.**

ANONYMOUS 8 A. *A tour through part of France, Switzerland and Italy*, London, 1827; *c.* **1823.**

ANONYMOUS 8 B. *Lion hunting; or a summer's ramble through parts of Flanders, Germany, and Switzerland*, Edinburgh, 1826; **1825.**

ANONYMOUS 8 C. *Edward and Alfred's Tour in France and Switzerland*, London, 1826; **1824.**

ANONYMOUS 9. *Voyage épisodique et anecdotique dans les Alpes par un parisien*, Paris, 1830; **1826.**

ANONYMOUS 9 A. *Souvenirs de voyage*, Paris, 1834; **1832, 1833.**

ANONYMOUS 9 B. *Journal de voyage d'un collégien*, Paris, 1837; **1835.**

ANONYMOUS 9 C. *Notes abroad and rhapsodies at home*, London, 1837; *c.* **1837.**

ANONYMOUS 9 D. *A traveller's thoughts*, London, 1837; *c.* **1837.**

ANONYMOUS 9 E. *A peep at the Continent: or six weeks' tour through parts of Belgium, Rhenish Prussia, Savoy, Switzerland and France*, Dublin, 1835; **1834.**

ANONYMOUS 10. In *A tour in Switzerland*, W. Chambers, Edinburgh, 1842; **1841.**

ANONYMOUS 10 A. *Recollections of General Garibaldi: or travels from Rome to Lucerne*, London, 1861; **1857.**

ANONYMOUS 10 B. *The summer tour of an invalid*, London, 1860; **1860.**

ANONYMOUS 10 C. *A three weeks' tour in Savoy and Switzerland*, Geneva, 1844; **1844.**

ANONYMOUS 11. *Travels in Switzerland, Italy and Dalmatia, by a lady*, Hastings, 1862; **1857.**

ANONYMOUS 11 A. *The Yankee Boy from home*, New York, 1864; **1861.**

ANONYMOUS 11 B. *Autumn rambles. By a lady*, Rochdale, 1863; **1862.**

ANONYMOUS 12. *A peep at the mountains: the journal of a lady*, Leicester n.d.; **1871.**

ANONYMOUS 13. *A Briton abroad*, London, 1878; *c.* **1878.**

ANSTED, D. T. *Scenery, Science and Art*, London, 1854; **1838.**

ARANTHON D'ALEX, V. *Vie*, Lyon, 1699; **1690.**

ARGYLL, GEORGE DOUGLAS, DUKE OF. *Autobiography and Memoirs*, London, 1906; **1843, 1844.**

ARNAUD, HENRI. *Histoire de la glorieuse rentrée*, n.p., 1710; **1689.**

ARNOLD, HOWARD PAYSON. *European Mosaic*, Boston, 1864; *c.* **1864.** *The Great Exhibition*, Boston, 1868; **1866.** *Gleanings from Pontresina*, Boston, 1880; *c.* **1880.**

ARNOLD, MATTHEW. *Matthew Arnold and France*, H. E. Sells, Cambridge, 1935; **1846.** *Letters of Matthew Arnold to Arthur Hugh Clough*, edited by H. F. Lowry, London, 1932; **1848, 1849.** *Letters of Matthew Arnold*, edited by G. H. E. Russell, London, 1895; **1857, 1858, 1859, 1865, 1871, 1880.**

ARNOLD, THOMAS. *Life and Correspondence*, edited by A. P. Stanley, London, 1844; **1829, 1839, 1840.**

ARRIVABENE, GIOVANNI. *Memorie della mia vita*, Firenze, 1874; **1838.**

ARUNDELL, ISABEL. *Sir Richard Burton's Wife*, J. Burton, London, 1942; **1858.** *The Romance of Isabel Lady Burton*, London, 1897; **1858.**

ASTLEY, SIR JOHN DUGDALE. *Fifty Years of My Life*, London, 1894; **1847, 1863.**

ATKINS, HENRY MARTIN. *Ascent to the Summit of Mont Blanc*, London, 1838; **1837.**

AUGERD, VICTOR. *Une excursion à Chamonix en 1790*, Bourg-en-Bresse, 1886; **1790.**

Alphabetical Section

AULDJO, JOHN. *Narrative of an Ascent to the Summit of Mont Blanc*, London, 1828; **1827.**

AVEBURY, LORD. *Life of Sir John Lubbock*, H. G. Hutchinson, London, 1914; **1868.**

BACHELIN, A. *Un jour au Creux du Van*, Neuchâtel, 1866; **1866.**

BADEN-POWELL, LORD. *Biography*, E. E. Reynolds, Oxford, 1942; **1931.**

BAGGE, HENRY. *Switzerland revisited by an Artist and an Author*, London, n.d.; **1913.**

BAGGESEN, JENS IMMANUEL. *Parthenais*, Hamburg, 1803; **1797.**

BAILLIE, MARIANNE. *First Impressions on a Tour on the Continent*, London, 1819; **1818.**

BAKEWELL, ROBERT. *Travels Comprising observations made during a residence in the Tarentaise and various parts of the Grecian and Pennine Alps and in Switzerland and Auvergne*, London, 1823; **1820.**

BAKUNIN, MICHAEL. *Michael Bakunin*, E. H. Carr, London, 1937; **1867, 1869, 1870, 1872, 1873, 1876.** *Michel Bakounine*, H. E. Kaminski, Paris, 1938; **1843, 1868, 1874.**

BALE, JOHN. *Acta Romanorum Pontificorum*, Basileae, 1558; **1553.**

BALL, B. L. *Three days on the White Mountains*, Boston, 1856; **1850.**

BALL, JOHN. 'Zermatt in 1845', *Peaks, Passes, and Glaciers*, London, 1859; **1845.** 'Obituary of John Ball', Proceedings of Royal Geographical Society. *Geographical Journal*, 1890; **1827.**

BALZAC, HONORÉ DE. In *Voyageurs illustres en Suisse*, C. Gos, Berne, 1937; **1832, 1836.** *Lettres à l'étrangère*, Paris, 1906; **1833, 1836, 1837.** 'Balzac à Genève', G. J. Aubry, *Revue de Paris*, 1 Avril, 1935; **1833, 1836, 1837, 1846.**

BANCROFT, G. *Life & Letters*, New York, 1908; **1821.**

BANCROFT, SQUIRE. *Mr. & Mrs. Bancroft on and off the Stage*, London, 1888; **1873, 1874, 1875, 1876, 1877, 1878, 1879, 1880, 1881, 1882, 1883, 1884.**

BARING-GOULD, S. *Early reminiscences 1834–64*, London, 1923; **1841.**

BARKER, SIR H. *Leaves from my Life*, London, 1927; *c.* **1902,** *c.* **1905.**

BARNARD, GEORGE. *Drawing from Nature*, London, 1865; *c.* **1858,** *c.* **1859.**

BARRÈS, JEAN-BAPTISTE. *Souvenirs d'un officier de la Grande Armée*, Paris, 1923; **1805.**

BARRINGTON, CHARLES. *Alpine Journal*, 11, 1882; **1858.**

BARROW, J. *Expeditions on the glaciers, including an ascent of Mont Blanc, Monte Rosa, Col du Géant*, London, 1864; **1862.**

BARROW, JOHN. *Tour in Austrian Lombardy, the Northern Tyrol and Bavaria*, London, 1841; **1840**

BARRY, MARTIN. *Ascent to the Summit of Mont Blanc*, London, 1838; **1834.**

BATEMAN, MRS. *A Summer's Tour through Belgium, up the Rhine and to the Lakes of Switzerland*, London, 1834; **1833.**

BATTERSEA, CONSTANCE, *Reminiscences*, London, 1922; **1867.**

BAUHIN, CASPAR. In *Historia stirpium Helvetiae*, A. von Haller, Bernae, 1768; **1577.**

BAUHIN, JOHANN. In *Historia stirpium Helvetiae*, A. von Haller, Bernae, 1768; **1563.**

BEAUFOY, MRS. MARK. 'A journey through the Oberland and to Chamonix', J. M. Thorington. *Alpine Journal*, 1928; **1787.**

BEAUMONT, ALBANIS. *Travels through the Lepontine Alps*, London, 1806; **1789.**

BEAUREGARD, HENRY COSTA DE. *Un homme d'autrefois*, Paris, 1877; **1796.**

BECHER, AUGUSTA. *Personal Reminiscences in India & Europe*, London, 1930; **1837.**

BECK, JEAN JOSEPH. *Bollettino del Club Alpino Italiano*, 1884; **1778.**

BECKFORD, PETER. *A Biography*, A. H. Higginson, London, 1937; **1764.**

BECKFORD, WILLIAM. *Travel Diaries*, edited by G. Chapman, London, 1928; **1777.** *Life and Letters of William Beckford*, L. Melville, London, 1910; **1783, 1785, 1786, 1794.** *Life*, T. W. Oliver, Oxford, 1937; **1792.** In *Voyage d'une Française en Suisse . . . .* Mme de Gauthier, Londres, 1790; **1789.**

BEDDOES, THOMAS LOVELL. *Letters*, Edited by Edmund Gosse, London, 1894; **1837.**

BÉDOYÈRE, HENRI DE LA. *Journal d'un voyage en Savoie et dans le midi de la France en 1804 et 1805*, Paris, 1849; **1805.**

BELL, ANDREW. *Life*, R. Southey, London, 1844; **1816.**

BELL, GERTRUDE. *Letters*, London, 1927; **1901, 1902, 1904.**

BELLI, FRANZESCO. 'Un ambasceria Veneta', *Bollettino storico della Svizzera Italiana*, 19, 1897; **1626.**

BELLOC, HILAIRE. *The Path to Rome*, London, 1902; **1901.**

BELLOT, M. *Annales Jean-Jacques Rousseau*, Genève, 7, 1911; **1823.**

BELLOWS, HENRY W. *The Old World in its New Face*, New York, 1868; **1867.**

BENEDICT, CLARE. *The Benedicts abroad*, London, n.d.; **1921.**

Benedict, Erastus C. *A run through Europe*, New York, 1860; *c.* **1860.**

Bennett, Arnold. *Journal*, London, 1930; **1908, 1910.**

Benson, Edward Frederick. *Our Family Affairs*, London, 1920; **1880, 1889, 1890, 1891.**

Benson, Edward White. *Life*, A. E. Benson. London, 1899; **1880, 1885, 1889, 1890, 1891, 1893.**

Bentivoglio, Cardinale. *Raccolta di lettere*, Londra, 1764; **1607.**

Benzenberg, Johann Friedrich. *Briefe geschrieben auf einer Reise durch die Schweiz im Jahr 1810*, Düsseldorf, 1811; **1810.**

Bernard of Clairvaux. *Life & Times*, J. C. Morison, London, 1863; **1125.**

Bernard, Richard Boyle. *Tour through some parts of France, Switzerland, Savoy, Germany and Belgium*, London, 1815; **1814.**

Bernoulli, Christoph. In *Leonhard's Taschenbuch für die Gesammte Mineralogie*, 7, 1813; **1812.**

Bernoulli, Jean. *Lettres sur différens sujets pendant le cours d'un voyage par l'Allemagne, la Suisse, la France méridionale et l'Italie*, Berlin, 1777; **1774.**

Bernstein, Eduard. *My years of exile*, London, 1921; **1878.**

Berry, M. *Journals & Correspondence*, London, 1865; **1783, 1784, 1803, 1818, 1820, 1822, 1823.**

Berthoud, Fritz. *Sur la montagne. Alpes & Jura*, Neuchâtel, 1865; **1845.**

Bertolotti, Davide. *Viaggio in Savoia*, Torino, 1828; **1827.**

Bessborough, Henrietta, Countess of. In *Private correspondence of Lord Granville Leveson-Gower*, London, 1916; **1821.**

Besson, Henri. *Manuel pour les savans et les curieux qui voyagent en Suisse*, Lausanne, 1786; **1777.**

Béthencourt, Général Antoine. *Campagne de l'armée de réserve*, De Cugnac, Paris, 1900; **1800.**

Binet-Hentsch, J. L. *Les Alpes de la Haute Engadine*, Genève, 1859; **1857.**

Bithray, E. *Switzerland and Italy*, London, 1883; *c.* **1883.**

Björnstahl, Jakob Jonas. *Briefe auf seiner ausländischen Reise*, Leipzig & Rostock, 1780–3; **1773.**

Blackie, John Stuart. *John Stuart Blackie*, A. M. Stoddart. London, 1895; **1879.**

Blackwell, Eardley J. In *Switzerland in 1854*, W. G. Heathman, London, 1855; **1854.**

BLAIKIE, THOMAS. *Journal de Thomas Blaikie. Excursions d'un botaniste écossais dans les Alpes et le Jura en 1775*, edited by L. Seylaz, Neuchâtel, 1935; **1775.**

BLAINVILLE, M. DE. *Travels through Holland, Germany, Switzerland, but especially Italy*, London, 1757; **1705, 1707.**

BLANC, CHARLES. *De Paris à Venise*, Paris, 1857; *c.* **1857.**

BLESSINGTON, COUNTESS OF. *The idler in Italy*, London, 1839; **1822.**

BLOCK, BARON VON. In *Travels of Count Stolberg*, London, 1796; **1791.** And in 'J. S. Wyttenbach und seine Freunde', H. Dübi, *Neujahrsblatt der literarischen Gesellschaft Bern auf das Jahr 1911*, Bern, 1910; **1791.**

BLOOMFIELD, GEORGIANA, BARONESS. *Reminiscences of Court and Diplomatic Life*, London, 1883; **1855.**

BLUNT, WILFRID SCAWEN. *Wilfrid Scawen Blunt*, E. Finch. London, 1938; **1858, 1886.**

BODDINGTON, MRS. *Slight Reminiscences of the Rhine, Switzerland, and a Corner of Italy*, London, 1834; *c.* **1826, 1830.**

BODMER, SAMUEL. 'Bernische Pioniere der Alpenkunde', J. H. Graf, *Jahrbuch des Schweizer Alpenclub*, 26, 1890; **1706.**

BOIGNE, ADÈLE DE. *Mémoires de la comtesse de Boigne*, Paris, 1907; **1793.**

BOMBELLES, MARQUIS DE. *Les dernières années du marquis et de la marquise de Bombelles.* Comte Fleury, Paris, 1906; **1793.**

BONAPARTE, LOUIS NAPOLÉON (NAPOLÉON III). *La jeunesse de Napoléon III*, Stéphane-Pol, Paris, s.d.; **1826.** *La société du second Empire*, Fleury et Sonolat, Paris, 1913; **1860.**

BONAPARTE, NAPOLÉON (NAPOLÉON I). *Correspondance de Napoléon Ier*, 3, lettre 2379, Paris, 1859; **1797.** *Avec Bonaparte de Genève à Bâle*, P. Grellet, Lausanne, 1946; **1797.** *Campagne de l'armée de réserve*, De Cugnac, Paris, 1900; **1800.**

BONIFACE OF BRUSSELS. *Boniface de Bruxelles*, A. Simon & R. Aubert, Bruxelles, 1945; **1231.**

BONINGTON, R. P. *Bonington*, A. Dubuisson, London, 1924; **1826.**

BONNER, MISS. *A Visit to the St. Bernard in May*, London, 1877; **1875.**

BONNEY, THOMAS GEORGE. *The Alpine Regions*, Cambridge, 1868; **1856, 1858, 1859, 1860, 1861, 1864, 1865, 1867.** *The making of the Alps*, London, 1912; **1856, 1858, 1859, 1860, 1861, 1864, 1865, 1867, 1868, 1870, 1873, 1874, 1875, 1878, 1880, 1881, 1883, 1885, 1889, 1891, 1893, 1895, 1896, 1897, 1900, 1901.** *Memories of a long life*, p.p., Cambridge, 1921; **1911.**

BONSTETTEN, KARL VIKTOR VON. *Briefe über ein Schweizerisches Hirtenland*, Basle, 1782; **1779.** *Briefe an Friederike Brun*, Frankfurt, 1829; **1794, 1798.** 'Briefe', *Eggers Magazin*, 1797–9; **1795.** *Briefe von Bonstetten an Matthisson*, Zürich, 1827; **1796.** 'Briefe über die italienischen Ämter Lugano, Mendrisio, Locarno, Valmaggia', *Schriften*, Kopenhagen, 1800; **1797.**

BOOTH, C. *The Salvation Army in Switzerland*, J. Butler, London, 1883; **1883.**

BORDIER, ANDRÉ CÉSAR. *Voyage pitoresque aux glacières de Savoie, fait en 1772*, Genève, 1773; **1772.**

BÖRNE, LUDWIG. 'Briefe aus der Schweiz', *Nachgelassene Schriften*, Mannheim, 1850; **1832, 1833.**

BOSWELL, JAMES. 'Private papers of James Boswell', prepared for press by G. Scott. *Boswell with Rousseau and Voltaire*, n.p., 1928; **1764.**

BOUFFLERS, CHEVALIER DE. *Lettres de Monsieur le Chevalier de Boufflers pendant un voyage en Suisse à Madame sa Mère*, s.l., 1771; **1764.**

BOUGY, A. DE. *Le Tour du Léman*, Paris, 1846; **1844.**

BOUHELIER, ST. GEORGES DE. *Voyage dans la Suisse d'autrefois*, Paris, 1940; **1893.**

BOURBONNE, CHARTRAIRE DE. 'Un voyage à Chamonix en 1780', *La Montagne*, 197, p. 323, 1926; **1780.**

BOURQUENOUD, F. 'Tournée dans les Alpes Fribourgeoises', *Le Conservateur Suisse*, 10, p. 124, Lausanne, 1857; **1813.**

BOURRIT, MARC-THÉODORE. *Description des aspects du Mont Blanc*, Lausanne, 1776; **1766, 1769, 1770, 1774.** *Description des glacières de Savoie*, Genève, 1773; **1770.** 'The Early History of the Col du Géant', H. F. Montagnier, *Alpine Journal*, 34, 1922; **1772.** *Nouvelle description des glacières etc.*, Genève, 1787; **1773, 1775, 1776, 1777, 1778, 1779, 1780, 1783.** *Itinéraire de Genève, Chamouni, etc.*, Genève, 1808; **1782, 1788.** In *Voyages dans les Alpes*, H.-B. de Saussure, Neuchâtel, 1796; **1784, 1785.** In *Briefe einer reisenden Dame aus der Schweiz*, A. H. von Krock, Frankfurt, 1787; **1786.** *Description des Cols etc.* Genève, 1803; **1787, 1789, 1790, 1792, 1793, 1795, 1797, 1803.** In *Letters during the Course of a Tour through Germany, Switzerland, and Italy*, R. Gray, London, 1794; **1791.** In *Erinnerungen von F. Matthisson*, Zurich, 1810; **1801.** In *Paccard wider Balmat*, H. Dübi, Bern, 1913; **1802.** 'Bourrit', *Biographie Universelle*, Michaud, **1812.**

BOUTERWECK, FRIEDRICH. *Schweizerbriefe an Cäcilie, geschrieben im Sommer 1794*, Berlin, 1795; **1794.**

BOVET, A. *Carnet d'un Touriste*, Neuchâtel, 1884; **1882.** *Récits d'un montagnard*, par Azeline, Paris, 1887; **1885,** *c.* **1887.** *Souvenirs d'un alpiniste*, par Azeline, Neuchâtel, 1891; **1888, 1889.**

BOVIER, L. *Impressions de route.* Bruxelles, 1906; **1905.**

BOWLES, W. L. *Poetical Works,* Edinburgh, 1855; **1787.**

BOYD, A. K. H. *The Autumn Holidays of a Country Parson,* London, 1865; *c.* **1865.**

BOYLE, HON. ROBERT. *Life.* T. Birch, London, 1744; **1641.** *Lismore Papers,* 2, ser. 4, p.p., 1888; **1641.**

BRACKENHOFER, ELIE. *Voyages en Suisse,* traduit par H. Lehe, Lausanne, 1930; **1643, 1646.**

BRADBURY, J. *Three Weeks from Home through France & Switzerland,* London, n.d.; **1866.**

BRAHMS, JOHANNES. *Johannes Brahms,* M. Kalbeck, Berlin, 1907–14; **1865, 1866, 1874, 1886, 1887, 1888.**

BRÄKER, ULRICH. *Leben und Schriften,* S. Voellmy, Basel, 1945; **1793.**

BRAND, THOMAS. 'Diary of Thomas Brand', A. W. Malkin, *Alpine Journal,* 32, 1918; **1780, 1786.**

BRANDES, GEORGE. *Recollections of my Childhood and Youth,* London, 1906; **1868, 1870.**

BRANTÔME, P. DE B. DE. In *Les sonnets suisses de Joachim du Bellay,* A. François, Lausanne, 1946; **1557.**

BRAUNSCHWEIGER, N. *Promenade durch die Schweiz,* Hamburg, 1793; **1786.**

BRAY, MRS. A. E. *The Mountains and Lakes of Switzerland,* London, 1851; **1839.**

BRECKINRIDGE, R. J. *Memoranda of Travel,* Baltimore, 1845; **1836.**

BREMER, FREDERIKA. *Two Years in Switzerland and Italy,* London, 1861; **1856, 1857.**

BREVAL, JOHN DURAND. *Remarks on Several Parts of Europe,* London, 1726; **1720, 1724.**

BREWSTER, SIR DAVID. *Home Life of Sir D. Brewster,* M. M. Gordon, Edinburgh, 1869; **1814.**

BRICHE, MME DE LA. *Les voyages en Suisse de Mme de la Briche,* Comte Pierre de Zurich, Neuchâtel, 1935; **1785, 1788.** 'Le Voyage de Mme de la Briche', *Revue de Paris,* 15 août, 1935; **1788.**

BRIDEL, LOUIS. 'Voyage dans le pays Grison en 1784', *Le Conservateur Suisse,* Lausanne, 1813, i, p. 240; **1779**: p. 148; **1784.** 'Itinéraire d'un voyage à pied dans une partie de la Suisse', *Le Conservateur Suisse,* 3, p. 273; Lausanne, 1813; **1796.** 'Fragment d'un voyage fait en juillet 1800 dans une partie des cantons dévastés', *Le Conservateur Suisse,* 4, Lausanne, 1814; **1800.** 'Course au St. Bernard en avril 1801', *Le Conservateur Suisse,* 5, Lausanne, 1814; **1801.**

BRIDEL, PHILIPPE. 'Petite course dans les Alpes en prose et en vers', *Le Conservateur Suisse*, 8, p. 394, Lausanne, 1817; **1780.** 'De Bex à Sion par le Mont Anzeindaz', *Le Conservateur Suisse*, 2, Lausanne, 1813; **1786.** *Course de Bâle à Bienne par les vallées du Jura*, Bâle, 1789; **1788.** 'Journal d'une course à pied dans l'intérieur de la Suisse en juillet 1790', *Le Conservateur Suisse*, 2, Lausanne, 1813; **1790.** 'Coup d'œil sur une contrée pastorale des Alpes', *Le Conservateur Suisse*, 4, Lausanne, 1814; **1797.** 'Promenade au lac de Lioson', *Le Conservateur Suisse*, 5, Lausanne, 1814; **1799.** 'Mélanges d'un voyageur dans les Alpes', *Le Conservateur Suisse*, 5, Lausanne, 1814; **1803, 1804.** 'Journal d'un pèlerinage à la vallée de Bagnes et au Grand St. Bernard', *Le Conservateur Suisse*, 10, Lausanne, 1857; **1818.**

BRIDGES, GEORGE WINDHAM. *Alpine Sketches by a Member of the University of Oxford*, London, 1814; **1814.**

BRIGG, M. A. *Iter Helveticum*, p.p., Keighley, 1887; **1886.**

BRIONNE, COMTESSE DE. In *Voyage historique et littéraire dans la Suisse occidentale*, Baron de Sinner, En Suisse, 1787; **1773.**

BRISSOT, J.-P. *Jeunesse de Brissot*. J. F.-Primo, Paris, 1932; **1782.**

BROCKEDON, WILLIAM. *Excursions in the Alps*, London, 1833; **1821, 1824, 1825.**

BROOKE, STOPFORD. *Life and Letters*, L. P. Jacks, London, 1917; **1858, 1871, 1876.**

BROOKS, PHILLIPS. *Letters of Travel*, London, 1893; **1866, 1870, 1877, 1882, 1883, 1885, 1890, 1892.**

BROUGHAM, HENRY, LORD. *Creevey Papers*, London, 1903; **1816.**

BROWN, EDWARD. *Travels*, London, 1753; **1663.**

BROWN, JOHN. *Letters*, D. W. Forrest, London, 1907; **1868.**

BROWN, T. GRAHAM. *Brenva*, London, 1944; **1926, 1927, 1928, 1929, 1930, 1931, 1932, 1933.**

BROWN, THOMAS EDWARD. *Letters*, edited by S. T. Irwin, London, 1900; **1874, 1881.**

BROWN, YEATS. *Alpine Journal*, 5, 1872; **1828.**

BROWNE, G. F. *Off the Mill*, London, 1895; **1863, 1866.** *Ice-caves of France and Switzerland*, London, 1865; **1861, 1864.** *Recollections of a Bishop*, London, 1915; **1864.**

BROWNE, J. D. H. *Stories from Switzerland*, London, 1852; **1852.**

BROWNING, OSCAR. *Memories of Sixty Years*, London, 1910; **1863, 1867, 1876, 1879, 1880.** *Memories of Later Years*, London, 1910; **1888.**

BROWNING, ROBERT. *Letters of Robert Browning*, edited by T. L. Hood, London, 1933; **1883, 1884, 1885, 1887.** *Life and Letters*, S. Orr, London, 1891; **1877, 1878.**

BRUCE, C. L. CUMMING. In *Proceedings of the Royal Society of Edinburgh*, 5, 1866; **1814.**

BRUN, FRIEDERIKE. *Prosaïsche Schriften*, Zürich, 1799; **1791.** *Tagebuch einer Reise durch die östliche, südliche und italienische Schweiz*, Kopenhagen, 1800; **1795.** *Episoden aus Reisen*, Zürich, 1806–9; **1796, 1801, 1802.**

BRUNNER, SAMUEL. 'Eine Fussreise vor 60 Jahren', A. Wäber, *Jahrbuch des Schweizer Alpenclub*, 27, 1891; **1829.** 'Ausflug ins Zermatt-Thal', *Flora*, 20, 1837; **1827, 1836.**

BRUSCHIUS, GASPAR. *Hodoeporicum*, Nicolas Reussner, Basle, 1580, *c.* **1559.**

BRYCE, JAMES VISCOUNT. *Memories of Travel*, London, 1923; **1884.**

BRYDGES, SIR EGERTON. *Recollections of Foreign Travel*, London, 1825; **1819.** *Letters from the Continent*, London, 1821; **1819.**

BRYDONE, PATRICK. *Tour through Sicily and Malta*, London, 1773; **1771.** 'Chronologie critique', L. J. Courtois, *Annales de la société Jean-Jacques Rousseau*, 15, Genève, 1923; **1765.**

BUCH, L. VON. *Gesammelte Schriften*, Berlin, 1867; **1800, 1802, 1803, 1812.**

BUCHON, J. A. C. *Quelques souvenirs de courses en Suisse*, Paris, 1836; **1821.**

BUCKINGHAM, JAMES SILK. *Belgium, the Rhine, Switzerland and Holland*, London, 1848; **1844.**

BUCKLAND, W. *Proceedings of the Geological Society*, 3, 1841; **1838.**

BULLAR, WILLIAM. *Letters from Abroad*, London, 1861; **1860.**

BULLARD, A. T. J. *Sights and Scenes in Europe*, St. Louis, 1852; **1850.**

BULLINGER, BALTHAZAR. In *Geschichte des Reisens in der Schweiz*, G. Peyer, Basel, 1885; **1757.**

BULWER, J. REDFORD. *Extracts from my Journal*, Norwich, 1853; **1852.**

BUNBURY, SIR CHARLES J. F. *Life*, H. Lyell, London, 1906; **1848.**

BUNBURY, SIR HENRY EDWARD. *Memoir and Literary Remains*, London, 1868; **1829.**

BUNSEN, CHRISTIAN, BARON. *Memoir*, London, 1868; **1839, 1840, 1856.**

BUNSEN, FRANCES, BARONESS. *Life and Letters*, A. J. C. Hare, London, 1879; **1840, 1841, 1865, 1870.**

BÜRDE, SAMUEL GOTTLIEB. *Erzählung einer gesellschaftlichen Reise durch einen Theil der Schweiz und des obern Italien*, Breslau, 1785; **1780.**

BURNABY, MRS. (*see* LE BLOND, Mrs., MAIN, Mrs.). *The High Alps in Winter*, London, 1883; **1883.**

BURNE-JONES, EDWARD. *Memorials*, London, 1904; **1862, 1878.**

BURNET, GILBERT. *Some Letters containing what seemed most remarkable in Switzerland, Italy, &c.*, Amsterdam, 1686; **1685, 1686.**

BURNET, WILLIAM. *Philosophical Transactions of the Royal Society of London*, 26, 1709; **1708.**

BURSER, JOACHIM. In *Catalogue of Manuscripts. Linnean Society of London*, S. Savage, London, 1937; *c.* **1620.**

BURTON, SIR RICHARD. *Life*, I. Burton, London, 1893; **1888, 1889, 1890.**

BURY, LADY CHARLOTTE. *Diary of a Lady in Waiting*, edited by A. F. Stewart, London, 1908; **1814.**

BUSINO, HORATIO. In *Notes and Queries*, M. Letts, series 12, 1, 1916; **1617.**

BUTLER, ARTHUR JOHN. *Memoir*, A. Quiller-Couch, London, 1917; **1857, 1897.**

BUTLER, GEORGE and JOSEPHINE. *Recollections of George Butler*, Josephine Butler, Bristol, n.d.; **1869, 1875, 1876, 1877, 1881, 1882, 1883, 1884, 1885, 1886, 1887, 1888, 1889.**

BUTLER, HENRY MONTAGU. *The Harrow Life of Henry Montagu Butler*, E. Graham, London, 1920; **1856, 1884.** *H. M. Butler*, J. R. M. Butler, London, 1925; **1888.**

BUTLER, SAMUEL. 'Our Tour', in *A First Year in Canterbury Settlement*, London, 1914; **1857.** *Alps and Sanctuaries*, London, 1881; **1879.** *Samuel Butler*, H. F. Jones, London, 1919; **1869, 1871, 1872, 1876, 1877, 1878, 1879, 1880, 1884, 1885, 1886, 1887, 1890, 1891, 1894, 1895, 1896, 1897, 1899, 1900, 1901.** 'Art in the valley of Saas', in *The Humour of Homer*, London, 1913; **1890.**

BUXTON, EDWARD NORTH. *Short Stalks*, London, 1892; **1863, 1865, 1874.**

BUXTON, SIR THOMAS FOWELL. 'The Col de Chermontane', *Peaks, Passes, and Glaciers*, 2, 1, London, 1862; **1861.**

BYERS, S. H. M. *Twenty Years in Europe*, Chicago, n.d.; **1869, 1872, 1879.**

BYRON, LORD. *Letters and Journals*, edited by R. E. Prothero, London, 1899; **1816.**

Cade, George. 'A tour in the Alps in 1800', J. Sowerby, *Alpine Journal*, 7, 1874–6; **1800.**

Cagliostro, Count. *Les vies du Comte de Cagliostro*, C. Photiades, Paris, 1932; **1787.**

Cairns, John. *Life and Letters.* A. R. Macewen, London, 1895; **1844.**

Calame, Alexandre. *Sa vie et son œuvre*, E. Rambert, Paris, 1884; **1835, 1840, 1851, 1854.**

Callow, William. *Autobiography*, London, 1908; **1838.**

Calvert, G. H. *Scenes and Thoughts in Europe*, New York, 1852; **1850.**

Cambry, Jacques. *Voyage pittoresque en Suisse et en Italie*, Paris, an IX; **1788.**

Campbell of Ardkinglas, Sir James. *Memoirs*, London, 1832; **1769.**

Camus, T. *Œuvres alpines*, Chamonix, s.d.; **1890, 1892.**

Candolle, Augustin Pyrame de. *Mémoires et souvenirs*, Genève, 1862; **1801, 1805, 1825, 1830, 1833.**

Canning, Stratford. *Life*, S. Lane Poole, London, 1888; **1814, 1815.**

Cappeler, M. A. *Pilati Montis Historia*, Basileae, 1767; **1717.**

Capper, Samuel James. *Shores and Cities of the Bodensee*, London, 1881; **1879.**

Cardano, Geronimo. *De propria vita*, Amstelodami, 1654; **1552.**

Carne, John. *Letters from Switzerland and Italy during a late tour*, London, 1834; **1826, 1827.**

Carnot, Lazare. *Mémoires*, Paris, 1863; **1797.**

Caroline, Princess of Wales. *Voyages and Travels of her Majesty Caroline Queen of Great Britain*, London, 1821; **1814.**

Carr, Alfred. *Adventures with my Alpenstock and Knapsack, or a Five Weeks Tour in Switzerland in 1874*, p.p., York, 1875; **1874.**

Carter, N. H. *Letters from Europe*, New York, 1827; **1826.**

Carus, C. G. *Reise durch Deutschland, Italien, und die Schweitz*, Leipzig, 1835; **1828.**

Casanova, Jacques. *Mémoires*, Paris, n.d.; **1750, 1760, 1769.** *Les aventures de Casanova en Suisse*, P. Grellet, Lausanne, 1919; **1760.**

Catani, J. B. 'Bemerkungen bei einer in Gesellschaft Herrn Pfarrer Pol durch die Montafunerberge in die Gebirge Fermunt in Julius 1780 angestellten Bergreise', *Der Sammler*, 3, Coire, 1781; **1780.**

CATANI, J. B., and POL, L. 'Bericht von einigen in den Gebirgen von St. Antönien angestellten Reisen', *Der Sammler*, 6, Coire, 1784; **1782, 1783.**

CATLOW, AGNES and MARIA. *Sketching Rambles*, London, 1861; **1856, 1857.**

CAVALIER, J. In *St-Saphorin*, S. S.-Michaud, p.p., Villette-Cully, 1935; **1704.**

CAVOUR, CAMILLO. *Lettere*, edited by L. Chiala, Torino, 1884; **1858, 1859.**

CAZENOVE, H. *A Narrative, in two parts: written in 1812*, London, 1813; **1803, 1804, 1810.**

CELLINI, BENVENUTO. *Vita*, Milano, 1805; **1537.**

CÉZANNE, PAUL. *Paul Cézanne*, G. Mack, Paris, 1938; **1891.**

CHAMBERLAIN, SIR AUSTEN. *Seen in Passing*, London, 1937; **1921.**

CHAMBERS, WILLIAM. *A Tour in Switzerland*, Edinburgh, 1842; **1841.**

CHAMIER, CAPTAIN. *My Travels, or an Unsentimental Journey through France, Switzerland, and Italy*, London, 1855; **1853.**

CHAMISSO, ADALBERT VON. 'Chamissos Schweizerreise im Jahre 1812', A. Bruckner, *Die Alpen*, 7, 1931; **1812.**

CHANDLER, RICHARD. *Travels in Asia Minor and Greece*, Oxford, 1825; **1786.**

CHAPMAN, F. S. *Memoirs of a Mountaineer*, London, 1945; **1930.**

CHAPUYS MONTLAVILLE, LOUIS ALCESTE DE. *Lettres sur la Suisse et le pays des Grisons*, Paris, 1826; **1823.**

CHARLES EDWARD, PRINCE. *Life & Times of Prince Charles Edward Stuart*, A. C. Ewald, London, 1875; **1756.**

CHARLES IV, EMPEROR. 'Jugendleben', *Die Geschichtschreiber*, 83, Leipzig, 1899; **1331.**

CHARPENTIER, J. DE. *Essai sur les glaciers*, Lausanne, 1841; **1815, 1821, 1834.**

CHATEAUBRIAND, FRANÇOIS RENÉ DE. *Voyage au Mont Blanc*, edited by G. Faure, Grenoble, 1920; **1805.** *Mémoires d'outre-tombe*, Paris, 1848–50; **1824, 1826, 1831, 1832.** 'Six Voyages en Italie', G. Faure, *Rev. des Deux Mondes*, 1915; **1822, 1828, 1833.** *Les cahiers de Mme. de Chateaubriand*, J. L. de Lacharrière, Paris, 1909; **1805.**

CHAVANNES, GAUDARD DE. *Journal d'un voyage de Genève à Londres en passant par la Suisse*, Lyon, 1783; **1760.**

CHEEVER, GEORGE BARRELL. *Wanderings of a Pilgrim in the Shadow of Mont-Blanc and the Jungfrau Alp*, Glasgow and London, 1846; *c.* **1845.**

Chênedollé, Charles de. In *Ces Monts affreux*, C.-E. Engel et C. Vallot, Paris, 1934; **1797.**

Chénier, André. 'Aux deux frères Trudaine', in *Élégies*, Paris, 1910; **1784.**

Chevalier, Casimir ('Duverney, Jacques'). *Un tour en Suisse*, Tours, 1866; **1862.**

Chorley, Henry Fothergill. *Autobiography, Memoir and Letters*, edited by H. G. Hewlett, London, 1873; **1841, 1847.**

Christen, Rodolphe. *The Story of an Artist's Life*, London, 1910; **1898.**

Christen, Wolfgang. 'Description des glacières, ou pour mieux dire, de la mer glaciale qui se trouve dans les Alpes de la Suisse', in 'Der Alpensinn', H. Dübi, *Neujahrsblatt der litterarischen Gesellschaft Bern auf das Jahr 1902*, Bern, 1901; **1740.**

Chytraeus, Nathan. *Hodoeporica, sive itineraria a diversis doctissimis viris*, Frankfurt a/M., 1575; *c.* **1575.**

Civiale, Aimé. *Les Alpes*, Paris, 1882; **1859, 1860, 1861, 1862, 1863, 1865, 1866.**

Clairmont, Claire. *Claire Clairmont*, R. Glynn Grylls, London, 1939; **1814.**

Clarke, Andrew. *Tour in France, Italy, and Switzerland during the Years 1840 and 1841*, London, 1843; **1841.**

Clarke, Edmund. 'Narrative of an Excursion to the Summit of Mont Blanc (with Sherwill, M.)', *New Monthly Magazine*, 16, 17, 1826; **1825.**

Clarke, Edward Daniel. *Life and Remains*, W. Otter, London, 1824; **1792, 1794.**

Clarke, James Freeman. *Eleven Weeks in Europe*, Boston, 1852; **1849.**

Clason, Francis Lewis. *The Case of Switzerland, Briefly Stated*, London, 1802; **1802.**

Clément, Jean-Maurice. 'Jean-Maurice Clément', O. Nicollier, *Die Alpen*, 14, 1938; **1788.**

Clifford, Lady de. *A Picturesque Tour through France, Switzerland, on the Banks of the Rhine, and through Parts of the Netherlands*, London, 1817; **1816.**

Clissold, Frederick. *Narrative of an Ascent to the Summit of Mont Blanc*, London, 1823; **1822.**

Cloncurry, Valentine Lawless, Lord. *Personal Recollections*, Dublin, 1850; **1792.**

Clough, Arthur Hugh. *Poems and Prose Remains of A. H. Clough*, edited by his wife, London, 1869; **1843, 1849, 1861.** *Memoir of Anne Jemima Clough*, London, 1897; **1846.**

Clowes, G. *Forty-six Days in Switzerland and the North of Italy*, London, 1856; **1856.**

Cobbett, J. P. *Journal of a Tour in Italy*, London, 1830; **1829.**

Cobden-Sanderson, Thomas James. *Journal*, London, 1926; **1883, 1888, 1897, 1898, 1901, 1902, 1903, 1904, 1905, 1909, 1911, 1914, 1920.**

Cockburn, James. *Swiss Scenery*, London, 1820; **1816.**

Coeurderoy, Ernest. *Œuvres, 1. Jours d'exile*, Paris, 1910; **1849.**

Coignet, J.-R. *Cahiers du capitaine Coignet*, Paris, 1883; **1800.**

Coke, Lady Mary. *Letters and Journals*, p.p., Edinburgh, 1892; **1769.**

Cole, Mrs. H. Warwick. *A Lady's Tour round Monte Rosa*, London, 1859; **1850, 1856, 1858.**

Coleman, Edmund Thomas. *Scenes from the Snowfields*, London, 1859; **1855, 1858.**

Collings, H. *Switzerland as I saw it*, London, n.d.; **1875.**

Collingwood, W. Gershom. *The Limestone Alps of Savoy*, Orpington, 1884; **1882.**

Collini, C. A. *Mon séjour auprès de Voltaire*, Paris, 1807; **1749, 1755.**

Colman, H. *European life and manners*, Boston, 1849; **1847.**

Colston, Marianne. *Journal of a Tour in France, Switzerland, and Italy*, Paris, 1822; **1820.**

Conan Doyle, Sir Arthur. *Memories and Adventures*, London, 1924; **1894.** *His Life and Art*, H. Pearson, London, 1943; **1893, 1895.**

Condamine, M. de la. *Journal of a Tour to Italy*, Dublin, 1763; **1756.**

Condé, Louis Joseph, Prince de. *Journal d'émigration*, edited by Comte de Ribes, Paris, 1921; **1789.**

Connaught, Arthur, Duke of. *H.R.H. the Duke of Connaught*, G. Aston, London, 1929; **1868.**

Conrad, Joseph. *Some Reminiscences*, London, 1912; **1873.**

Constant, Rosalie de. 'Rosalie de Constant et son voyage à Chamonix', C. de Severy, *Revue Historique Vaudoise*, 44, 1936; **1807.** In *Amitié ou Amour*, H. Bordeaux, Paris, 1932; *c.* **1807.**

Contat, L. *La Célimène de Thermidor*, Dussane, Paris, 1929; **1804.**

Conway, Martin. *Mountain Memories*, London, 1920; **1872, 1876, 1877, 1878, 1880, 1881, 1882, 1886, 1887, 1890.** *The Alps from End to End*, London, 1895; **1894.**

Cook, Joel. *A Holiday Tour in Europe*, Philadelphia, 1879; **1878.**

Cook, Theodore Andrea. *Notes on Tobogganing at St. Moritz*, London, 1896; **1894.**

Cook, Thomas. In *Grosse Welt und kleine Menschen,* F. N. Wagner, Zürich, 1942; **1864.**

Coolidge, W. A. B. *Alpine Studies,* London, 1912; **1868, 1869, 1870, 1871, 1872, 1874, 1875, 1876, 1879, 1888, 1890, 1893, 1896, 1897, 1899, 1900, 1902, 1905.**

Cooper, James Fenimore. *Excursions in Switzerland,* London, 1836; **1828.** *A Residence in France, with an Excursion up the Rhine, and a Second Visit to Switzerland,* London, 1836; **1832.**

Cope, J. P. *Bramshill,* London, 1938; **1931.**

Copleston, Edward. *Memoir,* London, 1851; **1814, 1816.**

Corot, Camille. *Œuvres,* A. Robaut, Paris, 1905; **1825, 1834, 1842.**

Corrie, George Elwes. *Memoir,* edited by M. Holroyd, Cambridge, 1890; **1821.**

Corson, John W. *Loiterings in Europe,* Dublin, 1849; **1846.**

Coryat, Thomas. *Coryat's Crudities,* London, 1611 (Glasgow, 1905); **1608.**

Costello, L. S. *A Tour to and from Venice,* London, 1846; **1845.**

Cotta, Bernhard. *Die Alpen,* Leipzig, 1851; **1843, 1849.**

Coulmann, J. J. *Reminiscences,* Paris, 1865; **1820, 1821.**

Coulton, G. G. *Fourscore Years,* London, 1943; **1897, 1902.**

Courbet, Gustave. *Courbet,* C. Leger, Paris, 1929; **1873.**

Courier, P.-L. *Lettres,* Paris, 1828; **1809.**

Cowell, Edward Byles. *Life and Letters,* G. Cowell, London, 1904; **1876.**

Coxe, Thomas. In *Berner Oberland in Sage und Geschichte,* A. Hartmann, Bern, 1915; **1690.** In *Notes and Queries,* M. Letts, series 12, 3, 1917; **1690.**

Coxe, William. *Travels in Switzerland,* London, 1791; **1776, 1779, 1785, 1786.**

Cozens, John Robert. 'The Drawings and Sketches of John Robert Cozens', C. V. Bell and J. Girtin, *Walpole Society,* 28, 1925; **1776.**

Crawford, Francis Marion. *My Cousin Francis Marion Crawford,* M. H. Elliott, London, 1934; **1872.**

Cuchetat, C. *Souvenirs d'une promenade en Suisse,* Paris, 1828; **1827.**

Cumming, W. F. *Notes of a Wanderer in Search of Health,* London, 1839; **1836.**

Curti, Léopold de. *Lettres sur la Suisse,* Altona, 1797; **1791.**

Custine, Astolphe de. *Mémoires et Voyages,* Paris, 1830; **1811.**

CUSTINE, DELPHINE, MARQUISE DE. *Memoirs*, G. Maugras and P. de Croze-Lemercier, London, 1912; **1811, 1826.**

CUTLER, H. O. *De glacier en glacier*, C. Pascal, Paris, s.d.; **1880.**

DARGAUD, J. M. *Voyage aux Alpes*, Paris, 1857; **1856.**

DARLEY, FELIX O. C. *Sketches Abroad with Pen and Pencil*, New York, 1868; **1866.**

DAUDET, ALPHONSE. *Lettres familiales*, L. Daudet, Paris, 1944; **1881, 1884.**

DAULLIA, E. *Voyage impressionniste en Suisse*, Paris, 1887; **1883.**

DAVALL, E. In *Memoir and Correspondence of J. E. Smith*, London, 1832; **1789.**

DAVIES, WALFORD. *A Biography*, H. C. Coles, London, 1942; **1893.**

DAVY, SIR HUMPHRY. *Life*, J. A. Paris, London, 1831; **1814.**

DEFELLER, ABBÉ. *Itinéraire*, Liége, 1820; **1777.**

DEGAS, EDGAR. *Lettres*, edited by M. Guérin, Paris, 1831; **1882, 1893.**

DEHANSY, CHARLES. *La Suisse à pied*, Paris, s.d.; *c.* **1864.**

DE LA BECHE, H. *Transactions of the Geological Society*, 1, 1824; **1819.**

DE LUC, GUILLAUME-ANTOINE. In *Lettres physiques et morales sur l'histoire de la terre et de l'homme*, J.-A. De Luc, La Haye, 1779; **1778.**

DE LUC, JEAN-ANDRÉ. In 'Relation inédite d'un voyage aux glacières de Savoie', L. Raulet, *Annuaire du Club Alpin Français*, 20, 1894; **1754.** *Recherches sur les modifications de l'atmosphère*, Genève, 1772; **1765, 1770.** *Relation de différents voyages dans les Alpes de Faucigny par Messieurs D. et D.*, P. G. Dentan, Maestricht, 1776; **1772.** *Lettres physiques et morales sur les Montagnes et sur l'histoire de la terre et de l'homme*, en Suisse, 1778; **1774.**

DENMAN, GEORGE. *Autobiographical notes*, p.p., London, 1897; **1844.**

DENT, CLINTON T. *Above the Snow Line*, London, 1885; **1870, 1871, 1872, 1873, 1878.**

DERBY, ELIZABETH, COUNTESS OF. *The Rocks of Meillerie*, London, 1779; **1768.**

DÉROULÈDE, PAUL. *La vie et la mort de Déroulède*, J. Tharaud, Paris, 1925; **1900.**

DESAIX, GENERAL. *Journal de voyage du général Desaix. Suisse et Italie (1797)*, publié par A. Chuquet, Paris, 1907; **1797.**

DESART, EARL OF. *A Page from the Past*, London, 1932; *c.* **1908.**

DESBAROLLES, ADOLPHE. *Un mois de voyage en Suisse*, Paris, 1840; **1839.** *Voyage d'un artiste en Suisse à 3 F. 50 par jour*, Paris, 1864; *c.* **1862.**

DESJOBERT, LUCIEN-CHARLES-FÉLIX. 'Un voyage en Suisse en 1777', edited by E. Rott, *Musée Neuchâtelois*, 1910; **1777.**

DES LOGES, CHR. *Voyage d'un convalescent dans le Département du Simplon*, n.p., 1813; *c.* **1813.**

DESMAREST, NICOLAS. 'Précis d'un mémoire sur le mouvement progressif des glaces dans les glaciers', *Observations sur la Physique*, 13, Paris, 1779; **1765.**

DESNOUES, ABBÉ. 'Mon émigration', *Annales religieuses d'Orléans*, Orléans, 1899; **1792.**

DESOR, ÉDOUARD. *Excursions et séjours dans les glaciers*, Neuchâtel, 1844; **1838, 1839, 1840, 1841, 1842, 1843.** *Nouvelles excursions et séjours dans les glaciers*, Neuchâtel, 1845; **1844.**

DÉTRÉ, E. *En Suisse! Impressions de deux bourgeois de Paris*, Paris, n.d.; **1876.**

DE VERE, AUBREY. *Recollections*, New York, 1897; **1839, 1843.**

DEVONSHIRE, GEORGIANA, DUCHESS OF. *The Face without a Frown*, I. Leveson Gower, London, 1945; **1792.** *The Passage of the Mountain of St. Gothard*, London, 1802; **1793.**

DICK, JAKOB. In *Epistolarum ab eruditis viris ad Alb. Hallerum scriptarum Pars I*, Bernae, 1774; **1763, 1766.** In *Historia Stirpium Helvetiae*, A. von Haller, Bernae, 1768; **1763.**

DICKENS, CHARLES. *Life*, J. Forster, London, 1873; **1844, 1845, 1846, 1853.** *Letters of Charles Dickens*, London, 1880–2; **1844.**

DICKINSON, G. LOWES. *G. Lowes Dickinson*, E. M. Forster, London, 1934; **1902.**

DIGBY, K. H. *The Temple of Memory*, London, 1875; *c.* **1820.**

D'INDY, VINCENT. *Vincent d'Indy*, Léon Vallas, Paris, 1946; **1882.**

DINO, DUCHESSE DE. *Memoirs*, edited by Princess Radziwill, London, 1909; **1835.**

DISRAELI, BENJAMIN. *Life*, W. F. Monypenny, London, 1910; **1826.**

DOBELL, SYDNEY. *Life and Letters*, London, 1878; **1851.**

DODD, —. *Cursory Notes of a Nine-weeks Tour*, p.p., Newcastle, 1834; **1833.**

DOLOMIEU, DÉODAT DE. *Déodat Dolomieu*, A. Lacroix, Paris, 1921; **1793, 1794, 1795, 1797.** *Journal du dernier voyage du citoyen Dolomieu dans les Alpes*, T. C. Bruun-Neergaard, Paris, 1802; **1801.**

DONIZETTI, GAETANO. *Donizetti*, G. Donati-Petteni, Milano, 1930; **1841.**

DORA D'ISTRIA, COMTESSE. *La Suisse allemande et l'ascension du Monsch*, Paris, Genève, 1856; **1855.**

DORÉ, GUSTAVE. *Life and Reminiscences*, B. Roosevelt, London, 1885; **1853.**

DORIGNY, C. *Voyage circulaire en Suisse en 10 jours*, Paris, 1877; *c.* **1877.**

DORNFORD, J. 'Mont Blanc', *New Monthly Magazine*, **1**, 1821; **1820.**

DOSTOYEVSKY, FEODOR. *Diary of Dostoyevsky's Wife*, edited by R. Fulop-Muller and F. Eckstein, London, 1928; **1867.** *Correspondance de Dostoyevski*, edited by J. W. Bienstock, Paris, 1908; **1868.**

DOUGLAS, A. *Notes of a Journey from Berne to England through France*, Kelso, n.d.; **1796.**

DOUGLAS, NORMAN. *Looking back*, London, 1934; **1888.**

DOUKHOVSKOY, BARBARA. *Diary of a Russian Lady*, London, 1917; **1884.**

DOWNES, GEORGE. *Letters from Continental Countries*, Dublin, 1832; **1825.**

DOWSING, WILLIAM. *Rambles in Switzerland with Reminiscences of the Great St. Bernard, Mont Blanc, and the Bernese Alps*, Kingston-upon-Hull, 1869; **1868.**

DRINKWATER, MISS. *Poetische Reise*, n.p., n.d.; **1837.**

DRUMMOND, A. T. K. *Scenes and Impressions in Switzerland and the North of Italy*, Edinburgh, 1853; **1852.**

DRUMMOND, HENRY. *Life*, G. Adam Smith, London, 1899; **1886, 1888.**

DUBOIS, A. *Croquis alpins*, Mons, 1883; **1881.**

DU BELLAY, JEAN, CARDINAL. In *Les sonnets suisses de Joachim Du Bellay*, A. François, Lausanne, 1946; **1553.**

DU BELLAY, JOACHIM. *Regrets*, Paris, 1910; **1557.** *Les sonnets suisses de Joachim Du Bellay*, A. François, Lausanne, 1946; **1557.**

DUCOMMUN, JULES-CÉSAR. *Une excursion au Mont Blanc*, Genève, 1859; **1858.**

DUCREST, MME. *Memoirs of Empress Josephine*, London, 1894; **1810.**

DUFF, MOUNTSTUART E. GRANT. *Notes from a Diary 1851–1872*, London, 1897; **1852, 1860, 1861, 1868, 1869, 1870, 1871.** *Notes from a Diary 1889–1891*, London, 1901; **1891.** *Notes from a Diary 1892–1895*, London, 1904; **1893.**

DUFOUR, GÉNÉRAL GUILLAUME HENRI. *Rapport général du commandant en chef des troupes fédérales sur l'armement et la campagne de 1847*, Berne, 1848; **1847.**

DUMAS, ALEXANDRE. *Impressions de voyage*, Paris, 1841; **1832.**

DUPIN, J. P. 'Voyage à Zermatt en août 1844', E. Thomas, *Die Alpen*, 18, 1942; **1844.**

DUPIN, MAURICE. In *Histoire de ma Vie*, George Sand, 1, Paris, 1856; **1799.**

DUPPA, R. *Miscellaneous Observations and Opinions on the Continent*, London, 1825; **1822.**

DURBIN, J. P. *Observations in Europe*, New York, 1844; **1842.**

DÜRER, ALBRECHT. In 'Neue Beiträge zur Dürerforschung', J. Meder, *Jahrbuch der kunsthistorischen Sammlungen des allerhöchsten Kaiserhauses*, Wien, 1912; **1492.**

DURHAM, W. E. *Summer Holidays in the Alps*, London, 1916; **1873, 1898, 1899, 1900, 1901, 1903, 1904, 1905, 1906, 1907, 1909, 1910, 1911, 1912, 1913, 1914.**

DURY, J. *John Dury*, J. Minton Batten, Chicago, 1944; **1654.**

DUVILLARD, LOUIS. 'De Lausanne à Iselle en 1826', *Revue Historique Vaudoise*, 41, 1933; **1826.**

DYKE, T. *Travelling Mems. during a Tour through Belgium, Rhenish Prussia, Germany, Switzerland.* London, 1834; **1832.**

DZIEDUSZYCKI, L. M. In *La Suisse et ses Amis*, C.-E. Engel, Neuchâtel, 1943; **1787.**

EARLE, P. *Memoirs*, Boston, 1898; **1838.**

EASTLAKE, LADY. *Journals and Correspondence*, edited by C. E. Smith, London, 1895; **1854, 1855, 1864.**

EDGEWORTH, MARIA. *Life and Letters*, A. J. C. Hare, London, 1894; **1820.**

ELIOT, GEORGE. *Life*, J. W. Cross, London, 1885; **1849, 1859, 1860.**

ELIZABETH, EMPRESS. *Elizabeth Empress of Austria*, C. Tschudi, London, 1901; **1898.**

ELLACOMBE, H. N. *A Memoir*, ed. A. W. Hill, London, 1919; **1889, 1893, 1897, 1898, 1899, 1903, 1907.**

ELLERTON, J. *Life & Writings*, H. Housman, London, 1896; **1884.**

ELLIOTT, HENRY. *Life*, J. Bateman, London, 1870; **1817, 1864.**

ELLIOTT, JULIUS. In *Life of Henry Elliott*, J. Bateman, London, 1870; **1868, 1869.**

EMERSON, RALPH WALDO. *A Memoir of R. W. Emerson*, J. E. Cabot, London, 1887; **1833.**

ENGELHARDT, CHRISTIAN MORITZ. *Naturschilderungen*, Basle, 1840; **1830, 1832, 1835, 1836, 1837, 1838, 1839.** *Das Monte Rosa und Matterhorn Gebirg*, Paris & Strassburg, 1852; **1840, 1841, 1842, 1848, 1849, 1850, 1851.** In *Geschichte des Reisens in der Schweiz*, G. Peyer, Basel, 1885; **1855.**

ENGHIEN, DUC D'. *Histoire des trois derniers princes de la maison de Condé*, J. Crétineau-Joly, Paris, 1867; **1797.**

EPTINGEN, HANS BERNHARD VON. *Schweizerischer Geschichtsforscher*, 7, 1828; **1460.**

ERASMUS OF ROTTERDAM. *Epistles*, ed. F. M. Nichols, London, 1918; **1509.** *Erasmus*, P. Smith, New York, 1923; **1522.**

ERSKINE, THOMAS. *Letters*, Edinburgh, 1877; **1823, 1826.**

ESCHER, HANS CONRAD. 'Geognostische Nachrichten über die Alpen in Briefen aus Helvetien', *Alpina*, 2, Winterthur, 1807; **1795.** 'Auszüge aus den Bemerkungen eines schweitzerschen Wanderers über einige der weniger bekannten Gegenden der Alpen', *Alpina*, 3, Winterthur, 1808; *c.* **1797.** 'Bergreischen auf den Niesen', *Alpina*, 3, Winterthur, 1808; **1805.** 'Kleine Bergreise auf die Sul oder Suleck', *Alpina*, 3, Winterthur, 1808; **1806.** In *Mittheilungen aus dem Gebiet der theoretischen Erdkunde*, J. Fröbel & O. Heer, Zürich, 1836; **1812, 1816.**

ESCHERNY, F. L. D'. In *Pèlerins de Motiers*, C. Guyot, Neuchâtel, 1936; **1764.** *Mélanges de littérature etc.*, Paris, 1811; **1764, 1765,** *c.* **1792.**

ESPINCHAL, COMTE D'. *Journal d'émigration*, edited by E. d'Hauterive, Paris, 1912; **1783, 1789, 1791.**

EUSTACE, J. C. *A Classical Tour through Italy*, London, 1815; **1802.**

EVELYN, JOHN. *Memoirs of John Evelyn comprising his Diary*, London, 1818; **1646.**

EVILL, WILLIAM. *A Winter Journey to Rome and back*, London, 1871; **1869.**

EWING, ALEXANDER. *Memoir*, A. J. Ross, London, 1877; **1855, 1864.**

EXCHAQUET, CHARLES-FRANÇOIS. 'The early history of the Col du Géant', H. F. Montagnier, *Alpine Journal*, 34, 1923; **1787.**

FABRICIUS, J. In *J. Simler*, W. A. B. Coolidge, Grenoble 1904; **1559.**

FAESCH, H. J. M. *Frühe Freunde des Tessins*, W. A. Vetterli, Zürich, 1946; **1682.**

FAIRBANKS, HENRY. *American Alpine Journal*, 2, p. 353, 1936; **1856.**

FARADAY, MICHAEL. *Life and Letters*, H. Bence Jones, London, 1870; **1814, 1835, 1841.**

FAWCETT, DOUGLAS. *Zermatt Dialogues*, London, 1931; *c.* **1931.**

FAWCETT, HENRY. *Life*, L. Stephen, London, 1885; **1872.**

FAYRER, SIR JOSEPH. *Recollections of My Life*, London, 1900; **1847, 1858.**

FEARNSIDE, W. G. *Tombleson's Rhine*, London, 1832; *c.* **1832.**

FÉE, A. L. A. *Promenade dans la Suisse occidentale*, Paris, 1835; **1829.**

FELLENBERG, EDMUND VON. *Doldenhorn und Weisse Frau*, Coblenz, 1863; **1859.**

FELLOWS, CHARLES. *Narrative of an Ascent to the Summit of Mont Blanc* (with Hawes, W.), London, 1828; **1827.**

FELTON, C. C. *Familiar Letters from Europe*, Boston, 1865; **1852.**

FERBER, JOHANN JAKOB. *Mineralogische & Metallurgische Bemerkungen in Neuchâtel, Franche Comté & Bourgogne*, Berlin, 1789; **1788.**

FERGUSON, A. *Biographical Sketch*, J. Small, Edinburgh, 1864; **1774.**

FERGUSON, F. *Wanderings in France & Switzerland*, London, 1869; **1863.**

FERGUSON, ROBERT. *Swiss Men and Swiss Mountains*, London, 1853; **1852.**

'FIELD, MICHAEL.' *Works and Days*, edited by T. & D. C. Sturge Moore, London, 1933; **1898.**

FINSLER, G. *Wanderungen und Feiertage*, Bern, n.d.; **1880, 1887, 1889, 1890, 1891, 1892.**

FISK, W. *Travels on the Continent of Europe*, New York, 1838; **1836.**

FISKE, J. *Life & Letters*, J. S. Clarke, Boston, 1917; **1874.**

FLAUBERT, GUSTAVE. *Notes de voyage*, Paris, 1912; **1845.**

FLECKER, JAMES ELROY. *Life*, G. Hodgson, Oxford, 1925; **1913, 1914.**

FLORIAN, J. P. C. DE. *Mémoires d'un jeune Espagnol*, Paris, 1923; **1765.** 'Claudine, Nouvelle Savoyarde', in *Œuvres complètes*, 3, Paris, 1874; **1788.**

FLOWER, WILLIAM HENRY. *Sir W. H. Flower*, C. J. Cornish, London, 1904; **1889, 1896.**

FONTANES, J. P. L. DE. *Correspondance de Fontanes et de Joubert*, publiéc par P. Tessonneau, Paris, 1943; **1787.**

FORBES, EDWARD. *Memoir*, G. Wilson & A. Geikie, London, 1861; **1835.**

FORBES, E. A. *A Woman's First Impressions of Europe*, New York, 1865; **1863.**

FORBES, JAMES DAVID. *Life & Letters*, edited by Tait, Sharp, & Adams Reilly, London, 1873; **1826.** *Travels through the Alps*, edited by W. A. B. Coolidge, London, 1900; **1832, 1839, 1841, 1842, 1843, 1844, 1846, 1850.**

FORBES, JOHN. *A Physician's Holiday or a Month in Switzerland*, London, 1850; **1848.**

FORBES, MURRAY. *The Diary of a Traveller over Alps and Appenines*, London, 1824; **1823.**

Forney, John W. *Letters from Europe*, Philadelphia, 1867; **1867.**

Forster, R. W. E. 'The Alps of Glarus', *Peaks, Passes, & Glaciers*, 1859; **1857.** 'From the Grütli to the Grimsel', *Peaks, Passes, & Glaciers*, ii, London, 1862; **1861.**

Foscolo, U. *Vita*, G. Pecchio, Città di Castello, 1915; **1815.**

Fowler, W. Warde. *A Year with the Birds*, London, 1886; **1884, 1886.**

Fox, Charles James. *Memoir of the Life of C. J. Fox*, R. B. Sheridan, London, 1808; **1768.** *Memorials and Correspondence of C. J. Fox*, Lord John Russell, London, 1857; **1788.**

Fox, Joseph Hoyland. *Holiday Memories*, p.p., Wellington, 1908: **1853, 1856, 1859, 1860, 1863, 1869, 1871, 1872, 1873, 1880, 1885, 1889, 1890, 1891, 1892, 1893, 1894, 1895, 1898, 1899, 1900, 1902, 1903, 1904, 1906, 1907.**

Frankland, E. *Proceedings of the Royal Society*, 22, London, 1874; **1873.**

Fraser, General Sir Thomas. *Recollections with Reflections*, Edinburgh, 1914; **1854.**

Frederick William III, King. *Le passage des alliés en Suisse*, W. Oechsli, Paris, 1912; **1814.**

Frénilly, Baron François Auguste de. *Recollections*, translated by A. Chuquet, London, 1909; **1787.**

Freshfield, Douglas. *Across Country from Thonon to Trent*, p.p., London, 1865; **1863, 1864.** *Italian Alps*, London, 1875; **1864, 1865, 1866, 1874.**

Freshfield, Mrs. Henry. *Alpine Byways*, London, 1861; **1859, 1860.** *A Summer Tour in the Grisons and Italian valleys of the Bernina*, London, 1862; **1861,**

Freygrabend, Dr. In *Travels in Switzerland*, W. Coxe, London, 1791; **1785.**

Fries, Hans. 'Die Geschichte des Splügenpasses', E. Walder, *Die Alpen*, 2, 1926; **1545.**

Fripp, George A. 'George A. Fripp & Alfred D. Fripp', H. Stuart Thompson, *Walker's Quarterly*, 25, London, 1828; **1834.**

Frisi, Paolo. *Opuscoli filosofici*, Milano, 1781; **1778.**

Fröbel, Julius. *Reise in die weniger bekannten Thäler auf der Nordseite der Penninischen Alpen*, Berlin, 1840; **1839.**

Fry, Sir Edward. *A Memoir*, A. Fry, Oxford, 1921; **1848.**

Fry, Elizabeth. *Memoir of the life of Elizabeth Fry*, London, 1848; **1839.**

Frye, W. E. *After Waterloo*, London, 1908; **1815, 1816, 1817.**

FUESSLI, JOHANN CONRAD. *Staats- und Erdbeschreibung der schweizerischen Eidgenosschaft*, Schaffhausen, 1772; **1767.**

FULTON, CHARLES CARROLL. *Europe viewed through American Spectacles*, Philadelphia, 1874; **1873.**

GAGNEBIN, A. *Abraham Gagnebin*, J. Thurmann, Porrentruy, 1851; **1726, 1761.**

GALLATIN, JAMES. *Diary*, London, 1914; **1815, 1822.**

GAMBETTA, LÉON. *Lettres de Gambetta*, ed. by D. Halévy & E. Pillias, Paris, 1938; **1869, 1872, 1876.**

GARCIN, JEAN-LAURENT. 'Biographie', P. Bridel, in *Le Conservateur Suisse*, 13, Lausanne, 1857; **1781.**

GARIBALDI, GIUSEPPE. *Garibaldi: Recollections of his Public and Private Life*, E. Melena, London, 1887; **1867.**

GASKELL, MRS. *Life*, A. S. Whitfield, London, 1929; **1864.**

GAUDIN, J.-F.-T. *Flora Helvetica*, Zürich, 1828–33; **1806, 1808, 1809, 1812.**

GAUTHIER, MME DE. *Voyage d'une Française en Suisse et en Franche-Comté depuis la révolution*, Londres 1790; **1789, 1790.**

GAUTIER, THÉOPHILE. In *Ces Monts sublimes*, C.-E. Engel & C. Vallot, Paris, 1936; **1850.** *Les vacances du Lundi; tableaux de montagnes*, Paris, 1888; **1868.**

GAY, J. In *Flora Helvetica*, J.-F.-T. Gaudin, Zürich, 1828–33, and in *Le major Roger*, C.-E. Engel, Neuchâtel, n.d.; **1820.**

GENLIS, MME DE. *Mémoires*, Paris, 1928; **1793.**

GENOUDE, EUGÈNE. *Voyage dans la Vendée et dans le midi de la France; suivi d'un voyage pittoresque en Suisse*, Paris, 1821; **1814.**

GEORGE, H. B. *The Oberland and its Glaciers*, London, 1866; **1865.**

GÉRARD DE NERVAL. *Voyage en Orient*, Paris, 1851; **1838.**

GERCKEN, PHILIPP WILHELM. *Reisen durch Schwaben, Baiern, die angränzende Schweiz, etc.*, Stendal, 1783–8; **1779.**

GERSDORF, BARON VON. In *Paccard wider Balmat*, H. Dübi, Bern, 1913; **1786.**

GESNER, CONRAD. 'Voyage de Conrad Gesner au Mont Pilate', *Le Conservateur Suisse*, 4, Lausanne, 1814; **1555.** In *Historia stirpium Helvetiae*, A. von Haller, Bernae, 1768; **1561.**

GESNER, JOHANN. In *Epistolarum ab eruditis viris ad Alb. Hallerum scriptarum, Pars I*, Bernae, 1774; **1726, 1730, 1731, 1735.**

GIBBON, EDWARD. *Miscellaneous Works*, London, 1814; **1753, 1758, 1763, 1764, 1783, 1793.** 'Journal de mon voyage dans quelques endroits de la Suisse', in *Historic Studies*, M. Read, London, 1895; **1755.** *Journal de Gibbon à Lausanne*, G. Bonnard, Lausanne, 1945; **1763.**

GIDE, ANDRÉ. *Œuvres Complètes*, Paris, 1935; **1894, 1912, 1917.**

GIORDANI, PIETRO. In *Early mountaineers*, F. Gribble, London, 1899; **1801.**

GIRDLESTONE, A. G. *The High Alps without Guides*, London, 1870; **1864, 1865, 1866, 1867, 1869.**

GLENBERVIE, LORD. *The Diaries of Sylvester Douglas*, edited by E. Bickley, London, 1828; **1816.**

GLOVER, S. *A Description of the Valley of Chamouni*, London, 1819; *c.* **1792.**

GOBAT, SAMUEL. *Life and Work*, London, 1884; **1823, 1843.**

GOBINEAU, COMTE ARTHUR DE. *Le Comte Arthur de Gobineau*, M. Lange, Strasbourg, 1924; **1851.**

GODEFFROY, C. *Notice sur les glaciers, les moraines, et les blocs erratiques des Alpes*, Paris & Genève, 1840; **1838.**

GODKIN, EDWIN LAWRENCE. *Life and Letters*, edited by R. Ogden, New York, 1907; **1861, 1892.**

GODLEY, A. D. *Reliquiae*, edited by C. R. L. Fletcher, Oxford, 1926; **1889, 1891.**

GODWIN, C. G. *Notes of a Ramble in Belgium, the Rhine, and Switzerland*, London, 1846; **1842.**

GOETHE, JOHANN WOLFGANG. *Goethes Schweizerreisen*, H. Wahl, Gotha, 1921; **1775, 1779, 1788, 1797.**

GOLDSMITH, OLIVER. *Life and Times of Oliver Goldsmith*, J. Forster, London, 1877; **1755.**

GONCOURT, EDMOND DE. *Journal*, Paris, 1891; **1874.**

GOODWIN, HARVEY. *Biographical Memoir*, H. D. Rawnsley, London, 1896; **1842.**

GORANI, COMTE JOSEPH. In *L'Italia e la Svizzera*, L. Mazzucchetti e A. Lohner, Milano, 1943; **1769.** 'Le Comte Gorani en Suisse', M. Monnier, *Bibliothèque Universelle*, 52, Genève, 1875; **1779, 1793, 1794.**

GOS, ALBERT. *Souvenirs d'un peintre de montagne*, Genève 1943; **1872, 1873, 1874, 1876.**

GOSSE, EDMUND. In *Switzerland Poetical & Pictorial*, Zürich, 1893; **1883.**

GOTTSCHALK, F. *Das Chamounithal am Fusse des Montblanc*, Halle, 1811; **1810.**

GOUGH, JOHN B. *Autobiography*, London, 1870; **1859.**

GOULD, EMILY BLISS. *Memorials*, L. W. Bacon, New York, 1879; **1860.**

GRANDE, CONSTANCE & JULIAN. *Constance Grande*, J. Grande, London, 1925; **1911, 1914.**

GRANT, HARRY ALLEN. *American Alpine Journal*, 2, p. 494, 1936; **1839.**

GRANT, JAMES. *Records of a Run through Continental Countries*, London, 1853; **1853.**

GRANT, GENERAL ULYSSES S. *Around the World with General Grant*, J. R. Young, New York, 1879; **1877.**

GRANVILLE, A. B. *Autobiography*, London, 1874; **1819.**

GRASS, CARL. *Fragmente von Wanderungen in der Schweiz*, Zürich, 1797; **1790, 1796.**

GRASSER, J. J. *Itinerarium historico-politicum per celebriores Helvetiae urbes.* Basileae, 1624; *c.* **1610.**

GRAVES, C. *Swiss Summer*, London, 1938; **1937.**

GRAY, ASA. *Letters*, London, 1893; **1839, 1850, 1869, 1881.**

GRAY, ROBERT. *Letters during the Course of a Tour through Germany, Switzerland and Italy*, London, 1794; **1791.** *Life*, London, 1876; **1827.**

GREELEY, HORACE. *Glances at Europe*, New York, 1851; **1851.**

GREEN, JOHN RICHARD. *Stray studies from England and Italy*, London, 1876; **1869.**

GREG, MRS. W. In *Notes of a Diary 1881–86.* M. E. Grant Duff, London, 1899; **1884.**

GREISCHE, COMTE ANATOLE SCITIVEAUX DE. *Un voyage en Suisse en 1849 du peintre Guérard*, Toulouse, 1933; **1849.**

GREVILLE, CHARLES. *Greville Memoirs*, London, 1875; **1830.**

GRIBBLE, FRANCIS. *Seen in passing*, London, 1929; **1892.**

GRIMM, SAMUEL HIERONYMUS. *Reise nach den Alpen*, Zürich, 1776; **1758.**

GROB, GREGORIUS. *Der Schweizer auf dem Rigiberg*, St. Gallen, 1795; *c.* **1789.**

GROTE, GEORGE. *Personal Life of George Grote*, London, 1873; **1834, 1837, 1847.**

GROVE, SIR GEORGE. *Life and Letters*, C. L. Graves, London, 1903; **1864, 1871, 1874, 1885, 1891.**

GRÜN, C. *Seize jours en Suisse*, Verviers, 1886; **1886.**

GRUNER, GOTTLIEB SIEGMUND. *Die Eisgebirge des Schweizerlandes*, Bern, 1760; **1756.**

GUALANDRIS, ANGELO. *Lettere odeporiche*, Venezia, 1780; **1775.**

GUETTARD, J.-E. *Mémoires de l'Académie Royale*, Paris, 1752; *c.* **1752.**

GÜGLINGEN, PAUL WALTER VON. In *Geschichte des mittelalterlichen Handels*, A. Schulte, Leipzig, 1900; **1481.**

GUIBERT, COMTE DE. *Voyages de Guibert dans diverses parties de la France et en Suisse*, Paris, 1806; **1784.**

GUILD, CURTIS. *Over the Ocean*, Boston, 1888; **1867**. *Abroad again*, Boston, 1888; **1873.**

GUILLAUME, DR. *Trois jours de vacances*, Neuchâtel, 1864; **1864.** *Autour de deux Lacs*, Neuchâtel, 1865; **1865.**

GÜSSFELDT, P. *In den Hochalpen*, Berlin, 1886; **1859, 1865, 1868, 1869, 1872, 1877, 1878, 1879, 1881, 1882, 1884, 1885**. *Der Mont Blanc*, Berlin, 1894; **1886, 1887, 1889, 1890, 1891, 1892, 1893.**

GUSTAVUS ADOLPHUS IV. *An Exiled King*. S. Elkan, London, 1913; **1815.**

GUTHRIE, THOMAS. *Autobiography and Memoir*, London, 1875; **1856, 1861.**

HACKAERT, JAN. *Unbekannte Schweizer Landschaften aus dem XVII. Jahrhundert*, S. Stelling-Michaud, Zürich, 1937; **1655.**

HACQUET, BALTHAZAR. *Physikalische-Politische Reise aus den Dinarischen durch die Julischen, Cärnischen, Rhätischen in die Norischen Alpen*, Leipzig, 1785; **1781.**

HADOW, G. *Grace Hadow*, H. Deneke, Oxford, 1946; **1922, 1923, 1924, 1925. 1926,** *c.* **1927, 1928.**

HAESELER, C. H. *Across the Atlantic*, Philadelphia, 1868; **1867.**

HAGEN, FRIEDRICH HEINRICH VON DER. *Briefe in die Heimat aus Deutschland, der Schweiz und Italien*, Breslau, 1818; **1816.**

HAGENBACH, J. J. In *Historia Stirpium Helvetiae*, A. von Haller, Bernae, 1768; *c.* **1620.**

HAGENBUCH, JOHANN KASPAR. 'Zur Schweizer Turistik im 18. Jahrhundert', A. Bruckner, *Die Alpen*, 7, 1931; **1727.**

HAGGARD, SIR RIDER. *The Days of My Life*, London, 1926; **1872.**

HAKE, GORDON. *Memoirs of Eighty Years*, London, 1892; **1831.**

HALDANE, ROBERT. *Memoirs of the Lives of Robert Haldane of Airthrey and of his Brother James Alexander Haldane*, A. Haldane, London, 1852; **1816.**

HALEM, G. A. VON. *Blicke auf einen Theil Deutschlands, der Schweiz, und Frankreichs bey einer Reise vom Jahre 1790*, Hamburg, 1791; **1790.**

HALIFAX, CHARLES LINDSEY, VISCOUNT. *Halifax*, J. G. Lockhart, London, 1935; **1879.**

HALL, BASIL. *Patchwork*, London, 1841; **1818.**

HALL, F. W. *Rambles in Europe*, New York, 1839; **1836.**

HALL, NEWMAN. *Autobiography*, London, 1898; **1854, 1865, 1878, 1880, 1884, 1887, 1889, 1891, 1894, 1897.**

HALLER, ALBRECHT VON. 'Albrecht von Hallers erste Alpenreise', W. von Arx, *Revue Helvétique*, 1, 1892; **1728.** 'Descriptio itineris Alpini suscepti M. Julio Anni 1731', *Tempe Helvetica*, 1, 1735; **1731.** *Relation d'un voyage de Albert de Haller dans l'Oberland Bernois*, H. Mettrier, Langres, 1906; **1732.** *Historia Stirpium Helvetiae*, Bernae, 1768; **1730, 1733, 1736, 1755, 1756, 1757, 1759, 1760, 1761.** *Iter Helveticum*, Gottingae, 1740; **1739.**

HAMEL, DR. 'Extract from "An Account of Two Late Attempts to ascend Mont Blanc",' *Annals of Philosophy*, 1821; **1820.**

HAMILTON, CLAYTON. *Wanderings*, New York, 1925; **1903.**

HAMILTON, HELEN. *Mountain Madness*, London, 1922; *c.* **1912.**

HAMMERTON, PHILIP GILBERT. *An Autobiography*, London, 1897; **1862.**

HANNINGTON, JAMES. *History of his Life and Work*, E. S. Dawson, London, 1887; **1863.**

HARCOURT, SIR WILLIAM. *Life*, A. G. Gardiner, London, 1923; **1857.** And in *From a Holiday Journal*, E. T. Cook, London, 1904; **1857.**

HARDMAN, SIR WILLIAM. *Letters & Memoirs*, edited by S. M. Ellis, London, 1925; **1863, 1864.**

HARDWICK, CHARLES. *Over the Alps by the St. Gothard*, n.p., n.d.; **1867.**

HARDY, J. F. In *Peaks, Passes, & Glaciers*, 2, 1, London, 1862; **1861.**

HARDY, THOMAS. *Later Years*, F. E. Hardy, London, 1930; **1897.**

HARE, AUGUSTUS J. C. *The Story of my Life*, London, 1900; **1854, 1857, 1863, 1884.**

HARE, AUGUSTUS WILLIAM. *Memorials of a Quiet Life*, A. J. C. Hare, London, 1872; **1797, 1817.**

HARE, LUCEBELLA. In *G. F. Whidborne*, p.p., Glasgow, 1917; **1856.**

HARE, LUCY ANNE. *Memorials of a Quiet Life*, A. J. C. Hare, London, 1872; **1863.**

HARE, MARIA. *Memorials of a Quiet Life*, A. J. C. Hare, London, 1872; **1834, 1857.**

HARRISON, FREDERIC. *Autobiographic Memoirs*, London, 1911; **1851.** *My Alpine Jubilee*, London, 1908; **1854, 1863, 1864, 1866, 1868.**

HARTE, BRET. *Letters*, London, 1926; **1879, 1895.**

HAUSSEZ, BARON D'. *Voyage d'un exilé*, Paris, 1835; *c.* **1834.** *Alpes et Danube*, Paris, 1857; *c.* **1835.**

HAVERGAL, FRANCES RIDLEY. *Memorials of F. R. Havergal*, London, n.d., and *Swiss Letters*, London, 1882; **1869, 1871, 1873, 1874, 1876.**

HAVERGAL, MARIA V. G. *Autobiography*, London, 1888; **1882.**

HAWTREY, STEPHEN. *History of the Hawtrey Family*, F. M. Hawtrey, London, 1903; **1855.**

HAYDEN, J. *A Sketch of a Tour in Switzerland*, London, 1859; **1857.**

HAYWARD, ABRAHAM. *Some Account of a Journey across the Alps*, London, n.d.; **1834.**

HAZLITT, WILLIAM. *Notes of a Journey through France and Italy*, London, 1826; **1825.**

HEADLEY, J. T. (with CHEEVER, G. B.). *Travels among Alpine Scenery*, London, 1855; **1845.**

HEARD, GEORGE W. *American Alpine Journal*, 3, p. 172, 1939; **1855.**

HEATHMAN, W. G. *Switzerland in 1854–5*, London, 1855; **1854.**

HEER, OSWALD. 'Geographische Verbreitung der Käfer in den Schweizeralpen', in *Mittheilungen aus dem Gebiet der theoretischen Erdkunde*, J. Fröbel & O. Heer, Zürich, 1834; **1833.** 'Über die nivale Flora der Schweiz', *Neue Denkschriften der allgemeinen schweizerischen Gesellschaft für die gesammten Naturwissenschaften*, 29, 1885; **1834, 1835.**

HEGEL, GEORG WILHELM FRIEDRICH. 'Supplement, "Leben",' in *Sämmtliche Werke*, edited by K. Rosenkranz, *Reisetagebuch Hegels durch die Berner Oberalpen*, Berlin, 1844; **1796.**

HEGER, THOMAS. *A Tour through part of the Netherlands, France, and Switzerland in the Year 1817*, London, 1820; **1817.**

HEGETSCHWEILER, JOHANN. *Reisen in dem Gebirgstock zwischen Glarus und Graubünden*, Zürich, 1825; **1819, 1820, 1822.**

HEGNER, ULRICH. *Auch ich war in Paris*, Berlin, 1828; **1801.** *Briefe aus dem Berner Oberlande*, Berlin, 1828; **1804.** *Berg-, Land- und Seereise*, Berlin, 1828; **1817.**

HEIGELIN, J. F. *Briefe über Graubünden*, Stuttgart, 1793; *c.* **1790.**

HEINSE, J. J. WILHELM. *W. Heinse Sämtliche Werke*, edited by J. Schüddekopf, Leipzig, 1909; **1780.**

HENNEZEL, BÉAT DE. 'Un voyage en Italie à la fin du XVIIIe siècle.' C. Gilliard, *Bibliothèque Universelle*, 73, Genève, 1914; **1794.**

HENTZNER, PAUL. *Itinerarium Germaniae etc.*, Noribergae, 1629; **1597, 1599.**

HÉRAULT DE SÉCHELLES. *Hérault de Séchelles*, E. Dard, Paris, 1907; **1790.**

HERBART, JOHANN FRIEDRICH. 'Bericht über eine Reise in die Alpen 1798', *Schweizer Alpenzeitung*, 2, 1883; **1798.**

HERBERT, HENRY. *A Fortnight's Journal*, London, 1838; **1837.**

HERMAN, ANDRÉ. *Vallons de l'Helvétie*, Paris, 1882; **1877.**

HERSCHEL, SIR JOHN. *Peaks, Passes, & Glaciers*, 2, II; London, 1862; **1821.**

HERVEY, CHARLES. *Recollections of the Continent*, Naples, 1839; **1838.**

HERVEY, FREDERICK AUGUSTUS. In 'Chronologie Critique', J. L. Courtois, *Annales de la société J.-J. Rousseau*, 15 Genève, 1923; **1765.** *The Earl Bishop*, W. S. Childe-Pemberton, London, 1925; **1766, 1770, 1779, 1793.**

HERVEY, WILLIAM. *Journals of the Hon. W. Hervey*, Bury St. Edmunds, 1906; **1766, 1773.**

HERZEN, ALEXANDER. *Erinnerungen*, Berlin, 1907; **1849.**

HESS, LUDWIG. *Jahrbuch des Schweizer Alpenclub*, 16, p. 437, 1881; **1792.**

HESSE, PRINCESS ALICE, GRAND DUCHESS OF. *Biographical Sketches and Letters*, London, 1884; **1865, 1867.**

HEUGH, H. *Notices of the State of Religion in Geneva & Belgium.* Glasgow, 1844; **1843.**

HEWAT, K. *My Diary, being Notes of a Continental Tour*, p.p. n.p.n.d.; **1878.**

HIESTAND, H. *Travels in Germany, Prussia & Switzerland*, New York, 1837; **1835.**

HINCHLIFF, THOMAS WOODBINE. *Summer Months among the Alps*, London, 1857; **1854, 1855, 1856.** *Peaks, Passes, & Glaciers*, London, 1859; **1857.**

HIRSCHFELD, C. C. L. *Briefe die Schweiz betreffend*, Leipzig, 1776; **1766.** *Neue Briefe über die Schweiz*, Kiel, 1785; **1783.**

HIRZEL-ESCHER, H. *Wanderungen in weniger bekannten Alpengegenden der Schweiz*, Zürich, 1829; **1822, 1823.**

HOBHOUSE, B. *Remarks on Several Parts of France, Italy etc.*, p.p., Bath, 1796; **1785.**

HOBHOUSE, JOHN CAM. *Recollections of a Long Life*, London, 1909; **1816, 1828.**

HOFFMANN, G. *Wanderungen in der Gletscherwelt*, Zürich, 1843; **1838.** *Berg- und Gletscher-Fahrten in den Hochalpen der Schweiz*, G. Studer, M. Ulrich, & J. J. Weilenmann, Zürich, 1859; **1844, 1847, 1848.**

HOG, ROGER. *Tour on the Continent in France, Switzerland and Italy*, London, 1824; **1817.**

HOGG, JOHN. *Letters from Abroad to a Friend at Cambridge*, London, 1844; **1824.**

HOGG, QUINTIN. *The Polytechnic and its Founder Quintin Hogg*, E. M. Wood, London, 1932; **1889.**

HOGG, THOMAS JEFFERSON. *Two hundred and nine Days*, London, 1827; **1825.**

HOLBEIN, H. *Holbein & his Time*, A. Wotlmann, London, 1872; **1517.**

HOLDEN, L. L. *A Summer Jaunt through the Old World*, Boston, 1879; **1878.**

HÖLDER, G. C. VON. *Meine Reise über den Gotthard nach den Borromäischen Inseln und Mailand; und von da zurück über das Val Formazza, die Grimsel und das Oberland im Sommer 1801*, Stuttgart, 1803; **1801.** *Meine Reise durch das Wallis und Pays de Vaud im Jahre 1803*, Stuttgart, 1805; **1803.**

HÖLDERLIN, FRIEDRICH. *F. Hölderlin*, F. Litzmann, Berlin, 1890; **1801.**

HOLL, FRANK. *Life and Work*, A. M. Reynolds, London, 1912; **1869.**

HOLLAND, SIR HENRY. *Recollections of Past Life*, London, 1872; **1814.**

HOLLAND, MARY SIBYLLA. *Letters*, London, 1898; **1880.**

HOLLIS, THOMAS. *Memoirs of Thomas Hollis*, London, 1780; **1748.**

HOLMAN, JAMES. *The Narrative of a Journey undertaken in the Years 1819, 1820, and 1821, through France, Savoy, Switzerland, etc.*, London, 1822; **1821.**

HOLMES, C. J. *Self & Partners*, London, 1936; **1903.**

HOLMES, MRS. DALKEITH. *A Ride on Horseback to Florence through France and Switzerland. By a Lady*, London, 1842; **1839.**

HOLMES, D. T. *A Scot in France and Switzerland*, Paisley, 1910; **1906.**

HOLMES, OLIVER WENDELL. *Life*, J. T. Morse, London, 1896; **1835.**

HOLROYD, MARIA JOSEPHA. *The Girlhood of Maria Josepha Holroyd (Lady Stanley of Alderley)*, edited by H. Adeane, London, 1897; **1791.**

HOLWORTHY, S. M. *Alpine Scrambles and Classic Rambles*, London, n.d.; **1882.**

HOOKHAM, THOMAS. *A Walk through Switzerland in September 1816*, London, 1818; **1816.**

HOPKINS, GERARD MANLEY. *Gerard Manley Hopkins*, G. J. Lahey, Oxford, 1930; **1868.** *Note Books*, Oxford, 1937; **1868.**

HORNBY, EMILY. *Mountaineering Records*, p.p., Liverpool, 1907; **1873, 1875, 1876, 1881, 1882, 1885.**

HORSLEY, JOHN WILLIAM. *I remember*, London, 1911; **1891, 1892.**

HORT, FENTON JOHN ANTHONY. *Life and Letters*, London, 1896; **1854, 1856, 1860, 1861, 1862, 1865, 1867, 1872, 1875, 1876, 1883, 1885, 1887, 1890, 1892.**

Hortense, Queen. *Memoirs*, edited by Prince Napoleon, London, 1922; **1810, 1815.** *Les saisons et les jours d'Arenenberg*, P. Grellet, Lausanne, 1944; **1815.**

Hottinger, J. H. 'Montium glacialium Helveticorum descriptio', *Appendix ad annum IX et X Decuriae Ephemeridum Academiae Caesaris Leopoldinae Naturae Curiosorum in Germania*, Nuremberg, 1706; **1703.**

Houghton, Richard Monckton Milnes, Lord. *Memorials of a Residence on the Continent*, London, 1838; **1829.**

Howard, John. *Life*, J. Field, London, 1850; **1776.**

Howard, General Oliver Otis. *Autobiography*, New York, 1907; **1884.**

Howell, James. *Epistolae Ho-elianae*, edited by J. Jacobs, London, 1890; **1621.**

Howitt, Mary. *An Autobiography*, London, 1889; **1870.**

Huber, J. J. In *Historia Stirpium Helvetiae*, A. von Haller, Bernae, 1768; **1738.**

Hudson, Charles. *Where there 's a Will there 's a Way*, London, 1856; **1853, 1855.** 'Days of Long Ago', J. P. Farrar, *Alpine Journal*, 32, 1920; **1859.**

Hughes, Hugh Price. *Life*, London, 1904; **1873, 1876, 1881, 1892, 1902.** *Story of My Life*, K. P. Hughes, London, 1945; **1887.**

Hugi, Franz Joseph. *Das Wesen der Gletscher*, Solothurn, 1842; **1827, 1830, 1832, 1836.** *Naturhistorische Alpenreise*, Solothurn, 1830; **1828, 1829.** In 'The early Swiss Pioneers of the Alps', H. Dübi, *Alpine Journal*, 33, 1920; **1831.**

Hugo, Victor. 'Fragment d'un voyage aux Alpes', *Revue des Deux Mondes*, 1831; **1825.** *Victor Hugo raconté par un témoin de sa vie*, Adèle Hugo, Bruxelles, 1863; **1825.** *Le Rhin. Alpes et Pyrénées*, Paris, n.d.; **1839.**

Hull, E. *Reminiscences of a Strenuous Life*, London, 1910; **1908.**

Humbolt, Alexander von. *Life*, K. Bruhns, London, 1873; **1795.**

Hunter, Sir William Wilson. *Life*, F. H. Skrine, London, 1901; **1867.**

Hutton, James. *Memoirs*, London, 1856; **1748.**

Hutton, R. H. *Holiday Rambles in Ordinary Places by a Wife and her Husband*, London, 1877; **1867, 1868, 1870.**

Huxley, Thomas Henry. *Life and Letters*, edited by L. Huxley, London, 1900; **1856, 1857, 1862, 1886, 1887, 1888, 1889.** And in *Memoir of the Duchess of Teck*, C. Kinloch Cooke, London, 1900; **1893.**

HUYGENS, CONSTANTIJN. 'Constantijn Huygens' Journaal van zijne Reis naar Venetie', J. A. Worp, *Bijdragen en Mededeelingen van het historisch Genootschap Utrecht*, 15, 1894; **1620.**

HUYGENS, CONSTANTIJN, JUNR. 'Journalen van Constantijn Huygens den Zoon', *Werken van het Historisch Genootschap Utrecht*, N.S. 46, 1888; **1650.**

ICHIKAWA, H. *Japanese Lady in Europe*, London, 1937; **1932.**

IFFLAND, A. W. *Blick in die Schweiz*, Leipzig, 1793; **1792.**

ILLINGWORTH, JOHN RICHARDSON. *Life and Work*, London, 1917; **1875, 1877, 1878.**

INGLIS, H. D. *Switzerland, the south of France and the Pyrenees*, London, 1837; **1830.**

IRVING, PETER. *American Alpine Journal*, 4, p. 463, 1942; **1807.**

IRVING, WASHINGTON. *Life & Letters*, P. M. Irving, London, 1862; **1805.** *Life*, S. T. Williams, New York, 1935; **1805.**

ISABEL, INFANTA CLARA EUGENIA. 'Correspondencia de la Infanta Doña Isabel', Villa. *Boletín de la Real Academia de la Historia*, 49, App. V, Madrid, 1906; **1599.**

JACKSON, EILEEN MONTAGUE. *Switzerland calling*, London, 1927; **1923, 1925.**

JACKSON, H. H. *New Monthly Magazine*, London, 1827; **1823.**

JACOBI, GEORG ARNOLD. *Briefe aus der Schweiz und Italien*, Zürich & Leipzig, 1796; **1791.**

JACOMB, FREDERICK WILLIAM. *Peaks, Passes, & Glaciers*, 2, 1, London, 1862; **1860, 1861.**

JAMESON, MRS. ANNA. *Letters and Friendship*, S. Erskine, London, 1915; **1821.** *Diary of an Ennuyée*, London, 1826; **1821.**

JAVELLE, ÉMILE. *Souvenirs d'un Alpiniste*, Lausanne, 1886; **1869, 1870, 1871, 1872, 1873, 1874, 1875, 1876, 1878, 1881, 1882.**

JEKYLL, GERTRUDE. *A Memoir*, F. Jekyll, London, 1934; **1873.**

JERSEY, COUNTESS OF. *Fifty-one Years of Victorian Life*, London, 1922; **1879.**

JETZLER, CHRISTOPH. In *J. H. Lambert deutscher gelehrter Briefwechsel*, Berlin, 1782–7; **1766.**

JEVONS, W. STANLEY, *Letters and Journal*, London, 1886; **1865.**

JOHN DE BREMBLE. *Lectures on the Study of Medieval and Modern History*, W. Stubbs, p. 128, Oxford, 1886; **1188.**

JOHNSON, JAMES. *Change of Air*, London, 1832; **1823, 1829.** *Pilgrimages to the Spas*, London, 1841; **1834.**

JOHNSTON, SIR HARRY. *The Story of my Life*, London, 1923; **1889, 1894, 1913.**

JONES, C. A. *The Foreign Freaks of Five Friends*, London, 1882; **1881.**

JONES, REV. HARRY. *The Regular Swiss Round*, London, 1865; **1862, 1863, 1864.**

JONES, J. V. *John Viriamu Jones*, E. B. Poulton, Oxford, 1911; **1887.**

JOPLING, L. *Twenty Years of my Life*, London, 1925; **1883.**

JOSEPH II, EMPEROR. *Kaiser Joseph II*, E. Benedikt, Wien, 1936; **1777.**

JOSEPHINE, EMPRESS. *Joséphine répudiée*, F. Masson, Paris, 1901; **1810.** *L'Impératrice Joséphine*, Baron de Méneval, Paris, 1910; **1810.**

JOWETT, BENJAMIN. *Life & Letters*, E. Abbott & L. Campbell, London, 1897; **1871, 1876.**

JOYCE, JAMES. *Biography*, H. Gorman, London, 1941; **1917.**

KARAMSIN, NIKOLAI. *Travels from Moscow through Prussia, Germany, Switzerland, France and England*, London, 1803; **1789.**

KASTHOFER, KARL. *Bemerkungen auf einer Alpenreise über den Susten, Gotthard, Bernardin, und über die Oberalp, Furka und Grimsel*, Aarau, 1822; **1821.** *Bemerkungen auf einer Alpenreise über den Brünig, Pragel, Kirzenberg und über die Flüela, den Maloya und Splügen*, Bern, 1825; **1822.**

KEAN, EDMUND. *Life*, F. W. Hawkins, London, 1869; **1818.**

KEATE, GEORGE. *George Keate Esq.*, K. G. Dapp, Philadelphia, 1939; **1756.**

KELPER, D. DE. *Quelques jours en Suisse*, Bruxelles, 1914; *c.* **1914.**

KELSALL, THOMAS FORBES. In *The Browning Box*, H. W. Donner, Oxford, 1935; **1868.**

KEMBLE, FANNY. *Further Records*, London, 1890; **1862,** *c.* **1871, 1873, 1877.** In *The Bancrofts on and off the Stage*, London, 1888; **1878.** And in *Essays in London*, Henry James, London, 1893.

KENNEDY, BENJAMIN E. *My Old Playground revisited*, London, 1882; **1881.**

KENNEDY, EDWARD SHIRLEY. *Where there's a Will there's a Way*, London, 1856; **1855.** 'The Pizzo Bernina', *Peaks, Passes, & Glaciers*, 2, 1, London, 1862; **1861.**

KENNEDY, THOMAS S. 'Zermatt and the Matterhorn in winter', *Alpine Journal*, 1, London, 1863; **1862.**

KENT, EDWARD, DUKE OF. *Edward, Duke of Kent*, D. Duff, London, 1938; **1818.**

KER, W. P. 'W. P. Ker', R. W. Chambers, *Proc. British Academy*, 11, 1923; **1922.** *Reliquiae*, A. D. Godley, Oxford, 1926; **1923.**

KEYSLER, JOHANN GEORG. *Travels through Germany, Bohemia, Hungary, Switzerland, Italy and Lorrain*, London, 1756; **1729.**

KING, S. W. *The Italian Valleys of the Pennine Alps*, London, 1858; **1855.**

KINGSFORD, ANNA MAY. *Her Life, Letters, Diary and Work*, E. Maitland, London, 1896; **1882.**

KINLOCH, FRANCIS. *Letters from Switzerland and France written during a Residence of between two and three Years in Different Parts of those Countries*, Boston, 1819, and London, 1821; **1804.**

KIRKLAND, MRS. *Holidays Abroad; or Europe from the West*, New York, 1849; **1848.**

KLEIST, HEINRICH VON. *Heinrich Kleist in der Schweiz*, T. Zolling, Stuttgart, 1882; **1802, 1803.**

KLOPSTOCK, F. *Kleine poetische & prosaische Werke*, Frankfurt, 1771; **1750.**

KLUCKER, CHRISTIAN. *Adventures of an Alpine Guide*, London, 1932; **1872, 1882, 1887, 1888, 1926.**

KNIGHTLEY OF FAWSLEY, LADY. *Journals* edited by J. Cartwright, London, 1915; **1871.**

KNIGHTON, SIR WILLIAM. *Memoirs*, London, 1838; **1833.**

KNOX, JOHN. *John Knox*, Lord Eustace Percy, London, 1937; **1554.**

KOHL, J. G. *Alpenreisen*, Dresden & Leipzig, 1849–51; **1846, 1847.**

KÖNIG, F. N. *Reise in die Alpen*, Bern, 1814; **1809.**

KOSCIUSKO, THADDEUS. *Bollettino Storico della Svizzera Italiana*, E. Motta, 5, p. 241, 1883; **1816.**

KOSSUTH, LOUIS. *Memories of my Exile*, London, 1880; **1859.**

KOTHARI, JEHANGIR H. *Impressions of a First Tour round the World*, p.p., London, 1889; **1883.**

KOTZEBUE, AUGUST VON. *Travels from Berlin through Switzerland to Paris in the Year 1804*, London, 1804; **1804.**

KROCK, ANNA HELENE VON. *Briefe einer reisenden Dame aus der Schweitz*, Frankfurt & Leipzig, 1787; **1786.**

KROPOTKIN, PETER. *Autour d'une vie.* Paris, 1921; **1872, 1876, 1881.**

KRÜDENER, JULIE DE. *The Lady of the Holy Alliance*, E. J. Knapton, New York, 1939; **1797, 1801, 1808, 1817.** In *Mme Récamier*, H. Noel Williams, London, 1901; **1815.**

KUGY, JULIUS. *Alpine Pilgrimage*, London, 1934; **1886, 1888, 1889, 1892, 1905, 1906.**

KÜTTNER, K. G. *Briefe eines Sachsen aus der Schweiz an seinen Freund in Leipzig*, Leipzig, 1785; **1776, 1778, 1779.**

La Borde, Jean Benjamin de. *Lettres sur la Suisse, adressées à Mme. de M. par un voyageur français en 1781*, Genève, 1783; **1781.**

Labrune (Reboulet &). *Voyage de Suisse, relation historique contenue en deux lettres, écrites par les Srs. Reboulet et Labrune à un de leurs amis de France*, La Haye, 1686; **1685.**

Lachenal, W. In *Historia Stirpium Helvetiae*, A. von Haller, Bernae, 1768; **1760.**

Lage de Volude, B.-S. de. *La marquise de Lage de Volude*, H. de Reinach-Fournmagne, Paris, 1908; **1789, 1797.**

Lagneau, Louis-Vivant. *Journal d'un chirurgien de la Grande Armée*, edited by E. Tattet, Paris, 1913; **1805.**

La Grandville, Ctesse de. *Souvenirs de voyage*, Paris, 1836; **1819, 1822.**

Laing, S. *Notes of a Traveller on the Social and Political State of France, Prussia, Switzerland, etc.*, London, 1842; **1839.**

Lalande, J. In *Magazin Encyclopédique*, 4, 1796; **1795.**

Lamartine, Alphonse de. *Mémoires inédits*, Paris, 1909; **1812, 1815.** *Correspondance*, Paris, 1874; **1824.** *Confidences*, Paris, 1897; **1815.** In *Un Genevois cosmopolite: Huber Saladin*, G. Fournet, Paris, 1932; **1841.** In *Les amours de Genève*, F. Fournier-Marcigny, Genève, 1943; **1820.**

Lambert, L. *Au pays blanc*, Bruxelles, 1922; **1911.**

Lambin, Denys. In *Les sonnets suisses de Joachim du Bellay*, A. François, Lausanne, 1946; **1552.**

Lamont, Martha Macdonald. *Impressions, Thoughts and Sketches during Two Years in France and Switzerland*, London, 1844; **1838.**

Lamprell, E. E. *A Fortnight in Switzerland for Five Guineas*, London, 1905; *c.* **1905.**

Lançon, Xavier ('Gallicus'). *Voyage en Suisse; souvenirs humoristiques*, Paris & Lyon, 1866; **1865.**

Langle, Marquis de. *A Picturesque Description of Switzerland*, London, n.d.; **1784.**

Langton, T. *Letters*, pp. Manchester, 1900; **1816, 1817.**

Laporte, Albert. *En Suisse, le sac au dos*, Paris, 1869; *c.* **1869.**

Larden, Walter. *Recollections of an Old Mountaineer*, London, 1910; **1880, 1882, 1883, 1884, 1885, 1886, 1887, 1889, 1890, 1891, 1893, 1894, 1895, 1896, 1897, 1898, 1899, 1900, 1901, 1902, 1903, 1904, 1905, 1906, 1907.**

La Roche, Sophie von. *Tagebuch einer Reise durch die Schweitz*, Altenburg, 1787; **1784.** *Erinnerungen aus meiner dritten Schweitzer-Reise*, Offenbach, 1793; **1791.**

LASCELLES, ROWLEY. *Sketch of a Descriptive Journey through Switzerland*, London, 1796; **1794.** *Sketch of a tour in Switzerland*, London, 1797; **1794.** *Memorandums of the Face of the Country in Switzerland*, London, 1799; **1794.** *Journal of a short excursion among the Swiss Landscapes made in the summer of the year ninety four*, London & Dublin, 1803; **1794.** *A general outline of the Swiss Landscapes*, London, 1812; **1794.**

LA TROBE, CHARLES JAMES. *The Alpenstock*, London, 1839; **1825, 1826, 1827.** *The Pedestrian*, London, 1832; **1830.**

LATROBE, J. H. B. *Hints for Six Months in Europe*, Philadelphia, 1869; **1868.**

LAUGHLIN, CLARA E. *Where it all comes true in Italy and Switzerland*, London, 1929; **1927.**

LA VALLÉE, J. *Voyage dans les départements de la France*, Paris, 1792; **1792.**

LAVELEYE, ÉMILE DE. 'Le Mont Rose', *Revue des Deux Mondes*, 57, Paris, 1865; **1862.** *Letters from Italy*, London, 1886; **1882.**

LAWRENCE, DAVID HERBERT. *Letters*, edited by A. Huxley, Leipzig, 1938; **1913.** *Not I but the Wind*, F. Lawrence, London, 1935; **1928.**

LEAF, WALTER. *Autobiography*, London, 1932; **1869.**

LEAKE, W. M. *Brief Memoir of the Life & Writings*, p.p., London, 1864; **1815.**

LEAR, EDWARD. *Letters*, edited by Lady Strachey, London, 1907; **1861.** *Later Letters*, edited by Lady Strachey, London, 1911; **1882.**

LE BLOND, MRS. AUBREY. (*See* MAIN, MRS., & BURNABY, MRS. FRED.) *Day in Day out*, London, 1928; **1890, 1897.**

LECCHI, GENERAL. *Campagne de l'Armée de Réserve*, De Cugnac, Paris, 1900; **1800.**

LECOURBE, GÉNÉRAL CLAUDE-JOSÈPHE. *Le Général Lecourbe*, Général Philebert, Paris, 1895; **1799.** *Der Feldzug der Division Lecourbe im schweizerischen Hochgebirge*, A. Gunther, Frauenfeld, 1895; **1799.**

LEE, ROBERT. *Life & Remains*, R. H. Story, London, 1870; **1856.**

LEFROY, W. *In Memoriam*, B. B. Gould, 1909; **1909.**

LEGGETT, BENJAMIN F. *A Tramp through Switzerland*, New York, 1887; *c.* **1887.**

LEJEUNE, DR. In *La Montagne*, 5, 1909; **1806.**

LELAND, C. G. *Memoirs*, London, 1893; **1846.**

LEMAISTRE, J. G. *Travels after the Peace of Amiens through Parts of France, Switzerland, Italy and Germany*, London, 1806; **1802.**

LE MESURIER, W. H. *An Impromptu Ascent of Mont Blanc*, London, 1882; **1881.**

LEMNIUS, SIMON. 'Iter Helveticum', in *Hodoeporicum*, N. Reussner, Basle, 1580; *c.* **1550.**

LENGEFELD, CHARLOTTE VON. *Charlotte von Lengefeld und ihre Freunde*, L. Urlichs, Stuttgart, 1860; **1783.**

LENIN, VLADIMIR ILYICH. *Lenin*, C. Hollis, London, 1938; **1904, 1911, 1915, 1916.**

LENZ, JAKOB MICHAEL REINHARD. *Jakob M. R. Lenz*, M. N. Rosanow, Leipzig, 1909; **1777.**

LE PAYS, RENÉ. *Annuaire du Club Alpin Français*, 1890–1; **1669.**

LEQUINIO, J. M. *Voyage dans le Jura*, Paris, An 9; *c.* **1799.**

LESCARBOT, MARC. *Le tableau de la Suisse*, Paris, 1618; **1612.**

LESCHEVIN, P. X. *Voyage à Genève & dans la vallée de Chamouni*, Paris, 1812; **1810.**

LESLIE, SIR JOHN. *An Experimental Enquiry into the Nature and Propagation of Heat*, London, 1804; **1796.**

LEVER, CHARLES. *Dr. Quicksilver*, L. Stevenson, London, 1939; **1847.**

LE VERT, O. W. *Souvenirs of Travel*, New York, 1857; **1853.**

LEWIS, SIR GEORGE CORNWALL. *Letters*, London, 1870; **1824.**

LEWIS, M. G. *Life and Correspondence*, London, 1839; **1816.**

LIDDELL, A. G. C. *Notes from the Life of an Ordinary Mortal*, London, 1911; **1865.**

LIDDELL, HENRY GEORGE. *A Memoir*, H. L. Thompson, London, 1899; **1843.**

LIDDIARD, WILLIAM. *A Three Months' Tour in Switzerland and France*, London, 1832; **1827.**

LIEBIG, J. VON. *Justus von Liebig & Christoph Friedrich Schönbein*, G. W. A. Kahlbaum & E. Thon, Leipzig, 1900; **1862.**

LIÉGEARD, STEPHEN. *A travers l'Engadine*, Paris, 1877; **1875.**

LIEVEN, PRINCESS. *Unpublished Diary*, H. Temperley, London, 1925; **1823.**

LINDEBERG, P. *Hodoeporicon itineris Veneti, Romani, Helvetici, et Rhenani.* Rostochii, 1586; *c.* **1586.**

LISMORE, JAMES DANIEL O'BRIEN, LORD. In *Les aventures de Casanova en Suisse*, P. Grellet, Lausanne, 1919; **1794.**

LISZT, FRANZ. *Essais und Reisebriefe eines Baccalaureus der Tonkunst*, Leipzig, 1881; **1836.** *Briefe*, edited by La Mara, Leipzig, 1899; **1853.** *Franz Liszt*, J. Kapp, Leipzig, 1909; **1836, 1853.** *Mémoires*, Comtesse d'Agoult, Paris, 1927; **1836.** *Une retraite romantique en Suisse*, R. Bory, Lausanne, 1925; **1836.**

Lithgow, William. *The Totall Discourse of the Rare Adventures and Painefull Peregrinations of Long Nineteene Years Travayles*, London, 1632 (Glasgow, 1906); **1613.**

Lloyd, Francis. *The Physiography of the Upper Engadine*, London, 1881; **1875.**

Locatelli, Sebastiano. *Voyage de France. Moeurs et coutumes françaises (1664–1665). Relation de Sébastien Locatelli, prêtre bolonais*, A. Vautier, Paris, 1905; **1665.**

Locke, D. R. *Nasby in Exile or 6 Months of Travel*, Boston, 1882; **1881.**

Lockyer, Sir Norman. *Life & Work*, T. M. Lockyer, London, 1928; **1868.**

Lodge, Eleanor C. *Terms & Vacations*, Oxford, 1938; **1894,** *c.* **1910.**

Lodge, Oliver. *Autobiography; Past Years.* London, 1931; **1893,** *c.* **1895.**

Lohmüller, Wilhelm. 'Die Eroberung des Berner Oberland durch den Ski', *Die Alpen*, 7, 1931; **1897.**

Longfellow, Henry Wadsworth. *Letters and Journal, Life of Henry Wadsworth Longfellow*, Boston & New York, 1891; **1836.**

Longman, William (& Trower, Henry). *Journal of Six Weeks Adventures in Switzerland, Piedmont, and the Italian Lakes*, London, 1856; **1856.**

Louis-Philippe. *Louis-Philippe*, R. Recouly, Paris, s.d.; **1793.**

Lowder, Charles. *An Autobiography*, London, 1881; **1863, 1864, 1868, 1874.**

Lowell, James Russell. *Letters*, edited by H. E. Scudder, London, 1901; **1873.**

Ludlow, Edmund. *Memoirs*, Oxford, 1894; **1660, 1662.**

Ludwig, Prince of Anhalt Köhten. In *Accessiones Historiae Anhaltinae*, J. C. Beckmann, Zerbst, 1716; **1598.**

Lunn, Arnold. *Mountains of Youth*, Oxford, 1925; **1892, 1902, 1908, 1909, 1911, 1912, 1914, 1916, 1917, 1918, 1920, 1921, 1923.** *Mountain Jubilee*, London, 1943; **1930, 1931, 1940.** *British Ski Year Book*, 11, 1945; **1945.**

Lunn, Sir Henry. *Chapters from my Life*, London, 1918; **1892.** *Nearing Harbour*, London, 1934; **1924.**

Lyell, Sir Charles. *Life, Letters, & Journal*, London, 1881; **1818, 1832, 1835, 1857, 1865.**

Lyttelton, E. *Memories & Hopes*, London, 1925; **1880, 1887, 1888.**

Lytton, Edward Bulwer, Lord. *The Student*, Paris, 1835; **1833.**

MAARTENS, MAARTEN. *Letters*, London, 1930; **1893.**

MABILLON, JEAN. 'Fragment relatif à la Suisse tiré d'un voyage plus étendu', L. Bridel, *Le Conservateur Suisse*, 12; Lausanne, 1857; **1683.**

MACAULAY, THOMAS BABINGTON. *Life & Letters*, London, 1881; **1853.**

MACDONALD, GREVILLE. *Reminiscences of a Specialist*, London, 1932; **1876.**

MACDONALD, MARSHAL. *La campagne de 1800 à l'armée des Grisons*, H. Leplus, Paris, 1908; **1800.**

MACFARREN, WALTER. *Memories: An Autobiography*, London, 1905; **1878.**

MACGREGOR, JOHN. *My Note Book*, London, 1835; **1834.** *John MacGregor (Rob Roy)*, E. Hodder, London, 1894; **1853, 1865.** *A Thousand Miles in the Rob Roy Canoe on Twenty Rivers and Lakes in Europe*, London, 1866; **1865.**

MACHIAVELLI, N. *Legazioni e Commissarie*, L. Passerini e G. Milanesi, Firenze e Roma, 1876; **1507.**

MACKINTOSH, SIR JAMES. *Memoirs*, London, 1836; **1814.**

MACNEVIN, WILLIAM JAMES. *A Ramble through Swisserland in the Summer and Autumn of 1802*, Dublin, 1803; **1802.**

MACQUOID, GILBERT S. *Up and Down*, London, 1890; **1886, 1887.**

MAGEE, WILLIAM CONNOR. *Life and Correspondence*, London, 1892; **1865.**

MAGGS, J. *Round Europe with the Crowd*, London, 1880; **1877.**

MAGNY, OLIVIER DE. In *Les sonnets suisses de Joachim Du Bellay*, A. François, Lausanne, 1946; **1556.**

MAIN, MRS. (*See* BURNABY, MRS., LE BLOND, MRS.) *High Life and Towers of Silence*, London, 1886; **1884, 1885.**

MAISTRE, X. DE. In *Amitié ou amour*, H. Bordeaux, Paris, 1932; **1799.**

MALBY, REGINALD A. *With Camera and Rucksack in Oberland and Valais*, London, n.d.; **1911, 1912.**

MALESHERBES, C. G. DE L. DE. In 'J. S. Wyttenbach', H. Dübi. *Neujahrsblatt der literarischen Gesellschaft*, Bern, 1911; **1776.**

MALKIN, A. T. 'Leaves from the diary of the late Mr. Malkin', *Alpine Journal*, 15, 1891; **1839, 1840, 1843, 1856.**

MALLET, GEORGE. *Lettres sur la route de Genève à Milan par le Simplon*, Paris & Genève, 1816; **1809.**

MALMESBURY, EARL OF. *Memoirs of an Ex-Minister*, London, 1884; **1828, 1832.**

MALTHUS, D. In 'Chronologie critique', J. L. Courtois. *Annales de la société J.-J. Rousseau*, 15, Genève, 1923; **1764.**

MAN, H. DE. *Après Coup*, Bruxelles, 1941; **1926.**

MANCINI, MARIE. *Une princesse romaine au 17e siecle*, L. Percy, Paris, 1896; **1661.** *Les illustres aventurières*, P. Camo, Paris, 1929; **1673.**

MANN, SIR HORACE. In *Eisgebirge des Schweizerlandes*, G. S. Gruner, Bern, 1760; **1723.**

MANNING, HENRY EDWARD, CARDINAL. *Life*, E. S. Purcell, London, 1896; **1847.**

MANSFIELD, KATHARINE. *Journal*, edited by J. M. Murry, Hamburg, 1933; **1921.**

MANZONI, GIULIETTA. *Carteggio di A. Manzoni*, Milano, 1912; **1830.**

MARCARD, H. M. *Reise durch die Französische Schweitz und Italien*, Hamburg, 1799; **1785.**

MARCET, WILLIAM. *Principal Southern and Swiss Health-resorts*, London, 1883; **1858, 1882.** *Proceedings of the Royal Society of London*, 27, 1878; **1875**, and 31, 1881; **1880.**

MARIE-AMÉLIE. *Journal*, Duchesse de Vendôme, Paris, 1943; **1825.**

MARIE-LOUISE, EMPRESS, *Récit d'une excursion de l'impératrice Marie Louise aux glaciers de Savoie*, Baron Méneval, Paris, n.d.; **1814.**

MAROT, CLÉMENT. *Œuvres*, Paris, 1881; **1542.**

MARRACKS, R. *How we did them in 17 days!* p.p. Truro, n.d.; *c.* **1873.**

MARRYAT, CAPTAIN FREDERICK. *Olla podrida*, London, 1840; **1836.**

MARSH, GEORGE PERKINS. *Life & Letters*, New York, 1888; **1854.**

MARSH, HERBERT. *Two Seasons in Switzerland*, London, 1895; **1892, 1893.**

MARSHALL HALL, MRS. 'Zermatt and the Weissthor in 1849', *Alpine Journal*, 9, 1880; **1849.**

MARTEL, PETER. *An Account of the Glaciers of the Alps in Savoy*, London, 1744; **1742.**

MARTI, B. In *J. Simler*, W. A. B. Coolidge, Grenoble, 1904; **1557.**

MARTINEAU, HARRIET. *Autobiography*, Boston, 1877; **1839.**

MARTINS, CHARLES. *Du Spitzbergue au Sahara*, Paris, 1864; **1841, 1844, 1863.**

MARTYN, THOMAS. *Sketch of a Tour through Swisserland*, London, 1787; **1779.** *Memoirs of John Martyn and of Thomas Martyn*, G. C. Gorham, London, 1830; **1778, 1779.**

MASSIE, J. W. *Recollections of a Tour. A Summer's Ramble in Belgium, Germany and Switzerland*, London, 1846; **1844.**

MATHEWS, W. 'The Mountains of Bagne', *Peaks, Passes, & Glaciers*, London, 1859; **1856, 1857.** 'The Col de Lys', *Peaks, Passes, & Glaciers*, 2, 1, London 1862; **1859.**

MATTHEWS, HENRY. *The Diary of an Invalid*, London, 1824; **1818.**

MATTHISSON, FRIEDRICH. *Briefe*, Zürich, 1795; **1788, 1789, 1790, 1791, 1792, 1793, 1794.** *Erinnerungen*, Zürich, 1810–15; **1787, 1790, 1794, 1795, 1801, 1804.** In *Bonstettens Briefe an Friederike Brun*, Frankfurt, 1829; **1822.**

MATZEWSKI, COUNT. *Blackwood's Magazine*, 19, 1818; **1818.**

MAUDE, THOMAS. *The Traveller's Lay, a Poem*, London, 1830; **1828.**

MAUGIRON, MARQUIS DE. 'Lettre inédite du Marquis de Maugiron', M. Paillon, *Revue Alpine*, 2, 1896; **1750.**

MAUPASSANT, GUY DE. *Au Soleil*, Paris, 1894; **1877.** *Lettres de Flaubert à sa nièce Caroline*, Paris, 1905; **1877.**

MAURICE, FREDERICK DENISON. *Life*, F. Maurice, London, 1884; **1840.**

MAXIMILIAN, DUKE OF BAVARIA. In *Die deutsche Schweizerbegeisterung*, E. Ziehen, Frankfurt a. M., 1922; **1593.**

MAXWELL, SIR HERBERT. *Evening Memories*, London, 1932; **1875.**

MAYER, CHARLES JOSEPH DE. *Voyage de M. de Mayer en Suisse*, Paris, 1786; **1784.**

MAYNARD, HENRI. 'The First Ascent of the Zermatt Breithorn', W. A. B. Coolidge, *Alpine Journal*, 15, 1891; **1813.**

MAYNE, JOHN. *Journal*, edited by J. M. Colles, London, 1909; **1814.**

MAYOL, SAINT. *Jahrbuch für Schweizergeschichte*, E. Oehlmann, 3, Zürich, 1878; **972.**

MAYR, JOHANN HEINRICH. *Der erste Winterkurgast im Oberengadin*, J. Robbi, Samaden, 1913; **1834.**

MAZARIN, HORTENSE MANCINI, DUCHESSE DE. *Les illustres aventurières*, P. Camo, Paris, 1929; **1668.**

MAZZINI, GIUSEPPE. *Mazzini*, G. O. Griffith, London, 1932; **1834, 1848, 1849, 1871.**

McCORMICK, JOSEPH. *A Sad Holiday*, London, 1865; **1865.**

McTAGGART, MRS. *Memoirs of a Gentlewoman*, London, 1830; **1789.**

McTEAR, ROBERT. *Notes of a Continental Tour and a Visit to Caprera*, Glasgow, 1865; **1864.**

MEDICI, COLONEL GIACOMO. In *Memoirs of Garibaldi*, A. Dumas, London, 1931; **1849.**

MEDWIN, T. 'Hazlitt in Switzerland', *Fraser's Magazine*, 19, 1839; **1825.** *Life of Shelley*, Oxford, 1913; **1818, 1820.** *Records of Shelley, Byron and the Author*, E. J. Trelawny, London, 1878; **1820.**

MEINERS, CHRISTOPH. *Briefe über die Schweitz*, Berlin, 1788; **1782, 1788.**

MEISNER, FRIEDRICH. *Alpenreise mit seinen Zöglingen*, Bern, 1801; **1800.**

MEISTER, LEONARD. *Kleine Reisen durch einige Schweizer Kantonen*, Bern, 1782; *c.* **1782.**

MENDELSSOHN-BARTHOLDY, FELIX. *Letters*, ed. G. Selden-Roth, New York, 1945; **1822.** *Letters from Italy and Switzerland*, London, 1864; **1831.** *Letters*, London, 1863; **1842, 1847.**

MERCIER, J. J. *Mountains & Lakes of Switzerland & Italy*, London, 1871; *c.* **1871.**

MERCIER, S. *Sa vie.* L. Béclard, Paris, 1903; **1781, 1784.**

MEREDITH, GEORGE. *Letters*, London, 1912; **1861, 1863.**

MÉRIMÉE, P. *Lettres à la ctesse de Boigne*, Paris, 1933; **1857.** *Lettres à une inconnue*, Paris, s.d.; **1858.**

MERIWETHER, L. *A Tramp Trip. How to see Europe on 50 Cents a Day*, New York, 1887; *c.* **1887.**

METTERNICH, PRINCE. *Aus Metternichs nachgelassenen Papieren*, Wien, 1880; **1815.**

MEYER, CONRAD FERDINAND. *Conrad Ferdinand Meyer*, A. Frey, Leipzig, 1908; **1836, 1838, 1857, 1858, 1859, 1866, 1867, 1869, 1870, 1871, 1872, 1873, 1878, 1879, 1884, 1885, 1886, 1887, 1889, 1890.**

MEYER, DANIEL. 'Kurzgefasstes Tagebuch einer kleinen Reise durch einen Theil von Bündten', *Alpina*, 3, Winterthur, 1809; **1806.**

MEYER, G. & R. *Reise auf die Eisgebirge des Kantons Bern*, H. Zschokke, Aarau, 1813; **1812.**

MEYER, J. H. *Mahlerische Reise in die Italienische Schweiz*, Zürich, 1793; **1789.**

MEYER, JOHANN RUDOLF. 'Reise auf den Jungfrau Gletscher', *Miszellen für die neueste Weltkunde*, 1811; **1811.**

MICHAELIS, ERNST HANS. 'Barometrische Höhenbestimmungen', *Mittheilungen aus dem Gebiet der Theoretischen Erdkunde*, J. Fröbel & O. Heer, Zürich, 1834; **1827, 1828.** 'Der erste bekannte Übergang über den Allalinpass', A. Wäber, *Jahrbuch des Schweizer Alpenclub*, 39, 1903; **1828.**

MICHAUD, JOSEPH. *Voyage littéraire au Mont Blanc*, Paris, 1791; **1787.**

MICHELET, JULES. *Voyages et séjours de Michelet en Italie*, T. Scharten, Paris, 1934; **1830.** *Sur les chemins de l'Europe*, 3, Paris, 1893; **1838.** *La Montagne*, Paris, 1867; **1865, 1867.** *L'Insecte*, Paris, 1858; **1856.** *Michelet et ses enfants*, E. Noël, Paris, 1878; **1843.**

MICKIEWICZ, ADAM. *Correspondance*, Paris, n.d.; **1840.**

MILFORD, JOHN. *Observations: Moral, Literary, and Antiquarian made during a Tour through the Pyrenees, South of France, Switzerland, the Whole of Italy, and the Netherlands*, London, 1818; **1814, 1815.**

MILMAN, ARTHUR. *Peaks, Passes, & Glaciers*, 2, 1, London, 1862; **1861.**

MILTON, JOHN. *John Milton on the Continent*, F. Byse, London, 1902; **1639.**

MINTO, LORD. 'Zermatt and the Breithorn in 1830', *Alpine Journal*, 16, 1892; **1830.**

MINUTOLI, MENU VON. *Reise durch einen Theil von Teutschland, Helvetien und Oberitalien, im Sommer 1803*, Berlin, 1804; **1803.**

MIRABEAU, GABRIEL-HONORÉ DE. *Mémoires*, Bruxelles, 1834; **1776.** *Vie intime et amoureuse de Mirabeau*, D. Meunier, Paris, 1933; **1776.**

MISSON, MAXIMILIEN. *Voyage d'Italie*, Amsterdam, 1743; **1688.**

MONCEY, GENERAL. *Campagne de l'armée de réserve*, De Cugnac, Paris, 1900; **1800.**

MONK, JAMES A. *A Week in Switzerland*, Pendleton, n.d.; **1887.**

MONKSWELL, MARY, LADY. *A Victorian Diarist*, London, 1944; **1873, 1887, 1889, 1891.** *A Victorian Diarist. Later Extracts*, London, 1946; **1901, 1902, 1907.**

MONRO, HAROLD. *The Chronicle of a Pilgrimage, Paris to Milan*, London, 1909; *c.* **1909.**

MONTAGU, LADY MARY. *Letters & Works*, London, 1887; **1741.**

MONTAGUE, CHARLES EDWARD. *A Memoir*, O. Elton, London, 1929; **1891.**

MONTAIGNE, MICHEL EYQUEM DE. *Journal du voyage de Michel de Montaigne en Italie par la Suisse et l'Allemagne*, Rome, 1774; **1580.**

MONTBEL, COMTE DE. *Souvenirs*, Paris, 1913; **1830.**

MONTÉMONT, ALBERT. *Tour over the Alps and in Italy*, London, 1823; **1820.**

MONTGOLFIER, E. A. DE. In *Le Mont Blanc. Route classique et voies nouvelles*, C.-E. Engel, Neuchâtel, s.d.; **1799.**

MONTYON, A. DE. *Auget de Montyon*, C. Guimbaud, Paris, 1909; **1792.**

MOORE, A. W. *The Alps in 1864*, p.p. (and Edinburgh, 1902); **1864, 1865, 1870, 1872.** 'On some Winter expeditions in the Alps', *Alpine Journal*, 4, 1870; **1866.**

MOORE, JOHN. *A View of Society and Manners in France, Switzerland, and Germany*, London, 1783; **1773.**

MOORE, THOMAS. *Memoirs, Journal & Correspondence*, edited by Lord J. Russell, London, 1853; **1819.**

MORGAN, JOHN. *American Alpine Journal*, 4, p. 460, 1942; **1763.**

MORGAN, JOHN MINTER. *A Tour through Switzerland and Italy in the Years 1846–1847*, London, 1850; **1846.**

MOROZZO DELLA ROCCA, COUNT. *Mémoires de l'Académie Royale des Sciences*, Turin, 1789; *c.* **1787.**

MORSE, SAMUEL B. *Letters and Journals*, Boston, 1914; **1831.**

MORTOFT, FRANCIS. 'His Book', edited by M. Letts, *Hakluyt Society*, ser. 2, 57, 1925; **1659.**

MORYSON, FYNES. *An Itinerary*, London, 1617 (Glasgow, 1905); **1592, 1595.**

MOSS, GERTRUDE E. *Happy Days in France and Italy*, p.p., Edinburgh, 1902; **1901.**

MOTLEY, JOHN LOTHROP. *Correspondence*, G. W. Curtis, London, 1889; **1855.**

MOULE, HENRY CARR GLYN. *Biography*, J. B. Harford & F. L. Macdonald, London, 1922; **1864, 1901.**

MOULINIÉ, C. E. F. *Promenades philosophiques & religieuses aux environs du Mont-Blanc*, Genève, 1820; **1814, 1815, 1817, 1819.**

MOULTON, LOUISE CHANDLER. *Lazy Tours in Spain and Elsewhere*, London, 1896; *c.* **1896.**

MOUNTAIN, ARMINE S. H. *Memoirs and Letters*, London, 1857; **1820, 1821, 1822.**

MUDDOCK, J. E. *Pages from an Adventurous Life*, London, 1908; **1879.**

MÜGGE, THEODORE. *Switzerland in 1847*, London, 1848; **1847.**

MUIRHEAD, LOCKHART. *Journals of Travels in Parts of the Late Austrian Low Countries, France, the Pays de Vaud, and Tuscany in 1787 and 1789*, London, 1803; **1787.**

MÜLLER, GEORGE. *Preaching Tours & Missionary Labours*, London, 1883; **1876, 1878.**

MÜLLER, JOHANN GEORG. *Reise durch etliche Cantone der Schweitz*, Zurich, 1790; **1789.**

MÜLLER, JOHANNES VON. 'Briefe an Carl Victor von Bonstetten'. In *Sämmtliche Werke*, 4, 13, Tübingen, 1810–12; **1773, 1774, 1775, 1778, 1779.** 'Tagebuch einer Schweizerreise'. In *Sämmtliche Werke*, 27, Tübingen, 1819; **1777.**

MÜLLER, W. L. *Flug von der Nordsee zum Montblank . . .*, Altona, 1821; **1819.**

MUMMERY, A. F. *My Climbs in the Alps and Caucasus*, London, 1895; **1879, 1880, 1881, 1887, 1892, 1893, 1894.**

MUNDT, THEODOR. *Spaziergänge und Weltfahrten, 3. Ausflug durch die Schweitz nach der Provence*, Altona, 1839; **1838.**

MUNRO, HECTOR ('SAKI'). *The Short Stories of Saki. Biography of Saki*, E. M. Munro, London, 1930; **1893.**

MÜNSTER, SEBASTIAN. *Cosmographia universalis*, Basileae, 1550; **1546.**

MÜNZER, JEROME. 'Jerome Münzer et son voyage dans le midi de la France', E. Déprez, *Annales du Midi*, 48, Toulouse, 1936; **1494.**

MURALT, JOHANN VON. *Philosophical Transactions of the Royal Society of London*, 4, 1669 and 8, 1673–4; **1668.** *Eydgnössischer Lust-Garten*, Zürich, 1715; *c.* **1666.**

MURCHISON, SIR RODERICK. *Life*, A. Geikie, London, 1875; **1816, 1848.**

MURITH, L. In *Description des Alpes Pennines et Rhétiennes*, M.-T. Bourrit, Genève, 1781; **1779.** *Guide du botaniste qui voyage dans le Valais*, Lausanne, 1810; **1803.**

MURRAY, JOHN. *A Glance at Some of the Beautiful Sublimities of Switzerland*, London, 1829; **1818, 1825.**

MURRAY, JOHN. *John Murray III*, J. Murray IV, London, 1919; **1837.**

MUSAFIR, CAPTAIN. *Rambles in Alpine Lands*, G. B. Malleson, London, 1884; **1863, 1864.**

MUSSET, ALFRED DE. *Correspondance*, L. Sèche, Paris, 1907; **1834.**

MUSSET-PATHAY, VICTOR ANTOINE DONATIEN. *Voyage en Suisse et en Italie fait avec l'armée de réserve*, Paris, an 8; **1800.**

MUSSOLINI, BENITO. *Mussolini in the Making*, G. Megaro, London, 1938; **1902, 1903, 1904.**

NAEF, EDUARD. 'Erinnerungen eines Skiveteranen', *Die Alpen*, 5, 1929; **1893.**

NAPIER, GENERAL CHARLES JAMES. *Life and Opinions*, W. Napier, London, 1857; **1819.**

NAVEZ, L. *Dans les Alpes*, Bruxelles, s.d., *c.* **1880.** *En Suisse*, Bruxelles, s.d., **1881.**

NECKER, L. A. In *H. B. de Saussure*, D. Freshfield, Genève, 1924; **1798.** *Proceedings of the Royal Society of Edinburgh*, 5, 1866; **1803, 1826, 1832, 1837.**

NEEDHAM, JOHN TURBERVILLE. *Observation des hauteurs faite avec le baromètre au mois d'Aoust 1751 sur une partie des Alpes*, Berne, 1760; **1751.**

NEUILLY, A.-A.-C. DE. *Dix années d'émigration*, Paris, 1941; **1799.**

NEWBERRY, J. *Julia Newberry's Diary*, London, n.d.; **1870, 1871.**

NICOLAI, FRIEDRICH. *Beschreibung einer Reise durch Deutschland und die Schweiz im Jahre 1781*, Berlin, 1783–96; **1781.**

NICOLL, LADY ROBERTSON. *Bells of Memory*, p.p., n.p., n.d.; **1881.**

NIETZSCHE, FRIEDRICH. *Gesammelte Briefe*, Leipzig, 1909; **1871, 1872, 1873, 1874, 1876, 1877, 1878, 1879, 1881, 1882, 1883, 1884, 1885, 1886, 1887, 1888.**

NIGHTINGALE, FLORENCE. *Life*, E. Cook, London, 1914; **1838.**

NIJINSKY, VASLAV. *Nijinsky*, R. Nijinsky, Hamburg, 1935; **1918.**

NODIER, CHARLES. 'Voyage à la Tête Noire', *Revue des Deux Mondes*, 1831; **1825.**

NOEL, BAPTIST W. *Notes of a Tour in Switzerland in the Summer of 1847*, London, 1848; **1847.**

NOEL, GERARD THOMAS. *Arvendel, or Sketches in Italy and Switzerland*, London, 1826; **1802.**

NOEL, RODEN. *A Little Child's Monument*, London, 1881; **1876.** *Songs of the Heights and Deeps*, London, 1885; **1876.**

NORMAN-NERUDA, L. *The Climbs of Norman-Neruda*, London, 1899; **1890, 1891.**

NORTH, MARIANNE. *Recollections of a Happy Life*, London, 1892; **1864.** *Further Recollections of a Happy Life*, London, 1893; **1860, 1865, 1870.**

NORTHBROOK, FRANCIS THORNHILL BARING, LORD. *Journals and Correspondence*, London, 1902; **1853.**

NORTHUMBERLAND, DUCHESS OF. *The Diaries of a Duchess*, J. Greig, London, 1926; **1772.**

OBERSON, GABRIEL. *Et les hommes fuiront vers les montagnes*, Neuchâtel, 1939; **1921, 1922, 1923, 1924, 1932, 1935.**

O'CONOR, MATTHEW. *Picturesque and Historical Recollections during a Tour through Belgium, Germany, France and Switzerland*, London, 1837; **1835.**

ODO DE ROUEN. In *Geschichte des mittelalterlichen Handels und Verkehrs zwischen Westdeutschland und Italien*, A. Schulte, Leipzig, 1900; **1254.**

O'FLANAGAN, J. R. *Impressions at Home & Abroad*, London, 1837; **1836.**

OLIPHANT, MRS. M. O. W. *Autobiography & Letters*, Edinburgh, 1899; **1890.**

OLIVIER, JUSTE. 'Some early Visits to Zermatt and Saas', W. A. B. Coolidge, *Alpine Journal*, 1907; **1843.**

OMAN, SIR C. *Things I have seen*, London, 1933; **1890.**

ORSINI, F. *Memoirs & Adventures*, Edinburgh 1857; **1854.**

OSTERWALD, SAMUEL FRÉDÉRIC D'. *Description des montagnes et des vallées qui font partie de la principauté de Neuchâtel et Valangin*, Neuchâtel, 1766; *c.* **1764.**

OWEN, JOHN. In *Travels through the Lepontine Alps*, A. Beaumont, London, 1806; **1612.**

OWEN, JOHN. *Travels into Different Parts of Europe in the Years 1791 and 1792*, London, 1796; **1791, 1792.**

OWEN, SIR RICHARD. *Life*, R. Owen, London, 1894; **1860.**

PACE, SIR RICHARD. *Richard Pace*, J. Wegg, London, 1932; **1515.**

PACKE, CHARLES. *The Spirit of Travel*, London, 1856; **1855.**

PADEREWSKY, IGNACY JAN. *Paderewsky*, C. Phillips, New York, 1934; **1897.**

PALGRAVE, FRANCIS TURNER. *His Journals and Memories of his Life*, G. F. Palgrave, London, 1899; **1886.**

PALMERSTON, LORD. In *Private Letters*, E. Gibbon, London, 1897; **1763.**

PANGE, F. DE. *Mme de Staël & F. de Pange*, Ctesse J. de Pange, Paris, 1925; **1786.**

PARACELSUS, PHILIP THEOPHRASTUS VON HOHENHEIM. 'De Morbis tartareis', 1537. In *Quellenbuch für die Gemeinde St. Moritz*, J. Robbi, Chur, 1910; **1535.**

PARKER, C. S. *More Ports, more Happy Places*, New York, 1926; **1923.**

PARKER, JOSEPH. *Life*, London, 1912; **1898.**

PARKER, THEODORE. *Life & Teachings*, London, 1877; **1844, 1859.**

PARKHURST, C. H. *My 40 Years in New York*, New York, 1923; *c.* **1885.**

PARKMAN, FRANCIS. *Life*, C. H. Farnham, London, 1909; **1844.**

PARLATORE, FILIPPO. *Viaggio alla catena del Monte Bianco*, Firenze, 1850; **1849.**

PARROT, FREDERIC. In *Der Monte Rosa*, L. von Welden, Wien, 1824; **1816.**

PARRY, HUBERT. *Life & Works*, C. L. Graves, London, 1926; **1889.**

PARS, WILLIAM. In *British Museum Catalogue of Prints and Drawings*, 1902; **1770.**

PARSONS, WILLIAM. *Travelling Recreations*, London, 1807; **1784.**

PASSERAT, J.-A. *Un juste proscrit*, P. Debongnie, Paris, 1938; **1807.**

PATIN, CHARLES. *Travels through Germany, Bohemia, Switzerland, Holland, and Other Parts of Europe*, London, 1701; **1669.**

PATMORE, EMILY HONORIA. *A Daughter of Coventry Patmore*, London, 1924; **1869.**

PATTESON, JOHN COLERIDGE. *Life*, C. M. Yonge, London, 1874; **1850.**

PAUL, CZAREVICH. *Paul Ier de Russie*, P. Morane, Paris, 1907; **1782.** In *Berner Oberland*, H. Hartmann, Interlaken, n.d.; **1782.**

PEABODY, ANDREW P. *Reminiscences of European Travel*, New York, 1868; **1866.**

PEAKE, ELIZABETH. *Pen Pictures of Europe*, Philadelphia, 1880; **1871.**

PELL, J. In *Protectorate of Cromwell*, R. Vaughan, London, 1839; **1656.**

PELLIKAN, KONRAD. *Das Chronikon des Konrad Pellikan*, B. Riggenbach, Basel, 1877; **1504.**

PENNANT, T. *Literary Life*, London, 1793; **1765.** *Tour on the Continent*, edited by G. R. de Beer, London, 1948; **1765.**

PENNELL, JOSEPH. 'Play & Work in the Alps', *Century Magazine*, n.s. 20, 1891; **1889.**

PENNINGTON, THOMAS. *Continental Excursions, or Tours into France, Switzerland, and Germany, in 1782, 1787, and 1789*, London, 1809; **1787, 1789.**

PENNY, THOMAS. In *English Naturalists from Meckam to Ray*, C. E. Raven, Cambridge, 1945; **1566.**

PESTALOZZI, MRS. CONRAD. *My Travels Abroad*, Zürich, 1856; **1846.**

PETRARCA, FRANCESCO. *Lettere*, edited by G. Fracassetti, Firenze, 1863; **1356.**

PEZAY, MASSON DE. *Les Soirées Helvétiennes, Alsaciennes et Francomtoises*, Amsterdam & Paris, 1771; *c.* **1771.**

PHILIP OF COLOGNE. In *The Alpine Passes*, J. E. Tyler, Oxford, 1930; **1176.**

PHILIPS, FRANCIS. *A Reading Party in Switzerland; with an Account of the Ascent of Mont Blanc*, London, 1851; **1851.**

PHILIPS, JOHN BURTON. *Continental Travel in 1802–3. The Story of an Escape*, Manchester, 1904; **1802, 1803.**

PIATTI, PIATTINO. *Bollettino storico della Svizzera Italiana*, 17, Bellinzona; **1468.**

PICARD, E. *Monseigneur le Mont Blanc*, Bruxelles, 1900; **1900.**

PICKERING, ANNA M. W. *Memoirs*, edited by S. Pickering, London, 1903; **1840.**

PICTET, ADOLPHE. *Une course à Chamonix*, Paris, 1872 (Genève, 1930); **1836.**

PICTET, MARC-AUGUSTE. 'Le voyage de H.-B. de Saussure autour du Mont Blanc en 1778', edited by E. Gaillard, *La Montagne*, 1934; **1778.**

Pilati di Tassullo, Carlo Anton. *Voyages en différens pays de l'Europe*, En Suisse, 1778; **1774.**

Pilley, Dorothy. *Climbing days*, London, 1935; **1920, 1921, 1922, 1923, 1924, 1927, 1928.**

Pini, Ermenegildo. *Memoria mineralogica sulla montagna e sui contorni di S. Gotardo*, Milano, 1783; **1782.**

Pitman, Marie J. *European Breezes*, Boston, 1882; *c.* **1882.**

Pius II, Aeneas Sylvius Piccolomini, Pope. 'The Commentaries of Pius II', *Smith College Studies*, Northampton, Mass., 1937; **1432, 1435.**

Pixérécourt, Gilbert de. 'Esquisses et fragments de voyage', in *Théâtre*, 7, Paris, 1843; **1833.**

Placidus à Spescha. *Placidus à Spescha*, F. Pieth & P. K. Hager, Bern, 1913; **1789, 1810, 1811, 1812, 1820.**

Platen-Hallermuende, Graf August von. *Die Tagebücher des Grafen August von Platen*, edited by G. Laubemann & L. Scheffler, Stuttgart, 1896; **1816.**

Platter, Felix. *Felix et Thomas Platter à Montpellier*, Montpellier, 1892; **1552.** *Autobiography*, edited by D. A. Fechter, Basel, 1840; **1562.**

Platter, Thomas. *Thomas Platter. Autobiography*, P. Monroe, New York, 1904; *c.* **1508,** *c.* **1514,** *c.* **1524, 1532.**

Playfair, John. *Works*, Edinburgh, 1822; **1816, 1817.**

Ploucquet, Wilhelm Gottfried. *Vertrauliche Erzählung einer Schweizerreise im Jahre 1786*, Tübingen, 1787; **1786.**

Plunket, Frederica. *Here and there among the Alps*, London, 1875; **1874.**

Pococke, R. *Description of the East*, London, 1743–5; **1741.**

Pol, Lucius. 'Bemerkungen bei einer Reise in Rhaetiens südöstlichen Gegenden', *Der Sammler*, 4, Chur, 1782; **1781.**

Polidori, John William. *Diary*, edited by W. Rossetti, London, 1911; **1816.**

Polier de Bottens. In *Nouvelle description des glacières*, M.-T. Bourrit, Genève, 1787; **1742.**

Pollen, Colonel. 'Une tentative d'ascension au Mont Blanc', H. F. Montagnier, *Revue Alpine*, 1, 1912; **1802.**

Pöllnitz, Charles Lewis, Baron de. *Memoirs*, London, 1738; **1720.**

Ponsonby, Henry. *His Life from his Letters*, A. Ponsonby, London, 1942; **1868.**

Ponsonby, John, Viscount. In *Berner Oberland in Sage und Geschichte*, H. Hartmann, Interlaken, n.d.; **1832.**

PONTÉCOULANT, L.-G. LE DOULCET DE. *Souvenirs historiques et parlementaires*, Paris, 1861; **1794**.

POWYS, LLEWELYN. *Letters*, edited by L. Wilkinson, London, 1943; **1910, 1936**. *Earth Memories*, London, 1934; **1911**.

PRENTISS, ELIZABETH. *Life & Letters*, edited by G. L. Prentiss, London, 1882; **1859**.

PRESTON-THOMAS, H. *Work & Play*, Edinburgh, 1909; **1861, 1864, 1866**.

PRESTWICH, SIR JOSEPH. *Life & Letters*, London, 1899; **1858**.

PRIME, S. I. *The Alhambra & the Kremlin*, New York, 1873; *c.* **1873**.

PRITCHARD, H. BADEN. *Tramps in the Tyrol*, London, 1874; *c.* **1874**.

PUMPELLY, RAPHAEL. *My Reminiscences*, New York, 1918; **1855, 1894**.

PUPIN, M. *From Immigrant to Inventor*, New York, 1922; **1885, 1894**.

PURTSCHELLER, L. *Über Fels & Firn*, München, 1901; **1884, 1887, 1888, 1898**.

QUEENSBERRY, MARQUESS OF. *The Spirit of the Matterhorn*, London, n.d.; **1876**.

QUERINI, ANGELO. *Giornale del viaggio nella Svizzera fatto di Angelo Querini, senatore Veneziano, nel 1777, descritto dal Dottore Girolamo Festari di Valdagno*, Venezia, 1834; **1777**.

QUINET, EDGAR. *Correspondance. Lettres à sa mère*. Paris, s.d.; **1823**. *Mémoires d'exil (Bruxelles-Oberland)*, Mme Edgar Quinet, Paris, 1868–70; **1857, 1858**.

RABELAIS, FRANÇOIS. *Tiers Livre*. And in *Les Sonnets suisses de Joachim Du Bellay*, A. François, Lausanne, 1946; *c.* **1541**.

RACOWITZA, HELENE VON. *Autobiography*, tr. by C. Mar, London, 1910; **1864, 1894**.

RAFFLES, THOMAS. *Letters during a Tour through Some Parts of France, Savoy, Switzerland, and Germany, and the Netherlands*, Liverpool, 1818; **1817**.

RAFFLES, W. W. *Zermatt with the Cols d'Érin and de Collon and an ascent to the summit of Mont Blanc*, p.p., n.p., 1854; **1854**.

RAMBERT, EUGÈNE. *De Schwyz à Schwyz par Sion, Ascensions et Flâneries*, Lausanne, 1888; **1874**. *Les Alpes Suisses*, Bâle & Genève, 1869; **1863, 1867, 1868**.

RAMBUTEAU, C.-P. DE. *Mémoires*, Paris, 1905; **1813**.

RAMOND DE CARBONNIÈRES, LOUIS ÉLISABETH. *Lettres sur l'état politique, civil et naturel de la Suisse, traduites de l'anglais de M. Coxe*, Paris, 1791; **1777.** *Observations sur les Alpes*, edited by H. Béraldi, Toulouse, 1929; **1777.**

RAMSAY, ANDREW CROMBIE. *A Memoir*, A. Geikie, London, 1895; **1852, 1858, 1861, 1862, 1873, 1881.**

RAMSAY, SIR JAMES. 'Recollections of the Engadine in 1872', *Alpine Journal*, 34, 1921; **1872.**

RANDOLPH, —. *Observations on the Present State of Denmark, Russia, and Switzerland*, London, 1784; **1778.**

RAOUL-ROCHETTE, DÉSIRÉ. *Lettres sur la Suisse*, Paris, 1823; **1819, 1820, 1821.** *Lettres sur la Suisse*, Paris, 1828; **1824, 1825.**

RATTI, ACHILLE (POPE PIUS XI). *Climbs on Alpine Peaks*, London, 1923; **1889.**

RAUWOLFF, LEONHART. In *Mr. Ray's Travels*, vol. ii, London, 1738; **1573.**

RAVEL, M. *Maurice Ravel par quelques-uns de ses familiers*, Paris, 1939; **1906.** *Maurice Ravel*, J. M. Leroy, Bruxelles, 1944; **1913.**

RAWNSLEY, H. D. *Flower Time in the Oberland*, Glasgow, 1904; **1903.**

RAY, JOHN. *Travels through the Low Countries, Germany, Italy and France*, London, 1673; **1663, 1665.**

RAYMOND, JOHN. *Mercurio Italico. An Itinerary Containing a Voyage made through Italy*, London, 1648; **1647.**

RAYNAL, G.-T. *L'Abbé Raynal*, A. Feugère, Angoulême, 1922; **1780.**

RAZOUMOWSKY, COMTE GRÉGOIRE DE. *Voyages minéralogiques dans le Gouvernement d'Aigle et une partie du Vallais*, Lausanne, 1784; **1783.**

READE, J. E. *Prose from the South*, London, 1846; *c.* **1846.**

REBMANN, H. R. *Ein neuw lustig ernsthafft poetisch Gastmal und Gespräch zweyer Bergen.* Bern, 1605; *c.* **1600.**

RECKITT, MAURICE B. *As it happened*, London, 1941; **1907, 1914.**

REICHARD, H. A. O. *Mahlerische Reise durch einen grossen Theil der Schweiz*, Gotha, 1827; **1792, 1802, 1811, 1817.**

RENAN, E. *Lettres*, Paris, s.d.; **1871, 1874.**

RENNIE, SIR JOHN. *Autobiography*, London, 1875; **1819.**

RENSSELAER, JEREMIAH VAN (& HOWARD, W.). 'Account of a journey to the summit of Mont Blanc', H. F. Montagnier, *Alpine Journal*, 33, 1921; **1819.**

RERESBY, SIR JOHN. *Travels and Memoirs*, London, 1818; **1656.**

REY, GUIDO. *Le Mont Cervin*, Paris, 1905; **1893.**

REY, W. *Les Grisons et la haute Engadine*, Genève, 1850; **1846.** *Les quatre sources de la Reuss au St. Gothard*, Paris, 1835; **1834.** *La source et le glacier du Rhône*, Paris, 1835; **1834.**

REYNIER, L. *Mémoires pour servir à l'histoire physique et naturelle de la Suisse*, I, Lausanne, 1788; *c.* **1788.** *Guide des voyageurs en Suisse*, Paris, 1790; *c.* **1788**

REYNOLDS, HENRY ROBERT. *Life & Letters*, London, 1898; **1847, 1853.**

RHELLICANUS, J. M. In *J. Simler*, W. A. B. Coolidge, Grenoble, 1904; **1536.**

RICHARDSON, F. ET ALIAE. *Swiss notes by five ladies*, Leeds, 1875; **1874.**

RICHARDSON, JOHN WIGHAM, *Memoirs*, p.p., Glasgow, 1911; **1857.**

RICKMAN, E. S. *The Diary of a Solitaire, or Sketch of a Pedestrian Excursion through Switzerland*, London, 1835; **1824.**

RICOU, J. D. In *Historia stirpium Helvetiae inchoata*, A. von Haller, Bernae, 1768; **1766.** In 'Un curé alsacien à Zermatt'. C.-E. Engel, *Die Alpen* (*Chronik des S.A.C.*), 1945; **1766.**

RIGBY, EDWARD. *Dr. Rigby's Letters from France etc. in 1789*, London, 1880; **1789.**

RILKE, RAINER MARIA. *Briefe*, Leipzig, 1937; **1919, 1920, 1921.**

RIMBAUD, JEAN-ARTHUR. *Lettres*, Paris, 1899; **1878.**

RIMSKY KORSAKOW, NIKOLAY ANDREYEVICH. *My Musical Life*, New York, 1942; **1872, 1891, 1900.**

RITCHIE, ANNE THACKERAY. *Letters*, London, 1924; **1875.**

RITCHIE, LEITCH. *Travelling Sketches in the North of Italy, the Tyrol, and on the Rhine*, London, 1832; *c.* **1832.**

RITZ, CÉSAR. *César Ritz*, M. L. Ritz, London, 1938; **1874.**

RIVETT-CARNAC, J. H. *Many Memories*, London, 1910; **1895, 1902.**

RIVINGTON, ALEXANDER. *Notes of Travel in Europe*, p.p., London, 1865; **1858, 1860, 1861, 1862, 1863.**

ROBERT, F. *Voyage dans les XIII cantons de la Suisse*, Paris, 1789; **1784.**

ROBINSON, HENRY CRABB. *Diary, Reminiscences and Correspondence*, London, 1869; **1820.**

ROBY, JOHN. *Seven Weeks in Belgium, Switzerland, Lombardy, Piedmont, Savoy, etc.*, London, 1838; **1835.**

ROCCA, HENRI DELLA. *Souvenirs*, Paris, 1902; **1835.**

ROCHEFOUCAULD D'ENVILLE, LOUIS ALEXANDRE, DUC DE LA. 'Relation inédite d'un voyage aux Glacières de Savoie fait en 1762 par un voyageur français', L. Raulet, *Annuaire du Club Alpin Français,* 20, 1894; **1762.**

ROGER, A. S. *Le Major Roger,* C.-E. Engel, Neuchâtel, 1935; **1811, 1828, 1829, 1830, 1831, 1832, 1833, 1834, 1835.**

ROGERS, C. K. *The Story of Two Lives,* p.p., Plimpton, 1932; **1881.**

ROGERS, SAMUEL. *Samuel Rogers and his contemporaries,* P. W. Claydon, London, 1889; **1814, 1821.**

ROGET, CATHERINE. *Travel in the Last Two Centuries of Three Generations,* S. R. Roget, London, 1921; **1783.**

ROGET, F. F. *Ski Runs in the High Alps,* London, 1913; **1909, 1910, 1911.**

ROGET, PETER MARK. *Travels in the Last Two Centuries of Three Generations,* S. R. Roget, London, 1921; **1803, 1844.**

ROHAN, HENRI, DUC DE. *Mémoires et lettres de Henri duc de Rohan, sur la guerre de la Valtelline,* Genève, 1758; **1635.**

ROHRDORF, CASPAR. *Reise über die Grindelwald-Viescher-Gletscher auf den Jungfrau-Gletscher und Ersteigung des Gletschers des Jungfrau-Berges.* Bern, 1828; **1828.**

ROLAND, MME. *Voyage en Suisse 1787,* edited by G. R. de Beer, Neuchâtel, 1937; **1787.**

ROLAND DE LA PLATIÈRE, J. M. *Lettres écrites de Suisse, d'Italie, de Sicile et de Malthe,* Amsterdam, 1780; **1769, 1774, 1776.**

ROLLAND, ROMAIN. *Romain Rolland vivant,* P. J. Jouve, Paris, 1920; **1916.**

ROMILLY, LADY ANNE. *Romilly-Edgworth Letters,* edited by J. H. Romilly, London, 1936; **1815.**

ROMILLY, SIR SAMUEL. *Memoirs of the life of Sir Samuel Romilly,* London, 1841; **1781, 1815.**

RONAT, G. *En Suisse,* Bruges, n.d.; *c.* **1892.**

RÖNTGEN, W. C. *Wilhelm Conrad Röntgen,* O. Glasser, London, 1933; **1921.**

ROOSEVELT, THEODORE. *Life,* H. Hagedorn, London, 1919; **1869.** *Roosevelt,* H. Pringle, London, 1932; **1881.**

ROQUE, M. DE LA. *Voyage d'un amateur des arts,* Amsterdam, 1783; **1776, 1778.**

ROSCOE, THOMAS. *The Tourist in Switzerland and Italy,* London, 1830; *c.* **1830.**

ROSE, F. HORACE. *A Caper on the Continent,* Maritzburg, 1913; **1911.**

ROSE, STEWART. *Letters from the North of Italy addressed to Henry Hallam*, London, 1819; **1817.**

ROSSETTI, CHRISTINA. *Life*, M. E. Saunders, London, 1930; **1865.**

ROSSETTI, WILLIAM. *Rossetti Papers*, London, 1903; **1864.**

ROSTAN, J. L. *The Alpine Missionary*, M. F. Sandars, London, 1869; **1842.**

ROTH, ABRAHAM. *Gletscherfahrten in den Berneralpen*, Berlin, 1861; **1856, 1858, 1860.** *Doldenhorn und Weisse Frau*, Coblenz, 1863; **1862.** *Finsteraarhornfahrt*, Berlin, 1863; **1861.**

ROTH, GOTTLIEB. In 'Eine Ehrenrettung', C. Egger, *Die Alpen*, 16, 1940; **1845.**

ROUSSEAU, JEAN-BAPTISTE. *Allégories: Sophronyme*, Paris, 1797; **1712.**

ROUSSEAU, JEAN-JACQUES. In *Chronologie critique*, J. L. Courtois, *Annales de la soc. J.-J. Rousseau*, 15, Genève, 1923; **1730, 1731, 1744, 1754, 1762**, I. *Confessions*, Paris, 1847; **1754, 1762, 1765.** *Correspondance Générale*, Paris, 1928; **1762, 1763, 1764, 1765.**

RUDOLF DE ST. TROND. In *Swiss Travel and Swiss Guide-Books*, W. A. B. Coolidge, London, 1889; **1128.**

RUMBOLD, SIR HORACE. *Recollections of a Diplomatist*, London, 1902; **1865, 1867.** *Further Recollections of a Diplomatist*, London, 1903; **1878.**

RUMFORD, COUNT. *Philosophical Transactions of the Royal Society*, 94, 1804; **1803.**

RUSKIN, JOHN. 'Ruskin and the Alps', A. L. Mumm, *Alpine Journal*, 32, 1919; **1833, 1835, 1842, 1844, 1845, 1846, 1849, 1851.** *Life of John Ruskin*, E. T. Cook, London, 1911; **1854, 1856, 1858, 1859, 1860, 1861, 1862, 1863, 1866, 1869, 1870, 1874, 1877, 1882, 1888.** *Works*, edited by E. T. Cook & A. Wedderburn, London, 1905; **1841, 1852, 1872, 1876.**

RUSSELL, GEORGE. *The Narrative of George Russell*, Oxford, 1935; **1852.**

RUSSELL, LORD JOHN. *Life*, S. Walpole, London, 1889; **1856.**

RUSSELL-KILLOUGH, COMTE HENRY. *Souvenirs d'un montagnard*, Pau, 1888; **1867.**

RYFF, ANDREAS. 'Andreas Ryffs Gotthardreise im Jahre 1587', A. Bruckner, *Die Alpen*, xii, 1937; **1587.** 'Die Gemmi. Eine Reise über dieselbe im Jahre 1591', D. A. Fechter, *Basler Taschenbuch auf das Jahr 1862*; **1591.** 'Das Reisebüchlein des Andreas Ryff', H. Trog, *Basler Jahrbuch*, 1891; **1599.**

Sabran, Mme de. *Correspondance inédite de la Comtesse de Sabran et du Chevalier de Boufflers*, Magnieu & Prat, Paris, 1875; **1778.** *Memoirs of the Marquise de Custine*, G. Maugras & P. de Croze-Lemercier, London, 1912; **1789, 1795.**

Safford, Daniel. *A Memoir*, Boston, 1861; **1846.**

Sainte-Beuve, C. A. de. *Correspondance générale*, edited by J. Bonnerot, Paris, 1936; **1837.** *Sainte-Beuve à l'Académie de Lausanne*, R. Bray, Lausanne, 1937; **1837, 1839.**

Saint John, Sir Frederick. *Reminiscences of a Retired Diplomat*, London, 1905; **1905.**

Saint-Maure, Charles de. *A new Journey through Greece, Ægypt, Palestine, Italy, Swisserland, Alsatia*, London, 1725; **1722.**

Sales, Saint François de. In *Tableau littéraire du Mont Blanc*, C. Vallot, Chambéry, 1930; **1606.**

Salis, Ulysses von. 'Fragment einiger Bemerkungen bei einer Reise in Bünden', *Der Sammler*, ii, Chur, 1780; *c.* **1780.** 'Reise durch Lugnetz bis in das St. Peters Thal oder Vals', *Der Sammler*, ii, Chur, 1780; *c.* **1780.** 'Reise von Worms bis auf Scanfs im Engadin durch das Livinerthal', *Der Sammler*, v, Chur, 1783; **1783.**

Salisbury, F. S. *Rambles in the Vaudese Alps*, London, 1916; **1908.**

Salis-Marschlins, Karl Ulysses von. 'Bemerkungen auf einer Reise durch einen Theil des Cantons Graubünden', *Der Neue Sammler*, iv, Chur, 1808; **1806.**

Sand, George. *Une Histoire d'amour*, P. Mariéton, Paris, 1903; **1834.** *Lettres d'un voyageur*, Paris, 1869; **1836.**

Sansom, J. *Travels from Paris through Switzerland & Italy*, London, 1807; **1801.**

Saussure, César de. *Lettres et voyages*, Lausanne, 1903; **1725.**

Saussure, Horace-Bénédict de. *Voyage dans les Alpes*, Neuchâtel, 1779–96; **1760, 1761, 1764, 1767, 1770, 1771, 1774, 1775, 1776, 1777, 1778, 1779, 1781, 1783, 1784, 1785, 1787, 1788, 1789, 1792.** *Lettres de H.-B. de Saussure à sa femme*, edited by E. Gaillard and H. F. Montagnier, Chambéry, 1937; **1770, 1775, 1777, 1786.** *Life of H.-B. de Saussure*, D. W. Freshfield, London, 1920; **1766, 1781, 1784.**

Sauvan, M. *Le Rhône*, Paris, 1829; **1828.**

Scheffel, Joseph Viktor. *Reisebilder*, Stuttgart, 1887, *Leben und Dichten*, J. Proelss, Berlin, 1887, and *Werke*, edited by F. Panzer, Berlin, n.d.; **1850, 1851, 1852, 1854, 1860, 1862, 1864.**

Schellinks, Willem. *Unbekannte Schweizer Landschaften aus dem XVII. Jahrhundert*, S. Stelling-Michaud, Zürich-Leipzig, 1937; **1665.**

SCHEUCHZER, JOHANN. In *Historia stirpium Helvetiae*, A. von Haller, Bernae, 1768; **1709.** In *Herbarium Diluvianum*, J. J. Scheuchzer, Lugduni Batavorum, 1723; **1709.**

SCHEUCHZER, JOHANN JAKOB. *Itinera per Helvetiae Alpinas regiones*, Lugduni Batavorum, 1723; **1702, 1703, 1704, 1705, 1706, 1707, 1709, 1710, 1711.**

SCHINER, M. *Description du département du Simplon*, Sion, 1812; *c.* **1812.**

SCHINZ, C. S. *Reise auf den Uetliberg*, Zürich, 1775; **1774.**

SCHINZ, HANS RUDOLF. In *Berner Oberland in Sage und Geschichte*, H. Hartmann, Interlaken, n.d.; **1763.** *Beyträge zur nähern Kenntniss des Schweitzerlandes*, Zürich, 1783–7; **1777.**

SCHLAGINTWEIT, A. *Neue Untersuchungen*, Leipzig, 1854; **1851.**

SCHLEGEL, AUGUST-WILHELM. *Auguste-Guillaume Schlegel et Mme. de Staël*, Comtesse Jean de Pange, Paris, 1938; **1807.**

SCHLEICHER, J. C. In *Voyages dans les Alpes*, H.-B. de Saussure, Neuchâtel, 1796; **1792.**

SCHMUZ, JOHANN. In *Geschichte des Reisens in der Schweiz*, G. Peyer, Basel, 1885; **1731.**

SCHOBERL, FREDERICK. *Picturesque Tour from Geneva to Milan by way of the Simplon*, London, 1820; *c.* **1811.**

SCHÖNBEIN, C. F. *Justus von Liebig & Christian Friedrich Schönbein*, G. W. A. Kahlbaum and E. Thon, Leipzig, 1900; **1860, 1861.**

SCHOPENHAUER, ARTHUR. *Leben*, W. Gwinner, Leipzig, 1874; **1804.**

SCHOPENHAUER, JOHANNA. *Reise von Paris durch das südliche Frankreich bis Chamouni*, Leipzig, 1831; **1804.**

SCHOTT, A. *Die deutschen Colonien in Piemont*, Stuttgart, 1842; **1839.**

SCHREIBER, LADY CHARLOTTE. *Journals*, London, 1911; **1869.**

SCHULTES, G. VON. *Skizze einer Wanderung durch einen Theil der Schweiz und des südlichen Deutschlands*, Bamberg & Würzburg, 1820; **1819.**

SCHURZ, CARL. *Reminiscences*, London, 1909; **1849, 1851.**

SCHUSTER, CLAUD. *Peaks and Pleasant Pastures*, Oxford, 1911; **1902, 1911.** *Men, Women & Mountains*, London, 1931; **1925, 1928.**

SCHÜTZ, KARL VON. *Reise von Linthal über die Limmernalp nach Briegels*, Zürich, 1812; **1811.**

SCOTT, JOHN. *Sketches of Manners, Scenery, &c., in the French Provinces, Switzerland and Italy*, London, 1821; **1818.**

SCOTT, JOHN BARBER. *An Englishman at Home and Abroad*, edited by E. Mann, London, 1930; **1817.**

SEDGWICK, ADAM. *Life & Letters*, edited by J. W. Clark and T. McK. Hughes, Cambridge, 1890; **1816.**

SEDGWICK, MISS. *Letters from Abroad*, London, 1841; **1839.**

SEEMUNDARSON, NICOLAS. In *The Alpine Passes*, J. E. Tyler, Oxford, 1930; **1151.**

SEGANTINI, GIOVANNI. *Schriften und Briefe*, Leipzig, 1909; **1886.**

SEIGNEUX DE CORREVON, GABRIEL. 'Voiage fait à la fin de juillet 1736 dans les Montagnes occidentales du Païs de Vaud', *Mercure Suisse (Journal Helvétique)*, Neuchâtel, juillet 1737; **1736.**

SELBORNE, ROUNDELL PALMER, LORD. *Memorials*, London, 1896; **1846, 1857, 1887.**

SÉMONVILLE, C. L. H. DE M. DE. *Novate*, A. Rufer, Zurich, 1941; **1793.**

SÉNANCOUR, ÉTIENNE PIVERT DE. *Obermann*, Paris, 1804; **1790.**

SENIOR, N. W. *Conversations*, London, 1880; **1861.**

SENNETT, A. R. *Fragments from Continental Journeyings*, London, 1903; **1898.**

SENNONES, VICOMTE DE. *Promenade sur le lac de Wallenstadt et dans le pays des Grisons*, Paris, 1827; **1826.**

SERERHARD, NICOLAUS. *Einfalte Delineation aller Gemeinden gemeiner dreyen Pündten*, edited by C. von Moor, Cur, 1872; *c.* **1742.**

SERGENT-MARCEAU, A. *Reminiscences of a Regicide*, M. L. M. Simpson, London, 1889; **1795.**

SERRANT, M. DE. In *Description des cols*, M. T. Bourrit, Genève, 1803; **1790.**

SEWELL, ELIZABETH MISSING. *A Journal kept during a Summer Tour*, London, 1852; **1851.**

SHAFTESBURY, LORD. *Life and Work of the Seventh Earl of Shaftesbury*, E. Hodder, London, 1886; **1846.**

SHALER, NATHANIEL. *Autobiography*, Boston & New York, 1909; **1867.**

SHAND, ALEXANDER INNES. *Old Time Travel*, London, 1903; *c.* **1854.**

SHARP, RICHARD. *Letters and Essays in Prose and Verse*, London, 1834; **1816, 1821, 1823.**

SHARP, SAMUEL. *Letters from Italy*, London, 1766; **1765.**

SHELLEY, FRANCES, LADY. *Diary*, edited by R. Edgcumb, London, 1912; **1816, 1853.**

SHELLEY, MRS. MARY. *Rambles in Germany and Italy*, London, 1844; **1840.**

SHELLEY, PERCY BYSSHE. *An Account of Shelley's Visits to France, Switzerland, and Savoy*, C. S. Elton, London, 1894; **1814.** *History of a Six Weeks' Tour*, M. Shelley, London, 1817; **1816.**

SHEPPARD, JOHN. *Letters after a Tour through Some Parts of France, Italy, Switzerland and Germany*, Edinburgh, 1817; **1816.**

SHERARD, W. In *Historia stirpium Helvetiae*, Haller, Bern, 1768; *c.* **1693.**

SHERER, COLONEL MOYLE. *Notes and Reflections during a Ramble in Germany*, London, 1826; **1825.**

SHERLOCK, MARTIN. *Letters from an English Traveller*, London, 1780; **1776.** *New Letters from an English Traveller*, London, 1780; **1779.**

SHERMAN, MRS. *The Pastor's Wife. A Memoir*, London, 1853; **1842.**

SHUCKBURGH, SIR GEORGE. 'Observations made in Savoy', *Philosophical Transactions of the Royal Society*, 67, 1777; **1775.**

SHUTTLEWORTH, ROBERT JAMES. 'Account of a botanical excursion in the Alps of the Canton of Valais', *Magazine of Zoology and Botany*, 2, 1838; **1835.**

SIDDONS, MRS. *The Incomparable Siddons*, C. Parsons, London, 1909; **1821.**

SIDGWICK, HENRY. *A Memoir*, London, 1906; **1869, 1880.**

SIGERIC OF CANTERBURY. *Memorials of St. Dunstan*, Rolls series 392, W. Stubbs, London, 1874; **990.**

SILLIMAN, BENJAMIN. *A Visit to Europe*, New York, 1853; **1851.**

SIMOND, L. *Voyage en Suisse*, Paris, 1824; **1817, 1818.**

SINCLAIR, J. D. *An Autumn in Italy*, Edinburgh, 1829; **1827.**

SINNER, FRIEDRICH. In 'Der Alpensinn', H. Dübi, *Neujahrsblatt der litterarischen Gesellschaft Bern auf das Jahr 1902*, Bern, 1901; **1753, 1755.**

SMILES, SAMUEL. *Autobiography*, London, 1905; **1881.**

SMITH, ALBERT. *The Story of Mont Blanc*, London, 1860; **1838, 1851, 1853.** *Mont Blanc Sideshow*, J. M. Thorington, Philadelphia, 1934; **1849.**

SMITH, G. ADAM. *Personal Memoir*, London, 1943; **1883, 1891, 1928, 1929.**

SMITH, J. ADAM. *Mountain Holidays*, London, 1946; **1929, 1934, 1935, 1936, 1938.**

SMITH, JAMES EDWARD. *A Sketch of a Tour on the Continent in the Years 1786 and 1787*, London, 1793; **1787.**

SMITH, JOHN. *A Month in France and Switzerland*, London, 1825; **1824.**

SMITH, JOHN DENHAM. *A Voice from the Alps*, Dublin, 1854; **1853.**

SMITH, J. MANTON. *Jottings on my Journeys in Switzerland*, p.p., London, 1896; **1896.**

SMITH, JOHN 'WARWICK'. 'John (Warwick) Smith', B. S. Long, *Walker's Quarterly*, 24, London, 1927; **1786.**

SMITH, L. A. *Personal Memoir*, London, 1943; **1889.**

SMITH, RICHARD. 'The Grand Tour of an Elizabethan', A. H. S. Yeames, *Papers of the British School at Rome*, 7, 1914; **1564.**

SMITH, WILLIAM. *Adventures with my Alpenstock & Carpet Bag*, Rochdale, 1864; **1864.**

SMYTH, ETHEL. *Impressions that remained*, London, 1919; **1882, 1886.** *What happened next*, London, 1940; **1897.**

SMYTHE, FRANK. *Climbs & Ski-runs*, London, 1929; **1922, 1925, 1927, 1928, 1929.** *An Alpine Journey*, London, 1934; **1934.** *Mountaineering Holiday*, London, 1940; **1939.**

SNEEDORF, N. *Briefe eines reisenden Dänen*, Züllichau, 1793; **1791.**

SNOECK, C. A. *Promenade aux Alpes*, s.l., s.d.; **1824.**

SNOW, ROBERT. *Memorials of a Tour on the Continent*, London, 1845; **1844.**

SOMERVILLE, MARY. *Personal Recollections*, London, 1874; **1817.**

SOUTHEY, ROBERT. *Life & Correspondence*, C. Southey, London, 1850; **1817.**

SPALLANZANI, LAZZARO. In 'Volta alpinista', M. Cermenati, *Bollettino del Club Alpino Italiano*, 32, 1899; **1779.**

SPAZIER, KARL. *Wanderungen durch die Schweiz*, Gotha, 1790; **1789.**

SPEER, STANHOPE TEMPLEMAN. *The Athenæum*, Nov. 1, 1845; **1845.**

SPENCER, HERBERT. *Autobiography*, London, 1904; **1853.**

SPENCER, LAVINIA, COUNTESS. *Letters of Sarah, Lady Lyttelton*, edited by Mrs. H. Wyndham, London, 1912; **1819.**

SPINOLA, H. DE. *Voyage de deux artistes en Suisse*, Limoges, 1838; *c.* **1838.**

SPOHR, LUDWIG. *Autobiography*, London, 1865; **1816, 1817.**

SPURGEON, C. H. *Autobiography*, London, 1894; **1865.**

STAËL, MME DE. *De l'Allemagne*, Paris & Londres, 1813; **1808.** *Dix années d'exil*, Londres, 1821; **1811, 1812.** *Mme. de Staël et la Suisse*, P. Kohler, Lausanne, 1916; **1807, 1815.**

STANDEN, R. S. *Continental Wayside Notes*, pp. n.p., 1865; **1857.**

STANHOPE, PHILIP. In *Letters to his Son*, Lord Chesterfield, London, 1774; **1747.**

STANHOPE, P. H., EARL. *Letters from Switzerland*, Carlsruhe, 1834; **1833.**

STANHOPE, WALTER. *Annals of a Yorkshire House*, A. M. W. Stirling, London, 1911; **1769.**

STANLEY, ARTHUR PENRHYN. *Life & Correspondence*, R. E. Prothero, London, 1893; **1840.**

STANLEY, EDWARD. *The Mauvais Pas. A Scene in the Alps, illustrating a Passage in the Novel 'Anne of Geierstein'*, Macclesfield, 1837; **1818.**

STANLEY, HENRY MORTON. *Autobiography*, London, 1909; **1890. 1891.**

STANLEY, SIR JOHN THOMAS. *The Early Married Life of Maria Josepha, Lady Stanley*, London, 1899; **1786.**

STAPFER, PHILIPP AUGUST. *A Picturesque Tour through the Oberland in the canton of Berne in Switzerland*, London, 1823; *c.* **1812.**

STARKE, MARIANNE. *Information and Directions for Travellers on the Continent*, London, 1824; **1817.**

STEIN, BARON VOM. *Freiherr vom Stein*, edited by E. Botzenhart, Berlin, 1935; **1820.**

STEIN, C. G. D. *Reise durch Baiern, Salzburg, Tirol, die Schweiz, und Württemberg*, Leipzig, 1829; **1827.**

STEINBRENNER, WILHELM LUDWIG. *Reise durch einige teutsche, schweizer, und französische Provinzen*, Göttingen, 1791; **1787.**

STENDHAL. *Vie de Henri Brulard*, Paris, 1890; **1800.** *Correspondance*, 1, Paris, 1933; **1800.** *Souvenirs d'Égotisme*, Paris, 1927; **1821.** *Mémoires d'un Touriste*, Paris, 1854; **1837.**

STEPHEN, LESLIE. *The Playground of Europe*, London, 1871; **1857, 1862, 1864, 1869,** *Life and Letters*, edited by F. W. Maitland, London, 1906; **1857, 1858, 1859, 1860, 1861, 1862, 1864, 1866, 1867, 1869, 1870, 1871, 1872, 1873, 1874, 1875, 1876, 1877, 1879, 1881, 1887, 1888, 1889, 1891, 1894.**

STETTLER, RUDOLF. 'Reise von Grund bei Hasle über das hintere Wetterhorn und den Lauteraargletscher auf die Grimsel', *Jahrbuch des Schweizer Alpen Club*, 31, 1896; **1795.**

STEVENSON, ROBERT LOUIS. *Swiss Notes*, London, 1923; **1880.** *Letters of Robert Louis Stevenson*, edited by S. Colvin, London, 1899; **1880, 1881.** *Robert Louis Stevenson at Davos*, W. J. Lockett, London, 1937; **1880, 1881.**

STEVENSON, SETH WILLIAM. *A Tour in France, Savoy, Northern Italy, Switzerland, Germany and the Netherlands*, London, 1827; **1825.**

STEWARTON. *The Belgian traveller, being a tour through Holland, France and Switzerland in the years 1804–5*, Middletown, Conn., 1807; **1805.**

STILLINGFLEET, B. *Literary Life*, London, 1811; **1741.**

STILLMAN, W. J. *The Autobiography of a Journalist*, London, 1901; **1860.**

STOCK, E. *My Recollections*, London, 1909; **1875, 1880, 1883, 1887.**

STOLBERG, FRIEDRICH LEOPOLD. *Travels through Germany, Switzerland, Italy and Sicily*, London, 1796; **1791.**

STORR, GOTTLIEB KONRAD CHRISTIAN. *Alpenreise*, Leipzig, 1784–6; **1781, 1784, 1785.**

STORY, WILLIAM WETMORE. *William Wetmore Story and His Friends*, Henry James, London, 1903; **1886.**

STOWE, HARRIET BEECHER. *Sunny Memories of Foreign Lands*, London, 1854; **1853.**

STRAVINSKY, I. *Igor Stravinsky*, A. Schaeffner, Paris, 1931; **1910, 1911, 1913, 1914, 1915, 1917, 1918.**

STRONG, AUGUST H. 'Swiss Mountaineering in 1859', *American Alpine Journal*, 5, 1945; **1859.**

STRUTT, MRS. ELIZABETH. *Domestic Residence in Switzerland*, London, 1842; **1835.**

STUDER, BERNHARD. 'On some phenomena of the diluvial epoch', *Edinburgh New Philosophical Journal*, 29, 1840; **1839.**

STUDER, GOTTLIEB. *Topographische Mittheilungen aus dem Alpengebirge*, Bern, 1843; **1839, 1840, 1841, 1842.** *Das Panorama von Bern*, Bern, 1850; **1843.** *Berg- und Gletscherfahrten in den hohen Alpen der Schweiz*, Zürich, 1852; **1852, 1854, 1856, 1858.** *Pontresina & Engelberg*, Bern, 1907; **1826, 1827, 1836, 1857, 1859, 1861, 1862, 1863.**

STUDER, GOTTLIEB SIEGMUND. In 'J. S. Wyttenbach', H. Dübi, *Neujahrsblatt der literarischen Gesellschaft Bern*, 1911; **1779.**

STUDER, SAMUEL EMANUEL. In 'J. S. Wyttenbach', H. Dübi, *Neujahrsblatt der literarischen Gesellschaft Bern*, 1911; **1778, 1783.**

STUMPF, JOHANN. 'Ein Reisebericht des Chronisten Stumpf', H. Escher, *Quellen zur Schweizer Geschichte*, 6, 1884; **1544.**

SULZBACH, PRINCE OF. In *Annals of Mont Blanc*, C. E. Mathews, London, 1898; **1727.**

SULZER, F. J. *Altes und Neues oder dessen litteralischen Reise durch Siebenbürgen, den Temeswarer Banat, Ungarn, Oesterreich, Bayern, Schwaben, Schweiz und Elsass*, n.p. 1782; **1782.**

SULZER, JOHANN GEORG. *Beschreibung der Merckwürdigkeiten welche er in einer Ao. 1742 gemachten Reise durch einige Orte des Schweizerlandes beobachtet hat*, Zürich, 1743; **1742.** *Beobachtungen und Anmerkungen auf einer i. J. 1775 und 1776 gethanen Reise aus Deutschland nach der Schweiz und Oberitalien*, Herausgegeben von Zimmermann, Bern & Winterthur, 1780; **1775, 1776.**

SUMNER, CHARLES. *Memoirs and Letters*, E. L. Pierce, London, 1893; **1857, 1858.**

SUVOROF, ALEXANDER. 'Der Zug Suvorofs durch die Schweiz', R. von Reding-Biberegg, *Der Geschichtsfreund*, 50, Stans, 1895; **1799.**

SWEENEY, J. N. *Switzerland in 1876*, London, 1877; **1876.**

SWINNERTON, FRANK. *Autobiography*, London, 1933; **1920.**

SYDNEY, ALGERNON. *Life and Times*, A. C. Ewald, London, 1873; **1663.**

SYMONDS, JOHN ADDINGTON. *John Addington Symonds, a Biography*, H. F. Brown, London, 1895; **1861, 1862, 1863, 1866, 1867, 1870, 1875, 1876, 1878, 1881, 1882, 1883, 1884, 1886, 1887, 1889.** *Letters & Papers of John Addington Symonds*, edited by H. F. Brown, London, 1923; **1868, 1869, 1871, 1873, 1876, 1879, 1882, 1887, 1890.** *Our Life in the Swiss Highlands*, London, 1892; **1877.** *Out of the past*, M. Symonds, London, 1925; **1864, 1867, 1868, 1869, 1877, 1878, 1880, 1885.**

TAFUR, PERO. *Travels and Adventures*, tr. M. Letts, London, 1926; **1438.**

TALBOT, ISRAEL TISDALE. *American Alpine Journal*, 3, p. 66, 1939; **1854.**

TALFOURD, THOMAS NOON. *Vacation Rambles*, London, 1851; **1841, 1842, 1843.** *Supplement to Vacation Rambles*, London, 1854; **1846.**

TALLEYRAND, CHARLES MAURICE, PRINCE DE. *Talleyrand*, G. Lacour-Gayet, Paris, 1931; **1825.**

TAPPAN, H. P. *A Step from the New World to the Old, and then back again*, New York, 1852; **1851.**

TAVERNIER, JEAN-BAPTISTE. *Jean-Baptiste Tavernier*, C. Joret, Paris, 1886; **1684.**

TAYLOR, BAYARD. *Views afoot*, London, 1871; **1845.**

TAYLOR, GENERAL SIR HERBERT. *The Taylor Papers*, London, 1913; **1792.**

TAYLOR, ISAAC. *Words and Places*, London, 1864; **1862.**

TAYLOR, MEADOWS. *The Story of My Life*, London, 1877; **1860.**

TCHAIKOVSKY, PETER ILJITCH. *Leben*, Moscow, 1901; **1877, 1878.**

TECK, MARY ADELAIDE, DUCHESS OF. *A Memoir of H.R.H. the Duchess of Teck*, C. Kinloch Cooke, London, 1900; **1859, 1883, 1884, 1887, 1889, 1890, 1893, 1894, 1896.**

TEIGNMOUTH, LORD. *Reminiscences of Many Years*, Edinburgh, 1878; **1816.**

TEN HAMME, J. D. DE. *Quinze jours en Suisse*, Bruxelles, 1869; **1868, 1869.**

TENNANT, CHARLES. *A Tour through Parts of the Netherlands, Holland, Germany, Switzerland, Savoy and France*, London, 1824; **1821.**

TENNYSON, ALFRED, LORD. *Alfred, Lord Tennyson*, Hallam, Lord Tennyson, London, 1897; **1846, 1869, 1873.**

THACKERAY, WILLIAM MAKEPEACE. *Thackeray, a Personality*, M. Elwin, London, 1932; **1853.** 'On a Lazy Idle *Boy*', *Cornhill Magazine*, 1860; **1859.** *A Collection of Letters*, London, 1887; **1851.** *Letters to an American Family*, London, 1904; **1853.**

THIOLY, F. *Zermatt et l'ascension du Mont Rose*, Genève, 1860; **1860.** *De Genève à Zermatt par la vallée d'Anniviers*, Genève, 1867; **1866.**

THOMAS, ABRAHAM. *Bex et ses environs*, E. Rambert, Lausanne, 1871; **1765.** In *Historia stirpium Helvetiae*, A. von Haller, Bernae, 1768; *c.* **1768.** *Le guide du botaniste qui voyage dans le Valais*, L. Murith, Lausanne, 1810; **1795.**

THOMAS, LOUIS. *Le guide du botaniste qui voyage dans le Valais*, L. Murith, Lausanne, 1810; **1806.**

THOMAS, PETER. In *Historia stirpium Helvetiae*, A. von Haller, Bernae, 1768; **1765.**

THOMPSON, S. P. *Life & Letters*, London, 1920; **1874, 1877, 1883, 1894, 1907, 1908, 1910, 1911, 1913.**

THOMSON, WILLIAM. *Two journeys through Italy and Switzerland*, London, 1835; **1824, 1826.**

THOU, JACQUES AUGUSTE DE. 'Fragments des voyages du président de Thou', L. Bridel, *Le Conservateur Suisse*, 9, Lausanne, 1856; **1589.**

TICKNOR, GEORGE. *Life, Letters and Journals*, London, 1876; **1817, 1836, 1837.**

TILLY, COMTE HENRI DE. *Ascensions aux cimes de l'Etna et du Mont Blanc*, Genève, 1835; **1834.**

TISDALL, JAMES THOMAS TOWNLEY. *The Marlay Papers*, edited by R. W. Bond, London, 1937; **1814.**

TISSOT, VICTOR. *Unknown Switzerland*, London, 1889; **1886.**

TOLLEMACHE, BEATRIX. *Engelberg and Other Verses*, London, 1890; *c.* **1890.**

TOLLEMACHE, LIONEL. *Old and Odd Memories*, London, 1908; **1871.**

TOLSTOI, LEO. *Private Diary*, edited by A. Maude, London, 1927; **1857.**

TÖPFFER, RODOLPHE. *Voyage aquatico-historico-romantico-comico-comique dans le Nord-Est*, Lausanne, 1937; **1826.** *Rodolphe Töpffer*, A. Blondel & P. Miraboud, Paris, 1886; **1828.** *Nouvelles Genevoises. Le Col d'Anterne*, Paris, 1841; **1830.** *Premiers voyages en zigzag*,

Paris, 1844; **1837, 1838, 1839, 1840, 1841.** *Nouveaux voyages en zigzag*, Paris, 1854; **1842.** *Derniers voyages en zigzag*, Genève, 1910; **1832, 1833, 1835, 1836.**

TORR, CECIL. *Small Talk at Wreyland*, Cambridge, 1918; **1869.**

TORR, JOHN. *Small Talk at Wreyland*, C. Torr, Cambridge, 1918; **1850.**

TORR, T. S. *Small Talk at Wreyland*, C. Torr, Cambridge, 1918; **1840, 1849.**

TOUR DU PIN, MARQUISE DE LA. *Journal d'une femme de cinquante ans*, Paris, 1924; **1790.**

TOUSEY, S. *Pages from over the Water*, New York, 1869; **1867.**

TOWNE, FRANCIS. 'Francis Towne, landscape painter', A. P. Oppé, *Walpole Society*, 8, 1920; **1781.**

TOWNSEND, GEORGE. *Journal of a Tour in Italy*, London, 1850; **1850.**

TRALLES, J. G. *Bestimmungen der Höhen . . .*, Bern, 1790; **1789.**

TRANCHANT DE LAVERNE, L. M. P. *Voyage d'un Observateur de la nature et de l'homme, dans les montagnes du canton de Fribourg, et dans diverses parties du Pays de Vaud en 1793*, Paris, an XII (1804); **1793.**

TRANT, CLARISSA. *Journal*, edited by C. G. Luard, London, 1925; **1815, 1825, 1826.**

TRELAWNEY, EDWARD JOHN. *Recollections of Shelley, Byron and the Author*, London, 1858; **1820.**

TREMBLAYE, CHEVALIER DE LA. *Bemerkungen eines reisenden Weltmannes auf einer Reise durch Frankreich, Sardinien, Malta, Sicilien, Italien, und die Schweiz*, Breslau, 1791; **1771.**

TRENCH, FRANCIS. *A Few Notes from Past Life*, Oxford, 1862; **1830.** *A Walk round Mont Blanc*, London, 1847; **1847.**

TRENCH, R. In *A Few Notes from Past Life*, Oxford, 1862; **1830.**

TROLLOPE, T. ADOLPHUS. *Impressions of a Wanderer in Italy, Switzerland, France and Spain*, London, 1850; **1848.** *Further Reminiscences*, London, 1889; **1869, 1870, 1872, 1879.**

TROTSKY, LEON. *My Life*, London, 1930; **1915.**

TROWER, FRED. *American Alpine Journal*, 5, p. 276, 1944; **1857.**

TSCHARNER, JOHANN BAPTIST VON. 'Die Bernina', *Schweizerisches Museum*, 5, Zürich, 1789 (München, 1936); **1786.**

TSCHUDI, AEGIDIUS. *Hauptschlüssel zu zerschidenen Alterthumen oder gründliche Theils-historische Theils-topographische Beschreibung von dem Ursprung, Landmarchen, Alten, Namen, und Muttersprachen Galliae Comatae*, Constanz, 1758; **1524.**

TUCKETT, FRANCIS FOX. *A Pioneer in the High Alps*, London, 1920; **1856, 1859, 1860, 1861, 1863, 1864, 1865, 1866, 1867, 1869, 1871, 1872, 1874.**

TUCKETT, LUCY. *How We spent the Summer, or a Voyage en zigzag in Switzerland and Tyrol with Some Members of the Alpine Club*, London, 1864; **1864.** *Pictures in Tyrol and Elsewhere*, London, 1867; **1864.** *Beaten Tracks*, London, 1866; **1865.**

TUPPER, MARTIN. *Paterfamilias' Diary of Everybody's Tour*, London, 1856; **1855.**

TURGENEV, IVAN. 'Anouchka', *Revue des Deux Mondes*, Paris, 1 Oct. 1858; **1840.** *Turgenev*, A. Yarmolinsky, London, 1926; **1840.**

TURNER, JOSEPH MALLORD WILLIAM. *Life*, A. J. Finberg, Oxford, 1939; **1802, 1841, 1842, 1844.** *Life*, W. Thornbury, London, 1877; **1836, 1843.**

TURNER, WILLIAM. *Turner on Birds*, A. H. Evans, Cambridge, 1903; **1541.** In *English Naturalists from Meckam to Ray*, C. E. Raven, Cambridge, 1945; **1541.**

TWAIN, MARK. *A Tramp Abroad*, Hartford (Conn.), 1880; **1878.** *Mark Twain, a Biography*, A. B. Payne, New York, 1912; **1878.** *Mark Twain's Note Book*, A. B. Payne, New York, 1935; **1897.**

TWEDDELL, JOHN. *Remains*, London, 1816; **1796.**

TWINING, R. *Selections from Papers of the Twining Family*, London, 1887; **1827.**

TYNDALL, JOHN. *New Fragments*, London, 1892; **1849, 1877.** *Glaciers of the Alps*, London, 1860; **1856, 1857, 1858, 1859.** *Hours of Exercise in the Alps*, London, 1871; **1860, 1861, 1862, 1863, 1864, 1865, 1866, 1867, 1868, 1869, 1870.** *The Forms of Water*, London, 1875; **1871, 1872.**

TZARA, T. In *Modern French Painters*, R. H. Wilenski, London, 1939; **1916.**

UKLANSKI, CARL THEODOR VON. *Einsame Wanderungen in die Schweiz*, Berlin, 1810; **1809.**

ULRICH, MELCHIOR. *Die Seitenthäler des Wallis und der Monte Rosa*, Zürich, 1850; **1847, 1848, 1849.** *Mittheilungen der Naturforschenden Gesellschaft in Zürich*, 5, 7, Zürich, 1851–3; **1850, 1852, 1853.**

UNDRELL, CAPT. J. 'An Account of an Ascent to the Summit of Mont Blanc', *Annals of Philosophy*, London, 1821; **1819.**

URLIN, RICHARD DENNY. *Journal and reminiscences*, p.p., n.p., n.d.; **1860, 1872, 1874, 1876, 1881, 1884, 1886, 1890, 1891.**

URQUHART, DAVID. *Some Chapters in the Life of a Victorian Knight-errant*, G. Robinson, Oxford, 1920; **1864.**

UWINS, THOMAS. *A Memoir*, Mrs. Uwins, London, 1858; **1824.**

VALÉRY, M. *Voyages historiques, littéraires et artistiques en Italie*, Paris, 1838; **1827.**

VAUGHAN, HERBERT, CARDINAL. *Letters*, edited by S. Leslie, London, 1942; **1869, 1885.**

VERGERIO, PIERPAOLO. In *History of the Reformation in Italy*, T. McCrie, Edinburgh, 1827; **1549.**

VERNET, JOSEPH. *Les Vernets*, L. Lagrange, Paris, 1864; **1778.** *Voyage à Genève*, P. X. Leschevin, Paris, 1812; **1778.**

VERNON, WILLIAM WARREN. *Recollections of Seventy-two Years*, London, 1917; **1840, 1844, 1858.**

VEUILLOT, LOUIS. *Les pèlerinages de Suisse*, Bruxelles, 1839; **1838.**

VICTORIA, QUEEN. *Life and Times of Queen Victoria*, London, 1901; **1868.** *Princess Louise Duchess of Argyll*, D. Duff, London, 1940; **1868.** *Henry Ponsonby*, A. Ponsonby, London, 1942; **1868.** *Social Gleanings*, M. Boyd, London, 1875; **1868.**

VIGÉE LE BRUN, ÉLISABETH LOUISE. *Souvenirs*, Paris, 1869; **1807, 1808.**

VIGNET, LOUIS. *Le fond du sac d'un vieux touriste*, Bourg, 1886–7; **1841, 1844, 1855, 1864, 1872.**

VIGNOLES, C. B. *Life*, O. J. Vignoles, London, 1889; **1854.**

VILLENEUVE, M. DE. *Les loisirs de M. de Villeneuve, ou voyage d'un habitant de Paris à l'est de la France, en Savoie et en Suisse*, J. J. Lemoine, Paris, 1827; **1824.**

VINCENT, J. N. In *Der Monte Rosa*, L. von Welden, Wien, 1824; **1819.**

VINNE, VINCENT LAURENTZ VAN DER. In *Unbekannte Schweizer Landschaften aus dem XVII. Jahrhundert*, S. Stelling-Michaud, Zürich-Leipzig, 1937; **1653.**

VIRIDET, MARC. *Passage du Roth-horn*, Genève, 1835; **1833.**

VIRIEUX, E. *L'Alpe d'or*, Genève, 1901; **1892, 1898.**

VIRUES, C. DE. In 'Personaggi celebri attraverso il Gottardo', *Bollettino Storico della Svizzera Italiana*, Bellinzona, 1892; **1604.**

VIZARD, JOHN. *Narrative of a Tour through France, Italy and Switzerland*, London, 1872; **1867.**

VIZETELLY, HENRY. *Glances back through Seventy Years*, London, 1893; **1852.**

VOGT, CARL. *Im Gebirg und auf den Gletschern*, Solothurn, 1843; **1841.**

VOLTA, ALESSANDRO. 'Alessandro Volta alpinista', M. Cermenati, *Bollettino del Club Alpino Italiano*, 32, 1899; **1777, 1787, 1801.**

VOLTAIRE. In *Mon séjour auprès de Voltaire*, C. A. Collini, Paris, 1807; **1756.**

WAASER, J. E. In *Staats- und Erdbeschreibung der Schweizerischen Eidgenossschaft*, J. C. Fuessli, Schaffhausen, 1772; **1744.**

WAGNER, J. J. *Historia naturalis Helvetiae curiosa*, Zürich, 1680; **1676.**

WAGNER, RICHARD. *Mein Leben*, München, 1911; **1849, 1850, 1851, 1852, 1853, 1854, 1856, 1858, 1859, 1864.** *Vie de R. Wagner*, A. de Pourtalès, Paris, 1932; **1857, 1866.**

WAHLENBERG, G. *De vegetatione et climate in Helvetia*, Zürich, 1813; **1812.**

WALDIE, JANE. *Sketches descriptive of Italy in 1816–17; with a Brief Account of Travels in Various Parts of France and Switzerland*, London, 1820; **1817.**

WALLACE, ALFRED RUSSEL. *My Life*, London, 1905; **1853, 1867, 1895.**

WALLACE, H. B. *Art & Scenery in Europe*, Philadelphia, 1857; **1850.**

WALPOLE, HORACE. *Letters*, Oxford, 1903; **1739.**

WALSER, GABRIEL. *Schweizergeographie*, Zürich, 1776; **1750, 1754.**

WALSH, COMTE THÉOBALD. *Notes sur la Suisse et une partie de l'Italie*, Paris, 1823; **1822.** *Voyage en Suisse, en Lombardie et en Piedmont*, Paris, 1834; *c.* **1833.**

WALTER, W. *Letters from the Continent*, Edinburgh, 1828; **1826, 1827.**

WARD, MARY. *Life*, M. C. E. Chambers, London, 1882; **1621.**

WARING, SAMUEL MILLER. *The Traveller's Fireside*, London, 1819; **1817, 1818.**

WARNER, C. D. *Saunterings*, Boston, 1873; *c.* **1869.**

WATERHOUSE, THEODORE. *Notes of his Life*, p.p., n.p., n.d.; **1877.**

WATKINS, THOMAS. *Travels through Switzerland, Italy, Sicily, etc.*, London, 1794; **1787.**

WATSON, PHILIPPA H. *Early Recollections*, p.p. London, 1931; **1865, 1869.**

WATT, JOACHIM VON. In *Josias Simler*, W. A. B. Coolidge, Grenoble, 1904; **1518.**

WATTENWYL, EMANUEL VON. In 'Der Alpensinn', H. Dübi, *Neujahrsblatt der litterarischen Gesellschaft Bern auf das Jahr 1902*, Bern, 1901; **1791.**

WEBER, CARL MARIA VON. *Carl Maria von Weber*, M. M. von Weber, Leipzig, 1864; **1811.**

WEBSTER, LADY E. *Journal of Lady Holland*, London, 1908; **1791, 1793.**

WEDGWOOD, TOM. *Tom Wedgwood, the First* Litchfield, London, 1903; **1796.**

WEILENMANN, J. J. *Berg- und Gletscherfahrten in* *Schweiz*, Zürich, 1859; **1857, 1858.** *Aus der F* 1872–6; **1855, 1857, 1858, 1859, 1863, 1864, 1** **1871, 1872, 1873, 1874.**

WEITBRECHT, JOHN JAMES. *Memoir*, London, 1854;

WELDEN, LUDWIG VON. In *Geographisch-historisch* *Beschreibung zu K. W. Kummer's Stereorama oder* *blanc Gebirges*, C. Ritter, Berlin, 1824; **1815.** *Der Mon* 1824; **1821, 1822.**

WELZENBACH, W. *Les ascensions de Willo Welzenbach,* **1923, 1924, 1925, 1926, 1927, 1929, 1930, 1931, 19**

WESTON, G. F. *Journal of a Tour in Europe and the Ea* 1894; **1844.**

WESTON, STEPHEN. *La Scava*; *or some account of an exca* *Roman villa . . . to which is added a journey to the Simplo* *sanne, and to Mont Blanc through Geneva*, London, 1818; *trimester in France & Switzerland*, London, 1821; **1820.**

WEY, WILLIAM. *Itineraries of William Wey*, London, 1857;

WHALEY, THOMAS 'BUCK'. *Memoirs*, edited by Sir E. Sullivan don, 1906; **1792.**

WHALLEY, THOMAS SEDGWICK. *Journals and Correspondence*, edit A. Wickham, London, 1863; **1784, 1786.**

WHATELY, RICHARD. *Life and Correspondence*, E. J. Whately, Lon 1866; **1839.**

WHERRY, GEORGE. *Alpine Notes and the Climbing Foot*, Cambrid 1896; **1891, 1892, 1893, 1895.** *Notes from a Knapsack*, Cambridg 1909; **1896, 1897, 1898.**

WHIDBORNE, G. F. *G. F. Whidborne*, p.p., Glasgow, 1917; **1913.**

WHITE, WALTER. *To Mont Blanc and back again*, London, 1854; **1853.**

WHYMPER, EDWARD. *Scrambles amongst the Alps*, London, 1871; **1860, 1862, 1863, 1864, 1865.** *Edward Whymper*, F. S. Smyth, London, 1940; **1860, 1862, 1863, 1864, 1865, 1866, 1874, 1893, 1894, 1895,**

WICKHAM, EDWARD CHARLES. *A Memoir*, L. Ragg, London, 1911; **1910.**

WICKHAM, WILLIAM. *Correspondence*, London, 1876; **1795, 1799.**

WIDMANN, J. V. *Spaziergänge in die Alpen*, Frauenfeld, 1896; **1882, 1883, 1885, 1887, 1888, 1890, 1892, 1895.** *Du schöne Welt*, Frauenfeld, 1919; **1901, 1902, 1904, 1906, 1911.**

WIELAND, OBERST. *Mein Sommer 1826*, Basle, 1827; **1826.**

WIGRAM, WOOLMORE. *Memoirs*, p.p., London, 1908; **1860, 1862, 1863.**

WILBERFORCE, SAMUEL, BISHOP. *Life*, R. G. Wilberforce, London, 1882; **1863.**

WILBRAHAM, EDWARD BOOTLE. 'Narrative of an ascent of Mont Blanc', *The Keepsake*, London, 1832; **1830.**

WILDE, OSCAR. *Life*, H. Pearson, London, 1946; **1899.** *Collection of original MSS. letters and books of Oscar Wilde*, Dulau & Co., London, 1929; **1899.**

WILDER, F. *The Continental Traveller being the Journal of an Economical Tourist to France, Switzerland & Italy*, London, 1833; *c.* **1833.**

WILKES, JOHN. *Correspondence*, London, 1805; **1765.**

WILKIE, D. *Life*, London, 1843; **1827.**

WILKINSON, JOSHUA LUCOCK. *The Wanderer; or Anecdotes and Incidents, the Result and Occurrences of a Ramble on foot through France, Germany and Italy in 1791 and 1793.* London, 1798; **1791.**

WILKINSON, BISHOP T. E. *Twenty Years of Continental Work and Travel.* London, 1906; **1886, 1887, 1888, 1889, 1890, 1891, 1893, 1894, 1895, 1897, 1898, 1899, 1901, 1902, 1903.**

WILKLEY, E. *Notes of a Ramble through France, Italy, Switzerland, etc.*, London, 1836; **1834.**

WILLA OF IVREA. 'Aus Liudprands Werken', *Geschichtsschreiber*, 29, Leipzig, 1890; **941.**

WILLIAMS, CHARLES J. B. *Memoirs*, London, 1884; **1829,** *c.* **1860,** *c.* **1867,** *c.* **1868.** 'Notes on alpine quarters for invalids', *British Medical Journal*, ii, 1869; **1862, 1869.**

WILLIAMS, HELEN MARIA. *A Tour in Switzerland*, London, 1798; **1794.**

WILLIAMS, H. W. *Travels in Italy, Greece, etc.*, Edinburgh, 1820; **1816.**

WILLIS, N. P. *Pencillings by the Way*, London, 1836; **1834.**

WILLS, ALFRED. *Wanderings among the High Alps*, London, 1856; **1850, 1852, 1853, 1854.** *The Eagle's Nest*, London, 1860; **1857, 1858.**

WILLS, M. H. *A Summer in Europe*, Philadelphia, 1876; **1875.**

WILSON, CLAUDE. *An Epitome of 50 Years' Climbing*, p.p., 1933; **1877.**

WILSON, DANIEL. *Letters from an Absent Brother*, London, 1827; **1823.**

WILSON, H. SCHÜTZ. *Alpine ascents and adventures*, London, 1878; **1869, 1871, 1872, 1873, 1874, 1875, 1876, 1877.**

WILSON, GENERAL SIR ROBERT. *Private Diary*, London, 1881; **1814.**

WINDHAM, WILLIAM. *An Account of the Glacieres or Ice Alps in Savoy*, London, 1744; **1741.**

WINDHAM, WILLIAM. *Diary*, London, 1866; **1788.**

WINKWORTH, STEPHEN. *Peaks, Passes, & Glaciers*, 2, 1, London, 1862; **1861.**

WINTER, J. B. *From Switzerland to the Mediterranean on foot*, London, 1922; **1919.**

WISE, A. T. TUCKER. *Wiesen as a health resort in early phthisis*, London, 1883; **1882.**

WITMER, T. B. *Wild Oats sown Abroad*, Philadelphia, 1872; *c.* **1851.**

WITTE, CARL. *Scenen aus meinen Reisen durch Deutschland, die Schweiz, Italien, einen Theil von Frankreich und Polen*, Mainz & Hamburg, 1804–5; **1792, 1804.**

WITTE, KARL. *Alpinisches und Transalpinisches*, Berlin, 1858; **1856.**

WOLFF, JOSEPH. *Missionary Journal and Memoir*, London, 1824; **1815, 1819.**

WOLFF, PIERRE-ÉTIENNE. 'Une traversée du Col du Lauteraar en 1846', H. Dübi, *Die Alpen*, 9, 1933; **1846.**

WOLLASTON, C. B. In *Journal of Mary Frampton*, edited by H. G. Mundy, London, 1886; **1791.**

WOOLSON, C. F. *Five Generations*, ed. C. Benedict, London, 1936; **1880, 1881, 1883.**

WORDSWORTH, CHRISTOPHER. *Journal of a tour in Italy*, London, 1863; **1862.**

WORDSWORTH, DOROTHY. *Journals*, London, 1897; **1820.**

WORDSWORTH, WILLIAM. *Descriptive Sketches taken during a Pedestrian Tour in the Italian, Grison, Swiss, and Savoyard Alps*, London, 1793; **1790.** *Letters of the Wordsworth Family*, edited by W. Knight, Boston, 1907; **1790.** *Memoirs of William Wordsworth*, C. Wordsworth, London, 1881; **1820.**

WOTTON, SIR HENRY. *Life and Letters*, Logan Pearsall Smith, London, 1907; **1593, 1604, 1616, 1623.**

WYNNE, ELIZABETH. *The Wynne Diaries*, London, 1940; **1791, 1792, 1793, 1794, 1815.**

WYSS, JOHANN RUDOLF. *Voyage dans l'Oberland Bernois*, Bern, 1817; **1814.**

WYSS, RUDOLF. 'Description d'un voyage de l'Oberland fait en 1757', in *Der Alpensinn*, H. Dübi, *Neujahrsblatt der litterarischen Gesellschaft Bern auf das Jahr 1902*, Bern, 1901; **1757.**

WYTTENBACH, JAKOB SAMUEL. 'Reise durch die Alpen und das Wallisland', *Bernerisches Magazin der Natur, Kunst, und Wissenschaften*, 1, (2), Bern, 1777; **1771.** 'Description d'un voyage fait en 1776 dans une partie des Alpes du canton de Berne', in *Vues remarquables des montagnes de la Suisse avec leur description*, Wagner, Berne, 1778; **1776.** In *Voyage dans l'Oberland Bernois*, J. R. Wyss, Berne, 1817; **1776.** 'J. S. Wyttenbach', H. Dübi, *Neujahrsblatt der literarischen Gesellschaft*, Bern, 1911; **1780, 1787, 1788, 1789, 1791, 1792.**

YATES, MRS. ASHTON. *Letters written during a Journey to Switzerland*, London, 1843; **1841.**

YATES, ELIZABETH. *High Holiday*, London, 1938; *c.* **1938.**

YEO, J. BURNEY. *Notes of a Season at St. Moritz in the Upper Engadine and of a Visit to the Baths of Tarasp*, London, 1870; **1869.** *Health Resorts*, London, 1882; **1869.**

YOSY, A. *Switzerland*, London, 1815; **1802,** *c.* **1805, 1812.**

YOUNG, CHARLES MAYNE. *Last Leaves from the Journal of J. C. Young*, London, 1878; **1821.**

YOUNG, GEOFFREY WINTHROP. *On High Hills*, London, 1927; **1896, 1898, 1899, 1900, 1902, 1904, 1905, 1906, 1907, 1909, 1910, 1911, 1912, 1914.**

YOUNG, JULIAN CHARLES. *A Memoir of Charles Mayne Young*, J. C. Young, London, 1871; **1838, 1853.**

YOUNGE, W. In *Memoir & Correspondence of J. E. Smith*, London, 1832; **1787.**

ZAPF, G. W. *Litterarische Reisen. Durch einen Theil von Baiern, Schwaben und die Schweiz*, Augsburg, 1796; **1781.**

ZELLER, CONRAD. In *Reise in die weniger bekannten Thäler auf der Nordseite der Penninischen Alpen*, J. Fröbel, Berlin, 1840; **1832.**

ZINCKE, F. BARHAM. *A Month in Switzerland*, London, 1873; **1872.** *Swiss allmends*, London, 1874; **1873.** *A Walk in the Grisons*, London, 1875; **1874.**

ZOLLIKOFER, CASPAR. 'Rückerinnerungen einer Reise durch die Appenzelleralpen', *Alpina*, 2, Winterthur, 1807; **1803.**

ZSIGMONDY, EMIL. *Im Hochgebirge*, Leipzig, 1889; **1882, 1884.**

ZUMSTEIN, JOSEPH. In *Der Monte Rosa*, L. von Welden, Wien, 1824; **1820.**

PRINTED IN GREAT BRITAIN
AT THE UNIVERSITY PRESS, OXFORD
BY CHARLES BATEY, PRINTER TO THE UNIVERSITY